Lewis Bodwell

Clifton Chapel Collection of Psalms, Hymns and Spiritual Songs

for public, social, and family worship and private devotions at the Sanitarium, Clift

Lewis Bodwell

Clifton Chapel Collection of Psalms, Hymns and Spiritual Songs
for public, social, and family worship and private devotions at the Sanitarium, Clift

ISBN/EAN: 9783337265816

Printed in Europe, USA, Canada, Australia, Japan

Cover: Foto ©Lupo / pixelio.de

More available books at **www.hansebooks.com**

"**Prayer and Supplication with Tha**

The

Clifton Chapel C

of

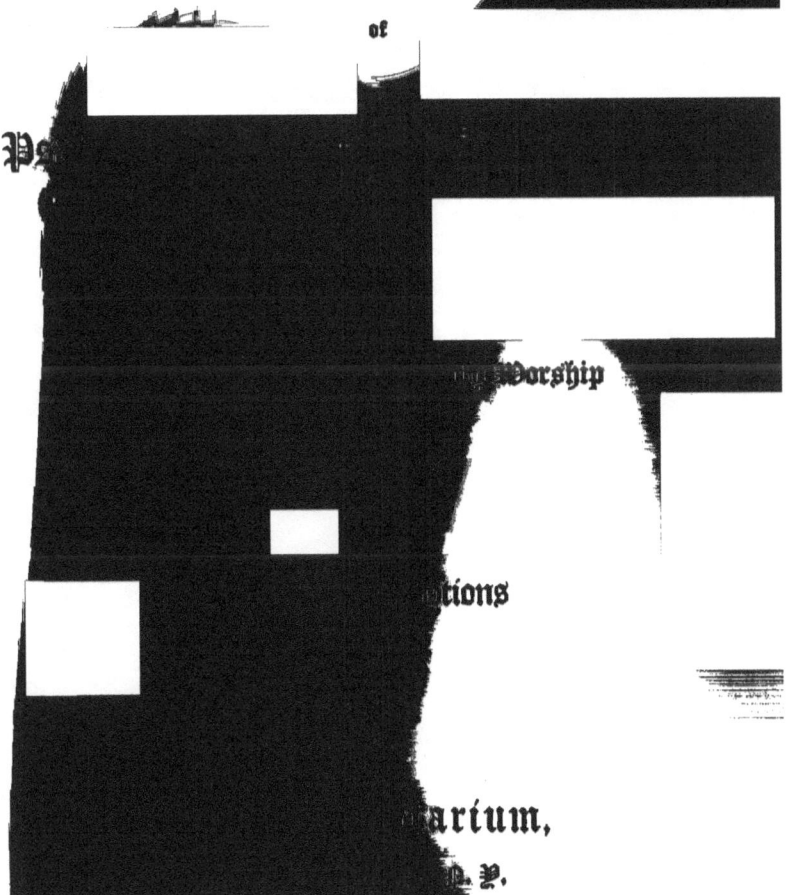

Preface.

The preparation of this volume has its warrant in the law which leads Christian families, congregations, and denominations often to change the old or prepare new works to help them in their worship. Peculiar views or conditions must be provided for by each in its own chosen way.

The Clifton Springs Sanitarium was established, and has always been conducted, on the principle that by proper spiritual conditions, bodily health can best be preserved, or restored when it becomes impaired. To every one coming for help, it is daily said: "Aiming in our treatment of disease to use in a liberal spirit all known remedial agents; and recognizing, as we do, the power of the mind over the body, and the salutary effects of a consistent, religious faith upon the sick, we hold it to be the first duty of the Institution to seek to bring its patients under the power and influence of the Word and Worship of GOD as a means of restoring mind and body to health." There is a continual presentation of the thought that God, the Giver of life, the Preserver of health, is the only Restorer when health has failed. That, all other things being equal, He will more surely give His special blessings to His loving, believing followers and friends than to those who are not such. That He is more likely to bestow His best gift on the child who asks, than upon the one who does not ask. And that nowhere does He more delight to bless, than where His people "assemble and meet together to render thanks for the great benefits received at His hands; to set forth His most worthy praise; to hear His most holy Word; and to ask those things which are requisite and necessary not only for the body but the soul." With fullest confidence in these principles, there has been unsparing effort made to supply and maintain all agencies which promised to bring in and promote true godliness. Among these is the Chapel, with its frequently returning hours of worship; always offered, often prescribed, and often proven to be the very help needed on the way to that health of body which mental peace and soul comfort always promote.

In these gatherings it is found that the Scriptures cannot be too constantly in mind and before the eye; and that for reasons sanitary as well as spiritual, Christian song should have, as it does, a more than usually prominent place. During a series of years, the long use of many excellent works only made more manifest a want which first found public expression in 1875, in a Circular to which were attached the names of men known in all the land, and honored by the whole Church, as well as by their own denominations; and who as friends and guests of the House knew well its needs and how to meet them. Their opinion and wish were thus stated: —

"A New Hymnal, adapted to the worship of the Sanitarium at Clifton Springs, has long been desired, and now is an imperative need. The services are so various, — embracing Family prayers each morning, Social meetings on four evenings of each week, and Public worship twice on each Sabbath; and so peculiar, — the congregation being composed of people of all denominations, and they being, for the most part, invalids — that no existing collection is adapted to our use."

To secure the help of many others, who were known to be in sympathy with the plan, the following request was also sent out: "As in Public, Social, and Family worship you have known our Chapel services, we believe that you have an interest in, as well as an acquaintance with, our wants. Feeling assured of this, Dr. Foster wishes to ask that you will join in the work of choosing what you think proper material

Preface.

for a Clifton Chapel Hymnal, by naming the first lines of favorite hymns, and the collection in which may be found the version you prefer. We do not ask for sacred poetry, however sweet, unless it is in actual use among the 'Songs of the Church.' Of these we do not seek any such as can only be properly rendered by a choir. Our request is simply for the 'psalms and hymns and spiritual songs' which you hear sung by congregations with spirit and profit. Of such will you direct us to those you would wish to find in any and every collection you may have occasion to use."

A hearty and loving interest was at once shown, by responses from all parts of the land and all branches of the Church; and with selections of many hundreds of the brightest gems of Christian Hymnology came also generous subscriptions paid in advance, to be returned in copies of the book when done.

The peculiar features of the book are in accord with the views and wishes of the one by whom it was planned and provided for its place and use in the Christian Institution whose planting has been his life work.

The unusually large number of Hymns seemed necessary for healthful variety, where there are regularly six hundred public services each year, and where members of all Christian bodies may justly expect to find much that is familiar and comforting by its associations with home worship.

To secure this in as wide a range of authorship, thought, and language as possible, and yet not make a volume too large for even an invalid's use, and also to avoid the cost of printing hundreds of verses only to be omitted at last; such carefully studied contractions were made of most of the longer hymns, as should in each retain one or the best of its thoughts, and yet usually leave only so much as could be sung without the hurried and imperfect abbreviations so often made by those who are called to lead in religious services. Thus, with no further remark, it may be taken for granted that nearly every hymn is only a part of the original poem.

As to alterations in language, it has been thought best that so much of the authors' work as was set over their names should be in their own words when they could be ascertained. But though much care and labor have been expended here; with the multitude of changes and the conflict of authorities, it is safe to conclude that but few hymns remain as originally written.

Again, in head-lines to mark the topic of each page; in texts to point out some leading thought of each hymn; and in Scripture readings suggested with every one; there is an effort to make more prominent the fact that the Word of God is the fountain of Christian song, as well as the leader of Christian thought. While in this part of the work no pains have been spared to secure the greatest possible variety and appropriateness of Scripture for every hymn and page, in selections which embody over Six Thousand quotations and references, certainly not all, and possibly not the best passages have been selected; yet it is believed that the path is pointed out, which willing minds and loving hearts may follow with the best results to themselves, the greatest pleasure to the Master, and the highest glory to God.

Thus designed by the founder of this Institution to meet its peculiar wants; commended, selected, and arranged by loving friends, to whom the House has proved a place of refreshing to body, soul, and spirit; this volume is offered with no claim that it surpasses or rivals any other. To none will it seem perfect; and few, if any, will see its imperfections more clearly than those who have labored longest to make it acceptable and useful. But it is their hope that, filling first the place for which it was specially designed, it may also find its way to every spot where in heart or home, in church or community, it may help to advance that Kingdom which is "righteousness and peace and joy in the Holy Ghost."

CLIFTON SPRINGS SANITARIUM, 1881.

Table of Contents.

	PAGE
I. PREFACE	iii
II. INDEX OF SUBJECTS	v
III. PSALMS AND HYMNS	1
IV. INDEX OF FIRST LINES OF HYMNS	291
V. INDEX OF FIRST LINES OF VERSES	301
VI. INDEX OF SCRIPTURE TEXTS	309
VII. INDEX OF AUTHORS	315

Index of Subjects.

The Deity.

THE FATHER.

	HYMN
HIS BEING	1-4
OMNIPOTENCE	5-10
OMNISCIENCE	11-13
OMNIPRESENCE	14-16
HOLINESS	17-22
JUSTICE AND TRUTH	23-28
LOVE	29-34
WORKS	35-40
CARE	41-46
IMMUTABILITY	47-52

THE SON.

HIS INCARNATION	53-61
CHARACTER	62-66
MINISTRY	67-72
TRIALS	73-78
CROSS	79-84
DEATH	85-87
BURIAL	88-90
RESURRECTION	91-96
EXALTATION	97-102
CORONATION	103-107
PRIESTHOOD	108-113

THE HOLY SPIRIT.

HIS PROMISED COMING	114-123

Personal Experience.

MAN.

IN SIN.

Lost	124-129
Ransomed	130-135
Called by The Father	136-141
The Saviour	142-147
The Spirit	148-153
Invited by Friends	154-158
Invited and Warned	159-173
Convicted	174-184

IN CHRIST.

Penitent	185-190
Believing	191-205
Praying	206-217
Praising	218-241
Justified	242-256
Adopted	257-262
Consecration	263-285
Sanctification	286-301

Index of Subjects.

GRACES.
Love for God 302-346
The Word 347-352
The Sabbath 353-366
The Sanctuary 367-372
Christians 373-378
Mankind 379-384
Faith, Hope, Charity 385-397

DUTIES.
Prayer 398-406
Watchfulness 407-412
Warfare 413-417
Work 418-433
Walk 434-445

DECLENSION.
Confessed 446-451
Deplored 452-457
Recall 458-473
Return 474-497
Relief 498-501

CHASTENINGS.
Sorrow 502-523
Comfort 524-547

DESIRE.
For God 548-569
Christ 570-608
Help 609-629
Guidance 630-639
Peace 640-649
Holiness 650-668

DEVOTIONS.
Morning 669-680
Morning to Evening 681-689
Evening 690-709

ATTAINMENTS.
Trust 710-742
Rest 743-781
Joy 782-807
Looking Heavenward 808-847

The Church.
HER FOUNDATION, Defence, Glory . . 848-857
FELLOWSHIP 858-883

HER ORACLES 884-900
HOME WORSHIP.
Morning 901-964
Evening 965-987
Children 988-1008

PUBLIC WORSHIP.
Invocation. The Father . 1009-1022
The Son . . 1023-1038
The Holy Spirit 1039-1048
Call to God's People . . . 1049-1058
All People 1059-1066
All Creatures . . . 1067-1069
Praises. The Lord Jesus Christ 1070-1104
The Triune God . 1105-1119
Doxologies . . . 1120-1141
Sabbath and Sanctuary . . 1142-1167
Sabbath Evening 1168-1193

ORDINANCES.
Baptism 1194-1199
Lord's Supper 1200-1222

MINISTRY   1223-1233

WORK.
Church Erection 1234-1243
Prayer for Reviving . . . 1244-1258
Temperance 1259-1269
Home Missions 1270-1279
Seamen 1280-1284
Israel 1285-1290
Foreign Missions 1291-1339

HOPE. Christ's Coming . . . 1340-1362

FASTS 1363-1373

FESTIVALS.
The Seasons 1374-1387
Thanksgiving 1388-1401
National 1402-1405

PILGRIMAGE.
Life 1406-1415
Death 1416-1441
Resurrection 1442-1447
Judgment 1448-1456

REST. Heaven 1457-1500

Clifton Chapel Collection.

"I am the Lord thy God."

1 " Canst thou by searching find out God?" **L. M.**
Gen. i. Acts xiv. 8–17. Ex. iii. 1–15.

1 GOD is the name my soul adores,
  Th' Almighty Three, th' Eternal One :
  Nature and grace, with all their powers,
  Confess the Infinite Unknown.

2 Thy voice produced the seas and spheres,
  Bade the waves roar, and planets shine ;
  But nothing like Thyself appears
  Through all these spacious works of Thine.

3 Still restless nature dies and grows ;
  From change to change the creatures run ;
  Thy being no succession knows,
  And all Thy vast designs are one.

4 Who can behold the blazing light ?
  Who can approach consuming flame ?
  None but Thy wisdom knows Thy might,
  None but Thy word can speak Thy name.
  Rev. Isaac Watts. (1674-1748.)

2 "The Eternal God." **L. M.**
Isa. xl. 12–31. Dan. iv. 34–37. Acts xvii. 22–31.

1 ETERNAL God ! Almighty Cause
  Of earth, and seas, and worlds unknown !
  All things are subject to Thy laws,
  All things depend on Thee alone.

2 Thy glorious being singly stands,
  Of all within itself possessed ;
  Controlled by none are Thy commands,
  Thou from Thyself alone art blessed.

3 To Thee alone ourselves we owe ;
  Let heaven and earth due homage pay ;
  All other gods we disavow,
  Deny their claims, renounce their sway.

4 Spread Thy great name through heathen lands ;
  Their idol deities dethrone ;
  Reduce the world to Thy command,
  And reign, as Thou art, God alone.
  Rev. Simon Browne. (1680-1732.)

3 "God is great, and we know Him not." **C. M.**
Ex. xl. 34, 35. Isa. vi. 1–5. Rev. iv.

1 How wondrous great, how glorious bright,
  Must our Creator be,
  Who dwells amidst the dazzling light
  Of vast infinity !

2 Our soaring spirits upward rise
  Toward the celestial throne ;
  Fain would we see the blessed Three,
  And the Almighty One.

3 Our reason stretches all its wings,
  And climbs above the skies ;
  But still how far beneath Thy feet
  Our grovelling reason lies !

4 Lord, here we bend our humble souls,
  And awfully adore ;
  For the weak pinions of our mind
  Can stretch a thought no more.
  Rev. Isaac Watts.

4 "Which was, and is, and is to come." **C. M.**
Ps. xc. Isa. xliv. Rev. i. 1–8.

1 GREAT God, how infinite art Thou !
  What worthless worms are we !
  Let the whole race of creatures bow,
  And pay their praise to Thee.

2 Thy throne eternal ages stood,
  Ere seas or stars were made ;
  Thou art the ever-living God,
  Were all the nations dead.

3 Eternity, with all its years,
  Stands present in Thy view ;
  To Thee there 's nothing old appears,
  Great God ! there 's nothing new.

4 Our lives through various scenes are drawn,
  And vexed with trifling cares ;
  While Thine eternal thought moves on
  Thine undisturbed affairs.
  Rev. Isaac Watts.

"The Lord God Omnipotent."

5 "Power belongeth unto God." C. M.
Ps. xviii. 7-15. Gen. vii. 11 to viii. 14. Rev. xix. 11-16.

1 THE Lord descended from above,
And bowed the heavens most high;
And underneath His feet He cast
The darkness of the sky.

2 On cherubim and seraphim
Full royally He rode,
And on the wings of mighty winds
Came flying all abroad.

3 He sat serene upon the floods,
Their fury to restrain;
And He, as sovereign Lord and King,
For evermore shall reign.
Thomas Sternhold. (-1549.)

6 "I am the Almighty God." L. M.
Rev. xi. 15-17. Deu. xi. 8-25. Ps. lxxvi.

1 THE Lord is King: lift up thy voice,
O earth, and all ye heavens rejoice!
From world to world the joy shall ring,
The Lord Omnipotent is King.

2 The Lord is King: who then shall dare
Resist His will, distrust His care,
Or murmur at His wise decrees,
Or doubt His royal promises?

3 The Lord is King: child of the dust,
The Judge of all the earth is just;
Holy and true are all His ways:
Let every creature speak His praise.

4 O, when His wisdom can mistake,
His might decay, His love forsake,
Then may His children cease to sing,
The Lord Omnipotent is King.
Josiah Conder. (1789-1855.)

7 "The winds and the sea obey Him!" C. M.
Josh. x. 12-14. Job xxxviii. 1-11. Mark iv. 35-41.

1 THE Lord our God is full of might;
The winds obey His will;
He speaks, and in His heavenly height
The rolling sun stands still.

2 Rebel, ye waves, and o'er the land
With threatening aspect roar:
The Lord uplifts His awful hand,
And chains you to the shore.

3 Howl, winds of night, your force combine:
Without His high behest,
Ye shall not in the mountain pine
Disturb the sparrow's nest.

4 Ye nations, bend, in reverence bend;
Ye monarchs, wait His nod;
And bid the choral song ascend,
To celebrate our God.
Henry K. White. (1785-1806.)

8 "The Lord, the Almighty." L. M.
Gen. i. Joel ii. Rev. xxi.

1 THE Lord, the God of glory, reigns,
In robes of majesty arrayed;
His rule omnipotence sustains,
And guides the worlds His hands have made.

2 Ere rolling worlds began to move,
Or ere the heavens were stretched abroad,
Thine awful throne was fixed above;
From everlasting Thou art God.

3 The Lord, the mighty God on high,
Controls the fiercely raging seas;
He speaks! and noise and tempest fly;
The waves sink down in gentle peace.
Miss Anne Steele. (1717-1778.)

9 "Upholding all things by the word of His power." C. M.
Isa. li. 4-16. Rev. xv. Job xxxvii.

1 THE Lord! how fearful is His name!
How wide is His command!
Nature, with all her moving frame,
Rests on His mighty hand.

2 A word of His almighty breath
Can swell or sink the seas;
Build the vast empires of the earth,
Or break them, as He please.

3 Immortal glory forms His throne,
And lights His awful robe;
Whilst with a smile, or with a frown,
He manages the globe.
Rev. Isaac Watts. (1674-1748.)

10 "He ruleth by His power forever." H. M.
Ps. xcii. Prov. viii. 22-31. Rev. iv.

1 THE Lord Jehovah reigns;
His throne is built on high;
The garments He assumes
Are light and majesty:
His glories shine with beams so bright,
No mortal eye can bear the sight.

2 The thunders of His hand
Keep the wide world in awe;
His wrath and justice stand
To guard His holy law;
And where His love resolves to bless,
His truth confirms and seals the grace.

3 Through all His ancient works
Surprising wisdom shines;
Confounds the powers of hell,
And breaks their cursed designs.
Strong is His arm, and shall fulfill
His great decrees, His sovereign will.
Rev. Isaac Watts.

"The eyes of the Lord are in every place."

11 "He that is perfect in knowledge."
Isa. xliv. 1-6. Jer. xxxii. 14-19. Heb. iv. 13

1 MIGHTY God, the First, the Last,
   What are ages in Thy sight
   But as yesterday when past,
   Or a watch within the night?

2 All that being ever knew,
   Down, far down, ere time had birth,
   Stands as clear within Thy view
   As the present things of earth.

3 In Thine all-embracing sight,
   Every change its purpose meets,
   Every cloud floats into light,
   Every woe its glory greets.

4 All that being e'er shall know,
   On, still on, through farthest years,
   All eternity can show,
   Bright before Thee now appears.
   Mrs. Elizabeth C. Gaskell. (1810-1855.)

12 "Thou art acquainted with all my ways." C. M.
Ps. cxxxix. Job xxxiv. 13-22. 1 John iii. 20.

1 IN all my vast concerns with Thee,
   In vain my soul would try
   To shun Thy presence, Lord, or flee
   The notice of Thine eye.

2 Thine all-surrounding sight surveys
   My rising and my rest,
   My public walks, my private ways,
   And secrets of my breast.

3 My thoughts lie open to the Lord,
   Before they're formed within;
   And ere my lips pronounce the word,
   He knows the sense I mean.

4 O wondrous knowledge, deep and high!
   Where can a creature hide?
   Within Thy circling arms I lie,
   Beset on every side.
   Rev. Isaac Watts. (1674-1748.)

13 "Thou knowest all things." L. M.
Ps. cviii. 1-6. 1 Chr. xxix. 10-18. Rev. xv. 1-4.

1 AWAKE, my tongue! thy tribute bring
   To Him who gave thee power to sing;
   Praise Him who is all praise above,
   The source of light, of truth, and love.

2 How vast His knowledge, how profound!
   A depth where all our thoughts are drowned;
   The stars He numbers, and their names
   He gives to all these heavenly flames.

3 Through each bright world above, behold
   Ten thousand thousand charms unfold;
   Earth, air, and mighty seas combine
   To speak his wisdom all-divine.
   Rev. John Needham. 1768.

14 "Thou art there." S. M.
Jer. xxiii. 16-24. Amos ix. 1-6. Mat. xviii. 20.

1 GOD of almighty power!
   How glorious are Thy ways!
   Angels Thy majesty adore,
   All creatures speak Thy praise.

2 Wherever earth is fair,
   Or brighter worlds extend,
   Almighty Sovereign, Thou art there,
   Creation's Lord and Friend.

3 Heaven is Thy glorious throne,
   Earth does Thy footstool seem;
   But souls redeemed Thou lov'st to own
   Thy richer diadem.

4 And while they bless Thy name,
   Hell trembles at Thy rod:
   Earth, heaven, and hell Thy power proclaim,
   All things proclaim Thee God!
   Author unknown. 1858.

15 "Whither shall I flee from Thy presence?" C. M.
Ps. cxlvii. 1 Kings xix. Acts xxvii.

1 JEHOVAH, God, Thy gracious power
   On every hand we see;
   O, may the blessings of each hour
   Lead all our thoughts to Thee.

2 If on the wings of morn we speed
   To earth's remotest bound,
   Thy hand will there our footsteps lead,
   Thy love our path surround.

3 Thy power is in the ocean deeps,
   And reaches to the skies;
   Thine eye of mercy never sleeps,
   Thy goodness never dies.

4 From morn till noon, till latest eve,
   Thy hand, O God, we see;
   And all the blessings we receive
   Proceed alone from Thee.
   Rev. John Thomson. (1782-1841.)

16 "I fill heaven and earth, saith the Lord." L. M.
Ps. xcvii. 1 Kings viii. 12-30. Eph. i. 23.

1 O DREADFUL glory that doth make
   Thick darkness round the heavenly throne,
   Through which no angel eye may break,
   Wherein the Lord doth dwell alone!

2 What secret place, what distant star,
   Is like, dread Lord, to Thine abode?
   Why dwellest Thou from us so far?
   We yearn for Thee, thou hidden God.

3 Vain searchers! but we need not mourn,
   We need not stretch our weary wings:
   Thou meetest us where'er we turn;
   Thou beamest, Lord, from all bright things!
   Thomas H. Gill. (1819-.)

"Thou only art holy."

17 "There is none holy as the Lord." **L. M.**
Ps. xcix. Heb. i. 12, 13. Mat. xix. 17.

1 HOLY as Thou, O Lord, is none;
Thy holiness is all Thine own;
A drop of that unbounded sea
Is ours, a drop derived from Thee.

2 And when thy purity we share,
Thine only glory we declare:
And, humbled into nothing, own,
Holy and pure is God alone.

3 Sole, self-existing God and Lord,
By all Thy heavenly hosts adored,
Let all on earth bow down to Thee,
And own Thy peerless majesty:

4 Thy power unparalleled confess,
Established on the Rock of peace;
The Rock that never shall remove,
The Rock of pure, almighty love.
Rev. Charles Wesley. (1708-1788.)

18 "Holy, holy, holy, is the Lord." **7.**
Rev. iv. 8-11. Isa. vi. Rom. xvi. 24-27.

1 HOLY, holy, holy Lord
God of hosts! when heaven and earth
Out of darkness, at Thy word,
Issued into glorious birth,
All Thy works before Thee stood,
And Thine eye beheld them good,
While they sang with sweet accord,
Holy, holy, holy Lord!

2 Holy, holy, holy! all
Heaven's triumphant choir shall sing,
When the ransomed nations fall
At the footstool of their King:
Then shall saints and seraphim,
Hearts and voices, swell one hymn,
Round the throne with full accord,
Holy, holy, holy Lord!
James Montgomery. (1771-1854.)

19 "Who is like Thee, glorious in holiness?" **C. M.**
Ex. xv. 1-11. Ps. cxlv. Rom. viii. 1-15.

1 O GOD, Thy power is wonderful,
Thy glory passing bright;
Thy wisdom, with its deep on deep,
A rapture to the sight.

2 Thy justice is the gladdest thing
Creation can behold;
Thy tenderness so meek, it wins
The guilty to be bold.

3 Yet more than all, and evermore,
Should we, Thy creatures, bless,
Most worshipful of attributes,
Thine awful holiness.
Rev. Frederick W. Faber. (1814-1863.)

20 "The heavens are not clean in His sight." **S. M.**
Ex. xix. 5-14. Deu. iv. 1-13. Rev. xv. 1-4.

1 EXALT the Lord our God,
And worship at His feet;
His nature is all holiness,
And mercy is His seat.

2 How holy is His name!
How terrible His praise!
Justice and truth and judgment join
In all His works of grace.

3 Exalt the Lord our God,
Whose grace is still the same;
Still He's a God of holiness,
And jealous for His name.
Rev. Isaac Watts. (1674-1748.)

21 "Holy and reverend is His name." **C. M.**
Ps. v. 1-8. Lev. xi. 44, 45. Mat. v. 8.

1 HOLY and reverend is the name
Of our eternal King:
"Thrice holy Lord!" the angels cry;
"Thrice holy!" let us sing.

2 The deepest reverence of the mind,
My soul, pay to thy God;
Lift, with thy hands, a holy heart,
To His sublime abode.

3 With sacred awe pronounce His name,
Whom words nor thoughts can reach;
A broken heart shall please Him more
Than the best forms of speech.

4 Thou holy God! preserve my soul
From all pollution free;
The pure in heart are Thy delight,
And they Thy face shall see.
Rev. John Needham. 1708.

22 "Thou art of purer eyes than to behold evil." **C. M.**
Job xxvi. Ps. cxlvii. Rev. v.

1 My God, how wonderful Thou art,
Thy majesty how bright;
How beautiful Thy mercy-seat
In depths of burning light.

2 How dread are Thine eternal years,
O Everlasting Lord;
By prostrate spirits day and night
Incessantly adored.

3 How beautiful, how beautiful,
The sight of Thee must be,
Thine endless wisdom, boundless power,
And awful purity.

4 Father of Jesus, love's reward,
What rapture will it be,
Prostrate before Thy throne to lie
And gaze, and gaze on Thee.
Rev. Frederick W. Faber.

"Just and true are Thy ways."

23 "Thou art just in all that is brought upon us." **L. M.**
Ps. xxv. 1-6. Isa. xlv. 5-19. John xiii. 3-11.

1 WAIT, O my soul, thy Maker's will,
Tumultuous passions, all be still,
Nor let a murmuring thought arise;
His ways are just, His counsels wise.

2 He in the thickest darkness dwells,
Performs His work, the cause conceals;
And though His footsteps are unknown,
Judgment and truth support His throne.

3 In heaven and earth, in air and seas,
He executes His wise decrees;
And by His saints it stands confessed
That what He does is ever best.

4 Then, O my soul, submissive wait;
With reverence bow before His seat;
And midst the terrors of His rod,
Trust in a wise and gracious God.
Rev. Benjamin Beddome. (1717-1705.)

24 "The Lord is righteous in all His ways." **L. M.**
Deu. x. 12-18. Job xxxvii. 10-23. Rev. xv.

1 JUST are Thy ways, and true Thy word,
Great Rock of my secure abode;
Who is a God beside the Lord?
Or where's a Refuge like our God?

2 'T is He that girds me with His might,
Gives me His holy sword to wield;
And while with sin and hell I fight,
Spreads His salvation for my shield.

3 He lives, and blessings crown His reign;
The God of my salvation lives;
The dark designs of hell are vain,
While heavenly peace my Father gives.
Rev. Isaac Watts. (1674-1748.)

25 "A God of truth, just and right is He." **L. M.**
Ps. xcvii. Gen. xviii. 20-33. Mat. xx. 1-16.

1 JEHOVAH reigns! let all the earth
In His just government rejoice;
Let all the isles, with sacred mirth,
In His applause unite their voice.

2 Darkness and clouds of awful shade
His dazzling glory shroud in state;
Judgment and righteousness are made
The habitation of His seat.

3 The seeds are sown of glorious light,
A future harvest for the just;
And gladness for the heart that's right,
To recompense its pious trust.

4 Rejoice, ye righteous, in the Lord;
Memorials of His holiness
Deep in your faithful breasts record,
And with your thankful tongues confess.
Tate and Brady. 1696.

26 "The paths of the Lord are mercy and truth." **L. M.**
Ps. lxxxix. Ex. xxxiv. 1-7. Rom. xi 26-36.

1 THINE, Lord, is wisdom, Thine alone;
Justice and truth before Thee stand;
Yet, nearer to Thy sacred throne,
Mercy withholds Thy lifted hand.

2 Each evening shows Thy tender love,
Each rising morn Thy plenteous grace;
Thy wakened wrath doth slowly move,
Thy willing mercy flies apace.

3 To Thy benign, indulgent care,
Father, this light, this breath, we owe;
And all we have, and all we are,
From Thee, great Source of being, flow.

4 Thrice Holy, Thine the kingdom is,
The power omnipotent is Thine;
And when created nature dies,
Thy never-ceasing glories shine.
Ernest Lange. (1650-1727.)
Tr. by Rev. John Wesley. (1703-1791.)

27 "The Lord, abundant in goodness and truth." **L. M.**
Ex. xxxiii. 12-23. Ps. xxxvi. 1 Tim. vi. 13-17.

1 HIGH in the heavens, eternal God,
Thy goodness in full glory shines;
Thy truth shall break through every cloud
That veils and darkens Thy designs.

2 Forever firm Thy justice stands,
As mountains their foundations keep;
Wise are the wonders of Thy hands;
Thy judgments are a mighty deep.

3 My God, how excellent Thy grace,
Whence all our hope and comfort springs!
The sons of Adam, in distress,
Fly to the shadow of Thy wings.

4 Life, like a fountain rich and free,
Springs from the presence of the Lord;
And, in Thy light, our souls shall see
The glories promised in Thy word.
Rev. Isaac Watts.

28 "The goodness of God endureth forever." **C. M.**
Ps. cvii. Jer. l. 1-20. Luke x. 21-37.

1 LET every tongue Thy goodness speak,
Thou sovereign Lord of all!
Thy strengthening hands uphold the weak,
And raise the poor that fall.

2 The Lord supports our tottering days,
And guides our giddy youth:
Holy and just are all His ways,
And all His words are truth.

3 His mercy never shall remove
From men of heart sincere;
He saves the souls whose humble love
Is joined with holy fear.
Rev. Isaac Watts.

"In this was manifested the love of God."

29 Ps. cvii. 1-9. "God is love." Deu. viii. 2, 3. Mat. vi. 25-34. **L. M.**

1 GIVE thanks to God, He reigns above;
  Kind are His thoughts, His name is Love;
  His mercy ages past have known,
  And ages long to come shall own.

2 He feeds and clothes us all the way,
  He guides our footsteps lest we stray;
  He guards us with a powerful hand,
  And brings us to the heavenly land.

3 O, let the saints with joy record
  The truth and goodness of the Lord:
  How great His works, how kind His ways!
  Let every tongue pronounce His praise.
  Rev. Isaac Watts. (1674-1748.)

30 1 John iv. 7-21. "The Lord God, merciful and gracious." Rom. xi. 33-36. Ex. xxxiii. 12-23. **8, 7.**

1 GOD is love; His mercy brightens
  All the path in which we rove;
  Bliss He wakes, and woe He lightens:
  God is wisdom, God is love.

2 Chance and change are busy ever;
  Man decays and ages move;
  But His mercy waneth never:
  God is wisdom, God is love.

3 E'en the hour that darkest seemeth
  Will His changeless goodness prove;
  From the mist His brightness streameth:
  God is wisdom, God is love.

4 He with earthly cares entwineth
  Hope and comfort from above;
  Everywhere His glory shineth:
  God is wisdom, God is love.
  Sir John Bowring. (1792-1872.)

31 Ps. ciii. "God ready to pardon, gracious and merciful." Micah vii. 18-20. Heb. viii. **L. M.**

1 THE Lord, how wondrous are His ways!
  How firm His truth, how large His grace!
  He takes His mercy for His throne,
  And thence He makes His glories known.

2 Not half so high His power hath spread
  The starry heavens above our head,
  As His rich love exceeds our praise,
  Exceeds the highest hopes we raise.

3 Not half so far hath nature placed
  The rising morning from the west,
  As His forgiving grace removes
  The daily guilt of those He loves.

4 But His eternal love is sure
  To all the saints, and shall endure:
  From age to age His truth shall reign;
  Nor children's children hope in vain.
  Rev. Isaac Watts.

32 Neh. ix. 7-17. "An everlasting love." Jonah iii. 2 Peter ii. 9. **C. M.**

1 THY ceaseless, unexhausted love,
  Unmerited and free,
  Delights our evil to remove,
  And help our misery.

2 Thou waitest to be gracious still;
  Thou dost with sinners bear;
  That, saved, we may Thy goodness feel,
  And all Thy grace declare.

3 Faithful, O Lord, Thy mercies are,
  A rock that cannot move:
  A thousand promises declare
  Thy constancy of love.
  Rev. Charles Wesley. (1708-1788.)

33 Ps. xcv. "God commendeth his love toward us." Eph. ii. 4-10. Ex. xxxiv. 1-7. **C. M.**

1 COME, ye that know and fear the Lord,
  And lift your souls above;
  Let every heart and voice accord,
  To sing that God is love.

2 This precious truth His word declares,
  And all His mercies prove;
  Jesus, the Gift of gifts, appears,
  To show that God is love.

3 Behold His patience lengthened out
  To those who from him rove,
  And calls effectual reach their hearts,
  To teach them God is love.

4 The work begun is carried on
  By power from heaven above;
  And every step, from first to last,
  Declares that God is love.
  Rev. George Burder. (1752-1832.)

34 Ps. lxix. 16-36. "The Father Himself loveth you." Lam. iii. John iii. 14-18. **8, 4.**

1 I CANNOT always trace the way
  Where Thou, Almighty One, dost move;
  But I can always, always say
  That God is love.

2 When fear her chilling mantle throws
  O'er earth, my soul to heaven above,
  As to her native home, upsprings,
  For God is love.

3 When mystery clouds my darkened path,
  I'll check my dread, my doubts reprove;
  In this my soul sweet comfort hath,
  That God is love.

4 Yes, God is love: a thought like this
  Can every gloomy thought remove,
  And turn all tears, all woes, to bliss,
  For God is love.
  Author unknown.

"The works of the Lord are great."

35 "Understood by the things that are made." **C. M.**
Ps. cxlvii. Gen. i. Heb. xi. 3.

1 ETERNAL Wisdom! Thee we praise,
Thee the creation sings;
With Thy loved name rocks, hills, and seas,
And heaven's high palace rings.

2 Thy hand, how wide it spread the sky!
How glorious to behold!
Tinged with a blue of heavenly dye,
And starred with sparkling gold.

3 Thy glories blaze all nature round,
And strike the gazing sight,
Through skies, and seas, and solid ground,
With terror and delight.

4 Infinite strength and equal skill
Shine through the worlds abroad;
Our souls with vast amazement fill,
And speak the builder, God.
Rev. Isaac Watts. (1674-1748.)

36 "God that made the world, and all things therein." **L. M.**
Ps. xix. Isa. xl. 12-31. Rom. i. 19, 20.

1 THE spacious firmament on high,
With all the blue ethereal sky,
And spangled heavens, a shining frame,
Their great Original proclaim.

2 Th' unwearied sun, from day to day,
Does his Creator's power display,
And publishes to every land
The work of an almighty hand.

3 Soon as the evening shades prevail,
The moon takes up the wondrous tale;
And nightly, to the listening earth,
Repeats the story of her birth:

4 Whilst all the stars that round her burn,
And all the planets in their turn,
Confirm the tidings as they roll,
And spread the truth from pole to pole.
Joseph Addison. (1672-1719.)

37 "I know that Thou canst do everything." **C. M.**
Job xxvi. Ps. cxxxvi. 1-9. Rev. x.

1 GREAT Ruler of all nature's frame,
We own Thy power divine;
We hear Thy breath in every storm,
For all the winds are Thine.

2 Wide as they sweep their sounding way,
They work Thy sovereign will;
And, awed by Thy majestic voice,
Confusion shall be still.

3 Thy mercy tempers every blast
To them that seek Thy face,
And mingles with the tempest's roar
The whispers of Thy grace.
Rev. Philip Doddridge. (1702-1751.)

38 "Lo, all these things worketh God." **L. M.**
Job viii. 3-22. Josh. xxiii. Rev. iii. 7-12.

1 O LORD, Thy mercy, my sure hope,
The highest orb of heaven transcends;
Thy sacred truth's unmeasured scope
Beyond the spreading sky extends.

2 Thy justice like the hills remains,
Unfathomed depths Thy judgments are;
Thy providence the world sustains,
The whole creation is Thy care.

3 Since of Thy goodness all partake,
With what assurance should the just
Thy sheltering wings their refuge make,
And saints to Thy protection trust.

4 Such guests shall to Thy courts be led,
To banquet on Thy love's repast;
And drink, as from a fountain's head,
Of joys that shall forever last.
Tate and Brady. 1696.

39 "God which worketh all in all." **C. M.**
Ps. lxxiv. 12-17. Job xxxvi. Acts xiv. 8-17.

1 THE Lord our God is Lord of all;
His station who can find?
I hear Him in the waterfall,
I hear Him in the wind.

2 He lives, He reigns, in every land,
From winter's polar snows
To where, across the burning sand,
The blazing meteor goes.

3 If in the gloom of night I shroud,
His face I cannot fly;
I see Him in the evening cloud,
And in the morning sky.

4 He bids His blasts the fields deform;
Then when His thunders cease,
He paints His rainbow on the storm,
And lulls the winds to peace.
Henry K. White. (1785-1806.)

40 "He hath shewed . . . the power of His works." **C. M.**
Ps. xlvii. 1 Kings xviii. 30-46. Acts xvii. 22-31.

1 GOD, in the high and holy place,
Looks down upon the spheres;
Yet, in His providence and grace,
To every eye appears.

2 He bows the heavens; the mountains stand
A highway for our God;
He walks amidst the desert land;
'Tis Eden where He trod.

3 The forests in His strength rejoice;
Hark! on the evening breeze,
As once of old, Jehovah's voice
Is heard among the trees.
James Montgomery. (1777-1854.)

"He that keepeth Israel."

41 "God is our refuge and strength."   **L. M.**
Ps. xlvi. Isa. xxxii. Rev. xxii. 1-5.

1 GOD is the Refuge of His saints,
   When storms of sharp distress invade;
   Ere we can offer our complaints,
   Behold Him present with His aid.

2 Let mountains from their seats be hurled
   Down to the deep, and buried there;
   Convulsions shake the solid world;
   Our faith shall never yield to fear.

3 Loud may the troubled ocean roar,
   In sacred peace our souls abide;
   While every nation, every shore,
   Trembles, and dreads the swelling tide.

4 There is a stream, whose gentle flow
   Supplies the city of our God;
   Life, love, and joy still gliding through,
   And watering our divine abode.
                 Rev. Isaac Watts. (1674-1748.)

42 "His work is perfect."   **L. M.**
Ps. xcix. Job xxvi. Acts xvii. 22-31.

1 JEHOVAH reigns: His throne is high,
   His robes are light and majesty;
   His glory shines with beams so bright,
   No mortal can sustain the sight.

2 His terrors keep the world in awe,
   His justice guards His holy law;
   His love reveals a smiling face,
   His truth and promise seal the grace.

3 Through all His works His wisdom shines,
   And baffles Satan's deep designs;
   His power is sovereign to fulfil
   The noblest counsels of His will.
                 Rev. Isaac Watts.

43 "The Lord, He is my fortress."   **8. 7.**
Ps. xci. 2 Sam. xxii. 17-33. Jude 20-25.

1 CALL Jehovah thy salvation,
   Rest beneath th' Almighty's shade;
   In His secret habitation
   Dwell, and never be dismayed.
   There no tumult can alarm thee,
   Thou shalt dread no hidden snare;
   Guile nor violence can harm thee,
   In eternal safeguard there.

2 From the sword, at noonday wasting,
   From the noisome pestilence,
   In the depth of midnight, blasting,
   God shall be thy sure defence:
   Since, with pure and warm affection,
   Thou on God hast set thy love,
   With the wings of His protection,
   He will shield thee from above.
                 James Montgomery. (1771-1854.)

44 "The Lord is thy keeper."   **L. M.**
Ps. cxxi. Jer. iii. 12-23. 2 Cor. i. 1-20.

1 UP to the hills I lift mine eyes,
   Th' eternal hills beyond the skies;
   Thence all her help my soul derives,
   There my Almighty Refuge lives.

2 He guides our feet, He guards our way,
   His morning smiles bless all the day;
   He spreads the evening veil, and keeps
   The silent hours while Israel sleeps.

3 Israel, a name divinely blest,
   May rise secure, securely rest;
   Thy holy Guardian's wakeful eyes
   Admit no slumber, nor surprise.
                 Rev. Isaac Watts.

45 "The floods lift up their waves."   **L. M.**
Ps. xciii. Eze. xxviii. 24-26. Rev. xv.

1 THE floods, O Lord, lift up their voice,
   The mighty floods lift up their roar;
   The floods in tumult loud rejoice,
   And climb in foam the sounding shore.

2 But mightier than the mighty sea,
   The Lord of glory reigns on high:
   Far o'er its waves we look to Thee,
   And see their fury break and die.
                 Bp. George Burgess. (1809-1855.)

46 "His ways past finding out."   **C. M.**
Job ix. 1-12. Ps. lxxvii. John xi.

1 GOD moves in a mysterious way
   His wonders to perform;
   He plants His footsteps in the sea,
   And rides upon the storm.
   Deep in unfathomable mines
   Of never-failing skill,
   He treasures up His bright designs,
   And works His sovereign will.

2 Ye fearful saints, fresh courage take:
   The clouds ye so much dread
   Are big with mercy, and shall break
   In blessings on your head.
   Judge not the Lord by feeble sense,
   But trust Him for His grace;
   Behind a frowning providence
   He hides a smiling face.

3 His purposes will ripen fast,
   Unfolding every hour;
   The bud may have a bitter taste,
   But sweet will be the flower.
   Blind unbelief is sure to err,
   And scan His work in vain;
   God is His own interpreter,
   And He will make it plain.
                 William Cowper. (1731-1800.)

"The same yesterday, and to=day, and forever."

47 "Thou art the same."   **C. M.**
Ps. cii. 11-28. Isa. li. 4-16. 2 Pet. iii. 5-14.

1 THROUGH endless years Thou art the same,
   O Thou eternal God ;
Ages to come shall know Thy name,
   And tell Thy works abroad.

2 Soon shall this goodly frame of things,
   Formed by Thy powerful hand,
Be, like a vesture, laid aside,
   And changed at Thy command.

3 But Thy perfections, all divine,
   Eternal as Thy days,
Through everlasting ages shine,
   With undiminished rays.

4 Our children's children, still Thy care,
   Shall own their fathers' God ;
To latest times Thy favor share,
   And spread Thy praise abroad.
Tate and Brady. 1696.

48 "I am the Lord, I change not."   **L. M.**
1 Tim. vi 15, 16. Ps. xciii. Heb. i. 1-12.

1 JEHOVAH reigns ! He dwells in light,
Girded with majesty and might :
The world, created by His hands,
Still on its first foundation stands.

2 But ere this spacious world was made,
Or had its first foundation laid,
Thy throne eternal ages stood,
Thyself the ever-living God.

3 Forever shall Thy throne endure ;
Thy promise stands forever sure ;
And everlasting holiness
Becomes the dwellings of Thy grace.
Rev. Isaac Watts. (1674-1748.)

49 "He will ever be mindful of His covenant."   **L. M.**
Ps. cxxxvi. 1 Chr. xvi. 8-36. James i. 17.

1 LORD of all being, throned afar,
Thy glory flames from sun and star ;
Centre and soul of every sphere,
Yet to each loving heart how near.

2 Sun of our life, Thy quickening ray
Sheds on our path the glow of day ;
Star of our hope, Thy softened light
Cheers the long watches of the night.

3 Our midnight is Thy smile withdrawn ;
Our noontide is Thy gracious dawn ;
Our rainbow arch Thy mercy's sign ;
All, save the clouds of sin, are Thine.

4 Lord of all life, below, above,
Whose light is truth, whose warmth is love,
Before Thy ever-blazing throne
We ask no lustre of our own.
Oliver W. Holmes. (1809--.)

50 "From everlasting to everlasting, Thou art God."   **C. M.**
Ps. xc. Deu. xxxiii. 26-29. 2 Thes. ii. 16, 17.

1 OUR God, our Help in ages past,
   Our Hope for years to come ;
Our Shelter from the stormy blast,
   And our eternal Home :

2 A thousand ages in Thy sight
   Are like an evening gone ;
Short as the watch that ends the night,
   Before the rising sun.

3 Under the shadow of Thy throne
   Thy saints have dwelt secure ;
Sufficient is Thine arm alone,
   And our defence is sure.

4 Before the hills in order stood,
   Or earth received her frame,
From everlasting Thou art God,
   To endless years the same.
Rev. Isaac Watts.

51 "With whom is no variableness."   **L. M.**
Ex. iii. 1-15. Ps. civ. Rev. xxii. 1-5.

1 WHAT is our God, or what His name,
Nor men can learn, nor angels teach ;
He dwells concealed in radiant flame,
Where neither eye nor thought can reach.

2 The spacious worlds of heavenly light.
Compared with Him, how short they fall !
They are too dark, and He too bright ;
Nothing are they, and God is all.

3 He spake the wondrous word, and lo !
Creation rose at His command ;
Whirlwinds and seas their limits know,
Bound in the hollow of His hand.

4 The tide of creatures ebbs and flows,
Measuring their changes by the moon :
No ebb His sea of glory knows ;
His age is one eternal noon.
Rev. Isaac Watts.

52 "The faithful God, which keepeth covenant."   **L. M.**
Ps. xlv. Hab. iii. Titus i. 1-3.

1 WITH glory clad, with strength arrayed,
The Lord that o'er all nature reigns,
The world's foundation strongly laid,
And the vast fabric still sustains.

2 How surely stablished is thy throne,
Which shall no change or period see !
For Thou, O Lord, and Thou alone,
Art God from all eternity.

3 Thy promise, Lord, is ever sure,
And they that in thy house would dwell,
That happy station to secure,
Must still in holiness excel.
Tate and Brady. 1696.

"Emmanuel."

53 "The Lord of hosts is with us." 7.
Isa. vii. 14. Mat. i. 23. 1 Tim. iii. 16 John i. 1.

1 GOD with us! O glorious name!
  Let it shine in endless fame;
  God and man in Christ unite;
  O mysterious depth and height!

2 God with us! amazing love
  Brought Him from His courts above;
  Now, ye saints, His grace admire,
  Swell the song with holy fire.

3 God with us! but tainted not
  With our father Adam's blot;
  Yet did He our sins sustain,
  Bear the guilt, the curse, the pain.

4 God with us! O wondrous grace!
  Let us see Him face to face;
  That we may Immanuel sing,
  As we ought, our God and King.
  Miss Sarah Slinn. 1770.

54 "There shall come out of Sion the Deliverer." C. M.
Isa. lxi. Luke iv. 1-21. Mal. iii. 1-6.

1 HARK, the glad sound! the Saviour comes,
  The Saviour promised long;
  Let every heart prepare a throne,
  And every voice a song.

2 On Him the Spirit, largely poured,
  Exerts His sacred fire;
  Wisdom and might, and zeal and love,
  His holy breast inspire.

3 He comes the pris'ners to release,
  In Satan's bondage held;
  The gates of brass before Him burst,
  The iron fetters yield.

4 He comes, from thickest films of vice
  To clear the mental ray;
  And on the eyeballs of the blind
  To pour celestial day.

5 He comes the broken heart to bind,
  The bleeding soul to cure:
  And with the treasures of His grace
  T' enrich the humble poor.

6 Our glad hosannas, Prince of Peace,
  Thy welcome shall proclaim,
  And heaven's eternal arches ring
  With Thy belovéd name.
  Rev. Philip Doddridge. (1702-1751.)

55 "Which was the Son of God." 7.
Luke ii. 1-14. Isa. ix. 6-7. Rev. v. 11-14.

1 BRIGHT and joyful is the morn,
  For to us a Child is born;
  From the highest realms of heaven
  Unto us a Son is given.
  On His shoulder He shall bear
  Power and majesty, and wear
  On His vesture and His thigh
  Names most awful, names most high.

2 Wonderful in counsel, He,
  The incarnate Deity,
  Sire of ages ne'er to cease,
  King of kings and Prince of Peace.
  Come and worship at His feet,
  Yield to Christ the homage meet;
  From His manger to His throne,
  Homage due to God alone.
  James Montgomery. (1771-1854.)

56 "Unto us a child is born." C. M.
Ps. lxxii. Dan. ii. 44. Luke i. 32, 33.

1 To us a Child of hope is born,
  To us a Son is given;
  Him shall the tribes of earth obey,
  Him all the hosts of heaven.

2 His name shall be the Prince of Peace,
  For evermore adored;
  The Wonderful, the Counsellor,
  The great and mighty Lord.

3 His power, increasing, still shall spread,
  His reign no end shall know;
  Justice shall guard His throne above,
  And peace abound below.
  Rev. John Morrison. (1749-1798.)

57 "Make a joyful noise unto the Lord." S. M.
Ps. xcviii. Rev. xi. 15-17. Mat. xxi. 1-16.

1 REJOICE in Jesus' birth,
  To us a Son is given;
  To us a Child is born on earth,
  Who made both earth and heaven.

2 He reigns above the sky,
  This universe sustains;
  The God supreme, the Lord most high,
  The king Messiah reigns.

3 The mighty God is He,
  Author of heavenly bliss,
  The Father of eternity,
  The glorious Prince of Peace.

4 His government shall grow,
  From strength to strength proceed,
  His righteousness the church o'erflow,
  And all the earth o'erspread.
  Rev. Charles Wesley. (1708-1788.)

"Emmanuel."

58 "The heavenly host praising God." 8, 7.
Luke ii. 1-14. Isa. ix. 1-7. Rev. xix. 11-16.

1 HARK, what mean those holy voices,
　　Sweetly warbling in the skies?
　Sure th' angelic host rejoices,
　　Loudest hallelujahs rise.

2 Listen to the wondrous story,
　　Which they chant in hymns of joy:
　"Glory in the highest, glory,
　　Glory be to God most high.

3 "Peace on earth, good-will from heaven,
　　Reaching far as man is found;
　Souls redeemed, and sins forgiven,
　　Loud our golden harps shall sound.

4 "Christ is born, the great Anointed;
　　Heaven and earth His glory sing:
　Glad receive whom God appointed
　　For your Prophet, Priest, and King.

5 "Hasten, mortals, to adore Him;
　　Learn His name and taste His joy:
　Till in heaven you sing before Him,
　　'Glory be to God most high.'"
　　　　　　　　Rev. John Cawood. (1775-1852.)

60 "God with us." 7.
Heb. i. 1-6. Micah v. 2, 3. Mal. iv. 2.

1 HARK, the herald angels sing:
　"Glory to the new-born King!
　Peace on earth, and mercy mild,
　God and sinners reconciled!"

2 Joyful, all ye nations, rise,
　Join the triumph of the skies;
　Universal nature, say,
　"Christ, the Lord, is born to-day!"

3 Veiled in flesh, the Godhead see,
　Hail th' incarnate Deity!
　Pleased as man with men t' appear,
　Jesus, our Immanuel here!

4 Hail the heavenly Prince of Peace,
　Hail the Sun of Righteousness!
　Light and life to all He brings,
　Risen with healing in His wings.

5 Mild He lays His glory by,
　Born that man no more may die;
　Born to raise the sons of earth,
　Born to give them second birth.
　　　　　　　　Rev. Charles Wesley. (1708-1788.)

59 "Glory to God in the highest." C. M.
Isa. xlix. 13. Micah iv. 1-7. Rev. xxi. 1-4.

1 IT came upon the midnight clear,
　　That glorious song of old,
　From angels bending near the earth,
　　To touch their harps of gold:
　"Peace on the earth, good-will to men
　　From heaven's all-gracious King."
　The world in solemn stillness lay
　　To hear the angels sing.

2 Still through the cloven skies they come,
　　With peaceful wings unfurled;
　And still their heavenly music floats
　　O'er all the weary world:
　Above its sad and lowly plains
　　They bend on hovering wing,
　And ever o'er its Babel sounds
　　The blessed angels sing.

3 For lo, the days are hastening on,
　　By prophet bards foretold,
　When with the ever-circling years
　　Comes round the age of gold:
　When peace shall over all the earth
　　Its ancient splendors fling,
　And the whole world give back the song
　　Which now the angels sing.
　　　　　　　　Rev. Edmund H. Sears. (1810-1876.)

61 "On earth peace, good-will toward men." C. M.
Mat. ii. 1-10. Luke ii. 25-32. Isa. xliv. 23.

1 CALM on the listening ear of night
　　Come heaven's melodious strains,
　Where wild Judea stretches far
　　Her silver-mantled plains.
　Celestial choirs from courts above
　　Shed sacred glories there;
　And angels, with their sparkling lyres,
　　Make music on the air.

2 Glory to God! the lofty strain
　　The realm of ether fills;
　How sweeps the song of solemn joy
　　O'er Judah's sacred hills!
　"Glory to God!" the sounding skies
　　Loud with their anthems ring:
　"Peace on the earth, good-will to men,
　　From heaven's eternal King."

3 This day shall Christian tongues be mute,
　　And Christian hearts be cold?
　O, catch the anthem that from heaven
　　O'er Judah's mountains rolled,
　When nightly burst from seraph-harps
　　The high and solemn lay,
　"Glory to God, on earth be peace;
　　Salvation comes to-day!"
　　　　　　　　Rev. Edmund H. Sears.

"The Word was God ... and the Word was made flesh."

62 "In the beginning was the Word." **L. M.**
John i. 1–14. Gen. i. 1–5. 1 Pet. i. 1–12.

1 ERE the blue heavens were stretched abroad,
From everlasting was the Word;
With God He was, the Word was God,
And must divinely be adored.

2 By His own power were all things made;
By Him supported, all things stand:
He is the whole creation's head,
And angels fly at His command.

3 But lo, He leaves those heavenly forms;
The Word descends and dwells in clay,
That He may hold converse with worms,
Dressed in such feeble flesh as they.

4 Mortals with joy beheld His face,
Th' eternal Father's only Son;
How full of truth, how full of grace,
When through His eyes the Godhead shone.

5 Archangels leave their high abode,
To learn new mysteries here, and tell
The love of our descending God,
The glories of Immanuel.

Rev. Isaac Watts. (1074-1748.)

63 "Before Abraham was, I am." **7. 6.**
Prov. viii. 22–31. Ps. ii. Col. i. 12 to ii. 10.

1 ERE God had built the mountains,
Or raised the fruitful hills,
Before He filled the fountains
That feed the running rills,
In me from everlasting
The wonderful I AM
Found pleasures never wasting,
And Wisdom is my name.

2 When like a tent to dwell in,
He spread the skies abroad,
And swathed about the swelling
Of ocean's mighty flood,
He wrought by weight and measure,
And I was with Him then;
Myself the Father's pleasure,
And mine the sons of men.

3 Thus wisdom's words discover
Thy glory and Thy grace,
Thou Everlasting Lover
Of our unworthy race.
Thy gracious eyes surveyed us
Ere stars were seen above;
In wisdom Thou hast made us,
And died for us in love.

William Cowper. (1731-1800.)

64 "Yet He opened not His mouth." **L. M.**
1 Pet. ii. 21–25. Ps. xxii. 23–31. Heb. v. 1–8.

1 How beauteous were the marks divine
That in Thy meekness used to shine,
That lit Thy lonely pathway, trod
In wondrous love, O Son of God!

2 O, who like Thee, so mild, so bright,
Thou Son of man, Thou Light of light,
O, who like Thee did ever go,
So patient, through a world of woe?

3 O, who like Thee so humbly bore
The scorn, the scoffs, of men before;
So meek, so lowly, yet so high,
So glorious in humility?

4 And death, that sets the prisoner free,
Was pang and scoff and scorn to Thee;
Yet love through all Thy torture glowed,
And mercy with Thy life-blood flowed.

Bp. Arthur C. Coxe. (1818—.)

65 "And took upon Him the form of a servant." **C. M.**
Isa. liii. Rom. v. 6–21. Lam. iii. 1–21.

1 How condescending and how kind
Was God's eternal Son!
Our misery reached His heavenly mind,
And pity brought Him down.

2 He sunk beneath our heavy woes
To raise us to His throne;
There's ne'er a gift His hand bestows
But cost His heart a groan.

3 This was compassion like a God,
That when the Saviour knew
The price of pardon was His blood,
His pity ne'er withdrew.

4 Now, though He reigns exalted high,
His love is still as great;
Well He remembers Calvary,
Nor lets His saints forget.

Rev. Isaac Watts.

66 "There is none like unto Thee." **C. M.**
John vi. 38–51. Luke xxiii. 33–46. Ps. xl. 7, 8.

1 O LORD, when we the path retrace
Which Thou on earth hast trod,
To man Thy wondrous love and grace,
Thy faithfulness to God;

2 Thy love, by man so sorely tried,
Proved stronger than the grave:
The very spear that pierced Thy side
Drew forth the blood to save. ·

3 Faithful amidst unfaithfulness,
Midst darkness only light,
Thou didst Thy Father's name confess,
And in His will delight.

James G. Deck. (1808—.)

"Who went about doing good and healing."

67 "Who did no sin." C. M.
John xiii. 1-15. Mat. xxvii. 1-31. Ps. xxii.

1 BEHOLD where, in the Friend of man,
Appears each grace divine;
The virtues, all in Jesus met,
With mildest radiance shine.

2 To spread the rays of heavenly light,
To give the mourner joy,
To preach glad tidings to the poor,
Was His divine employ.

3 Midst keen reproach and cruel scorn,
Patient and meek He stood.
His foes, ungrateful, sought His life;
He labored for their good.

4 In the last hour of deep distress,
Before His Father's throne,
With soul resigned, He bowed, and said,
"Thy will, not Mine, be done!"
Rev. William Enfield. (1741-1797.)

68 "A man of sorrows and acquainted with grief." C. M.
Mat. viii. 19, 20. Ps. xxxviii. John xix. 38-42.

1 A PILGRIM through this lonely world,
The blesséd Saviour passed;
A mourner all His life was He,
A dying Lamb at last.

2 That tender heart that felt for all,
For all its life-blood gave;
It found on earth no resting-place,
Save only in the grave.

3 Dead to the world with Him who died
To win our hearts, our love,
We, risen with our risen Head,
In spirit dwell above.
Sir Edward Denny. (1796-.)

69 "He had done no violence" L. M.
Isa. liii. 7. Luke xxii. 47-53. John iv. 27-34.

1 WHENE'ER the angry passions rise,
And tempt our thoughts or tongues to strife,
To Jesus let us lift our eyes,
Bright pattern of the Christian life.

2 O how benevolent and kind!
How mild, how ready to forgive!
Be this the temper of our mind,
And these the rules by which we live.

3 To do His heavenly Father's will
Was His employment and delight;
Humility and holy zeal
Shone through His life, divinely bright.

4 Dispensing good where'er He came,
The labors of His life were love:
O, if we love the Saviour's name,
Let His divine example move.
Miss Anne Steele. (1717-1778.)

70 "Grace is poured into Thy lips." L. M.
Luke iv. 16-22. Isa. lxi. Prov. viii.

1 How sweetly flowed the gospel's sound
From lips of gentleness and grace,
When listening thousands gathered round,
And joy and reverence filled the place.

2 From heaven He came, of heaven He spoke,
To heaven He led His followers' way;
Dark clouds of gloomy night He broke,
Unveiling an immortal day.

3 "Come, wanderers, to my Father's home;
Come, all ye weary ones, and rest:"
Yes, sacred Teacher, we will come,
Obey Thee, love Thee, and be blest.

4 Decay, then, tenements of dust!
Pillars of earthly pride, decay!
A nobler mansion waits the just,
And Jesus has prepared the way.
Sir John Bowring. (1792-1872.)

71 "To comfort all that mourn." L. M.
Luke xvii. 11-19. Mat. xv. 21-31. Isa. xxvi. 1-12.

1 WHEN, like a stranger on our sphere,
The lowly Jesus sojourned here,
Where'er He went affliction fled,
And sickness reared her drooping head.

2 His touch the outcast leper healed,
His lips the sinner's pardon sealed;
The palsied frame, the crippled limb,
Felt virtue going forth from Him.

3 Through paths of loving kindness brought,
May all our work in Him be wrought;
In His great name, let us dispense
The crumbs of our benevolence.
James Montgomery. (1771-1854.)

72 "He that is mighty hath done ... great things." L. M.
Mat. xi. 1-6. Luke xxiii. 44-56. Ps. xxiv. 7-10.

1 BEHOLD! the blind their sight receive;
Behold! the dead awake and live;
The dumb speak wonders, and the lame
Leap, like the hart, and bless His name.

2 Thus doth th' eternal Spirit own
And seal the mission of the Son;
The Father vindicates His cause,
While He hangs bleeding on the cross.

3 He dies! the heavens in mourning stood;
He rises, the triumphant God!
Behold the Lord ascending high,
No more to bleed, no more to die!

4 Hence, and forever, from my heart,
I bid my doubts and fears depart;
And to those hands my soul resign
Which bear credentials so divine.
Rev. Isaac Watts. (1674-1748.)

"He was oppressed and He was afflicted."

73 "Sorrowful even unto death." 7.
Mark xiv. 32-42. 1 Pet. iv. 12-14. Lam. iii. 55-66.

1 MANY woes had Christ endured,
   Many sore temptations met,
Patient and to pains inured ;
   But the sorest trial yet
Was to be sustained in thee,
   Gloomy, sad Gethsemane.

2 Came at length the dreadful night ;
   Vengeance, with its iron rod,
Stood, and with collected might
   Bruised the harmless Lamb of God.
See, my soul, thy Saviour see,
   Prostrate in Gethsemane.
Rev. Joseph Hart. (1712-1768.)

74 "A place called Gethsemane." 8. 6.
John xviii. 1, 2. Mat. xxvi. 36-46. Ps. lxxxviii.

1 BEYOND where Kidron's waters flow,
   Behold the suffering Saviour go
     To sad Gethsemane !
His countenance is all divine,
Yet grief appears in every line.

2 He bows beneath the sins of men,
He cries to God, and cries again,
     In sad Gethsemane ;
He lifts His mournful eyes above,
"My Father, can this cup remove ?"

3 With gentle resignation still,
He yielded to His Father's will,
     In sad Gethsemane ;
"Behold Me here, Thine only Son,
And, Father, let Thy will be done !"
Rev. Samuel F. Smith. (1808-.)

75 "And fell on His face and prayed." L. M.
Luke xxii. 39-46. Ps. xxii. Heb. v. 7-10.

1 'T IS midnight, and on Olive's brow
The star is dimmed that lately shone ;
'T is midnight, in the garden now
The suffering Saviour prays alone.

2 'T is midnight, and, from all removed,
Immanuel wrestles lone with fears ;
E'en the disciple that He loved
Heeds not his Master's grief and tears.

3 'T is midnight, and for others' guilt
The Man of sorrows weeps in blood ;
Yet He who hath in anguish knelt
Is not forsaken by His God.

4 'T is midnight, and from ether plains
Is borne the song that angels know ;
Unheard by mortals are the strains
That sweetly soothe the Saviour's woe.
Rev. William B. Tappan. (1794-1849.)

76 "When the morning was come." L. M.
Mat. xxvii. 1-31. Luke xxii. 63-71. Zech. xiii.

1 THE morning dawns upon the place
   Where Jesus spent the night in prayer ;
Through yielding glooms behold His face !
   Nor form nor comeliness is there.

2 Brought forth to judgment, now He stands
   Arraigned, condemned, at Pilate's bar ;
Here, spurned by fierce prætorian bands,
   There, mocked by Herod's men of war.

3 He bears their buffeting and scorn,
   Mock homage of the lip, the knee,
The purple robe, the crown of thorn,
   The scourge, the nail, the accursèd tree.

4 No guile within His mouth is found ;
   He neither threatens nor complains :
Meek as a lamb for slaughter bound,
   Dumb 'midst His murderers He remains.
James Montgomery. (1771-1854.)

77 "He hath borne our griefs." L. M.
1 Cor. ii. 2-10. 1 Pet. ii. 21-25. Ps. cxlii.

1 O LORD, when faith with fixèd eyes
Beholds Thy wondrous sacrifice,
Love rises to an ardent flame,
And we all other hope disclaim.

2 With cold affections, who can see
The thorns, the scourge, the nails, the tree ;
The flowing tears, the crimson sweat,
The bleeding hands and head and feet ?

3 The sorrow, shame, and death were Thine,
And all the stores of wrath divine ;
Ours are the pardon, life, and bliss :
What love can be compared to this ?
Author unknown.

78 "Behold the man!" L. M.
John xix. 1-16. Mat. xxvi. 51-75. Isa. liii.

1 BEHOLD the Man ! how glorious He !
Before His foes He stands unawed ;
And without wrong or blasphemy,
He claims equality with God.

2 Behold the Man ! by all condemned,
Assaulted by a host of foes ;
His person and His claim contemned,
A Man of sufferings and of woes.

3 Behold the Man ! He stands alone ;
His foes are ready to devour ;
Not one of all His friends will own
Their Master in this trying hour.

4 Behold the Man ! a King He is ;
His throne is built in heaven above ;
And there the people who are His
Shall see His face and sing His love.
Rev. Thomas Kelly. (1769-1855.)

"Who ... endured the cross."

79 "All we like sheep have gone astray." **S. M.**
Isa. liii. Matt. xviii. 11-14. Mark xv. 1-32.

1 LIKE sheep we went astray,
  And broke the fold of God;
  Each wandering in a different way,
  But all the downward road!

2 How dreadful was the hour
  When God our wanderings laid,
  And did at once His vengeance pour
  Upon the Shepherd's head.

3 How glorious was the grace
  When Christ sustained the stroke!
  His life and blood the Shepherd pays,
  A ransom for the flock.

4 But God shall raise His head
  O'er all the sons of men;
  And make Him see a numerous seed,
  To recompense His pain.
  Rev. Isaac Watts. (1674-1748.)

80 "He hath carried our sorrows." **L. M.**
John i. 29-41. Heb. ix. 13-28. Zech. xii. 10.

1 BEHOLD the sin-atoning Lamb,
  With wonder, gratitude, and love;
  To take away our guilt and shame,
  See Him descending from above.

2 Our sins and griefs on Him were laid;
  He meekly bore the mighty load;
  Our ransom-price He fully paid,
  In groans and tears, in sweat and blood.

3 To save a guilty world He dies;
  Sinners, behold the bleeding Lamb!
  To Him lift up your longing eyes,
  And hope for mercy in His name.
  Rev. John Fawcett. (1770-1817.)

81 "By wicked hands crucified and slain." **L. M.**
Mat. xxvii. 27-50. 1 Pet. iii. 18. Zech. xiii. 6.

1 O COME, and mourn with me awhile;
  O come ye to the Saviour's side;
  O come, together let us mourn;
  Jesus, our Lord, is crucified.

2 Have we no tears to shed for Him,
  While soldiers scoff and Jews deride?
  Ah, look how patiently He hangs!
  Jesus, our Lord, is crucified.

3 How fast His hands and feet are nailed!
  His throat with parching thirst is dried;
  His failing eyes are dimmed with blood,
  Jesus, our Lord, is crucified.

4 Seven times He spake, seven words of love;
  And all three hours His silence cried
  For mercy on the souls of men!
  Jesus, our Lord, is crucified.
  Rev. Frederick W. Faber. (1814-1863.)

82 "Stricken, smitten of God, and afflicted." **8. 7.**
Luke xxiii. 33-38. Acts iii. 13-15. Ex. xii.

1 "STRICKEN, smitten, and afflicted,"
  See Him dying on the tree!
  'T is the Christ by man rejected;
  Yes, my soul, 't is He, 't is He!

2 Mark the sacrifice appointed!
  See who bears the awful load!
  'T is the Word, the Lord's Anointed,
  Son of man and Son of God.

3 Lamb of God, for sinners wounded,
  Sacrifice to cancel guilt,
  None shall ever be confounded
  Who on Him their hope have built.
  Rev. Thomas Kelly. (1769-1855.)

83 "Whom ye have crucified." **L. M.**
John xix. 1-18. Rom. xi. 26-36. Isa. lix. 16-21.

1 YE that pass by, behold the Man,
  The Man of griefs condemned for you!
  The Lamb of God, for sinners slain,
  Weeping to Calvary pursue.

2 His sacred limbs they stretch, they tear;
  With nails they fasten to the wood
  His sacred limbs, exposed and bare.
  Or only covered with His blood.

3 See, there, His temples crowned with thorn,
  His bleeding hands extended wide;
  His streaming feet transfixed and torn,
  The fountain gushing from His side!

4 O Thou dear suffering Son of God,
  How doth Thy heart to sinners move!
  Sprinkle on us Thy precious blood,
  And melt us with Thy dying love.
  Rev. Charles Wesley. (1708-1788.)

84 "My God, why hast Thou forsaken me?" **L. M.**
Ps. xxii. 1. Mark xv. 33-38. Luke xxiii. 46.

1 FROM Calvary a cry was heard,
  A bitter and heart-rending cry;
  My Saviour, every mournful word
  Bespeaks Thy soul's deep agony.

2 A horror of great darkness fell
  On Thee, Thou spotless, holy One!
  And all the swarming hosts of hell
  Conspired to tempt God's only Son.

3 The scourge, the thorns, the deep disgrace,
  These Thou couldst bear, nor once repine;
  But when Jehovah veiled His face,
  Unutterable pangs were Thine.

4 Let the dumb world its silence break,
  Let pealing anthems rend the sky;
  Awake, my sluggish soul, awake!
  He died, that we might never die.
  Rev. John W. Cunningham. (1780-1831.)

"He made His grave with the wicked."

85 "Father, into Thy hands I commend my spirit." **C. M.**
Mat. xxvii. 35-53. Acts ii. 22-24. Ps. xxx.

1 BEHOLD the Saviour of mankind
   Nailed to the shameful tree;
How vast the love that Him inclined
   To bleed and die for thee!

2 Hark, how He groans, while nature shakes,
   And earth's strong pillars bend!
The temple's vail in sunder breaks,
   The solid marbles rend.

3 'T is done, the precious ransom's paid;
   "Receive my soul!" He cries.
See where He bows His sacred head,
   He bows His head, and dies.

4 But soon He'll break death's envious chain,
   And in full glory shine:
O Lamb of God, was ever pain,
   Was ever love, like Thine?
                    Rev. Samuel Wesley. (1662-1735.)

86 "It is finished." **8. 7. 4.**
John xix. 25-30. 2 Cor. v. 15-21. Ex. xii.

1 HARK! the voice of love and mercy
   Sounds aloud from Calvary;
See! it rends the rocks asunder,
   Shakes the earth, and veils the sky.
      "It is finished!"
   Hear the dying Saviour cry.

2 "It is finished!" O what pleasure
   Do these charming words afford!
Heavenly blessings, without measure,
   Flow to us through Christ, the Lord.
      "It is finished!"
   Saints! the dying words record.
                    Rev. Jonathan Evans. (1740-1890.)

87 "He bowed His head and gave up the ghost." **L. M.**
John xvii. 1-4. Heb. x. 7-14. Dan. ix. 26.

1 "'Tis finished!" so the Saviour cried,
   And meekly bowed His head, and died.
"'T is finished!" yes, the race is run,
   The battle fought, the victory won.

2 'T is finished! all that heaven decreed
   And all the ancient prophets said
Is now fulfilled, as was designed,
   In Me, the Saviour of mankind.

3 'T is finished! this My dying groan
   Shall sins of every kind atone;
Millions shall be redeemed from death
   By this My last expiring breath.

4 'T is finished! let the joyful sound
   Be heard through all the nations round;
'T is finished! let the echo fly
   Through heaven and hell, through earth and
      sky.
                    Rev. Samuel Stennett. (1727-1795.)

88 "Come, see the place where the Lord lay." **C. M.**
Mark xvi. 1-7. 1 Cor. xv. 55. Hos. xiii. 14.

1 COME, see the place where Jesus lies:
   The last sad rite is done;
With aching hearts and weeping eyes,
   The faithful few are gone.

2 By the sealed stone with grounded spears
   The guards their vigils keep;
They wist not other eyes than theirs
   Watch o'er the Saviour's sleep.

3 All heaven above, all hell beneath,
   Bright hope and blank dismay,
Look on to see if grisly Death
   Can hold his mighty prey.

4 'T is done! O Death, thy Victor-Guest
   Hath smoothed thy visage grim!
O Grave, thou place of blessèd rest
   To all who sleep in Him!
                    Rev. Thomas E. Hankinson. (1805-1843.)

89 "And that He was buried." **7.**
Mat. xxvii. 57-66. Mark xv. 47. Isa. liii. 9.

1 PAIN and toil are over now:
   Bring the spice and bring the myrrh;
Fold the limb and bind the brow,
   In the rich man's sepulchre.

2 Sin hath bruised the Victor's heel;
   Roll the stone and guard it well;
Bring the Roman's boasted seal,
   Bring his stanchest sentinel.

3 Yet the morning's purple ray
   Shall present a glorious sight:
Stone by angels rolled away,
   Guard of angels robed in white.
                    Mrs. Cecil F. Alexander. (1823-.)

90 "There laid they Jesus." **8. 7. 7.**
Luke xxiii. 50-56. John xix. 41, 42. Ps. xc. 14-16.

1 ALL is o'er, the pain, the sorrow,
   Human taunts and fiendish spite;
Death shall be despoiled to-morrow
   Of the prey he grasps to-night;
Yet once more to seal his doom,
Christ must sleep within the tomb.

2 Close and still the cell that holds Him,
   While in brief repose He lies;
Deep the slumber that enfolds Him,
   Veiled awhile from mortal eyes;
Slumber such as needs must be
After hard-won victory.

3 Now to-night, with plaintive voicing,
   Chant His requiem soft and low;
Loftier strain of loud rejoicing
   From to-morrow's harps shall flow:
"Death and hell at length are slain,
Christ hath triumphed, Christ doth reign."
                    Rev. John Moultrie. (1790-1874.)

"He rose again."

91 "The angel of the Lord ... rolled back the stone." **7.**
Mat. xxviii. 1-8. 1 Tim. iii. 16. Isa. lii. 9-15.

1 ANGEL, roll the rock away ;
Death, yield up thy mighty prey !
See, He rises from the tomb,
Glowing with immortal bloom.

2 'T is the Saviour : angels, raise
Fame's eternal trump of praise ;
Let the world's remotest bound
Hear the joy-inspiring sound.

3 Shout, ye saints, in rapturous song,
Let the strains be sweet and strong ;
Shout the Son of God, this morn,
From His sepulchre new-born.
Rev. Thomas Scott. (1700-1776.)

92 "I am He that liveth and was dead." **H. M.**
Mark xvi. 1-8. Ps. xvi. 8-11. Acts ii. 22-31.

1 THE happy morn is come,
    The Saviour leaves the grave ;
    His glorious work is done,
    Almighty now to save :
Captivity is captive led,
Since Jesus liveth that was dead.

2 Christ hath the ransom paid,
    The glorious work is done ;
    On Him our help is laid,
    The victory is won :
Captivity is captive led,
Since Jesus liveth that was dead.
Rev. Thomas Havels. (1725-1820.)

93 "Whom God hath raised up." **8. 6.**
Luke xxiv. 1-9. Heb. ii. 1-9. Ps. lxxii. 15-19.

1 THE morning purples all the sky,
The air with praises rings ;
Defeated hell stands sullen by,
The world exulting sings.
    Glory to God ! our glad lips cry ;
    All glory be to God Most High !

2 While He, the King all strong to save,
Rends the dark doors away,
And through the breaches of the grave
Strides forth into the day,
    Glory to God ! our glad lips cry ;
    All glory be to God Most High !

3 The shining angels cry, "Away
With grief, no spices bring ;
Not tears, but songs, this joyful day,
Should greet the rising King ! "
    Glory to God ! our glad lips cry ;
    All glory be to God Most High.
Ambrose of Milan. (340-397.)
Tr. by Rev. Alexander R. Thompson. (1822-.)

94 "O Grave, where is thy victory ? " **7.**
Mat. xxviii. 5-7. Ps. xviii. 46-50. 1 Cor. xv. 1-20.

1 "CHRIST, the Lord, is risen to-day ! "
Sons of men and angels, say ;
Raise your joys and triumphs high ;
*Sing, ye heavens, and earth, reply.

2 Love's redeeming work is done ;
Fought the fight, the battle won ;
Lo, our Sun's eclipse is o'er ;
Lo, He sets in blood no more.

3 Vain the stone, the watch, the seal,
Christ hath burst the gates of hell ;
Death in vain forbids His rise :
Christ has opened paradise.

4 Lives again our glorious King !
"Where, O Death, is now thy sting ? "
Once He died our souls to save ;
Where 's thy victory, boasting Grave ?
Rev. Charles Wesley. (1708-1788.)

95 "He is not here." **S. M.**
Luke xxiv. 34. Rom. vi 8, 9. Ps. xlvii. 5.

1 "THE Lord is risen indeed ! "
Then is His work performed ;
The Captive-Surety now is freed,
And death, our foe, disarmed.

2 "The Lord is risen indeed ! "
Then hell has lost his prey ;
With Him is risen the ransomed seed,
To reign in endless day.

3 "The Lord is risen indeed ! "
He lives, to die no more ;
He lives, the sinner's cause to plead,
Whose curse and shame He bore.

4 "The Lord is risen indeed ! "
Attending angels, hear ;
Up to the courts of heaven, with speed,
The joyful tidings bear.
Rev. Thomas Kelly. (1769-1855.)

96 "He is risen." **8, 7, 4.**
John xx. 1-10. Ps. xxiv. Eph. iv. 8-10.

1 COME, ye saints, look here and wonder :
See the place where Jesus lay ;
He has burst His bands asunder,
He has borne our sins away :
    Joyful tidings,
Yes, the Lord is risen to-day.

2 Jesus triumphs ! Countless legions
Come from heaven to meet their King ;
Soon, in yonder blesséd regions,
They shall join His praise to sing :
    Songs eternal
Shall through heaven's high arches ring.
Rev. Thomas Kelly.

"The Lord is exalted; ... He dwelleth on high."

97 "Thou hast ascended on high." L. M.
Luke xxiii. 27-49. Mark xvi. 1-19. Ps. lxviii. 18.

1 HE dies, the Friend of sinners dies !
    Lo, Salem's daughters weep around !
 A solemn darkness veils the skies,
    A sudden trembling shakes the ground.

2 Here's love and grief beyond degree,
    The Lord of glory dies for men ;
 But, lo, what sudden joys we see !
    Jesus, the dead, revives again.

3 The rising God forsakes the tomb,
    Up to His Father's court He flies ;
 Cherubic legions guard Him home,
    And shout Him welcome to the skies.
                    Rev. Isaac Watts. (1674-1748.)
                    Alt. by Rev. John Wesley. (1703-1791.)

98 "And the King of glory shall come in." 6. 4.
2 Chr. vi. 41. Acts ii. 22-36. Rev. xiv. 1-5.

1 RISE, glorious Conqueror, rise
    Into Thy native skies ;
        Assume Thy right ;
 And where in many a fold
 The clouds are backward rolled,
 Pass through those gates of gold,
        And reign in light.

2 Victor o'er death and hell,
 Cherubic legions swell
        The radiant train ;
 Praises all heaven inspire ;
 Each angel sweeps his lyre,
 And claps his wings of fire,
        Thou Lamb once slain.

3 Enter, Incarnate God !
 No feet but Thine have trod
        The serpent down.
 Blow the full trumpets, blow,
 Wider yon portals throw ;
 Saviour, triumphant, go,
        And take Thy crown.
                    Matthew Bridges. (1800-1852.)

99 "God is gone up with a shout." C. M.
Ps. xlvii. Acts i. 1-9. Heb. ii. 1-9.

1 O FOR a shout of sacred joy
    To God, the sovereign King !
 Let every land their tongues employ,
    And hymns of triumph sing.

2 Jesus, our God, ascends on high ;
    His heavenly guards around
 Attend Him rising through the sky,
    With trumpets' joyful sound.
                    Rev. Isaac Watts.

100 "Thou hast led captivity captive." L. M.
John xx. 17-25. Col. ii. 15. Ps. xxiv. 7-10.

1 OUR Lord is risen from the dead,
    Our Jesus is gone up on high ;
 The powers of hell are captive led,
    Dragged to the portals of the sky.

2 There His triumphal chariot waits,
    And angels chant the solemn lay :
 "Lift up your heads, ye heavenly gates,
    Ye everlasting doors, give way.

3 "Loose all your bars of massy light,
    And wide unfold the ethereal scene ;
 He claims these mansions as His right ;
    Receive the King of Glory in."
                    Rev. Charles Wesley. (1708-1788.)

101 "Alive for evermore." 6. 4.
Rev. iv. 1 Pet. iii. 22. Ps. ii.

1 ARCHANGELS, fold your wings ;
 Seraphs, keep mute the strings
        Of all your lyres.
 The Lamb of God is slain.
 But see ! He lives again,
 O'er earth and heaven to reign :
        Wake all your choirs.

2 Bow down in gloom, ye skies,
 The Lamb for sinners dies ;
        He dies, in love.
 Now lift your voices high,
 Ye powers of earth and sky ;
 He lives, no more to die,
        He reigns above.

3 Worthy is He alone
 To fill the Father's throne,
        And share His praise :
 Slain to redeem our race,
 Blest Jesus, full of grace,
 In heaven now take Thy place,
        Ancient of days !
                    Sir Samuel E. Brydges. (1762-1837.)

102 "He is the King of glory." 8. 7.
Heb. ix. 24-28. Isa. lxiii. 1-7. Rev. xix. 1-16.

1 SEE, the Conqueror mounts in triumph,
    See the King in royal state,
 Riding on the clouds His chariot,
    To His heavenly palace gate !
 Hark, the choirs of angel voices
    Joyful alleluias sing,
 And the portals high are lifted
    To receive their heavenly King.
                    Bp. Christopher Wordsworth. (1807-.)

"Thou ... hast crowned Him with glory and honor."

103 "King of kings and Lord of lords." 8. 7. 4.
Isa. lxiii. 1-6. Zech. ii. 10-13. Acts v. 30, 31.

1 LOOK, ye saints, the sight is glorious,
　See the Man of sorrows now ;
　From the fight returned victorious,
　　Every knee to Him shall bow :
　　　Crown Him, crown Him ;
　　Crowns become the Victor's brow.

2 Crown the Saviour, angels, crown Him ;
　Rich the trophies Jesus brings ;
　In the seat of power enthrone Him,
　　While the vault of heaven rings :
　　　Crown Him, crown Him,
　　Crown the Saviour King of kings.

3 Hark, those bursts of acclamation ;
　Hark, those loud triumphant chords ;
　Jesus takes the highest station,
　　O what joy the sight affords !
　　　Crown Him, crown Him,
　　King of kings and Lord of lords.
　　　　　　　Rev. Thomas Kelly. (1769-1835.)

104 "On His head a golden crown." 7.
Rev. i. 1 Cor. xv. 24-28. Ps. ii.

1 CROWNS of glory, ever bright,
　Rest upon the Victor's head ;
　Crowns of glory are His right,
　His, "who liveth and was dead."

2 His the fight, the arduous toil,
　His the honors of the day,
　His the glory and the spoil :
　Jesus bears them all away.

3 Now proclaim His deeds afar,
　Fill the world with His renown :
　His alone the Victor's car,
　His the everlasting crown.
　　　　　　　Rev. Thomas Kelly.

105 "The Lamb ... in the midst of the throne." S. M.
Rev. v. Heb. xii. 1-3. Ps. cx.

1 THRONED high is Jesus now,
　Upon His heavenly seat ;
　The kingly crown is on His brow,
　The saints are at His feet.

2 In shining white they stand,
　A great and countless throng ;
　A palmy sceptre in each hand,
　On every lip a song.

3 They sing the Lamb of God,
　Once slain on earth for them ;
　The Lamb, through whose atoning blood
　Each wears his diadem.
　　　　　　　Rev. Thomas J. Judkin. (1788-1871.)

106 "Perfect through sufferings." C. M.
Mat. xxvii. 29-33. Isa. liii. Rom. viii. 14-19.

1 THE head that once was crowned with
　　　thorns
　Is crowned with glory now ;
　A royal diadem adorns
　　The mighty Victor's brow.

2 The highest place that heaven affords
　Is to our Jesus given ;
　The King of kings and Lord of lords,
　　He reigns o'er earth and heaven :

3 The joy of all who dwell above,
　The joy of all below,
　To whom He manifests His love,
　　And grants His name to know.

4 To them the cross, with all its shame,
　With all its grace, is given ;
　Their name, an everlasting name,
　　Their joy, the joy of heaven.

5 The cross He bore is life and health,
　Though shame and death to Him ;
　His people's hope, His people's wealth,
　　Their everlasting theme.
　　　　　　　Rev. Thomas Kelly.

107 "Seen of angels." C. M.
Rev. xix. 1-16. 1 Tim. iii. 16. Ps. lxviii. 17, 18.

1 BEYOND the glittering, starry skies,
　　Far as th' eternal hills,
　There, in the boundless worlds of light,
　　Our dear Redeemer dwells.
　Immortal angels, bright and fair,
　　In countless armies shine ;
　At His right hand, with golden harps,
　　They offer songs divine.

2 In all His toils and dangerous paths,
　　They did His steps attend ;
　Oft paused, and wondered how at last
　　This scene of love would end.
　As on the torturing tree He hung,
　　And darkness veiled the sky,
　They saw, aghast, that awful sight,
　　The Lord of glory die.

3 Anon He bursts the gates of death,
　　And quells the tyrant's power ;
　They saw the illustrious Conqueror rise,
　　And hailed the blessèd hour.
　They thronged His chariot up the sky,
　　And bore Him to His throne ;
　Then swept their golden harps, and cried,
　　" The glorious work is done ! "
　　　　　　　Rev. James Fanch. 1776.
　　　　Alt. by Rev. Daniel Turner. (1710-1798.)

"Jesus made a High Priest forever."

108 "A merciful and faithful High Priest." **L. M.**
Heb. iv. 14-16. Luke vii. 11-23. Zech. vi. 9-15.

1 WHERE high the heavenly temple stands,
  The house of God not made with hands,
  A great High Priest our nature wears,
  The Patron of mankind appears.

2 He who for men in mercy stood,
  And poured on earth His precious blood,
  Pursues in heaven His plan of grace,
  The guardian God of human race.

3 Though now ascended up on high,
  He bends on earth a brother's eye ;
  Partaker of the human name,
  He knows the frailty of our frame.

4 Our fellow-sufferer yet retains
  A fellow-feeling of our pains ;
  He sympathizes in our grief,
  And to the sufferer sends relief.
  Michael Bruce. (1746-1767.)

109 "He Himself hath suffered being tempted." **C. M.**
Heb. v. 1-9. Phil. ii. 5-11. Isa. xlii. 1-4.

1 WITH joy we meditate the grace
  Of our High Priest above ;
  His heart is made of tenderness,
  His bosom glows with love.

2 Touched with a sympathy within,
  He knows our feeble frame ;
  He knows what sore temptations mean,
  For He hath felt the same.

3 He, in the days of feeble flesh,
  Poured out His cries and tears ;
  And, in His measure, feels afresh
  What every member bears.

4 He 'll never quench the smoking flax,
  But raise it to a flame ;
  The bruiséd reed He never breaks,
  Nor scorns the meanest name.
  Rev. Isaac Watts. (1674-1748.)

110 "The High Priest of our profession." **C. M.**
Heb. vi. 19, 20. Ex. xxviii. 9-12. Rev. iii. 1-5.

1 Now let our cheerful eyes survey
  Our great High Priest above ;
  And celebrate His constant care,
  And sympathetic love.

2 The names of all His saints He bears
  Deep graven on His heart ;
  Nor shall the meanest Christian say
  That he hath lost his part.

3 Those characters shall fair abide,
  Our everlasting trust,
  When gems and monuments and crowns
  Are mouldered down to dust.
  Rev. Philip Doddridge. (1702-1751.)

111 "The Mediator of the new testament." **C. M.**
Deu. xviii. 15-19. Heb. ii. 14-18. Ps. cx.

1 WE bless the Prophet of the Lord,
  That comes with truth and grace ;
  Jesus, Thy Spirit and Thy word
  Shall lead us in Thy ways.

2 We reverence our High Priest above,
  Who offered up His blood,
  And lives to carry on His love
  By pleading with our God.

3 We honor our exalted King ;
  How sweet are His commands !
  He guards our souls from hell and sin
  By His almighty hands.
  Rev. Isaac Watts.

112 "By His own blood He entered in." **C. M.**
Eph. ii. 4-22. 1 Cor. i. 18-31. Ps. iii.

1 DEAREST of all the names above,
  My Jesus and my God,
  Who can resist Thy heavenly love,
  Or trifle with Thy blood ?

2 'T is by the merits of Thy death
  Thy Father smiles again ;
  'T is by Thine interceding breath
  The Spirit dwells with men.

3 While Jews on their own law rely,
  And Greeks of wisdom boast,
  I love the Incarnate Mystery,
  And there I fix my trust.
  Rev. Isaac Watts.

113 "He ever liveth to make intercession." **L. M.**
Rev. i. 18. Heb. ix 11-28. Ps. xvii.

1 HE lives, the great Redeemer lives,
  What joy the blest assurance gives !
  And now, before His Father, God,
  Pleads the full merits of His blood.

2 Repeated crimes awake our fears,
  And justice armed with frowns appears ;
  But in the Saviour's lovely face
  Sweet mercy smiles, and all is peace.

3 Hence, then, ye black, despairing thoughts !
  Above our fears, above our faults,
  His powerful intercessions rise,
  And guilt recedes, and terror dies.

4 In every dark, distressful hour,
  When sin and Satan join their power,
  Let this dear hope repel the dart,
  That Jesus bears us on His heart.

5 Great Advocate, Almighty Friend,
  On Him our humble hopes depend ;
  Our cause can never, never fail,
  For Jesus pleads, and must prevail.
  Miss Anne Steele. (1717-1778.)

"The Holy Ghost, whom the Father will send."

114 "I will send Him unto you." 8. 6. 4.
John xvi. Mat. iii. 13-17. Eze. xxxvi. 27.

1 OUR blest Redeemer, ere He breathed
    His tender last farewell,
  A Guide, a Comforter, bequeathed
    With us to dwell.

2 He came in semblance of a dove
    With sheltering wings outspread,
  The holy balm of peace and love
    On earth to shed.

3 He came sweet influence to impart,
    A gracious, willing guest,
  While He can find one humble heart
    Wherein to rest.

4 And His that gentle voice we hear,
    Soft as the breath of even,
  That checks each thought, that calms each fear,
    And speaks of heaven.

5 And every virtue we possess,
    And every victory won,
  And every thought of holiness,
    Are His alone.

Miss Harriet Auber. (1773-1862.)

115 "The manifestation of the Spirit." C. M.
Ex. xix. 16-19. Hab. iii. 3, 4. Acts ii. 1-4.

1 WHEN God of old came down from heaven,
    In power and wrath He came;
  Before His feet the clouds were riven,
    Half darkness and half flame.
  But when He came the second time,
    He came in power and love;
  Softer than gale at morning prime,
    Hovered His holy Dove.

2 The fires that rushed on Sinai down
    In sudden torrents dread
  Now gently light, a glorious crown,
    On every sainted head.
  And as, on Israel's awestruck ear
    The voice exceeding loud,
  The trump that angels quake to hear,
    Thrilled from the deep, dark cloud.

3 So, when the Spirit of our God
    Came down His flock to find,
  A voice from heaven was heard abroad,
    A rushing mighty wind.
  It fills the church of God, it fills
    The sinful world around;
  Only in stubborn hearts and wills
    No place for it is found.

Rev. John Keble. (1792-1866.)

116 "The Holy Ghost ... given unto us." 7.
John xiv. 16. Acts x. 34-43. Isa. xliv. 3.

1 GRANTED is the Saviour's prayer,
  Sent the gracious Comforter,
  Promise of our parting Lord,
  Jesus, to His heaven restored.

2 Christ, who now gone up on high,
  Captive leads captivity,
  While His foes from Him receive
  Grace, that God with man may live.

3 God, the everlasting God,
  Makes with mortals His abode;
  Whom the heavens cannot contain,
  He vouchsafes to dwell in man.

4 Never will He thence depart,
  Inmate of a humble heart;
  Carrying on His work within,
  Striving till He cast out sin.

5 There He helps our feeble moans,
  Deepens our imperfect groans;
  Intercedes in silence there,
  Sighs the unutterable prayer.

Rev. Charles Wesley. (1708-1788.)

117 "A sound ... as of a rushing mighty wind." C. M.
Gen. i. 2. Acts iv. 31-33. Rom. viii. 1-26.

1 No track is on the sunny sky,
    No footprints on the air;
  Jesus hath gone; the face of earth
    Is desolate and bare.
  That Upper Room is heaven on earth:
    Within its precincts lie
  All that earth has of faith, or hope,
    Or heaven-born charity.

2 He comes! He comes! that mighty Breath
    From heaven's eternal shores;
  His uncreated freshness fills
    His Bride, as she adores.
  One moment, and the Spirit hung
    O'er all with dread desire;
  Then broke upon the heads of all
    In cloven tongues of fire.

3 The Spirit came into the church
    With His unfailing power;
  He is the living heart that beats
    Within her at this hour.
  Most tender Spirit, mighty God,
    Sweet must Thy presence be,
  If loss of Jesus can be gain,
    So long as we have Thee!

Rev. Frederick W. Faber. (1814-1853.)

"The Holy Ghost fell on them."

118 "They were all filled with the Holy Ghost." **C. M.**
Acts iv. Isa. liv. 11–13. John xiv. 15–31.

1 HE'S come : let every knee be bent,
All hearts new joy resume ;
Sing, ye redeemed, with one consent,
"The Comforter is come."

2 What greater gift, what greater love,
Could God on man bestow ?
Angels for this rejoice above,
Let man rejoice below.

3 Hail, blessed Spirit ! may each soul
Thy sacred influence feel ;
Do Thou each sinful thought control,
And fix our wavering zeal.

4 Thou to the conscience dost convey
Those checks which we should know ;
Thy motions point to us the way,
Thou giv'st us strength to go.
Author unknown.

119 "Cloven tongues like as of fire." **8. 7.**
Acts ii. 1 Cor. iii. 16. Isa. lvii. 15.

1 DAY divine, when, sudden streaming,
To the Lord's first lovers came
Glory new and treasures teeming,
Mighty gifts and tongues of flame.
Day to happy souls commended,
When the Holy Ghost was given,
When the Comforter descended,
And brought down the joy of heaven.

2 Sure, the Holy Ghost is dwelling
With the souls that holier grow ;
Signs most glorious, all excelling,
Witness brightest we may show :
Hope that makes ashamèd never,
Perfect peace that passeth thought,
Mighty joy that stayeth ever,
Love divine that changeth not.
Thomas H. Gill. (1819–.)

120 "On all them which heard the word." **C. M.**
Acts x. 34–48. Joel ii. 28–32. John xvi. 12–15.

1 LET songs of praises fill the sky ;
Christ, our ascended Lord,
Sends down His Spirit from on high,
According to His word.

2 The Spirit, by His heavenly breath,
New life creates within ;
He quickens sinners from the death
Of trespasses and sin.

3 The things of Christ the Spirit takes,
And to our heart reveals ;
Our bodies He His temple makes,
And our redemption seals.
Rev. Thomas Cotterill. (1779–1823.)

121 "The unity of the Spirit in the bond of peace." **C. M.**
Gal. v. 22. Rom. viii. 1–27. Neh. ix. 20.

1 SPIRIT of peace, celestial Dove,
How excellent Thy praise !
How rich the gift of Christian love
Thy gracious power displays !

2 Sweet as the dew on hill and flower,
That silently distils,
At evening's soft and balmy hour,
On Zion's fruitful hills ;

3 So, with mild influence from above,
Shall promised grace descend ;
Till universal peace and love
O'er all the earth extend.
Rev. Henry F. Lyte. (1793–1847.)

122 "The Spirit beareth witness." **7. 6.**
1 Cor. ii. 2 Thes. ii. 13–17. Isa. li. 9–12.

1 GOD of all consolation,
The Holy Ghost Thou art ;
Thy secret inspiration
Hath told it to my heart :
The blessing I inherit,
Through Jesus' prayer bestowed,
The Comforter, the Spirit,
The true, eternal God.

2 With God the Son and Saviour,
With God the Father one,
The tokens of His favor
Are now to man made known.
An antepast of heaven
Thou dost in me reveal,
Attest my sins forgiven,
And my salvation seal.
Rev. Charles Wesley. (1708–1788.)

123 "Righteousness and peace, and joy." **L. M.**
Zech. iv. 6. Rom. xv. 13. Eph. iii. 16.

1 ETERNAL Spirit, we confess
And sing the wonders of Thy grace ;
Thy power conveys our blessings down
From God the Father and the Son.

2 Enlightened by Thy heavenly ray,
Our shades and darkness turn to day ;
Thine inward teachings make us know
Our danger and our refuge too.

3 Thy power and glory work within,
And break the chains of reigning sin ;
Do our imperious lusts subdue,
And form our wretched hearts anew.

4 The troubled conscience knows Thy voice :
Thy cheering words awake our joys ;
Thy words allay the stormy wind,
And calm the surges of the mind.
Rev. Isaac Watts. (1674–1748.)

"None that doeth good; no, not one."

124 "They are all gone aside." **C. M.**
Ps. xiv. Gen. vi. 5–13. Rom. iii. 10–23.

1 THE Lord, from His celestial throne,
Looked down on things below,
To find the man that sought His grace,
Or did His justice know.

2 By nature all are gone astray,
Their practice all the same;
There's none that fears his Maker's hand,
There's none that loves His name.

3 Such seeds of sin, that bitter root,
In every heart are found;
Nor can they bear diviner fruit
Till grace refine the ground.
Rev. Isaac Watts. (1674-1748.)

125 "That which is born of the flesh is flesh." **L. M.**
Ps. li. Eph. i. Jude.

1 LORD, I am vile, conceived in sin,
And born unholy and unclean;
Sprung from the man whose guilty fall
Corrupts the race and taints us all.

2 Soon as we draw our infant breath,
The seeds of sin grow up for death;
The law demands a perfect heart,
But we're defiled in every part.

3 No bleeding bird nor bleeding beast,
Nor hyssop-branch, nor sprinkling priest,
Nor running brook, nor flood, nor sea,
Can wash the dismal stain away.

4 Jesus, my God, Thy blood alone
Hath power sufficient to atone;
Thy blood can make me white as snow;
No Jewish types could cleanse me so.
Rev. Isaac Watts.

126 "Our bones are dried and our hope is lost." **L. M.**
Eze. xxxvii. 1–10. Ex. xxxii. 1–28. 1 Thes. v.

1 LOOK down, O Lord, with pitying eye:
See Adam's race in ruin lie;
Sin spreads its trophies o'er the ground,
And scatters slaughtered heaps around.

2 Thy ministers are sent in vain
To prophesy upon the slain;
In vain they call, in vain they cry,
Till Thine almighty aid is nigh.

3 But if Thy Spirit deign to breathe,
Life spreads through all the realms of death;
Dry bones obey Thy powerful voice,
They move, they waken, they rejoice.

4 So when Thy trumpet's awful sound
Shall shake the heavens and rend the ground,
Dead saints shall from their tombs arise,
And spring to life beyond the skies.
Rev. Philip Doddridge. (1702-1751.)

127 "When we were yet without strength." **L. M.**
1 Cor. i. 18–31. Rom. vii. 5–25. Jer. xxxiii. 9–16.

1 BURIED in shadows of the night,
We lie, till Christ restores the light;
Wisdom descends to heal the blind,
And chase the darkness of the mind.

2 Our guilty souls are drowned in tears,
Till His atoning blood appears;
Then we awake from deep distress,
And sing the Lord our Righteousness.

3 Jesus beholds where Satan reigns,
Binding his slaves in heavy chains;
He sets the prisoners free, and breaks
The iron bondage from our necks.
Rev. Isaac Watts.

128 "There is none that understandeth." **C. M.**
Ps. lxxv. Job xviii. Rom. i. 18–32.

1 How helpless guilty nature lies,
Unconscious of its load!
The heart, unchanged, can never rise
To happiness and God.

2 Can aught, beneath a power divine,
The stubborn will subdue?
'T is Thine, Almighty Spirit, Thine,
To form the heart anew.

3 'T is Thine the passions to recall,
And upward bid them rise;
To make the scales of error fall
From reason's darkened eyes;

4 To chase the shades of death away,
And bid the sinner live;
A beam of heaven, a vital ray,
'T is Thine alone to give.
Miss Anne Steele. (1717-1778.)

129 "Ye were sometime darkness." **S. M.**
2 Cor. iv. 1–7. Acts xxvi. 12–18. Isa. xli. 5–10.

1 How heavy is the night
That hangs upon our eyes,
Till Christ, with His reviving light,
Over our souls arise!

2 Our guilty spirits dread
To meet the wrath of heaven;
But, in His righteousness arrayed,
We see our sins forgiven.

3 Unholy and impure
Are all our thoughts and ways;
His hands infected nature cure,
With sanctifying grace.

4 The powers of hell agree
To hold our souls in vain:
He sets the sons of bondage free,
And breaks the curséd chain.
Rev. Isaac Watts.

"A ransom for all."

130 "The redemption that is in Christ." **S. M.**
Rom. ii. 1-16. Lev. iii. 1-8. 1 Thes. v. 1-10.

1 GOD'S holy law transgressed
   Speaks nothing but despair ;
   Convinced of guilt, with grief oppressed
   We find no comfort there.

2 Not all our groans and tears,
   Nor works which we have done,
   Nor vows, nor promises, nor prayers,
   Can e'er for sin atone.

3 Relief alone is found
   In Jesus' precious blood :
   'T is this that heals the mortal wound,
   And reconciles to God.

4 This is salvation's source
   And all our hopes arise
   From Him who, hanging on the cross,
   A spotless victim dies.

Rev. Benjamin Beddome. (1717-1795.)

131 "Wherewith shall I come before the Lord?" **L. M.**
Jer. xii. 1-5. Eze. xx. 27-44. 2 Cor. v. 13-21.

1 How shall the sons of men appear,
   Great God, before Thine awful bar ?
   How may the guilty hope to find
   Acceptance with th' Eternal Mind ?

2 Not vows, nor groans, nor broken cries,
   Not the most costly sacrifice,
   Not infant blood, profusely spilt,
   Will expiate a sinner's guilt.

3 Thy blood, dear Jesus, Thine alone,
   Hath sovereign virtue to atone ;
   Here we will rest our only plea,
   When we approach, great God, to Thee.

Rev. Samuel Stennett. (1727-1795.)

132 "How should man be just with God ?" **S. M.**
Isa. xlv. 5-9. Jer. xiii. 15-21. Rom. ix. 15-26.

1 AH, how shall fallen man
   Be just before his God ?
   If He contend in righteousness,
   We sink beneath His rod.

2 If He our ways should mark,
   With strict inquiring eyes,
   Could we, for one of thousand faults,
   A just excuse devise ?

3 The mountains, in Thy wrath,
   Their ancient seats forsake ;
   The trembling earth deserts her place,
   Her rooted pillars shake.

4 Ah, how shall guilty man
   Contend with such a God !
   None, none can meet Him and escape,
   But through the Saviour's blood.

Rev. Isaac Watts. (1674-1748.)

133 "He is the propitiation for our sins." **L. M.**
Dan. ix. 1-19. Neh. i. Rom. i. 19-32.

1 DEEP in the dust before Thy throne,
   Our guilt and our disgrace we own ;
   Great God, we own th' unhappy name
   Whence sprung our nature and our shame.

2 But whilst our spirits, filled with awe,
   Behold the terrors of Thy law,
   We sing the honors of Thy grace,
   That sent to save our ruined race.

3 We sing Thine everlasting Son,
   Who joined our nature to His own ;
   Adam the second, from the dust,
   Raises the ruins of the first.

4 Where sin did reign and death abound,
   There have the sons of Adam found
   Abounding life ; there glorious grace
   Reigns through the Lord our Righteousness.

Rev. Isaac Watts.

134 "Grace did much more abound." **L. M.**
Ps. lxxxix. 46-52. Acts xvi. 25-31. Rev. i. 10-18.

1 WHAT shall the dying sinner do,
   That seeks relief for all his woe ?
   Can souls, all o'er defiled with sin,
   Make their own powers and passions clean ?

2 In vain we search, in vain we try,
   Till Jesus brings His gospel nigh ,
   'T is there such power and glory dwell
   As save rebellious souls from hell.

3 This is the pillar of our hope,
   That bears our fainting spirits up ;
   We read the grace, we trust the word,
   And find salvation in the Lord.

Rev. Isaac Watts.

135 "While we were yet sinners Christ died for us." **C. M.**
Acts iii. 13-26. Mark i. 1-13. Eze. iv.

1 AND did the Holy and the Just,
   The Sovereign of the skies,
   Stoop down to wretchedness and dust,
   That guilty worms might rise ?

2 Yes, the Redeemer left His throne,
   His radiant throne on high :
   Surprising mercy, love unknown,
   To suffer, bleed, and die.

3 He took the dying traitor's place,
   And suffered in his stead ;
   For man, O miracle of grace,
   For man the Saviour bled.

4 Dear Lord, what heavenly wonders dwell
   In Thine atoning blood !
   By this are sinners snatched from hell,
   And rebels brought to God.

Miss Anne Steele. (1717-1778.)

"The mighty God ... hath spoken and called."

136 "Let him that is athirst come." **L. M.**
Isa. lv. John vii. 37-39. Rev. xxii. 17.

1 "Ho, every one that thirsts, draw nigh:"
'T is God invites the fallen race.
"Mercy and free salvation buy,
Buy wine, and milk, and gospel grace.

2 "Come to the living waters, come;
Sinners, obey your Maker's call;
Return, ye weary wanderers, home,
And find My grace is free for all.

3 "Nothing ye in exchange shall give,
Leave all you have and are behind;
Frankly the gift of God receive,
Pardon and peace in Jesus find."
Rev. John Wesley. (1703-1791.)

137 "A fountain for sin and for uncleanness." **8. 7. 7.**
Eze. xlvii. 1-12. Acts xxvi. 9-29. Isa. xxv. 6-9.

1 Come to Calvary's holy mountain,
Sinners ruined by the fall;
Here a pure and healing fountain
Flows to you, to me, to all,
In a full, perpetual tide,
Opened when our Saviour died.

2 Come, in sorrow and contrition,
Wounded, impotent, and blind;
Here the guilty, free remission,
Here the troubled, peace may find;
Health this fountain will restore,
He that drinks shall thirst no more.

3 He that drinks shall live forever;
'T is a soul-renewing flood.
God is faithful; God will never
Break His covenant in blood,
Signed when our Redeemer died,
Sealed when He was glorified.
James Montgomery. (1771-1854.)

138 "Come unto me all ye that labor." **L. M.**
Mat. xi. 28-30. Ps. xxxvii. 1-11. 1 Pet. v. 7.

1 "Come hither, all ye weary souls,
Ye heavy-laden sinners, come:
I 'll give you rest from all your toils,
And raise you to My heavenly home.

2 "They shall find rest that learn of Me;
I 'm of a meek and lowly mind;
But passion rages like the sea,
And pride is restless as the wind.

3 "Blest is the man whose shoulders take
My yoke, and bear it with delight;
My yoke is easy to his neck,
My grace shall make the burden light."
Rev. Isaac Watts. (1674-1748.)

139 "Return ye now every one from his evil way." **C. M.**
Heb. iii. 7-13. Job xv. 17-30 Isa. xlv. 22-25.

1 Sinners, the voice of God regard,
'T is mercy speaks to-day;
He calls you by His sovereign word
From sin's destructive way.

2 Bow to the sceptre of His word,
Renouncing every sin;
Submit to Him, your sovereign Lord,
And learn His will divine.

3 His love exceeds your highest thoughts;
He pardons like a God;
He will forgive your numerous faults,
Through a Redeemer's blood.
Rev. John Fawcett. (1739-1817.)

140 "Take my yoke upon you." **8. 7. 4.**
Jer. iii. 12-25. Hos. xiii. 9-14. James iv. 7-17.

1 Come, ye souls by sin afflicted,
Bowed with fruitless sorrow down,
By the perfect law convicted,
Through the cross behold the crown.
Look to Jesus;
Mercy flows through Him alone.

2 Take His easy yoke, and wear it;
Love will make obedience sweet;
Christ will give you strength to bear it,
While His wisdom guides your feet
Safe to glory,
Where His ransomed captives meet.

3 Sweet as home to pilgrims weary,
Light to newly-opened eyes,
Or full springs in deserts dreary,
Is the rest the cross supplies;
All who taste it
Shall to rest immortal rise.
Rev. Joseph Swain. (1761-1796.)

141 "Come ye near unto me." **L. M.**
Jer. xxxi. 18-34. Hos. xi. Luke xv. 11-24.

1 Return, O wanderer, return,
And seek an injured Father's face;
Those warm desires that in thee burn
Were kindled by reclaiming grace.

2 Return, O wanderer, return:
He hears thy deep repentant sigh;
He saw thy softened spirit mourn,
When no intruding ear was nigh.

3 Return, O wanderer, return,
And wipe away the falling tear;
'T is God who says, "No longer mourn!"
'T is mercy's voice invites thee near.
Rev. William B. Collyer. (1782-1854.)

"Jesus said, ... Come and follow me."

142 "Come ... all ye that are ... heavy laden." 7.
Mat. xi. 28-30. Jer. iii. 12-23. Acts iii. 19-26

1 COME, says Jesus' sacred voice,
    Come, and make My paths your choice;
    I will guide you to your home;
    Weary pilgrim, hither come.

2 Ye who, tossed on beds of pain,
    Seek for ease, but seek in vain;
    Ye by fiercer anguish torn,
    In remorse for guilt who mourn,

3 Hither come, for here is found
    Balm that flows for every wound,
    Peace that ever shall endure,
    Rest eternal, sacred, sure.
            Mrs. Anna L. Barbauld. (1743-1825.)

143 "Hear, and your soul shall live." 7.
Luke xiv. 15-24. Phil. ii. 9-11. Isa. xlv. 1-3

1 FROM the cross uplifted high,
    Where the Saviour deigns to die,
    What melodious sounds I hear,
    Bursting on my ravished ear!
    "Love's redeeming work is done;
    Come and welcome, sinner, come.

2 "Spread for thee, the festal board
    See with richest dainties stored;
    To thy Father's bosom pressed,
    Yet again a child confessed,
    Never from His house to roam;
    Come and welcome, sinner, come.

3 "Sprinkled now with blood the throne;
    Why beneath thy burdens groan?
    On My piercéd body laid,
    Justice owns the ransom paid.
    Bow the knee, and kiss the Son;
    Come and welcome, sinner, come."
            Rev. Thomas Hawels. (1732-1820.)

144 "Wisdom crieth without." 8. 7.
Prov. i. 20-23. Mat. xxi. 33-39. Isa. xlviii. 1-18

1 Now the Saviour standeth, pleading,
    At the sinner's bolted heart;
    Now in heaven He's interceding,
    Taking there the sinner's part.
    Sinner, hear your God and Saviour,
    Hear His gracious voice to-day;
    Turn from all your vain behavior,
    O repent, return, and pray!

2 Now He's waiting to be gracious,
    Now He stands and looks on thee:
    See what kindness, love, and pity
    Shine around on you and me.
    Come, for all things now are ready,
    Yet there's room for many more:
    O ye blind, ye lame and needy,
    Come to wisdom's boundless store!
            Author unknown.

145 "Ho, every one that thirsteth, come." C. M.
John vii. 37-39. Rev. xxi 6, 7. Amos v. 1-15.

1 THE Saviour calls, let every ear
    Attend the heavenly sound;
    Ye doubting souls, dismiss your fear,
    Hope smiles reviving round.

2 For every thirsty, longing heart,
    Here streams of bounty flow,
    And life and health and bliss impart,
    To banish mortal woe.

3 Ye sinners, come, 't is mercy's voice,
    The gracious call obey;
    Mercy invites to heavenly joys,
    And can you yet delay?
            Miss Anne Steele. (1717-1778.)

146 "I stand at the door and knock." 7, 8. 7.
Rev. iii. 14-22. Prov. viii. 1-17. Can. v. 2-6.

1 KNOCKING, knocking, who is there?
    Waiting, waiting, O how fair!
    'T is a Pilgrim, strange and kingly;
    Never such was seen before.
    Ah, my soul, for such a wonder
    Wilt thou not undo the door?

2 Knocking, knocking, still He's there,
    Waiting, waiting, wondrous fair;
    But the door is hard to open,
    For the weeds and ivy-vine,
    With their dark and clinging tendrils,
    Ever round the hinges twine.

3 Knocking, knocking; what, still there?
    Waiting, waiting, grand and fair;
    Yes, the piercéd hand still knocketh,
    And beneath the crownéd hair
    Beam the patient eyes, so tender,
    Of thy Saviour, waiting there.
            Mrs. Harriet E. B. Stowe. (1812-)
            Arr. by C. Guest.

147 "Come, for all things are now ready." C. M.
Mat. xxii. 1-10. Prov. ix. 1-12 Gen. xlv. 1-11.

1 YE wretched, hungry, starving poor,
    Behold a royal feast;
    Where mercy spreads her bounteous store
    For every humble guest.

2 See, Jesus stands with open arms;
    He calls, He bids you come.
    Guilt holds you back, and fear alarms,
    But see, there yet is room;

3 Room in the Saviour's bleeding heart:
    There love and pity meet;
    Nor will He bid the soul depart
    That trembles at His feet.
            Miss Anne Steele.

"Hear what the Spirit saith."

148 "The Spirit and the Bride say, Come." S. M.
Rev. xxii. 17-20. Joel ii. 21-32. Isa. xlii.

1 THE Spirit, in our hearts,
  Is whispering, "Sinner, come;"
The Bride, the church of Christ, proclaims
  To all His children, "Come."

2 Let him that heareth say
  To all about him, "Come;"
Let him that thirsts for righteousness
  To Christ, the fountain, come.

3 Yes, whosoever will,
  O let him freely come,
And freely drink the stream of life;
  'T is Jesus bids him come.

  Bp. Henry U. Onderdonk. (1789-1858.)

149 "To-day, if ye will hear His voice." 6, 4.
Heb. iii. 7-15. Luke xix. 41-44. 1 Sam. xii.

1 TO-DAY the Saviour calls:
  Ye wanderers come;
O ye benighted souls,
  Why longer roam?

2 To-day the Saviour calls:
  O, hear Him now;
Within these sacred walls
  To Jesus bow.

3 To-day the Saviour calls:
  For refuge fly;
The storm of justice falls,
  And death is nigh.

4 The Spirit calls to-day:
  Yield to His power;
O grieve Him not away,
  'T is mercy's hour.

  Rev. Samuel F. Smith. (1808-.)

150 "I came not to call the righteous." L. M.
Rev. iii. 1-12. John vii. 37-39. Zeph. iii. 1-20.

1 JUST as thou art, without one trace
Of love, or joy, or inward grace,
Or meetness for the heavenly place,
O guilty sinner, come, now come.

2 Thy sins I bore on Calvary's tree,
The stripes, thy due, were laid on Me,
That peace and pardon might be free;
O wretched sinner, come, now come.

3 Come, leave thy burden at the cross,
Count all thy gains but empty dross;
My grace repays all earthly loss:
O needy sinner, come, now come.

4 "The Spirit and the Bride say, Come;"
Rejoicing saints reëcho, "Come;"
Who faints, who thirsts, who will, may come;
Thy Saviour bids thee come, now come.

  Rev. Russell S. Cook. (1814-1864.)

151 "Come, eat of my bread." L. M.
Mat. xxii. 1-10. Luke xv. 1-10. Prov. ix. 1-12.

1 SINNERS, obey the gospel word,
Haste to the supper of my Lord;
Be wise to know your gracious day;
All things are ready, come away.

2 Ready the Father is to own
And kiss His late-returning son;
Ready your loving Saviour stands,
And spreads for you His bleeding hands.

3 The Father, Son, and Holy Ghost
Are ready, with Their shining host;
All heaven is ready to resound,
"The dead's alive, the lost is found!"

  Rev. Charles Wesley. (1708-1788.)

152 "Look unto me, and be ye saved." L. M.
Mat. xi. 28-30. Rev. ii. 1-7. 1 Kings viii. 46 to x. 5.

1 COME, weary souls, with sin distrest,
The Saviour offers heavenly rest;
The kind, the gracious call obey,
And cast your gloomy fears away.

2 Here mercy's boundless ocean flows,
To cleanse your guilt and heal your woes;
Pardon, and life, and endless peace,
How rich the gift, how free the grace!

  Miss Anne Steele. (1717-1778.)

153 "Turn you at my reproof." 7.
Eze. xxxiii. 10-19. Hos. xi. Mat. xxiii. 34-39.

1 SINNERS, turn, why will you die?
God, your Maker, asks you, Why?
God, who did your being give,
Made you with Himself to live:
He the fatal cause demands,
Asks the work of his own hands.
Why, ye thankless creatures, why,
Will ye cross His love, and die?

2 Sinners, turn, why will you die?
God, your Saviour, asks you, Why?
God, who did your souls retrieve,
Died Himself, that you might live.
Will you let Him die in vain,
Crucify your Lord again?
Why, ye ransomed sinners, why,
Will you slight His grace, and die?

3 Sinners, turn, why will you die?
God, the Spirit, asks you, Why?
God, who all your lives hath strove,
Wooed you to embrace His love.
Will you not the grace receive?
Will you still refuse to live?
Why, ye long-sought sinners, why,
Will you grieve your God, and die?

  Rev. Charles Wesley.

"Rise, He calleth thee."

154 "Yet there is room." C. M.
Luke xiv. 15-24. Joel ii. 12-32. James iv. 7-17.

1 COME, sinner, to the gospel feast,
  O come without delay ;
  For there is room in Jesus' breast
  For all who will obey.

2 There's room in God's eternal love
  To save thy precious soul ;
  Room in the Spirit's grace above
  To heal and make thee whole.

3 There's room within the church, redeemed
  With blood of Christ divine ;
  Room in the white-robed throng convened,
  For that dear soul of thine.

4 There's room around thy Father's board
  For thee and thousands more ;
  O come, and welcome, to the Lord,
  Yea, come this very hour.
  Author unknown.

155 "Seek ye the Lord while He may be found." S. M.
Hos. xi. Deu. xi. 1-25. John v. 24-40.

1 AND canst thou, sinner, slight
  The call of love divine ?
  Shall God with tenderness invite,
  And gain no thought of thine ?

2 Wilt thou not cease to grieve
  The Spirit from thy breast,
  Till He thy wretched soul shall leave,
  With all thy sins oppressed ?

3 To-day, a pard'ning God
  Will hear the suppliant pray ;
  To-day, a Saviour's cleansing blood
  Will wash thy guilt away.
  Mrs. Ann B. Hyde. (-1872.)

156 "Without money and without price." L. M.
Mat. xxii. 1-10. Acts ii. 38-40. Prov. viii.

1 COME, sinners, to the gospel feast,
  Let every soul be Jesus' guest ;
  Ye need not one be left behind,
  For God hath bidden all mankind.

2 Sent by my Lord, on you I call ;
  The invitation is to all :
  Come, all the world ; come, sinner, thou ;
  All things in Christ are ready now.

3 My message as from God receive,
  Ye all may come to Christ and live :
  O let His love your hearts constrain,
  Nor suffer Him to die in vain.

4 See Him set forth before your eyes
  That precious, bleeding sacrifice ;
  His offered benefits embrace,
  And freely now be saved by grace.
  Rev. Charles Wesley. (1708-1788.)

157 "Repent ye, therefore." 7.
Zech. xiii. Isa. lix. Acts iii. 12-26.

1 HEARTS of stone, relent, relent ;
  Break, by Jesus' cross subdued ;
  See His body, mangled, rent,
  Covered with His flowing blood.
  Sinful soul, what hast thou done ?
  Crucified the eternal Son !

2 Yes, thy sins have done the deed :
  Driven the nails that fixed Him there,
  Crowned with thorns His sacred head,
  Pierced Him with a soldier's spear,
  Made His soul a sacrifice ;
  For a sinful world He dies.

3 Wilt thou let Him die in vain,
  Still to death pursue our God,
  Open all His wounds again,
  Trample on His precious blood ?
  No, with all my sins I'll part ;
  Saviour, take my broken heart.
  John Krüger. 1610.
  Tr. by Rev. Charles Wesley.

158 "Come thou with us." 8. 3.
Num. x. 29-36. Ps. xxxiv. 8-22. John i. 43-51.

1 WE'RE travelling home to heaven above,
    Will you go ?
  To sing the Saviour's dying love,
    Will you go ?
  Millions have reached that blest abode,
  Anointed kings and priests to God,
  And millions more are on the road,
    Will you go ?

2 Ye weary, heavy-laden, come,
    Will you go ?
  In the blest house there still is room,
    Will you go ?
  The Lord is waiting to receive,
  If thou wilt on Him now believe,
  He'll give thy troubled conscience ease,
    Come, believe.

3 The way to heaven is straight and plain,
    Will you go ?
  Repent, believe, be born again,
    Will you go ?
  The Saviour cries aloud to thee,
  "Take up thy cross and follow Me,
  And thou shalt My salvation see,
    Come to Me."
  Author unknown.

"Turn ye, for why will ye die?"

159 "Let the wicked forsake his way." C. M.
Zech. i. 2-4. Hos. vi. 1-6. Luke xv. 11-24.

1 RETURN, O wanderer, to thy home,
   Thy Father calls for thee ;
   No longer now an exile roam
   In guilt and misery.

2 Return, O wanderer, to thy home,
   Thy Saviour calls for thee ;
   "The Spirit and the Bride say, Come ;"
   O now for refuge flee !

3 Return, O wanderer, to thy home,
   'T is madness to delay ;
   There are no pardons in the tomb,
   And brief is mercy's day.
                        Thomas Hastings. (1790-1872.)

160 "Refuse not Him that speaketh." L. M.
Rev. iii. 20-22. Mat. xxiii. 34-39. Prov. i. 20-33.

1 BEHOLD, a Stranger 's at the door ;
   He gently knocks, has knocked before ;
   Has waited long, is waiting still :
   You treat no other friend so ill.

2 But will He prove a friend indeed ?
   He will, the very Friend you need ;
   The Man of Nazareth, 't is He,
   With garments dyed at Calvary.

3 O lovely attitude ! He stands
   With melting heart and laden hands ;
   O matchless kindness ! and He shows
   This matchless kindness to His foes.

4 Admit Him ere His anger burn ;
   His feet departed ne'er return ;
   Admit Him, or the hour 's at hand
   When, at His door, denied you 'll stand.
                        Rev. Joseph Grigg. (1728-1768.)

161 "Now is the day of salvation." S. M.
2 Cor. v. 10 to vi. 2. Luke xiv. 16-24. Isa. lv.

1 Now is th' accepted time,
   Now is the day of grace ;
   O sinners, come without delay,
   And seek the Saviour's face.

2 Now is th' accepted time,
   The Saviour calls to-day ;
   To-morrow it may be too late,
   Then why should you delay ?

3 Now is th' accepted time,
   The gospel bids you come ;
   And every promise in His word
   Declares there yet is room.
                        John Dobell. (1737-1840.)

162 "All things are ready." S. M.
Mat. xxii. 1-14. Rev. ii. 18-29. Prov. ix. 1-12.

1 "ALL things are ready," come ;
   Come to the supper spread ;
   Come rich and poor, come old and young,
   Come, and be richly fed.

2 "All things are ready," come ;
   The door is open wide ;
   O feast upon the love of God,
   For Christ, His Son, has died.

3 "All things are ready," come ;
   All hindrance is removed ;
   And God, in Christ, His precious love
   To fallen man has proved.

4 "All things are ready," come ;
   To-morrow may not be ;
   O sinner, come, the Saviour waits
   This hour to welcome thee.
                        Albert Midlane. (1825-.)

163 "One thing is needful." L. M.
1 John ii. 15-17. 1 Pet. iv. 7-17. Ecc. xii.

1 WHY will ye waste on trifling cares
   That life which God's compassion spares,
   While, in the various range of thought,
   The one thing needful is forgot ?

2 Shall God invite you from above,
   Shall Jesus urge His dying love,
   Shall troubled conscience give you pain,
   And all these pleas unite in vain ?

3 Not so your eyes will always view
   Those objects which you now pursue ;
   Not so will heaven and hell appear,
   When death's decisive hour is near.

4 Almighty God, Thy grace impart ;
   Fix deep conviction on each heart ;
   Nor let us waste on trifling cares
   That life which Thy compassion spares.
                        Rev. Philip Doddridge. (1702-1751.)

164 "Grieve not the Holy Spirit." L. M.
Isa. xlv. 20-25. Ps. xcv. 8-11. Luke xiii. 24-35.

1 SAY, sinner, hath a voice within
   Oft whispered to thy secret soul,
   Urged thee to leave the ways of sin,
   And yield thy heart to God's control ?

2 Sinner, it was a heavenly voice,
   It was the Spirit's gracious call ;
   It bade thee make the better choice,
   And haste to seek in Christ thine all.

3 Spurn not the call to life and light,
   Regard in time the warning kind ;
   That call thou mayst not always slight,
   And yet the gate of mercy find.
                        Mrs. Ann B. Hyde. (-1872.)

"Turn ye, for why will ye die?"

165 "Can thine heart endure?" S. M.
Rev. iv. Mat. xxv. 31-46. Jer. xii. 5.

1 AND will the Judge descend,
  And must the dead arise,
  And not a single soul escape
  His all-discerning eyes?

2 How will my heart endure
  The terrors of that day,
  When earth and heaven before His face,
  Astonished, shrink away?

3 Ye sinners, seek His grace,
  Whose wrath ye cannot bear;
  Fly to the shelter of His cross,
  And find salvation there.
                    Rev. Philip Doddridge. (1702-1751.)

166 "Haste thee, escape." 7.
Heb. iii. 7-15. James iv. 7-17. Num. xxi. 4-9.

1 HASTEN, sinner, to be wise!
  Stay not for the morrow's sun:
  Wisdom, if thou still despise,
  Harder is she to be won.

2 Hasten, mercy to implore!
  Stay not for the morrow's sun,
  Lest thy season should be o'er
  Ere this evening's stage be run.

3 Hasten, sinner, to return!
  Stay not for the morrow's sun,
  Lest thy lamp should fail to burn
  Ere salvation's work is done.

4 Hasten, sinner, to be blessed!
  Stay not for the morrow's sun,
  Lest perdition thee arrest,
  Ere the morrow is begun.
                    Rev. Thomas Scott. (1700-1775.)

167 "God...commandeth all men...to repent." C. M.
Acts xvii. Mark i. 14-22. Eze. xxxiii. 1-20.

1 "REPENT!" the voice celestial cries,
  Nor longer dare delay;
  The wretch that scorns the mandate dies,
  And meets a fiery day.

2 No more the sovereign eye of God
  O'erlooks the crimes of men;
  His heralds are dispatched abroad
  To warn the world of sin.

3 Together in His presence bow,
  And all your guilt confess;
  Accept the offered Saviour now,
  Nor trifle with the grace.

4 Amazing love, that yet will call,
  And yet prolong our days!
  Our hearts, subdued by goodness, fall,
  And weep, and love, and praise.
                    Rev. Philip Doddridge.

168 "Repent and turn yourselves." 7.6. P.
John vi. 44-58 Jer xv Gen xix 1-17

1 DYING souls, fast bound in sin,
  Trembling and repining,
  With no ray of light divine
  On your pathway shining,
  Why in darkness wander on,
  Filled with consternation?
  Jesus lives; in Him alone
  Can you find salvation.

2 Prostrate bow, confess your guilt,
  Own your lost condition;
  Yield to Him whose blood was spilt
  Unreserved submission.
  Then no more in anguish groan;
  See His mediation;
  Jesus lives; in Him alone
  Can you find salvation.

3 Linger not in all the plain,
  Vengeance is pursuing;
  'Mid the dying and the slain,
  Save your souls from ruin.
  Flee to Him who can atone,
  Flee from condemnation;
  Jesus lives; in Him alone
  Can you find salvation.
                    Thomas Hastings. (1784-1872.)

169 "And the door was shut." 8.5.
Rev. iii. 14-22. Mat. xxv. 1-13. Prov. i. 20-23.

1 IN the silent midnight watches,
  List, thy bosom door,
  How it knocketh, knocketh, knocketh,
  Knocketh evermore.

2 Say not 't is thy pulse is beating:
  'T is thy heart of sin;
  'T is thy Saviour knocks, and crieth,
  Rise, and let Me in!

3 Jesus waiteth, waiteth, waiteth,
  But thy door is fast;
  Grieved, away thy Saviour goeth:
  Death breaks in at last.

4 Then 't is thine to stand entreating
  Christ to let thee in;
  At the gate of heaven beating,
  Wailing for thy sin.

5 Nay, alas, thou foolish virgin,
  Hast thou then forgot?
  Jesus waited long to know thee,
  But He knows thee not.
                    Bp. Arthur C. Coxe. (1818-.)

"Turn ye, for why will ye die?"

170 "Behold, now is the day of salvation."   **6. 4. P.**
Ecc. xii. 1-8. Ps. xcv. 7-11. Luke xii. 40-58. 1 Kings ix. 1-9.

1 CHILD of sin and sorrow, filled with dismay,
Wait not for to-morrow, yield thee to-day;
Heaven bids thee come, while yet there's room:
Child of sin and sorrow, hear and obey.

2 Child of sin and sorrow, why wilt thou die?
Come while thou canst borrow help from on high;
Grieve not that love which from above,
Child of sin and sorrow, would bring thee nigh.

3 Child of sin and sorrow, thy moments glide
Like the flitting arrow or the rushing tide;
Ere time is o'er Heaven's grace implore;
Child of sin and sorrow, in Christ confide.
                    Thomas Hastings. (1784-1872.)

171 "Turn yourselves... so iniquity shall not be your ruin."   **11.**
Eze. xxxiii. 1-11. Amos v. 1-15. Luke xiii. 24-35. 2 Pet iii.

1 O TURN ye, O turn ye, for why will ye die,
When God in great mercy is coming so nigh?
Now Jesus invites you, the Spirit says, "Come!"
And angels are waiting to welcome you home.

2 In riches, in pleasures, what can you obtain
To soothe your affliction, or banish your pain;
To bear up your spirit when summoned to die,
Or waft you to mansions of glory on high?

3 Why will you be starving, and feeding on air?
There's mercy in Jesus, enough and to spare;
If still you are doubting, make trial and see,
And prove that His mercy is boundless and free.
                    Rev. Josiah Hopkins. (1786-1862.)

172 "Up, get you out of this place."   **11.**
Gen. xix. 12-22. John iv. 1-14. Jer. ii. 1-13. Isa. lviii. 1-11.

1 DELAY not, delay not; O sinner, draw near;
The waters of life are now flowing for thee;
No price is demanded, the Saviour is here,
Redemption is purchased, salvation is free.

2 Delay not, delay not; why longer abuse
The love and compassion of Jesus, thy God?
A fountain is opened, how canst thou refuse
To wash and be cleansed in His pardoning blood?

3 Delay not, delay not; the Spirit of grace,
Long grieved and resisted, may take His sad flight,
And leave thee in darkness to finish thy race,
To sink in the vale of eternity's night.
                    Thomas Hastings.

173 "Come into the ark."   **10.**
Mat. xi. 28-30. Luke xv. 11-24. Jer. xxi. 8-14. 2 Sam xii. 13.

1 COME, heavy laden one, sighing for rest,
Come as a weary bird flies to her nest;
Now the accepted time, now is the day,
Come to the mercy-seat, why wilt thou stay?
Hark, 't is thy Saviour's voice calling to thee,
Come, heavy laden one, "come unto Me."

2 Linger not, linger not, come while 't is day,
Come while the shades of night close on thy way.
Life is a fleeting dream, soon 't will be o'er;
Turn from its fading joys, wander no more.
                    Author unknown.

"I habe done wickedly."

174 "Of whom I am chief." C. M.
1 Cor. xv. 8-11. 1 Tim. i. 12, 13. Ps. xxxviii.

1 I SEE the crowd in Pilate's hall,
I mark their wrathful mien;
Their shouts of "Crucify!" appall,
With blasphemy between.

2 And of that shouting multitude
I feel that I am one,
And in that din of voices rude
I recognize my own.

3 I see the scourges tear His back,
I see the piercing crown,
And of that crowd who smite and mock
I feel that I am one.

4 Around yon cross the throng I see,
Mocking the sufferer's groan;
Yet still my voice it seems to be,
As if I mocked alone.

5 'T was I that shed the sacred blood,
I nailed Him to the tree,
I crucified the Christ of God,
I joined the mockery.

6 Yet not the less that blood avails
To cleanse away my sin,
And not the less that cross prevails
To give me peace within.
Rev. Horatius Bonar. (1808-.)

175 "I have called, and ye refused." L. M.
Rev. iii. John v. 39-47. Eze. xxxiii. 1-19.

1 GOD calling yet! shall I not hear?
Earth's pleasures shall I still hold dear?
Shall life's swift passing years all fly,
And still my soul in slumber lie?

2 God calling yet! shall I not rise?
Can I His loving voice despise,
And basely His kind care repay?
He calls me still; can I delay?

3 God calling yet! and shall He knock,
And I my heart the closer lock?
He still is waiting to receive,
And shall I dare His Spirit grieve?

4 God calling yet! and shall I give
No heed, but still in bondage live?
I wait, but He does not forsake;
He calls me still; my heart, awake!

5 God calling yet! I cannot stay;
My heart I yield without delay.
Vain world, farewell, from thee I part;
The voice of God hath reached my heart.
Gerhard Tersteegen. (1697-1769.)
Tr. by Miss Jane Borthwick. (1820-.)

176 "I have sinned against the Lord God." 7.
Ps. li. Luke xxii. 54-62. 1 John i. 8-10.

1 DEPTH of mercy, can there be
Mercy still reserved for me?
Can my God His wrath forbear,
Me, the chief of sinners, spare?

2 I have long withstood His grace,
Long provoked Him to His face;
Would not hearken to His calls,
Grieved Him by a thousand falls.

3 Now incline me to repent,
Let me now my sins lament;
Now my foul revolt deplore,
Weep, believe, and sin no more.

4 Kindled His relentings are,
Me He now delights to spare;
Cries, "How shall I give thee up?"
Lets the lifted thunder drop.

5 There for me the Saviour stands,
Shows His wounds and spreads His hands.
God is love, I know, I feel;
Jesus weeps, and loves me still.
Rev. Charles Wesley. (1708-1788.)

177 "God be merciful to me a sinner." L. M.
Luke xviii. 9-14. Mat. viii. Lev. xiii. 45, 46.

1 WITH broken heart and contrite sigh,
A trembling sinner, Lord, I cry;
Thy pardoning grace is rich and free;
O God, be merciful to me!

2 I smite upon my troubled breast,
With deep and conscious guilt oppressed;
Christ and His cross my only plea,
O God, be merciful to me!

3 Far off I stand with tearful eyes,
Nor dare uplift them to the skies;
But Thou dost all my anguish see,
O God, be merciful to me!

4 Nor alms, nor deeds, that I have done
Can for a single sin atone;
To Calvary alone I flee,
O God, be merciful to me!
Rev. Cornelius Elven. (1797-.)

178 "Lord, to whom shall we go?" S. M.
John vi. 67-69. Isa. lxiv. Acts ix. 1-6.

1 AH, what avails my strife,
My wandering to and fro;
Thou hast the words of endless life;
Ah, whither should I go?

2 Lord, at Thy feet I fall,
I groan to be set free;
I fain would now obey the call,
And give up all for Thee.
Rev. Charles Wesley.

"I have done wickedly."

179 "Against Thee only have I sinned." **S. M.**
Ps. cxxxix. 1-18. Job x. 1-10. Acts xvi. 25-31.

1 AH, whither should I go,
   Burdened, and sick, and faint?
   To whom should I my trouble show,
   And pour out my complaint?

2 My Saviour bids me come;
   Ah, why do I delay?
   He calls the weary sinner home,
   And yet from Him I stay.

3 What is it keeps me back,
   From which I cannot part,
   Which will not let the Saviour take
   Possession of my heart?

4 Searcher of hearts, in mine
   Thy trying power display;
   Into its darkest corners shine,
   And take the veil away.
                  Rev. Charles Wesley. (1708-1788.)

180 "Sin hath reigned unto death." **C. M.**
Rom. iii. 1-26. Isa. lv. Zech. ix. 9-17.

1 How sad our state by nature is!
   Our sin, how deep it stains!
   And Satan binds our captive minds
   Fast in his slavish chains.

2 But there's a voice of sovereign grace
   Sounds from the sacred word;
   "Ho, ye despairing sinners, come,
   And trust upon the Lord."

3 My soul obeys th' almighty call,
   And runs to this relief;
   I would believe Thy promise, Lord,
   O help my unbelief.

4 A guilty, weak, and helpless worm,
   On Thy kind arms I fall:
   Be Thou my Strength and Righteousness,
   My Jesus, and my all.
                  Rev. Isaac Watts. (1674-1748.)

181 "My sins are not hid from Thee." **7.**
Hos. xiv. Rom. vii. Gen. viii. 1-12.

1 DOES the gospel word proclaim
   Rest for those that weary be?
   Then, my soul, put in thy claim,
   Sure that promise speaks to thee.

2 In the ark the weary dove
   Found a welcome resting-place;
   Thus my spirit longs to prove
   Rest in Christ, the Ark of grace.

3 Tempest-tossed I long have been,
   And the flood increases fast;
   Open, Lord, and take me in,
   Till the storm be overpast.
                  Rev. John Newton. (1725-1807.)

182 "I acknowledge my transgressions." **C. M.**
Heb. x. 19-22. Ps. xxxiv. 17-22. Lev. v. 1-19.

1 APPROACH, my soul, the mercy-seat,
   Where Jesus answers prayer;
   There humbly fall before His feet,
   For none can perish there.

2 Thy promise is my only plea,
   With this I venture nigh;
   Thou callest burdened souls to Thee,
   And such, O Lord, am I.

3 Bowed down beneath a load of sin,
   By Satan sorely prest,
   By war without, and fears within,
   I come to Thee for rest.

4 Be Thou my Shield and Hiding-place,
   That, sheltered near Thy side,
   I may my fierce accuser face,
   And tell him Thou hast died.
                  Rev. John Newton.

183 "Without God in the world." **C. M.**
Gen. xxviii. 16-22. Job xxiii. 2 Cor. iii. 7-18.

1 GOD is in this and every place;
   But O how dark and void
   To me! 'tis one great wilderness,
   This earth, without my God.

2 Empty of Him who all things fills,
   Till He His light impart,
   Till He His glorious self reveals,
   The veil is on my heart.

3 Regard me with a gracious eye,
   The long-sought blessing give;
   And bid me, at the point to die,
   Behold Thy face and live.
                  Rev. Charles Wesley.

184 "A friend of publicans and sinners." **L. M.**
Rom. v. 1-11. Mat. xv. 21-31. Ps. li.

1 JESUS, the sinner's Friend, to thee,
   Lost and undone, for aid I flee;
   Weary of earth, myself, and sin,
   Open Thine arms and take me in.

2 Pity and heal my sin-sick soul,
   'T is Thou alone canst make me whole;
   Dark, till in me Thine image shine,
   And lost, I am, till Thou art mine.

3 At last I own it cannot be
   That I should fit myself for Thee;
   Here, then, to Thee I all resign,
   Thine is the work, and only Thine.

4 What shall I say Thy grace to move?
   Lord, I am sin, but Thou art love:
   I give up every plea beside,
   Lord, I am lost, but Thou hast died.
                  Rev. Charles Wesley.

"I... repent in dust and ashes."

185 "Blot out my transgressions" **L. M.**
Ps. xxv. Dan. ix 1-19. John xxi 15-17

1 O THOU that hear'st when sinners cry,
Though all my crimes before Thee lie,
Behold me not with angry look,
But blot their mem'ry from Thy book.

2 Create my nature pure within,
And form my soul averse to sin;
Let Thy good Spirit ne'er depart,
Nor hide Thy presence from my heart.

3 I cannot live without Thy light,
Cast out and banished from Thy sight;
Thy holy joys, my God, restore,
And guard me, that I fall no more.

4 Though I have grieved Thy Spirit, Lord,
His help and comfort still afford;
And let a wretch come near Thy throne,
To plead the merits of Thy Son.

Rev. Isaac Watts. (1674-1748.)

186 "Cast me not away from Thy presence." **L. M.**
Ps. li 1-13. 2 Chr. xxxiv. 14-28. Mark x. 46-52.

1 SHOW pity, Lord, O Lord, forgive:
Let a repenting rebel live:
Are not Thy mercies large and free?
May not a sinner trust in Thee?

2 O wash my soul from every sin,
And make my guilty conscience clean;
Here on my heart the burden lies,
And past offences pain mine eyes.

3 My lips with shame my sins confess,
Against Thy law, against Thy grace;
Lord, should Thy judgments grow severe,
I am condemned, but Thou art clear.

4 Yet save a trembling sinner, Lord,
Whose hope, still hovering round Thy word,
Would light on some sweet promise there,
Some sure support against despair.

Rev. Isaac Watts.

187 "The sacrifices of God are a broken spirit." **L. M.**
Ps. li. 12-19. Job xlii. 1-6. Mat. xx. 30-34.

1 A BROKEN heart, my God, my King,
Is all the sacrifice I bring;
The God of grace will ne'er despise
A broken heart for sacrifice.

2 My soul lies humbled in the dust,
And owns Thy dreadful sentence just;
Look down, O Lord, with pitying eye,
And save the soul condemned to die.

3 Then will I teach the world Thy ways,
Sinners shall learn Thy sovereign grace;
I'll lead them to my Saviour's blood,
And they shall praise a pard'ning God.

Rev. Isaac Watts.

188 "Hide Thy face from my sins" **C. M.**
Luke xviii 9-14. Titus iii. 3-7 Ps lxxxvi

1 PROSTRATE, dear Jesus, at Thy feet,
A guilty rebel lies,
And upwards to Thy mercy-seat
Presumes to lift his eyes.

2 If tears of sorrow would suffice
To pay the debt I owe,
Tears should from both my weeping eyes
In ceaseless torrents flow.

3 But no such sacrifice I plead
To expiate my guilt;
No tears but those which Thou hast shed,
No blood but Thou hast spilt.

4 Think of Thy sorrows, dearest Lord,
And all my sins forgive;
Justice will well approve the word
That bids the sinner live.

Rev. Samuel Stennett. (1727-1795.)

189 "Take not Thy Holy Spirit from me." **L. M.**
Lam. iii. 41-66. Ex. xxxii. Heb. iii. 7 to iv. 7.

1 STAY, Thou insulted Spirit, stay,
Though I have done Thee such despite;
Nor cast the sinner quite away,
Nor take Thine everlasting flight.

2 Though I have most unfaithful been
Of all who e'er Thy grace received,
Ten thousand times Thy goodness seen,
Ten thousand times Thy goodness grieved.

3 Yet, O, the chief of sinners spare,
In honor of my great High Priest;
Nor in Thy righteous anger swear
To exclude me from Thy people's rest.

4 Now, Lord, my weary soul release,
Upraise me with Thy gracious hand,
And guide into Thy perfect peace,
And bring me to the promised land.

Rev. Charles Wesley. (1708-1788.)

190 "Unto Thee will I cry, O Lord, my Rock." **C. M.**
Luke xviii. 35-43. Acts xxii. 6-16. Ps. xiii.

1 O JESUS, Saviour of the lost,
My Rock and Hiding-Place,
By storms of sin and sorrow tost,
I seek Thy sheltering grace.

2 Guilty, forgive me, Lord, I cry,
Pursued by foes, I come;
A sinner, save me, or I die;
An outcast, take me home.

3 Once safe in Thine almighty arms,
Let storms come on amain;
There danger never, never harms,
There death itself is gain.

Rev. Edward H. Bickersteth. (1825-.)

"Lord, I believe; help Thou mine unbelief."

191 "Lord, remember me." Luke xxiii. 39–43. Heb. vii. 25–28. Job xiii. **C. M.**

1 JESUS, Thou art the sinner's Friend;
　As such I look to Thee;
　Now, in the fulness of Thy love,
　　O Lord, remember me.

2 Remember Thy pure word of grace,
　Remember Calvary;
　Remember all Thy dying groans,
　　And then remember me.

3 Thou wondrous Advocate with God,
　I yield myself to Thee;
　While Thou art sitting on Thy throne,
　　Dear Lord, remember me.

4 Lord, I am guilty, I am vile,
　But Thy salvation's free;
　Then, in Thine all-abounding grace,
　　Dear Lord, remember me.

5 And when I close my eyes in death,
　When creature-helps all flee,
　Then, O my dear Redeemer, God,
　　I pray, remember me.
　　　　　Rev. Richard Burnham. (1749-1810.)

192 "Thou hast the words of eternal life." 1 Pet. i. 18–25. Titus iii. 4–7. Isa. lxiv. 6–12. **L. M.**

1 JUST as I am, without one plea,
　But that Thy blood was shed for me,
　And that Thou bid'st me come to Thee,
　　O Lamb of God, I come, I come!

2 Just as I am, and waiting not
　To rid my soul of one dark blot,
　To Thee, whose blood can cleanse each spot,
　　O Lamb of God, I come, I come!

3 Just as I am, though tossed about
　With many a conflict, many a doubt,
　Fightings and fears within, without,
　　O Lamb of God, I come, I come!

4 Just as I am, poor, wretched, blind,
　Sight, riches, healing of the mind,
　Yea, all I need, in Thee to find.
　　O Lamb of God, I come, I come!

5 Just as I am, Thou wilt receive,
　Wilt welcome, pardon, cleanse, relieve;
　Because Thy promise I believe,
　　O Lamb of God, I come, I come!
　　　　　Miss Charlotte Elliott. (1789-1871.)

193 "O Lord, deliver my soul." Mark x. 46–52. Heb. ix. 11–28. Jer. xiv. 7–22. **8. 6.**

1 O THOU that hear'st the prayer of faith,
　Wilt Thou not save a soul from death,
　　That casts itself on Thee?
　I have no refuge of my own,
　But fly to what my Lord hath done
　　And suffered once for me.

2 Slain in the guilty sinner's stead,
　His spotless righteousness I plead,
　　And His availing blood:
　Thy merit, Lord, my robe shall be,
　Thy merit shall atone for me,
　　And bring me near to God.

3 Then snatch me from eternal death,
　The Spirit of adoption breathe,
　　His consolations send;
　By Him some word of life impart,
　And sweetly whisper to my heart,
　　"Thy Maker is thy Friend."

4 The king of terrors then would be
　A welcome messenger to me,
　　That bids me come away;
　Unclogged by earth, or earthly things,
　I'd mount upon his sable wings,
　　To everlasting day.
　　　　　Rev. Augustus M. Toplady. (1740-1778.)

194 "I believe that Thou art the Christ." Acts xvi. 25–34. Mark ix. 23, 24. Ps. xxxi. **7. 6. 8.**

1 LAMB of God, for sinners slain,
　　To Thee I humbly pray;
　Heal me of my grief and pain,
　　O take my sins away.
　From this bondage, Lord, release,
　　No longer let me be oppressed:
　Jesus, Master, seal my peace,
　　And take me to Thy breast.

2 Wilt Thou cast a sinner out
　　Who humbly comes to Thee?
　No, my God, I cannot doubt
　　Thy mercy is for me.
　Let me then obtain the grace,
　　And be of paradise possessed:
　Jesus, Master, seal my peace,
　　And take me to Thy breast.

3 Worldly good I do not want,
　　Be that to others given;
　Only for Thy love I pant,
　　My all in earth and heaven.
　This the crown I fain would seize,
　　The good wherewith I would be blest:
　Jesus, Master, seal my peace,
　　And take me to Thy breast.
　　　　　Rev. Charles Wesley. (1708-1788.)

"Lord, I believe; help Thou mine unbelief."

195 "Jesus, Son of David, have mercy on me." Mark x. 46-52. Acts ix. 1-6. Ps. xxxviii. **8. 7.**

1 JESUS, full of all compassion,
   Hear Thy humble suppliant's cry ;
   Let me know Thy great salvation,
   See, I languish, faint, and die.

2 Guilty, but with heart relenting,
   Overwhelmed with helpless grief,
   Prostrate at Thy feet repenting,
   Send, O send me quick relief.

3 Saved ! The deed shall spread new glory
   Through the shining realms above ;
   Angels sing the pleasing story,
   All enraptured with Thy love.

   Rev. Daniel Turner. (1710-1708.)

196 "I come . . . to do Thy will, O my God." Phil. iii. 8-14. Acts xxii. 1-21. Isa. xxxv. 8-10. **L. M.**

1 JESUS, my all, to heaven is gone,
   He whom I fix my hopes upon ;
   His track I see, and I 'll pursue
   The narrow way till Him I view.

2 This is the way I long have sought,
   And mourned because I found it not ;
   My grief a burden long has been,
   Because I was not saved from sin.

3 The more I strove against its power,
   I felt its weight and guilt the more ;
   Till late I heard my Saviour say,
   "Come hither, soul, I am the way."

4 Lo, glad I come, and Thou, blest Lamb,
   Shalt take me to Thee as I am;
   Nothing but sin have I to give,
   Nothing but love shall I receive.

5 Then will I tell to sinners round
   What a dear Saviour I have found ;
   I 'll point to Thy redeeming blood,
   And say, " Behold the way to God."

   Rev. John Cennick. (1717-1755.)

197 "In Thee do I put my trust." 1 Cor. iv. 4-14. John vi. 66-69. Ps. cxix. 17-32. **7.**

1 I AM coming to the cross,
   I am poor, and weak, and blind ;
   I am counting all but dross,
   I shall full salvation find.

   I am trusting, Lord, in Thee,
   Blest Lamb of Calvary ;
   Humbly at Thy cross I bow,
   Save me, Jesus, save me now.

2 Here I give my all to Thee,
   Friends, and time, and earthly store ;
   Soul and body Thine to be,
   Wholly Thine for evermore.

   Rev. William McDonald. (1820-.)

198 "Master, I will follow Thee." Acts xxvi. 9-19. Luke xxiii. 33-42. Ps. cviii. 1-6. **8. 6.**

1 LORD, Thou hast won, at length I yield ;
   My heart, by mighty grace compelled,
   Surrenders all to Thee.
   Against Thy terrors long I strove,
   But who can stand against Thy love ?
   Love conquers even me.

2 If Thou hadst bid Thy thunders roll,
   And lightnings flash to blast my soul,
   I still had stubborn been ;
   But mercy has my heart subdued,
   A bleeding Saviour I have viewed,
   And now I hate my sin.

3 Now, Lord, I would be Thine alone ;
   Come, take possession of Thine own,
   For Thou hast set me free.
   Released from Satan's hard command,
   See all my powers in waiting stand,
   To be employed by Thee.

   Rev. John Newton. (1725-1807.)

199 "I will put thee in a cleft of the rock." Isa. xxvi. 4. Ex. xxxiii. 22. Num. xx. 11. John xix. 34. **7.**

1 ROCK of Ages, cleft for me,
   Let me hide myself in Thee ;
   Let the water and the blood,
   From Thy riven side which flowed,
   Be of sin the double cure,
   Cleanse me from its guilt and power.

2 Not the labors of my hands
   Can fulfil Thy law's demands ;
   Could my zeal no respite know,
   Could my tears forever flow,
   All for sin could not atone,
   Thou must save, and Thou alone.

3 Nothing in my hand I bring,
   Simply to Thy cross I cling;
   Naked, come to Thee for dress,
   Helpless, look to Thee for grace ;
   Foul, I to the Fountain fly,
   Wash me, Saviour, or I die.

4 While I draw this fleeting breath,
   When my eyelids close in death,
   When I soar to worlds unknown,
   See Thee on Thy judgment throne,
   Rock of Ages, cleft for me,
   Let me hide myself in Thee.

   Rev. Augustus M. Toplady. (1740-1778.)

"Lord, I believe; help Thou mine unbelief."

200 "A broken and a contrite heart." 8, 7.
Luke xv. 11–32. Hos. xi. Ps. ci.

1 TAKE my heart, O Father, take it,
   Make and keep it all Thine own;
   Let thy Spirit melt and break it,
   This proud heart of sin and stone.

2 Father, make it pure and lowly,
   Fond of peace and far from strife;
   Turning from the paths unholy
   Of this vain and sinful life.

3 Ever let Thy grace surround it,
   Strengthen it with power divine,
   Till Thy cords of love have bound it;
   Make it to be wholly Thine.

4 May the blood of Jesus heal it,
   And its sins be all forgiven;
   Holy Spirit, take and seal it,
   Guide it in the path to heaven.
   Author unknown.

201 "Give... thy servant an understanding heart." L. M.
John ix. 24–38. 2 Cor. i. 5–22. Ezra ix. 5 to x. 1.

1 LORD, take my heart, and let it be
   Forever closed to all but Thee;
   Seal Thou my breast, and let me wear
   That pledge of love forever there.

2 How blest are they who still abide
   Close sheltered in Thy bleeding side;
   Who thence their life and strength derive,
   And by Thee move, and in Thee live!

3 What are our works but sin and death,
   Till Thou Thy quickening spirit breathe?
   Thou giv'st the power Thy grace to move;
   O wondrous grace, O boundless love!
   Nicolaus L. Zinzendorf. (1700–1760.)
   Tr. by Rev. John Wesley. (1703–1791.)

202 "Thy righteousness,... Thine only." S. M.
1 Pet. i. 17–25. 1 Cor. x. 23–31. Ps. cxi.

1 GOD of almighty love,
   By whose sufficient grace
   I lift my heart to things above,
   And humbly seek Thy face,
   Through Jesus Christ the Just
   My faint desires receive,
   And let me in Thy goodness trust,
   And to Thy glory live.

2 Whate'er I say or do,
   Thy glory be my aim;
   My offerings all be offered through
   The ever-blesséd name.
   Jesus, my single eye
   Be fixed on Thee alone;
   Thy name be praised on earth, on high
   Thy will by all be done.
   Rev. Charles Wesley. (1708–1788.)

203 "By whom the world is crucified unto me." L. M.
Gal. vi. 14. Mark xv. 22–39. Ps. cxvi. 12–19.

1 WHEN I survey the wondrous cross
   On which the Prince of Glory died,
   My richest gain I count but loss,
   And pour contempt on all my pride.

2 Forbid it, Lord, that I should boast,
   Save in the death of Christ, my God:
   All the vain things that charm me most,
   I sacrifice them to His blood.

3 See, from His head, His hands, His feet,
   Sorrow and love flow mingled down:
   Did e'er such love and sorrow meet,
   Or thorns compose so rich a crown?

4 Were the whole realm of nature mine,
   That were a present far too small:
   Love so amazing, so divine,
   Demands my soul, my life, my all.
   Rev. Isaac Watts. (1674–1748.)

204 "What things were gain... I counted loss." L. M.
Phil. iii. 4–11. 2 Cor. iv. 7–18. Jer. xx. 23, 24.

1 No more, my God, I boast no more
   Of all the duties I have done;
   I quit the hopes I held before,
   To trust the merits of Thy Son.

2 Now for the love I bear His name,
   What was my gain I count my loss;
   My former pride I call my shame,
   And nail my glory to His cross.

3 Yes, and I must and will esteem
   All things but loss for Jesus' sake;
   O may my soul be found in Him,
   And of His righteousness partake.
   Rev. Isaac Watts.

205 "Have mercy upon me and hear my prayer." 7.
Luke xxiii. 33–42. 1 Tim. i. 12–15. Job xix.

1 THOU, who didst on Calvary bleed,
   Thou, who dost for sinners plead,
   Help me in my time of need,
   Jesus, Saviour, hear my cry.
   In my darkness and my grief,
   With my heart of unbelief,
   I, who am of sinners chief,
   Jesus, lift to Thee mine eye.

2 Foes without and fears within,
   With no plea Thy grace to win;
   But that Thou canst save from sin,
   Jesus, to Thy cross I fly.
   There on Thee I cast my care,
   There to Thee I raise my prayer,
   Jesus, save me from despair,
   Save me, save me, or I die.
   Rev. James D. Burns. (1823–1864.)

"Behold, he prayeth."

206 "O Lord, heal me." 7.
Ps. li. Mat. xx. 30-34. Rom. viii. 15-26.

1 HOLY Father, hear my cry;
  Holy Saviour, bend Thine ear;
  Holy Spirit, come Thou nigh;
  Father, Saviour, Spirit, hear!

2 Father, save me from my sin;
  Saviour, I Thy mercy crave;
  Gracious Spirit, make me clean;
  Father, Son, and Spirit, save!

3 Father, let me taste Thy love;
  Saviour, fill my soul with peace;
  Spirit, come my heart to move;
  Father, Son, and Spirit, bless!

4 Father, Son, and Spirit, Thou
  One Jehovah, shed abroad
  All Thy grace within me now;
  Be my Father and my God!

  Rev. Horatius Bonar. (1808-.)

207 "Let us also walk in the Spirit." C. M.
Ps. lvi. 1 John iv. 1-6. Eph. ii. 19-22.

1 COME, Holy Ghost, my soul inspire;
  This one great gift impart,
  What most I need and most desire,
  An humble, holy heart.

2 Bear witness I am born again,
  My many sins forgiven;
  Nor let a gloomy doubt remain
  To cloud my hope of heaven.

3 More of myself grant I may know,
  From sin's deceit be free,
  In all the Christian graces grow,
  And live alone to Thee.

  Rev. Asahel Nettleton. (1783-1844.)

208 "Praying in the Holy Ghost." 7.
John xvi. 1-15. Rom. xiv. 17. Isa. xlviii. 16, 17.

1 HOLY Ghost, with light divine,
  Shine upon this heart of mine;
  Chase the shades of night away,
  Turn the darkness into day.

2 Holy Ghost, with power divine,
  Cleanse this guilty heart of mine;
  Long has sin, without control,
  Held dominion o'er my soul.

3 Holy Ghost, with joy divine,
  Cheer this saddened heart of mine;
  Bid my many woes depart,
  Heal my wounded, bleeding heart.

4 Holy Spirit, all divine,
  Dwell within this heart of mine;
  Cast down every idol-throne,
  Reign supreme, and reign alone.

  Rev. Andrew Reed. (1787-1862.)

209 "It is the Spirit that quickeneth." 7.
Ps. lxxxvi. Luke xi. 1-13. 2 Chr. i. 7-12.

1 FATHER, who didst fashion me
  Image of Thyself to be,
  Fill me with Thy love divine,
  Let my every thought be Thine.

2 Holy Jesus, may I be
  Dead and buried here with Thee;
  And, by love inflamed, arise
  Unto Thee a sacrifice.

3 Thou who dost all gifts impart,
  Shine, sweet Spirit, in my heart;
  Best of gifts, Thyself, bestow,
  Make me burn Thy love to know.

4 God, the blessed Three in One,
  Dwell within my heart alone;
  Thou dost give Thyself to me,
  May I give myself to Thee.

  Le Mans Breviary.
  Tr. by Rev. Sir Henry W. Baker. (1821-.)

210 "He . . . shall show it unto you." L. M.
Ps. xliii. Neh. ix. 19-21. Gal. v. 13-18.

1 COME, Holy Spirit, heavenly Dove,
  My sinful maladies remove;
  Be Thou my Light, be Thou my Guide,
  O'er every thought and step preside.

2 The light of truth to me display,
  That I may know and choose my way;
  Plant holy fear within my heart,
  That I from God may ne'er depart.

3 Lead me to Christ, the living Way,
  Nor let me from His pastures stray;
  Lead me to heaven, the seat of bliss,
  Where pleasure in perfection is.

  Rev. Simon Browne. (1680-1732.)

211 "The Spirit helpeth our infirmities." C. M.
John i. 1-5. Isa. xliv. 3-5. Mat. v. 13-16.

1 COME, mighty Spirit, penetrate
    This heart and soul of mine;
  And my whole being with Thy grace
    Pervade, O Life Divine!

2 As the clear air surrounds the earth,
    Thy grace around me roll;
  As the fresh light pervades the air,
    So pierce and fill my soul.

3 As from the cloud drops down in love
    The precious summer rain,
  So from Thyself pour down the flood
    That freshens all again.

4 Thus life within our lifeless hearts
    Shall make its glad abode,
  And we shall shine in beauteous light,
    Filled with the light of God.

  Rev. Horatius Bonar.

"Behold he prayeth."

212 " Lord, that I may receive my sight." **8, 7.**
Luke xviii. Acts ix. 1-22. 2 Kings vi. 8-17.

1 LORD, I know Thy grace is nigh me,
    Though Thyself I cannot see ;
Jesus, Master, pass not by me,
    Son of David, pity me.

2 While I sit in weary blindness,
    Longing for the blessèd light,
Many taste Thy loving-kindness ;
    " Lord, I would receive my sight."

3 I would see Thee and adore Thee,
    And Thy word the power can give ;
Hear the sightless soul implore Thee,
    Let me see Thy face and live.

4 Ah, what touch is this that thrills me,
    What this burst of strange delight ?
Lo, the rapturous vision fills me,
    This is Jesus, this is sight!
                    Rev. Hervey D. Ganse. (1822-.)

213 " Not disobedient to the heavenly vision." **C. M.**
John ix. 24-38. Luke xix. 1-9. Ps. cxvi. 7-19.

1 WELCOME, O Saviour, to my heart,
    Possess Thine humble throne ;
Bid every rival hence depart,
    And claim me for Thine own.

2 The world and Satan I forsake,
    To Thee I all resign ;
My longing heart, O Jesus, take,
    And make it all divine.
                    Rev. Hugh Bourne. (1772-1852.)

214 " Who loved me and gave Himself for me." **7.**
Rom. v. 6-21. John i. 35-51. Ps. lxxi.

1 JESUS, Lamb of God, for me,
    Thou, the Lord of Life, didst die ;
Whither, whither, but to Thee
    Can a trembling sinner fly ?
Death's dark waters o'er me roll,
Save, O save my sinking soul!

2 Never bowed a martyred head
    Weighed with equal sorrow down ;
Never blood so rich was shed,
    Never king wore such a crown.
To Thy cross and sacrifice
Faith now lifts her tearful eyes.

3 While with broken heart I kneel,
    Sinks the inward storm to rest ;
Life, immortal life, I feel
    Kindled in my throbbing breast.
Thine forever Thine, I am ;
Glory to the bleeding Lamb!
                    Rev. Ray Palmer. (1808-.)

215 " Father, forgive them." **L. M.**
John xix. 28-30. Eph. ii. 11-15. Isa. lix. 12-21.

1 I HEAR a voice that comes from far,
    From Calvary it sounds abroad ;
It soothes my soul and calms my fear,
    It speaks of pardon bought with blood.

2 And is it true that many fly
    The sound that bids my soul rejoice,
And rather choose with fools to die
    Than turn an ear to mercy's voice ?

3 With such, I own, I once appeared,
    But now I know how great their loss ;
For sweeter sounds were never heard
    Than mercy utters from the cross.
                    Rev. Thomas Kelly. (1769-1855.)

216 " Grace, mercy, and peace from God." **9. 6. 8.**
Zech. xii. 9-14. Isa. xlv. 22-25. Heb. ix. 11-28.

1 BY faith I view my Saviour dying
    On the tree, on the tree ;
To every nation He is crying,
    Look to me, look to me.
He bids the guilty now draw near,
Repent, believe, dismiss their fear ;
Hark, hark, what precious words I hear :
    Mercy's free, mercy's-free.

2 Jesus, the Lord of Life, hath spoken
    Peace to me, peace to me ;
Now all my chains of sin are broken,
    I am free, I am free.
Soon as I in His name believed,
His pardoning grace my soul received,
And was from sin and death retrieved,
    Mercy's free, mercy's free.
                    R. Jukes. 1842.

217 " Whereas I was blind, now I see." **7. 6.**
John iii. 14-18. Mat. viii. 1-17. Num. xxi. 4-9.

1 How lost was my condition,
    Till Jesus made me whole!
There is but one Physician
    Can cure a sin-sick soul.
Next door to death He found me,
And snatched me from the grave,
To tell to all around me
    His wondrous power to save.

2 A dying, risen Jesus,
    Seen by the eye of faith,
At once from anguish frees us,
    And saves the soul from death.
Come, then, to this Physician,
    His help He'll freely give ;
He makes no hard condition,
    'T is only, look and live!
                    Rev. John Newton. (1725-1807.)

39

"I will magnify Him with thanksgiving."

218 "He hath put a new song in my mouth." **L. M.**
Ps. lxxxix. 1-15. Luke i. 46-55. Rev. iv

1 Now to the Lord a noble song !
  Awake, my soul, awake, my tongue ;
  Hosanna to th' eternal name,
  And all His boundless love proclaim.

2 See where it shines in Jesus' face,
  The brightest image of His grace !
  God, in the person of His Son,
  Has all His mightiest works outdone.

3 Grace! 't is a sweet, a charming theme ;
  My thoughts rejoice at Jesus' name :
  Ye angels, dwell upon the sound ;
  Ye heavens, reflect it to the ground.

4 O may I live to reach the place
  Where He unveils His lovely face ;
  Where all His beauties you behold,
  And sing His name to harps of gold !
  Rev. Isaac Watts. (1674-1748.)

219 "Unto thee, O Lord, will I sing." **L. M.**
Ps. xviii. 1-18. Eph. i. 3-12. 2 Cor. i. 3-7.

1 O BLESSÈD God, to Thee I raise
  My voice in thankful hymns of praise ;
  And when my voice shall silent be,
  My silence shall be praise to Thee.

2 For voice and silence both impart
  The filial homage of my heart ;
  And both alike are understood
  By Thee, Thou Parent of all good ;

3 Whose grace is all unsearchable,
  Whose care for me no tongue can tell ;
  Who loves my loudest praise to hear,
  And loves to bless my voiceless prayer.
  Author unknown.

220 "My lips shall praise Thee." **C. M.**
Isa. xlix. 13-17. Luke i. 68-75. Rev. v. 6-10.

1 BEGIN, my tongue, some heavenly theme,
  And speak some boundless thing,
  The mighty works, or mightier name,
  Of our eternal King.

2 Tell of His wondrous faithfulness,
  And sound His power abroad ;
  Sing the sweet promise of His grace,
  And the performing God.

3 His very word of grace is strong
  As that which built the skies ;
  The voice that rolls the stars along
  Speaks all the promises.

4 O might I hear Thy heavenly tongue
  But whisper, "Thou art mine!"
  Those gentle words should raise my song
  To notes almost divine.
  Rev. Isaac Watts.

221 "I will bless Thy name forever and ever." **C. M.**
Ps cxlvi Heb xiii 14, 15. Rev xiv. 1-3.

1 YES, I will bless Thee, O my God,
  Through all my mortal days,
  And to eternity prolong
  Thy vast, Thy boundless praise.

2 Nor shall my tongue alone proclaim
  The honors of my God :
  My life, with all its active powers,
  Shall spread Thy praise abroad.

3 Nor will I cease Thy praise to sing
  When death shall close mine eyes ;
  My thoughts shall then to nobler heights
  And sweeter raptures rise.

4 There shall my lips, in endless praise,
  Their grateful tribute pay ;
  The theme demands an angel's tongue,
  And an eternal day.
  Rev. Ottiwell Heginbotham. (1744-1768.)

222 "While I live will I praise the Lord." **L. M.**
Ps. lxvi. 13-20. Rom. xii. 1. 2 Cor. 6-18.

1 GOD of my life, through all its days
  My grateful powers shall sound Thy praise ;
  The song shall wake with opening light,
  And warble to the silent night.

2 When anxious cares would break my rest,
  And griefs would tear my throbbing breast,
  Thy tuneful praises, raised on high,
  Shall check the murmur and the sigh.

3 When death o'er nature shall prevail,
  And all my powers of language fail,
  Joy through my swimming eyes shall break,
  And mean the thanks I cannot speak.

4 But O when that last conflict 's o'er,
  And I am chained to earth no more,
  With what glad accents shall I rise
  To join the music of the skies !
  Rev. Philip Doddridge. (1702-1751.)

223 "I will sing of mercy." **7.**
Ps. c. Heb. i. 1-12. Rom. v. 8-11.

1 SING, my soul, His wondrous love,
  Who, from yon bright throne above,
  Ever watchful o'er our race,
  Still to man extends His grace.

2 God, the merciful and good,
  Bought us with the Saviour's blood ;
  And, to make our safety sure,
  Guides us by His Spirit pure.

3 Sing, my soul, adore His name,
  Let His glory be thy theme ;
  Praise Him till He calls thee home,
  Trust His love for all to come.
  Author unknown.

"I will magnify Him with thanksgiving."

224 "Thou art exalted as head above all." 8. 7.
Ps. cxlviii. Isa. xlix. 13-23. Mat. xxi. 8-16.

1 MIGHTY God, while angels bless Thee,
   May a mortal sing Thy name?
Lord of men, as well as angels,
   Thou art every creature's theme.
Lord of every land and nation,
   Ancient of eternal days,
Sounded through the wide creation,
   Be Thy just and lawful praise.

2 For the grandeur of Thy nature,
   Grand beyond a seraph's thought;
For the wonders of creation,
   Works with skill and kindness wrought;
For Thy providence, that governs
   Through Thine empire's wide domain,
Wings an angel, guides a sparrow,
   Blesséd be Thy gentle reign.

3 For Thy rich. Thy free redemption,
   Bright, though veiled in darkness long,
Thought is poor, and poor expression,
   Who can sing that wondrous song?
Brightness of the Father's glory,
   Shall Thy praise unuttered lie?
Break, my tongue, such guilty silence,
   Sing the Lord who came to die.
                    Rev. Robert Robinson. (1735-1790.)

225 "With the precious blood of Christ." C. M.
Zech. xiii. 1-9. John xix. 30-42. 1 John i.

1 THERE is a fountain filled with blood
   Drawn from Emmanuel's veins;
And sinners, plunged beneath that flood,
   Lose all their guilty stains.

2 The dying thief rejoiced to see
   That fountain in his day;
And there have I, as vile as he,
   Washed all my sins away.

3 Dear dying Lamb, Thy precious blood
   Shall never lose its power,
Till all the ransomed church of God
   Be saved, to sin no more.

4 E'er since, by faith, I saw the stream
   Thy flowing wounds supply,
Redeeming love has been my theme,
   And shall be till I die.

5 Then, in a nobler, sweeter song,
   I'll sing thy power to save,
When this poor lisping, stammering tongue
   Lies silent in the grave.
                    William Cowper. (1731-1800.)

226 "My soul shall be joyful in the Lord." 8. 7.
Ps. cvii. Isa. lxiii. 7-14. 2 Cor. xii. 1-11.

1 LORD, with glowing heart I'd praise Thee
   For the bliss Thy love bestows,
For the pardoning grace that saves me,
   And the peace that from it flows.
Help, O God, my weak endeavor,
   This dull soul to rapture raise:
Thou must light the flame, or never
   Can my love be warmed to praise.

2 Praise, my soul, the God that sought thee,
   Wretched wanderer, far astray;
Found thee lost, and kindly brought thee
   From the paths of death away.
Praise, with love's devoutest feeling,
   Him who saw thy guilt-born fear,
And, the light of hope revealing,
   Bade the blood-stained cross appear.

3 Lord, this bosom's ardent feeling
   Vainly would my lips express;
Low before thy footstool kneeling,
   Deign Thy suppliant's prayer to bless.
Let Thy grace, my soul's chief treasure,
   Love's pure flame within me raise:
And since words can never measure,
   Let my life show forth Thy praise.
                    Francis S. Key. (1799-1843.)

227 "Sing... His praise from the end of the earth." C. M.
Rev. v. 9-14. Isa. xliv. 21-28. Ps. cl.

1 O FOR a thousand tongues to sing
   My great Redeemer's praise;
The glories of my God and King,
   The triumphs of His grace!

2 My gracious Master and my God,
   Assist me to proclaim,
To spread through all the earth abroad,
   The honors of Thy name.

3 Jesus, the name that charms our fears,
   That bids our sorrows cease;
'T is music in the sinner's ears,
   'T is life, and health, and peace.

4 He breaks the power of cancelled sin,
   He sets the pris'ner free;
His blood can make the foulest clean,
   His blood availed for me.

5 He speaks, and, listening to His voice,
   New life the dead receive;
The mournful, broken hearts rejoice,
   The humble poor believe.
                    Rev. Charles Wesley. (1708-1788.)

"I will magnify Him with thanksgiving."

228 "My soul, which Thou hast redeemed." 8, 7, 4.
Isa. xii. Ps. xl. 1 Pet. i. 12-17.

1 O THOU God of my salvation,
　My Redeemer from all sin,
Moved by Thy divine compassion,
Who hast died my heart to win,
　　I will praise Thee :
Where shall I Thy praise begin?

2 Though unseen, I love the Saviour,
He hath brought salvation near;
Manifests His pardoning favor ;
And when Jesus doth appear,
　　Soul and body
Shall His glorious image bear.

3 While the angel choirs are crying,
Glory to the great I AM,
I with them will still be vying,
Glory, glory to the Lamb !
　　O how precious,
Is the sound of Jesus' name !
Rev. Thomas Olivers. (1725-1799.)

229 "Unto the Son, Thy throne . . . is forever." L. M.
Ps. xlv. Heb. i. 1-12. Acts ii. 22-36.

1 Now be my heart inspired to sing
The glories of my Saviour King ;
Jesus, the Lord, how heavenly fair
His form, how bright His beauties are !

2 O'er all the sons of human race,
He shines with a superior grace ;
Love from His lips divinely flows,
And blessings all His state compose.

3 God, Thine own God, has richly shed
His oil of gladness on Thy head ;
And with His sacred Spirit blest
His first-born Son above the rest.
Rev. Isaac Watts. (1674-1748.)

230 "Praise the Lord, O my soul." 8, 7, 4.
Dan. iv. 34-37. Ps. ciii. Rom. vi. 1-18.

1 PRAISE, my soul, the King of heaven,
To His feet thy tribute bring ;
Ransomed, healed, restored, forgiven,
Evermore His praises sing :
　　Alleluia ! Alleluia !
Praise the everlasting King.

2 Father-like, He tends and spares us,
Well our feeble frame He knows ;
In His hands He gently bears us,
Rescues us from all our foes :
　　Alleluia ! Alleluia !
Praise with us the God of grace.
Rev. Henry F. Lyte. (1793-1847.)
Alt. by Rev. Sir He ry W. Baker. (1: -1877.)

231 "Make His praise glorious." 8, 6.
Ps. lxvi. 1 Pet. ii. 6-15. Eph. i.

1 O COULD I speak the matchless worth,
O could I sound the glories forth,
Which in my Saviour shine,
I 'd soar and touch the heavenly strings,
And vie with Gabriel while he sings
In notes almost divine.

2 I 'd sing the precious blood He spilt,
My ransom from the dreadful guilt
Of sin and wrath divine ;
I 'd sing His glorious righteousness,
In which all-perfect, heavenly dress
My soul shall ever shine.

3 I 'd sing the characters He bears,
And all the forms of love He wears,
Exalted on His throne ;
In loftiest songs of sweetest praise,
I would to everlasting days
Make all His glories known.

4 Well, the delightful day will come
When my dear Lord will bring me home,
And I shall see His face ;
Then, with my Saviour, Brother, Friend,
A blest eternity I 'll spend,
Triumphant in His grace.
Rev. Samuel Medley. (1738-1799.)

232 "A name which is above every name." H. M.
Isa. ix. 6. Jer. xxiii. 6. Mat. i. 21-23.

1 JOIN all the glorious names
Of wisdom, love, and power
That ever mortals knew,
That angels ever bore :
All are too mean to speak His worth,
Too mean to set my Saviour forth.

2 Great Prophet of my God,
My tongue would bless Thy name ;
By Thee the joyful news
Of our salvation came :
The joyful news of sins forgiven,
Of hell subdued, and peace with heaven.

3 My dear Almighty Lord,
My Conqueror and my King,
Thy sceptre and Thy sword,
Thy reigning grace, I sing :
Thine is the power ; behold, I sit,
In willing bonds, beneath Thy feet.
Rev. Isaac Watts.

42

"I will magnify Him with thanksgiving."

233 "The Lord merciful and gracious." **S. M.**
Eph. ii. 4-10. 2 Tim. i. 9, 10. Zech. iv. 6, 7.

1 GRACE! 't is a charming sound,
  Harmonious to mine ear;
Heaven with the echo shall resound,
  And all the earth shall hear.

2 Grace first contrived a way
  To save rebellious man;
And all the steps that grace display,
  Which drew the wondrous plan.

3 Grace led my wandering feet
  To tread the heavenly road;
And new supplies each hour I meet,
  While pressing on to God.
  Rev. Philip Doddridge. (1702-1751.)

234 "As sheep going astray, but are now returned." **S. M.**
Ps. cxix. 169-176. Ez. xxxiv. 11-24. Luke xv.

1 I WAS a wandering sheep,
    I did not love the fold;
  I did not love my Shepherd's voice,
    I would not be controlled.
  I was a wayward child,
    I did not love my home;
  I did not love my Father's voice,
    I loved afar to roam.

2 The Shepherd sought His sheep,
    The Father sought His child;
  They followed me o'er vale and hill,
    O'er deserts waste and wild.
  They found me nigh to death,
    Famished and faint and lone;
  They bound me with the bands of love,
    They saved the wandering one.

3 Jesus my Shepherd is,
    'T was He that loved my soul;
  'T was He that washed me in His blood,
    'T was He that made me whole.
  'T was He that sought the lost,
    That found the wandering sheep;
  'T was He that brought me to the fold,
    'T is He that still doth keep.

4 No more a wandering sheep,
    I love to be controlled;
  I love my tender Shepherd's voice,
    I love the peaceful fold.
  No more a wayward child,
    I seek no more to roam;
  I love my heavenly Father's voice,
    I love, I love His home!
  Rev. Horatius Bonar. (1808-.)

235 "The brightness of His glory." **C. M.**
Ps. viii. Dan. vii. 9-14. Heb. i. 1-12.

1 FATHER, how wide Thy glory shines,
    How high Thy wonders rise!
  Known through the earth by thousand signs,
    By thousand through the skies.
  Those mighty orbs proclaim Thy power,
    Their motions speak Thy skill;
  And on the wings of every hour
    We read Thy patience still.

2 But when we view Thy strange design
    To save rebellious worms,
  Where vengeance and compassion join
    In their divinest forms,
  Here the whole Deity is known;
    Nor dares a creature guess
  Which of the glories brightest shone,
    The justice or the grace.

3 Now the full glories of the Lamb
    Adorn the heavenly plains;
  Bright seraphs learn Immanuel's name,
    And try their choicest strains.
  O may I bear some humble part
    In that immortal song;
  Wonder and joy shall tune my heart,
    And love command my tongue.
  Rev. Isaac Watts. (1674-1748.)

236 "All Judah rejoiced at the oath." **L. M.**
Ps. cxxxviii. 2 Chr. i. 7-12. Mark i. 16-20.

1 O HAPPY day, that fixed my choice
  On Thee, my Saviour and my God:
  Well may this glowing heart rejoice,
  And tell its raptures all abroad.

2 O happy bond, that seals my vows
  To Him who merits all my love;
  Let cheerful anthems fill His house,
  While to that sacred shrine I move.

3 'T is done, the great transaction 's done;
  I am my Lord's, and He is mine;
  He drew me, and I followed on,
  Charmed to confess the voice divine.

4 Now rest, my long-divided heart,
  Fixed on this blissful centre, rest;
  With ashes who would grudge to part,
  When called on angels' bread to feast?

5 High Heaven, that heard the solemn vow,
  That vow renewed shall daily hear,
  Till in life's latest hour I bow,
  And bless in death a bond so dear.
  Rev. Philip Doddridge.

"I will magnify Him with thanksgiving."

237 "A refuge from the storm." L. M.
Isa. xxxii. Eze. xxxiv. 6-15. Acts iii. 12-26.

1 HAIL, sovereign Love, that first began
The scheme to rescue fallen man ;
Hail, matchless, free, eternal grace,
That gave my soul a hiding-place.

2 Against the God that rules the sky
I fought with hand uplifted high ;
Despised His rich, abounding grace,
Too proud to seek a hiding-place.

3 Indignant Justice stood in view ;
To Sinai's fiery mount I flew :
But Justice cried, with frowning face,
"This mountain is no hiding-place."

4 Vain every hope, until I heard
The voice of mercy in Thy word,
Proclaiming free redeeming grace,
And Jesus as my hiding-place.
Rev. Jehoida Brewer. (1752-1817.)

238 "I will declare what He hath done for my soul." 8. 6.
Ps. cxlviii. 2 Sam. xxii. 1-18. Acts iii. 1-9.

1 BEGIN, my soul, th' exalted lay,
Let each enraptured thought obey,
And praise th' Almighty's name ;
Lo, heaven and earth, and seas and skies,
In one melodious concert rise,
To swell th' inspiring theme.

2 Let man, by nobler passions swayed,
The feeling heart, the judging head,
In heavenly praise employ ;
Spread His tremendous name around,
Till heaven's broad arch rings back the sound,
The general burst of joy.
Rev. John Ogilvie. (1733-1814.)

239 "I am as a wonder unto many." 8. 7.
1 Tim. i. 12-15. Luke viii. 36-50. Isa. xii.

1 HAIL, my ever-blessèd Jesus !
Only Thee I wish to sing ;
To my soul Thy name is precious,
Thou my Prophet, Priest, and King.
O what mercy flows from heaven,
O what joy and happiness !
Love I much, I 've much forgiven ;
I 'm a miracle of grace.

2 Once with Adam's race in ruin,
Unconcerned in sin I lay.
Swift destruction still pursuing,
Till my Saviour passed that way ;
Witness, all ye host of heaven,
My Redeemer's tenderness.
Love I much, I 've much forgiven ;
I 'm a miracle of grace.
John Wingrove. 1905.

240 "Bless the Lord, O my soul" S. M.
Ps ciii. Job xxxiii. 14-33 2 Cor i 3-5

1 O BLESS the Lord, my soul,
His grace to thee proclaim ;
And all that is within me join
To bless His holy name.

2 O bless the Lord, my soul,
His mercies bear in mind ;
Forget not all His benefits,
Who is to thee so kind.

3 He pardons all thy sins,
Prolongs thy feeble breath ;
He healeth thine infirmities,
And ransoms thee from death.

4 He feeds thee with His love,
Upholds thee with His truth ;
And, like the eagle's, He renews
The vigor of thy youth.

5 Then, bless the Lord, my soul,
His grace, His love proclaim ;
Let all that is within me join
To bless His holy name.
Rev. Isaac Watts. (1674-1748.)

241 "Make me to hear joy and gladness." 8. 7.
Ps. xlviii. 1 Sam. vii. 3-12. Heb. vi

1 COME, Thou Fount of every blessing,
Tune my heart to sing Thy grace ;
Streams of mercy, never ceasing,
Call for songs of loudest praise.
Teach me some melodious sonnet,
Sung by flaming tongues above ;
Praise the mount, I 'm fixed upon it,
Mount of God's unchanging love.

2 Here I raise my Ebenezer,
Hither by Thy help I 'm come ;
And I hope, by Thy good pleasure,
Safely to arrive at home.
Jesus sought me, when a stranger,
Wandering from the fold of God ;
He, to rescue me from danger,
Interposed His precious blood.

3 O to grace how great a debtor
Daily I 'm constrained to be !
Let that grace now, like a fetter,
Bind my wandering heart to Thee.
Prone to wander, Lord, I feel it,
Prone to leave the God I love ;
Here 's my heart, O take and seal it,
Seal it from Thy courts above.
Rev. Robert Robinson. (1735-1790.)

"Being justified freely by His grace."

242 "With His stripes we are healed." H. M.
Eph. ii. 8-22. Rom. vi. 4-23. Isa. liii. 4, 5.

1 THY works, not mine, O Christ,
  Speak gladness to this heart;
  They tell me all is done,
  They bid my fear depart:
    To whom save Thee, who canst alone
    For sin atone, Lord, shall I flee?

2 Thy wounds, not mine, O Christ,
  Can heal my bruiséd soul;
  Thy stripes, not mine, contain
  The balm that makes me whole:
    To whom save Thee, who canst alone
    For sin atone, Lord, shall I flee?

3 Thy cross, not mine, O Christ,
  Has borne the awful load
  Of sins that none in heaven
  Or earth could bear but God:
    To whom save Thee, who canst alone
    For sin atone, Lord, shall I flee?

4 Thy death, not mine, O Christ,
  Has paid the ransom due;
  Ten thousand deaths like mine
  Would have been all too few:
    To whom save Thee, who canst alone
    For sin atone, Lord, shall I flee?
          Rev. Horatius Bonar. (1808-.)

243 "Being justified by His blood." 8,
Ps. xxxi. Rom. viii. 1-4. Acts xii. 1-17.

1 AND can it be that I should gain
    An interest in the Saviour's blood?
  Died He for me, who caused His pain,
    For me, who Him to death pursued?
  Amazing love! how can it be
    That Thou, my Lord, shouldst die for me?

2 Long my imprisoned spirit lay
    Fast bound in sin and nature's night.
  Thine eye diffused a quick'ning ray:
    I woke; the dungeon flamed with light;
  My chains fell off, my heart was free;
  I rose, went forth, and followed Thee.

3 No condemnation now I dread,
    Jesus, with all in Him, is mine;
  Alive in Him, my living Head,
    And clothed in righteousness divine,
  Bold I approach th' eternal throne,
  And claim the crown, through Christ, my own.
          Rev. Charles Wesley. (1708-1788.)

244 "Old things are passed away." C. M.
Rom. xii. Acts iv. 31-35. Josh. xxiv. 14, 15.

1 LET worldly minds the world pursue,
    It has no charms for me;
  Once I admired its trifles, too,
    But grace has set me free.

2 Its pleasures now no longer please,
    No more content afford;
  Far from my heart be joys like these,
    Now I have seen the Lord.

3 As by the light of opening day
    The stars are all concealed,
  So earthly pleasures fade away
    When Jesus is revealed.

4 Creatures no more divide my choice,
    I bid them all depart;
  His name and love and gracious voice
    Have fixed my roving heart.
          Rev. John Newton. (1725-1807.)

245 "Blessed are the pure in heart." S. M.
Ps. xxxii. Rom. iv. 1-16. 1 John i. 6-9.

1 O BLESSÉD souls are they
    Whose sins are covered o'er;
  Divinely blest, to whom the Lord
    Imputes their guilt no more.

2 They mourn their follies past,
    And keep their hearts with care;
  Their lips and lives without deceit
    Shall prove their faith sincere.

3 While I concealed my guilt,
    I felt the festering wound;
  Till I confessed my sins to Thee,
    And ready pardon found.
          Rev. Isaac Watts. (1674-1748.)

246 "In Him we live." L. M.
Col. ii. 1-17. Rom. viii. 31-39. Ps. lix. 16, 17.

1 MY soul complete in Jesus stands,
  It fears no more the law's demands;
  The smile of God is sweet within,
  Where all before was guilt and sin.

2 My soul at rest in Jesus lives,
  Accepts the peace His pardon gives;
  Receives the grace His death secured,
  And pleads the anguish He endured.

3 My soul its every foe defies,
  And cries, 'T is God that justifies!
  Who charges God's elect with sin?
  Shall Christ, who died their peace to win?

4 A song of praise my soul shall sing,
  To our eternal, glorious King;
  Shall worship humbly at His feet,
  In whom alone it stands complete.
          Mrs. Grace W. Hinsdale. 1855.

"Being justified freely by His grace."

247 "Being justified by faith." 6, 7, 5.
John xv. 1-11. Luke xii. 35-40. Isa. liv.

1 I HEAR the Saviour say,
   Thy strength indeed is small ;
   Child of weakness, watch and pray,
   Find in me thine all in all.

  Jesus paid it all,
    All to Him I owe ;
  Sin had left a crimson stain,
    He washed it white as snow.

2 Lord, now indeed I find
   Thy power, and Thine alone,
   Can change the leper's spots,
   And melt the heart of stone.

3 For nothing good have I
   Whereby Thy grace to claim ;
   I 'll wash my garment white
   In the blood of Calvary's Lamb.

4 And when before the throne
   I stand in Him complete,
   I 'll lay my trophies down,
   All down at Jesus' feet.

   Mrs. Elvira M. Hall. (1818-.)

248 "I will be glad and rejoice in Thee." S. M.
Ps. lxxi. Acts v. 29-42. 2 Cor. xii. 1-10.

1 DEAR Lord and Master mine,
   Thy happy servant see ;
   My Conqueror, with what joy divine
   Thy captive clings to Thee.
   I love Thy yoke to wear,
   To feel Thy gracious bands ;
   Sweetly restrained by Thy care,
   And happy in Thy hands.

2 No bar would I remove,
   No bond would I unbind ;
   Within the limits of Thy love
   Full liberty I find.
   I would not walk alone,
   But still with Thee, my God ;
   At every step my blindness own,
   And ask of Thee the road.

3 Dear Lord and Master mine,
   Still keep Thy servant true ;
   My Guardian and my Guide divine,
   Bring, bring Thy pilgrim through.
   My Conqueror and my King,
   Still keep me in Thy train ;
   And with Thee Thy glad captive bring,
   When Thou return'st to reign.

   Thomas H. Gill. (1819-.)

249 "The riches of His grace." C. M.
Dan. ix. 3-10. Neh. i. 5-11. 1 Cor. xv. 8-10.

1 ALL that I was, my sin, my guilt,
   My death, was all my own ;
   All that I am, I owe to Thee,
   My gracious God, alone.

2 The evil of my former state
   Was mine, and only mine ;
   The good in which I now rejoice
   Is Thine, and only Thine.

3 The darkness of my former state,
   The bondage, all was mine ;
   The light of life, in which I walk,
   The liberty, is Thine.

4 Thy grace first made me feel my sin,
   It taught me to believe ;
   Then, in believing, peace I found,
   And now I live, I live.

5 All that I am, ev'n here on earth,
   All that I hope to be
   When Jesus comes and glory dawns,
   I owe it, Lord, to Thee.

   Rev. Horatius Bonar. (1808-.)

250 "Therefore my heart is glad." C. M.
Mat. xi. 28-30. Acts xxvi. 9-29. Isa. xlviii. 1-17.

1 I HEARD the voice of Jesus say,
   " Come unto me and rest ;
   Lay down, thou weary one, lay down
   Thy head upon my breast."
   I came to Jesus as I was,
   Weary and worn and sad ;
   I found in Him a resting-place,
   And He has made me glad.

2 I heard the voice of Jesus say,
   " Behold, I freely give
   The living water ; thirsty one,
   Stoop down, and drink, and live."
   I came to Jesus, and I drank
   Of that life-giving stream ;
   My thirst was quenched, my soul revived,
   And now I live in Him.

3 I heard the voice of Jesus say,
   " I am this dark world's Light ;
   Look unto me ; thy morn shall rise,
   And all thy day be bright."
   I looked to Jesus, and I found
   In Him my Star, my Sun ;
   And in that light of life I 'll walk
   Till travelling days are done.

   Rev. Horatius Bonar.

"Being justified freely by His grace."

251 "The Lord turned and looked upon Peter." **C. M.**
Acts xxii. 1-15. Luke xxiii. 26-49. Zech. xii. 9, 10.

1 IN evil long I took delight,
  Unawed by shame or fear,
Till a new object struck my sight,
  And stopped my wild career.

2 I saw One hanging on a tree,
  In agonies and blood ;
Who fixed His languid eyes on me,
  As near His cross I stood.

3 Sure, never till my latest breath
  Can I forget that look ;
It seemed to charge me with His death,
  Though not a word He spoke.

4 A second look He gave, that said,
  "I freely all forgive ;
This blood is for thy ransom paid,
  I die that thou mayst live."

5 Thus, while His death my sin displays
  In all its blackest hue,
Such is the mystery of grace,
  It seals my pardon, too.
                    Rev. John Newton. (1725-1807.)

252 "Who gave Himself a ransom." **L. M.**
Gal. vi. 14. 1 Cor. ii. 2-8. Dan. vii. 9-14.

1 O THE sweet wonders of that cross,
Where my Redeemer loved and died !
Her noblest life my spirit draws
From His dear wounds and bleeding side.

2 I would forever speak His name
In sounds to mortal ears unknown ;
With angels join to praise the Lamb,
And worship at His Father's throne.
                    Rev. Isaac Watts. (1674-1748.)

253 "Christ died for our sins." **C. M.**
Rom. v. 6-21. John iii. 14-21. Job xxxiii. 14-26.

1 GREAT God, when I approach Thy throne,
  And all Thy glory see,
This is my stay, and this alone,
  That Jesus died for me.

2 How can a soul condemned to die
  Escape the just decree ?
Helpless and full of sin am I,
  But Jesus died for me.

3 Burdened with sin's oppressive chain,
  O how can I get free ?
No peace can all my efforts gain,
  But Jesus died for me.

4 And Lord, when I behold Thy face,
  This must be all my plea :
Save me by Thy almighty grace,
  For Jesus died for me.
                    Author unknown.

254 "Not having mine own righteousness." **L. M.**
Phil. iii. 7-13. Rev. iii. 17-22. Isa. lxi. 10, 11.

1 JESUS, Thy blood and righteousness
My beauty are, my glorious dress ;
'Midst flaming worlds, in these arrayed,
With joy shall I lift up my head.

2 When from the dust of death I rise,
To claim my mansion in the skies,
E'en then this shall be all my plea,
" Jesus hath lived, hath died, for me."

3 This spotless robe the same appears
When ruined nature sinks in years ;
No age can change its constant hue,
Thy blood preserves it ever new.

4 O let the dead now hear Thy voice,
Now bid Thy banished ones rejoice ;
Their beauty this, their glorious dress,
Jesus, Thy blood and righteousness.
            Nicolaus L. Zinzendorf. (1700-1760.)
            Tr. by Rev. John Wesley. (1703-1791.)

255 "Life through His name." **C. M.**
Isa. ix. 6. Mat. i. 21. John i. 4. Rev. xix. 16.

1 THERE is a name I love to hear,
  I love to sing its worth ;
It sounds like music in mine ear,
  The sweetest name on earth.

2 It tells me of a Saviour's love,
  Who died to set me free ;
It tells me of His precious blood,
  The sinner's perfect plea.
                    Rev. Frederick Whitfield. (1829-.)

256 "Thou art my portion, O Lord." **L. M.**
Col. i. 12-20. 1 Cor. i. 23-31. Ps. xxvii.

1 FOUNTAIN of grace, rich, full, and free,
What need I that is not in Thee ?
Full pardon, strength to meet the day,
And peace which none can take away.

2 Doth sickness fill my heart with fear,
'T is sweet to know that Thou art near ;
Am I with dread of justice tried,
'T is sweet to know that Christ hath died.

3 In life, Thy promises of aid
Forbid my heart to be afraid ;
In death, peace gently veils the eyes :
Christ rose, and I shall surely rise.

4 O all-sufficient Saviour, be
This all-sufficiency to me ;
Nor pain, nor sin, nor death can harm
The weakest shielded by Thine arm.
                    James Edmeston. (1791-1867.)

"Ye have received the Spirit of adoption."

257 "My Father and your Father." C. M.
Gal. iv. 1-7. Ps. lxxxix. 15-34. Mal. iii. 16-18.

1 MY Father, God! how sweet the sound,
    How tender and how dear !
  Not all the melody of heaven
    Could so delight the ear.

2 Come, sacred Spirit, seal the name
    On my expanding heart,
  And show that in Jehovah's grace
    I share a filial part.

3 Cheered by a signal so divine,
    Unwavering I believe;
  My spirit "Abba, Father," cries,
    Nor can the sign deceive.
        Rev. Philip Doddridge. (1702-1751.)

258 "Who also maketh intercession for us." H. M.
Isa. i. 15-27. Jer. iii. 12-19. Heb. ix. 11-15.

1 ARISE, my soul, arise,
    Shake off thy guilty fears ;
  The bleeding Sacrifice
    In my behalf appears :
  Before the throne my Surety stands,
  My name is written on His hands.

2 The Father hears Him pray,
    His dear anointed One ;
  He cannot turn away
    The presence of His Son :
  His Spirit answers to the blood,
  And tells me I am born of God.

3 My God is reconciled,
    His pardoning voice I hear ;
  He owns me for His child,
    I can no longer fear :
  With confidence I now draw nigh,
  And "Father, Abba, Father !" cry.
        Rev. Charles Wesley. (1708-1788.)

259 "Lord God of Israel, our Father." C. M.
Heb. xiii. 15. Rom. ix. 18-26. Deu. xxxii. 1-14.

1 COME, shout aloud the Father's grace,
    And sing the Saviour's love ;
  Soon shall you join the glorious theme
    In loftier strains above.

2 God, the eternal, mighty God,
    To dearer names descends ;
  Calls you His treasure and His joy,
    His children and His friends.

3 My Father, God! and may these lips
    Pronounce a name so dear ?
  Not thus could heaven's sweet harmony
    Delight my listening ear.
        Rev. Ottiwell Heginbotham. (1744-1768.)

260 "Was lost and is found." L. M.
Luke xv. 11-32. 1 Pet. ii. 2 Chr. xxxiii. 1-20.

1 THE wanderer no more will roam,
  The lost one to the fold hath come,
  The prodigal is welcomed home,
    O Lamb of God, in Thee.

2 Though clothed with shame, by sin defiled,
  The Father hath embraced His child,
  And I am pardoned, reconciled,
    O Lamb of God, in Thee.

3 Now shall my famished soul be fed,
  A feast of love for me is spread,
  I feed upon the children's bread,
    O Lamb of God, in Thee.

4 Yea, in the fulness of His grace,
  He puts me in the children's place,
  Where I may gaze upon His face,
    O Lamb of God, in Thee.
        Mrs. Mary J. Walker. 1847.

261 "They are the sons of God." S. M.
1 John iii. 1-3. Gal. iii. 16 to iv. 5. Hos. i. 10.

1 BEHOLD what wondrous grace
    The Father hath bestowed
  On sinners of a mortal race,
    To call them sons of God!

2 Nor doth it yet appear
    How great we must be made ;
  But when we see our Saviour here,
    We shall be like our Head.

3 A hope so much divine
    May trials well endure,
  May purge our souls from sense and sin,
    As Christ, the Lord, is pure.
        Rev. Isaac Watts. (1674-1748.)

262 "As obedient children." C. M.
1 John iii. Rom. viii. 1-17. 2 Sam. vii. 1-14.

1 GRACE, like an uncorrupted seed,
    Abides and reigns within ;
  Immortal principles forbid
    The sons of God to sin.

2 They find access, at every hour,
    To God within the veil ;
  Hence they derive a quickening power,
    And joys that never fail.

3 Lord, I address Thy heavenly throne,
    Call me a child of Thine ;
  Send down the Spirit of Thy Son,
    To form my heart divine.

4 There shed Thy choicest love abroad,
    And make my comforts strong ;
  Then shall I say, " My Father, God,"
    With an unwavering tongue.
        Rev. Isaac Watts.

"Consecrated ... unto the Lord."

263 "What shall I render unto the Lord?" **C. M.**
Ps. cxvi. 1 Kings viii. 54–56. Luke xix. 1–9.

1 WHAT shall I render to my God
  For all His kindness shown?
  My feet shall visit Thine abode,
  My songs address Thy throne.

2 Among the saints that fill Thy house,
  My offerings shall be paid;
  There shall my zeal perform the vows
  My soul in anguish made.

3 How happy all Thy servants are!
  How great Thy grace to me!
  My life, which Thou hast made Thy care,
  Lord, I devote to Thee.

4 Now I am Thine, forever Thine,
  Nor shall my purpose move;
  Thy hand hath loosed my bonds of pain,
  And bound me with Thy love.

5 Here in Thy courts I leave my vow,
  And Thy rich grace record;
  Witness, ye saints, who hear me now,
  If I forsake the Lord.
  Rev. Isaac Watts. (1674–1748.)

264 "I will walk before the Lord." **S. M.**
1 Cor. vi. 19, 20. 2 Cor. iv. 1–10. 2 Chr. xxx.

1 LORD, in the strength of grace,
  With a glad heart and free,
  Myself, my residue of days,
  I consecrate to Thee.

2 Thy ransomed servant, I
  Restore to Thee Thine own;
  And from this moment live or die,
  To serve my God alone.
  Rev. Charles Wesley. (1708–1788.)

265 "Thine hands have made me." **S. M.**
2 Sam. xxii. 17–51. Col. i. 16–29. Eph. ii. 8–22.

1 MY Maker and my King,
  To Thee my all I owe;
  Thy sovereign bounty is the spring
  Whence all my blessings flow.

2 The creature of Thy hand,
  On Thee alone I live;
  My God, Thy benefits demand
  More praise than life can give.

3 Shall I withhold Thy due,
  And shall my passions rove?
  Lord, form this wretched heart anew,
  And fill it with Thy love.

4 O let Thy grace inspire
  My soul with strength divine;
  Let all my powers to Thee aspire,
  And all my days be Thine.
  Miss Anne Steele. (1717–1778.)

266 "And serve Him with a perfect heart." **L. M.**
Josh. xxiv. 14–24. Mat. v. 1–16. 1 Pet. ii.

1 Now I resolve, with all my heart,
  With all my powers, to serve the Lord;
  Nor from His precepts e'er depart,
  Whose service is a rich reward.

2 O be His service all my joy!
  Around let my example shine,
  Till others love the blest employ,
  And join in labors so divine.

3 Be this the purpose of my soul,
  My solemn, my determined choice,
  To yield to His supreme control,
  And in His kind commands rejoice.

4 O may I never faint nor tire,
  Nor wandering leave His sacred ways;
  Great God, accept my soul's desire,
  And give me strength to live Thy praise.
  Miss Anne Steele.

267 "O Lord, truly I am Thy servant." **H. M.**
Ps. xl. Luke v. 1–11, 27, 28. Rom. v. 1–18.

1 MY soul and all its powers,
  Thine, wholly Thine, shall be;
  All, all my happy hours
  I consecrate to Thee.
  Me to Thine image now restore,
  And I shall praise Thee evermore.

2 Long as I live beneath,
  To Thee, O let me live;
  To Thee my every breath
  In thanks and praises give.
  Whate'er I have, whate'er I am,
  Shall magnify my Maker's name.
  Rev. Charles Wesley.

268 "I will call upon Him as long as I live." **C. M.**
Ps. cxix. 10–16. 2 Chr. xxix. 1–10. Heb. x.

1 MY God, accept my heart this day,
  And make it always Thine,
  That I from Thee no more may stray,
  No more from Thee decline.

2 Before the cross of Him who died,
  Behold, I prostrate fall;
  Let every sin be crucified,
  Let Christ be all in all.

3 May the dear blood, once shed for me,
  My blest atonement prove,
  That I, from first to last, may be
  The purchase of Thy love.

4 Let every thought and work and word
  To Thee be ever given;
  Then life shall be Thy service, Lord,
  And death the gate of heaven.
  Matthew Bridges. (1800–1852.)

49

"Consecrated ... unto the Lord."

269 "A living sacrifice, holy, acceptable." **8.**
Ps. cxvi. 12–19. Hos. vi. 1–6. 2 Cor. xi. 16–23.

1 O GOD, what offering shall I give
   To Thee, the Lord of earth and skies?
   My spirit, soul, and flesh receive,
   A holy, living sacrifice:
   Small as it is, 'tis all my store;
   More shouldst Thou have if I had more.

2 Now, then, my God, Thou hast my soul,
   No longer mine, but Thine, I am:
   Guard thou Thine own, possess it whole,
   Cheer it with hope, with love inflame.
   Thou hast my spirit; there display
   Thy glory to the perfect day.

3 Thou hast my flesh, Thy hallowed shrine,
   Devoted solely to Thy will:
   Here let Thy light forever shine,
   This house still let Thy presence fill.
   O Source of life, live, dwell, and move
   In me, till all my life be love.

4 Lord, arm me with Thy Spirit's might;
   Since I am called by Thy great name,
   In Thee let all my thoughts unite,
   Of all my works be Thou the aim;
   Thy love attend me all my days,
   And my sole business be Thy praise.
   Rev. Joachim Lange. (1670-1744.)
Tr. by Rev. John Wesley. (1703-1791.)

270 "In God is my salvation." **S. M.**
Isa. xxvi. 1–13. Rom. vi. 2 Tim. iii. 10 to iv. 8.

1 O LORD, Thou art my Lord,
   My Portion and Delight;
   All other lords I now reject,
   And cast them from my sight.

2 Thy sovereign right I own,
   Thy glorious power confess;
   Thy law shall ever rule my heart,
   While I adore Thy grace.

3 Too long my feet have strayed
   In sin's forbidden way;
   But since Thou hast my soul reclaimed,
   To Thee my vows I'll pay.

4 My soul, to Jesus joined
   By faith and hope and love,
   Now seeks to dwell among Thy saints,
   And rest with them above.

5 Accept, O Lord, my heart,
   To Thee myself I give;
   Nor suffer me from hence to stray,
   Or cause Thy saints to grieve.
   Rev. Benjamin Beddome. (1717-1795.)

271 "Return unto thy rest, O my soul." **C. M.**
Ps. cxvi. 1–9. Deu. viii. 7–10. 2 John 3–12.

1 RETURN, my soul, unto thy rest,
   From God no longer roam;
   His hand hath bountifully blest,
   His goodness calls thee home.

2 What shall I render unto Thee,
   My Saviour, in distress,
   For all Thy benefits to me,
   So great and numberless?

3 This will I do for Thy love's sake,
   And thus Thy power proclaim:
   The cup of Thy salvation take,
   And call upon Thy name.

4 Thou God of covenanted grace,
   Hear and record my vow,
   While in Thy courts I seek Thy face,
   And at Thine altar bow:

5 Henceforth to Thee myself I give,
   With single heart and eye,
   To walk before Thee while I live,
   And bless Thee when I die.
   James Montgomery. (1771-1854.)

272 "Let Thy tender mercies come unto me." **8. 7.**
Luke xv. 11–32. Ps. li. 1–17. Judg. x. 10–16.

1 TAKE me, O my Father, take me,
   Take me, save me, through Thy Son;
   That which Thou wouldst have me make me,
   Let Thy will in me be done.
   Long from Thee my footsteps straying,
   Thorny proved the way I trod;
   Weary come I now, and praying,
   Take me to Thy love, my God.

2 Fruitless years with grief recalling,
   Humbly I confess my sin;
   At Thy feet, O Father, falling,
   To Thy household take me in.
   Freely now to Thee I proffer
   This relenting heart of mine;
   Freely life and soul I offer,
   Gift unworthy love like Thine.

3 Once the world's Redeemer, dying,
   Bore our sins upon the tree;
   On that sacrifice relying,
   Now I look in hope to Thee.
   Father, take me; all forgiving,
   Fold me to Thy loving breast;
   In Thy love forever living,
   I must be forever blest.
   Rev. Ray Palmer. (1808-.)

"Consecrated ... unto the Lord."

273 "But I follow after." 8. 7.
Mark i. 16-20. Luke xviii. 28. Ps. cxix. 57-64.

1 JESUS, I my cross have taken,
  All to leave, and follow Thee ;
Naked, poor, despised, forsaken,
  Thou, from hence, my all shalt be.
Perish, every fond ambition,
  All I 've sought, and hoped, and known,
Yet how rich is my condition,
  God and heaven are still my own !

2 Let the world despise and leave me,
  They have left my Saviour, too ;
Human hearts and looks deceive me,
  Thou art not, like man, untrue ;
And while Thou shalt smile upon me,
  God of wisdom, love, and might,
Foes may hate and friends may shun me,
  Show Thy face, and all is bright.

3 Go, then, earthly fame and treasure !
  Come disaster, scorn, and pain !
In Thy service, pain is pleasure,
  With Thy favor, loss is gain :
I have called Thee "Abba, Father !"
  I have stayed my heart on Thee :
Storms may howl, and clouds may gather,
  All must work for good to me.

4 Man may trouble and distress me,
  'T will but drive me to Thy breast ;
Life with trials hard may press me,
  Heaven will bring me sweeter rest.
O 't is not in grief to harm me,
  While Thy love is left to me ;
O 't were not in joy to charm me,
  Were that joy unmixed with Thee.
      Rev. Henry F. Lyte. (1793-1847.)

274 "That I may apprehend." 8. 7.
2 Cor. vi. 13 to vii. 1. 1 Thes. iv. Ps. xviii. 1-19.

1 TAKE, my soul, thy full salvation,
  Rise o'er sin, and fear, and care ;
Joy to find in every station
  Something still to do or bear.
Think what Spirit dwells within thee,
  What a Father's smile is thine,
What a Saviour died to win thee :
  Child of heaven, shouldst thou repine ?

2 Haste thee on from grace to glory,
  Armed by faith, and winged by prayer ;
Heaven's eternal day 's before thee,
  God's own hand shall guide thee there.
Soon shall close thy earthly mission,
  Swift shall pass thy pilgrim days,
Hope soon change to glad fruition,
  Faith to sight, and prayer to praise.
      Rev. Henry F. Lyte.

275 "I will freely sacrifice to Thee." 6. 4. P.
Rom. xi 22-36. Luke vii. 36-50. Ps. ci.

1 SAVIOUR, Thy dying love
    Thou gavest me,
  Nor should I aught withhold,
    Dear Lord, from Thee ;
  In love my soul would bow,
    My heart fulfil its vow,
  Some offering bring Thee now,
    Something for Thee.

2 At the blest mercy-seat,
    Pleading for me,
  My feeble faith looks up,
    Jesus, to Thee ;
  Help me the cross to bear,
    Thy wondrous love declare,
  Some song to raise, or prayer,
    Something for thee.

3 Give me a faithful heart,
    Likeness to Thee,
  That each departing day
    Henceforth may see
  Some work of love begun,
    Some deed of kindness done,
  Some wand'rer sought and won,
    Something for Thee.

4 All that I am and have,
    Thy gifts so free,
  In joy, in grief, through life,
    Dear Lord, for Thee ;
  And when Thy face I see,
    My ransomed soul shall be,
  Through all eternity,
    Something for Thee.
      Rev. Sylvester D. Phelps. (1816-.)

276 "My heart trusted in Him." L. M.
Ps. xxiv. Isa. vi. 1-8. Acts viii. 26-39.

1 LIFT up your heads, ye mighty gates !
  Behold, the King of Glory waits ;
  The King of kings is drawing near,
  The Saviour of the world is here.

2 Fling wide the portals of your heart,
  Make it a temple, set apart ;
  So shall your Sovereign enter in,
  And new and nobler life begin.

3 Redeemer, come ! I open wide
  My heart to Thee : here, Lord, abide !
  Let me Thine inner presence feel,
  Thy grace and love in me reveal.
      Rev. George Weissel. (1590-1635.)
      Tr. by Miss Catherine Winkworth. (1825-.)

"Consecrated ... unto the Lord."

277 "With my whole heart have I sought Thee." **8. 7. 4.**
Mark x. 28-30. 1 Cor. iii. 16, 17. Gen. xviii. 1-8.

1 WELCOME, welcome, dear Redeemer,
   Welcome to this heart of mine :
   Lord, I make a full surrender,
      Every power and thought be Thine,
         Thine entirely,
   Through eternal ages Thine.

2 Known to all to be Thy mansion,
   Earth and hell will disappear,
   Or in vain attempt possession,
      When they find the Lord is near ;
         Shout, O Zion,
   Shout, ye saints, the Lord is here !
   Rev. William Mason. (1725-1797.)

278 "Jesus Christ and Him crucified." **7. 6. 8.**
Ecc. xii. 1-7. 1 Cor. ii. Phil. iii.

1 VAIN, delusive world, adieu,
   With all of creature good ;
   Only Jesus I pursue,
   Who bought me with His blood.
   All thy pleasures I forego,
   I trample on thy wealth and pride :
   Only Jesus will I know,
   And Jesus crucified.

2 Other knowledge I disdain,
   'T is all but vanity ;
   Christ, the Lamb of God, was slain,
   He tasted death for me.
   Me to save from endless woe,
   The sin-atoning Victim died :
   Only Jesus will I know,
   And Jesus crucified.

3 Him to know is life and peace,
   And pleasure without end ;
   This is all my happiness,
   On Jesus to depend,
   Daily in His grace to grow,
   Ever in His faith abide :
   Only Jesus will I know,
   And Jesus crucified.

4 O that I could all invite
   This saving truth to prove ;
   Show the length, the breadth, the height,
   And depth of Jesus' love !
   Fain I would to sinners show
   The blood by faith alone applied :
   Only Jesus will I know,
   And Jesus crucified.
   Rev. Charles Wesley. (1708-1788.)

279 "And hast redeemed us to God." **7. 6.**
1 Cor. vi. 20. 2 Cor. v. 14, 15. Jer. xxxi. 33, 34.

1 No more my own, Lord Jesus ;
   Bought with Thy precious blood,
   I give Thee but Thine own, Lord,
   That long Thy love withstood.
   I give the life Thou gavest,
   My present, future, past ;
   My joys, my fears, my sorrows,
   My first hope and my last.

2 I give the love, the sweetest
   Thy goodness grants to me ;
   Take it, and make it meet, Lord,
   For offering to Thee.
   Smile, and the very shadows
   In Thy blest light shall shine ;
   Take Thou my heart, Lord Jesus,
   For Thou hast made it Thine.

3 O deathless love that bought me,
   O price beyond my ken ;
   O life that hides my own life
   E'en from my fellow-men,
   Now fashion, form, and fill me
   With light and love divine ;
   So, one with Thee, Lord Jesus,
   I 'm Thine, forever Thine.
   Miss Anna Shipton.

280 "For all is Thine." **L. M.**
Acts ix. 1-6. Luke xix. 1-10. Ps. cxvi. 12-19.

1 My gracious Lord, I own Thy right
   To every service I can pay,
   And call it my supreme delight
   To hear Thy dictates and obey.

2 What is my being, but for Thee,
   Its sure support, its noblest end ;
   Thine ever-smiling face to see,
   And serve the cause of such a Friend ?

3 I would not breathe for worldly joy,
   Or to increase my worldly good ;
   Nor future days or powers employ,
   To spread a sounding name abroad.

4 'T is to my Saviour I would live,
   To Him who for my ransom died ;
   Nor could untainted Eden give
   Such bliss as blossoms at His side.

5 His work my hoary age shall bless,
   When youthful vigor is no more ;
   And my last hour of life confess
   His love hath animating power.
   Rev. Philip Doddridge. (1702-1751.)

"Consecrated ... unto the Lord."

281 "I am Thine; save me." S. M.
1 Cor. xii. 12-27. Rom. xiv. 7, 8. Ps. lxxi.

1 DEAR Saviour, I am Thine,
  By everlasting bands ;
  My name, my heart, I would resign,
  My soul is in Thy hands.

2 To Thee I still would cleave
  With ever-growing zeal ;
  Let millions tempt me Christ to leave,
  They never shall prevail.

3 His Spirit shall unite
  My soul to Him, my Head ;
  Shall form me to His image bright,
  And teach His paths to tread.

4 Death may my soul divide
  From this abode of clay,
  But love shall keep me near His side
  Through all the gloomy way.
  Rev. Philip Doddridge. (1702-1751.)

282 "I am Thine, and all that I have." C. M.
1 John ii. 24, 25. John xvii. Deu. viii. 1-18.

1 "THE promise of my Father's love
   Shall stand forever good!"
  He said, and gave His soul to death,
  And sealed the grace with blood.

2 To this dear covenant of Thy word
  I set my worthless name ;
  I seal th' engagement to my Lord,
  And make my humble claim.

3 Thy light, and strength, and pard'ning grace,
  And glory shall be mine ;
  My life and soul, my heart and flesh,
  And all my powers are Thine.
  Rev. Isaac Watts. (1674-1748.)

283 "All Mine are Thine, and Thine are Mine." L. M.
Acts xvi. 25-34. Phil. i. 21-30. Ps lxxxvi.

1 LORD, I am Thine, entirely Thine,
  Purchased and saved by blood divine ;
  With full consent Thine I would be,
  And own Thy sovereign right in me.

2 Grant one poor sinner more a place
  Among the children of Thy grace ;
  A wretched sinner, lost to God,
  But ransomed by Immanuel's blood.

3 Thine would I live, Thine would I die,
  Be Thine through all eternity ;
  The vow is past beyond repeal,
  Now will I set the solemn seal.

  Here at that cross where flows the blood
  That bought my guilty soul for God,
  Thee my new Master now I call,
  And consecrate to Thee my all.
  Rev. Samuel Davies. (1724-1761.)

284 "He was seen of me also." C. M.
Ps. xlv. Mat. xvii. 1-8. Heb. i. 1-6.

1 MAJESTIC sweetness sits enthroned
  Upon the Saviour's brow ;
  His head with radiant glories crowned,
  His lips with grace o'erflow.

2 He saw me plunged in deep distress,
  He flew to my relief ;
  For me He bore the shameful cross,
  And carried all my grief.

3 To Him I owe my life and breath,
  And all the joys I have ;
  He makes me triumph over death,
  He saves me from the grave.

4 To heaven, the place of His abode,
  He brings my weary feet ;
  Shows me the glories of my God,
  And makes my joy complete.

5 Since from His bounty I receive
  Such proofs of love divine,
  Had I a thousand hearts to give,
  Lord, they should all be Thine.
  Rev. Samuel Stennett. (1727-1795.)

285 "I have willingly offered all." 7.
Ps. lxiii Rom. vi. 1-18 Acts x. 25-48

1 FATHER, Son, and Holy Ghost,
  One in Three, and Three in One,
  As by the celestial host,
  Let Thy will on earth be done ;
  Praise by all to Thee be given,
  Glorious Lord of earth and heaven.

2 If so poor a worm as I
  May to Thy great glory live,
  All my actions sanctify,
  All my words and thoughts receive ;
  Claim me for Thy service, claim
  All I have and all I am.

3 Take my soul and body's powers,
  Take my memory, mind, and will,
  All my goods and all my hours,
  All I know, and all I feel,
  All I think, or speak, or do ;
  Take my heart, but make it new.

4 Now, O God, Thine own I am,
  Now I give Thee back Thine own ;
  Freedom, friends, and health, and fame,
  Consecrate to Thee alone :
  Thine I live, thrice happy I ;
  Happier still if Thine I die.
  Rev. Charles Wesley. (1708-1788.)

"This is the will of God, your sanctification."

286 *"Lord, not my feet only."* **C. M.**
Eph. i. 15-23. Lev. xix. 2. 1 Pet. ii. 1-11

1 WHAT is our calling's glorious hope,
　But inward holiness?
For this to Jesus I look up,
　I calmly wait for this.

2 I wait till He shall touch me clean,
　Shall life and power impart;
Give me the faith that casts out sin,
　And purifies the heart.

3 When Jesus makes my heart His home,
　My sin shall all depart;
And lo, He saith, I quickly come,
　To fill and rule Thy heart.

4 Be it according to Thy word,
　Redeem me from all sin;
My heart would now receive Thee, Lord;
　Come in, my Lord, come in!
　　　　　　Rev. Charles Wesley. (1708-1788.)

287 *"Create in me a clean heart."* **7.**
2 Cor. iv. 1-10. Rom. viii. 1-10. Ps. xlii.

1 HOLY Lamb, who Thee receive,
Who in Thee begin to live.
Day and night they cry to Thee,
As thou art, so let us be!
Jesus, see my panting breast;
See, I pant in Thee to rest.

2 Gladly would I now be clean,
Cleanse me now from every sin;
Fix, O fix my wavering mind,
To Thy cross my spirit bind;
Earthly passions far remove,
Swallow up my soul in love.
　　　　Mrs. Anna S. Dober. (1713-1739.)
　　　　Tr. by Rev. John Wesley. (1703-1791.)

288 *"I will wash mine hands in innocency."* **L. M.**
2 Chr. vi. 18-31. Hag. ii. 1-9. Col. i.

1 AND will th' offended God again
Return, and dwell with sinful men?
Will He, within this bosom, raise
A living temple to His praise?

2 The joyful news transports my breast;
All hail, I cry, thou heavenly Guest!
Lift up your heads, ye powers within,
And let the King of glory in!

3 Enter, with all Thy heavenly train;
Here live, and here forever reign;
Thy sceptre o'er my passions sway,
Let love command, and I'll obey.

4 Reason and conscience shall submit,
And pay their homage at Thy feet;
To Thee I'll consecrate my heart,
And bid each rival thence depart.
　　　　Rev. Samuel Stennett. (1727-1795.)

289 *"Holy in all manner of conversation."* **S. M.**
Ps. cxix. 113-120. Mat v 17-20. Rom xii

1 THE thing my God doth hate,
　That I no more may do;
Thy creature, Lord, again create,
　And all my soul renew.

2 That blessèd law of Thine,
　Jesus, to me impart;
The Spirit's law of life divine,
　O write it on my heart!

3 Thy nature be my law,
　Thy spotless sanctity;
And sweetly every moment draw
　My happy soul to Thee.

4 Soul of my soul, remain!
　Who didst for all fulfil,
In me, O Lord, fulfil again
　Thy heavenly Father's will.
　　　　　　Rev. Charles Wesley.

290 *"Lord, I have hoped for Thy salvation."* **C. M.**
Ps. lxxiii. 25-28. Isa. xxvi. 1-9. 2 Cor. vi.

1 THY name to me, Thy nature grant,
　This, only this, be given;
Nothing beside my God I want,
　Nothing in earth or heaven.

2 The bliss Thou hast for me prepared
　No longer be delayed;
Come, my exceeding great Reward,
　For whom I first was made.

3 Come, Father, Son, and Holy Ghost,
　And seal me Thine abode;
Let all I am in Thee be lost,
　Let all be lost in God.
　　　　　　Rev. Charles Wesley.

291 *"Wash me, and I shall be whiter than snow."* **L. M.**
John xv. 7-16. James i. 2 Chr. i. 7-12.

1 AND dost Thou say, "Ask what Thou
　　wilt"?
Lord, I would seize the golden hour;
I pray to be released from guilt,
And freed from sin and Satan's power.

2 More of Thy presence, Lord, impart;
More of Thine image let me bear;
Erect Thy throne within my heart,
And reign without a rival there.

3 Give me to read my pardon sealed,
And from Thy joy to draw my strength;
To have Thy boundless love revealed
In all its height and breadth and length.

4 Grant these requests; I ask no more,
But to Thy care the rest resign;
Sick or in health, or rich or poor,
All shall be well if Thou art mine.
　　　　Rev. John Newton. (1725-1807.)

"This is the will of God, your sanctification."

292 "My soul waiteth for the Lord." 7. 6. 8.
2 Cor. xii. 1-10. Mat. viii. Ps. cix. 21-31.

1 EVER fainting with desire,
  For Thee, O Christ, I call;
Thee I restlessly require,
  I want my God, my All.
Jesus, dear redeeming Lord,
  I wait Thy coming from above:
Help me, Saviour, speak the word,
  And perfect me in love.

2 Thou my Life, my Treasure be,
  My Portion here below;
Nothing would I seek but Thee,
  Thee only would I know;
My exceeding great Reward,
  My heaven on earth, my heaven above:
Help me Saviour, speak the word,
  And perfect me in love.

3 Grant me now the bliss to feel
  Of those that are in Thee;
Son of God, Thyself reveal,
  Engrave Thy name on me.
As in Heaven, be here adored,
  And let me now the promise prove:
Help me, Saviour, speak the word,
  And perfect me in love.
              Rev. Charles Wesley. (1706-1788.)

294 "I will lift up my hands in Thy name." H. M.
Jer. xiv. 7, 8. Luke xxiv. 13-29. 2 Cor. vi.

1 COME, my Redeemer, come,
  And deign to dwell with me;
Come, make my heart Thy home,
  And bid Thy rivals flee.
Come, my Redeemer, quickly come,
And make my heart Thy lasting home.

2 Exert Thy mighty power,
  And banish all my sin;
In this auspicious hour,
  Bring all Thy graces in.
Come, my Redeemer, quickly come,
And make my heart Thy lasting home.

3 Rule Thou in every thought
  And passion of my soul,
Till all my powers are brought
  Beneath Thy full control.
Come, my Redeemer, quickly come,
And make my heart Thy lasting home.

4 Then shall my days be Thine,
  And all my heart be love;
And joy and peace be mine,
  Such as are known above.
Come, my Redeemer, quickly come,
And make my heart Thy lasting home.
              Rev. Andrew Reed. (1787-1862.)

293 "My soul thirsteth for Thee." 8.
Eph. iii. 14-21. Col. iii. 1-17. Isa. xxvi. 1-13.

1 THOU hidden love of God, whose height,
  Whose depth unfathomed no man knows,
I see from far Thy beauteous light,
  Inly I sigh for Thy repose;
My heart is pained, nor can it be
At rest till it finds rest in Thee.

2 Is there a thing beneath the sun
  That strives with Thee my heart to share?
Ah, tear it thence, and reign alone,
  The Lord of every motion there;
Then shall my heart from earth be free,
When it hath found repose in Thee.

3 Each moment draw from earth away
  My heart, that lowly waits Thy call;
Speak to my inmost soul, and say,
  "I am thy Love, thy God, thy All!"
To feel Thy power, to hear Thy voice,
To taste Thy love, be all my choice.
              Gerhard Tersteegen. (1697-1769.)
              Tr. by Rev. John Wesley. (1703-1791.)

295 "Wash me thoroughly from mine iniquity." 8. 6.
Rom. vi. 1-18. Mat. v. 3-9. Ps. xlii.

1 SAVIOUR, on me the grace bestow,
  That, with Thy children, I may know
My sins on earth forgiven;
  Give me to prove the kingdom mine,
And taste, in holiness divine,
  The happiness of heaven.

2 Me with that restless thirst inspire,
  That sacred, infinite desire,
And feast my hungry heart;
  Less than Thyself cannot suffice;
My soul for all Thy fulness cries,
  For all Thou hast and art.

3 Jesus, the crowning grace impart;
  Bless me with purity of heart,
That now beholding Thee,
  I soon may view Thy open face,
On all Thy glorious beauties gaze,
  And God forever see.
              Rev. Charles Wesley.

"This is the will of God, your sanctification."

296 "He that calleth you... also will do it." C. M.
1 Cor. iii. 16, 17. Ps. iii. Ex. xl. 17-38.

1 THY presence, Lord, the place shall fill,
　My heart shall be Thy throne ;
　Thy holy, just, and perfect will
　Shall in my flesh be done.

2 I thank Thee for the present grace,
　And now in hope rejoice ;
　In confidence to see Thy face,
　And always hear Thy voice.

3 I have the things I ask of Thee ;
　What more shall I require ?
　That still my soul may restless be,
　And only Thee desire.

4 Thy only will be done, not mine,
　But make me, Lord, Thy home ;
　Come as Thou wilt, I that resign,
　But O, my Jesus, come!
　　　　Rev. Charles Wesley. (1708-1788.)

297 "I will delight myself in Thy statutes." C. M.
Ps. xl. 1-8. John iv. 34-38. Phil. iv. 6-8.

1 BEHOLD, I come with joy to do
　The Master's blessed will ;
　My Lord in outward works pursue,
　And serve His pleasure still.

2 Though careful, without care I am,
　Nor feel my happy toil,
　Preserved in peace by Jesus' name,
　Supported by His smile.

3 Rejoicing thus my faith to show,
　His service my reward ;
　While every work I do below,
　I do it to the Lord.
　　　　Rev. Charles Wesley.

298 "He led them forth by the right way." S. M.
Rom. xiv. 7, 8. 2 Cor. v. 14, 15. Ps. ci.

1 JESUS, I live to Thee,
　The loveliest and best ;
　My life in Thee, Thy life in me,
　In Thy blest love I rest.

2 Jesus, I die to Thee,
　Whenever death shall come ;
　To die in Thee is life to me,
　In my eternal home.

3 Whether to live or die,
　I know not which is best ;
　To live in Thee is bliss to me,
　To die is endless rest.

4 Living or dying, Lord,
　I ask but to be Thine ;
　My life in Thee, Thy life in me,
　Makes heaven forever mine.
　　　　Rev. Henry Harbaugh. (1816-1867.)

299 "Satisfied when I awake with Thy likeness." C. M.
Rom. vi.1 1-21. Ps. xci. John viii. 28-36.

1 O LORD, impart Thyself to me,
　No other good I need ;
　When Thou, the Son, shalt make me free,
　I shall be free indeed.

2 I cannot rest till in Thy blood
　I full redemption have ;
　But Thou, through whom I come to God,
　Canst to the utmost save.

3 From sin, the guilt, the power, the pain,
　Thou wilt redeem my soul :
　Lord, I believe, and not in vain ;
　My faith shall make me whole.

4 I too with Thee shall walk in white ;
　With all Thy saints shall prove
　The length, and depth, and breadth, and height,
　Of everlasting love.
　　　　Rev. Charles Wesley.

300 "Now the God of peace... make you perfect." L. M.
Gen. xvii. 1. Mat. v. 48. 2 Pet. i. 2-11.

1 HE wills that I should holy be :
　That holiness I long to feel ;
　That full divine conformity
　To all my Saviour's righteous will.

2 On Thee, O God, my soul is stayed,
　And waits to prove Thine utmost will ;
　The promise by Thy mercy made
　Thou canst, thou wilt, in me fulfil.

3 No more I stagger at Thy power,
　Or doubt Thy truth, which cannot move ;
　Hasten the long-expected hour,
　And bless me with Thy perfect love.
　　　　Rev. Charles Wesley.

301 "That ye may stand... complete." L. M.
Col. ii. 1-10. John i. 15-18. Jer. xxxiii. 9-16.

1 COMPLETE in Thee ! no work of mine
　May take, dear Lord, the place of Thine ;
　Thy blood has pardon bought for me,
　And I am now complete in Thee.

2 Complete in Thee ! no more shall sin
　Thy grace has conquered, reign within ;
　Thy voice will bid the tempter flee,
　And I shall stand complete in Thee.

3 Complete in Thee ! each want supplied,
　And no good thing to me denied ;
　Since Thou, my portion, Lord, wilt be,
　I ask no more, complete in Thee.

4 Dear Saviour, when, before Thy bar,
　All tribes and tongues assembled are,
　Among Thy chosen may I be
　At Thy right hand, complete in Thee.
　　　　Rev. Aaron R. Wolfe. (1821-.)

"I love the Lord."

302 1 John iv. 7-21. 2 Cor. v. 14-21. Deu. vii. 6-9. "He first loved us." C. M.

1 My God, I love Thee : not because
   I hope for heaven thereby ;
   Nor yet because who love Thee not
   Must die eternally.

2 Thou, O my Jesus, Thou didst me
   Upon the cross embrace ;
   For me didst bear the nails and spear,
   And manifold disgrace.

3 Then why, O blessèd Jesus Christ,
   Should I not love Thee well ?
   Not for the hope of winning heaven,
   Nor of escaping hell;

4 Not with the hope of gaining aught,
   Not seeking a reward ;
   But as Thyself hast lovèd me,
   O ever-loving Lord.

5 So would I love Thee, dearest Lord,
   And in Thy praise will sing,
   Solely because Thou art my God,
   And my eternal King.

   Rev. Edward Caswall. (1814-1878.)

303 1 John iv. 1-10. 1 Cor. ii. 1-12. Ps. lxiii. "Thou knowest that I love Thee." L. M.

1 Jesus, I love Thee evermore,
   For Thou hast loved me, Lord, before ;
   I have no freedom but to be
   A willing servant, Lord, to Thee.

2 Let memory, then, no thought retain
   Except the glory of Thy reign ;
   Nor let my mind desire below
   Aught but the love of Christ to know.

3 I cannot have a wish or thought,
   Except to love Thee as I ought ;
   What by Thy gracious gift is mine
   With joy I freely make it Thine.

   Erastus C. Benedict. (1800-.)

304 John xxi. 15-17. Luke vii. 36-50. Ps. xviii. "I will love Thee, O Lord, my strength." 8. 7. 7.

1 I will love Thee, all my Treasure,
   I will love Thee, all my Strength ;
   I will love Thee without measure,
   And will love Thee right at length :
   I will love Thee, Light Divine,
   Till I die, and find Thee mine.

2 I will love in joy or sorrow,
   Crowning joy, will love Thee well ;
   I will love to-day, to-morrow,
   While I in this body dwell :
   I will love Thee, Light Divine,
   Till I die, and find Thee mine.

   Johann A. Scheffler. (1624-1677.)
   Tr. by Miss Jane Borthwick. (1825-.)

305 Phil. iii. 7-11. Eph. iii. Jer. ix. 23, 24. "O Thou whom my soul loveth!" 7.

1 Blessèd Saviour, Thee I love,
   All my other joys above ;
   All my hopes in Thee abide,
   Thou my Hope, and naught beside :
   Ever let my glory be
   Only, only, only Thee.

2 Once again beside the cross,
   All my gain I count but loss ;
   Earthly pleasures fade away,
   Clouds they are that hide my day :
   Hence, vain shadows ! let me see
   Jesus, crucified for me.

3 From beneath that thorny crown
   Trickle drops of cleansing down ;
   Pardon from Thy piercèd hand
   Now I take, while here I stand :
   Only then I live to Thee,
   When Thy wounded side I see.

4 Blessèd Saviour, Thine am I,
   Thine to live and Thine to die ;
   Height, or depth, or earthly power,
   Ne'er shall hide my Saviour more :
   Ever shall my glory be
   Only, only, only Thee.

   Rev. George Duffield, Jr. (1818-.)

306 2 Cor. xi. Heb. vii. 19 to viii. 6. Job xix. 25. "We will remember Thy love." C. M.

1 According to Thy gracious word,
   In meek humility,
   This will I do, my dying Lord,
   I will remember Thee.

2 Gethsemane can I forget,
   Or there Thy conflict see,
   Thine agony and bloody sweat,
   And not remember Thee ?

3 When to the cross I turn mine eyes,
   And rest on Calvary,
   O Lamb of God, my Sacrifice,
   I must remember Thee :

4 Remember Thee, and all Thy pains,
   And all Thy love to me ;
   Yea, while a breath, a pulse, remains,
   Will I remember Thee.

5 And when these failing lips grow dumb,
   And mind and memory flee,
   When Thou shalt in Thy kingdom come,
   Jesus, remember me.

   James Montgomery. (1771-1854.)

"I love the Lord."

307 "To know the love of Christ." L. M.
Ps. lxxxi. Deu. xxxii. 1-14. Acts xxi. 10-13.

1 OF Him who did salvation bring,
　I could forever think and sing ;
　Though sin and sorrow wound my soul,
　Jesus, Thy balm will make it whole.

2 'T is Thee I love ; for Thee alone
　I shed my tears and make my moan ;
　Where'er I am, where'er I move,
　I meet the object of my love.

3 Insatiate to this Spring I fly ;
　I drink, and yet am ever dry.
　Ah, who against Thy charms is proof ?
　Ah, who that loves can love enough ?

　　　　Bernard of Clairvaux. (1091-1153.)
　　　Tr. by Rev. Anthony W. Boehm. (1673-1722.)

308 "Whom, having not seen, ye love." C. M.
1 Pet. i. Isa. xxxiii. 15-24. Ps. lxxiii. 25.

1 JESUS, these eyes have never seen
　That radiant form of Thine ;
　The veil of sense hangs dark between
　Thy blessèd face and mine.

2 I see Thee not, I hear Thee not,
　Yet art Thou oft with me ;
　And earth hath ne'er so dear a spot
　As where I meet with Thee.

3 Like some bright dream that comes unsought,
　When slumbers o'er me roll,
　Thine image ever fills my thought,
　And charms my ravished soul.

4 Yet, though I have not seen, and still
　Must rest in faith alone,
　I love Thee, dearest Lord, and will,
　Unseen, but not unknown.

5 When death these mortal eyes shall seal,
　And still this throbbing heart,
　The rending veil shall Thee reveal,
　All glorious as Thou art.
　　　　　　Rev. Ray Palmer. (1808-..)

309 "Whom have I in heaven but Thee?" L. M.
Ps. xvi. John xx. 1-16. 1 Pet. ii. 6-25.

1 JESUS, my Lord, my chief Delight,
　For Thee I long, for Thee I pray,
　Amid the shadows of the night,
　Amid the business of the day.

2 Thou art the glorious Gift of God
　To sinners weary and distressed ;
　The first of all His gifts bestowed,
　And certain pledge of all the rest.

3 The precious jewel I would keep,
　And lodge it deep within my heart ;
　At home, abroad, awake, asleep,
　It never should from thence depart.
　　　　　Rev. Benjamin Beddome. (1717-1795.)

310 "My exceeding joy." C. M.
John xxi. 15-17. 2 Cor. xii. 1-10. Deu. x. 12-22.

1 Do not I love Thee, O my Lord ?
　Behold my heart and see ;
　And turn each cursèd idol out
　That dares to rival Thee.

2 Do not I love Thee from my soul ?
　Then let me nothing love ;
　Dead be my heart to every joy,
　When Jesus cannot move.

3 Is not Thy name melodious still
　To mine attentive ear ?
　Doth not each pulse with pleasure bound
　My Saviour's voice to hear ?

4 Hast Thou a lamb in all Thy flock
　I would disdain to feed ?
　Hast Thou a foe before whose face
　I fear Thy cause to plead ?

5 Thou know'st I love Thee, dearest Lord,
　But O, I long to soar
　Far from the sphere of mortal joys,
　And learn to love Thee more.
　　　　　Rev. Philip Doddridge. (1702-1751.)

311 "Thou hast redeemed me, O Lord." 8. P.
Ps. cxviii. 5-21. Eph. ii. 4-17. Rev. v.

1 MY gracious Redeemer I love,
　His praises aloud I 'll proclaim,
　And join with the armies above,
　To shout His adorable name.
　To gaze on His glories divine
　Shall be my eternal employ,
　And feel them incessantly shine
　My boundless, ineffable joy.

2 He freely redeemed, with His blood,
　My soul from the confines of hell,
　To live on the smiles of my God,
　And in His sweet presence to dwell ;
　To shine with the angels of light,
　With saints and with seraphs to sing,
　To view, with eternal delight,
　My Jesus, my Saviour, my King.
　　　　　Rev. Benjamin Francis. (1734-1799.)

312 "None upon earth I desire besides Thee." 7.
Ps. civ. John i. 1-14. Col. i. 16 to ii. 7.

1 EARTH has nothing sweet or fair,
　Lovely forms or beauties rare,
　But before my eyes they bring
　Christ, of beauty Source and Spring.

2 Lord of all that 's fair to see,
　Come, reveal Thyself to me ;
　Let me 'mid Thy radiant light
　See Thine unveiled glories bright.
　　　　　Johann A. Scheffler. (1624-1677.)
　　　　　Tr. by Miss Frances E. Cox.

"I love the Lord."

313 "My glory and the lifter up of mine head." **S. M.**
Ps. lxiii. Jer. xxxi. 10-14. Eph. i. 15-23.

1 MY God, my Life, my Love!
  To Thee, to Thee I call;
  I cannot live if Thou remove,
  For Thou art all in all.

2 Not all the harps above
  Can make a heavenly place,
  If God His residence remove,
  Or but conceal His face.

3 Nor earth, nor all the sky,
  Can one delight afford;
  No, not a drop of real joy,
  Without Thy presence, Lord.

4 Thou art the sea of love,
  Where all my pleasures roll;
  The circle where my passions move,
  And centre of my soul.
                    Rev. Isaac Watts. (1674-1748.)

314 "Because He hath heard my voice" **C. M.**
Ps. xviii. 1-6. 1 John iv. 9, 10. John x. 13-38.

1 I LOVE the Lord; He heard my cries,
  And pitied every groan:
  Long as I live, when troubles rise,
  I'll hasten to His throne.

2 I love the Lord; He bowed His ear,
  And chased my grief away:
  O let my heart no more despair,
  While I have breath to pray.

3 The Lord beheld me sore distressed;
  He bade my pains remove:
  Return, my soul, to God, thy Rest,
  For thou hast known His love.
                    Rev. Isaac Watts.

315 "The memory of Thy great goodness." **C. M.**
Ps. cxlvii. Josh. xxiv. Eph. iii.

1 SWEET is the memory of Thy grace,
  My God, my heavenly King!
  Let age to age Thy righteousness,
  In sounds of glory, sing.

2 God reigns on high, but ne'er confines
  His goodness to the skies;
  Through the whole earth His bounty shines,
  And every want supplies.

3 With longing eyes, Thy creatures wait
  On Thee for daily food;
  Thy liberal hand provides their meat,
  And fills their mouths with good.

4 How kind are Thy compassions, Lord,
  How slow Thine anger moves!
  But soon He sends His pardoning word
  To cheer the souls He loves.
                    Rev. Isaac Watts.

316 "From Him cometh my salvation." **C. M.**
Ps. lxiii. 25-28. Hab. iii. 17-19. Col. i. 10, 11.

1 GOD, my Supporter and my Hope,
  My Help forever near,
  Thine arm of mercy held me up
  When sinking in despair.

2 Were I in heaven without my God,
  'T would be no joy to me;
  And while this earth is my abode
  I long for none but Thee.

3 What if the springs of life were broke,
  And flesh and heart should faint?
  God is my soul's eternal Rock,
  The Strength of every saint.

4 But to draw near to Thee, my God,
  Shall be my sweet employ:
  My tongue shall sound Thy works abroad,
  And tell the world my joy.
                    Rev. Isaac Watts.

317 "So panteth my soul after Thee." **8. 7.**
1 Pet. i. 3-9. Ps. cxviii. 5-21. Jer. xvii. 7-14.

1 I WOULD love Thee, God and Father,
  My Redeemer and my King;
  I would love Thee, for, without Thee,
  Life is but a bitter thing.

2 I would love Thee; look upon me,
  Ever guide me with Thine eye.
  I would love Thee; if not nourished
  By Thy love, my soul would die.

3 I would love Thee, I have vowed it;
  On Thy love my heart is set;
  While I love Thee, I will never
  My Redeemer's blood forget.
                    Madame Jeanne M. B. de la M. Guyon. (1648-1717.)

318 "Our eyes wait upon the Lord." **L. M.**
Ps. cxvi. Isa. lv. ii. 13, 14. Phil. iii. 4-14.

1 GREAT God, indulge my humble claim!
  Thou art my Hope, my Joy, my Rest;
  The glories that compose Thy name
  Stand all engaged to make me blest.

2 Thou Great and Good, Thou Just and Wise,
  Thou art my Father and my God;
  And I am Thine by sacred ties,
  Thy son, Thy servant, bought with blood.

3 With heart and eyes and lifted hands,
  For Thee I long, to Thee I look;
  As travellers in thirsty lands
  Pant for the cooling water-brook.

4 I'll lift my hands, I'll raise my voice,
  While I have breath to pray or praise:
  This work shall make my heart rejoice,
  And spend the remnant of my days.
                    Rev. Isaac Watts.

"I love the Lord."

319 1 Pet. ii. 1-10. "He is precious." Phil. iii. 7-14. Ps. cxxxviii   C. M.

1 JESUS, I love Thy charming name,
'T is music to mine ear ;
Fain would I sound it out so loud
That earth and heaven should hear.

2 Yes, Thou art precious to my soul,
My Transport and my Trust;
Jewels to Thee are gaudy toys,
And gold is sordid dust.

3 All my capacious powers can wish
In Thee doth richly meet ;
Not to mine eyes is light so clear,
Nor friendship half so sweet.

4 Thy grace still dwells upon my heart,
And sheds its fragrance there ;
The noblest balm of all its wounds,
The cordial of its care.

5 I 'll speak the honors of Thy name
With my last laboring breath ;
Then, speechless, clasp Thee in mine arms,
The antidote of death.

Rev. Philip Doddridge. (1702-1751.)

321 Job xxviii. 12-28. "By whom are all things." Prov. iii. 13-35. John xiv 6-31.   C. M.

1 I 'VE found the pearl of greatest price,
My heart doth sing for joy;
And sing I must, for Christ is mine,
Christ shall my song employ.

2 Christ is my Prophet, Priest, and King :
A Prophet full of light,
My great High Priest before the throne,
My King of heavenly might.

3 For He indeed is Lord of lords,
And He the King of kings ;
He is the Sun of Righteousness,
With healing in His wings.

4 Christ is my Peace : He died for me,
For me He gave His blood ;
And as my wondrous Sacrifice
Offered Himself to God.

5 Christ Jesus is my All in all,
My Comfort and my Love ;
My Life below, and He shall be
My Joy and Crown above.

Rev. John Mason. (-1694.)

320 Mat. i. 21-25. "Above...every name that is named." Isa. ix. 6. Jer. xxiii. 5, 6.   C. M.

1 How sweet the name of Jesus sounds
In a believer's ear !
It soothes his sorrows, heals his wounds,
And drives away his fear.
It makes the wounded spirit whole,
And calms the troubled breast ;
'T is manna to the hungry soul,
And to the weary rest.

2 Dear name, the Rock on which I build,
My Shield and Hiding-place ;
My never-failing Treasury, filled
With boundless stores of grace,
Jesus, my Shepherd, Husband, Friend,
My Prophet, Priest, and King:
My Lord, my Life, my Way, my End,
Accept the praise I bring.

3 Weak is the effort of my heart,
And cold my warmest thought ;
But when I see Thee as Thou art,
I 'll praise Thee as I ought.
Till then I would Thy love proclaim
With every fleeting breath ;
And may the music of Thy name
Refresh my soul in death.

Rev. John Newton. (1725-1807.)

322 John i. 14-34. "He hath borne it upon Him." Mat. viii. 17. Isa. liii. 4-8.   7, 6.

1 I LAY my sins on Jesus,
The spotless Lamb of God ;
He bears them all, and frees us
From the accursèd load.
I bring my guilt to Jesus,
To wash my crimson stains
White, in His blood most precious,
Till not a stain remains.

2 I lay my wants on Jesus,
All fullness dwells in Him ;
He heals all my diseases,
He doth my soul redeem.
I lay my griefs on Jesus,
My burdens and my cares ;
He from them all releases,
He all my sorrows shares.

3 I long to be like Jesus,
Meek, loving, lowly, mild;
I long to be like Jesus,
The Father's holy child.
I long to be with Jesus,
Amid the heavenly throng,
To sing, with saints, His praises,
To learn the angels' song.

Rev. Horatius Bonar. (1808-.)

"I love the Lord."

323 "Perfect love casteth out fear." **6. 4.**
1 John iv. 17-19. Phil. ii. 9-11. Ps. lxi.

1 JESUS, Thy name I love
  All other names above,
    Jesus, my Lord !
  Oh, Thou art all to me ;
  Nothing to please I see,
  Nothing apart from Thee,
    Jesus, my Lord !

2 Thou, blessèd Son of God,
  Hast bought me with Thy blood,
    Jesus, my Lord !
  O how great is Thy love,
  All other loves above,
  Love that I daily prove,
    Jesus, my Lord !

3 When unto Thee I flee,
  Thou wilt my Refuge be,
    Jesus, my Lord !
  What need I now to fear,
  What earthly grief or care,
  Since Thou art ever near,
    Jesus, my Lord !

4 Soon Thou wilt come again ;
  I shall be happy then,
    Jesus, my Lord !
  Then Thine own face I 'll see,
  Then I shall like Thee be,
  Then evermore with Thee,
    Jesus, my Lord !

James G. Deck. (1806-.)

324 "The Lord our righteousness." **C. M.**
Ps. lxxi. 15-24. John xiii. 3-10. 1 John i.

1 JESUS, Thou art my Righteousness,
    For all my sins were Thine ;
  Thy death hath bought of God my peace,
    Thy life hath made Him mine.

2 My dying Saviour and my God,
    Fountain for guilt and sin,
  Sprinkle me ever with Thy blood,
    And cleanse and keep me clean.

3 Wash me, and make me thus Thine own ;
    Wash me, and mine Thou art ;
  Wash me, but not my feet alone,
    My hands, my head, my heart.

4 The atonement of Thy blood apply,
    Till faith to sight improve ;
  Till hope in full fruition die,
    And all my soul be love.

Rev. Charles Wesley. (1708-1788.)

325 "My soul thirsteth for God." **8. 6.**
Rom. viii. 35-39. Eph. iii. 14-19. Zeph. iii.

1 O LOVE divine, how sweet thou art !
  When shall I find my willing heart
    All taken up by thee ?
  I thirst, I faint, I die, to prove
  The greatness of redeeming love,
    The love of Christ to me.

2 Stronger His love than death or hell ;
  Its riches are unsearchable ;
    The first-born sons of light
  Desire in vain its depths to see ;
  They cannot reach the mystery,
    The length, and breadth, and height.

3 God only knows the love of God ;
  O that it now were shed abroad
    In this poor, stony heart !
  For love I sigh, for love I pine :
  This only portion, Lord, be mine,
    Be mine this better part.

Rev. Charles Wesley.

326 "This is the way." **L. M.**
John xiv. 4-6. Heb. ix. 8-15. Zech. i.

THOU art the Way ; and he who sighs,
  Amid this starless waste of woe,
To find a pathway to the skies,
  A light from heaven's eternal glow,
By Thee must come, Thou Gate of love,
  Through which the saints undoubting trod,
Till faith discovers, like the dove,
  An ark, a resting-place in God.

Author unknown.

327 "Blessed be the Lord, my strength." **8.**
John xxi. 15-17. Luke vii. 36-50. Ps. xviii. 1-6.

1 I THANK Thee, uncreated Sun,
    That Thy bright beams on me have shined ;
  I thank Thee, who hast overthrown
    My foes, and healed my wounded mind ;
  I thank Thee, whose enlivening voice
  Bids my freed heart in Thee rejoice.

2 Give to mine eyes refreshing tears ;
    Give to my heart chaste, hallowed fires ;
  Give to my soul, with filial fears,
    The love that all heaven's host inspires,
  That all my powers, with all their might,
  In Thy sole glory may unite.

3 Thee will I love, my Joy, my Crown ;
    Thee will I love, my Lord, my God ;
  Thee will I love, beneath Thy frown
    Or smile, Thy sceptre or Thy rod.
  What though my flesh and heart decay ?
  Thee shall I love in endless day !

Johann A. Scheffler. (1624-1677.)
Tr. by Rev. John Wesley. (1703-1791.)

"I love the Lord."

328 "Greater love hath no man." Eph. iii. 14-19. Rom. viii. 25-39. Ps. ciii.   8.

1 JESUS, Thy boundless love to me
   No thought can reach, no tongue declare ;
   O knit my thankful heart to Thee,
   And reign without a rival there.
   Thine wholly, Thine alone, I am ;
   Be Thou alone my constant flame.

2 O grant that nothing in my soul
   May dwell but Thy pure love alone ;
   O may Thy love possess me whole,
   My Joy, my Treasure, and my Crown.
   Strange fires far from my soul remove ;
   My every act, word, thought, be love.

3 Unwearied may I this pursue,
   Dauntless to the high prize aspire ;
   Hourly within my breast renew
   This holy flame, this heavenly fire ;
   And day and night be all my care
   To guard this sacred treasure there.
Rev. Paul Gerhardt. (1606-1676.)
Tr. by Rev. John Wesley. (1703-1791.)

329 "There is no fear in love." 1 Cor. xiii. John xvii. Zeph. iii. 14-20.   8.

1 O LOVE, how cheering is thy ray !
   All pain before thy presence flies ;
   Care, anguish, sorrow, melt away,
   Where'er thy healing beams arise.
   O Jesus, nothing may I see,
   Nothing desire or seek, but Thee !

2 In suffering be Thy love my peace,
   In weakness be Thy love my power ;
   And when the storms of life shall cease,
   Jesus, in that important hour,
   In death as life be Thou my Guide,
   And save me, who for me hast died.
Rev. Paul Gerhardt.
Tr. by Rev. John Wesley.

330 "He is like a refiner's fire." Phil. iii. 7-14. Ps. cxix. 81-88. Mal. iii. 1-4.   C. M.

1 JESUS, Thine all-victorious love
   Shed in my heart abroad ;
   Then shall my feet no longer rove,
   Rooted and fixed in God.

2 Refining Fire, go through my heart,
   Illuminate my soul ;
   Scatter Thy life through every part,
   And sanctify the whole.

3 My steadfast soul, from falling free,
   Shall then no longer move ;
   While Christ is all the world to me,
   And all my heart is love.
Rev. Charles Wesley. (1708-1788.)

331 "I have chosen you." John xv. 1-16. 1 John iv. 9, 10. Deu. vii. 6-9.   7, 6.

1 'T IS not that I did choose Thee,
   For, Lord, that could not be ;
   This heart would still refuse Thee,
   But Thou hast chosen me.
   Thou from the sin that stained me
   Hast made me pure and free ;
   Of old Thou hast ordained me,
   That I should live to Thee.

2 'T was sovereign mercy called me,
   And taught my opening mind ;
   The world had else enthralled me,
   To heavenly glories blind.
   My heart owns none above Thee,
   For Thy rich grace I thirst ;
   This knowing, if I love Thee,
   Thou must have loved me first.
Josiah Conder. (1780-1855.)

332 "Blessed be His glorious name." Isa. ix. 6. Luke ii. 14. Col. i. 1-20.   L. M.

1 SWEETER sounds than music knows
   Charm me in Immanuel's name ;
   All her hopes my spirit owes
   To His birth, and cross, and shame.

2 When He came, the angels sung,
   "Glory be to God on high !"
   Lord, unloose my stammering tongue ;
   Who should louder sing than I ?

3 O my Saviour, Shield, and Sun,
   Shepherd, Brother, Lord, and Friend,
   Every precious name in one,
   I will love Thee without end !
Rev. John Newton. (1725-1807.)

333 "I forgave thee all that debt." Ps. cxvi. John xxi. Isa. xxxiii. 15-24.   C. M.

1 O JESUS, Jesus, dearest Lord !
   Forgive me if I say,
   For very love, Thy sacred name
   A thousand times a day.

2 For Thou to me art All in all,
   My Honor and my Wealth,
   My heart's Desire, my body's Strength,
   My soul's eternal Health.

3 Burn, burn, O love, within my heart,
   Burn fiercely night and day,
   Till all the dross of earthly loves
   Is burned, and burned away.

4 O Light in darkness, Joy in grief,
   O heaven begun on earth,
   Jesus, my Love, my Treasure, who
   Can tell what Thou art worth ?
Rev. Frederick W. Faber. (1814-1863.)

"I love the Lord."

334 "None other name." L. M.
Acts iv. 12. Jer. xxiii. 5, 6. Ps. lxxxix. 24-29.

1 THERE is none other name than Thine,
 Jehovah Jesus, name divine,
 On which to rest for sins forgiven,
 For peace with God, for hope of heaven.

2 There is none other name than Thine,
 When cares and fears and griefs are mine,
 That, with a gracious power, can heal
 Each care and fear and grief I feel.

3 There is none other name than Thine,
 When called my spirit to resign,
 To bear me through that latest strife,
 And ev'n in death to be my life.

4 Name above every name! thy praise
 Shall fill the remnant of my days:
 Jehovah Jesus, name divine,
 Rock of salvation, Thou art mine!
Author unknown.

335 "Mary sat at Jesus' feet." L. M.
Ps. xlii. Luke x. 38-42. John ix. 13-38.

1 JESUS, my heart within me burns
 To tell Thee all its conscious love;
 And from earth's low delight it turns,
 To taste a joy like that above.

2 Though oft these lips my love have told,
 They still the story would repeat;
 To me the rapture ne'er grows old
 That thrills me, bending at Thy feet.

3 I breathe my words into Thine ear,
 I seem to fix mine eyes on Thine;
 And, sure that Thou dost wait to hear,
 I dare in faith to call Thee mine.

4 Reign Thou sole Sovereign of my heart,
 My all I yield to Thy control;
 O let me never from Thee part,
 Thou best Belovéd of my soul!
Rev. Ray Palmer. (1808-.)

336 "He is altogether lovely." C. M.
Phil. ii. 9-11. Heb. viii. Ps. lxxii.

1 O JESUS, Thou the beauty art
 Of angel worlds above;
 Thy name is music to the heart,
 Enchanting it with love.

2 O Jesus, Saviour, hear the sighs
 Which unto Thee I send;
 To Thee my inmost spirit cries,
 My being's Hope and End.

3 Stay with us, Lord, and with Thy light
 Illume the soul's abyss;
 Scatter the darkness of our night,
 And fill the world with bliss.
Rev. Edward Caswall. (1814-1878.)

337 "That I may know Him." C. M.
Ps. clv. 33, 34. 1 Pet. i. 3-13. Eph. iii. 14-21.

1 JESUS, the very thought of Thee
 With sweetness fills my breast;
 But sweeter far Thy face to see,
 And in Thy presence rest.

2 Nor voice can sing, nor heart can frame,
 Nor can the memory find,
 A sweeter sound than Thy blest name,
 O Saviour of mankind!

3 O Hope of every contrite heart,
 O Joy of all the meek,
 To those who fall how kind Thou art,
 How good to those who seek!

4 But what to those who find? Ah, this
 Nor tongue nor pen can show:
 The love of Jesus, what it is,
 None but His loved ones know.

5 Jesus, our only Joy be Thou,
 As Thou our Prize wilt be;
 Jesus, be Thou our Glory now,
 And through eternity!
Rev. Edward Caswall.

338 "Cause Thy face to shine." 8. P.
Job xxxiii. 3-10. Hab. iii. 17-19. Rom. viii. 35-39.

1 How tedious and tasteless the hours
 When Jesus no longer I see!
 Sweet prospects, sweet birds, and sweet flowers
 Have lost all their sweetness with me.
 The midsummer sun shines but dim,
 The fields strive in vain to look gay;
 But when I am happy in Him,
 December's as pleasant as May.

2 His name yields the richest perfume,
 And sweeter than music His voice;
 His presence disperses my gloom,
 And makes all within me rejoice.
 I should, were He always thus nigh,
 Have nothing to wish or to fear;
 No mortal so happy as I,
 My summer would last all the year.

3 Content with beholding His face,
 My all to His pleasure resigned,
 No changes of season or place
 Would make any change in my mind.
 While blessed with a sense of His love,
 A palace a toy would appear;
 And prisons would palaces prove,
 If Jesus would dwell with me there.
Rev. John Newton. (1725-1807.)

"I love the Lord."

339 "My songs in the house of my pilgrimage." 7, 6.
Ps. cxlv. Luke viii. 38, 39. John iv. 28-42.

1 I LOVE to tell the story
   Of unseen things above,
Of Jesus and His glory,
   Of Jesus and His love.
I love to tell the story,
   Because I know it's true;
It satisfies my longings
   As nothing else would do.

   I love to tell the story:
     'T will be my theme in glory,
   To tell the old, old story
     Of Jesus and His love.

2 I love to tell the story:
   More wonderful it seems
Than all the golden fancies
   Of all our golden dreams.
I love to tell the story:
   'T is pleasant to repeat
What seems each time I tell it
   More wonderfully sweet.

3 I love to tell the story:
   For those who know it best
Seem hungering and thirsting
   To hear it, like the rest;
And when, in scenes of glory,
   I sing the new, new song,
'T will be the old, old story,
   That I have loved so long.

             Miss Katherine Hankey. 1865.

---

340 "The cross of our Lord Jesus Christ." 8, 7.
Heb. xii. 1-14. Mat. xxvii. 54, 55. Cant. ii. 1-14.

1 SWEET the moments, rich in blessing,
   Which before the cross I spend;
Life and health and peace possessing,
   From the sinner's dying Friend.

2 Here it is I find my heaven,
   While upon the Lamb I gaze;
Love I much, I've much forgiven;
   I'm a miracle of grace.

3 Love and grief my heart dividing,
   With my tears His feet I'll bathe;
Constant still, in faith abiding,
   Life deriving from His death.

4 Lord, in ceaseless contemplation
   Fix my thankful heart on Thee,
Till I taste Thy full salvation,
   And Thine unveiled glories see.

           Rev. James Allen. (1734-1804.)
        Alt. by Hon. and Rev. Walter Shirley. (1725-1786.)

---

341 "Who... desired to hear the word of God." 7, 6.
Acts xiii. 42, viii. 31. John i. 1-5. Ps. cxix. 25-32

1 TELL me the old, old story
   Of unseen things above,
Of Jesus and His glory,
   Of Jesus and His love.
Tell me the story simply,
   As to a little child,
For I am weak and weary,
   And helpless and defiled.

   Tell me the old, old story,
   Tell me the old, old story,
   Tell me the old, old story,
     Of Jesus and His love.

2 Tell me the story slowly,
   That I may take it in,
That wonderful redemption,
   God's remedy for sin.
Tell me the story softly,
   With earnest tones, and grave;
Remember, I'm the sinner
   Whom Jesus came to save.

3 Tell me the same old story,
   When you have cause to fear
That this world's empty glory
   Is costing me too dear.
Yes, and when that world's glory
   Is dawning on my soul,
Tell me the old, old, story:
   "Christ Jesus makes thee whole."

            Miss Katherine Hankey. 1835.

---

342 "His name alone is excellent." 8, 7.
Phil. ii. 9-11. 1 Tim. vi. 12-16. Isa. ix. 6, 7.

1 TAKE the name of Jesus with you,
   Child of sorrow and of woe;
It will joy and comfort give you;
   Take it, then, where'er you go.

   Precious name, O how sweet,
     Hope of earth, and joy of heaven;
   Precious name, O how sweet,
     Hope of earth and joy of heaven!

2 Take the name of Jesus ever,
   As a shield from every snare;
If temptations round you gather,
   Breathe that holy name in prayer.

3 At the name of Jesus bowing,
   Falling prostrate at His feet,
King of kings in heaven we'll crown Him,
   When our journey is complete.

            Mrs. Lydia Baxter. (1809-1874.)

"I love the Lord."

343 Mal iv 2. "A sun and shield" 2 Sam. xxiii. 4 Rev. xxi 22-26. 7, 6.

1 O BLESSÉD Sun, whose splendor
　Dispels the shades of night;
　O Jesus, my Defender,
　My soul's supreme Delight!
　All day I hear resounding
　　A voice with silver tone,
　Which speaks of grace abounding
　　Through God's eternal Son.

2 A deep and heavenly feeling
　　Oft seizes on my breast;
　Ah, here is balm for healing,
　　Here only is true rest.
　Though fortune should bereave me
　　Of all I love the best,
　If Christ His love still leave me,
　　I freely give the rest.

3 Thy love it was which sought me,
　　Thyself unsought by me,
　And to the haven brought me,
　　Where I would gladly be.
　The things which once distressed me
　　My heart no longer move,
　Since this sweet truth impressed me,
　　That I possess Thy love.
　　　　　Rev. Carl J. P. Spitta. (1801-1859.)
　　　　　　Tr. by Richard Massie.

344 "I am not ashamed of the gospel of Christ." L. M.
　　　Mark viii. 34-38. Rom. i. 16. Ps. xxxiv.

1 JESUS, and shall it ever be,
　A mortal man ashamed of Thee?
　Ashamed of Thee, whom angels praise,
　Whose glories shine through endless days?

2 Ashamed of Jesus! just as soon
　Let midnight be ashamed of noon;
　'T is midnight with my soul, till He,
　Bright Morning Star, bid darkness flee.

3 Ashamed of Jesus! that dear Friend,
　On whom my hopes of heaven depend!
　No; when I blush, be this my shame,
　That I no more revere His name.

4 Ashamed of Jesus! yes, I may,
　When I've no guilt to wash away;
　No tear to wipe, no good to crave,
　No fear to quell, no soul to save.

5 Till then, nor is my boasting vain,
　Till then I boast a Saviour slain;
　And O may this my glory be,
　That Christ is not ashamed of me!
　　　　Rev. Joseph Grigg. (1728-1768.)
　　　　Alt. by Rev. Benjamin Francis. (1734-1799.)

345 Luke x. 38-42. "My beloved is mine." Phil. iii. 4-14. Ps. lxxiii. 25, 26. 6, 4.

1 FADE, fade, each earthly joy,
　　Jesus is mine;
　Break, every tender tie,
　　Jesus is mine.
　Dark is the wilderness,
　Earth has no resting-place,
　Jesus alone can bless,
　　Jesus is mine.

2 Tempt not my soul away,
　　Jesus is mine;
　Here would I ever stay,
　　Jesus is mine.
　Perishing things of clay,
　Born but for one brief day,
　Pass from my heart away;
　　Jesus is mine.

3 Farewell, ye dreams of night,
　　Jesus is mine;
　Lost in this dawning bright,
　　Jesus is mine.
　All that my soul has tried,
　Left but a dismal void,
　Jesus has satisfied;
　　Jesus is mine.

4 Farewell, mortality,
　　Jesus is mine;
　Welcome, eternity,
　　Jesus is mine.
　Welcome, O loved and blest,
　Welcome, sweet scenes of rest,
　Welcome, my Saviour's breast;
　　Jesus is mine.
　　　　Mrs. Catharine J. Bonar. (1808-.)

346 Ps. cxv. 9-18. "Thou art my God; I will praise Thee." C. M.
　　　　Lam. iii. 22-32. Phil. iv. 4-9.

1 ETERNAL Source of joys divine,
　　To Thee my soul aspires;
　O could I say, The Lord is mine,
　　'T is all my soul desires.

2 My Hope, my Trust, my Life, my Lord,
　　Assure me of Thy love;
　O speak the kind, transporting word,
　　And bid my fears remove.

3 Then shall my thankful powers rejoice,
　　And triumph in my God,
　Till heavenly rapture tune my voice
　　To spread Thy praise abroad.
　　　　Miss Anne Steele. (1717-1778.)

"I love Thy commandments above gold."

347 Ps. cxix. 97. Rom. vii. 12-22. 2 Tim. iii. 14-17. "How love I Thy law!" C. M.

1 O HOW I love Thy holy law!
'T is daily my delight;
And thence my meditations draw
Divine advice by night.

2 How doth Thy word my heart engage,
How well employ my tongue,
And, in my tiresome pilgrimage,
Yields me a heavenly song!

3 Am I a stranger, or at home,
'T is my perpetual feast;
Not honey dropping from the comb
So much allures the taste.

4 When nature sinks and spirits droop,
Thy promises of grace
Are pillars to support my hope,
And there I write Thy praise.
Rev. Isaac Watts. (1674-1748.)

348 Ps. cxix. 113. Prov. viii. 1-21. John xvi. 13-15. "Therein do I delight." L. M.

1 I LOVE the sacred book of God;
No other can its place supply;
It points me to the saints' abode,
It gives me wings and bids me fly.

2 Sweet book! in thee mine eyes discern
The image of my absent Lord;
From thine illumined page I learn
The joys His presence will afford.

3 I know His Spirit breathes in thee,
To animate His people here;
May thy sweet truths prove life to me,
Till in His presence I appear.
Rev. Thomas Kelly. (1769-1855.)

349 Ps. cxix. 89. Acts viii. 26-39. John vi. 63. "Thy word have I hid in mine heart." C. M.

1 LORD, I have made Thy word my choice,
My lasting heritage:
There shall my noblest powers rejoice,
My warmest thoughts engage.

2 I 'll read the histories of Thy love,
And keep Thy laws in sight,
While through the promises I rove
With ever fresh delight.

3 'T is a broad land of wealth unknown,
Where springs of life arise,
Seeds of immortal bliss are sown,
And hidden glory lies.

4 The best relief that mourners have,
It makes our sorrows blest;
Our fairest hope beyond the grave,
And our eternal rest.
Rev. Isaac Watts.

350 Ps. cxix. 129. Prov vi. 23. Heb. iv. 12-16 "Thy word was ... the rejoicing of mine heart" 8.

1 I LOVE the volumes of Thy word;
What light and joy those leaves afford
To souls benighted and distressed!
Thy precepts guide my doubtful way,
Thy fear forbids my feet to stray,
Thy promise leads my heart to rest.

2 From the discoveries of Thy law
The perfect rules of life I draw;
These are my study and delight.
Not honey so invites the taste;
Nor gold, that hath the furnace passed,
Appears so pleasing to the sight.

3 Thy threatenings wake my slumbering eyes,
And warn me where my danger lies;
But 't is Thy blessed gospel, Lord,
That makes my guilty conscience clean,
Converts my soul, subdues my sin,
And gives a free but large reward.
Rev. Isaac Watts.

351 Ps. cxix. 20. Isa. xl. 10-31. 2 Pet. i. "Wondrous things out of Thy law." L. M.

1 Now let my soul, eternal King,
To Thee its grateful tribute bring;
My knee, with humble homage, bow,
My tongue perform its solemn vow.

2 All nature sings Thy boundless love,
In worlds below and worlds above;
But in Thy blessèd word I trace
Diviner wonders of Thy grace.

3 There what delightful truths I read!
There I behold the Saviour bleed:
His name salutes my listening ear,
Revives my heart, and checks my fear.

4 There Jesus bids my sorrows cease,
And gives my lab'ring conscience peace;
Raises my grateful passions high,
And points to mansions in the sky.
Rev. Ottiwell Heginbotham. (1744-1768.)

352 Ps. cxix. 5. 2 Chr. xxxiv. Acts xvii. 1-11. "I will keep Thy statutes." C. M.

1 O THAT Thy statutes every hour
Might dwell upon my mind!
Thence I derive a quickening power,
And daily peace I find.

2 To meditate Thy precepts, Lord,
Shall be my sweet employ;
My soul shall ne'er forget Thy word,
Thy word is all my joy.
Rev. Isaac Watts.

"A day in Thy courts is better than a thousand."

353 "Unto Thee lift I up mine eyes." **L. M.**
Ps. cxviii. 24-29. Isa. lvi. 2-7. Mark vi. 2.

1 MY opening eyes with rapture see
   The dawn of Thy returning day;
   My thoughts, O God, ascend to Thee,
   While thus my early vows I pay.

2 O bid this trifling world retire,
   And drive each carnal thought away;
   Nor let me feel one vain desire,
   One sinful thought, through all the day.

3 Then to Thy courts when I repair,
   My soul shall rise on joyful wing;
   The wonders of Thy love declare,
   And join the strains which angels sing.
   James Hutton. (1715-1795.)

354 "And call the Sabbath...honorable." **H. M.**
Ps. cxxii. Gen. ii. 1-3. Mat. iii. 16.

1 WELCOME, delightful morn,
   Thou day of sacred rest,
   I hail thy kind return;
   Lord, make these moments blest.
   From the low train of mortal toys,
   I soar to reach immortal joys.

2 Now may the King descend,
   And fill His throne of grace;
   Thy sceptre, Lord, extend,
   While saints address Thy face;
   Let sinners feel Thy quickening word,
   And learn to know and fear the Lord.

3 Descend, celestial Dove,
   With all Thy quickening powers;
   Disclose a Saviour's love,
   And bless these sacred hours;
   Then shall my soul new life obtain,
   Nor Sabbaths e'er be spent in vain.
   Hayward. 1805.

355 "The holy of the Lord." **S. M.**
Ps. xcv. Luke xxiv. 1-9. Mark ix. 5.

1 WELCOME, sweet day of rest
   That saw the Lord arise;
   Welcome to this reviving breast
   And these rejoicing eyes.

2 The King Himself comes near,
   And feasts His saints to-day;
   Here we may sit, and see Him here,
   And love, and praise, and pray.

3 My willing soul would stay
   In such a frame as this,
   And sit and sing herself away
   To everlasting bliss.
   Rev. Isaac Watts. (1674-1748.)

356 "In the Spirit on the Lord's day." **8. 6.**
Ps. lxxxiv. Isa. lviii. 13, 1; Acts xiii. 14-39.

1 THE festal morn, my God, is come,
   That calls me to Thy sacred dome,
   Thy presence to adore:
   My feet the summons shall attend,
   With willing steps Thy courts ascend,
   And tread the hallowed floor.

2 With holy joy I hail the day
   That warns my thirsting soul away;
   What transports fill my breast!
   For lo, my great Redeemer's power
   Unfolds the everlasting door,
   And leads me to His rest.

3 E'en now, to my expecting eyes,
   The heaven-built towers of Salem rise;
   E'en now, with glad survey,
   I view her mansions, that contain
   Th' angelic forms, an awful train,
   And shine with cloudless day.

4 Mother of cities, o'er thy head
   Bright peace, with healing wings outspread,
   For evermore shall dwell:
   Let me, blest seat, my name behold
   Among thy citizens enrolled,
   And bid the world farewell.
   Rev. James Merrick. (1720-1769.)

357 "The Lord blessed the Sabbath day." **L. M.**
Ps. lxvi. 8-20. Ex. xxxi. 13-17. John. xx. 19

1 DEAR is the hallowed morn to me,
   When Sabbath bells awake the day,
   And, by their sacred minstrelsy,
   Call me from earthly cares away.

2 And dear to me the wingéd hour
   Spent in Thy hallowed courts, O Lord;
   To feel devotion's soothing power,
   And catch the manna of Thy word.

3 And dear to me the loud Amen
   Which echoes through the blest abode;
   Which swells, and sinks, and swells again,
   Dies on the walls, but lives to God.

4 Oft when the world, with iron hands,
   Has bound me in its six days' chain,
   This bursts them, like the strong man's bands,
   And lets my spirit loose again.

5 Then, dear to me the Sabbath morn,
   The village bells, the shepherd's voice:
   These oft have found my heart forlorn,
   And always bid that heart rejoice.
   Rev. John W. Cunningham. (1780-1861.)

"A day in Thy courts is better than a thousand."

358 "Not doing thine own ways." L. M.
Ps. xcii.   Nch. viii. 1-10.   Heb xiii. 12-21.

1 SWEET is the work, my God, my King,
To praise Thy name, give thanks, and sing;
To show Thy love by morning light,
And talk of all Thy truth at night.

2 Sweet is the day of sacred rest,
No mortal cares shall seize my breast;
O may my heart in tune be found,
Like David's harp of solemn sound.

3 My heart shall triumph in my Lord,
And bless His works and bless His word;
Thy works of grace, how bright they shine;
How deep Thy counsels, how divine!

4 Lord, I shall share a glorious part,
When grace hath well refined my heart,
And fresh supplies of joy are shed,
Like holy oil, to cheer my head.

5 Then shall I see, and hear, and know
All I desired or wished below;
And every power find sweet employ,
In that eternal world of joy.
Rev. Isaac Watts. (1674-1748.)

359 "The goodness of Thy house." L. M.
Ps. lxxxiv.   Isa. lvi. 5-7.   Heb. xii. 22-24.

1 How pleasant, how divinely fair,
O Lord of hosts, Thy dwellings are;
With long desire my spirit faints,
To meet th' assemblies of Thy saints.

2 My flesh would rest in Thine abode,
My panting heart cries out for God;
My God, my King, why should I be
So far from all my joys and Thee?

3 Blest are the saints who sit on high,
Around Thy throne of majesty;
Thy brightest glories shine above,
And all their work is praise and love.

4 Blest are the souls who find a place
Within the temple of Thy grace;
There they behold Thy gentler rays,
And seek Thy face, and learn Thy praise.

5 Blest are the men whose hearts are set
To find the way to Zion's gate;
God is their Strength, and, through the road,
They lean upon their Helper, God.

6 Cheerful they walk, with growing strength,
Till all shall meet in heaven at length;
Till all before Thy face appear,
And join in nobler worship there.
Rev. Isaac Watts.

360 "Blessed are they that dwell in Thy house." 7.
Ps. xcv. 2-7.   Isa. lx. 19, 20   Heb x. 19-25

1 PLEASANT are Thy courts above,
In the land of light and love;
Pleasant are Thy courts below,
In this land of sin and woe.
O my spirit longs and faints
For the converse of Thy saints,
For the brightness of Thy face,
For Thy fulness, God of grace!

2 Happy souls, their praises flow,
Even in this vale of woe;
Waters in the desert rise,
Manna feeds them from the skies.
On they go from strength to strength,
Till they reach Thy throne at length;
At Thy feet adoring fall,
Who hast led them safe through all.

3 Lord, be mine this prize to win,
Guide me through a world of sin;
Keep me by Thy saving grace,
Give me at Thy side a place.
Sun and Shield alike Thou art,
Guide and guard my erring heart;
Grace and glory flow from Thee,
Shower, O shower them, Lord, on me.
Rev. Henry F. Lyte. (1793-1847.)

361 "I was glad." 6, 8.
Ps. cxxii.   Isa. ii. 1-5.   Eph. ii. 11-22.

1 How pleased and blest was I
To hear the people cry,
"Come, let us seek our God to-day!"
Yes, with a cheerful zeal,
We haste to Zion's hill,
And there our vows and honors pay.

2 Zion, thrice happy place,
Adorned with wondrous grace,
And walls of strength embrace thee round:
In thee our tribes appear,
To pray, and praise, and hear
The sacred gospel's joyful sound.

3 May peace attend thy gate,
And joy within thee wait,
To bless the soul of every guest.
The man that seeks thy peace,
And wishes thine increase,
A thousand blessings on him rest!

4 My tongue repeats her vows,
"Peace to this sacred house!"
For there my friends and kindred dwell;
And since my glorious God
Makes thee His blest abode,
My soul shall ever love thee well.
Rev. Isaac Watts.

"A day in Thy courts is better than a thousand."

362 "The seventh day is the Sabbath." 8. 6.
Ps. lxxxiv. 2 Chr. xxix. 29-36. Heb. vi.

1 WELCOME, sweet day, of days the best,
The time of holy mirth and rest :
To God's own house repair,
To hear His word and see His face,
To learn His will and sing His grace,
To join in praise and prayer.

2 This is employment all divine ;
My soul, the blest assembly join,
And from the world retire :
Go, bow before thy Maker's throne,
Thy risen Saviour's glories own,
And fan devotion's fire.

3 Forget the trifles here below,
The shining heap, the gaudy show,
Vain mirth and worldly cares :
On wings of strong devotion rise,
Pass every cloud, pass all the skies,
And soar above the stars.

4 To God direct thy steady flight,
Great fund of bliss and source of light,
And there delight thine eyes :
View every shining wonder o'er,
With glad, transported heart adore,
And feast in Paradise.
Rev. Simon Browne. (1680-1732.)

363 "The Sabbath of rest." L. M.
Ps. cxvi. 7, 8. Isa. lviii. 13, 14. Heb. iv. 9, 10.

1 ANOTHER six days' work is done,
Another Sabbath is begun ;
Return, my soul, enjoy thy rest,
Improve the day thy God hath blessed.

2 Come, bless the Lord, whose love assigns
So sweet a rest to wearied minds ;
Provides an antepast of heaven,
And gives this day the food of seven.

3 O that our thoughts and thanks may rise,
As grateful incense, to the skies ;
And draw from heaven that sweet repose,
Which none but he that feels it knows.

4 This heavenly calm within the breast
Is the dear pledge of glorious rest,
Which for the church of God remains,
The end of cares, the end of pains.

5 In holy duties, let the day,
In holy pleasures, pass away ;
How sweet the Sabbath thus to spend,
In hope of one that ne'er shall end !
Rev. Joseph Stennett. (1663-1713.)

364 "Let us go up to Zion." C. M.
Ps. cxxii. Isa. lxii. Acts xiii. 44-49.

1 How did my heart rejoice to hear
My friends devoutly say,
"In Zion let us all appear,
And keep the solemn day ! "

2 I love her gates, I love the road ;
The church, adorned with grace,
Stands like a palace built for God,
To show His milder face.

3 My soul shall pray for Zion still,
While life or breath remains ;
There my best friends, my kindred, dwell,
There God, my Saviour, reigns.
Rev. Isaac Watts. (1674-1748.)

365 "A feast unto the Lord." C. M.
Gen. ii. 1-3. Mat. xxviii. Rev. i. 10-20.

1 BLEST day of God, most calm, most bright,
The first and best of days ;
The laborer's rest, the saint's delight,
A day of mirth and praise.

2 My Saviour's face did make thee shine,
His rising did thee raise ;
This made thee heavenly and divine
Beyond the common-days.

3 My Lord on thee His name did fix,
Which makes thee rich and gay ;
Amid His golden candlesticks
My Saviour walks this day.

4 This day must I 'fore God appear,
For, Lord, the day is Thine ;
O let me spend it in Thy fear,
Then shall the day be mine.
Rev. John Mason. (-1694.)

366 "I will direct my prayer unto Thee." C. M.
Ps. v. 1-3. Mark i. 35. Col. iv. 2.

1 LORD, in the morning Thou shalt hear
My voice ascending high ;
To Thee will I direct my prayer,
To Thee lift up mine eye :

2 Up to the hills where Christ is gone
To plead for all His saints ;
Presenting at His Father's throne
Our songs and our complaints.

3 Now to Thy house will I resort,
To taste Thy mercies there ;
I will frequent Thy holy court,
And worship in Thy fear.

4 O may Thy Spirit guide my feet
In ways of righteousness ;
Make every path of duty straight
And plain before my face.
Rev. Isaac Watts.

"A day in Thy courts is better than a thousand."

367 "How amiable are Thy tabernacles!" **C. M.**
Ps. xlviii. 1 Chr. xxix. 2 Tim. iv. 6-8.

1 O GOD of hosts, the mighty Lord,
How lovely is the place
Where Thou, enthroned in glory, show'st
The brightness of Thy face!

2 My longing soul faints with desire
To view Thy blest abode;
My panting heart and flesh cry out
For Thee, the living God.
Nahum Tate. (1652-1715.)

368 "Bring me unto Thy holy hill." **H. M.**
Ps. lxvi. 1 Kings viii. 22-30. Heb. xiii. 14-21.

1 Now to Thy sacred house
With joy I turn my feet,
Where saints, with morning vows,
In full assembly meet:
Thy power divine shall there be shown,
And from Thy throne Thy mercy shine.

2 O send Thy light abroad;
Thy truth, with heavenly ray,
Shall lead my soul to God,
And guide my doubtful way:
I'll hear Thy word with faith sincere,
And learn to fear and praise the Lord.

3 Here reach Thy bounteous hand,
And all my sorrows heal;
Here health and strength divine,
O make my bosom feel:
Like balmy dew shall Jesus' voice
My heart rejoice, my strength renew.

4 Now in Thy holy hill,
Before Thine altar, Lord,
My harp and song shall sound
The glories of Thy word:
Henceforth, to Thee, O God of grace,
A hymn of praise my life shall be.
Rev. Timothy Dwight. (1752-1817.)

369 "Out of Zion... God hath shined." **C. M.**
Ps. xcvi. 6-13. Isa. lvi. 5-7. Mat. xvii. 1-9.

1 My soul, how lovely is the place
To which Thy God resorts!
'T is heaven to see His smiling face,
Though in His earthly courts.

2 There the great Monarch of the skies
His saving power displays,
And light breaks in upon our eyes
With kind and quickening rays.

3 With His rich gifts the heavenly Dove
Descends and fills the place,
While Christ reveals His wondrous love,
And sheds abroad His grace.
Rev. Isaac Watts. (1674-1748.)

370 "My soul longeth... for the courts of the Lord." **H. M.**
Ps. xxvi. 6-8. Ex. xxv. 17-22. Rev. xiv. 1-5.

1 To spend one sacred day
Where God and saints abide
Affords diviner joy
Than thousand days beside;
Where God resorts, I love it more
To keep the door, than shine in courts.

2 The Lord His people loves;
His hand no good withholds
From those His heart approves,
From pure and pious souls.
Thrice happy he, O God of hosts,
Whose spirit trusts alone in Thee.
Rev. Isaac Watts.

371 "I will come into Thine house." **7.**
Ps xliii. 3, 4. 1 Kings viii 54-61. Heb. xii. 18-24.

1 To Thy temple I repair;
Lord, I love to worship there,
When within the veil I meet
Christ before the mercy-seat.

2 While Thy glorious praise is sung,
Touch my lips, unloose my tongue,
That my joyful soul may bless
Thee, the Lord, my Righteousness.

3 While the prayers of saints ascend,
God of love, to mine attend;
Hear me, for Thy Spirit pleads,
Hear, for Jesus intercedes.

4 While I hearken to Thy law
Fill my soul with humble awe,
Till Thy gospel bring to me
Life and immortality.
James Montgomery. (1771-1854.)

372 "Beautiful for situation." **S. M.**
Ps. lxxxiv. 2 Chr. vi. 1-21. Heb. viii.

1 How charming is the place
Where my Redeemer, God,
Unveils the beauties of His face,
And sheds His love abroad.

2 Not the fair palaces,
To which the great resort,
Are once to be compared with this,
Where Jesus holds His court.

3 Here, on the mercy-seat,
With radiant glory crowned,
Our joyful eyes behold Him sit,
And smile on all around.

4 Give me, O Lord, a place
Within Thy blest abode,
Among the children of Thy grace,
The servants of my God.
Rev. Samuel Stennett. (1727-1795.)

"Love to all the saints."

373 "Whither thou goest I will go." **7.**
Ruth i. 16, 17.   Mat. viii. 19-22.   Heb. xi. 24-26.

1 PEOPLE of the living God,
  I have sought the world around,
  Paths of sin and sorrow trod,
  Peace and comfort nowhere found.
  Now to you my spirit turns,
    Turns, a fugitive unblest ;
  Brethren, where your altar burns,
    O receive me into rest.

2 Lonely I no longer roam,
    Like the cloud, the wind, the wave ;
  Where you dwell shall be my home,
    Where you die shall be my grave.
  Mine the God whom you adore,
    Your Redeemer shall be mine ;
  Earth can fill my heart no more,
    Every idol I resign.
              James Montgomery.   (1771-1854.)

374 "Love the brotherhood." **L. M.**
Phil. i. 1-11.   Rom. xvi.   Ex. xxxii. 30-32.

1 Now, by the love of Christ, my God,
  His sharp distress, His sore complaints ;
  By His last groans, His dying blood,
  I charge my soul to love the saints.

2 Tender and kind be all our thoughts,
  Through all our lives let mercy run ;
  So God forgives our numerous faults,
  For the dear sake of Christ, his Son.
              Rev. Isaac Watts.   (1674-1748.)

375 "Above my chief joy." **S. M.**
Ps. cxxxvii.   Isa. lxii.   Acts xx. 28-35.

1 I LOVE Thy kingdom, Lord,
    The house of Thine abode,
  The church our blest Redeemer saved
    With His own precious blood.

2 I love Thy church, O God,
    Her walls before Thee stand,
  Dear as the apple of Thine eye,
    And graven on Thy hand.

3 For her my tears shall fall,
    For her my prayers ascend ;
  To her my cares and toils be given,
    Till toils and cares shall end.

4 Beyond my highest joy
    I prize her heavenly ways,
  Her sweet communion, solemn vows,
    Her hymns of love and praise.

5 Sure as Thy truth shall last,
    To Zion shall be given
  The brightest glories earth can yield,
    And brighter bliss of heaven.
              Rev. Timothy Dwight.   (1752-1817.)

376 "That we love the children of God." **C. M.**
Heb. xi. 13-16.   Num. xiv.   Josh. xiv. 6-14.

1 RISE, O my soul, pursue the path
    By ancient worthies trod ;
  Aspiring, view those holy men
    Who lived and walked with God.

2 Though dead, they speak in reason's ear,
    And in example live ;
  Their faith and hope and mighty deeds
    Still fresh instruction give.

3 'T was through the Lamb's most precious
      blood
  They conquered every foe ;
  And to His power and matchless grace
    Their crowns and honors owe.

4 Lord, may I ever keep in view
    The patterns Thou hast given ;
  And ne'er forsake the blessed path
    Which led them safe to heaven.
              Rev. John Needham.   1768.

377 "Blessed in His deed." **L. M.**
1 John ii. 1-10.   Gal. vi. 1-10.   Deu. xv. 1-18.

1 BLEST is the man whose spirit shares
  A suffering brother's wants and cares ;
  The Lord will visit him in grief,
  And bring his trials sweet relief.

2 The sinner's Friend delights to see
  His people kind and good as He ;
  And bids them each with each unite
  To make their common burden light.
              Rev. Henry F. Lyte.   (1793-1847.)

378 "Where thou diest will I die." **L. M.**
Ps. lxxxiv.   Dan. ix. 3-19.   John xvii.

1 JESUS, from whom all blessings flow,
  Great Builder of Thy church below,
  If now Thy Spirit move my breast,
  Hear, and fulfil Thine own request.

2 The few that truly call Thee Lord,
  And wait Thy sanctifying word,
  And Thee their utmost Saviour own,
  Unite and perfect them in one.

3 From every sinful wrinkle free,
  Redeemed from all iniquity,
  The fellowship of saints make known,
  And O, my God, may I be one !

4 This only thing do I require,
  Thou know'st 't is all my heart's desire :
  Freely what I receive to give,
  The servant of Thy church to live.

5 Confirm the prayer, the seed impart,
  And speak the answer to my heart :
  The word hath passed Thy lips, and I
  Shall with Thy people live and die.
              Rev. Charles Wesley.   (1708-1788.)

"Love toward all men."

379 " Blessed are the merciful." C. M.
Ps. xli. 1-3. Job xxix. Mat. v. 7-9.

1 BLEST is the man whose softening heart
  Feels all another's pain,
  To whom the supplicating eye
  Was never raised in vain;

2 Whose breast expands with generous warmth,
  A stranger's woes to feel,
  And bleeds in pity o'er the wound
  He wants the power to heal.

3 He spreads His kind supporting arms
  To every child of grief;
  His secret bounty largely flows,
  And brings unasked relief.

4 To gentle offices of love
  His feet are never slow;
  He views, through mercy's melting eye,
  A brother in a foe.

5 Peace from the bosom of his God
  The Lord to him will give;
  And when he kneels before the throne
  His trembling soul shall live.
  Mrs. Anna L. Barbauld. (1743-1825.)

380 " They shall obtain mercy." C. M.
Ps. cxxvi. 6. Luke xxi. 1-3. Mat. xix. 27-30.

1 THE seeds which piety and love
  Have scattered here below
  In the fair fertile fields above
  To ample harvests grow.

2 The mite my willing hands can give
  At Jesus' feet I lay;
  Grace shall the humble gift receive,
  And heaven at large repay.
  Rev. Philip Doddridge. (1702-1751.)

381 " A good man showeth favor." C. M.
Ex. xxiii. Job xxxi. 13-22. 2 Cor. ix. 6-15.

1 HAPPY is he that fears the Lord,
  And follows His commands;
  Who lends the poor without reward,
  Or gives with liberal hands.

2 As pity dwells within his breast
  To all the sons of need,
  So God shall answer his request
  With blessings on his seed.

3 No evil tidings shall surprise
  His well-established mind;
  His soul to God, his Refuge flies,
  And leaves his fears behind.

4 In times of general distress,
  Some beams of light shall shine,
  To show the world his righteousness,
  And give him peace divine.
  Rev. Isaac Watts. (1674-1748.)

382 " Do good unto all men." L. M.
John xv. 12-17. 1 John iv. Deu. xv. 1-18.

1 O WHAT stupendous mercy shines
  Around the Majesty of heaven!
  Rebels He deigns to call His sons,
  Their souls renewed, their sins forgiven.

2 Go imitate the grace divine,
  The grace that blazes like a sun;
  Hold forth your fair though feeble light,
  Through all your lives let mercy run.

3 Upon your bounty's willing wings
  Swift fly your gifts and charity;
  The hungry feed, the naked clothe,
  To pain and sickness health apply.

4 Pity the weeping widow's woe,
  And be her counsellor and stay;
  Adopt the fatherless, and smooth
  To useful, happy life his way.

5 When all is done, renounce your deeds,
  Renounce self-righteousness with scorn;
  Thus will you glorify your God,
  And thus the Christian name adorn.
  Rev. Thomas Gibbons. (1720-1785.)

383 " Unto the upright there ariseth light." L. M.
Ps. cxii. Deu. xxiv. 10-22. James i. 21-27.

1 THRICE happy man, who fears the Lord,
  Loves His commands, and trusts His word!
  Honor and peace his days attend,
  And blessings to his seed descend.

2 Compassion dwells upon his mind,
  To works of mercy still inclined;
  He lends the poor some present aid,
  Or gives them, not to be repaid.

3 His soul, well fixed upon the Lord,
  Draws heavenly courage from His word;
  Amid the darkness light shall rise,
  To cheer his heart and bless his eyes.
  Rev. Isaac Watts.

384 " The children of the Highest." L. M.
Mat. x. 40-42. Heb. vi. 10. 1 Sam. xv. 22.

1 ONE cup of healing oil and wine,
  One offering laid on mercy's shrine,
  Is thrice more grateful, Lord, to Thee,
  Than lifted eye or bended knee.

2 In true and inward faith we trace
  The source of every outward grace;
  Within the pious heart it plays,
  A living fount of joy and praise.

3 Kind deeds of peace and love betray
  Where'er the stream has found its way;
  But where these spring not rich and fair,
  The stream has never wandered there.
  Rev. William H. Drummond. (1772-1850.)

"Faith is ... the evidence of things not seen."

385 "All things are possible to him that believeth." **L. M.**
Rom. x. 4-17. John iii. 5-18. Job xiii. 14-16.

1 FAITH is a living power from heaven
Which grasps the promise God has given;
A trust that cannot be o'erthrown,
Securely fixed on Christ alone.

2 Faith finds in Christ whate'er we need
To save and strengthen, guide and feed;
Strong in His grace, it joys to share
His cross, in hope His crown to wear.

3 Faith to the conscience whispers peace,
And bids the mourner's sighing cease;
By faith the children's right we claim,
And call upon our Father's name.

4 Faith feels the Spirit's kindling breath
In love and hope that conquer death;
Faith brings us to delight in God,
And blesses e'en His smiting rod.
Author unknown.

386 "The author and finisher of our faith." **L. M.**
Heb. xi. 1-10. Mat. ix. 18-31. 2 Kings vi. 15-17.

1 AUTHOR of faith, eternal Word,
Whose Spirit breathes the active flame;
Faith, like its finisher and Lord,
To-day, as yesterday, the same,

2 By faith we know Thee strong to save;
Save us, a present Saviour Thou;
Whate'er we hope by faith we have,
Future and past subsisting now.

3 The things unknown to feeble sense,
Unseen by reason's glimmering ray,
With strong commanding evidence
Their heavenly origin display.

4 Faith lends its realizing light,
The clouds disperse, the shadows fly;
Th' Invisible appears in sight,
And God is seen by mortal eye.
Rev. Charles Wesley. (1708-1788.)

387 "Joy and peace in believing." **L. M.**
Gal. ii. 16-21. Mat. vi. 24-34. Jer. xvii. 7, 8.

1 By faith in Christ I walk with God,
With heaven, my journey's end, in view;
Supported by His staff and rod,
My road is safe and pleasant too.

2 Though snares and dangers throng my path,
And earth and hell my course withstand,
I triumph over all by faith,
Guarded by His almighty hand.

3 With Him sweet converse I maintain;
Great as He is, I dare be free
To tell Him all my grief and pain,
And He reveals His love to me.
Rev. John Newton. (1725-1807.)

388 "By grace ... through faith." **C. M.**
Eph. ii. 4-22. 1 Cor. xv. 1-14. Micah vii. 18-20.

1 O GIFT of gifts, O grace of faith!
My God, how can it be
That Thou, who hast discerning love,
Shouldst give that gift to me?

2 Ah, grace, into unlikeliest hearts
It is thy boast to come;
The glory of thy light to find
In darkest spots a home.

3 The crowd of cares, the weightiest cross,
Seem trifles less than light;
Earth looks so little and so low
When faith shines full and bright.

4 O happy, happy that I am!
If thou canst be, O faith,
The treasure that thou art in life,
What wilt thou be in death?
Rev. Frederick W. Faber. (1814-1863.)

389 "Furtherance and joy of faith." **C. M.**
Gen. xv. 1-6. Dan. iii. 8-18. Rom. iv.

1 FATHER of Jesus Christ, my Lord,
My Saviour, and my Head,
I trust in Thee, whose powerful word
Hath raised Him from the dead.

2 Faith, mighty faith, the promise sees,
And looks to that alone;
Laughs at impossibilities,
And cries, "It shall be done!"

3 Obedient faith, that waits on Thee,
Thou never wilt reprove;
But Thou wilt form Thy Son in me,
And perfect me in love.
Rev. Charles Wesley.

390 "We which have believed do enter into rest." **C. M.**
1 Pet. i. 2 Cor. iv. 13 to v. 8. Ex. xii 21-27.

1 FAITH adds new charms to earthly bliss,
And saves me from its snares;
Its aid in every duty brings,
And softens all my cares.

2 The wounded conscience knows its power
The healing balm to give;
That balm the saddest heart can cheer,
And make the dying live.

3 Wide it unveils celestial worlds,
Where deathless pleasures reign,
And bids me seek my portion there,
Nor bids me seek in vain;

4 Shows me the precious promise, sealed
With the Redeemer's blood,
And helps my feeble hope to rest
Upon a faithful God.
Rev. Daniel Turner. (1710-1798.)

"And now abideth faith, hope, charity."

391 1 Cor. xiii. 1 John iii. 11-24. Lev. xix. 9-18. "These three." **L. M.**

1 FAITH, hope, and charity, these three,
 Yet is the greatest charity:
 Father of lights, these gifts impart
 To mine and every human heart.

2 Faith, that in prayer can never fail;
 Hope, that o'er doubting must prevail;
 And charity, whose name above
 Is God's own name, for "God is love."

3 The morning star is lost in light,
 Faith vanishes at perfect sight;
 The rainbow passes with the storm,
 And hope with sorrow's fading form;

4 But charity, serene, sublime,
 Beyond the range of death and time,
 Like the blue sky's all-'bounding space,
 Holds heaven and earth in its embrace.
 James Montgomery. (1771-1854.)

392 Mat. v. 3-12, 43-48. Gal. v. 13-23. Ps. cxxviii. "The greatest of these is charity." **C. M.**

1 HAPPY the heart where graces reign,
 Where love inspires the breast;
 Love is the brightest of the train,
 And strengthens all the rest.

2 Knowledge, alas! 't is all in vain,
 And all in vain our fear;
 Our stubborn sins will fight and reign,
 If love be absent there.

3 This is the grace that lives and sings,
 When faith and hope shall cease;
 'T is this shall strike our joyful strings
 In the sweet realms of bliss.
 Rev. Isaac Watts. (1674-1748.)

393 1 John iv. 7-21. Mat. xix. 16-24. Isa. l. 11-17. "And have not charity, I am nothing." **L. M.**

1 HAD I the tongues of Greeks and Jews,
 And nobler speech than angels use,
 If love be absent, I am found,
 Like tinkling brass, an empty sound.

2 Were I inspired to preach and tell
 All that is done in heaven and hell,
 Or could my faith the world remove,
 Still I am nothing without love.

3 Should I distribute all my store
 To feed the bowels of the poor,
 Or give my body to the flame
 To gain a martyr's glorious name;

4 If love to God and love to men
 Be absent, all my hopes are vain;
 Nor tongues, nor gifts, nor fiery zeal,
 The work of love can e'er fulfil.
 Rev. Isaac Watts.

394 Mark xii. 28-33. John xv. Ex. xxxii 30-32. "Every one that loveth is born of God." **8. 7.**

1 MEEK and lowly, pure and holy,
 Chief among the blessèd three,
 Turning sadness into gladness,
 Heaven-born art thou, Charity!
 Pity dwelleth in thy bosom,
 Kindness reigneth o'er thy heart;
 Gentle thoughts alone can sway thee,
 Judgment hath in thee no part.

2 Hoping ever, failing never,
 Though deceived, believing still;
 Long abiding, all confiding
 To the heavenly Father's will.
 Never weary of well-doing,
 Never fearful of the end;
 Claiming all mankind as brothers,
 Thou dost all alike befriend.
 Author unknown.

395 Isa. lvii. 15-19. Ps. cxxxviii. Luke xviii. 9-17. "With him also of ... humble spirit." **C. M.**

1 THY home is with the humble, Lord,
 The simple are the blest;
 Thy lodging is in child-like hearts,
 Thou makest there Thy rest.

2 Dear Comforter, eternal Love,
 If Thou wilt stay with me
 Of lowly thoughts and simple ways,
 I'll build a house for Thee.

3 Who made this breathing heart of mine
 But Thou, my heavenly Guest?
 Let no one have it, then, but Thee,
 And let it be Thy rest.
 Rev. Frederick W. Faber. (1814-1863.)

396 Mat. viii. 19, 20. 1 Cor. ii. 9-16. Ps. lxii. "I will wait on Thy name." **7.**

LORD, forever at Thy side
 May my place and portion be;
 Strip me of the robe of pride,
 Clothe me with humility.
 Meekly may my soul receive
 All Thy Spirit hath revealed;
 Thou hast spoken, I believe,
 Though the prophecy were sealed.
 James Montgomery.

397 Ps. xv. 1 John iii. 1-3. 2 Cor. vi. 17, 18. "He that hath clean hands and a pure heart." **S. M.**

1 BLEST are the pure in heart,
 For they shall see our God;
 The secret of the Lord is theirs,
 Their soul is Christ's abode.

2 Still to the lowly soul
 He doth Himself impart;
 And for His cradle and His throne
 Chooseth the pure in heart.
 Rev. John Keble. (1792-1867.)

"Praying always with all prayer."

398 "Ask, and it shall be given you." **L. M.**
Mat. vii. 7-11. James v. 14-20. Jer. xxix. 11-14.

1 PRAYER is appointed to convey
  The blessings God designs to give :
  Long as they live should Christians pray ;
  They learn to pray when first they live.

2 If pain afflict, or wrongs oppress ;
  If cares distract, or fears dismay ;
  If guilt deject, if sin distress,
  In every case, still watch and pray.

3 'T is prayer supports the soul that 's weak :
  Though thought be broken, language lame,
  Pray, if thou canst or canst not speak,
  But pray with faith in Jesus' name.

4 Depend on Him, thou canst not fail ;
  Make all thy wants and wishes known.
  Fear not, His merits must prevail ;
  Ask but in faith, it shall be done.
    Rev. Joseph Hart. (1712-1768.)

399 "He heareth us." **C. M.**
Ps. cxxxix. 1-9. Dan. iv. 34-37. 1 John v. 14.

1 THERE is an eye that never sleeps,
  Beneath the wing of night ;
  There is an ear that never shuts,
  When sink the beams of light.

2 There is an arm that never tires,
  When human strength gives way ;
  There is a love that never fails,
  When earthly loves decay.

3 That eye is fixed on seraph throngs,
  That arm upholds the sky ;
  That ear is filled with angel songs,
  That love is throned on high.

4 But there 's a power which man can wield,
  When mortal aid is vain,
  That eye, that arm, that love, to reach,
  That listening ear to gain.

5 That power is prayer, which soars on high,
  Through Jesus, to the throne,
  And moves the hand which moves the world,
  To bring salvation down.
    Rev. John A. Wallace. (1802-1870.)

400 "Continuing instant in prayer." **L. M.**
Luke xviii. 39. 2 Kings xix. 15-37. Gen. xxviii.

1 WHAT various hindrances we meet,
  In coming to a mercy-seat ;
  Yet who that knows the worth of prayer
  But wishes to be often there ?

2 Prayer makes the darkened cloud withdraw,
  Prayer climbs the ladder Jacob saw ;
  Gives exercise to faith and love,
  Brings every blessing from above.
    William Cowper. (1731-1800.)

401 "Behold, he prayeth." **C. M.**
Heb. x. 19-22. Luke xviii. 10-14. 2 Chr. vii.

1 PRAYER is the soul's sincere desire,
  Uttered or unexpressed ;
  The motion of a hidden fire
  That trembles in the breast.

2 Prayer is the burden of a sigh,
  The falling of a tear,
  The upward glancing of an eye,
  When none but God is near.

3 Prayer is the simplest form of speech
  That infant lips can try ;
  Prayer the sublimest strains that reach
  The Majesty on high.

4 Prayer is the contrite sinner's voice
  Returning from his ways,
  While angels in their songs rejoice,
  And cry, "Behold, he prays ! "

5 Prayer is the Christian's vital breath,
  The Christian's native air,
  His watchword at the gates of death ;
  He enters heaven with prayer.

6 O Thou, by whom we come to God,
  The Life, the Truth, the Way,
  The path of prayer Thyself hast trod ;
  Lord, teach us how to pray.
    James Montgomery. (1771-1854.)

402 "The Spirit . . . maketh intercession." **C. M.**
Rom. viii. 14-26. Zech. xii. 10. Luke vii. 36-50.

1 PRAYER is the breath of God in man,
  Returning whence it came ;
  Love is the sacred fire within,
  And prayer the rising flame.

2 It gives the burdened spirit ease,
  And soothes the troubled breast ;
  Yields comfort to the mourners here,
  And to the weary rest.

3 When God inclines the heart to pray,
  He hath an ear to hear ;
  To Him there 's music in a groan,
  And beauty in a tear.

4 The humble suppliant cannot fail
  To have his wants supplied,
  Since He for sinners intercedes,
  Who once for sinners died.
    Rev. Benjamin Beddome. (1717-1795.)

"Praying always with all prayer."

403   "Ask what I shall give thee."   S. M.
Heb. iv. 14-16. Mat. vii. 7-11. 1 Kings iii. 4-14.

1 BEHOLD the throne of grace !
    The promise calls me near ;
    There Jesus shows a smiling face,
    And waits to answer prayer.

2 That rich atoning blood,
    Which sprinkled round I see,
    Provides for those who come to God,
    An all-prevailing plea.

3 My soul, ask what thou wilt ;
    Thou canst not be too bold ;
    Since His own blood for thee He spilt,
    What else can He withhold ?

4 Thine image, Lord, bestow,
    Thy presence and Thy love ;
    I ask to serve Thee here below,
    And reign with Thee above.

5 Teach me to live by faith ;
    Conform my will to Thine ;
    Let me victorious be in death,
    And then in glory shine.
                 Rev. John Newton. (1725-1807.)

404   "Unto Thee will I pray."   L. M.
Ps. civ. 33, 34. Isa. xl. 31. Acts xvi. 13-15.

1 MY God, is any hour so sweet,
    From blush of morn to evening star,
    As that which calls me to Thy feet,
    The hour of prayer ?

2 Blest is that tranquil hour of morn,
    And blest that solemn hour of eve,
    When, on the wings of prayer upborne,
    The world I leave.

3 Then is my strength by Thee renewed ;
    Then are my sins by Thee forgiven ;
    Then dost Thou cheer my solitude
    With hopes of heaven.

4 No words can tell what sweet relief
    Here for my every want I find ;
    What strength for warfare, balm for grief,
    What peace of mind.

5 Hushed is each doubt, gone every fear ;
    My spirit seems in heaven to stay ;
    And e'en the penitential tear
    Is wiped away.

6 Lord, till I reach that blissful shore,
    No privilege so dear shall be
    As thus my inmost soul to pour
    In prayer to Thee.
                 Miss Charlotte Elliott. (1789-1871.)

405   "I will bless the Lord at all times."   L. M.
Ps. c. John xx. 19-31. Mat xvii. 1-9

1 BLEST hour, when mortal man retires
    To hold communion with his God ;
    To send to heaven his warm desires,
    And listen to the sacred word.

2 Blest hour, when God Himself draws nigh,
    Well pleased His people's voice to hear ;
    To hush the penitential sigh,
    And wipe away the mourner's tear.

3 Blest hour, for where the Lord resorts
    Foretastes of future bliss are given ;
    And mortals find His earthly courts
    The house of God, the gate of heaven.

4 Hail, peaceful hour, supremely blest
    Amid the hours of worldly care ;
    The hour that yields the spirit rest,
    That sacred hour, the hour of prayer.

5 And when my hours of prayer are past,
    And this frail tenement decays,
    Then may I spend in heaven at last
    A never-ending hour of praise.
                 Rev. Thomas Raffles. (1788-1863.)

406   "Under His shadow with great delight."   L. M.
Mat. vi. 6-13. Ps. cxxxiv. Deu. xxxiv. 1-7.

1 SWEET hour of prayer, sweet hour of prayer,
    That calls me from a world of care,
    And bids me, at my Father's throne,
    Make all my wants and wishes known :
    In seasons of distress and grief,
    My soul has often found relief,
    And oft escaped the tempter's snare,
    By thy return, sweet hour of prayer.

2 Sweet hour of prayer, sweet hour of prayer,
    Thy wings shall my petition bear
    To Him, whose truth and faithfulness
    Engage the waiting soul to bless :
    And since He bids me seek His face,
    Believe His word, and trust His grace,
    I 'll cast on Him my every care,
    And wait for thee, sweet hour of prayer.

3 Sweet hour of prayer, sweet hour of prayer,
    May I thy consolation share,
    Till, from Mount Pisgah's lofty height,
    I view my home, and take my flight.
    This robe of flesh I 'll drop, and rise
    To seize the everlasting prize ;
    And shout, while passing through the air,
    Farewell, farewell, sweet hour of prayer !
                 Rev. William W. Walford. 1846.

"Watching thereunto with all perseverance."

407 "Take ye heed, watch and pray." C. M.
Mat. xxvi. 36-41. 2 Pet. iii. Eze. xxxiii. 1-9.

1 THE Saviour bids thee watch and pray
Through life's momentous hour;
And grants the Spirit's quickening ray
To those who seek His power.

2 The Saviour bids thee watch and pray,
Maintain a warrior's strife:
O Christian, hear His voice to-day;
Obedience is thy life.

3 The Saviour bids thee watch and pray:
For soon the hour will come
That calls thee from the earth away
To thy eternal home.

4 The Saviour bids thee watch and pray:
O hearken to His voice,
And follow where He leads the way,
To heaven's eternal joys!
Thomas Hastings. (1790-1872.)

408 "Not as though I had already attained." 7. 5.
Eph. vi. 2 Tim. iii. 14 to iv. 5. Eze. iii. 16-21.

1 CHRISTIAN, seek not yet repose,
Cast thy dreams of ease away;
Thou art in the midst of foes,
Therefore watch and pray.

2 Gird thy heavenly armor on,
Wear it ever, night and day;
Near thee lurks the evil one,
Therefore watch and pray.

3 Listen to thy sorrowing Lord,
Him thou lovest to obey;
It is He who speaks the word,
Therefore watch and pray.

4 Watch, for thou thy guard must keep;
Pray, for God must speed thy way;
Narrow is the road, and steep,
Therefore watch and pray.
Rev. William W. How. (1823-.)

409 "Preserve me, O God." C. M.
Ps. liv. Mat. vi. 9-13. Rom. vii. 7-25.

1 ALAS, what hourly dangers rise!
What snares beset my way!
To heaven O let me lift mine eyes,
And hourly watch and pray.

2 O gracious God, in whom I live,
My feeble efforts aid;
Help me to watch, and pray, and strive,
Though trembling and afraid.

3 O keep me in Thy heavenly way,
And bid the tempter flee;
And let me never, never stray
From happiness and Thee.
Miss Anne Steele. (1717-1778.)

410 "Watch, therefore." S. M.
Mat. xxv. 1-13. Rev. iii. 1-6. Num. iii.

1 YE servants of the Lord,
Each in His office wait,
Observant of His heavenly word,
And watchful at His gate.

2 Let all your lamps be bright,
And trim the golden flame;
Gird up your loins as in His sight,
For awful is His name.

3 Watch! 'tis your Lord's command;
And while we speak He's near:
Mark the first signal of His hand,
And ready all appear.

4 O happy servant he,
In such a posture found!
He shall his Lord with rapture see,
And be with honor crowned.
Rev. Philip Doddridge. (1702-1751.)

411 "Awake, thou that sleepest!" L. M.
Eph. v. 14-16. 1 Thes. v. 1-11. Neh. iv.

1 AWAKE, my soul, lift up thine eyes;
See where thy foes against thee rise,
In long array, a numerous host:
Awake, my soul, or thou art lost.

2 Thou tread'st upon enchanted ground,
Perils and snares beset thee round;
Beware of all, guard every part,
But most the traitor in thy heart.

3 Come, then, my soul, now learn to wield
The weight of thine immortal shield;
Put on the armor from above
Of heavenly truth and heavenly love.

4 The terror and the charm repel,
The powers of earth and powers of hell;
The Man of Calvary triumphed here;
Why should His faithful followers fear?
Mrs. Anna L. Barbauld. (1743-1825.)

412 "Let us watch and be sober." S. M.
1 Cor. ix. 23-27. 1 Tim. vi. 11-21. Prov. xiii.

1 MY soul, be on thy guard,
Ten thousand foes arise;
And hosts of sins are pressing hard,
To draw thee from the skies.

2 O watch, and fight, and pray;
The battle ne'er give o'er;
Renew it boldly every day,
And help divine implore.

3 Ne'er think the victory won,
Nor lay thine armor down:
Thine arduous work will not be done,
Till thou obtain the crown.
George Heath. (1781-.)

"That thou ... war a good warfare."

413 "These are they which follow the Lamb." C. M.
Isa. lxiii. 1-6. Mark viii. 34-38. Heb. xi. 33-40.

1 THE Son of God goes forth to war,
  A kingly crown to gain ;
His blood-red banner streams afar :
  Who follows in His train ?
Who best can drink His cup of woe,
  Triumphant over pain,
Who patient bears His cross below,
  He follows in His train.

2 The martyr first, whose eagle eye
  Could pierce beyond the grave,
Who saw his Master in the sky,
  And called on Him to save :
A glorious band, the chosen few
  On whom the Spirit came ;
Twelve valiant saints, their hope they knew,
  And mocked the cross and flame.

3 A noble army, men and boys,
  The matron and the maid,
Around the throne of God rejoice,
  In robes of light arrayed :
They climbed the steep ascent of heaven
  Through peril, toil, and pain :
O God, to us may grace be given
  To follow in their train.

Bp. Reginald Heber. (1783–1826.)

414 "Go forward." 7. 6.
Ex. xiv. 15-31. Josh. i. 1-9. Acts ix. 1-18.

1 Go forward, Christian soldier,
  Beneath His banner true ;
The Lord Himself, thy Leader,
  Shall all thy foes subdue.
His love foretells thy trials,
  He knows thine hourly need ;
He can with bread of heaven
  Thy fainting spirit feed.

2 Go forward, Christian soldier,
  Fear not the secret foe ;
Far more are o'er thee watching
  Than human eyes can know.
Trust only Christ, thy Captain,
  Cease not to watch and pray ;
Heed not the treacherous voices
  That lure thy soul astray.

3 Go forward, Christian soldier,
  Fear not the gathering night ;
The Lord has been thy shelter,
  The Lord will be thy Light.
When morn His face revealeth,
  Thy dangers all are past ;
O pray that faith and virtue
  May keep thee to the last.

Rev. Laurence Tuttiett. (1825–.)

415 "The good fight of faith." C. M.
Rom. i. 1-16. 2 Tim. ii. 1-14. 2 Sam. x. 7-14.

1 AM I a soldier of the cross,
  A follower of the Lamb,
And shall I fear to own His cause,
  Or blush to speak His name ?

2 Must I be carried to the skies
  On flowery beds of ease,
While others fought to win the prize,
  And sailed through bloody seas ?

3 Are there no foes for me to face ?
  Must I not stem the flood ?
Is this vile world a friend to grace,
  To help me on to God ?

4 Sure, I must fight, if I would reign ;
  Increase my courage, Lord !
I'll bear the toil, endure the pain,
  Supported by Thy word.

Rev. Isaac Watts. (1674–1748.)

416 "Be strong in the Lord." L. M.
Ps. cxliv. Eze. ii. 1-7. 2 Tim. iv. 1-8.

1 STAND up, my soul ! shake off thy fears,
  And gird the gospel armor on ;
March to the gates of endless joy,
  Where thy great Captain-Saviour's gone.

2 Hell and thy sins resist thy course,
  But hell and sin are vanquished foes ;
Thy Jesus nailed them to the cross,
  And sung the triumph when He rose.

3 Then let my soul march boldly on,
  Press forward to the heavenly gate ;
There peace and joy eternal reign,
  And glittering robes for conquerors wait.

4 There shall I wear a starry crown,
  And triumph in almighty grace,
While all the armies of the skies
  Join in my glorious Leader's praise.

Rev. Isaac Watts.

417 "And having done all, to stand." L. M.
Eph. vi. 1 Tim. vi. 11-18. 1 Sam. xvii. 38-47.

1 THE Christian warrior, see him stand
  In the whole armor of his God ;
The Spirit's sword is in his hand,
  His feet are with the gospel shod.

2 In panoply of truth complete,
  Salvation's helmet on his head,
With righteousness, a breastplate meet,
  And faith's broad shield before him spread.

3 Thus strong in his Redeemer's strength,
  Sin, death, and hell he tramples down ;
Fights the good fight ; and wins at length,
  Through mercy, an immortal crown.

James Montgomery. (1771–1854.)

"I must work the works of Him that sent me."

418 "Laborers together with God." L. M.
John iv. 34-38. Heb. x. 7-25. Ecc. iii. 1-15.

1 Go, labor on; spend and be spent,
   Thy joy to do the Father's will :
   It is the way the Master went ;
   Should not the servant tread it still ?

2 Go, labor on ; 't is not for naught ;
   Thine earthly loss is heavenly gain :
   Men heed thee, love thee, praise thee, not ;
   The Master praises ; what are men ?

3 Go, labor on ; enough, while here,
   If He shall praise thee, if He deign
   Thy willing heart to mark and cheer :
   No toil for Him shall be in vain.

4 Toil on, and in thy toil rejoice :
   For toil comes rest, for exile home ;
   Soon shalt thou hear the Bridegroom's voice,
   The midnight peal : " Behold, I come ! "
   Rev. Horatius Bonar. (1808-.)

419 "Go work to-day in my vineyard." 8, 7.
Isa. vi. Mat. xxii. 1-10. Luke x. 1-20.

1 HARK, the voice of Jesus calling,
   Who will go and work to-day ?
   Fields are white, and harvests waiting,
   Who will bear the sheaves away ?
   Loud and long the Master calleth,
   Rich reward He offers free ;
   Who will answer, gladly saying,
   " Here am I, send me, send me ! "

2 Let none hear you idly saying,
   " There is nothing I can do,"
   While the souls of men are dying,
   And the Master calls for you.
   Take the task He gives you gladly,
   Let His work your pleasure be ;
   Answer quickly, when He calleth,
   " Here am I, send me, send me ! "
   Rev. Daniel March. (1816-.)

420 "Not slothful in business." L. M.
Luke xiv. 16-23. Mat. v. 13-20. Ecc. ix. 7-10.

1 Go, labor on, while it is day ;
   The world's dark night is hastening on ;
   Speed, speed thy work, cast sloth away !
   It is not thus that souls are won.

2 Men die in darkness at your side,
   Without a hope to cheer the tomb ;
   Take up the torch, and wave it wide,
   The torch that lights time's thickest gloom.

3 Toil on, faint not ; keep watch, and pray ;
   Be wise the erring soul to win ;
   Go forth into the world's highway,
   Compel the wanderer to come in.
   Rev. Horatius Bonar.

421 "When no man can work" 7, 6.
Ecc. xi. 6 to xii. 7. John v. 17-36. Mat. x. 1-23.

1 WORK, for the night is coming,
   Work through the morning hours ;
   Work while the dew is sparkling,
   Work 'mid springing flowers.
   Work when the day grows brighter,
   Work in the glowing sun ;
   Work, for the night is coming,
   When man's work is done.

2 Work, for the night is coming,
   Work through the sunny noon ;
   Fill brightest hours with labor,
   Rest comes sure and soon.
   Give every flying minute
   Something to keep in store ;
   Work, for the night is coming,
   When man works no more.

3 Work, for the night is coming,
   Under the sunset skies ;
   While their bright tints are glowing,
   Work, for the daylight flies.
   Work till the last beam fadeth,
   Fadeth to shine no more ;
   Work while the night is darkening,
   When man's work is o'er.
   Rev. Sidney Dyer. (1814-.)

422 "That sow beside all waters." S. M.
Ecc. xi. 1-6. Ps. cxxvi. Heb. vi. 9-20.

1 Sow in the morn thy seed,
   At eve hold not thy hand ;
   To doubt and fear give thou no heed,
   Broadcast it o'er the land.

2 Beside all waters sow,
   The highway furrows stock ;
   Drop it where thorns and thistles grow,
   Scatter it on the rock.

3 The good, the fruitful ground
   Expect not here nor there ;
   O'er hill and dale alike 't is found ;
   Go forth, then, everywhere.

4 And duly shall appear,
   In verdure, beauty, strength,
   The tender blade, the stalk, the ear,
   And the full corn at length.

5 Thou canst not toil in vain ;
   Cold, heat, the moist and dry,
   Shall foster and mature the grain
   For garners in the sky.
   James Montgomery. (1771-1854.)

"I must work the works of Him that sent me."

423 "In the morning sow thy seed." S. M.
James iv. 13-17.   1 John ii.   Job vii. 1-10.

1 MAKE haste, O man, to live,
   For thou so soon must die;
   Time hurries past thee like the breeze;
   How swift its moments fly!

2 Make haste, O man, to do
   Whatever must be done;
   Thou hast no time to lose in sloth,
   Thy day will soon be gone.

3 Up, then, with speed, and work;
   Fling ease and self away;
   This is no time for thee to sleep,
   Up, watch, and work and pray.

4 Make haste, O man, to live,
   Thy time is almost o'er;
   O sleep not, dream not, but arise,
   The Judge is at the door.
   Rev. Horatius Bonar. (1808-.)

424 "With what measure ye mete." C. M.
2 Cor. ix. 6-15.   Prov. xi. 23-31.   Deu. xv. 7-10.

1 MAKE channels for the streams of love,
   Where they may broadly run;
   And love has overflowing streams,
   To fill them every one.

2 But if at any time we cease
   Such channels to provide,
   The very founts of love for us
   Will soon be parched and dried.

3 For we must share, if we would keep
   That blessing from above;
   Ceasing to give, we cease to have:
   Such is the law of love.
   Bp. Richard C. Trench. (1807-.)

425 "A cup of cold water only." C. M.
Mat. x. 40-42.   Mark xii. 41-44.   Lev. xiv. 9, 10.

1 SCORN not the slightest word or deed,
   Nor deem it void of power;
   There's fruit in each wind-wafted seed
   That waits its natal hour.

2 A whispered word may touch the heart,
   And call it back to life;
   A look of love bid sin depart,
   And still unholy strife.

3 No act falls fruitless; none can tell
   How vast its power may be,
   Nor what results infolded dwell
   Within it, silently.

4 Work on, despair not; bring thy mite,
   Nor care how small it be;
   God is with all that serve the right,
   The holy, true, and free.
   Author unknown.

426 "So laboring, ye ought to support the weak." S. M.
1 Thes. v. 14-28.   Acts xx.   Lev. xxv. 25-42.

1 LABORER of Christ, arise,
   And gird you for the toil;
   The dew of promise from the skies
   Already cheers the soil.

2 Go where the sick recline,
   Where mourning hearts deplore;
   And where the sons of sorrow pine
   Dispense your hallowed store.

3 Be faith which looks above,
   With prayer, your constant guest;
   And wrap the Saviour's changeless love
   A mantle round your breast.

4 So shall you share the wealth
   That earth may ne'er despoil,
   And the blest gospel's saving health
   Repay your arduous toil.
   Mrs. Lydia H. H. Sigourney. (1791-1865.)

427 "Well done, good and faithful." S. M.
Ps. i.   Luke x. 17-24.   James v. 7-11.

1 HAPPY the man who knows
   His Master to obey;
   Whose life of care and labor flows
   Where God points out the way.

2 He riseth to his task
   Soon as the word is given;
   Nor waits, nor doth a question ask,
   When orders come from heaven.

3 Nothing he calls his own,
   Nothing he hath to say;
   His feet are shod for God alone,
   And God alone obey.
   Rev. Thomas C. Upham. (1799-1872.)

428 "He shall ... come again with rejoicing." 8. 7.
Ps. cxxvi.   Ecc. xi. 1-6.   Mat. xiii. 1-8.

1 HE that goeth forth with weeping,
   Bearing precious seed in love,
   Never tiring, never sleeping,
   Findeth mercy from above.
   Soft descend the dews of heaven,
   Bright the rays celestial shine;
   Precious fruits will thus be given,
   Through an influence all divine.

2 Sow thy seed, be never weary,
   Let no fears thy soul annoy;
   Be the prospect ne'er so dreary,
   Thou shalt reap the fruits of joy.
   Lo, the scene of verdure brightening,
   See the rising grain appear;
   Look again! the fields are whitening,
   For the harvest time is near.
   Thomas Hastings. (1784-1872.)

"I must work the works of Him that sent me."

429 "So run that ye may obtain." C. M.
Heb. xii. 2 Cor. xi. 21 to xii. 9. Ex. xiv. 15-31.

1 AWAKE, my soul, stretch every nerve,
  And press with vigor on;
  A heavenly race demands thy zeal,
  And an immortal crown.

2 A cloud of witnesses around
  Hold thee in full survey;
  Forget the steps already trod,
  And onward urge thy way.

3 'T is God's all-animating voice
  That calls thee from on high;
  'T is His own hand presents the prize
  To thine aspiring eye.

4 Blest Saviour, introduced by Thee,
  Have I my race begun;
  And, crowned with victory, at Thy feet
  I 'll lay my honors down.
        Rev. Philip Doddridge. (1702-1751.)

430 "Let him . . . take up his cross daily." C. M.
Luke ix. 23-27. Mat. xxvii. 24-32. Jer. viii. 21.

1 MUST Jesus bear the cross alone,
  And all the world go free?
  No; there 's a cross for every one,
  And there 's a cross for me.

2 How happy are the saints above,
  Who once went sorrowing here!
  But now they taste unmingled love,
  And joy without a tear.

3 The consecrated cross I 'll bear
  Till death shall set me free,
  And then go home my crown to wear,
  For there 's a crown for me.
        Thomas Shepherd. (1665-1739.)

431 "About my Father's business." S. M.
2 Tim. iv. 1-5. Acts xx. 18-35. Ps. xxxix. 1-7.

1 A CHARGE to keep I have,
  A God to glorify;
  A never-dying soul to save,
  And fit it for the sky;

2 To serve the present age,
  My calling to fulfil,
  O may it all my powers engage
  To do my Master's will.

3 Arm me with jealous care,
  As in Thy sight to live;
  And O Thy servant, Lord, prepare
  A strict account to give.

4 Help me to watch and pray,
  And on Thyself rely;
  Assured, if I my trust betray,
  I shall forever die.
        Rev. Charles Wesley. (1708-1788.)

432 "Serving the Lord." C. M.
Mark vi. 1-3. Phil. i. 21-30. Neh. v. 14-19.

1 SON of the carpenter, receive
  This humble work of mine;
  Worth to my meanest labor give,
  By joining it to Thine.

2 Servant, at once, and Lord of all,
  While dwelling here below,
  Thou didst not scorn our earthly toil
  And weariness to know.

3 Thy bright example I pursue,
  To Thee in all things rise;
  And all I think, or speak, or do,
  Is one great sacrifice.

4 Careless through outward cares I go,
  From all distraction free;
  My hands are but engaged below,
  My heart is still with Thee.

5 O when wilt Thou, my life, appear?
  Then gladly will I cry,
  "'T is done, the work Thou gav'st me here,
  'T is finished, Lord," and die.
        Rev. Charles Wesley.

433 "To His labor until the evening." 7. 6. 5.
Acts xvi. 11-40. Luke x. 1-17. Ps. xc.

1 ONE more day's work for Jesus,
  One less of life for me;
  But heaven is nearer,
  And Christ is dearer,
  Than yesterday to me.
  His love and light
  Fill all my soul to-night.

‖: One more day's work for Jesus, :‖
  One less of life for me.

2 One more day's work for Jesus,
  How glorious is my King!
  'T is joy, not duty,
  To speak His beauty.
  My soul mounts on the wing
  At the mere thought
  How Christ my life has bought.

3 O bless'ed work for Jesus,
  O rest at Jesus' feet!
  There toil seems pleasure,
  My wants are treasure,
  And pain for Him is sweet.
  Lord, if I may,
  I 'll serve another day.
        Miss Anna B. Warner.

"The Lord sent thee on a journey."

434 "I press toward the mark for the prize." **8. 7.**
2 Cor. iv. 1-10. Mat. xxvi. 36-42. Ps. xci.

1 ONWARD, Christian, though the region
Where thou art be drear and lone;
God has set a guardian legion
Very near thee; press thou on!

2 By the thorn-road, and none other,
Is the mount of vision won;
Tread it without shrinking, brother;
Jesus trod it; press thou on!

3 Be this world the wiser, stronger,
For thy life of pain and peace;
While it needs thee, O no longer
Pray thou for thy quick release.

4 Pray thou, Christian, daily, rather,
That thou be a faithful son;
By the prayer of Jesus, "Father,
Not my will, but Thine, be done!"
Rev. Samuel Johnson. (1822-.)

435 "We shall reap if we faint not." **7.**
Rev. ii. 8-10. 1 Pet. v. 8-11. Ps. xxvii.

1 FAINT not, Christian! though the road
Leading to thy blest abode
Darksome be, and dangerous too;
Christ, thy Guide, will bring thee through.

2 Faint not, Christian! though the world
Has its hostile flag unfurled;
Hold the cross of Jesus fast,
Thou shalt overcome at last.

3 Faint not, Christian! though within
There's a heart so prone to sin;
Christ, the Lord, is over all,
He'll not suffer thee to fall.

4 Faint not, Christian! look on high;
See the harpers in the sky:
Patient, wait, and thou wilt join
Chant with them of love divine.
Rev. James H. Evans. (1785-1840.)

436 "We glory in tribulations also." **7.**
James i. 2-4. Mat. v. 10-12. Ps. xciv. 12-15.

1 'TIS my happiness below,
Not to live without the cross,
But the Saviour's power to know,
Sanctifying every loss.

2 Trials must and will befall;
But, with humble faith, to see
Love inscribed upon them all,
This is happiness to me.

3 Trials make the promise sweet,
Trials give new life to prayer;
Trials bring me to His feet,
Lay me low, and keep me there.
William Cowper. (1731-1800.)

437 "As He is in the light." **C. M.**
John xii. 35, 36. Eph. v. 8-20. Isa. ii. 1-5.

1 WALK in the light! so shalt thou know
That fellowship of love
His Spirit only can bestow
Who reigns in light above.

2 Walk in the light! and thou shalt find
Thy heart made truly His
Who dwells in cloudless light enshrined,
In whom no darkness is.

3 Walk in the light! and thou shalt own
Thy darkness passed away,
Because that light hath on thee shone
In which is perfect day.

4 Walk in the light! and e'en the tomb
No fearful shade shall wear;
Glory shall chase away its gloom,
For Christ hath conquered there.

5 Walk in the light! thy path shall be
Peaceful, serene, and bright;
For God, by grace, shall dwell in thee,
And God Himself is Light.
Bernard Barton. (1784-1849.)

438 "As a good soldier of Jesus Christ." **L. M.**
1 Tim. vi. 11-21. 2 Tim. ii. 1 Sam. xiv. 1-23.

1 FIGHT the good fight with all thy might,
Christ is Strength, and Christ thy Right;
Lay hold on life, and it shall be
Thy joy and crown eternally.

2 Run the straight race through God's good grace,
Lift up thine eyes, and seek His face;
Life with its way before us lies,
Christ is the Path, and Christ the Prize.

3 Cast care aside; upon thy Guide
Lean, and His mercy will provide;
Lean, and the trusting soul shall prove
Christ is its Life, and Christ its Love.

4 Faint not nor fear, His arms are near;
He changeth not, and thou art dear:
Only believe, and thou shalt see
That Christ is All in all to thee.
Rev. John S. B. Monsell. (1811-1875.)

439 "Bringing his sheaves with him." **S. M.**
Ps. cxxvi. Jer. xxxi. 6-14. Gal. vi. 7-14.

1 THE harvest dawn is near,
The year delays not long;
And he who sows with many a tear
Shall reap with many a song.

2 Sad to his toil he goes,
His seed with weeping leaves;
But he shall come at twilight's close,
And bring his golden sheaves.
Bp. George Burgess. (1809-1866.)

"The Lord sent thee on a journey."

440 "The Lord delivereth him." C. M.
1 Thes. v. Rom. viii. 12-21. Ps. cxxxviii.

1 REJOICE, believer, in the Lord,
   Who makes your cause His own;
   The hope that's built upon His word
   Can ne'er be overthrown.

2 Though many foes beset your road,
   And feeble is your arm,
   Your life is hid with Christ in God,
   Beyond the reach of harm.

3 Weak as you are, you shall not faint,
   Or, fainting, shall not die;
   For God, the strength of every saint,
   Will aid you from on high.

4 Though sometimes unperceived by sense,
   Faith sees Him always near,
   A Guide, a Glory, a Defence;
   Then what have you to fear?

5 As surely as Christ overcame
   And triumphed once for you,
   So surely you that love His name
   Shall triumph in Him, too.
   Rev. John Newton. (1725-1807.)

441 "I have given you an example." L. M.
Acts x. 36-43. 2 Cor. ix. 6-11. Prov. xi. 24-31.

1 WHEN Jesus dwelt in mortal clay,
   What were His works from day to day
   But miracles of power and grace,
   That spread salvation through our race?

2 Teach us, O Lord, to keep in view
   Thy pattern, and Thy steps pursue;
   Let alms bestowed, let kindness done,
   Be witnessed by each rolling sun.

3 That man may last, but never lives,
   Who much receives, but nothing gives,
   Whom none can love, whom none can thank,
   Creation's blot, creation's blank;

4 But he who marks, from day to day,
   In generous acts his radiant way
   Treads the same path the Saviour trod,
   The path to glory and to God.
   Rev. Thomas Gibbons. (1720-1785.)

442 "Our conversation is in heaven." C. M.
Ps. i. 1-3. Mat. v. 3-12. Heb. xii. 1-24.

1 How happy every child of grace
   Who knows his sins forgiven!
   This earth, he cries, is not my place,
   I seek my place in heaven:

2 A country far from mortal sight,
   Yet O by faith I see
   The land of rest, the saints' delight,
   The heaven prepared for me.
   Rev. Charles Wesley. (1708-1788.)

443 "A stranger and a sojourner with you." C. M.
Heb. xi. 1-16. 1 Pet. ii. 11-25. Isa. xxxv.

1 A STRANGER in the world below,
   I calmly sojourn here;
   Nor can its happiness or woe
   Provoke my hope or fear.

2 Its evils in a moment end,
   Its joys as soon are past;
   But O the bliss to which I tend
   Eternally shall last.

3 To that Jerusalem above
   With singing I repair;
   While in the flesh, my hope and love,
   My heart and soul, are there.
   Rev. Charles Wesley.

444 "They that seek the Lord shall not want." C. M.
Ps. lxii. Gen. i. 26-28. 2 Cor. v. 14.

1 O HOW the thought of God attracts
   And draws the heart from earth,
   And sickens it of passing shows
   And dissipating mirth!

2 God only is the creature's home,
   Though long and rough the road;
   Yet nothing less can satisfy
   The love that longs for God.

3 A trusting heart, a yearning eye,
   Can win their way above;
   If mountains can be moved by faith,
   Is there less power in love?

4 How little of that road, my soul,
   How little hast thou gone!
   Take heart, and let the thought of God
   Allure thee further on.
   Rev. Frederick W. Faber. (1814-1862.)

445 "Blessed be the name of the Lord." C. M.
Ps. liv. Hab. iii. 17-19. 2 Tim. iv. 6-18.

1 FATHER, whate'er of earthly bliss
   Thy sovereign hand denies,
   Accepted at Thy throne of grace,
   Let this petition rise:

2 Give me a calm, a thankful heart,
   From every murmur free;
   The blessings of Thy grace impart,
   And let me live to Thee.

3 Let the sweet hope that Thou art mine
   My life and death attend;
   Thy presence through my journey shine,
   And crown my journey's end.
   Miss Anne Steele. (1717-1778.)

83

"Turned back from the Lord."

446 "O that I were as in months past." C. M.
Job xxix. Ps. cxix. 145-152. Heb. vi.

1 SWEET was the time when first I felt
The Saviour's pardoning blood
Applied to cleanse my soul from guilt,
And bring me home to God.

2 Soon as the morn the light revealed,
His praises tuned my tongue ;
And when the evening shades prevailed,
His love was all my song.

3 In prayer my soul drew near the Lord,
And saw His glory shine ;
And when I read His holy word
I called each promise mine.

4 But now, when evening shade prevails,
My soul in darkness mourns ;
And when the morn the light reveals,
No light to me returns.

5 Rise, Saviour ! help me to prevail,
And make my soul Thy care ;
I know Thy mercy cannot fail,
Let me that mercy share.
Rev. John Newton. (1725-1807.)

447 "Let us not sleep, as do others." C. M.
Prov. vi. 6-11. Rom. xiii. 11-14. 1 Cor. ix.

1 MY drowsy powers, why sleep ye so ?
Awake, my sluggish soul !
Nothing has half thy work to do,
Yet nothing's half so dull.

2 We, for whom God, the Son, came down,
And labored for our good,
How careless to secure that crown,
He purchased with His blood !

3 Lord, shall we lie so sluggish still,
And never act our parts ?
Come, holy Dove, from th' heavenly hill,
And sit and warm our hearts.
Rev. Isaac Watts. (1674-1748.)

448 "Thou knowest my foolishness." C. M.
Ps. xliii. Rom. vii. 7-25. Jonah ii.

1 WHY is my heart so far from Thee,
My God, my chief Delight,
Why are my thoughts no more by day
With Thee, no more by night ?

2 Why should my foolish passions rove ?
Where can such sweetness be
As I have tasted in Thy love,
As I have found in Thee ?

3 Wretch that I am, to wander thus,
In chase of false delight !
Let me be fastened to Thy cross,
Rather than lose Thy sight.
Rev. Isaac Watts.

449 "When His candle shined upon my head" 7.
Ps. xxii. Gal iv 15, 16. Acts xxvi 1-23

1 ONCE I thought my mountain strong,
Firmly fixed, no more to move ;
Then Thy grace was all my song,
Then my soul was filled with love.
Those were happy, golden days,
Sweetly spent in prayer and praise.

2 Little then myself I knew,
Little thought, of Satan's power ;
Now I feel my sins anew,
Now I feel the stormy hour.
Sin has put my joys to flight,
Sin has changed my day to night.

3 Saviour, shine and cheer my soul,
Bid my dying hopes revive ;
Make my wounded spirit whole,
Far away the tempter drive.
Speak the word, and set me free ;
Let me live alone to Thee.
Rev. John Newton.

450 "Let my cry come unto Thee." C. M.
Ps. vi. Mat. xxvi. 57-75. John xxi. 15-17.

1 TIMES without number have I prayed,
This only once forgive ;
Relapsing when Thy hand was stayed,
And suffered me to live.

2 Yet now the kingdom of Thy peace,
Lord, to my heart restore ;
Forgive my vain repentances,
And bid me sin no more.
Rev. Charles Wesley. (1708-1788.)

451 "Lord, is it I ?" 8. 6.
Ps. xxvi. Mat. xxv. 31-46. 2 Pet iii.

1 WHEN Thou, my righteous Judge, shalt come
To fetch Thy ransomed people home,
Shall I among them stand ?
Shall such a worthless worm as I,
Who sometimes am afraid to die,
Be found at Thy right hand ?

2 I love to meet among them now,
Before Thy gracious feet to bow,
Though vilest of them all ;
But can I bear the piercing thought,
What if my name should be left out,
When Thou for them shalt call !

3 Prevent, prevent it by Thy grace ;
Be Thou, dear Lord, my Hiding-place,
In this th' accepted day ;
Thy pardoning voice O let me hear,
To still my unbelieving fear ;
Nor let me fall, I pray.
Selina Shirley, Countess of Huntingdon. (1707-1791.)

"I will be sorry for my sin."

452 Ps. cxxx. "And wept bitterly." Acts xxii. 3-20. Gal. i. 10-24. **C. M.**

1 WITH tears of anguish I lament,
  Here at Thy feet, my God,
My passion, pride, and discontent,
  And vile ingratitude.

2 Sure there was ne'er a heart so base,
  So false, as mine has been;
So faithless to its promises,
  So prone to every sin.

3 How long, dear Saviour, shall I feel
  These struggles in my breast?
When wilt Thou bow my stubborn will,
  And give my conscience rest?

4 Break, sovereign grace, O break the charm,
  And set the captive free;
Reveal, almighty God, Thine arm,
  And haste to rescue me.

Rev. Samuel Stennett. (1727-1795.)

453 "In the day of my trouble I sought the Lord." Hos. xiv. Luke xv. 11-34. Rom. xi. 29-36. **C. M.**

1 How oft, alas, this wretched heart
  Has wandered from the Lord!
How oft my roving thoughts depart,
  Forgetful of His word!

2 Yet sovereign mercy calls, "Return!"
  Dear Lord, and may I come?
My vile ingratitude I mourn;
  O take the wanderer home.

3 Thy pardoning love, so free, so sweet,
  Dear Saviour, I adore;
O keep me at Thy sacred feet,
  And let me rove no more.

Miss Anne Steele. (1717-1778.)

454 Ps. cxvi. 1-8. Heb. x. 19-39. 2 Chr. xxxiii. 1-19. "Let me not wander." **L. M.**

1 RETURN, my roving heart, return,
  And chase these shadowy forms no more;
Seek out some solitude, to mourn,
  And thy forsaken God implore.

2 And Thou, my God, whose piercing eye
  Distinct surveys each deep recess,
In these abstracted hours draw nigh,
  And with Thy presence fill the place.

3 Through all the mazes of my heart,
  My search let heavenly wisdom guide;
And still its radiant beams impart,
  Till all be searched and purified.

4 Then, with the visits of Thy love,
  Vouchsafe my inmost soul to cheer;
Till every grace shall join to prove
  That God has fixed His dwelling there.

Rev. Philip Doddridge. (1702-1751.)

455 Luke xix. 41-44. "For these things I weep." Heb. v. 7-10. Hos. vi. **S. M.**

1 DID Christ o'er sinners weep,
  And shall our cheeks be dry?
Let floods of penitential grief
  Burst forth from every eye.

2 The Son of God in tears
  Angels with wonder see:
Be thou astonished, O my soul;
  He shed those tears for thee.

3 He wept that we might weep;
  Each sin demands a tear;
In heaven alone no sin is found,
  And there's no weeping there.

Rev. Benjamin Beddome. (1717-1795.)

456 Ps. cxix. 33-40. "I abhor myself." 2 Kings xx. 1 Cor. xiii. 1-10. **C. M.**

1 LONG have I seemed to serve Thee, Lord,
  With unavailing pain;
Fasted, and prayed, and read Thy word,
  And heard it preached in vain.

2 To please Thee, thus at length I see,
  Vainly I hoped and strove;
For what are outward things to Thee,
  Unless they spring from love?

3 Where am I now, or what my hope?
  What can my weakness do?
Jesus, to Thee my soul looks up;
  'T is Thou must make it new.

Rev. Charles Wesley. (1708-1788.)

457 Micah vi. 6-9. "We have an Advocate with the Father." Mat. xxvi. 57-75. 1 John i. **8.**

1 WEARY of wandering from my God,
  And now made willing to return,
I hear, and bow me to the rod:
  Not without hope, for Him I mourn;
I have an Advocate above,
A Friend before the throne of love.

2 O Jesus, full of pardoning grace,
  More full of grace than I of sin,
Yet once again I seek Thy face;
  Open Thine arms, and take me in;
And freely my backslidings heal,
And love the faithless sinner still.

3 Thou know'st the way to bring me back,
  My fallen spirit to restore;
O for thy truth and mercy's sake,
  Forgive, and bid me sin no more;
The ruins of my soul repair,
And make my heart a house of prayer.

Rev. Charles Wesley.

"Return unto me, and I will return unto you."

458 "Inquire ye; return, come." 7.
Luke ii. 25-38. Isa. xlii. 5-16. Ps. lxxxix. 15-18.

1 YE that in His courts are found,
  Listening to the joyful sound,
  Lost and helpless as ye are,
  Sons of sorrow, sin, and care,
  Glorify the King of kings,
  Take the peace the gospel brings.

2 Turn to Christ your longing eyes,
  View His bloody sacrifice ;
  See in Him your sins forgiven,
  Pardon, holiness, and heaven :
  Glorify the King of kings,
  Take the peace the gospel brings.
  Rev. Rowland Hill. (1744-1833.)

459 "Strengthen ye the weak hands." 7. 6. P.
Mat. xi 28-30. Mal. i.i. 7-18. Acts ii. 22-39.

1 DROOPING souls, no longer mourn,
    Jesus still is precious ;
  If to Him you now return,
    Heaven will be propitious.
  Jesus now is passing by,
    Calling wanderers near Him ;
  Drooping souls, you need not die,
    Go to Him, and hear Him.

2 He has pardons, full and free,
    Drooping souls to gladden ;
  Still He cries, " Come unto me,
    Weary, heavy laden ! "
  Though your sins, like mountains high,
    Rise, and reach to heaven,
  Soon as you on Him rely,
    All shall be forgiven.

3 Precious is the Saviour's name,
    All His saints adore Him ;
  He to save the dying came,
    Prostrate, bow before Him ;
  Wandering sinners, now return ;
    Contrite souls, believe Him ;
  Jesus calls you, cease to mourn ;
    Worship Him, receive Him.
  Thomas Hastings. (1784-1872.)

460 "Incline your ear and come." S. M.
Deu. xxiii. 21-23. Isa. xvi. 1-5. Acts iii. 13-26.

1 COME, take His offers now,
    From every sin depart :
  Perform thy oft-repeated vow,
    And render Him thy heart.

2 Repent, return, receive
    The grace through Jesus given ;
  Sure, if with God on earth we live,
    We live with God in heaven.
  Rev. Charles Wesley. (1708-1788.)
Alt. by Rev. Nehemiah Adams. (1806-.)

461 "Follow thou me." 6.
John x. 11-18. 1 John iii. 16-24. Isa. l. 6.

1 I GAVE my life for thee,
    My precious blood I shed,
  That thou mightst ransomed be,
    And quickened from the dead :
  I gave, I gave my life for thee,
  What hast thou given for me ?

2 My Father's house of light,
    My glory-circled throne,
  I left, for earthly night,
    For wand'rings sad and lone :
  I left, I left it all for thee,
  Hast thou left aught for me ?

3 I suffered much for thee,
    More than thy tongue can tell,
  Of bitterest agony,
    To rescue thee from hell :
  I 've borne, I 've borne it all for thee,
  What hast thou borne for me ?

4 And I have brought to thee,
    Down from my home above,
  Salvation full and free,
    My pardon and my love ;
  I bring, I bring rich gifts to thee,
  What hast thou brought to me ?
  Miss Frances R. Havergal. (1836-1879.)

462 "Casting all your care upon Him." S. M.
Ps. lv. 22. 1 John v. 1-15. Deu. xxx. 1-14.

1 How gentle God's commands,
    How kind His precepts are !
  " Come, cast your burdens on the Lord,
    And trust His constant care."

2 Why should this anxious load
    Press down your weary mind ?
  Haste to your heavenly Father's throne,
    And sweet refreshment find.
  Rev. Philip Doddridge. (1702-1751.)

463 "Cast thy burden upon the Lord." 7.
1 Pet. v. 7. Isa. xli. 10-14. Deu. xxxi. 1-8.

1 CAST thy burden on the Lord,
  Only lean upon His word ;
  Thou shalt soon have cause to bless
  His eternal faithfulness.

2 Cast thy burden at His feet,
  Linger at His mercy-seat ;
  He will lead thee by the hand
  Gently to the better land.

3 He will gird thee by His power,
  In thy weary, fainting hour ;
  Lean, then, loving, on His word,
  Cast thy burden on the Lord.
  Rev. Rowland Hill.
Alt. by George Rawson. (1807-.)

"Return unto me, and I will return unto you."

464 "Turn you to the stronghold." 8. 7. P.
Ps. xi. Josh. xx. Luke xv. 11-24.

1 FLEE as a bird to your mountain,
   Thou who art weary of sin;
Go to the clear flowing fountain,
   Where you may wash and be clean.
Fly, for the avenger is near thee;
   Call, and the Saviour will hear thee:
He in His bosom will bear thee,
   O thou who art weary of sin!

2 He will protect thee forever,
   Wipe every falling tear;
He will forsake thee O never,
   Sheltered so tenderly there.
Haste, then, the hours are flying;
   Spend not the moments in sighing;
Cease from thy sorrow and crying;
   The Saviour will wipe every tear.

Mrs. Mary S. B. Dana. (1810-.)

465 "Seek the Lord, and ye shall live." 7.
Jer. iii. 12-23. Isa. xlv. 20-25. Rev. iii.

1 PILGRIM, burdened with thy sin,
   Come the way to Zion's gate;
There, till mercy lets thee in,
   Knock, and weep, and watch, and wait:
Knock, He knows the sinner's cry;
   Weep, He loves the mourner's tears;
Watch, for saving grace is nigh;
   Wait, till heavenly light appears.

2 Hark, it is the Bridegroom's voice:
   "Welcome, pilgrim, to thy rest!"
Now within the gate rejoice,
   Safe, and sealed, and bought, and blest:
Safe from all the lures of vice;
   Sealed by signs the chosen know;
Bought by love, and life the price;
   Blest the mighty debt to owe.

Rev. George Crabbe. (1754-1832.)

466 "That in me ye might have peace." 8.
John xiv. 27-31. Jer. viii. 18-22. Isa. liv.

1 PEACE, troubled soul, whose plaintive moan
   Hath taught each scene the note of woe;
Cease thy complaint, suppress thy groan,
   And let thy tears forget to flow:
Behold, the precious balm is found,
   Which lulls thy pain, which heals thy wound.

2 Come, freely come, by sin opprest;
   Unburden here thy weighty load;
Here find thy refuge and thy rest,
   Safe in the mercy of thy God:
Thy God's thy Saviour, glorious word!
   O hear, believe, and bless the Lord.

Hon. and Rev. Walter Shirley. (1725-1786.)

467 "When he looketh upon it he shall live." 7.
Isa. li. Zech. ix. 12-17. John iii. 14-17.

1 WEARY sinner, keep thine eyes
   On th' atoning Sacrifice;
View Him bleeding on the tree,
   Pouring out His life for thee.

2 Surely Christ thy griefs hath borne;
   Weeping soul, no longer mourn;
Now by faith the Son embrace,
   Plead His promise, trust His grace.

3 Cast thy guilty soul on Him,
   Find Him mighty to redeem;
At His feet thy burden lay,
   Look thy doubts and care away.

Author unknown.

468 "The Master is come and calleth for thee." 7.
John xxi. 15-17. Isa. xlix. 13-23. Rom. viii. 31-39.

1 HARK, my soul! it is the Lord,
   'T is thy Saviour, hear His word;
Jesus speaks, and speaks to thee:
   "Say, poor sinner, lov'st thou me?

2 "I delivered thee, when bound,
   And, when wounded, healed thy wound;
Sought thee wandering, set thee right,
   Turned thy darkness into light.

3 "Mine is an unchanging love,
   Higher than the heights above,
Deeper than the depths beneath,
   Free and faithful, strong as death.

4 "Thou shalt see my glory soon,
   When the work of grace is done;
Partner of my throne shalt be;
   Say, poor sinner, lov'st thou me?"

William Cowper. (1731-1800.)

469 "Draw nigh unto God." L. M.
Mat. xi. 28-30. Isa. xxvi. 9-21. Ps. xvi.

1 WITH tearful eyes I look around;
   Life seems a dark and stormy sea;
Yet 'midst the gloom I hear a sound,
   A heavenly whisper, "Come to me!"

2 When against sin I strive in vain,
   And cannot from its yoke get free,
Sinking beneath the heavy chain,
   The words arrest me, "Come to me!"

3 "Come, for all else must fail and die;
   Earth is no resting-place for thee;
Heavenward direct thy weeping eye;
   I am thy portion; come to me!"

4 O voice of mercy, voice of love,
   In conflict, grief, and agony,
Support me, cheer me from above,
   And gently whisper, "Come to me!"

Miss Charlotte Elliott. (1789-1871.)

"Return unto me, and I will return unto you."

470 "Ye shall find rest to your souls." 11, 10.
Joel ii. 12-14. Jer. xxx. 4-22. Isa. lxvi. 5-13. John xi.

1 COME, ye disconsolate, where'er ye languish,
 Come to the mercy-seat, fervently kneel;
 Here bring your wounded hearts, here tell your anguish;
 Earth has no sorrows that Heaven cannot heal.

2 Joy of the desolate, Light of the straying,
 Hope of the penitent, fadeless and pure,
 Here speaks the Comforter, tenderly saying,
 Earth has no sorrows that Heaven cannot cure.

3 Here see the Bread of Life; see waters flowing
 Forth from the throne of God, pure from above;
 Come to the feast prepared; come, ever knowing
 Earth has no sorrows but Heaven can remove.
Thomas Moore. (1770-1852.)
Thomas Hastings. (1784-1872.) v. 2.

471 "I will give you rest." 11, 10.
Isa. xxvi. 20, 21. Jer. vi. 16. John xiv. 1-13. Mat. xi. 28-30.

1 COME unto me when shadows darkly gather,
 When the sad heart is weary and distressed,
 Seeking for comfort from your heavenly Father;
 Come unto me, and I will give you rest.

2 Large are the mansions in thy Father's dwelling,
 Glad are the homes that sorrows never dim;
 Sweet are the harps in holy music swelling,
 Soft are the tones which raise the heavenly hymn.

3 There, like an Eden blossoming in gladness,
 Bloom the fair flowers the earth too rudely pressed;
 Come unto me all ye who droop in sadness,
 Come unto me, and I will give you rest.
Mrs. Catharine H. Esling. (1812-)

472 "Return, ... for I am merciful, saith the Lord." 12, 11.
Acts ii. 23-39. Hos. xi. Ps. xxxiv. 8-22. Jer. iii. 12-23.

1 O COME to the merciful Saviour that calls you,
 O come to the Lord, who forgives and forgets;
 Though dark be the fortune on earth that befalls you,
 There's a bright home above, where the sun never sets.

2 O come, then, to Jesus, whose arms are extended
 To fold His dear children in closest embrace;
 O come, for your exile will shortly be ended,
 And Jesus will show you His beautiful face.

3 Then come to the Saviour, whose mercy grows brighter
 The longer you look at the depths of His love;
 And fear not, 't is Jesus, and life's cares grow lighter,
 As you think of the home and the glory above.
Rev. Frederick W. Faber. (1814-1863.)

473 "Turn, ... and I will bring you to Zion." 12, 11.
2 Sam. xii. 13. Luke xxiii. 43. John xviii. 17-27. 1 Cor. xv. 9.

1 HAVE you sinned as none else in the world have before you?
 Are you blacker than all other creatures in guilt?
 O fear not, and doubt not! the mother who bore you
 Loves you less than the Saviour whose blood you have spilt.

2 Come, come to His feet, and lay open your story
 Of suffering and sorrow, of guilt and of shame;
 For the pardon of sin is the crown of His glory,
 And the joy of our Lord to be true to His name.
Rev. Frederick W. Faber.

"I will arise and go to my father."

474 "Look Thou upon me and be merciful." 7. 6. 8.
Luke xxii. 54-62. Acts iii. 12-26. Ps. li.

1 JESUS, let Thy pitying eye
  Call back a wandering sheep;
  False to Thee, like Peter, I
  Would fain, like Peter, weep.
  Let me be by grace restored ;
  On me be all long-suffering shown ;
  Turn, and look upon me, Lord,
  And break my heart of stone.

2 Saviour, Prince, enthroned above,
  Repentance to impart,
  Give me, through Thy dying love,
  The humble, contrite heart ;
  Give what I have long implored,
  A portion of Thy grief unknown ;
  Turn, and look upon me, Lord,
  And break my heart of stone.

3 See me, Saviour, from above,
  Nor suffer me to die ;
  Life, and happiness, and love,
  Drop from Thy gracious eye.
  Speak the reconciling word,
  And let Thy mercy melt me down ;
  Turn, and look upon me, Lord,
  And break my heart of stone.

4 Look, as when Thy languid eye
  Was closed that we might live ;
  "Father," at the point to die,
  My Saviour prayed, " Forgive ! "
  Surely with that dying word
  He turns, and looks, and cries, 'T is done !
  O my bleeding, loving Lord,
  Thou break'st my heart of stone.

Rev. Charles Wesley. (1708-1788.)

475 "Hide not Thy face from me." C. M.
Mal. iv. 2-6. Ps. xxxvi. 5-10. Eph. v. 8-20.

1 ETERNAL Sun of Righteousness,
  Display Thy beams divine,
  And cause the glory of Thy face
  Upon my heart to shine.

2 Light in Thy light O may I see,
  Thy grace and mercy prove,
  Revived, and cheered, and blessed by Thee,
  The God of pardoning love.

3 Lift up Thy countenance serene,
  And let Thy happy child
  Behold, without a cloud between,
  The Godhead reconciled.

Rev. Charles Wesley.

476 "If any man open the door . . . I will come in." 7. 6.
Rev. iii. 14-22. Luke xii. 35-40. Prov. viii.

1 O JESUS, Thou art standing
  Outside the fast-closed door,
  In lowly patience waiting
  To pass the threshold o'er :
  Shame on us, Christian brethren,
  His name and sign who bear,
  O shame, thrice shame upon us,
  To keep Him standing there.

2 O Jesus, Thou art knocking :
  And lo, that hand is scarred,
  And thorns Thy brow encircle,
  And tears Thy face have marred.
  O love that passeth knowledge,
  So patiently to wait !
  O sin that hath no equal,
  So fast to bar the gate !

3 O Jesus, Thou art pleading
  In accents meek and low,
  " I died for you, my children,
  And will ye treat me so ? "
  O Lord, with shame and sorrow
  We open now the door :
  Dear Saviour, enter, enter,
  And leave us nevermore.

Rev. William W. How? (1823-.)

477 "Restore unto me the joy of Thy salvation." C. M.
Hos. xiv. Mal. iii. 7-18. Mat. viii.

1 O THOU, whose tender mercy hears
  Contrition's humble sigh ;
  Whose hand, indulgent, wipes the tears
  From sorrow's weeping eye.

2 See, low before Thy throne of grace,
  A wretched wanderer mourn :
  Hast Thou not bid me seek Thy face ?
  Hast Thou not said, " Return " ?

3 And shall my guilty fears prevail
  To drive me from Thy feet ?
  O let not this dear refuge fail,
  This only safe retreat !

4 Absent from Thee, my Guide, my Light,
  Without one cheering ray,
  Through dangers, fears, and gloomy night,
  How desolate my way !

5 O shine on this benighted heart,
  With beams of mercy shine ;
  And let Thy healing voice impart
  A taste of joy divine.

Miss Anne Steele. (1717-1778.)

"I will arise and go to my father."

478 "Make haste to help me, O Lord." Ps. lxx. Neh. iv. 1-6. Mark xiv. 32-42. 7.

1 HASTEN, Lord, to my release,
  Haste to help me, O my God!
  Foes, like arméd bands, increase;
  Turn them back the way they trod.

2 Dark temptations round me press,
  Evil thoughts my soul assail;
  Doubts and fears, in my distress,
  Rise, till flesh and spirit fail.

3 Thou mine only Helper art,
  My Redeemer from the grave;
  Strength of my desiring heart,
  Do not tarry, haste to save.
            James Montgomery. (1771-1854.)

479 "Redeem me, and be merciful unto me." Isa. xxxviii. Ps. vi. Heb. xii. 11-24. 7.

1 GENTLY, gently lay Thy rod
  On my sinful head, O God;
  Stay Thy wrath, in mercy stay,
  Lest I sink before its sway.

2 Heal me, for my flesh is weak;
  Heal me, for Thy grace I seek;
  This my only plea I make,
  Heal me for Thy mercy's sake.

3 Who, within the silent grave,
  Shall proclaim Thy power to save?
  Lord, my sinking soul reprieve;
  Speak, and I shall rise and live.

4 Lo, He comes, He heeds my plea!
  Lo, He comes, the shadows flee!
  Glory round me dawns once more;
  Rise, my spirit, and adore!
            Rev. Henry F. Lyte. (1793-1847.)

480 "Neither by the blood of goats and calves." Heb. ix. 11-14. 2 Cor. v. 14-21. Lev. xvi. 15-22. S. M.

1 NOT all the blood of beasts
  On Jewish altars slain
  Could give the guilty conscience peace,
  Or wash away the stain.

2 But Christ, the heavenly Lamb,
  Takes all our sins away;
  A Sacrifice of nobler name
  And richer blood than they.

3 My faith would lay her hand
  On that dear head of Thine,
  While like a penitent I stand,
  And there confess my sin.

4 My soul looks back to see
  The burdens Thou didst bear,
  When hanging on the curséd tree,
  And hopes her guilt was there.
            Rev. Isaac Watts. (1674-1748.)

481 "Thou art the God of my salvation." Ps. xxxviii. Eph. ii. 4-22. Heb. x. 1-22. 7. 6. 8.

1 GOD of my salvation, hear,
  And help me to believe;
  Simply do I now draw near,
  Thy blessing to receive.
  Full of guilt, alas, I am,
  But to Thy wounds for refuge flee;
  Friend of sinners, spotless Lamb,
  Thy blood was shed for me.

2 Standing now as newly slain,
  To Thee I lift mine eye,
  Balm of all my grief and pain,
  Thy blood is always nigh:
  Now as yesterday the same
  Thou art, and wilt forever be;
  Friend of sinners, spotless Lamb,
  Thy blood was shed for me.

3 Nothing have I, Lord, to pay,
  Nor can Thy grace procure;
  Empty send me not away,
  For I, Thou know'st, am poor.
  Dust and ashes is my name,
  My all is sin and misery;
  Friend of sinners, spotless Lamb,
  Thy blood was shed for me.
            Rev. Charles Wesley. (1708-1788.)

482 "Blot out all mine iniquities." Ps. li Luke xviii. 13-43. Acts xvi. 27-34. S. M.

1 HAVE mercy, Lord, on me,
  As Thou wert ever kind;
  Let me, oppressed with loads of guilt,
  Thy wonted mercy find.

2 Against Thee, Lord, alone,
  And only in Thy sight,
  Have I transgressed, and though condemned,
  Must own Thy judgment right.

3 Blot out my crying sins,
  Nor me in anger view;
  Create in me a heart that's clean,
  An upright mind renew.

4 Withdraw not Thou Thy help,
  Nor cast me from Thy sight;
  Nor let Thy Holy Spirit take
  His everlasting flight.

5 The joy Thy favor gives
  Let me, O Lord, regain,
  And Thy free Spirit's firm support
  My fainting soul sustain.
            Tate and Brady. 1696.

"I will arise and go to my Father."

483 "Have mercy on me, . . . thou Son of David." 8. 7.
Ps. lxxxvi. John iv. 39-47. Acts x. 1-22.

1 LORD, I hear of showers of blessing,
   Thou art scattering full and free ;
Showers, the thirsty land refreshing ;
   Let some droppings fall on me :
      Even me, even me,
   Let some droppings fall on me!

2 Have I long in sin been sleeping,
   Long been slighting, grieving Thee ;
Has the world my heart been keeping,
   O forgive and rescue me :
      Even me, even me,
   O forgive and rescue me!

3 Pass me not, this lost one bringing,
   Satan's slave Thy child shall be ;
All my heart to Thee is springing ;
   Blessing others, O bless me :
      Even me, even me,
   Blessing others, O bless me!

   Mrs. Elizabeth Codner. 1860.

484 "Pass not away . . . from Thy servant." 8. 7.
Gen. xxvii. 30-33. Mark x. 46-52. Ps. li.

1 PASS me not, O gracious Father,
   Sinful though my heart may be ;
Thou mightst curse me, but the rather
   Let Thy mercy light on me :
      Even me, even me,
   Let Thy mercy light on me.

2 Pass me not, O tender Saviour,
   Let me love and cling to Thee ;
I am longing for Thy favor ;
   When Thou comest, call for me :
      Even me, even me,
   When Thou comest, call for me!

3 Pass me not, O mighty Spirit,
   Thou canst make the blind to see ;
Witnesser of Jesus' merit,
   Speak the word of power to me :
      Even me, even me,
   Speak the word of power to me!

4 Love of God, so pure and changeless,
   Blood of Christ, so rich and free,
Grace of God, so strong and boundless,
   Magnify them all in me :
      Even me, even me,
   Magnify them all in me!

   Mrs. Elizabeth Codner. 1860.

485 "I flee unto Thee to hide me." C. M.
Luke xv. Ps. xxxviii. 2 Chr. xxxiv. 14-28.

1 My head is low, my heart is sad,
   My feet with travel torn ;
Yet, O my Saviour, Thou art glad
   To see Thy child return.

2 It was Thy love that homeward led,
   Thine arm that upward stayed ;
It is Thy hand which on my head
   Is now in mercy laid.

3 O Saviour, in this broken heart
   Confirm the trembling will
Which longs to reach Thee where Thou art,
   Rest in Thee and be still.

4 Within that bosom which hath shed
   Both tears and blood for me,
O let me hide this aching head,
   Once pressed and blessed by Thee.

   Rev. John S. B. Monsell. (1811-1875.)

486 "I will cry unto God most high." L. M.
Eph. ii. 1 Pet. iv. 14. Ps xxviii.

1 GOD of my life, Thy boundless grace
   Chose, pardoned, and adopted me ;
My Rest, my Home, my Dwelling-place :
   Father, I come, I come to Thee.

2 Jesus, my Hope, my Rock, my Shield,
   Whose precious blood was shed for me,
Into Thy hands my soul I yield :
   Saviour, I come, I come to Thee.

3 Spirit of glory and of God,
   Long hast Thou deigned my Guide to be ;
Now be Thy comfort sweet bestowed :
   My God, I come, I come to Thee.

   Author unknown.

487 "Thou art my refuge and my portion." L. M.
Ps. xxx. Acts xxii. 6-21. Isa. lvii. 15.

1 ETERNAL Father, when to Thee,
   Beyond all worlds, by faith I soar,
Before Thy boundless majesty
   I stand in silence, and adore.

2 But Saviour, Thou art by my side,
   Thy voice I hear, Thy face I see ;
Thou art my Friend, my daily Guide :
   God over all, yet God with me.

3 And Thou, great Spirit, in my heart
   Dost make Thy temple day by day ;
The Holy Ghost of God Thou art,
   Yet dwellest in this house of clay.

4 Blest Trinity, in whom alone
   All things created move or rest,
High in the heavens Thou hast Thy throne,
   Thou hast Thy throne within my breast.

   Rev. Hervey D. Ganse. (1822-.)

"I will arise and go to my father."

488 "Uphold me with Thy free Spirit." **L. M.**
John xiv. 15-26. 1 Cor. ii. 9-16. Neh. ix. 20.

1 COME, blesséd Spirit, Source of light,
  Whose power and grace are unconfined;
  Dispel the gloomy shades of night,
  The thicker darkness of the mind.

2 To mine illumined eyes display
  The glorious truths Thy word reveals;
  Cause me to run the heavenly way,
  Thy book unfold, and loose the seals.

3 Thine inward teachings make me know,
  The mysteries of redeeming love,
  The emptiness of things below,
  And excellence of things above.

4 While through this dubious maze I stray,
  Spread, like the sun, Thy beams abroad,
  To show the dangers of the way,
  And guide my feeble steps to God.
  Rev. Benjamin Beddome. (1717-1795.)

489 "Thy light and Thy truth, let them lead me." **L. M.**
Phil. iv. 6, 7. 1 John v. 6-12. Isa. xxx. 14-20.

1 COME, Holy Spirit, calm my mind,
  And fit me to approach my God;
  Remove each vain, each worldly thought,
  And lead me to Thy blest abode.

2 Hast Thou imparted to my soul
  A living spark of heavenly fire,
  O kindle now the sacred flame,
  Teach it to burn with pure desire.

3 A brighter faith and hope impart,
  And let me now the Saviour see:
  O soothe and cheer my burdened heart,
  And bid my spirit rest in Thee.
  Author unknown.

490 "The Spirit which is of God." **7.**
John xvi. 7-15. Titus iii 4-7. Ps. cxix. 169-176.

1 GRACIOUS Spirit, Dove divine!
  Let Thy light within me shine;
  All my guilty fears remove,
  Fill me full of heaven and love.

2 Speak Thy pardoning grace to me,
  Set the burdened sinner free;
  Lead me to the Lamb of God,
  Wash me in His precious blood.

3 Life and peace to me impart,
  Seal salvation on my heart;
  Breathe Thyself into my breast,
  Earnest of immortal rest.

4 Let me never from Thee stray,
  Keep me in the narrow way;
  Fill my soul with joy divine,
  Keep me, Lord, forever Thine.
  John Stocker. 1776.

491 "It is the Spirit that beareth witness." **8.**
John vi. 63. Rom. viii. 1-16. 2 Chr. i. 7-12.

1 COME, Holy Ghost, all quickening Fire,
  Come, and in me delight to rest;
  Drawn by the lure of strong desire,
  O come and consecrate my breast:
  The temple of my soul prepare,
  And fix Thy sacred presence there.

2 My Peace, my Life, my Comfort, now,
  My Treasure and my All Thou art;
  True Witness of my sonship Thou,
  Engraving pardon on my heart:
  Seal of my sins in Christ forgiven,
  Earnest of love, and Pledge of heaven.

3 Come, then, my God, mark out Thine heir,
  Of heaven a larger earnest give;
  With clearer light Thy witness bear,
  More sensibly within me live:
  Let all my powers Thy entrance feel,
  And deeper stamp Thyself the seal.
  Rev. Charles Wesley. (1708-1788.)

492 "By His Spirit that dwelleth in you." **C. M.**
Mat. ix. 14, 15. Eph. i. 13, 14. Isa. xl. 27-31.

1 WHY should the children of a King
  Go mourning all their days?
  Great Comforter, descend and bring
  Some tokens of Thy grace.

2 Dost Thou not dwell in all the saints,
  And seal the heirs of heaven?
  When wilt Thou banish my complaints,
  And show my sins forgiven?

3 Assure my conscience of her part
  In the Redeemer's blood;
  And bear Thy witness with my heart
  That I am born of God.

4 Thou art the Earnest of His love,
  The Pledge of joys to come;
  And Thy soft wings, celestial Dove,
  Will safe convey me home.
  Rev. Isaac Watts. (1674-1748.)

493 "The Spirit searcheth all things." **C. M.**
John iv. 24. Acts v. 1-11. Ps. cxxxix.

1 GOD is a Spirit, just and wise;
  He sees our inmost mind;
  In vain to heaven we raise our cries,
  And leave our hearts behind.

2 Lord, search my thoughts, and try my ways,
  And make my soul sincere;
  Then shall I stand before Thy face,
  And find acceptance there.
  Rev. Isaac Watts.

"I will arise and go to my father."

494 "In the presence of God for us." 7, 6.
Mat. xxvii. 26-50. Heb. ii. 9-18. Isa. liii. 12.

1 O BLESSÉD feet of Jesus,
  Weary with seeking me,
  Stand at God's bar of judgment,
  And intercede for me.
  O hands that were extended
  Upon the awful tree,
  Hold up those precious nail-prints
  Which intercede for me.

2 O side from whence the spear-point
  Brought blood and water free,
  For healing and for cleansing,
  Now intercede for me.
  O head so deeply piercéd
  With thorns which sharpest be,
  Bend low before Thy Father,
  And intercede for me.

3 O sacred heart, such sorrows
  This world may never see,
  As those which are Thy warrant
  To intercede for me.
  O loving, risen Saviour,
  From death and sorrow free,
  Though throned in endless glory,
  Still intercede for me.

Miss Margaret E. Winslow. (1836-.)

495 "He bare the sin of many." 7.
John xix. 17. Col. i. 9-20. Isa. liii. 14, 15.

1 WHITHER, with this crushing load,
  Over Salem's dismal road,
  All Thy body suffering so,
  O my God, where dost Thou go?

  Whither, Jesus, goest Thou?
  Son of God, what doest Thou?
  On this city's "Dolorous Way,"
  With that cross, O Sufferer, say!

2 Tell me, fainting, dying Lord,
  Dost Thou of Thine own accord
  Bear this cross; or did Thy foes,
  'Gainst Thy will, this load impose?

3 Patient Sufferer! how can I
  See Thee faint, and fall, and die;
  Galled, and pressed, and crushed, and ground,
  By this cross upon Thee bound?

4 Trembling arm and staggering limb,
  Visage marred, eyes dark and dim;
  Tongue all parched, and faint at heart,
  Bruised and sore in every part.

Vedanayagam, a Tamil Christian. 1774.
Tr. by Rev. Edward Webb. (1819-.)

496 "I will pray the Father." L. M.
1 John i. 1 to ii. 2. Heb. vii. 19-28. Ezra ix. 5-15.

1 O THOU, the contrite sinner's Friend,
  Who, loving, lov'st them to the end!
  On this alone my hopes depend,
  That Thou wilt plead for me, for me.

2 When, weary in the Christian race,
  Far off appears my resting-place,
  And, fainting, I mistrust Thy grace,
  Then, Saviour, plead for me, for me.

3 When I have erred and gone astray,
  Afar from Thine and wisdom's way,
  And see no glimmering guiding ray,
  Still, Saviour, plead for me, for me.

4 When Satan, by my sins made bold,
  Strives from Thy cross to loose my hold,
  Then, with Thy pitying arms, enfold,
  And plead, O plead for me, for me.

5 When the full light of heavenly day
  Reveals my sins in dread array,
  Say Thou hast washed them all away;
  O say Thou plead'st for me, for me.

Miss Charlotte Elliott. (1789-1871.)

497 "My God will hear me." 7, 8. P.
Rev. iii. 20-22. John xx. 19-29. Cant. v. 2.

1 LISTEN, listen, He is there,
  Knocking, knocking, worn with care:
  'T is the kingly One, the Stranger,
  He who came from glory down;
  Cradled once in Bethl'em's manger,
  Wearing now of thorns a crown.

2 Listen, listen, thee He seeks;
  Knocking, knocking; yes, He speaks:
  What, poor soul, dost thou not know Him?
  With night dews His locks are wet;
  Surely, thou wilt kindness show Him;
  What thou ow'st dost thou forget?

3 Listen, listen, at the door,
  Knocking, knocking, o'er and o'er:
  "Sinner, sinner, long I've sought thee!"
  This He says to you and me.
  "On the cross, with blood I've bought thee,
  Wilt thou not my follower be?"

4 Listen, listen, still the same;
  Knocking, knocking, 't was thy name;
  Hark His accents, soft and tender!
  Yes, I will unbar the door:
  Enter, I make full surrender;
  Reign within me, evermore.

Rev. Jeremiah E. Rankin. (1828-.)

"He restoreth my soul."

498 "Neither is there salvation in any other." **C. M.**
John vi. 66–69. Luke vii. 36–50. Ps. cvi. 43–48

1 WHEN, wounded sore, the stricken soul
   Lies bleeding and unbound,
   One only hand, a piercéd hand,
   Can salve the sinner's wound.

2 When sorrow swells the laden breast,
   And tears of anguish flow,
   One only heart, a broken heart,
   Can feel the sinner's woe.

3 When penitence has wept in vain
   Over some foul, dark spot,
   One only stream, a stream of blood,
   Can wash away the blot.

4 'T is Jesus' blood that washes white,
   His hand that brings relief;
   His heart that's touched with all our joys,
   And feeleth for our grief.

5 Lift up Thy bleeding hand, O Lord,
   Unseal that cleansing tide;
   We have no shelter from our sin
   But in Thy wounded side.
                Mrs. Cecil F. Alexander. (1823–.)

499 "Not by works... which we have done." **7.**
Titus iii. 4–7. Eph. ii. 4–22. Isa. lxiii. 7 to lxiv. 8.

1 CHOSEN not for good in me,
   Wakened up from wrath to flee,
   Hidden in the Saviour's side,
   By the Spirit sanctified,
   Teach me, Lord, on earth to show,
   By my love, how much I owe.

2 Oft I walk beneath the cloud,
   Dark as midnight's gloomy shroud;
   But, when fear is at the height,
   Jesus comes, and all is light:
   Blesséd Jesus, bid me show
   Doubting saints how much I owe.

3 When in flowery path I tread,
   Oft by sin I 'm captive led;
   Oft I fall, but still arise;
   Jesus comes, the tempter flies:
   Bless'd Saviour, bid me show
   Weary sinners all I owe.

4 Oft the nights of sorrow reign,
   Weeping, sickness, sighing, pain;
   But a night Thine anger burns,
   Morning comes, and joy returns:
   God of comforts, bid me show
   To Thy poor how much I owe.
                Rev. Robert M. McCheyne. (1813–1843.)

500 "Thou savest me from violence." **C. M.**
Mark xv. 33–39. Isa. liii. Acts ii. 36–47

1 ALAS, and did my Saviour bleed,
   And did my Sovereign die?
   Would He devote that sacred head
   For such a worm as I?

2 Was it for crimes that I had done
   He groaned upon the tree?
   Amazing pity, grace unknown,
   And love beyond degree!

3 Well might the sun in darkness hide,
   And shut his glories in,
   When Christ, the mighty Maker, died
   For man, the creature's sin.

4 Thus might I hide my blushing face,
   While His dear cross appears:
   Dissolve, my heart, in thankfulness,
   And melt, mine eyes, to tears.

5 But drops of grief can ne'er repay
   The debt of love I owe:
   Here, Lord, I give myself away;
   'T is all that I can do.
                Rev. Isaac Watts. (1674–1748.)

501 "Thou hast delivered my soul from death." **7. 6. 8.**
Ps. lxxxv. Luke xxii. 54–62. John xxi. 15–17.

1 LORD, and is Thine anger gone,
   And art Thou pacified?
   After all that I have done,
   Dost Thou no longer chide?
   Let Thy love my heart constrain,
   And all my restless passions sway;
   Keep me, lest I turn again
   Out of the narrow way.

2 See my utter helplessness,
   And leave me not alone;
   O preserve in perfect peace,
   And seal me for Thine own.
   More and more Thyself reveal,
   Thy presence let me always find;
   Comfort, and confirm, and heal,
   My feeble, sin-sick mind.

3 As the apple of Thine eye,
   Thy weakest servant keep;
   Help me at Thy feet to lie,
   And there forever weep.
   Tears of joy mine eyes o'erflow,
   That I have any hope of heaven;
   Much of love I ought to know,
   For I have much forgiven.
                Rev. Charles Wesley. (1708–1788.)

"The Lord hath chastened me sore."

502 "I besought the Lord thrice." **L. M.**
2 Cor. xii. 1-10. Job i. Prov. iii. 11, 12.

1 I ASKED the Lord that I might grow
  In faith, and love, and every grace ;
Might more of His salvation know,
  And seek more earnestly His face.
'T was He who taught me thus to pray,
  And He, I trust, has answered prayer;
But it has been in such a way
  As almost drove me to despair.

2 I hoped that in some favored hour,
  At once He 'd answer my request,
And, by His love's constraining power,
  Subdue my sins, and give me rest.
Instead of this, He made me feel
  The hidden evils of my heart,
And let the angry powers of hell
  Assault my soul in every part.

3 "Lord, why is this ?" I trembling cried.
  "Wilt Thou pursue Thy worm to death ?"
" 'T is in this way," the Lord replied,
  " I answer prayer for grace and faith.
These inward trials I employ,
  From self and pride to set thee free ;
And break thy schemes of earthly joy,
  That thou mayst seek thine all in me."
Rev. John Newton. (1725-1807.)

503 "I was dumb . . . because Thou didst it." **S. M.**
Job ii. 1-10. 1 Sam. iii. 11-18. Heb. xii. 3-11.

1 IT is Thy hand, my God,
  My sorrow comes from Thee ;
I bow beneath Thy chastening rod,
  'T is love that bruises me.

2 I would not murmur, Lord,
  Before Thee I am dumb ;
Lest I should breathe one murmuring word,
  To Thee for help I come.

3 My God, Thy name is Love ;
  A Father's hand is Thine ;
With tearful eyes I look above,
  And cry, "Thy will be mine !"

4 I know Thy will is right,
  Though it may seem severe ;
Thy path is still unsullied light,
  Though dark it may appear.

5 Here my poor heart can rest ;
  My God, it cleaves to Thee ;
Thy will is love, Thine end is best,
  All work for good to me.
James G. Deck. (1806.-)

504 "Lord, save us ; we perish." **C. M.**
John vi. 66-69. Mat. xiv. 14-33. Ps. xlvi.

1 JESUS, in sickness and in pain
  Be near to succor me,
My sinking spirit still sustain ;
  To Thee I turn, to Thee.

2 When cares and sorrows thicken round,
  And nothing bright I see,
In Thee alone can help be found ;
  To Thee I turn, to Thee.

3 Should strong temptations fierce assail,
  As if to ruin me,
Then in Thy strength will I prevail,
  While still I turn to Thee.

4 Through all my pilgrimage below,
  Whate'er my lot may be,
In joy or sadness, weal or woe,
  Jesus, I 'll turn to Thee.
Rev. Thomas H. Gallaudet. (1789-1851.)

505 "In all points tempted like as we." **L. M.**
Heb. ii. 14-18. John xi. 11-38. Isa. xlii. 1-7.

1 MY sufferings all to Thee are known,
  Tempted in every point like me ;
Regard my grief, regard Thine own ;
  Jesus, remember Calvary !

2 Art Thou not touched with human woe ?
  Hath pity left the Son of man ?
Dost Thou not all my sorrows know,
  And claim a share in all my pain ?

3 Thou wilt not break a bruiséd reed,
  Or quench the smallest spark of grace,
Till through the soul Thy power is spread,
  Thy all-victorious righteousness.
Rev. Charles Wesley. (1708-1788.)

506 "Be merciful unto me, and raise me up." **S. M.**
Mat. ix. Isa. xli. 10-14. 2 Kings iv. 8-37.

1 FEAR not, poor weary one,
  But struggle bravely yet ;
Toil on until thy task is done,
  Until thy sun is set.

2 Though many are thy cares,
  And many are thy fears,
The loving Christ thy burden shares,
  And wipes away thy tears.

3 No distant Christ is He,
  And one that doth not know ;
But watches close and constantly
  The path which thou dost go.

4 'T is when thy heart is tried,
  'T is in thine hour of grief,
He standeth ever at thy side,
  And ever brings relief.
Rev. Thomas C. Upham. (1799-1872.)

"The Lord hath chastened me sore."

507 "God...giveth strength and power." S. M.
John xv. 1-11. Isa. xxvi. 20. Rom. iii. 21-26.

1 MAN'S wisdom is to seek
  His strength in God alone ;
  And ev'n an angel would be weak
  Who trusted in his own.

2 Retreat beneath His wings,
  And in His grace confide:
  This more exalts the King of kings
  Than all your works beside.

3 In Jesus is our store ;
  Grace issues from His throne ;
  Whoever says, "I want no more,"
  Confesses he has none.
  William Cowper. (1731-1800.)

508 "The Lord shall guide thee." 8.
Ps. xxxvii. Luke xii. 22-34. Job xxii. 21-30.

1 LEAVE God to order all thy ways,
  And hope in Him, whate'er betide ;
  Thou'lt find Him in the evil days
  Thy all-sufficient Strength and Guide.
  Who trusts in God's unchanging love
  Builds on the Rock that naught can move.

2 What can these anxious cares avail,
  These never-ceasing moans and sighs ;
  What can it help us to bewail
  Each painful moment as it flies ?
  Our cross and trials do but press
  The heavier for our bitterness.

3 Only thy restless heart keep still,
  And wait in cheerful hope ; content
  To take whate'er His gracious will,
  His all-discerning love, hath sent.
  Doubt not our inmost wants are known
  To Him who chose us for His own.

4 He knows when joyful hours are best,
  He sends them as He sees it meet ;
  When thou hast borne the fiery test,
  And art made free from all deceit,
  He comes to thee all unaware,
  And makes thee own His loving care.
  George Neumarck. (1021-1081.)

509 "Your heavenly Father knoweth." L. M.
Phil. iv. 6. Prov. xvi. 1-9. Isa. xxxviii.

1 HAST thou within a care so deep,
  It chases from thine eyelids sleep ?
  Implore the Lord that naught may be
  A shade between Himself and thee.

2 Whate'er the care that breaks thy rest,
  Whate'er the wish that swells thy breast,
  Spread before God that wish, that care,
  And change anxiety to prayer.
  Author unknown.

510 "And He healed them all." 8. 7.
Isa. lv. 1-3. Ps. ciii. Mat. xi. 28-30.

1 COME to Jesus ! Are you lonely ?
  Solace sweet will He afford.
  Lean on Jesus, Jesus only ;
  Come and find a loving Lord.

2 He is waiting ; will you leave Him
  Pleading at your heart in vain ?
  He is willing, O believe Him !
  He may never call again.

3 Are you sick ? His word can heal you ;
  Are you weary with the strife ?
  Are you hungry ? He can fill you
  With the heavenly bread of life.

4 Come, O come this day, and try it!
  Jesus' words are proved and true ;
  Take His gift, you cannot buy it ;
  He has waited long for you.
  Miss Anna Shipton.

511 "Why art thou cast down, O my soul?" 8. 7.
Isa. l. 5-10. Ps. xlii. Heb. x. 32-39.

1 O MY soul, what means this sadness ?
  Wherefore art thou thus cast down ?
  Let thy griefs be turned to gladness,
  Bid thy restless fears begone.

2 Though ten thousand ills beset thee,
  From without and from within,
  Jesus saith He'll ne'er forget thee,
  But will save from hell and sin.

3 Though distresses now attend thee,
  And thou tread'st the thorny road,
  His right hand shall still defend thee ;
  Soon He'll bring thee home to God.
  Rev. John Fawcett. (1739-1817.)

512 "The Lord is my light and my salvation." 7. 6.
Ps. xxvii. Ex. xv. 1-18. Mat. vi. 25-34.

1 GOD is my strong Salvation ;
  What foe have I to fear ?
  In darkness and temptation,
  My Light, my Help, is near.
  Though hosts encamp around me,
  Firm to the fight I stand ;
  What terror can confound me,
  With God at my right hand ?

2 Place on the Lord reliance ;
  My soul, with courage wait ;
  His truth be thine affiance,
  When faint and desolate.
  His might thy heart shall strengthen,
  His love thy joy increase ;
  Mercy thy days shall lengthen ;
  The Lord will give thee peace.
  James Montgomery. (1771-1854.)

"The Lord hath chastened me sore."

513 "Lead me to the Rock that is higher than I." **C. M.**
Isa. xxvi. 1–12.   Ps. cxviii.   Acts xx. 24.

1 IN time of fear, when trouble's near,
   I look to Thine abode;
Though helpers fail, and foes prevail,
   I'll put my trust in God.

2 And what is life, 'mid toil and strife?
   What terror has the grave?
Thine arm of power, in peril's hour,
   The trembling soul will save.

3 In darkest skies, though storms arise,
   I will not be dismayed;
O God of light and boundless might,
   My soul on Thee is stayed.

Thomas Hastings. (1784-1872.)

514 "When my heart is overwhelmed." **S. M.**
Ps. lxi.   Mal. iii. 16–18.   2 Cor. i. 3–10.

1 WHEN, overwhelmed with grief,
   My heart within me dies,
Helpless, and far from all relief,
   To heaven I lift mine eyes.

2 O lead me to the Rock
   That's high above my head,
And make the covert of Thy wings
   My shelter and my shade.

3 Within Thy presence, Lord,
   Forever I'll abide;
Thou art the Tower of my defence,
   The Refuge where I hide.

4 Thou givest me the lot
   Of those that fear Thy name;
If endless life be their reward,
   I shall possess the same.

Rev. Isaac Watts. (1674-1748.)

515 "Himself likewise took part in the same." **C. M.**
Ps. lxxxvi.   Heb. v. 1–9.   Mat. xv. 32–39.

1 THERE is no sorrow, Lord, too light
   To bring in prayer to Thee;
There is no anxious care too slight
   To wake Thy sympathy.

2 Thou who hast trod the thorny road
   Wilt share each small distress;
The love which bore the greater load
   Will not refuse the less.

3 There is no secret sigh we breathe
   But meets Thine ear divine;
And every cross grows light beneath
   The shadow, Lord, of Thine.

4 Life's ills without, sin's strife within,
   The heart would overflow, .
But for that love which died for sin,
   That love which wept with woe.

Mrs. Jane F. Crewdson. (1800-1863.)

516 "I would seek unto God." **8. 6. 8.**
1 Sam. iii. 11–18.   Job i. 13–22.   James i. 1–12.

1 WHEN I can trust my all with God,
   In trial's fearful hour,
Bow, all resigned, beneath His rod,
   And bless His sparing power,
A joy springs up amid distress,
A fountain in the wilderness.

2 O to be brought to Jesus' feet,
   Though sorrows fix me there,
Is still a privilege; and sweet
   The energies of prayer,
Though sighs and tears its language be,
If Christ be nigh, and smile on me.

3 Then, blessèd be the hand that gave;
   Still blessèd when it takes;
Blessèd be He who smites to save,
   Who heals the heart He breaks:
Perfect and true are all His ways,
Whom heaven adores, and death obeys.

Josiah Conder. (1789-1855.)

517 "God is a refuge." **S. M.**
Ps. xlvi.   Mat. xiv. 12.   Heb. ii. 14–18..

1 IN every trying hour
   My soul to Jesus flies;
I trust in His almighty power
   When swelling billows rise.

2 His comforts bear me up;
   I trust a faithful God;
The sure foundation of my hope
   Is in my Saviour's blood.

Author unknown.

518 "For that He . . . is compassed with infirmity." **8.**
Heb. iv. 14–16.   John xi. 11–38.   Ps. cix. 21–31.

1 WHEN gathering clouds around I view,
And days are dark, and friends are few,
On Him I lean who not in vain
Experienced every human pain;
He sees my wants, allays my fears,
And counts and treasures up my tears.

2 When sorrowing o'er some stone I bend,
Which covers what was once a friend,
And from his voice, his hand, his smile,
Divides me for a little while,
Thou, Saviour, mark'st the tears I shed,
For Thou didst weep o'er Lazarus dead.

3 And O, when I have safely past
Through every conflict but the last,
Still, still unchanging, watch beside
My painful bed, for Thou hast died;
Then point to realms of cloudless day,
And wipe the latest tear away.

Sir Robert Grant. (1785-1838.)

"The Lord hath chastened me sore."

519 "Look upon mine affliction." 8, 7.
Ps. xliii. 1 Cor. x. 13. 2 Cor. i. 1-10.

1 GOD of mercy and compassion,
    Look with pity on my pain ;
  Hear a mournful, broken spirit
    Prostrate at Thy feet complain.
  Many are my foes, and mighty ;
    Strength to conquer I have none ;
  Nothing can uphold my goings,
    But Thy blessèd self alone.

2 Saviour, look on Thy belovèd,
    Triumph over all my foes ;
  Turn to heavenly joy my mourning,
    Turn to gladness all my woes.
  Live or die, or work or suffer,
    Let my weary soul abide,
  In all changes whatsoever,
    Sure and steadfast by Thy side.
                                    Author unknown.

520 "O my Father,... Thy will be done." 8, 6.
Luke xxii. 39-43. Acts xxi. 10-14. Ps. cxix. 81-88.

1 "FATHER, Thy will, not mine, be done!"
  So prayed on earth Thy suffering Son,
      So in His name I pray :
  The spirit fails, the flesh is weak ;
  Thy help in agony I seek ;
      O take the cup away.

2 If such be not Thy sovereign will,
  Thy wiser purpose then fulfil ;
      My wishes I resign :
  Into Thy hands my soul commend,
  On Thee for life or death depend ;
      Thy will be done, not mine.
                    James Montgomery. (1771-1854.)

521 "Is any ... afflicted? let him pray." L. M.
Ps. ix. Isa. xli. 17-21. Heb. vii. 25-28.

1 GOD of my life, to Thee I call !
  Afflicted, at Thy feet I fall ;
  When the great water-floods prevail,
  Leave not my trembling heart to fail.

2 Friend of the friendless and the faint,
  Where should I lodge my deep complaint ?
  Where but with Thee, whose open door
  Invites the helpless and the poor ?

3 Did ever mourner plead with Thee,
  And Thou refuse that mourner's plea ?
  Does not the word still fixed remain
  That none shall seek Thy face in vain ?

4 Poor though I am, despised, forgot,
  Yet God, my God, forgets me not ;
  And he is safe, and must succeed,
  For whom the Lord vouchsafes to plead.
                    William Cowper. (1731-1800.)

522 "I stretch forth my hands unto Thee." 7, 6.
Ps. xxxv. Jer. xvi. 19. John xvi. 23-33.

1 IN time of tribulation,
    Hear, Lord, my feeble cries ;
  With humble supplication
    To Thee my spirit flies.
  My heart with grief is breaking,
    Scarce can my heart complain ;
  Mine eyes, with tears kept waking,
    Still watch and weep in vain.

2 Hath God cast off forever ?
    Can time His truth impair ?
  His tender mercy never
    Shall I presume to share ?
  Hath He His loving-kindness
    Shut up in endless wrath ?
  No ; this is mine own blindness,
    That cannot see His path.

3 I call to recollection
    The years of His right hand,
  And, strong in His protection,
    Again through faith I stand.
  Through the wild sea Thou leddest
    Thy chosen flock of yore ;
  Still on the waves Thou treadest,
    And Thy redeemed pass o'er.
                                James Montgomery.

523 "Thou art my hiding-place." C. M.
Ps. lxxvii. Job xxiii. Luke viii. 22-56.

1 DEAR Refuge of my weary soul,
    On Thee, when sorrows rise,
  On Thee, when waves of trouble roll,
    My fainting hope relies.

2 To Thee I tell each rising grief,
    For Thou alone canst heal ;
  Thy word can bring a sweet relief
    For every pain I feel.

3 But O, when gloomy doubts prevail,
    I fear to call Thee mine ;
  The springs of comfort seem to fail,
    And all my hopes decline.

4 Yet, gracious God, where shall I flee ?
    Thou art my only trust :
  And still my soul would cleave to Thee,
    Though prostrate in the dust.

5 Thy mercy-seat is open still ;
    Here let my soul retreat,
  With humble hope attend Thy will,
    And wait beneath Thy feet.
                        Miss Anne Steele. (1717-1778.)

"Comforted of God."

524 "Peace I leave with you." 6. 4.
John xiv. 27-31. Rom. v. 1-11. Isa. lvii. 15-19.

1 PEACE, peace, I leave with you,
My peace I give to you;
Trust to my care!
Thus the Redeemer said,
And bowed His sacred head,
Lone in the garden shade,
Wrestling in prayer.

2 Peace, peace, I leave with you,
My peace I give to you,
Perfect and pure;
Not as the world doth give,
Words that the soul deceive;
Ye who in me believe
Shall rest secure.

3 Peace, peace, I leave with you,
My peace I give to you,
Though foes invade;
All power is given to me,
I will your refuge be,
Now and eternally;
Be not dismayed!

Thomas Hastings. (1784-1872.)

525 "I will not leave you comfortless." 6.
Gen. xxviii. 10-22. Ex. iii. 1-12. Mat. xxviii. 20.

1 ALONE! yet not alone,
For Thou, my God, art nigh;
Thou wilt not leave Thy child
In this lone desert wild,
Alone, for Thee to sigh.

2 Alone! yet not alone,
With Jesus by my side:
"I love thee," hear Him say;
"I'm with thee day by day,
And shall with thee abide."

3 Alone! yet not alone;
The Comforter has come;
He fills my heart with peace,
Bids every trouble cease,
And gently guides me home.

Author unknown.

526 "Wait thou only upon God." L. M.
Ps. lxii. Jer. xxx. 7-22. 1 Cor. i. 30, 31.

1 MY soul, for help on God rely,
On Him alone thy trust repose:
My Rock and Health will strength supply,
To bear the shock of all my foes.

2 God does His saving health dispense,
And flowing blessings daily send;
He is my Fortress and Defence,
On Him my soul shall still depend.

Tate and Brady. 1696.

527 "In returning and rest ye shall be saved." 8. 5. 3.
Isa. l. 10. Mat. xi. 28-30. Job xxxiii.

1 ART thou weary, art thou languid,
Art thou sore distrest?
"Come to me," saith One, "and, coming,
Be at rest!"

2 Hath He marks to lead me to Him,
If He be my guide?
"In His feet and hands are wound-prints,
And His side."

3 Is there diadem, as monarch,
That His brow adorns?
"Yea, a crown in very surety,
But of thorns!"

4 If I still hold closely to Him,
What hath He at last?
"Sorrow vanquished, labor ended,
Jordan past!"

5 If I ask Him to receive me,
Will He say me nay?
"Not till earth and not till heaven
Pass away!"

Stephen of St. Sabas. (72?-794.)
Tr. by Rev. John M. Neale. (1818-1866.)

528 "The Lord will bless His people with peace." C. M.
Ps. xxix. 1 Kings xix. 1-18. Acts xxvii. 1-25.

1 UNITE, my roving thoughts, unite,
In silence soft and sweet;
And thou, my soul, sit gently down
At Thy great Sovereign's feet.

2 Jehovah's awful voice is heard,
Yet gladly I attend;
For, lo, the everlasting God
Proclaims Himself my Friend.

3 Harmonious accents to my soul
The sounds of peace convey;
The tempest at His word subsides,
And winds and seas obey.

Rev. Philip Doddridge. (1702-1751.)

529 "Goodness and mercy shall follow me." C. M.
2 Cor. i. 1-4. 2 Sam. xii. 16-23. Neh. ix. 7-31.

1 AND can my heart aspire so high,
To say, "My Father, God!"
Lord, at Thy feet I fain would lie,
And learn to kiss the rod.

2 I would submit to all Thy will,
For Thou art good and wise;
Let every anxious thought be still,
Nor one faint murmur rise.

3 Thy love can cheer the darksome gloom,
And bid me wait serene,
Till hopes and joys immortal bloom,
And brighten all the scene.

Miss Anne Steele. (1717-1778.)

"Comforted of God."

530 "Who comforteth us in all our tribulation." S. M.
Ps. xlvi. Jer. xvii. 7–14. John vi. 68, 69.

1 THOU very present Aid
In suffering and distress,
The soul which still on Thee is stayed
Is kept in perfect peace.
The soul by faith reclined
On the Redeemer's breast,
'Midst raging storms exults to find
An everlasting rest.

2 Sorrow and fear are gone,
Whene'er Thy face appears ;
It stills the sighing orphan's moan,
And dries the widow's tears.
It hallows every cross ;
It sweetly comforts me ;
And makes me now forget my loss,
And lose myself in Thee.

3 Jesus, to whom I fly,
Doth all my wishes fill ;
In vain the creature streams are dry,
I have the Fountain still.
Stripped of my earthly friends,
I find them all in One,
And peace, and joy that never ends,
And heaven, in Christ alone.
Rev. Charles Wesley. (1708–1788.)

531 "Light is sown for the righteous." L. M.
Ps. lxxiii. 13–28. Dan. ix. 4–10. James i. 16–25.

1 WHEN darkness long has veiled my mind,
And smiling day once more appears,
Then, my Redeemer, then I find
The folly of my doubts and fears.

2 Straight I upbraid my wandering heart,
And blush that I should ever be
Thus prone to act so base a part,
Or harbor one hard thought of Thee.

3 O let me then at length be taught,
What I am still so slow to learn,
That God is love, and changes not,
Nor knows the shadow of a turn.

4 Sweet truth, and easy to repeat !
But when my faith is sharply tried,
I find myself a learner yet,
Unskilful, weak, and apt to slide.

5 But O my Lord, one look from Thee
Subdues the disobedient will ;
Drives doubt and discontent away,
And Thy rebellious worm is still.
William Cowper. (1731–1800.)

532 "Afterward ... the peaceable fruit." L. M.
Rom. v. 1–11. Heb. xii. 1–11. Prov. iii. 1–13.

1 I BLESS Thee, Lord, for sorrows sent
To break the dream of human power ;
For now my shallow cistern's spent,
I find Thy fount, and thirst no more.

2 I take Thy hand, and fears grow still ;
Behold Thy face, and doubts remove ;
Who would not yield his wavering will
To perfect truth and boundless love ?

3 That truth gives promise of a dawn,
Beneath whose light I am to see,
When all these blinding vails are drawn,
This was the wisest path for me.

4 That love this restless soul doth teach
The strength of Thy eternal calm ;
And tune its sad and broken speech,
To sing e'en now the angels' psalm.
Author unknown.

533 "The Lord is ... my fortress." L. M.
Ps. xci. Jer. xx. 10–13. Phil. iv. 12–20.

1 HE that hath made his refuge God
Shall find a most secure abode ;
Shall walk all day beneath His shade,
And there, at night, shall rest his head.

2 Then will I say, " My God, Thy power
Shall be my fortress and my tower ;
I, that am formed of feeble dust,
Make Thine almighty arm my trust."
Rev. Isaac Watts. (1674–1748.)

534 "He leadeth me." L. M.
Ps. xxiii. Neh. ix. 7–20. John x. 1–16.

1 HE leadeth me, O blessèd thought,
O words with heavenly comfort fraught ;
Whate'er I do, where'er I be,
Still 't is God's hand that leadeth me.
He leadeth me, He leadeth me,
By His own hand He leadeth me ;
His faithful follower I would be,
For by His hand He leadeth me.

2 Sometimes 'mid scenes of deepest gloom,
Sometimes where Eden's bowers bloom,
By waters still, o'er troubled sea,
Still 't is His hand that leadeth me.

3 Lord, I would clasp Thy hand in mine,
Nor ever murmur nor repine ;
Content, whatever lot I see,
Since 't is my God that leadeth me.

4 And when my task on earth is done,
When, by Thy grace the victory's won,
E'en death's cold wave I will not flee,
Since God through Jordan leadeth me.
Rev. Joseph H. Gilmore. (1834–.)

"Comforted of God."

535 "As many as I love I rebuke and chasten." **12. 11.**
Phil. iii. 4-14. Acts xxvi. 4-29. Ps. ciii. 1-18. 2 Sam. xxiii. 1-5.

1 O SAVIOUR, whose mercy, severe in its kindness,
   Hath chastened my wanderings, and guided my way,
  Adored be the power that hath pitied my blindness,
   And weaned me from phantoms that smiled to betray.

2 I thought that the course of the pilgrim to heaven
   Would be bright as the summer, and glad as the morn,
  Thou showedst me the path ; it was dark and uneven ;
   All rugged with rock, and all tangled with thorn.

3 Subdued and instructed, at length, to Thy will,
   My hopes and my wishes, my all, I resign ;
  O give me a heart that can wait and be still,
   Nor know of a wish or a pleasure but Thine.
                                       Sir Robert Grant. (1785-1838.)

536 "In everything give thanks." **11. 12.**
Heb. xii. 6-11. 2 Cor. xii. 1-10. Ps. cxviii. Job i. 13 to ii. 10.

1 FOR what shall I praise Thee, my God and my King,
  For what blessings the tribute of gratitude bring ?
  Shall I praise Thee for pleasure, for health, or for ease,
  For the sunshine of youth, for the garden of peace ?

2 For this I should praise ; but if only for this,
  I should leave half untold the donation of bliss :
  I thank Thee for sickness, for sorrow and care,
  For the thorns I have gathered, the anguish I bear ;

3 For nights of anxiety, watching, and tears,
  A present of pain, a prospective of fears ;
  I praise Thee, I bless Thee, my Lord and my God,
  For the good and the evil Thy hand hath bestowed.
                                    Mrs. Caroline F. Wilson. (1787-1846.)

537 "My heart shall not fear." **12. 11.**
Ps. lvi. Deu. xxxiii. 26-29. 1 Cor. xv. 20-28. Acts xx. 25.

1 WHILE Thou, O my God, art my Help and Defender,
   No cares can o'erwhelm me, no terrors appall ;
  The wiles and the snares of this world will but render
   More lively my hope in my God and my All.

2 Yes, Thou art my Refuge in sorrow and danger,
   My Strength when I suffer, my Hope when I fall,
  My Comfort and Joy in this land of the stranger,
   My Treasure, my Glory, my God, and my All.

3 To Thee, dearest Lord, will I turn without ceasing,
   Though grief may oppress me, or sorrow befall,
  And love Thee till death, my blest spirit releasing,
   Secures to me Jesus, my God and my All.
                                          Rev. William Young. (-1757.)

538 "The Lamb . . . shall lead them." **11. 10.**
Ps. xxiii. Jer. xxiii. 1-6. Heb. xiii. 20, 21. 2 Tim. iv. 6-8.

1 THE Lord is my Shepherd : He makes me repose
  Where the pastures in beauty are growing ;
  He leads me afar from the world and its woes,
  Where in peace the still waters are flowing.

2 He strengthens my spirit ; He shows me the path
  Where the arms of His love shall enfold me ;
  And when I walk through the dark valley of death,
  His rod and His staff will uphold me.
                                                       Knox.

"Comforted of God."

539 "Thy mercy, O Lord, endureth." C. M.
Prov. iii. 1–12. Heb. xii. 1–11. Rom v 1–5.

1 O THOU whose mercy guides my way,
   Though now it seems severe,
Forbid my unbelief to say
   There is no mercy here.

2 O grant me to desire the pain,
   That comes in kindness down,
More than the world's supremest gain,
   Succeeded by a frown.

3 Then, though Thou bend my spirit low,
   Love only shall I see;
The very hand that strikes the blow
   Was wounded once for me.
            James Edmeston. (1791–1857.)

540 "Thy loving-kindness is before mine eyes." 6.
Mark x. 28–31. Mat. iv. 18–22. Josh. xlv. 6–15.

1 MY Jesus, as Thou wilt!
   O may Thy will be mine!
Into Thy hand of love
   I would my all resign.
Through sorrow or through joy,
   Conduct me as Thine own,
And help me still to say,
   My Lord, Thy will be done!

2 My Jesus, as Thou wilt!
   All shall be well for me;
Each changing future scene
   I gladly trust with Thee.
Straight to my home above
   I travel calmly on,
And sing, in life or death,
   My Lord, Thy will be done!
            Rev. Benjamin Schmolke. (1672–1737.)
            Tr. by Miss Jane Borthwick. (1825–.)

541 "Wherefore doth a living man complain?" L. M.
James i. 1–12. Mal. iii. 1–4. Ps. lxxvii.

1 WHY should I murmur or repine,
   O Lamb of God, who bled for me?
What are my griefs compared with Thine,
   Thy tears, Thy groans, Thine agony?

2 If Thou the furnace dost employ,
   Thou sittest as refiner near,
To purge away the base alloy,
   Till Thine own image bright appear.

3 Though oft Thy way is in the sea,
   Thy footsteps in the wingéd storm;
Though crested billows threaten me,
   Love slumbers in their frowning form.

4 Submissive would I kiss the rod,
   Needful each stroke I humbly own:
Help me to trust Thee, O my God,
   If now Thy wisdom be unknown.
            Author unknown.

542 "All things are of God." C. M.
Ps. xxxi. Job v. 1–16. Phil iii. 7–21.

1 MY times of sorrow and of joy,
   Great God, are in Thy hand;
My chief enjoyments come from Thee,
   And go at Thy command.

2 O Lord, shouldst Thou withhold them all,
   Yet would I not repine;
Before they were by me possessed,
   They were entirely Thine.

3 Nor would I drop a murmuring word,
   If all the world were gone,
But seek substantial happiness
   In Thee, and Thee alone.
            Rev. Benjamin Beddome. (1717–1795.)

543 "Let Him do what seemeth Him good." C. M.
Acts xxi. 10–14. 2 Sam. xii. 16–23. Job i. 13–21.

1 ONE prayer I have, all prayers in one,
   When I am wholly Thine:
Thy will, my God, Thy will be done,
   And let that will be mine.

2 All-wise, almighty, and all-good,
   In Thee I firmly trust;
Thy ways, unknown or understood,
   Are merciful and just.

3 May I remember that to Thee
   Whate'er I have I owe;
And back, in gratitude, from me
   May all Thy bounties flow.

4 And though Thy wisdom takes away,
   Shall I arraign Thy will?
No, let me bless Thy name, and say,
   "The Lord is gracious still."
            James Montgomery. (1771–1854.)

544 "Remember me, O my God, for good." C. M.
Neh. xiii. 2 Chr. vi. 24–42. Luke xxiii. 39–43.

1 O THOU from whom all goodness flows,
   I lift my heart to Thee;
In all my sorrows, conflicts, woes,
   Dear Lord, remember me.

2 When groaning on my burdened heart
   My sins lie heavily,
Thy pardon speak, new peace impart;
   In love remember me.

3 Temptations sore obstruct my way,
   And ills I cannot flee;
O give me strength, Lord, as my day;
   For good remember me.

4 Distrest with pain, disease, and grief,
   This feeble body see;
Grant patience, rest, and kind relief;
   Hear and remember me.
            Rev. Thomas Hawels. (1720–1820.)

"Comforted of God."

545 "They looked unto Him, and were lightened." **11.**
Heb. xii. 1-11. Luke xxiv. 13-38. John xiv. 1-3. Ps. xvii.

1 O EYES that are weary and hearts that are sore,
  Look off unto Jesus, now sorrow no more!
  The light of His countenance shineth so bright
  That here, as in heaven, there need be no night.

2 While looking to Jesus, my heart cannot fear;
  I tremble no more when I see Jesus near;
  I know that His presence my safeguard will be,
  For, "Why are you troubled?" He saith unto me.

3 Still looking to Jesus, O may I be found,
  When Jordan's dark waters encompass me round;
  They bear me away in His presence to be;
  I see Him still nearer whom always I see.

4 Then, then shall I know the full beauty and grace
  Of Jesus, my Lord, when I stand face to face;
  Shall know how His love went before me each day,
  And wonder that ever my eyes turned away.
  Author unknown.

546 "God is faithful." **10.**
Luke xxii. 39-46. Acts xx. 17-37. Job i. Ps. xxi.

1 BOWED with a burden none can weigh save Thee,
  Strength of my life, on Thee I cast my care;
  My heart must prove its own infirmity,
  But what shall move me if my God be there?

2 Bright be my prospect as I pass along:
  An ardent service at the cost of all;
  Love by untiring ministry made strong,
  And ready for the first, the softest call.

3 Yes, "God is faithful," and my lot is cast;
  O not myself to serve, my own to be:
  Light of my life, the darkness now is past,
  And I beneath the cross can work for Thee.
  Miss Anna L. Waring. (1820-.)

547 "The voice of joy and the voice of gladness." **12. 8. 9.**
Ps. lxxxiv. Jer. xvii. 7, 8. Rom. v. 1-11. Gal. v. 22-26.

1 I HAVE entered the valley of blessing, so sweet,
  And Jesus abides with me there;
  And His Spirit and blood make my cleansing complete,
  And His perfect love casteth out fear.
      O come to this valley of blessing, so sweet,
        Where Jesus will fulness bestow;
      And believe and receive and confess Him,
        That all His salvation may know.

2 There is peace in the valley of blessing, so sweet,
    And plenty the land doth impart;
  And there's rest for the weary-worn traveller's feet,
    And joy for the sorrowing heart.

3 There's a song in the valley of blessing, so sweet
    That angels would fain join the strain,
  As with rapturous praises we bow at His feet,
    Crying, "Worthy the Lamb that was slain!"
  Mrs. Annie Wittenmeyer. 1868.

"My soul thirsteth for God."

548 "O that I knew where I might find Him!" **C. M.**
Job xxiii. 3-10. Ps lxxvii. John xi 20-32

1 O THAT I knew the secret place
  Where I might find my God !
  I'd spread my wants before His face,
  And pour my woes abroad.

2 He knows what arguments I'd take
  To wrestle with my God :
  I'd plead for His own mercy's sake,
  And for my Saviour's blood.

3 Arise, my soul, from deep distress,
  And banish every fear ;
  He calls thee to His throne of grace,
  To spread thy sorrows there.
  Rev. Isaac Watts. (1674-1748.)

549 "I wait for the Lord ; my soul doth wait." **C. M.**
Ex. xxv. 17-22. Ps. cxix. 41-48. Heb. x.

1 MY God, 't is to Thy mercy-seat
  My soul for shelter flies ;
  'T is here I find a safe retreat,
  When storms and tempests rise.

2 My cheerful hope can never die,
  If Thou, my God, art near ;
  Thy grace can raise my comforts high,
  And banish every fear.

3 My great Protector, and my Lord !
  Thy constant aid impart ;
  And let Thy kind, Thy gracious word
  Sustain my trembling heart.

4 O never let my soul remove
  From this divine retreat ;
  Still let me trust Thy power and love,
  And dwell beneath Thy feet.
  Miss Anne Steele. (1717-1778.)

550 "Search me, O God, and know my heart." **L. M.**
Ps. xliii. 1 Cor. iii. 9-17. Titus ii. 11-14.

1 MY God, permit me not to be
  A stranger to myself and Thee ;
  Amidst a thousand thoughts I rove,
  Forgetful of my highest love.

2 Why should my passions mix with earth,
  And thus debase my heavenly birth ?
  Why should I cleave to things below,
  And let my God, my Saviour, go ?

3 Call me away from flesh and sense ;
  One sovereign word can draw me thence ;
  I would obey the voice divine,
  And all inferior joys resign.

4 Be earth, with all her scenes, withdrawn ;
  Let noise and vanity be gone ;
  In secret silence of the mind,
  My heaven, and there my God, I find.
  Rev. Isaac Watts.

551 "What wilt thou, . . . and what is thy request ?" **7.**
Luke xi. 9-15. Est. v. 1-4. 1 Kings viii. 22-30

1 COME, my soul, thy suit prepare,
  Jesus loves to answer prayer ;
  He Himself has bid thee pray,
  Therefore will not say thee nay.
  Thou art coming to a King,
  Large petitions with thee bring ;
  For His grace and power are such,
  None can ever ask too much.

2 With my burden I begin :
  Lord, remove this load of sin ;
  Let Thy blood, for sinners spilt,
  Set my conscience free from guilt.
  Lord, I come to Thee for rest,
  Take possession of my breast ;
  There Thy blood-bought right maintain,
  And without a rival reign.

3 While I am a pilgrim here,
  Let Thy love my spirit cheer ;
  As my Guide, my Guard, my Friend,
  Lead me to my journey's end.
  Show me what I have to do,
  Every hour my strength renew ;
  Let me live a life of faith,
  Let me die Thy people's death.
  Rev. John Newton. (1725-1807.)

552 "I have longed for Thy salvation." **8. 9.**
Ps. xxv. Heb. vi. Ex. xxxiii. 12-23

1 MY prayer to the promise shall cling,
  I will not give heed to a doubt ;
  For I ask for the one needful thing,
  Which I cannot be happy without :
  A spirit of lowly repose
  In the love of the Lamb that was slain ;
  A heart to be touched with His woes,
  And a care not to grieve Him again ;

2 The peace that my Saviour has bought,
  The cheerfulness nothing can dim ;
  The love that can bring every thought
  Into perfect obedience to Him ;
  The wisdom His mercy to own
  In the way He directs me to take ;
  To glory in Jesus alone,
  And to love and do good for His sake.

3 Thy word has commanded my prayer,
  Thy Spirit has taught me to pray ;
  And all my unholy despair
  Is ready to vanish away.
  All this Thou hast offered to me
  In the promise whereon I will rest ;
  For faith, O my Saviour, in Thee,
  Is the substance of all my request.
  Miss Anna L. Waring. (1820-.)

"My soul thirsteth for God."

553 "Let Thy glory appear." 7.
John xvii. 1-10. Phil. ii. 5-15. Ps. lxvii.

1 FATHER of eternal grace,
  Glorify Thyself in me;
  Meekly beaming in my face,
  May the world Thine image see.

2 Happy only in Thy love,
  Poor, unfriended, or unknown,
  Fix my thoughts on things above,
  Stay my heart on Thee alone.

3 Humble, holy, all resigned
  To Thy will, Thy will be done;
  Give me, Lord, the perfect mind
  Of Thy well-belovéd Son.

4 Counting gain and glory loss,
  May I tread the path He trod;
  Die with Jesus on the cross,
  Rise with Him to Thee, my God!
      James Montgomery. (1771-1854.)

554 "Draw me; we will run after Thee." 8.
Ps. xviii. 16-36. Jer. xxxi. 1-9. Rev. iii. 7-13.

1 O DRAW me, Father, after Thee,
  So shall I run and never tire;
  With gracious words still comfort me;
  Be Thou my hope, my sole desire.
  Free me from every weight; nor fear
  Nor sin can come, if Thou art here.

2 In suffering be Thy love my peace,
  In weakness be Thy love my power;
  And when the storms of life shall cease,
  My God, in that important hour,
  In death as life be Thou my Guide,
  And bear me through death's whelming tide.
      Bp. Christopher Wordsworth. (1837-.)

555 "I will look unto the Lord." C. M.
James i. 17, 18. Acts xvii. 24-28. Isa. xxvi.

1 FATHER, to Thee my soul I lift;
  My soul on Thee depends,
  Convinced that every perfect gift
  From Thee alone descends.

2 Mercy and grace are Thine alone,
  And power and wisdom too;
  Without the Spirit of Thy Son,
  We nothing good can do.

3 Thou all our works in us hast wrought;
  Our good is all divine;
  The praise of every virtuous thought
  And righteous word is Thine.

4 From Thee, through Jesus, we receive
  The power on Thee to call,
  In whom we are, and move, and live;
  Our God is all in all.
      Rev. Charles Wesley. (1708-1788.)

556 "But Thou, Lord, knowest me." L. M.
Ps. cxxxix. Job xxxiv. 21-25. 1 Cor. iv. 5.

1 LORD, Thou hast searched and seen me
       through;
  Thine eye commands with piercing view
  My rising and my resting hours,
  My heart and flesh, with all their powers.

2 My thoughts before they are my own
  Are to my God distinctly known;
  He knows the words I mean to speak
  Ere from my opening lips they break.

3 Within Thy circling power I stand;
  On every side I find Thy hand;
  Awake, asleep, at home, abroad,
  I am surrounded still with God.

4 O may these thoughts possess my breast,
  Where'er I rove, whete'er I rest;
  Nor let my weaker passions dare
  Consent to sin, for God is there.
      Rev. Isaac Watts. (1674-1748.)

557 "Deal bountifully with Thy servant." 8. 6.
Ps. lvii. Acts xxi. 1-14. 2 Cor. vi. 1-10.

1 MY heart is fixed, O God, my Strength,
       My heart is strong to bear;
  I will be joyful in Thy love,
       And peaceful in Thy care.
  Deal with me, for my Saviour's sake,
       According to His prayer.

2 Deep unto deep may call; but I
       With peaceful heart will say,
  Thy loving-kindness has a charge
       No waves can take away;
  And let the storm that speeds me home
       Deal with me as it may!
      Miss Anna L. Waring. (1820-.)

558 "Let me fall now into the hand of the Lord." C. M.
Isa. l. 5-10. 1 Sam. iii. 1-18. Titus ii. 11-14.

1 O LORD, my best desire fulfil,
       And help me to resign
  Life, health, and comfort to Thy will,
       And make Thy pleasure mine.

2 Why should I shrink at Thy command,
       Whose love forbids my fears;
  Or tremble at the gracious hand
       That wipes away my tears?

3 No, let me rather freely yield;
       What most I prize to Thee,
  Who never hast a good withheld,
       Or wilt withhold, from me.

4 Thy favor all my journey through
       Thou art engaged to grant;
  What else I want, or think I do,
       'T is better still to want.
      William Cowper. (1731-1800.)

"My soul thirsteth for God."

559 "Grant me Thy law graciously." L. M.
Luke xi. 1-13. 1 Pet. iv. 12-19. Job ii. 1-10.

1 MY Father, when I come to Thee,
  I would not only bend the knee,
  But with my spirit seek Thy face,
  With my whole heart desire Thy grace.

2 I plead the name of Thy dear Son,
  All He has said, all He has done;
  O may I feel His love for me
  Who died from sin to set me free!

3 To guide me, Lord, be ever nigh;
  My sins forgive, my wants supply;
  With favor crown my youthful days,
  And my whole life shall speak Thy praise.

4 Thy Holy Spirit, Lord, impart;
  Impress Thy likeness on my heart;
  Let me obey Thy truth in love,
  Till raised to dwell with Thee above.

Author unknown.

560 "Thou that liftest me up." S. M.
Ps. xxxvi. 5-10. Isa. xxvi. 1-9. 1 Pet. ii. 1-10.

1 MY God, permit my tongue
  This joy, to call Thee mine;
  And let my early cries prevail
  To taste Thy love divine.

2 In wakeful hours at night
  I call my God to mind;
  I think how wise Thy counsels are,
  And all Thy dealings kind.

3 Since Thou hast been my Help,
  To Thee my spirit flies;
  And on Thy watchful providence
  My cheerful hope relies.

Rev. Isaac Watts. (1674-1748.)

561 "All to the glory of God." S. M.
Col. iii. 1-17. 1 Cor. x. 23-31. Ps. cxli.

1 TEACH me, my God and King,
  In all things Thee to see,
  And what I do in anything,
  To do it as for Thee;

2 To scorn the senses' sway,
  While still to Thee I tend:
  In all I do be Thou the way,
  In all be Thou the end.

3 All may of Thee partake;
  Nothing so small can be
  But draws, when acted for Thy sake,
  Greatness and worth from Thee.

4 If done to obey Thy laws,
  E'en servile labors shine;
  Hallowed is toil, if this the cause,
  The meanest work divine.

Rev. George Herbert. (1593-1632.)

562 "Examine me, O Lord, and prove me" C. M.
Ps. cxlii. 1 Kings iii. 5-15. Phil. iv

1 SEARCHER of hearts, from mine erase
  All thoughts that should not be,
  And in its deep recesses trace
  My gratitude to Thee.

2 Hearer of prayer, O guide aright
  Each word and deed of mine;
  Life's battle teach me how to fight,
  And be the victory Thine.

3 Giver of all, for every good
  In the Redeemer came,
  For raiment, shelter, and for food,
  I thank Thee in His name.

4 Father and Son and Holy Ghost,
  Thou glorious Three in One,
  Thou knowest best what I need most,
  And let Thy will be done.

George P. Morris. (1802-1864.)

563 "Not as I will, but as Thou wilt." 8, 4.
2 Sam. xv. 13-26. Acts xxi. 1-14. John xviii.

1 MY God and Father, while I stray
  Far from my home, on life's rough way,
  O teach me from my heart to say,
  Thy will be done.

2 If but my fainting heart be blest
  With Thy sweet Spirit for its guest,
  My God, to Thee I leave the rest:
  Thy will be done.

3 Renew my will from day to day;
  Blend it with Thine, and take away
  All that now makes it hard to say,
  Thy will be done.

Miss Charlotte Elliott. (1789-1871.)

564 "I will not let Thee go except Thou bless me." 7.
Gen. xxxii. Mark x. 46-52. Luke xviii. 1-14.

1 LORD, I cannot let Thee go
  Till a blessing Thou bestow;
  Do not turn away Thy face,
  Mine's an urgent, pressing case.

2 Once a sinner, near despair,
  Sought Thy mercy-seat by prayer;
  Mercy heard and set him free:
  Lord, that mercy came to me.

3 Thou hast helped in every need,
  This emboldens me to plead;
  After so much mercy past,
  Canst Thou let me sink at last?

4 No; I must maintain my hold;
  'T is Thy goodness makes me bold;
  I can no denial take
  When I plead for Jesus' sake.

Rev. John Newton. (1725-1807.)

"My soul thirsteth for God."

565 "With my soul have I desired Thee."
Ps. lxiii. Isa. xxvi. 1–9. Phil. iii. 7–14.   **6.**

1 I FEEL within a want,
  Forever burning there ;
  What I so thirst for grant,
  O Thou that hearest prayer!

2 This is the thing I crave :
  A likeness to Thy Son ;
  This would I rather have
  Than call the world my own.

3 'T is my most fervent prayer ;
  Be it more fervent still ;
  Be it my highest care,
  Be it my settled will.
                Rev. William H. Furness. (1802–.)

566 "Mine eyes are ever toward the Lord."   **S. M.**
Ps. cxxxix. 1–18. Mark ix. 1–10. John xv. 1–10.

1 STILL, still with Thee, my God,
  I would desire to be :
  By day, by night, at home, abroad,
  I would be still with Thee.

2 With Thee when dawn comes in,
  And calls me back to care ;
  Each day returning to begin
  With Thee, my God, in prayer.

3 With Thee amid the crowd
  That throngs the busy mart ;
  To hear Thy voice, 'mid clamor loud,
  Speak softly to my heart.

4 With Thee when day is done,
  And evening calms the mind ;
  The setting as the rising sun
  With Thee my heart would find.

5 With Thee when darkness brings
  The signal of repose,
  Calm in the shadow of Thy wings,
  Mine eyelids I would close.

6 With Thee, in Thee, by faith
  Abiding I would be ;
  By day, by night, in life, in death,
  I would be still with Thee.
                Rev. James D. Burns. (1823–1864.)

567 "Unto Thee, O Lord, do I lift up my soul."   **C. M.**
Ps. xlii. Isa. lviii. John iv. 10–15.

1 As pants the hart for cooling streams,
  When heated in the chase,
  So pants my soul, O Lord, for Thee,
  And Thy refreshing grace.

2 For Thee, the Lord, the living Lord,
  My thirsty soul doth pine :
  O when shall I behold Thy face,
  Thou majesty divine ?
                Tate and Brady. 1696.
                Alt. by Rev. Henry F. Lyte. (1793–1847.)

568 "My meditation of Him shall be sweet."   **C. M.**
John xx. 19–22. Acts i. 12–14. Dan. vi. 1–10.

1 FAR from the world, O Lord, I flee,
  From strife and tumult far ;
  From scenes where Satan wages still
  His most successful war.
  The calm retreat, the silent shade,
  With prayer and praise agree,
  And seem by Thy sweet bounty made
  For those who follow Thee.

2 There, if Thy Spirit touch the soul,
  And grace her mean abode,
  O with what peace, and joy, and love,
  She communes with her God !
  There, like the nightingale, she pours
  Her solitary lays ;
  Nor asks a witness of her song,
  Nor thirsts for human praise.

3 Author and Guardian of my life,
  Sweet Source of love divine,
  And all harmonious names in one,
  My Saviour, Thou art mine !
  What thanks I owe Thee, and what love,
  A boundless, endless store,
  Shall echo through the realms above,
  When time shall be no more !
                William Cowper. (1731–1800.)

569 "Precious are Thy thoughts unto me."   **C. M.**
Rev. iii. 7–12. Isa. xliii. 1–21. Ps. lxxi.

1 LORD, am I precious in Thy sight ?
  Lord, wouldst Thou have me Thine ?
  May it be given me to delight
  The majesty divine ?

2 Lord, dost Thou sweetly urge and press
  My soul Thy heaven to win ?
  Lord, dost Thou love my holiness ?
  Lord, dost Thou hate my sin ?

3 O Holy Spirit, dost Thou mourn
  When I from Thee depart ?
  Dost Thou rejoice when I return,
  And give Thee back my heart ?

4 O happy heaven, where Thine embrace
  I never more shall leave ;
  Nor ever cast away Thy grace,
  Nor once Thy Spirit grieve !

5 O let me, Lord, each grace possess
  That makes Thy heaven more bright,
  And bring the humble holiness
  That gives my God delight !
                Author unknown.

"Looking unto Jesus."

570 "I live by the faith of the Son of God." 7.
Gal. ii. 20.   John i. 36.   Acts iii. 15.   Isa. ix. 7.

1 Son of God, to Thee I cry!
　By the holy mystery
　Of Thy dwelling here on earth,
　By Thy pure and holy birth,
　Lord, Thy presence let me see,
　Manifest Thyself to me.

2 Lamb of God, to Thee I cry!
　By Thy bitter agony,
　By Thy pangs to us unknown,
　By Thy spirit's parting groan,
　Lord, Thy presence let me see,
　Manifest Thyself to me.

3 Prince of Life, to Thee I cry!
　By Thy glorious majesty,
　By Thy triumph o'er the grave,
　Meek to suffer, strong to save,
　Lord, Thy presence let me see,
　Manifest Thyself to me.

4 Lord of Glory, God most high,
　Man exalted in the sky,
　With Thy love my bosom fill,
　Prompt me to perform Thy will:
　Then Thy glory I shall see;
　Thou wilt bring me home to Thee.
　　　　　Bp. Richard Mant.   (1776-1848)

571 "Forsake me not, O Lord." 6. 4.
John xv. 1-5.   Ex. xxxiii. 12-15.   Ps. lxxxvi.

1 I need Thee every hour,
　Most gracious Lord;
　No tender voice like Thine
　Can peace afford.

　I need Thee, O I need Thee!
　Every hour I need Thee;
　O bless me now, my Saviour,
　I come to Thee!

2 I need Thee every hour,
　Stay Thou near by;
　Temptations lose their power
　When Thou art nigh.

3 I need Thee every hour,
　In joy or pain;
　Come quickly and abide,
　Or life is vain.

4 I need Thee every hour;
　Teach me Thy will,
　And Thy rich promises
　In me fulfil.
　　　　　Mrs. Annie S. Hawks.   (1835-.)

572 "Lord, ... bid me come unto Thee." 7.
Ps. cxxx.   Isa. xxv.   Mat. viii. 23-27.

1 Jesus, Lover of my soul,
　Let me to Thy bosom fly,
　While the nearer waters roll,
　While the tempest still is high.
　Hide me, O my Saviour, hide,
　Till the storm of life is past;
　Safe into the haven guide;
　O receive my soul at last.

2 Other refuge have I none,
　Hangs my helpless soul on Thee;
　Leave, ah, leave me not alone,
　Still support and comfort me.
　All my trust on Thee is stayed,
　All my help from Thee I bring;
　Cover my defenceless head
　With the shadow of Thy wing.

3 Wilt Thou not regard my call?
　Wilt Thou not accept my prayer?
　Lo, I sink, I faint, I fall!
　Lo, on Thee I cast my care.
　Reach me out Thy gracious hand;
　While I of Thy strength receive,
　Hoping against hope I stand,
　Dying, and behold I live!

4 Thou, O Christ, art all I want;
　More than all in Thee I find;
　Raise the fallen, cheer the faint,
　Heal the sick, and lead the blind.
　Just and holy is Thy name,
　I am all unrighteousness;
　False and full of sin I am,
　Thou art full of truth and grace.

5 Plenteous grace with Thee is found,
　Grace to cover all my sin;
　Let the healing streams abound,
　Make and keep me pure within.
　Thou of life the Fountain art,
　Freely let me take of Thee;
　Spring Thou up within my heart,
　Rise to all eternity.
　　　　　Rev. Charles Wesley.   (1708-1788.)

573 "All my springs are in Thee." L. M.
Phil. iii. 1-14.   Ps. lxxiii. 13-28.   John iv 1-15

1 O Jesus, if in days gone by
　My heart hath loved the world too well,
　It needs more love, for love of Thee
　To bid this cherished world farewell.

2 Take all the light away from earth,
　Take all that men can love from me;
　Let all I lean upon give way,
　That I may lean on naught but Thee.
　　　　　Rev. Frederick W. Faber.   (1814-1863.)

"Looking unto Jesus."

574 "This is the rest . . . and this is the refreshing." **C. M.**
Mat. ix. 18-3S. 1 John i. Ps. xxviii

1 JESUS, the sinner's rest Thou art,
    From guilt, and fear, and pain ;
  While Thou art absent from the heart
    We look for rest in vain.

2 O when wilt Thou my Saviour be ?
    O when shall I be clean ;
  The true eternal Sabbath see,
    A perfect rest from sin ?

3 The consolations of Thy word
    My soul have long upheld ;
  The faithful promise of the Lord
    Shall surely be fulfilled.

4 I look to my incarnate God
    Till He His work begin ;
  And wait till His redeeming blood
    Shall cleanse me from all sin.

Rev. Augustus M. Toplady. (1740-1778.)

575 "My hope is in Thee." **C. M.**
Mat. vi. 9-13. John xiv. 1-14. Ps. cxix. 49-56.

1 JESUS, the Life, the Truth, the Way,
    In whom I now believe,
  As taught by Thee, in faith I pray,
    Expecting to receive.

2 Thy will by me on earth be done,
    As by the powers above,
  Who always see Thee on Thy throne,
    And glory in Thy love.

3 I ask in confidence the grace
    That I may do Thy will,
  As angels, who behold Thy face,
    And all Thy words fulfil.

Rev. Charles Wesley. (1708-1788.)

576 "I sought the Lord." **6.**
Ps. cxix. 25-32. Lam. iii. 18-40. Luke xix. 1-10.

1 MY spirit longs for Thee
    Within my troubled breast,
  Unworthy though I be
    Of so divine a guest.
  Of so divine a guest
    Unworthy though I be,
  Yet has my heart no rest
    Unless it come from Thee.

2 Unless it come from Thee,
    In vain I look around ;
  In all that I can see
    No rest is to be found.
  No rest is to be found
    But in Thy blessèd love :
  O let my wish be crowned,
    And send it from above.

John Byrom. (1601-1763.)

577 "In quiet resting-places." **C. M.**
Mark iv. 35-41. Ps. lvii Isa. xxxii. 1-3.

1 Now to the haven of Thy breast,
    O Son of man, I fly ;
  Be Thou my Refuge and my Rest,
    For O the storm is high.

2 Protect me from the furious blast ;
    My Shield and Shelter be ;
  Hide me, my Saviour, till o'erpast
    The storm of sin I see.

3 As welcome as the water-spring
    Is to a barren place,
  Jesus, descend on me, and bring
    Thy sweet, refreshing grace.

4 As o'er a parched and weary land
    A rock extends its shade,
  So hide me, Saviour, with Thy hand,
    And screen my naked head.

Rev. Charles Wesley.

578 "All my desire is before Thee." **C. M.**
Rom. vii. 9-25. Phil. i. 19-26 Ps. xxv.

1 WHEN, O dear Jesus, when shall I
    Behold Thee all serene,
  Blest in perpetual Sabbath day,
    Without a veil between ?

2 Assist me while I wander here,
    Amidst a world of cares ;
  Incline my heart to pray with love,
    And then accept my prayers.

3 Thy Spirit, O my Father, give
    To be my Guide and Friend ;
  To light my path to ceaseless joys,
    To Sabbaths without end.

Rev. John Cennick. (1717-1755.)

579 "Hearken unto the voice of my cry." **C. M.**
Mal. iv. 2 Sam. xxiii. 1-4. John i. 1-14.

1 O SUN of Righteousness, arise,
    With healing in Thy wing ;
  To my diseased, my fainting soul
    Life and salvation bring.

2 These clouds of pride and sin dispel,
    By Thy all-piercing beam ;
  Lighten mine eyes with faith ; my heart
    With holy hope inflame.

3 My mind, by Thy all-quick'ning power,
    From low desires set free ;
  Unite my scattered thoughts, and fix
    My love entire on Thee.

4 Father, Thy long-lost son receive ;
    Saviour, Thy purchase own ;
  Blest Comforter, with peace and joy
    Thy new-made creature crown.

Rev. John Wesley. (1703-1791.)

"Looking unto Jesus."

580 "Keep me as the apple of the eye." 7. 6.
1 Pet. i. 3-9. John x. 27-30. 1 Sam. ii. 1-9.

1 O LAMB of God, still keep me
   Near to Thy wounded side;
'T is only there in safety
   And peace I can abide.
What foes and snares surround me!
   What doubts and fears within!
The grace that sought and found me
   Alone can keep me clean.

2 'T is only in Thee hiding,
   I know my life secure;
Only in Thee abiding,
   The conflict can endure.
Thine arm the victory gaineth
   O'er every hateful foe;
Thy love my heart sustaineth
   In all its care and woe.

3 Soon shall my eyes behold Thee
   With rapture, face to face;
One half hath not been told me
   Of all Thy power and grace.
Thy beauty, Lord, and glory,
   The wonders of Thy love,
Shall be the endless story
   Of all Thy saints above.

James G. Deck. (1808-.)

581 "Without me ye can do nothing." L. M.
Ps. lxxiii. 23-28. Luke x. 38-42. John xv. 1-5.

1 JESUS, engrave it on my heart
That Thou the one thing needful art;
I could from all things parted be,
But never, never, Lord, from Thee.

2 Needful is Thy most precious blood
To reconcile my soul to God;
Needful is Thy indulgent care,
Needful Thy all-prevailing prayer.

3 Needful Thy presence, dearest Lord,
True peace and comfort to afford;
Needful Thy promise to impart
Fresh life and vigor to my heart.

4 Needful art Thou, my Guide, my Stay,
Through all life's dark and weary way;
Nor less in death Thou 'lt needful be
To bring my spirit home to Thee.

5 Then, needful still, my God, my King,
Thy name eternally I'll sing;
Glory and praise be ever His,
The one thing needful Jesus is!

Rev. Samuel Medley. (1738-1799.)

582 "Hide me under the shadow of Thy wings." 7. 6.
Isa. xxvi. 9-13. John v. 1-15. Eph. iii.

1 I NEED Thee, precious Jesus,
   For I am full of sin;
My soul is dark and guilty,
   My heart is dead within.
I need the cleansing fountain,
   Where I can always flee,
The blood of Christ most precious,
   The sinner's perfect plea.

2 I need Thee, precious Jesus,
   For I am very poor;
A stranger and a pilgrim,
   I have no earthly store.
I need the love of Jesus
   To cheer me on my way,
To guide my doubting footsteps,
   To be my strength and stay.

3 I need Thee, precious Jesus,
   I need a friend like Thee;
A friend to soothe and pity,
   A friend to care for me.
And with Thy blood-bought children,
   My joy shall ever be
To sing Thy praises, Jesus,
   To gaze, my Lord, on Thee.

Rev. Frederick Whitfield. (1829-.)

583 "Our Lord Jesus Christ direct our way." 7.
Mark x. 13-16. Ps. cxxx. Eph. i.

1 JESUS, merciful and mild,
Lead me as a helpless child;
On no other arm but Thine
Would my weary soul recline.

2 Thou canst fit me, by Thy grace,
For the heavenly dwelling-place;
All Thy promises are sure,
Ever shall Thy love endure.

3 Then what more could I desire?
How to greater bliss aspire?
All I need in Thee I see;
Thou art all in all to me.

4 Jesus, Saviour all divine,
Hast Thou made me truly Thine?
Hast Thou bought me by Thy blood,
Reconciled my heart to God?

5 Hearken to my tender prayer,
Let me Thine own image bear;
Let me love Thee more and more,
Till I reach heaven's blissful shore.

Thomas Hastings. (1784-1872.)

"Looking unto Jesus."

584 "Be not far from me." Luke x. 38-42. John x. 27-30. Ps. xxvii. **L. M.**

1 O THAT I could forever dwell
   With Mary at my Saviour's feet,
   And view the form I love so well,
   And all His tender words repeat.

2 The world shut out from all my soul,
   And heaven brought in with all its bliss,
   O is there aught, from pole to pole,
   One moment to compare with this?

3 This is the hidden life I prize,
   A life of penitential love,
   When most my follies I despise,
   And raise the highest thoughts above.

4 Thus would I live till nature fail,
   And all my former sins forsake;
   Then rise to God within the vail,
   And of eternal joys partake.
   Rev. Andrew Reed. (1787-1862.)

585 "I count all things but loss." Mat. xix. 16-26. Rom. xii. 1, 2. Job i. 13 to ii. 10. **C. M.**

1 AND must I part with all I have,
   My dearest Lord, for Thee?
   It is but right, since Thou hast done
   Much more than this for me.

2 Yes, let it go! one look from Thee
   Will more than make amends
   For all the losses I sustain
   Of credit, riches, friends.

3 Ten thousand worlds, ten thousand lives,
   How worthless they appear,
   Compared with Thee, supremely good,
   Divinely bright and fair!

4 Saviour of souls; could I from Thee
   A single smile obtain,
   The loss of all things I could bear,
   And glory in my gain.
   Rev. Benjamin Beddome. (1717-1795.)

586 "Jesus only." Ps. cxxii. Mat. vi. 5-13. Luke ix. 28-36. **L. M.**

1 FAR from my thoughts, vain world, be gone,
   Let my religious hours alone;
   Fain would mine eyes my Saviour see;
   I wait a visit, Lord, from Thee.

2 My heart grows warm with holy fire,
   And kindles with a pure desire:
   Come, my dear Jesus, from above,
   And feed my soul with heavenly love.

   Blest Jesus, what delicious fare,
   How sweet thine entertainments are!
   Never did angels taste above
   Redeeming grace and dying love.
   Rev. Isaac Watts. (1674-1748.)

587 "Lord, it is good ... to be here." Mat. xvii. 1-9. 2 Pet. i. 16-18. Ex. xxxiv. 29-35. **L. M.**

1 O MASTER, it is good to be
   High on the mountain here with Thee,
   Where stand revealed to mortal gaze
   Those glorious saints of other days:
   Here, where the apostle's heart of rock
   Is nerved against temptation's shock;
   Here, where on eagle's wings we move
   With Him whose last, best creed is love.

2 O Master, it is good to be
   Entranced, enwrapt, alone with Thee,
   And watch Thy glistering raiment glow
   Whiter than Hermon's whitest snow;
   The human lineaments that shine
   Irradiant with a light divine;
   Till we too change from grace to grace,
   Gazing on that transfigured face.
   Rev. Arthur P. Stanley. (1815-1881.)

588 "The Lord is ... mine inheritance." Ps. lxxxvi. 10-13. Isa. xxvi. 7-9. 2 Cor. i. 1-12. **C. M.**

1 O COULD I find, from day to day,
   A nearness to my God,
   Then should my hours glide sweet away,
   And live upon Thy word.

2 Lord, I desire with Thee to live,
   Anew from day to day,
   In joys the world can never give,
   Nor ever take away.

3 O Jesus, come and rule my heart,
   And I'll be wholly Thine;
   And never, never more depart,
   For Thou art wholly mine.
   Benjamin Cleveland. 1790.

589 "With Thee is the fountain of light." Zech. xiii. 1 Cor. xv. 10, 11. 1 Pet. i. 17-23. **7.**

1 BLESSÉD Fountain, full of grace,
   Grace for sinners, grace for me!
   To this source alone I trace
   What I am and hope to be:
   What I am, as one redeemed,
   Saved and rescued by the Lord;
   Hating what I once esteemed,
   Loving what I once abhorred;

2 What I hope to be, erelong,
   When I take my place above,
   When I join the heavenly throng,
   When I see the God of love.
   Then I hope like Him to be,
   Who redeemed His saints from sin,
   Whom I now obscurely see,
   Through a vail that stands between.
   Rev. Thomas Kelly. (1769-1855.)

"Looking unto Jesus."

590 "Lead me in a plain path." 8. P.
Ps. lxxx. Ex. xxxiii. 18-23. John x. 27-29.

1 THOU Shepherd of Israel, and mine,
   The Joy and Desire of my heart,
For closer communion I pine;
   I long to reside where Thou art.
The pasture I languish to find,
   Where all who their Shepherd obey
Are fed, on Thy bosom reclined,
   And screened from the heat of the day.

2 'T is there, with the lambs of Thy flock,
   There only, I covet to rest;
To lie at the foot of the rock,
   Or rise to be hid in Thy breast.
'T is there I would always abide,
   And never a moment depart,
Concealed in the cleft of Thy side,
   Eternally held in Thy heart.
               Rev. Charles Wesley. (1709-1788.)

591 "Christ is all and in all." L. M.
1 Cor. i. 18 to ii. 2. Gal. vi. 14-17. Ps. lxxi.

1 MY precious Lord, for Thy dear name
   I bear the cross, despise the shame;
Nor do I faint, while Thou art near:
   I lean on Thee; how can I fear?

2 No other name but Thine is given
   To cheer my soul, in earth or heaven;
No other wealth will I require,
   No other friend can I desire.

3 Yea, into nothing would I fall
   For Thee alone, my all in all;
To feel Thy love my only joy,
   To tell Thy love my sole employ.
               Author unknown.

592 "The health of my countenance." 8. 7. P.
Jer. viii. 22. Mat. ix. 10-13. Luke viii. 26-56.

1 THE great Physician now is near,
   The sympathizing Jesus:
He speaks the drooping heart to cheer,
   O hear the voice of Jesus!

   Sweetest note in seraph song,
   Sweetest name on mortal tongue,
   Sweetest carol ever sung,
   Jesus, blessèd Jesus!

2 His name dispels my guilt and fear,
   No other name but Jesus;
O how my soul delights to hear
   The precious name of Jesus!

3 And when to that bright world above
   We rise to see our Jesus,
We 'll sing around the throne of love
   His name, the name of Jesus.
               Rev. William Hunter. (1811-1877.)

593 "Be Thou my strong rock." 7.
Ps. xviii. 1-32. Isa. xxvi. 1-13. Mat. vii. 24-27.

1 LORD, Thou art my Rock of strength,
   And my home is in Thine arms;
Thou wilt send me help at length,
   And I feel no wild alarms.

2 Sin nor death can pierce the shield
   Thy defence has o'er me thrown;
Up to Thee myself I yield,
   And my sorrows are Thine own.

3 When my trials tarry long,
   Unto Thee I look and wait;
Knowing none, though keen and strong,
   Can my trust in Thee abate.

4 Let Thy mercy's wings be spread
   O'er me, keep me close to Thee;
In the peace Thy love doth shed
   Let me dwell eternally.

5 Be my All; in all I do
   Let me only seek Thy will.
Where the heart to Thee is true
   All is peaceful, calm, and still.
               Rev. August H. Franke. (1663-1727.)
               Tr. by Miss Catherine Winkworth. (1829-)

594 "He careth for you." 8. 7.
Heb. vii. 15-25. Mat. xii. 46-50. Ps. lxi.

1 YES, for me, for me He careth
   With a brother's tender care;
Yes, with me, with me He shareth
   Every burden, every fear.
Yes, o'er me, o'er me He watcheth,
   Ceaseless watcheth, night and day;
Yes, e'en me, e'en me He snatcheth
   From the perils of the way.

2 Yes, for me He standeth pleading
   At the mercy-seat above;
Ever for me interceding,
   Constant in untiring love.
Yes, in me abroad He sheddeth
   Joys unspeakable, love and light;
And to cover me He spreadeth
   His paternal wing of might.

3 Yes, in me, in me He dwelleth;
   I in Him, and He in me!
And my empty soul He filleth,
   Here and through eternity.
Thus I wait for His returning,
   Singing all the way to heaven;
Such the joyful song of morning,
   Such the tranquil song of even.
               Rev. Horatius Bonar. (1808-)

"Looking unto Jesus."

595 C. M.
"Then will I go ... unto God."
Ps. lxxiii. 25-28. John ix. 35-38. Mat. xiv. 1-12.

1 To whom, my Saviour, shall I go,
  If I depart from Thee?
  My Guide through all this vale of woe,
  And more than all to me.

2 The world reject Thy gentle reign,
  And pay Thy death with scorn;
  O they could plait Thy crown again,
  And sharpen every thorn!

3 But I have felt Thy dying love
  Breathe gently through my heart,
  To whisper hope of joys above,
  And can we ever part?

4 Ah, no; with Thee I'll walk below,
  My journey to the grave:
  To whom, my Saviour, shall I go,
  When only Thou canst save?
  Author unknown.

598 L. M.
"Keep me from the snares laid for me."
Ex. xxxiii. 12-23. Ps. cxlii. Luke ix. 57, 58

1 BE with me, Lord, where'er I go,
  Teach me what Thou wouldst have me do;
  Suggest whate'er I think or say,
  Direct me in the narrow way.

2 Prevent me, lest I harbor pride,
  Lest I in mine own strength confide;
  Show me my weakness; let me see
  I have my power, my all, from Thee.

3 Enrich me always with Thy love;
  My kind Protector ever prove;
  Thy signet put upon my breast,
  And let Thy Spirit on me rest.

4 O may I never do my will,
  But Thine, and only Thine fulfil;
  Let all my time and all my ways
  Be spent and ended to Thy praise.
  Rev. John Cennick. (1717-1755.)

596 11. 8.
"I sought Him whom my soul loveth."
Cant. i. Job xxiii. 3-10. Ps. cxliii. John x. 11-28.

1 O THOU in whose presence my soul takes delight,
  On whom in affliction I call;
  My Comfort by day, and my Song in the night,
  My Hope, my Salvation, my All!

2 Where dost Thou, at noontide, resort with Thy sheep,
  To feed on the pastures of love?
  Say, why in the valley of death should I weep,
  Or alone in the wilderness rove?

3 O why should I wander an alien from Thee,
  Or cry in the desert for bread?
  Thy foes will rejoice when my sorrows they see,
  And smile at the tears I have shed.

4 The joy of Thy presence, dear Shepherd, restore;
  I pant for the light of Thy face;
  An alien no longer, I'll wander no more,
  But dwell in my Saviour's embrace.
  Rev. Joseph Swain. (1761-1796.)

597 S. M.
"In Thee, O Lord, do I hope."
Ps. xxv. Josh. xiv. 6-14. Rom. x. 11-13.

1 MINE eyes and my desire
  Are ever to the Lord;
  I love to plead His promises,
  And rest upon His word.

2 O keep my soul from death,
  Nor put my hope to shame;
  For I have placed my only trust
  In my Redeemer's name.

3 With humble faith I wait
  To see Thy face again;
  Of Israel it shall ne'er be said,
  "He sought the Lord in vain."
  Rev. Isaac Watts. (1674-1748.)

599 C. M.
"Sweet is Thy voice."
Ps. lxxxv. Mat. viii. 5-17. John xii. 20-36.

1 AH, Jesus, let me hear Thy voice
  Fall gently on mine ear;
  Thy voice alone can soothe my grief,
  And charm away my fear.

2 Ah, Jesus, let me see Thy face
  Beaming with truth and love;
  I ask no other heaven below,
  No other heaven above.

3 Ah, Jesus, let me feel Thy grace;
  Now hear my earnest cry;
  If Thou art absent, O behold!
  I droop, I faint, I die.
  Rev. Andrew Reed. (1787-1862.)

"Looking unto Jesus."

600 "Abide with us, for it is toward evening." 10.
Luke xxiv. 13-29. Jer. xiv. 1-9. Gen. xviii. 1-5. 2 Cor. vi. 16-18.

1 ABIDE with me ; fast falls the eventide ;
The darkness deepens ; Lord, with me abide !
When other helpers fail, and comforts flee,
Help of the helpless, O abide with me !

2 Swift to its close ebbs out life's little day ;
Earth's joys grow dim, its glories pass away ;
Change and decay in all around I see ;
O Thou who changest not, abide with me !

3 Not a brief glance I beg, a passing word ;
But as Thou dwell'st with Thy disciples, Lord,
Familiar, condescending, patient, free,
Come, not to sojourn, but abide, with me.

Rev. Henry F. Lyte. (1793-1847.)

601 "I am continually with Thee." 10.
1 Kings iii. 3-15. Ps. xxxi. 1 Cor. iii. 1 John v 12-20.

1 I NEED Thy presence every passing hour ;
What but Thy grace can foil the tempter's power ?
Who like Thyself my Guide and Stay can be ?
Through cloud and sunshine, O abide with me !

2 I fear no foe, with Thee at hand to bless ;
Ills have no weight, and tears no bitterness ;
Where is death's sting ? where, grave, thy victory ?
I triumph still, if Thou abide with me.

3 Hold Thou Thy cross before my closing eyes ;
Shine through the gloom, and point me to the skies ;
Heaven's morning breaks, and earth's vain shadows flee ;
In life, in death, O Lord, abide with me !

Rev. Henry F. Lyte.

602 "My Lord, pass not away,...I pray Thee." 11.
2 Chr. vi. 41, 42. Ps. liv. John xiv. 1-18. Rev. iii. 20-22.

1 COME, Jesus, Redeemer, abide Thou with me ;
Come, gladden my spirit, that waiteth for Thee ;
Thy smile every shadow shall chase from my heart,
And soothe every sorrow, though keen be the smart.

2 Without Thee but weakness, with Thee I am strong ;
By day Thou shalt lead me, by night be my Song ;
Though dangers surround me, I still every fear,
Since Thou, the Most Mighty, my Helper, art near.

3 Thy love, O how faithful, so tender, so pure !
Thy promise, faith's anchor, how steadfast and sure !
That love, like sweet sunshine, my cold heart can warm,
That promise make steady my soul in the storm.

4 Breathe, breathe on my spirit, oft ruffled, Thy peace ;
From restless, vain wishes bid Thou my heart cease ;
In Thee all its longings henceforward shall end,
Till glad to Thy presence my soul shall ascend.

5 O then, blessèd Jesus, who once for me died,
Made clean in the fountain that gushed from Thy side,
I shall see Thy full glory, Thy face shall behold,
And praise Thee forever with raptures untold.

Rev. Ray Palmer. (1808-.)

"Looking unto Jesus."

603 "Teach me to do Thy will." **C. M.**
John xiii. 1-15. Rom. xv. 1-6. 2 Kings iv. 8-27.

1 LORD, as to Thy dear cross we flee,
   And plead to be forgiven,
So let Thy life our pattern be,
   And form our souls for heaven.

2 Help us, through good report and ill,
   Our daily cross to bear ;
Like Thee, to do our Father's will,
   Our brethren's griefs to share.

3 Let grace our selfishness expel,
   Our earthliness refine ;
And kindness in our bosoms dwell
   As free and true as Thine.

4 If joy shall at Thy bidding fly,
   And grief's dark day come on,
We, in our turn, would meekly cry,
   " Father, Thy will be done !"
Rev. John H. Gurney. (1802-1862.)

604 "Bringing into captivity every thought." **7.**
Rom. vii. 14-25. Heb. xiii. 20, 21. Ps. xxv.

1 PRINCE of Peace, control my will,
   Bid this struggling heart be still ;
Bid my fears and doubtings cease,
Hush my spirit into peace.

2 Thou hast bought me with Thy blood,
   Opened wide the gate to God ;
Peace I ask ; but peace must be,
Lord, in being one with Thee.

3 May Thy will, not mine, be done ;
   May Thy will and mine be one ;
Chase these doubtings from my heart,
Now Thy perfect peace impart.

4 Saviour, at Thy feet I fall ;
   Thou my Life, my God, my All !
Let Thy happy servant be
One for evermore with Thee !
Mrs. Mary S. B. Dana. (1810-.)

605 "Made conformable unto His death." **C. M.**
Phil. iii. 8-14. Eph. iv. 1-16. Ps. cxxxi.

1 JESUS, my Life, Thyself apply,
   Thy Holy Spirit breathe ;
My vile affections crucify,
   Conform me to Thy death.

2 Reign in me, Lord ; Thy foes control,
   Who would not own Thy sway ;
Diffuse Thine image through my soul,
   Shine to the perfect day.

3 Scatter the last remains of sin,
   And seal me Thine abode ;
O make me glorious all within,
   A temple built by God !
Rev. Charles Wesley. (1708-1788.)

606 "Let this mind be in you." **L. M.**
1 Pet. ii. 21-23. Luke vi. 12-40. Isa. xlii 1-9.

1 MY dear Redeemer and my Lord,
   I read my duty in Thy word ;
But in Thy life the law appears
Drawn out in living characters.

2 Such was Thy truth, and such Thy zeal,
   Such deference to Thy Father's will,
Such love and meekness, so divine,
I would transcribe, and make them mine.

3 Cold mountains and the midnight air
   Witnessed the fervor of Thy prayer ;
The desert Thy temptations knew,
Thy conflict and Thy victory, too.

4 Be Thou my Pattern ; make me bear
   More of Thy gracious image here ;
Then God, the Judge, shall own my name
Amongst the followers of the Lamb.
Rev. Isaac Watts. (1674-1748.)

607 "My soul followeth hard after Thee." **L. M.**
Isa. xxvi. 8, 9. Mat. viii. 19-22. 2 Cor. i. 8-18.

1 THOU Lamb of God, Thou Prince of Peace,
   For Thee my thirsty soul doth pine ;
My longing heart implores Thy grace ;
O make me in Thy likeness shine !

2 With fraudless, even, humble mind,
   Thy will in all things may I see ;
In love be every wish resigned,
And hallowed my whole heart to Thee.

3 When pain o'er my weak flesh prevails,
   With lamb-like patience arm my breast ;
When grief my wounded soul assails,
In lowly meekness may I rest.

4 Close by Thy side still may I keep,
   Howe'er life's various currents flow ;
With steadfast eye mark every step,
And follow where my Lord doth go.
Christian F. Richter. (1676-1711.)
Tr. by Rev. John Wesley. (1703-1791.)

608 "I in them." **C. M.**
1 Pet. i. 2 Pet. i. 1-11. Ps. cxix. 169-176.

1 JESUS hath died that I might live,
   Might live to God alone ;
In Him eternal life receive,
   And be in spirit one.

2 Give me Thyself ; from every boast,
   From every wish, set free ;
Let all I am in Thee be lost,
   But give Thyself to me.

3 Thy gifts, alas, cannot suffice,
   Unless Thyself be given ;
Thy presence makes my paradise,
   And where Thou art is heaven.
Rev. Charles Wesley.

"Lord, be Thou my helper."

609 "In Thee is my trust." Mark iv. 36-41. Ps. lxxvii. 2 Chr. xx. **6. 4.**

1 SAVIOUR, I look to Thee!
   Be not Thou far from me,
   'Mid storms that lower:
On me Thy care bestow,
Thy loving-kindness show,
Thine arms around me throw,
   This trying hour.

2 Saviour, I look to Thee!
   Feeble as infancy,
   Gird up my heart:
Author of life and light,
Thou hast an arm of might,
Thine is the sovereign right,
   Thy strength impart.

3 Saviour, I look to Thee!
   Let me Thy fulness see,
   Save me from fear:
While at Thy cross I kneel,
All my backslidings heal,
And a free pardon seal,
   My soul to cheer.

4 Saviour, I look to Thee!
   Thine shall the glory be,
   Hearer of prayer:
Thou art my only aid,
On Thee my soul is stayed;
Naught can my heart invade,
   While Thou art near.

Thomas Hastings. (1784-1872.)

610 "My help and my deliverer." Phil. iv. 12, 13. Ps. cxxx. Job xxxvi. 1-15. **S. M.**

1 JESUS, my Strength, my Hope!
   On Thee I cast my care;
With humble confidence look up,
   And know Thou hear'st my prayer.

2 Give me on Thee to wait,
   Till I can all things do;
On Thee, almighty to create,
   Almighty to renew.

3 I rest upon Thy word;
   The promise is for me;
My succor and salvation, Lord,
   Shall surely come from Thee.

4 But let me still abide,
   Nor from my hope remove,
Till Thou my patient spirit guide
   Into Thy perfect love.

Rev. Charles Wesley. (1708-1788.)

611 "Renew a right spirit within me." Ps. cxix. 57-64. Eph. vi. 10-18. 2 Chr. xxxiv. **S. M.**

1 I WANT a heart to pray,
   To pray and never cease;
Never to murmur at Thy stay,
   Or wish my sufferings less.
This blessing, above all,
   Always to pray, I want;
Out of the deep on Thee to call,
   And never, never faint.

2 I want a sober mind,
   A self-renouncing will,
That tramples down, and casts behind,
   The baits of pleasing ill;
A soul inured to pain,
   To hardship, grief, and loss;
Bold to take up, firm to sustain,
   The consecrated cross.

3 I want, with all my heart,
   Thy pleasure to fulfil;
To know myself, and what Thou art,
   And what Thy perfect will;
To give Thee every thought,
   And all my wants to see:
I want, alas, what want I not,
   When Thou art not in me?

Rev. Charles Wesley.

612 "Arise, O Lord; save me." Ps. cxix. 33-40. Rom. xii. 1 Kings iii. 3-15. **L. M.**

1 ETERNAL beam of Light Divine,
Fountain of unexhausted love,
In whom the Father's glories shine,
Through earth beneath and heaven above!

2 Jesus, the weary wanderer's rest,
Give me Thy easy yoke to bear;
With steadfast patience arm my breast,
With spotless love and lowly fear.

3 Thankful I take the cup from Thee,
Prepared and mingled by Thy skill;
Though bitter to the taste it be,
Powerful the wounded soul to heal.

4 Be Thou, O Rock of Ages, nigh!
So shall each murmuring thought be gone,
And grief, and fear, and care shall fly,
As clouds before the midday sun.

5 Speak to my warring passions, "Peace;"
Say to my trembling heart, "Be still;"
Thy power my strength and fortress is,
For all things serve Thy sovereign will.

Rev. Charles Wesley.

"Lord, be Thou my helper."

613 " My soul melteth ; . . . strengthen Thou me." **L. M.**
Ps. cxix. 145-152. Eph. iv. 1 Thess. v. 14-28.

1 LORD, fill me with an humble fear;
 My utter helplessness reveal;
 Satan and sin are always near,
 Thee may I always nearer feel.

2 O that to Thee my constant mind
 Might with an even flame aspire;
 Pride in its earliest motions find,
 And mark the risings of desire.

3 O that my tender soul might fly
 The first abhorred approach of ill;
 Quick as the apple of an eye
 The slightest touch of sin to feel.

4 Till Thou anew my soul create,
 Still may I strive, and watch, and pray;
 Humbly and confidently wait,
 And long to see the perfect day.
 Rev. Charles Wesley. (1708-1788.)

614 " Let Thy salvation . . . set me up on high." **S. M.**
Ps. cxl. 1-7. Luke xv. Mark ix. 14-24.

1 JESUS, my Lord, attend
 Thy feeble creature's cry;
 And show Thyself the sinner's Friend,
 And set me up on high.

2 From hell's oppressive power
 My struggling soul release;
 And to Thy Father's grace restore,
 And to Thy perfect peace.
 Rev. Charles Wesley.

615 " Quicken Thou me in Thy way." **C. M.**
Acts xxiv. 10-16. 1 Cor. ix. 19-27. Ps. xxxii.

1 I WANT a principle within
 Of jealous, godly fear;
 A sensibility of sin,
 A pain to feel it near.

2 I want the first approach to feel
 Of pride, or fond desire;
 To catch the wandering of my will,
 And quench the kindling fire.

3 From Thee that I no more may part,
 No more Thy goodness grieve,
 The filial awe, the fleshly heart,
 The tender conscience give.

4 If to the right or left I stray,
 That moment, Lord, reprove;
 And let me weep my life away
 For having grieved Thy love.

5 O may the least omission pain
 My well-instructed soul,
 And drive me to the blood again
 Which makes the wounded whole.
 Rev. Charles Wesley.

616 "O my strength, haste Thee to help me!" **8. 6.**
Ps. xii. 2 Cor. iv. Eph. vi. 10-18.

1 HELP, Lord, to whom for help I fly,
 And still my tempted soul stand by
 Throughout the evil day;
 The sacred watchfulness impart,
 And keep the issues of my heart,
 And stir me up to pray.

2 My soul with Thy whole armor arm;
 In each approach of sin, alarm,
 And show the danger near:
 Surround, sustain, and strengthen me,
 And fill with godly jealousy
 And sanctifying fear.
 Rev. Charles Wesley.

617 "O keep my soul, and deliver me." **S. M.**
Mat. xiv. 23-31. 2 Cor. xii. 1-10. Ps. xvii.

1 THOU seest my feebleness,
 Jesus, be Thou my Power,
 My Help and Refuge in distress,
 My Fortress and my Tower.

2 Give me to trust in Thee;
 Be Thou my sure Abode:
 My Horn, and Rock, and Buckler be,
 My Saviour and my God.

3 Myself I cannot save,
 Myself I cannot keep,
 But strength in Thee I surely have,
 Whose eyelids never sleep.

4 My soul to Thee alone
 Now therefore I commend:
 Thou, Jesus, love me as Thine own,
 And love me to the end.
 Rev. Charles Wesley.

618 " Be Thou my strong habitation." **L. M.**
Phil. iii. 7-14. 1 Cor. iii. 11-23. Ps. lxxiii. 25-28.

1 MY Hope, my All, my Saviour, Thou!
 To Thee, lo, now my soul I bow;
 I feel the bliss Thy wounds impart,
 I find Thee, Saviour, in my heart.

2 Be Thou my Strength, be Thou my Way;
 Protect me through my life's short day;
 In all my acts may wisdom guide,
 And keep me, Saviour, near Thy side.

3 Correct, reprove, and comfort me;
 As I have need, my Saviour be;
 And if I would from Thee depart,
 Then clasp me, Saviour, to Thy heart.

4 In fierce temptation's darkest hour,
 Save me from sin and Satan's power;
 Tear every idol from Thy throne,
 And reign, my Saviour, reign alone.
 Bp. Thomas Coke. (1747-1814.)

"Lord, be Thou my helper."

619 "Strengthen Thou me according to Thy word." 7.
2 Cor. xi. 17-30.   Mat. v. 11-16.   Ps. lxxi.

1 JESUS, Master, whom I serve,
  Though so feebly and so ill,
  Strengthen hand and heart and nerve,
  All Thy bidding to fulfil.
  Open Thou mine eyes to see
  All the work Thou hast for me.

2 Lord, Thou needest not, I know,
  Service such as I can bring;
  Yet I long to prove and show
  Full allegiance to my King.
  Thou an honor art to me,
  Let me be a praise to Thee.

3 Jesus, Master, wilt Thou use
  One who owes Thee more than all?
  As Thou wilt; I would not choose;
  Only let me hear Thy call.
  Jesus, let me always be
  In Thy service glad and free.

Miss Frances R. Havergal.   (1836-1879.)

620 "O Lord, heal me, and I shall be healed." 7. 6. P.
Eph ii.   Luke xxiii. 33-43.   Zech. xiii.

1 JESUS, keep me near the cross:
  There a precious fountain,
  Free to all, a healing stream,
  Flows from Calvary's mountain.

2 Near the cross! O Lamb of God,
  Bring its scenes before me;
  Help me walk from day to day,
  With its shadows o'er me.

Mrs. Frances J. C. Van Alstyne.   (1833-.)

621 "Whose I am and whom I serve." 7.
Ps. lxxiii.   Isa. xxvi. 1-13.   Mat. x. 16-42.

1 JESUS, Master, whose I am,
  Purchased Thine alone to be,
  By Thy blood, O spotless Lamb,
  Shed so willingly for me.
  Let my heart be all Thine own,
  Let me live to Thee alone.

2 Other lords have long held sway;
  Now Thy name alone to bear,
  Thy dear voice alone obey,
  Is my daily, hourly prayer.
  Whom have I in heaven but Thee?
  Nothing else my joy can be.

3 Jesus, Master, I am Thine;
  Keep me faithful, keep me near;
  Let Thy presence in me shine
  All my homeward way to cheer.
  Jesus, at Thy feet I fall,
  O be Thou my all in all.

Miss Frances R. Havergal.

622 "Save me, and I shall be saved." L. M.
John xx. 24-29.   Acts viii. 26-37.   Ps. xxxii.

1 JESUS, in whom the Godhead's rays
  Beam forth with mildest majesty,
  I see Thee full of truth and grace,
  And come for all I want to Thee.

2 Save me from pride, the plague expel;
  Jesus, Thine humble self impart:
  O let Thy mind within me dwell,
  O give me lowliness of heart.

3 Enter Thyself, and cast out sin;
  Thy spotless purity bestow:
  Touch me, and make the leper clean;
  Wash me, and I am white as snow.

Rev. Charles Wesley.   (1708-1788.)

623 "Draw nigh unto my soul;... deliver me." L. M.
Mat. vi. 25-34.   Ps. xxxvii. 25-40.   Isa. xxx. 15-21.

1 JESUS, my Saviour, Brother, Friend,
  On whom I cast my every care,
  On whom for all things I depend,
  Inspire, and then accept, my prayer.

2 If I have tasted of Thy grace,
  The grace that sure salvation brings;
  If with me now Thy Spirit stays,
  And, hov'ring, hides me in His wings;

3 Still let Him with my weakness stay,
  Nor for a moment's space depart;
  Evil and danger turn away,
  And keep, till He renews, my heart.

4 If to the right or left I stray,
  His voice behind me may I hear:
  Return, and walk in Christ, thy Way;
  Fly back to Christ, for sin is near.

Rev. Charles Wesley.

624 "Lord, save me." S. M.
John ix. 1-11.   2 Cor. xii. 1-10.   Ps. lxx.

1 JESUS, my Truth, my Way,
  My sure, unerring Light,
  On Thee my feeble steps I stay,
  Which Thou wilt guide aright.

2 My Wisdom and my Guide,
  My Counsellor Thou art;
  O never let me leave Thy side,
  Or from Thy paths depart.

3 I lift mine eyes to Thee,
  Thou gracious, bleeding Lamb,
  That I may now enlightened be,
  And never put to shame.

4 Never will I remove
  Out of Thy hands my cause;
  But rest in Thy redeeming love,
  And hang upon Thy cross.

Rev. Charles Wesley.

"Lord, be Thou my helper."

625   "Love is the fulfilling of the law."   **L. M.**
Acts i. 1-14. 2 Tim. i. 6-12. Ps. cxliii.

1 O THOU who camest from above,
   The pure celestial fire t' impart,
   Kindle a flame of sacred love
   On the mean altar of my heart.

2 There let it for Thy glory burn,
   With inextinguishable blaze;
   And trembling to its Source return,
   In humble love and fervent praise.

3 Jesus, confirm my heart's desire
   To work, and speak, and think for Thee;
   Still let me guard the holy fire,
   And still stir up Thy gift in me.

4 Ready for all Thy perfect will,
   My acts of faith and love repeat,
   Till death Thy endless mercies seal,
   And make the sacrifice complete.
             Rev. Charles Wesley. (1708-1788.)

626   "Thy love is better than wine."   **S. M.**
Rom. xii. 1 Cor. viii. Ps. li. 7-19.

1 JESUS, I fain would find
   Thy zeal for God in me;
   Thy yearning pity for mankind,
   Thy burning charity;

2 In me Thy Spirit dwell,
   In me Thy bowels move:
   So shall the fervor of my zeal
   Be the pure flame of love.
             Rev. Charles Wesley.

627   "O Lord, open Thou my lips."   **C. M.**
Ps. ix. 1-11. Eze. xxxvi. 25-27. Eph. iv. 1-23.

1 O FOR a heart to praise my God,
   A heart from sin set free;
   A heart that always feels Thy blood
   So freely spilt for me:

2 A heart resigned, submissive, meek,
   My dear Redeemer's throne,
   Where only Christ is heard to speak,
   Where Jesus reigns alone:

3 A humble, lowly, contrite heart,
   Believing, true, and clean;
   Which neither life nor death can part
   From Him that dwells within:

4 A heart in every thought renewed,
   And full of love divine;
   Perfect and right and pure and good,
   A copy, Lord, of Thine.

5 Thy nature, dearest Lord, impart;
   Come quickly from above;
   Write Thy new name upon my heart,
   Thy new, best name of Love.
             Rev. Charles Wesley.

628   "Rooted and grounded in love."   **S. M.**
Ps. xviii. 27-50. 1 Pet. iv. 1-5. Phil. ii. 1-15.

1 EQUIP me for the war,
   And teach my hands to fight;
   My simple, upright heart prepare,
   And guide my words aright.
   Control my every thought,
   My whole of sin remove;
   Let all my works in Thee be wrought,
   Let all be wrought in love.

2 O arm me with the mind,
   Meek Lamb, that was in Thee;
   And let my knowing zeal be joined
   With perfect charity.
   With calm and tempered zeal
   Let me enforce Thy call,
   And vindicate Thy gracious will,
   Which offers life to all.

3 O may I love like Thee,
   In all Thy footsteps tread;
   Thou hatest all iniquity,
   But nothing Thou hast made.
   O may I learn the art
   With meekness to reprove;
   To hate the sin with all my heart,
   But still the sinner love.
             Rev. Charles Wesley.

629   "Make Thy way straight before my face."   **L. M.**
Ps. cxxxix. Isa. i. 10-27. Rev. ii. 1-11.

1 O THOU to whose all-searching sight
   The darkness shineth as the light,
   Search, prove my heart; it pants for Thee;
   O burst these bonds, and set it free!

2 Wash out its stains, refine its dross,
   Nail my affections to the cross;
   Hallow each thought; let all within
   Be clean as Thou, my Lord, art clean.

3 If in this darksome wild I stray,
   Be Thou my Light, be Thou my Way;
   No foes, no violence, I fear,
   No fraud while Thou, my God, art near.

4 When rising floods my soul o'erflow,
   When sinks my heart in waves of woe,
   Jesus, Thy timely aid impart,
   And raise my head and cheer my heart.

5 Saviour, where'er Thy steps I see,
   Dauntless, untired, I follow Thee;
   O let Thy hand support me still,
   And lead me to Thy holy hill.
             Gerhard Tersteegen. (1697-1769.)
             Tr. by *Rev. John Wesley.* (1703-1791.)

"Lead me, O Lord."

630 "By the springs of water shall He guide." 8, 7, 4.
Ex. xxxiii. 12-23. Nch. ix. 7-25. Heb. xi.

1 GUIDE me, O Thou great Jehovah,
   Pilgrim through this barren land;
I am weak, but Thou art mighty,
   Hold me with Thy powerful hand.
      Bread of heaven,
   Feed me now and evermore.

2 Open now the crystal fountain,
   Whence the healing streams do flow;
Let the fiery, cloudy pillar
   Lead me all my journey through.
      Strong Deliverer,
   Be Thou still my Strength and Shield.

3 When I tread the verge of Jordan,
   Bid my anxious fears subside;
Death of death, and hell's destruction,
   Land me safe on Canaan's side.
      Songs of praises
   I will ever give to Thee.

4 Musing on my habitation,
   Musing on my heavenly home,
Fills my heart with holy longing;
   Come, Lord Jesus, quickly come.
      Vanity is all I see;
   Lord, I long to be with Thee.
               Rev. Peter Williams. (1719-1796.)
         Alt. by Rev. William Williams. (1717-1791.)

631 "For Thy name's sake ... guide me." 7.
Ps. cxix. 113-128. Phil. iv. 6-13. Mat. x. 16-39.

1 HEAVENLY Father, to whose eye
   Future things unfolded lie,
Through the desert where I stray,
   Let Thy counsels guide my way.

2 Lord, uphold me day by day,
   Shed a light upon my way;
Guide me through perplexing snares,
   Care for me in all my cares.

3 All I ask for is enough;
   Only when the way is rough,
Let Thy rod and staff impart
   Strength and courage to my heart.

4 Should Thy wisdom, Lord, decree
   Trials long and sharp for me,
Pain or sorrow, care or shame,
   Father, glorify Thy name!

5 Let me neither faint nor fear,
   Feeling still that Thou art near;
In the course my Saviour trod,
   Tending still to Thee, my God!
               Josiah Conder. (1780-1855.)

632 "Show me Thy ways, O Lord." L. M.
Ps. xvii. John x. 1-28. Job xlii.

1 GOD of my life, whose gracious power
   Through varied deaths my soul hath led,
Or turned aside the fatal hour,
   Or lifted up my sinking head,

2 In all my ways Thy hand I own,
   Thy ruling providence I see;
Assist me still my course to run,
   And still direct my paths to Thee.

3 Whither, O whither should I fly
   But to my loving Saviour's breast!
Secure within Thine arms to lie,
   And safe beneath Thy wings to rest.

4 I have no skill the snare to shun,
   But Thou, O Christ, my Wisdom art;
I ever into ruin run,
   But Thou art greater than my heart.

5 Foolish and impotent and blind,
   Lead me a way I have not known;
Bring me where I my heaven may find,
   The heaven of loving Thee alone.
               Rev. Charles Wesley. (1708-1782.)

633 "Lead me in the way everlasting." C. M.
Ps. cxix. 1-16. Jer. xxxi. 27-34. James i.

1 O THAT the Lord would guide my ways
   To keep his statutes still;
O that my God would grant me grace
   To know and do His will!

2 O send Thy spirit down to write
   Thy law upon my heart;
Nor let my tongue indulge deceit,
   Or act the liar's part.

3 Order my footsteps by Thy word,
   And make my heart sincere;
Let sin have no dominion, Lord,
   But keep my conscience clear.

4 Make me to walk in Thy commands,
   'T is a delightful road;
Nor let my head, or heart, or hands,
   Offend against my God.
               Rev. Isaac Watts. (1674-1748.)

634 "Hold up my goings in Thy paths." L. M.
Ps. liv. Jer. i. 6-19. Eph. i.

1 UPHOLD me, Lord, too prone to stray,
   Uphold me in Thy narrow way;
From sin and folly bid me flee,
   And turn from all who turn from Thee.

2 The cloud and pillar of Thy word,
   Be this my guide, my comfort, Lord;
By day, by night, at hand to bless,
   And lead me through the wilderness.
               Rev. Henry F. Lyte. (1793-1847.)

"Lead me, O Lord."

635 "Teach me Thy way, O Lord, and lead me." 6.
Job xxiii. 3–10. 2 Sam. vii. Acts xxi. 10–14.

1 THY way, not mine, O Lord,
  However dark it be!
Lead me by Thine own hand;
  Choose out the path for me.
I dare not choose my lot;
  I would not, if I might;
Choose Thou for me, my God,
  So shall I walk aright.

2 The kingdom that I seek
  Is Thine: so let the way
That leads to it be Thine,
  Else I must surely stray.
Take Thou my cup, and fill
  With joy or sorrow fill,
As best to Thee may seem;
  Choose Thou my good and ill.

3 Choose Thou for me my friends,
  My sickness or my health;
Choose Thou my cares for me,
  My poverty or wealth.
Not mine, not mine, the choice,
  In things or great or small;
Be Thou my Guide, my Strength,
  My Wisdom, and my All.
            Rev. Horatius Bonar. (1808–.)

636 "O send out Thy light!" 10. 4.
Ps. xxvii. Ex. xiii. 21, 22. John i. 1–14.

1 LEAD, kindly Light, amid the encircling gloom,
  Lead Thou me on;
The night is dark, and I am far from home;
  Lead Thou me on.
Keep Thou my feet; I do not ask to see
The distant scene; one step enough for me.

2 I was not ever thus, nor prayed that Thou
    Shouldst lead me on;
I loved to choose and see my path; but now
    Lead Thou me on!
I loved the garish day, and, spite of fears,
Pride ruled my will. Remember not past
    years!

3 So long Thy power has blest me, sure it still
    Will lead me on
O'er moor and fen, o'er crag and torrent, till
    The night is gone,
And with the morn those angel faces smile
Which I have loved long since, and lost
    a while!
            Rev. John H. Newman. (1801–.)

637 "Thou that leadest Joseph like a flock." 7.
Eze. xxxiv. 11–16. Ps. xxiii. John x. 11–16.

1 To Thy pastures fair and large,
  Heavenly Shepherd, lead Thy charge;
And my couch, with tenderest care,
  Mid the springing grass prepare.

2 When I faint with summer's heat,
  Thou shalt guide my weary feet
To the streams that, still and slow,
  Through the verdant meadows flow.

3 Safe the dreary vale I tread,
  By the shades of death o'erspread,
With Thy rod and staff supplied,
  This my guard, and that my guide.

4 Constant to my latest end,
  Thou my footsteps shalt attend;
And shalt bid Thy hallowed dome
  Yield me an eternal home.
            Rev. James Merrick. (1720–1769.)

638 "Order my steps in Thy Word." L. M.
Ps. xvi. John xiv. 1–6. Mat. xiv. 22–33.

1 JESUS, I fain would walk in Thee,
  From nature's every path retreat;
Thou art my Way; my Leader be,
  And set upon the rock my feet.

2 Uphold me, Saviour, or I fall;
  O reach me out Thy gracious hand!
Only on Thee for help I call,
  Only by faith in Thee I stand.
            Rev. Charles Wesley. (1708–1788.)

639 "I have chosen the way of truth." 7.
Luke viii. 38, 39. Eze. xxxvi. 32–38. Ps. lxxiii. 23–28.

1 SAVIOUR, more than life to me,
  I am clinging, clinging close to Thee;
Let Thy precious blood applied
  Keep me ever, ever near Thy side.

  Every day, every hour,
  Let me feel Thy cleansing power;
  May Thy tender love to me
  Bind me closer, closer, Lord, to Thee.

2 Through this changing world below
  Lead me gently, gently as I go;
Trusting Thee, I cannot stray;
  I can never, never lose my way.

3 Let me love Thee more and more,
  Till this fleeting, fleeting life is o'er;
Till my soul is lost in love,
  In a brighter, brighter world above.
            Mrs. Frances J. C. Van Alstyne. (1823–.)

121

"The Lord of peace Himself ... give peace."

640 "The Lord grant you may find rest." 7.
Ps. cxxxi. Mat. xviii. 1-14. 1 Pet. v. 4-10.

1 QUIET, Lord, my froward heart;
 Make me teachable and mild,
Upright, simple, free from art;
 Make me as a weanéd child:
From distrust and envy free,
Pleased with all that pleases Thee.

2 What Thou shalt to-day provide
 Let me as a child receive;
What to-morrow may betide
 Calmly to Thy wisdom leave:
'Tis enough that Thou wilt care;
Why should I the burden bear?

3 As a little child relies
 On a care beyond his own:
Knows he's neither strong nor wise,
 Fears to move one step alone:
Let me thus with Thee abide,
As my Father, Guard, and Guide.

4 Thus preserved from Satan's wiles,
 Safe from dangers, free from fears,
May I live upon Thy smiles,
 Till the promised hour appears,
When the sons of God shall prove
All their Father's boundless love.
Rev. John Newton. (1725-1807.)

641 "Lead me in Thy truth." L. M.
Rom. vii. 13-25. Mark ix. 14-24. Ps. cxix. 1-8.

1 O THAT my load of sin were gone!
 O that I could at last submit
At Jesus' feet to lay it down,
 To lay my soul at Jesus' feet!

2 Rest for my soul I long to find;
 Saviour of all, if mine Thou art,
Give me Thy meek and lowly mind,
 And stamp Thine image on my heart.

3 Break off the yoke of inbred sin,
 And fully set my spirit free;
I cannot rest till pure within,
 Till I am wholly lost in Thee.

4 Fain would I learn of Thee, my God,
 Thy light and easy burden prove;
The cross all stained with hallowed blood,
 The labor of Thy dying love.

5 I would, but Thou must give the power,
 My heart from every sin release;
Bring near, bring near the joyful hour,
 And fill me with Thy perfect peace.
Rev. Charles Wesley. (1708-1788.)

642 "That I might rest." 8. P.
Ps. cxliii. Lam. v. Mark vi. 45-51.

1 ENCOMPASSED with clouds of distress,
 Just ready all hope to resign,
I pant for the light of Thy face,
 And fear it will never be mine.
Disheartened with waiting so long,
 I sink at Thy feet with my load;
All plaintive I pour out my song,
 And stretch forth my hands unto God.

2 Shine, Lord, and my terrors shall cease;
 The blood of atonement apply;
And lead me to Jesus for peace,
 The Rock that is higher than I.
Almighty to rescue Thou art;
 Thy grace is my shield and my tower;
O gladden my desolate heart,
 Let this be the day of Thy power!
Rev. Augustus M. Toplady. (1740-1778.)

643 "A good conscience." L. M.
2 Cor. i. 12-14. Acts xxiv. 10-16. Ps. cxx.

1 SWEET peace of conscience, heavenly guest,
 Come, fix Thy mansion in my breast!
Dispel my doubts, my fears control,
 And heal the anguish of my soul.

2 Come, smiling hope and joy sincere,
 Come, make your constant dwelling here!
Still let your presence cheer my heart,
 Nor sin compel you to depart.

3 Thou God of hope and peace divine,
 O make these sacred pleasures mine!
Forgive my sins, my fears remove,
 And send the tokens of Thy love.
Rev. Ottiwell Heginbotham. (1744-1768.)

644 "Thou hast wrought all our works in us." C. M.
Heb. iv. 4-10. Isa. xxx. 15-29. Ps. xvii.

1 MY Saviour, Thou hast promised rest,
 O give it now to me;
The rest of ceasing from myself,
 To find my all in Thee.

2 O Lord, I seek a holy rest,
 A victory over sin;
I seek that Thou alone shouldst reign
 O'er all, without, within.

3 In quietness and confidence,
 Saviour, my strength shall be;
And "Take me, else I cannot come!"
 Is still my cry to Thee.

4 Work in me, Lord, till on my soul
 Eternal light shall break,
And in Thy likeness, perfected,
 I satisfied shall wake.
Author unknown.

"The Lord of peace Himself ... give peace."

645 *"His soul shall dwell at ease."* **C. M.**
Ps. cxii. Mark ix. 14-27. Mat. xvii. 14-20.

1 LORD, I believe ; Thy power I own,
   Thy word I would obey ;
   I wander comfortless and lone,
   When from Thy truth I stray.

2 Lord, I believe ; but oft, I know,
   My faith is cold and weak :
   My weakness strengthen, and bestow
   The confidence I seek.

3 Yes, I believe ; and only Thou
   Canst give my soul relief :
   Lord, to Thy truth my spirit bow ;
   "Help Thou mine unbelief !"
   Rev. John R. Wreford. 1837.

646 *"I will trust in the covert of Thy wings."* **L. M.**
Ps. xxv. Micah vii. 7-20. Rom. v.

1 UNDER Thy wings, my God, I rest,
   Under Thy shadow safely lie ;
   By Thy own strength in peace possessed,
   While dreaded evils pass me by.

2 With strong desire I here can stay
   To see Thy love its work complete ;
   Here I can wait a long delay,
   Reposing at my Saviour's feet.

3 My place of lowly service, too,
   Beneath Thy sheltering wings I see ;
   For all the work I have to do
   Is done through strengthening rest in
   ⋅ Thee.

4 I would not rise this rest above ;
   I do not mourn my low estate ;
   Sure of my riches in Thy love,
   I feel it good to trust and wait.
   Miss Anna L. Waring. (1820-.)

647 *"Lord, Thou wilt ordain peace."* **C. M.**
Heb. iv. 1 John ii. Micah iv.

1 LORD, I believe a rest remains
   To all Thy people known ;
   A rest where pure enjoyment reigns,
   And Thou art loved alone :

2 A rest where all our soul's desire
   Is fixed on things above ;
   Where fear and sin and grief expire,
   Cast out by perfect love.

3 O that I now the rest might know,
   Believe, and enter in !
   Now, Saviour, now the power bestow,
   And let me cease from sin.

4 Remove this hardness from my heart,
   This unbelief remove ;
   To me the rest of faith impart,
   The Sabbath of Thy love.
   Rev. Charles Wesley. (1708-1788.)

648 *"That Thou mayest give him rest."* **8.**
Rom. viii. 31-39. James ii. 14-26. Ps. xl. 5-10.

1 NONE loves me, Saviour, with Thy love ;
   None else can meet such deeds as min- ;
   O grant me, as Thou shalt approve,
   All that befits a child of Thine !
   From every fear and doubt release,
   And give me confidence and peace.

2 Give me a faith shall never fail,
   One that shall always work by love ;
   And then, whatever foes assail,
   They shall but higher courage move
   More boldly for the truth to strive,
   And more by faith in Thee to live.

3 A heart that, when my days are glad,
   May never from Thy way decline ;
   And when the sky of life grows sad,
   May still submit its will to Thine :
   A heart that loves to trust in Thee,
   A patient heart create in me !
   Author unknown.

649 *"Mine eyes are unto Thee."* **6. 4.**
Luke xxiii. 39-43. Heb. xii. 1-4. Isa. xlv. 22-25.

1 MY faith looks up to Thee,
   Thou Lamb of Calvary,
   Saviour divine !
   Now hear me while I pray ;
   Take all my guilt away ;
   O let me from this day
   Be wholly Thine !

2 May Thy rich grace impart
   Strength to my fainting heart ;
   My zeal inspire ;
   As Thou hast died for me,
   O may my love to Thee
   Pure, warm, and changeless be,
   A living fire !

3 While life's dark maze I tread,
   And griefs around me spread,
   Be Thou my Guide ;
   Bid darkness turn to day,
   Wipe sorrow's tears away,
   Nor let me ever stray
   From Thee aside.

4 When ends life's transient dream,
   When death's cold, sullen stream
   Shall o'er me roll,
   Blest Saviour, then, in love,
   Fear and distrust remove ;
   O bear me safe above,
   A ransomed soul !
   Rev. Ray Palmer. (1808-.)

"Follow ... holiness."

650 "Peace ... to him that is near." 6, 4.
Gen. xxviii. Job xxiii. 3-12. 1 Thes. iv. 8-18.

1 NEARER, my God, to Thee,
   Nearer to Thee:
   E'en though it be a cross
   That raiseth me,
   Still all my song shall be,
   Nearer, my God, to Thee,
   Nearer to Thee.

2. Though like the wanderer,
   The sun gone down,
   Darkness be over me,
   My rest a stone,
   Yet in my dreams I'd be
   Nearer, my God, to Thee,
   Nearer to Thee.

3 There let the way appear
   Steps unto heaven ;
   All that Thou send'st to me,
   In mercy given ;
   Angels to beckon me
   Nearer, my God, to Thee,
   Nearer to Thee.

4 Then, with my waking thoughts
   Bright with Thy praise,
   Out of my stony griefs
   Bethel I'll raise ;
   So by my woes to be
   Nearer, my God, to Thee,
   Nearer to Thee.

5 Or if on joyful wing
   Cleaving the sky,
   Sun, moon, and stars forgot,
   Upwards I fly,
   Still all my song shall be,
   Nearer, my God, to Thee,
   Nearer to Thee.
   Mrs. Sarah F. Adams. (1805-1848.)

651 "My soul breaketh for the longing." C. M.
Ps. lxiii. Gen. xxxii. 24-30. 2 Tim. i. 1-12.

1 MY God, I know, I feel Thee mine,
   And will not quit my claim,
   Till all I have is lost in Thine,
   And all renewed I am.

2 I hold Thee with a trembling hand,
   And will not let Thee go,
   Till steadfastly by faith I stand,
   And all Thy goodness know.

3 No longer then my heart shall mourn,
   While, sanctified by grace,
   I only for Thy glory burn,
   And always see Thy face.
   Rev. Charles Wesley. (1708-1788.)

652 "Grant me the thing that I long for." 10,
Eph. i. 2 Cor. xi. 19 to xii. 10. Ps. xxvii.

1 NOT what I am, O Lord,
   But what Thou art :
   That, that alone,
   Can be my soul's true rest.
   Thy love, not mine,
   Bids fear and doubt depart,
   And stills the tempest
   Of my tossing breast.

2 Girt with that love of God
   On every side ;
   Breathing that love
   As heaven's own healing air,
   I work or wait,
   Still following my Guide,
   Braving each foe,
   Escaping every snare.

3 'T is what I know of Thee,
   My Lord and God,
   That fills my soul with peace,
   My lips with song.
   Thou art my Health, my Joy,
   My Staff and Rod ;
   Leaning on Thee,
   In weakness I am strong.

4 More of Thyself,
   O show me hour by hour;
   More of Thy love and truth,
   Incarnate Word !
   More of Thyself
   In all Thy grace and power ;
   More of Thy glory,
   O my God and Lord !
   Rev. Horatius Bonar. (180?-.)

653 "My flesh longeth for Thee." 8. 6.
Isa. xl. 8-31. Deu. viii. 7-10. Rev. xix. 1-16.

1 O GLORIOUS hope of perfect love !
   It lifts me up to things above ;
   It bears on eagles' wings ;
   It gives my ravished soul a taste,
   And makes me for some moments feast
   With Jesus' priests and kings.

2 Rejoicing now in earnest hope,
   I stand, and from the mountain top
   See all the land below :
   Rivers of milk and honey rise,
   And all the fruits of paradise
   In endless plenty grow.

3 A land of corn, and wine, and oil,
   Favored with God's peculiar smile,
   With every blessing blest ;
   There dwells the Lord our Righteousness,
   And keeps His own in perfect peace
   And everlasting rest.
   Rev. Charles Wesley.

"Follow ... holiness."

654 "And Enoch walked with God." C. M.
Ps. ci. Micah iv. 1-5. Rom vii. 7 to viii. 4.

1 O FOR a closer walk with God,
   A calm and heavenly frame ;
   A light to shine upon the road
   That leads me to the Lamb !

2 What peaceful hours I once enjoyed ;
   How sweet their memory still !
   But they have left an aching void
   The world can never fill.

3 Return, O holy Dove, return,
   Sweet messenger of rest :
   I hate the sins that made Thee mourn,
   And drove Thee from my breast.

4 The dearest idol I have known,
   Whate'er that idol be,
   Help me to tear it from Thy throne,
   And worship only Thee.
                         William Cowper. (1731-1800.)

655 "With my soul have I desired Thee." L. M.
Ps. cxix. 57-64. Prov. iii 13-26. Rom. vi.

1 IN vain the world's alluring smile
   Would my unwary heart beguile ;
   To nobler bliss my soul aspires ;
   Come, Lord, and fill these vast desires !

2 O let Thy sacred word impart
   Its healing influence to my heart ;
   With power, and light, and love divine,
   Assure my soul that Thou art mine.

3 Then shall my joyful spirit rise,
   On wings of faith, above the skies ;
   And dwell forever near Thy throne,
   In joys to mortal thought unknown.
                         Miss Anne Steele. (1717-1778.)

656 "O that I had wings like a dove !" C. M.
Ps. cxliii. Isa. xl. 28-31. 2 Cor. iv. 16-18.

1 THE bird let loose in Eastern skies,
   When hastening fondly home,
   Ne'er stoops to earth her wing, nor flies
   Where idle warblers roam ;

2 But high she shoots, through air and light,
   Above all low delay,
   Where nothing earthly bounds her flight,
   Nor shadow dims her way.

3 So grant me, Lord, from every care
   And stain of passion free,
   Aloft, through virtue's purer air,
   To hold my course to Thee.

4 No sin to cloud, no lure to stay,
   My soul, as home she springs ;
   Thy sunshine on her joyful way,
   Thy freedom in her wings.
                         Thomas Moore. (1779-1852.)

657 "I have stretched out my hands unto Thee." 8.
Ps. xlii. Ex. xvii. 1-6. 2 Pet. iii. 8-18.

1 As, panting in the sultry beam,
   The hart desires the cooling stream,
   So to Thy presence, Lord, I flee ;
   So longs my soul, O God, for Thee :
   Athirst to taste Thy living grace,
   And see Thy glory, face to face.

2 Ah, why, by passing clouds opprest,
   Should vexing thoughts distract thy breast ?
   Turn, turn to Him, in every pain,
   Whom suppliants never sought in vain :
   Thy Strength, in joy's ecstatic day ;
   Thy Hope, when joy has passed away.
                         John Bowdler. (1783-1815.)

658 "It is good for me to draw near to God." 6.
Ps. lxxiii. Job xlii. 1-6. Acts xxvi. 1-29.

1 I DID Thee wrong, my God,
   I wronged Thy truth and love ;
   I fretted at the rod,
   Against Thy power I strove.
   Come nearer, nearer still ;
   Let not Thy light depart ;
   Bend, break, this stubborn will,
   Dissolve this iron heart.

2 Less wayward let me be,
   More pliable and mild ;
   In glad simplicity
   More like a trustful child.
   Less, less of self each day,
   And more, my God, of Thee ;
   O keep me in the way,
   However rough it be.

3 Less of the flesh each day,
   Less of the world and sin ;
   More of Thy Son, I pray,
   More of Thyself within.
   More moulded to Thy will,
   Lord, let Thy servant be ;
   Higher and higher still,
   Liker and liker Thee.
                         Rev. Horatius Bonar. (1808--.)

659 "That I may dwell in the house of the Lord." C. M.
Ps. xc. 1 Chr. xvii. John xv. 1-9.

1 GRANT me within Thy courts a place,
   Among Thy saints a seat ;
   Forever to behold Thy face,
   And worship at Thy feet :

2 In Thy pavilion to abide,
   When storms of trouble blow ;
   And in Thy tabernacle hide,
   Secure from every foe.
                         James Montgomery. (1771-1854.)

"Follow ... holiness."

660 "To increase and abound in love." **6. 4.**
Phil. iii. 7-14.   John xxi. 15-17.   Ps. lxiii. 1-8.

1 MORE love to Thee, O Christ,
　　More love to Thee!
　Hear Thou the prayer I make
　　On bended knee;
　This is my earnest plea:
　More love, O Christ, to Thee,
　　More love to Thee!

2 Once earthly joy I craved,
　　Sought peace and rest;
　Now Thee alone I seek;
　　Give what is best.
　This all my prayer shall be:
　More love, O Christ, to Thee,
　　More love to Thee!

3 Then shall my latest breath
　　Whisper Thy praise;
　This be the parting cry
　　My heart shall raise;
　This still its prayer shall be:
　More love, O Christ, to Thee,
　　More love to Thee!
　　　　Mrs. Elizabeth P. Prentiss.   (1819-1860.)

661 "I will abide in Thy tabernacle." **10. 6.**
Ps. cxix. 89-104.   Acts xxii. 1-21.   1 Pet. i.

1 　I AM Thine, O Lord;
　　　I have heard Thy voice,
　　And it told Thy love to me;
　　　But I long to rise
　　　In the arms of faith,
　　And be closer drawn to Thee.

　　Draw me nearer, nearer, blessèd Lord,
　　　To the cross where Thou hast died;
　　Draw me nearer, nearer, blessèd Lord,
　　　To Thy precious, bleeding side.

2 　Consecrate me now
　　　To Thy service, Lord,
　　By the power of grace divine;
　　　Let my soul look up
　　　With a steadfast hope,
　　And my will be lost in Thine.

3 　There are depths of love
　　　That I cannot know
　　Till I cross the narrow sea;
　　　There are heights of joy
　　　That I may not reach
　　Till I rest in peace with Thee.
　　　　Mrs. Frances J. C. Van Alstyne.   (1823-..)

662 "I will gain the strength of the Lord." **6. 4.**
Num. ix. 15-23.   Ex. xvii. 1-6.   Gal. ii. 19-21.

1 SAVIOUR, I follow on,
　　Guided by Thee;
　Seeing not yet the hand
　　That leadeth me.
　Hushed be my heart and still,
　Fear I no further ill;
　　Only to meet Thy will
　　　My will shall be.

2 Riven the rock for me,
　　Thirst to relieve;
　Manna from heaven falls
　　Fresh every eve.
　Never a want severe
　Causeth my eye a tear,
　But Thou dost whisper near,
　　"Only believe!"

3 Saviour, I long to walk
　　Closer with Thee;
　Led by Thy guiding hand
　　Ever to be;
　Constantly near Thy side,
　Quickened and purified;
　Living for Him who died
　　Freely for me!
　　　　Rev. Charles S. Robinson.   1862.

663 "Love made perfect." **C. M.**
Ps. cxix. 25-32, 89-96.   Eph. iii.   Rom. viii.

1 DEEPEN the wound Thy hands have made
　　In this weak, helpless soul,
　Till mercy, with its balmy aid,
　　Descend to make me whole.

2 I see th' exceeding broad command,
　　Which all contains in one;
　Enlarge my heart to understand
　　The mystery unknown.

3 O that with all Thy saints I might
　　By sweet experience prove
　What is the length and breadth and height
　　And depth of perfect love!
　　　　Rev. Charles Wesley.   (1708-1788.)

664 "Of the abundance of the heart." **L. M.**
Mat. xii. 35-37.   James iii.   Prov. xv. 1-3.

1 WHAT! never speak one evil word,
　Or rash, or idle, or unkind?
　O how shall I, most gracious Lord,
　This mark of true perfection find?

2 Thy sinless mind in me reveal;
　Thy Spirit's plenitude impart;
　And all my spotless life shall tell
　Th' abundance of a loving heart.
　　　　Rev. Charles Wesley.

"Follow ... holiness."

665 "More to be desired." 2 Pet. i. 1–11. Col. i. 9–20. Isa. xl. 28–31.   **6. 5.**

1 PURER yet and purer
   I would be in mind ;
   Dearer yet and dearer
   Every duty find.
   Hoping still, and trusting
   God without a fear ;
   Patiently believing
   He will make all clear.

2 Calmer yet and calmer
   Trial bear, and pain ;
   Surer yet and surer
   Peace at last to gain.
   Suff'ring still and doing,
   To His will resigned,
   And to God subduing
   Heart and will and mind.

3 Higher yet and higher
   Out of clouds and night ;
   Nearer yet and nearer
   Rising to the light :
   Light serene and holy,
   Where my soul may rest ;
   Purified and lowly,
   Sanctified and blest.
   Author unknown.

666 "In the likeness of His resurrection." Phil. ii. 1–13. Rom. vi. 1–14. Ps. lxiii.   **7.**

1 MORE like Jesus would I be !
   Let my Saviour dwell in me ;
   Fill my soul with peace and love,
   Make me gentle as a dove.

2 More like Jesus while I go,
   Pilgrim, in this world below ;
   Poor in spirit would I be :
   Let my Saviour dwell in me.

3 He will teach me how to live,
   All my sinful thoughts forgive ;
   Pure in heart I still would be :
   Let my Saviour dwell in me.

4 More like Jesus when I pray,
   More like Jesus day by day ;
   May I rest me by His side,
   Where the tranquil waters glide.

5 Born of Him, through grace renewed,
   By His love my will subdued,
   Rich in faith I still would be :
   Let my Saviour dwell in me.
   Mrs. Frances J. C. Van Alstyne. (1820–.)

667 "Reaching forth." Ps. cxxxii. 2 Chr. xxx. 1–23. 1 Pet. iii. 8–15.   **8.**

1 IN all extremes, Lord, Thou art still
   The mount whereto my hopes do flee ;
   O make my soul detest all ill,
   Because so much abhorred by Thee :
   Lord, let Thy gracious trials show
   That I am just, or make me so.

2 Fountain of light, and living breath,
   Whose mercies never fail or fade,
   Fill me with life that hath no death,
   Fill me with light that hath no shade :
   Appoint the remnant of my days
   To see Thy power and sing Thy praise.

3 O Thou who sitt'st in heaven and seest
   My deeds without, my thoughts within,
   Be Thou my Prince, be Thou my Priest,
   Command my soul, and cure my sin :
   How bitter my afflictions be
   I care not, so I rise to Thee.

4 What I possess or what I crave
   Brings no content, great God, to me,
   If what I would or what I have
   Be not possessed and blest in Thee :
   What I enjoy, O make it mine,
   In making me, that have it, Thine.
   John Quarles. (–1665.)

668 "Unto those things which are before." Jer. xv. 15–21. Ps. cxix. 169–176. Rev. iii. 7–13.   **C. M.**

1 MY Saviour, on the word of truth,
   In earnest hope, I live :
   I ask for all the precious things
   Thy boundless love can give.

2 In holy expectation held,
   Thy strength my heart shall stay ;
   For Thy right hand will never let
   My trust be cast away.

3 Thou knowest that I am not blest
   As Thou wouldst have me be,
   Till all the peace and joy of faith
   Possess my soul in Thee.

4 It is not as Thou wilt with me,
   Till humbled in the dust,
   I know no place in all my heart
   Wherein to put my trust ;

5 Until I find, O Lord, in Thee,
   The lowly and the meek,
   That fulness which Thy own redeemed
   Go nowhere else to seek.
   Miss Anna L. Waring. (1820–.)

"My voice shalt Thou hear in the morning."

669 "Early will I seek Thee." L. M.
Ps. cviii. Isa. xxv. Gal. vi. 2-10.

1 O GOD, my God, my All Thou art!
   Ere shines the dawn of rising day,
   Thy sovereign light within my heart,
   Thy all-enlivening power, display.

2 For Thee my thirsty soul doth pant,
   While in this desert land I live;
   And, hungry as I am, and faint,
   Thy love alone can comfort give.

3 More dear than life itself, Thy love
   My heart and tongue shall still employ;
   And to declare Thy praise will prove
   My peace, my glory, and my joy.

4 In blessing Thee with grateful songs,
   My happy life shall glide away;
   The praise that to Thy name belongs,
   Hourly, with lifted hands, I'll pay.
   Author unknown.
   Tr. by Rev. John Wesley. (1703-1791.)

670 "In the morning shall my prayer prevent Thee." L. M.
Ps. lxiii. 1 Kings xviii. 30-46. 2 Cor. xi. 16-31.

1 O GOD, Thou art my God alone!
   Early to Thee my soul shall cry,
   A pilgrim in a land unknown,
   A thirsty land, whose springs are dry.

2 Yet, through this rough and thorny maze,
   I follow hard on Thee, my God;
   Thy hand unseen upholds my ways;
   I safely tread where Thou hast trod.

3 Thee, in the watches of the night,
   When I remember on my bed,
   Thy presence makes the darkness light;
   Thy guardian wings are round my head.

4 Better than life itself Thy love,
   Dearer than all beside to me;
   For whom have I in heaven above,
   Or what on earth, compared with Thee?
   James Montgomery. (1771-1854.)

671 "In Thy light." L. M.
Ps. cxli. Job i. 1-5. 2 Cor. vi. 1-10.

1 MY GOD, accept my early vows,
   Like morning incense in Thy house;
   And let my nightly worship rise,
   Sweet as the evening sacrifice.

2 Watch o'er my lips, and guard them, Lord,
   From every rash and heedless word;
   Nor let my feet incline to tread
   The guilty path where sinners lead.

3 O may the righteous, when I stray,
   Smite and reprove my wandering way;
   Their gentle words, like ointment shed,
   Shall never bruise, but shield my head.
   Rev. Isaac Watts. (1674-1748.)

672 "Day unto day uttereth speech." L. M.
Gen. i. 1-18. Col. iii. 1 Pet. ii. 1-12.

1 GOD of the morning, at whose voice
   The cheerful sun makes haste to rise,
   And like a giant doth rejoice
   To run his journey through the skies;

2 O, like the sun, may I fulfil
   Th' appointed duties of the day;
   With ready mind and active will
   March on, and keep my heavenly way.
   Rev. Isaac Watts.

673 "The day-spring from on high." 7.
John i. 1-9. Mal. iv. 2-6. Ps. xxvii.

1 CHRIST, whose glory fills the skies,
   Christ, the true, the only Light,
   Sun of Righteousness, arise,
   Triumph o'er the shades of night:
   Day-spring from on high, be near;
   Day-star, in my heart appear.

2 Dark and cheerless is the morn,
   Unaccompanied by Thee;
   Joyless is the day's return,
   Till Thy mercy's beams I see:
   Till they inward light impart,
   Glad my eyes and warm my heart.

3 Visit then this soul of mine,
   Pierce the gloom of sin and grief;
   Fill me, Radiancy divine,
   Scatter all my unbelief:
   More and more Thyself display,
   Shining to the perfect day.
   Rev. Charles Wesley. (1708-1788.)

674 "I awaked, for the Lord sustained me." S. M.
Ps. xix. Isa. xxxviii. 9-21. Luke xix. 1-10.

1 SEE how the morning sun
   Pursues his shining way;
   And wide proclaims his Maker's praise
   With every bright'ning ray.

2 Thus would my rising soul
   Its heavenly Parent sing,
   And to its great Original
   The humble tribute bring.

3 Serene I laid me down,
   Beneath His guardian care;
   I slept, and I awoke, and found
   My kind Preserver near.

4 My life I would anew
   Devote, O Lord, to Thee;
   And in Thy service I would spend
   A long eternity.
   Miss Elizabeth Scott. 1764.

"My voice shalt Thou hear in the morning."

675 "In the morning will I look up."
Ps. xcii. Isa. xii. 2 John. **7.**

1 THOU, who dost my life prolong,
Kindly aid my morning song ;
Thankful, from my couch I rise,
To the God that rules the skies.

2 Thou hast kept me through the night;
'T was Thy hand restored the light ;
Lord, Thy mercies still are new,
Plenteous as the morning dew.

3 Still my feet are prone to stray ;
O preserve me through the day ;
Dangers everywhere abound,
Sins and snares beset me round.

4 Gently, with the dawning ray,
On my soul Thy beams display ;
Sweeter than the smiling morn,
Let Thy cheering light return.
Author unknown.

676 "I myself will awake early." **C. M.**
Ps. xxv. Gen. xxviii. 16-22. Rev. iii. 1-6.

1 AWAKE, my soul, to meet the day ;
Unfold thy drowsy eyes,
And burst the heavy chain that binds
Thine active faculties.

2 God's guardian shield was round me spread
In my defenceless sleep :
Let Him have all my waking hours
Who doth my slumbers keep.

3 Pardon, O God, my former sloth,
And arm my soul with grace ;
As, rising, now I seal my vows
To prosecute Thy ways.
Rev. Philip Doddridge. (1702-1751.)

677 "Daily shall He be praised." **L. M.**
Ps. v. Isa. lii. 1-10. Eph. v. 14-21.

1 AWAKE, my soul, and with the sun
Thy daily stage of duty run ;
Shake off dull sloth, and joyful rise
To pay thy morning sacrifice.

2 Wake, and lift up thyself, my heart,
And with the angels bear thy part,
Who, all night long, unwearied sing
High praise to the eternal King.

3 Lord, I my vows to Thee renew ;
Disperse my sins as morning dew ;
Guard my first springs of thought and will,
And with Thyself my spirit fill.

4 Direct, control, suggest, this day,
All I design, or do, or say ;
That all my powers, with all their might,
In Thy sole glory may unite.
Bp. Thomas Ken. (1637-1711.)

678 "Awake up, my glory." **C. M.**
Ps. cviii. 1-6. Ex. xxx. 1-10. John xii. 35-50.

1 AGAIN, from calm and sweet repose,
I rise to hail the dawn ;
Again my waking eyes unclose
To view the smiling morn.

2 Glory to Thee, eternal Lord !
O teach my heart to pray ;
And thy blest Spirit's help afford,
To guide me through the day.

3 Let every thought and word accord
With Thy most holy will ;
Each deed the precepts of Thy word
With pious aim fulfil.

4 From danger, sin, and every ill
My constant Guardian prove ;
O sanctify my heart, and fill
With thoughts of holy love.
Rev. Charles Philpot. 1871.

679 "Awake, psaltery and harp." **C. M.**
Ps. xix. Rom. xii. Eph. iv.

1 ONCE more, my soul, the rising day
Salutes thy waking eyes ;
Once more, my voice, thy tribute pay
To Him who rules the skies.

2 Night unto night His name repeats,
The day renews the sound,
Wide as the heaven on which He sits
To turn the seasons round.

3 Great God, let all my hours be Thine
Whilst I enjoy the light ;
Then shall my sun in smiles decline,
And bring a peaceful night.
Rev. Isaac Watts. (1674-1748.)

680 "That I may daily perform my vows." **L. M.**
Ps. cxxiii. Micah iv. 4, 5. Col. ii. 6-23.

1 FORTH in Thy name, O Lord, I go,
My daily labor to pursue ;
Thee, only Thee, resolved to know,
In all I think, or speak, or do.

2 The task Thy wisdom hath assigned
O let me cheerfully fulfil ;
In all my works Thy presence find,
And prove Thy good and perfect will.

3 Give me to bear Thine easy yoke,
And every moment watch and pray ;
And still to things eternal look,
And hasten to Thy glorious day.

4 Fain would I still for Thee employ
Whate'er Thy bounteous grace hath given,
And run my course with even joy,
And closely walk with Thee to heaven.
Rev. Charles Wesley. (1708-1788.)

"Evening and morning and at noon will I pray."

681 "With my spirit... will I seek Thee early." **C. M.**
Ps. lxiii. 2 Chr. xxxv. 1–18. Luke vii. 36–50.

1 EARLY, my God, without delay,
   I haste to seek Thy face;
   My thirsty spirit faints away,
   Without Thy cheering grace.

2 Not all the blessings of a feast
   Can please my soul so well
   As when Thy richer grace I taste,
   And in Thy presence dwell.

3 Not life itself, with all its joys,
   Can my best passions move,
   Or raise so high my cheerful voice,
   As Thy forgiving love.

4 Thus, till my last expiring day,
   I'll bless my God and King;
   Thus will I lift my hands to pray,
   And tune my lips to sing.
   Rev. Isaac Watts. (1674-1748.)

682 "I awaked,... and my sleep was sweet." **L. M.**
Lam. iii. 22–41. Deu. xxxiii. 1 Thes. v. 5–28.

1 MY God, how endless is Thy love!
   Thy gifts are every evening new;
   And morning mercies from above
   Gently distil like early dew.

2 Thou spread'st the curtains of the night,
   Great Guardian of my sleeping hours;
   Thy sovereign word restores the light,
   And quickens all my drowsy powers.

3 I yield my powers to Thy command;
   To Thee I consecrate my days;
   Perpetual blessings from Thy hand
   Demand perpetual songs of praise.
   Rev. Isaac Watts.

683 "My prayer unto the God of my life." **7.**
Ps. iv. Dan. vi. 1–11. Acts vii. 55–60.

1 IN this calm, impressive hour,
   Let my prayer ascend on high;
   God of mercy, God of power,
   Hear me, when to Thee I cry:
   Hear me from Thy lofty throne,
   For the sake of Christ, Thy Son.

2 With the morning's early ray,
   While the shades of night depart,
   Let Thy beams of light convey
   Joy and gladness to my heart:
   Now o'er all my steps preside,
   And for all my wants provide.
   Thomas Hastings. (1784-1872.)

684 "Thou knowest... mine uprising." **C. M.**
Ps. cxlv. Ecc. iii. 1–15. 1 Thes. iv.

1 ON Thee, each morning, O my God,
   My waking thoughts attend;
   In Thee are founded all my hopes,
   In Thee my wishes end.

2 My soul, in pleasing wonder lost,
   Thy boundless love surveys;
   And, fired with grateful zeal, prepares
   A sacrifice of praise.

3 God leads me through the maze of sleep,
   And brings me safe to light;
   And, with the same paternal care,
   Conducts my steps till night.

4 When evening slumbers press mine eyes,
   With His protection blest,
   In peace and safety I commit
   My wearied limbs to rest.

5 My spirit, in His hand secure,
   Fears no approaching ill;
   For, whether waking or asleep,
   The Lord is with me still.
   Rev. Andrew Kippis. (1725-1795.)

685 "And Thy salvation all the day." **8.**
Ps. v. Rom. xiv. 7–13. 2 Tim. ii. 1–13.

1 WHEN, streaming from the eastern skies,
   The morning light salutes mine eyes,
   O Sun of Righteousness divine,
   On me with beams of mercy shine;
   Chase the dark clouds of guilt away,
   And turn my darkness into day.

2 And when to heaven's all-glorious King
   My morning sacrifice I bring,
   And, mourning o'er my guilt and shame,
   Ask mercy in my Saviour's name,
   Then, Jesus, cleanse me with Thy blood,
   And be my Advocate with God.

3 When each day's scenes and labors close,
   And wearied nature seeks repose,
   With pard'ning mercy richly blest,
   Guard me, my Saviour, while I rest;
   And as each morning sun shall rise,
   O lead me onward to the skies.

4 And at my life's last setting sun,
   My conflicts o'er, my labors done,
   Jesus, Thy heavenly radiance shed,
   To cheer and bless my dying bed;
   And from death's gloom my spirit raise,
   To see Thy face, and sing Thy praise.
   William Shrubsole, Jr. (1770-1829.)

"Evening and morning and at noon will I pray."

686 "Unto Thee will I sing."
Ps. cxlvi. Phil. iv. 4-9. 1 Thes. v. 16-28. **7. 6.**

1 To Thee, my God and Saviour,
  My heart exulting sings;
  Rejoicing in Thy favor,
  Almighty King of kings!
  I'll celebrate Thy glory,
  With all Thy saints above,
  And tell the joyful story
  Of Thy redeeming love.

2 Soon as the morn, with roses,
  Bedecks the dewy east,
  And when the sun reposes
  Upon the ocean's breast,
  My voice, in supplication,
  Well-pleaséd Thou shalt hear:
  O grant me Thy salvation,
  And to my soul draw near.

3 By Thee through life supported,
  I pass the dangerous road,
  With heavenly hosts escorted,
  Up to their bright abode;
  There, cast my crown before Thee,
  Now all my conflicts o'er,
  And day and night adore Thee:
  What can an angel more?

  Thomas Hastings. (1784-1872.)

687 "I laid me down and slept; I awaked."
Ps. lv. 16-23. Ecc. xi. 1 Pet. i. 13-25. **L. M.**

1 In sleep's serene oblivion laid,
  I safely passed the silent night;
  Again I see the breaking shade,
  I drink again the morning light.

2 New-born, I bless the waking hour,
  Once more, with awe, rejoice to be;
  My conscious soul resumes her power,
  And springs, my guardian God, to Thee.

3 O guide me through the various maze
  My doubtful feet are doomed to tread;
  And spread Thy shield's protecting blaze,
  When dangers press around my head.

4 A deeper shade will soon impend,
  A deeper sleep mine eyes oppress;
  Yet then Thy strength shall still defend,
  Thy goodness still delight to bless.

5 That deeper shade shall break away,
  That deeper sleep shall leave mine eyes;
  Thy light shall give eternal day,
  Thy love, the rapture of the skies.

  John Hawkesworth. (1715-1773.)

688 "I am still with Thee."
Ps. cxxxix. John xv. 4-10. Mark ix. 2-10. **11. 10.**

1 Still, still with Thee
  When purple morning breaketh,
  When the bird waketh,
  And the shadows flee;
  Fairer than morning,
  Lovelier than the daylight,
  Dawns the sweet consciousness,
  I am with Thee.

2 Alone with Thee,
  Amid the mystic shadows,
  The solemn hush
  Of nature newly born;
  Alone with Thee,
  In breathless adoration,
  In the calm dew
  And freshness of the morn.

3 When sinks the soul,
  Subdued by toil, to slumber,
  Its closing eye
  Looks up to Thee in prayer,
  Sweet the repose
  Beneath Thy wings o'ershading,
  But sweeter still
  To wake and find Thee there.

4 So shall it be
  At last, in that bright morning,
  When the soul waketh,
  And life's shadows flee;
  O in that hour,
  Fairer than daylight dawning,
  Shall rise the glorious thought,
  I am with Thee.

  Mrs. Harriet E. B. Stowe. (1812-.)

689 "I have cried day and night unto Thee."
Ps. v. Rom. xii. Gen. xxviii. 16-22. **7.**

1 In the morning hear my voice,
  Let me in Thy light rejoice;
  God, my Sun, my strength renew,
  Send Thy blessing down like dew.

2 Through the duties of the day,
  Grant me grace to watch and pray;
  Live as always seeing Thee,
  Knowing Thou, God, seest me.

3 When the round of care is run,
  And the stars succeed the sun,
  Songs of prayer with praise unite,
  Crown the day, and hail the night.

  James Montgomery. (1771-1854.)

"And the lifting up of my hands as the evening sacrifice."

690 "Let my prayer be...as incense." **L. M.**
Ps. iv. Job xi. 13-20. Acts xiii. 38, 39.

1 GREAT God, to Thee my evening song
  With humble gratitude I raise ;
  O let Thy mercy tune my tongue,
  And fill my heart with lively praise.

2 My days, unclouded as they pass,
  And every gently rolling hour,
  Are monuments of wondrous grace,
  And witness to Thy love and power.

3 Seal my forgiveness in the blood
  Of Jesus ; His dear name alone
  I plead for pardon, gracious God,
  And kind acceptance at Thy throne.

4 Let this blest hope mine eyelids close ;
  With sleep refresh my feeble frame ;
  Safe in Thy care may I repose,
  And wake with praises to Thy name.

  Miss Anna Steele. (1717-1778.)

691 "Thou, Lord, only makest me dwell in safety." **L. M.**
Ps. cxlv. Eph. v. Acts xxvii. 19-36.

1 ALL praise to Thee, my God, this night,
  For all the blessings of the light ;
  Keep me, O keep me, King of kings,
  Beneath Thine own almighty wings.

2 Forgive me, Lord, for Thy dear Son,
  The ill that I this day have done ;
  That with the world, myself, and Thee,
  I, ere I sleep, at peace may be.

3 When in the night I sleepless lie,
  My soul with heavenly thoughts supply ;
  Let no ill dreams disturb my rest,
  No powers of darkness me molest.

4 O may my soul on Thee repose,
  And may sweet sleep mine eyelids close ;
  Sleep, that shall me more vigorous make,
  To serve my God when I awake.

  Bp. Thomas Ken. (1637-1711.)

692 "I have called daily upon Thee." **8. 6. 8.**
Ps. xc. John xx. 19-31. Phil. iv. 4-9.

1 LORD of my life, whose tender care
  Hath led me on till now,
  Here, lowly, at the hour of prayer,
  Before Thy throne I bow :
  I bless Thy gracious hand, and pray
  Forgiveness for another day.

2 With prayer my humble praise I bring,
  For mercies day by day ;
  Lord, teach my heart Thy love to sing,
  Lord, teach me how to pray ;
  All that I have, I am, to Thee
  I offer, through eternity.

  Author unknown.

693 "He knoweth the way I take." **C. M.**
Ps. lv. 16-18. Heb. vi. 10-20. Ecc. iii. 1-15.

1 THE twilight falls, the night is near ;
  I fold my work away,
  And kneel to One who bends to hear
  The story of the day.

2 The old, old story ; yet I kneel
  To tell it at Thy call ;
  And cares grow lighter as I feel
  That Jesus knows them all.

3 Thou knowest all ; I lean my head,
  My weary eyelids close ;
  Content and glad awhile to tread
  This path, since Jesus knows.

4 And He has loved me : all my heart
  With answering love is stirred,
  And every anguished pain and smart
  Finds healing in the word.

5 So here I lay me down to rest,
  As nightly shadows fall,
  And lean confiding on His breast
  Who knows and pities all.

  Author unknown.

694 "When thou liest down, thou shalt not be afraid." **7.**
Ps. civ. 23-35. Mat. xiv. 14-23. John iii. 1-17.

1 Now from labor and from care
  Evening hours have set me free ;
  In the work of praise and prayer,
  Lord, I would converse with Thee :
  O behold me from above,
  Fill me with a Saviour's love.

2 For the blessings of this day,
  For the mercies of this hour,
  For the gospel's cheering ray,
  For the Spirit's quickening power,
  Grateful notes to Thee I raise :
  O accept the song of praise.

  Thomas Hastings. (1784-1872.)

695 "Thou art with me." **C. M.**
Ps. xxxi. Ezra ix. 5-10. Heb. x. 1-14.

1 LORD, Thou wilt hear me when I pray ;
  I am forever Thine ;
  I fear before Thee all the day,
  Nor would I dare to sin.

2 I pay this evening sacrifice ;
  And when my work is done,
  Great God, my faith and hope relies
  Upon Thy grace alone.

3 Thus with my thoughts composed to peace,
  I'll give mine eyes to sleep ;
  Thy hand in safety keeps my days,
  And will my slumbers keep.

  Rev. Isaac Watts. (1674-1748.)

"And the lifting up of my hands as the evening sacrifice."

696 " Are they not all ministering spirits?" **8. P.**
Ps. lxxi. Mat. xiv. 15-33. Acts xii. 1-10.

1 INSPIRER and hearer of prayer,
   Thou Shepherd and Guardian of Thine,
My all to Thy covenant care
   I, sleeping and waking, resign.
If Thou art my Shield and my Sun,
   The night is no darkness to me,
And, fast as my moments roll on,
   They bring me but nearer to Thee.

2 Thy ministering spirits descend,
   And watch while Thy saints are asleep;
By day and by night they attend,
   The heirs of salvation to keep.
Bright seraphs, despatched from the throne,
   Fly swift to their stations assigned;
And angels elect are sent down
   To guard the redeemed of mankind.

3 Thy worship no interval knows;
   Their fervor is still on the wing;
And while they protect my repose,
   They chant to the praise of my King.
I, too, at the season ordained,
   Their chorus forever shall join,
And love and adore, without end,
   Their gracious Creator, and mine.
                        Rev. Augustus M. Toplady. (1740-1778.)

697 " I will both lay me down in peace and sleep." **S. M.**
Ecc. xi. 6 to xii. 7. Ps. xvii. John xvii.

1 THE day is past and gone,
   The evening shades appear;
O may I ever keep in mind
   The night of death draws near.

2 I lay my garments by,
   Upon my bed to rest;
So death will soon remove me hence,
   And leave my soul undressed.

3 Lord, keep me safe this night,
   Secure from all my fears;
May angels guard me while I sleep,
   Till morning light appears.

4 And when I early rise,
   To view th' unwearied sun,
May I set out to win the prize,
   And after glory run:

5 That when my days are past,
   And I from time remove,
Lord, I may in Thy bosom rest,
   The bosom of Thy love.
                        Rev. John Leland. (1754-1841.)

698 " Sleep on now, and take your rest." **8. P.**
Ps. cxxi. Neh. ix. 6-25. Eph. iv. 1-16.

1 WHAT though my frail eyelids refuse
   Continual watching to keep,
And, punctual as midnight renews,
   Demand the refreshment of sleep?
A sovereign Protector I have,
   Unseen, yet forever at hand;
Unchangeably faithful to save,
   Almighty to rule and command.

2 From evil secure, and its dread,
   I rest, if my Saviour is nigh;
And songs His kind presence indeed,
   Shall in the night season supply.
He smiles, and my comforts abound,
   His grace as the dew shall descend,
And walls of salvation surround
   The soul He delights to defend.

3 Kind Author, and Ground of my hope,
   Thee, Thee for my God I avow;
My glad Ebenezer set up,
   And own Thou hast helped me till now;
I muse on the years that are past,
   Wherein my defence Thou hast proved;
Nor wilt Thou relinquish at last
   A sinner so signally loved.
                        Rev. Augustus M. Toplady.

699 " In Thy presence is fulness of joy." **C. M.**
Ps. xl. Mark vi. 30-32. Heb. iv.

1 I LOVE to steal awhile away
   From every cumbering care,
And spend the hours of setting day
   In humble, grateful prayer.

2 I love in solitude to shed
   The penitential tear,
And all His promises to plead
   Where none but God is near.

3 I love to think on mercies past,
   And future good implore,
And all my cares and sorrows cast
   On Him whom I adore.

4 I love by faith to take a view
   Of brighter scenes in heaven;
The prospect doth my strength renew,
   While here by tempests driven.

5 Thus, when life's toilsome day is o'er,
   May its departing ray
Be calm as this impressive hour,
   And lead to endless day.
                        Mrs. Phebe H. Brown. (1783-1861.)

"And the lifting up of my hands as the evening sacrifice."

700 "I cry... in the night season." 8. 7.
Luke xxiv. 28-32. Gen. xix. 1-3. Ps. xvi.

1 TARRY with me, O my Saviour,
  For the day is passing by;
See, the shades of evening gather,
  And the night is drawing nigh.
Deeper, deeper grow the shadows,
  Paler now the glowing west;
Swift the night of death advances;
  Shall it be the night of rest?

2 Lonely seems the vale of shadow,
  Sinks my heart with troubled fear;
Give me faith for clearer vision,
  Speak Thou, Lord, in words of cheer.
Let me hear Thy voice behind me,
  Calming all these wild alarms;
Let me, underneath my weakness,
  Feel the everlasting arms.

3 Feeble, trembling, fainting, dying,
  Lord, I cast myself on Thee;
Tarry with me through the darkness;
  While I sleep still watch by me.
Tarry with me, O my Saviour;
  Lay my head upon Thy breast
Till the morning; then awake me,
  Morning of eternal rest.

Mrs. Caroline S. Smith. 1855.

701 "Who giveth songs in the night." C. M.
Ps. cxli. Isa. xxv. 1-9. 1 Thes. v. 1-10.

1 DREAD Sovereign, let my evening song
    Like holy incense rise;
  Assist the offerings of my tongue
    To reach the lofty skies.

2 Through all the dangers of the day
    Thy hand was still my guard;
  And still to drive my wants away
    Thy mercy stood prepared.

3 Perpetual blessings from above
    Encompass me around;
  But O how few returns of love
    Hath my Creator found!

4 Lord, with this guilty heart of mine,
    To Thy dear cross I flee;
  And to Thy grace my soul resign,
    To be renewed by Thee.

5 Sprinkled afresh with pardoning blood,
    I lay me down to rest,
  As in the embraces of my God,
    Or on my Saviour's breast.

Rev. Isaac Watts. (1674-1748.)

702 "The night shineth as the day." L. M.
Isa. lx. 19, 20. Ps. xxvii. Eph. iii. 14-21.

1 SUN of my soul, Thou Saviour dear,
  It is not night if Thou be near;
  O may no earth-born cloud arise
  To hide Thee from Thy servant's eyes.

2 When the soft dews of kindly sleep
  My wearied eyelids gently steep,
  Be my last thought, how sweet to rest
  Forever on my Saviour's breast!

3 Abide with me from morn till eve,
  For without Thee I cannot live;
  Abide with me when night is nigh,
  For without Thee I dare not die.

4 If some poor wandering child of Thine
  Have spurned to-day the voice divine,
  Now, Lord, the gracious work begin;
  Let him no more lie down in sin.

5 Watch by the sick; enrich the poor
  With blessings from Thy boundless store;
  Be every mourner's sleep to night,
  Like infant's slumbers, pure and light.

6 Come near and bless us when we wake,
  Ere through the world our way we take,
  Till in the ocean of Thy love
  We lose ourselves in heaven above.

Rev. John Keble. (1792-1866.)

703 "In the night His song shall be with me." C. M.
Ps. cxlv. John vi. 15-37. 2 Pet. iii.

1 HAIL, tranquil hour of closing day;
    Begone, disturbing care;
  And look, my soul, from earth away
    To Him who heareth prayer.

2 How sweet the tear of penitence
    Before His throne of grace,
  While to the contrite spirit's sense
    He shows His smiling face!

3 How sweet, through long-remembered years,
    His mercies to recall,
  And, pressed with wants, and griefs, and fears,
    To trust His love for all!

4 How sweet to look, in thoughtful hope,
    Beyond this fading sky,
  And hear Him call His children up
    To His fair home on high!

5 Calmly the day forsakes our heaven
    To dawn beyond the west;
  So let my soul, in life's last even,
    Retire to glorious rest.

Rev. Leonard Bacon. (1802-)

"And the lifting up of my hands as the evening sacrifice."

704 "In the way the Lord led me." L. M.
Acts xxvi. 1-22. Ps. xvi. 1 Sam. vii. 3-12.

1 THUS far the Lord hath led me on,
  Thus far His power prolongs my days ;
  And every evening should make known
  Some fresh memorials of His grace.

2 I lay my body down to sleep ;
  Peace is the pillow for my head,
  While well-appointed angels keep
  Their watchful stations round my bed.

3 Faith in His name forbids my fear ;
  O may Thy presence ne'er depart ;
  And, in the morning, make me hear
  The love and kindness of Thy heart.

4 Thus, when the night of death shall come,
  My flesh shall rest beneath the ground ;
  And wait Thy voice to rouse my tomb,
  With sweet salvation in the sound.
  Rev. Isaac Watts. (1674-1748.)

705 "In the field until even." L. M.
Mark vi. 30-32. John xx. 24-29. Ps. xxxii.

1 THE busy scenes of day are fled,
  The evening shades invite to rest ;
  May I repose my weary head,
  Reclining on my Saviour's breast.

2 Jesus, to Thee an evening song
  My soul, in gratitude, would raise ;
  O could I mount and join that throng,
  I 'd vie with angels in Thy praise.

3 With tears of joy I 'd sing the God,
  Who wept and groaned and died for me ;
  Then hide beneath that precious blood,
  Which freely flowed on Calvary.
  Author unknown.

706 "The Lord will lighten my darkness." 8. 7.
Ps. lxi. Gen. xxviii. 10-22. Acts xxvii.

1 HEAR my prayer, O Heavenly Father,
  Ere I lay me down to sleep :
  Bid Thine angels, pure and holy,
  Round my bed their vigil keep.

2 Great my sins are, but Thy mercy
  Far outweighs them every one ;
  Down before the cross I cast them,
  Trusting in Thy help alone.

3 Keep me through this night of peril,
  Underneath its boundless shade ;
  Take me to Thy rest, I pray Thee,
  When my pilgrimage is made.

4 Pardon all my past transgressions,
  Give me strength for days to come ;
  Guide and guard me with Thy blessing,
  Till Thine angels bid me home.
  Miss Harriet Parr. 1850.

707 "The shadows of the evening are stretched out." 8. 7.
Ps. lxxvii. 10-20. Zech. xiv. 6-11. Heb. xi. 13-16.

1 SILENTLY the shades of evening
  Gather round my lowly door ;
  Silently they bring before me
  Faces I shall see no more.

2 O the lost, the unforgotten,
  Though the world be oft forgot,
  O the shrouded and the lonely,
  In our hearts they perish not ;

3 Living in the silent hours
  Where our spirits only blend :
  They, unlinked with earthly trouble,
  We, still hoping for its end.

4 How such holy memories cluster,
  Like the stars when storms are past !
  Pointing up to that far heaven
  We may hope to gain at last.
  Christopher C. Cox. (1816-.)

708 "To meditate at the evening tide." 7.
Ps. cxliii. Dan. ix. 21-23. Acts x. 19-33.

1 SOFTLY now the light of day
  Fades upon my sight away ;
  Free from care, from labor free,
  Lord, I would commune with Thee.

2 Thou, whose all-pervading eye
  Naught escapes, without, within,
  Pardon each infirmity,
  Open fault, and secret sin.

3 Soon for me the light of day
  Shall forever pass away :
  Then, from sin and sorrow free,
  Take me, Lord, to dwell with Thee.
  Bp. George W. Doane. (1799-1859.)

709 "My flesh also shall rest in hope." L. M.
Ps. lv. 16-19. Dan. vi. 1-11. 1 Cor. xv. 51-58.

1 SAVIOUR, when night involves the skies,
  My soul, adoring, turns to Thee :
  Thee, self-abased in mortal guise,
  And wrapt in shades of death for me.

2 On Thee my waking raptures dwell,
  When crimson gleams the east adorn :
  Thee, victor of the grave and hell,
  Thee, source of life's eternal morn.

3 When noon her throne in light arrays,
  To Thee my soul triumphant springs :
  Thee, throned in glory's endless blaze,
  Thee, Lord of lords, and King of kings.

4 O'er earth, when shades of evening steal,
  To death and Thee my thoughts I give :
  To death, whose power I soon must feel,
  To Thee, with whom I trust to live.
  Rev. Thomas Gisborne. (1758-1846.)

"I will trust, and not be afraid."

710 "Show me now Thy way." **C. M.**
1 Kings viii. 22-30. Ex. xxiv. Luke ix. 28-35.

1 I WOULD commune with Thee, my God;
 E'en to Thy seat I come;
 I leave my joys, I leave my sins,
 And seek in Thee my home.

2 I stand upon the mount of God,
 With sunlight in my soul;
 I see the storm in vales beneath,
 I hear the thunders roll.

3 But I am calm with Thee, my God,
 Beneath these glorious skies;
 And to the height on which I stand
 Nor storms nor clouds can rise.

4 O this is life, O this is joy,
 My God, to find Thee so;
 Thy face to see, Thy voice to hear,
 And all Thy love to know.

Author unknown.

711 "One thing have I desired of the Lord." **C. M.**
Ps. lxxiii. 25-28. John vi. 47-69. 1 John iv.

1 MY God, my Portion, and my Love,
 My everlasting All,
 I've none but Thee in heaven above,
 Or on this earthly ball.

2 Were I possessor of the earth,
 And called the stars my own,
 Without Thy graces and Thyself
 I were a wretch undone.

3 Let others stretch their arms like seas,
 . And grasp in all the shore;
 Grant me the visits of Thy face,
 And I desire no more.

Rev. Isaac Watts. (1674-1748.)

712 "I beseech Thee, show me Thy glory." **C. M.**
Luke xxiv. 13-32. Ps. xxv. 1 Kings xix.

1 TALK with me, Lord: Thyself reveal,
 While here o'er earth I rove;
 Speak to my heart, and let it feel
 The kindling of Thy love.

2 With Thee conversing, I forget
 All time, and toil, and care;
 Labor is rest, and pain is sweet,
 If Thou, my God, art here.

3 Here, then, my God, vouchsafe to stay,
 And make my heart rejoice;
 My bounding heart shall own Thy sway,
 And echo to Thy voice.

4 Thou callest me to seek Thy face:
 'T is all I wish to seek:
 To attend the whispers of Thy grace,
 And hear Thee inly speak.

Rev. Charles Wesley. (1708-1788.)

713 "And the Lord said, . . . Come up to me." **S. M.**
1 John i. 1-7. Ps. ciii. 1-18. John xv. 9-16.

1 OUR Heavenly Father calls,
 And Christ invites us near;
 With both our friendship shall be sweet,
 And our communion dear.

2 God pities all my griefs;
 He pardons every day;
 Almighty to protect my soul,
 And wise to guide my way.

3 Jesus, my living Head,
 I bless Thy faithful care:
 Mine Advocate before the throne,
 And my Forerunner there.

4 Here fix. my roving heart,
 Here wait, my warmest love,
 Till the communion be complete
 In nobler scenes above.

Rev. Philip Doddridge. (1702-1751.)

714 "To behold the beauty of the Lord." **C. M.**
Ps. xxvii. Micah vii. 7-20. John xii. 35-50.

1 THE Lord of glory is my light,
 And my salvation, too;
 God is my strength, nor will I fear
 What all my foes can do.

2 One privilege my heart desires:
 O grant me an abode
 Among the churches of Thy saints,
 The temples of my God.

3 There shall I offer my requests,
 And see Thy beauty still;
 Shall hear Thy messages of love,
 And there inquire Thy will.

Rev. Isaac Watts.

715 "I . . . meditate on Thee in the night watches." **C. M.**
Ps. lxiii. Mat. xiv. 22-33. Acts xxvii. 20-44.

1 'T WAS in the watches of the night
 I thought upon Thy power;
 I kept Thy lovely face in sight,
 Amid the darkest hour.

2 While I lay resting on my bed
 My thoughts arose on high;
 My God, my Life, my Hope, I said,
 Bring Thy salvation nigh.

3 I strive to mount Thy holy hill,
 And climb the heavenly road;
 And Thy right hand upholds me still,
 When I commune with God.

4 Thy mercy stretches o'er my head
 The shadow of Thy wing;
 My heart rejoices in Thine aid,
 And I Thy praises sing.

Rev. Isaac Watts.

"I will trust, and not be afraid."

716 Ps. lxxi. 1 Sam. xvii. 32–37. 2 Tim. iv. 6–8. "I shall not be moved." **C. M.**

1 IN Thee I put my steadfast trust,
   Defend me, Lord, from shame ;
   Incline Thine ear, and save my soul,
   For righteous is Thy name.

2 Be Thou my strong Abiding-place,
   To which I may resort ;
   Thy promise, Lord, is my defence,
   Thou art my rock and fort.

3 My steadfast and unchanging hope
   Shall on Thy power depend ;
   And I in grateful songs of praise
   My time to come will spend.
   Tate and Brady. 1696.

717 Heb. xii. 5–7. Deu. viii. 1–10. Ps. lxxxix. 15–29. "I said, Thou art my God." **C. M.**

1 My God, my Father, blissful name,
   O may I call Thee mine ?
   May I with sweet assurance claim
   A portion so divine ?

2 This only can my fears control,
   And bid my sorrows fly ;
   What harm can ever reach my soul
   Beneath my Father's eye ?

3 Whate'er Thy providence denies
   I calmly would resign,
   For Thou art good, and just, and wise :
   O bend my will to Thine.

4 Whate'er Thy sacred will ordains,
   O give me strength to bear ;
   And let me know my Father reigns,
   And trust His tender care.

5 Thy sovereign ways are all unknown
   To my weak, erring sight ;
   Yet let my soul adoring own
   That all Thy ways are right.
   Miss Anne Steele. (1717–1778.)

718 Job xi. 7–12. Ps. xxxvi. 5–10. Rev. xv. "Thy footsteps are not known." **L. M.**

1 LORD, how mysterious are Thy ways !
   How blind are we, how mean our praise !
   Thy steps can mortal eyes explore ?
   'T is ours to wonder and adore.

2 Great God, I would not ask to see
   What in my coming life shall be ;
   Enough for me if love divine,
   At length, through every cloud shall shine.

3 Are darkness and distress my share,
   Then let me trust Thy guardian care ;
   If light and bliss attend my days,
   Then let my future hours be praise.
   Miss Anne Steele.

719 Ps. xxxi. 1–17. Ecc. iii. 1–8. Rom. viii. 35–39. "All my ways are before Thee." **7.**

1 SOVEREIGN Ruler of the skies,
   Ever gracious, ever wise,
   All my times are in Thy hand,
   All events at Thy command.

2 Times of sickness, times of health,
   Times of penury and wealth ;
   Times of trial and of grief,
   Times of triumph and relief ;

3 Times the tempter's power to prove,
   Times to taste a Saviour's love :
   All must come, and last, and end,
   As shall please my heavenly Friend.

4 Thee at all times will I bless ;
   Having Thee, I all possess ;
   How can I bereavéd be,
   Since I cannot part with Thee ?
   Rev. John Ryland. (1753–1825.)

720 2 Sam. xxiii. 1–7. Jer. xxxiii. Heb. xiii. 20, 21. "The foundation of God standeth sure." **C. M.**

1 My God, the covenant of Thy love
   Abides forever sure,
   And in its matchless grace I feel
   My happiness secure.

2 I welcome all Thy sovereign will,
   For all that will is love ;
   And when I know not what Thou dost,
   I wait the light above.

3 Thy covenant, in the darkest gloom,
   Shall be my strength and stay ;
   Shall cheer my passage to the tomb,
   And guide to endless day.
   Rev. Philip Doddridge. (1702–1751.)

721 Job v. 17–27. Rom. xi. 26–36. 1 Cor. xv. "Thou art my hope." **C. M.**

1 ALMIGHTY Father of mankind,
   On Thee my hopes remain ;
   And when the day of trouble comes
   I shall not trust in vain.

2 In early days Thou wast my Guide,
   And of my youth the Friend ;
   And as my days began with Thee,
   With Thee my days shall end.

3 I know the Power in whom I trust,
   The arm on which I lean ;
   He will my Saviour ever be
   Who has my Saviour been.

4 Therefore in life I 'll trust in Thee,
   In death I will adore ;
   And after death will sing Thy praise,
   When time shall be no more.
   Michael Bruce. (1746–1767.)

"I will trust, and not be afraid."

722 "All things that pertain unto life and godliness." **8.**
Isa. xlv. 15-25. Col. i. 12-20. Eph. i

1 THOU hidden Source of calm repose,
　Thou all-sufficient Love divine,
　My Help and Refuge from my foes,
　　Secure I am while Thou art mine;
　And lo, from sin, and grief, and shame,
　I hide me, Jesus, in Thy name.

2 Thy mighty name salvation is,
　And keeps my happy soul above;
　Comfort it brings, and power, and peace,
　　And joy, and everlasting love.
　To me, with Thy dear name, are given
　Pardon, and holiness, and heaven.

3 Jesus, my All in all Thou art,
　　My Rest in toil, my Ease in pain;
　The Medicine of my broken heart,
　　In war, my Peace, in loss, my Gain;
　My Smile, beneath the tyrant's frown,
　In shame, my Glory and my Crown:

4 In want, my plentiful Supply,
　　In weakness, my almighty Power;
　In bonds, my perfect Liberty,
　　My Light, in Satan's darkest hour;
　In grief, my Joy unspeakable;
　My Life in death, my All in all.
　　　　　　Rev. Charles Wesley. (1708-1788.)

723 "Ask anything in my name, I will do it." **8, 4.**
Rom. vii. 7-25. Mat. ix. 28-30. Ps. cxliii.

1 JESUS, my Saviour, look on me,
　　For I am weary and opprest;
　I come to cast myself on Thee:
　　Thou art my Rest.

2 Look down on me, for I am weak,
　　I feel the toilsome journey's length;
　Thine aid omnipotent I seek:
　　Thou art my Strength.

3 I am bewildered on my way,
　　Dark and tempestuous is the night;
　O send Thou forth some cheering ray;
　　Thou art my Light.

4 Standing alone on Jordan's brink,
　　In that tremendous latest strife,
　Thou wilt not suffer me to sink:
　　Thou art my Life.

5 Thou wilt my every want supply,
　　E'en to the end, whate'er befall;
　Through life, in death, eternally,
　　Thou art my All.
　　　　　　Rev. John R. Macduff. 1853.

724 "What Thou wilt." **L. M.**
Acts xxi. 1-14. Gen. v. 18-24. Deu. xxxiv. 1-7.

1 JUST when Thou wilt, O Master, call!
　Or at the noon or evening fall,
　Or in the dark or in the light:
　Just when Thou wilt, it must be right.

2 Just when Thou wilt, O Saviour, come!
　Take me to dwell in Thy bright home:
　Or when the snows have crowned my head,
　Or ere it hath one silver thread.

3 Just when Thou wilt, Thy time is best!
　Thou shalt appoint my hour of rest;
　Marked by the Sun of perfect love,
　Shining unchangeably above.

4 Just when Thou wilt! No choice for me:
　Life is a gift to use for Thee;
　Death is a hushed and glorious tryst
　With Thee, my King, my Saviour Christ.
　　　　　　Miss Frances R. Havergal. (1836-1879.)

725 "I can do all things through Christ." **L. M.**
Phil. iv. 12, 13. 2 Cor. xii. Ps. lxii.

1 LET me but hear my Saviour say,
　" Strength shall be equal to thy day;"
　Then I rejoice in deep distress,
　Leaning on all-sufficient grace.

2 I glory in infirmity,
　That Christ's own power may rest on me;
　When I am weak, then am I strong;
　Grace is my shield and Christ my song.

3 I can do all things, or can bear
　All sufferings, if my Lord be there;
　Sweet pleasures mingle with the pains,
　While His kind hand my soul sustains.
　　　　　　Rev. Isaac Watts. (1074-1748.)

726 "No good thing will He withhold." **C. M.**
Ps. cxxxix. 1-18. Job i. 13 to ii. 10. Rev. iii. 1-6.

1 SINCE all the varying scenes of time
　　God's watchful eye surveys,
　O who so wise to choose our lot,
　　Or to appoint our ways?

2 Good, when He gives, supremely good,
　　Nor less when He denies;
　E'en crosses from His sovereign hand
　　Are blessings in disguise.

3 Why should we doubt a Father's love,
　　So constant and so kind?
　To His unerring, gracious will
　　Be every wish resigned.

4 In Thy fair book of life divine,
　　My God, inscribe my name;
　There let it fill some humble place,
　　Beneath my Lord, the Lamb.
　　　　　　Rev. James Hervey. (1714-1758.)

"I will trust, and not be afraid."

727 "My soul trusteth in Thee." L. M.
Ps. lxii. Micah vii. 7-20. Col. iii. 1-4.

1 MY spirit looks to God alone,
My rock and refuge is His throne ;
In all my fears, in all my straits,
My soul on His salvation waits.

2 Trust Him, ye saints, in all your ways,
Pour out your hearts before His face;
When helpers fail, and foes invade,
God is our all-sufficient aid.

3 For sovereign power reigns not alone ;
Grace is a partner of the throne;
Thy grace and justice, mighty Lord,
Shall well divide our last reward.
Rev. Isaac Watts. (1674-1748.)

728 "The Lord is on my side." 8, 7, 4.
Ps. lvi. Rom. viii. 28-39. 2 Chr. xxxii. 1-8.

1 GOD is for me ! O how glorious !
Who the weakest saint can harm ?
He will make that saint victorious,
Held and sheltered by His arm.
God is for me :
Nothing shall my soul alarm.

2 Wonderful the gift He gave me,
Lost without a hope or claim ;
Matchless mercy, when, to save me,
Christ the Lord of Glory came !
God is for me :
Thanks eternal to His name.

3 Promises, how great and precious,
Cheer and gladden all my way ;
Peace and comfort, sweet and gracious,
Keep me in their blessed sway.
God is for me,
Guides and guards me day by day.

4 How His goodness round me brightens !
His enfolding love I share ;
Present help each burden lightens,
Never fails His tender care.
God is for me :
Nothing shall my trust impair.
Rev. Sylvester D. Phelps. (1816-.)

729 "None...that trust in Him shall be desolate." L. M.
2 Cor. vi. 4-10. Ps. xc. Rom. xiv. 7, 8.

1 IF life in sorrow must be spent,
So be it ; I am well content;
And meekly wait my last remove,
Desiring only trustful love.

2 No bliss I 'll seek, but to fulfil
In life, in death, Thy perfect will ;
No succor in my woes I want,
But what my Lord is pleased to grant.
Madame Jeanne M. D. de la M. Guyon. (1648-1717.)

730 "Though He slay me, yet will I trust in Him." 8, 6.
Hab. iii. 17-19. Deu. xxxii. 9-14. Acts v. 40-42.

1 ALTHOUGH the vine its fruit deny,
The budding fig-tree droop and die,
No oil the olive yield,
Yet will I trust me in my God ;
Yea, bend rejoicing to His rod,
And by His grace be healed.

2 Though fields, in verdure once arrayed,
By whirlwinds desolate be laid,
Or parched by scorching beam,
Still in the Lord shall be my trust,
My joy; for, though His frown is just,
His mercy is supreme.

3 Though from the fold the flock decay,
Though herds lie famished o'er the lea
And round the empty stall,
My soul above the wreck shall rise ;
Its better joys are in the skies ;
There God is all in all.

4 In God my Strength, howe'er distrest,
I yet will hope, and calmly rest,
Nay, triumph in His love :
My lingering soul, my tardy feet,
Free as the hind He makes, and fleet,
To speed my course above.
Bp. Henry U. Onderdonk. (1789-1858.)

731 "My Father, Thou art the guide of my youth." C. M.
Ps. xxiii. Isa. xl. 1-11. John x. 1-16.

1 THE Lord Himself, the mighty Lord,
Vouchsafes to be my Guide;
The Shepherd, by whose constant care
My wants are all supplied.

2 In tender grass He makes me feed,
And gently there repose ;
Then leads me to cool shades, and where
Refreshing water flows.

3 He does my wandering soul reclaim,
And, to His endless praise,
Instruct with humble zeal to walk
In His most righteous ways.

4 I pass the gloomy vale of death,
From fear and danger free ;
For there His aiding rod and staff
Defend and comfort me.

5 Since God doth thus His wondrous love
Through all my life extend,
That life to Him I will devote,
And in His temple spend.
Tate and Brady. 1696.

"I will trust, and not be afraid."

732 "I shall not want." S. M.
Ps. xxiii. Luke xii. 22-32. Isa. xliii. 1-7

1 THE Lord my Shepherd is,
   I shall be well supplied;
Since He is mine, and I am His,
   What can I want beside?

2 He leads me to the place
   Where heavenly pasture grows;
Where living waters gently pass,
   And full salvation flows.

3 While He affords His aid,
   I cannot yield to fear;
Though I should walk through death's dark shade,
   My Shepherd's with me there.

4 In spite of all my foes
   Thou dost my table spread;
My cup with blessings overflows,
   And joy exalts my head.

5 The bounties of Thy love
   Shall crown my following days;
Nor from Thy house will I remove,
   Nor cease to speak Thy praise.
                    Rev. Isaac Watts. (1674-1748.)

733 "Unto God would I commit my cause." H. M.
Ps. cxxi. 2 Tim. i. 1-12. Heb. vi. 13-20.

1 UPWARD I lift mine eyes,
   From God is all my aid;
The God that built the skies,
   And earth and nature made:
      God is the Tower
         To which I fly;
      His grace is nigh
         In every hour.

2 My feet shall never slide,
   And fall in fatal snares,
Since God, my Guard and Guide,
   Defends me from my fears:
      Those wakeful eyes,
         That never sleep,
      Shall Israel keep
         When dangers·rise.

3 Hast Thou not given Thy word
   To save my soul from death?
And I can trust my Lord
   To keep my mortal breath:
      I'll go and come,
         Nor fear to die,
      Till from on high
         Thou call me home.
                             Rev. Isaac Watts.

734 "O Lord God, Thou art my trust." C. M.
Ps. cxviii. John xi. 21-27. 2 Cor. v. 14-17.

1 How can I sink with such a prop
   As my eternal God,
Who bears the earth's huge pillars up,
   And spreads the heavens abroad?

2 How can I die, while Jesus lives,
   Who rose and left the dead?
Pardon and grace my soul receives
   From my exalted Head.

3 All that I am, and all I have,
   Shall be forever Thine;
Whate'er my duty bids me give
   My cheerful hands resign.
                    Rev. Isaac Watts.

735 "He is able also to save." L. M.
Job xxiii. Ps. cxxiii. 1 John ii. 1, 2.

1 WHERE is my God? Does He retire
   Beyond the reach of humble sighs?
Are these weak breathings of desire
   Too languid to ascend the skies?

2 Look up, my soul, with cheerful eye:
   See where the great Redeemer stands,
The glorious Advocate on high,
   With precious incense in His hands!

3 He sweetens every humble groan,
   He recommends each broken prayer:
Recline thy hope on Him alone,
   Whose power and love forbid despair.
                    Miss Anne Steele. (1717-1778.)

736 "He maketh me to lie down in green pastures." 8.
Eze. xxxiv. 11-16. Isa. xl. 1-11. John x. 1-16.

1 THE Lord my pasture shall prepare,
And feed me with a shepherd's care;
His presence shall my wants supply,
And guard me with a watchful eye;
My noonday walks He shall attend,
And all my midnight hours defend.

2 When in the sultry glebe I faint,
Or on the thirsty mountain pant,
To fertile vales and dewy meads
My weary, wandering steps he leads,
Where peaceful rivers, soft and slow,
Amid the verdant landscape flow.

3 Though in the paths of death I tread,
With gloomy horrors overspread,
My steadfast heart shall fear no ill,
For Thou, O Lord, art with me still:
Thy friendly crook shall give me aid,
And guide me through the dreadful shade.
                    Joseph Addison. (1672-1719.)

"I will trust, and not be afraid."

737 John x. 27-29. Rom. viii. 31-39. Ps. cxxiv. "I trust in Thy word." C. M.

1 FIRM as the earth Thy gospel stands,
   My Lord, my hope, my trust!
 If I am found in Jesus' hands,
   My soul can ne'er be lost.

2 His honor is engaged to save
   The meanest of His sheep;
 All that His heavenly Father gave
   His hands securely keep.

3 Nor death, nor hell, shall e'er remove
   His fav'rites from His breast;
 In the dear bosom of His love
   They must forever rest.
         Rev. Isaac Watts. (1674-1748.)

738 Eph. ii. 19-22. Isa. liii. Mat. vii. 24-27. "My rock and my fortress." 8.

1 MY hope is built on nothing less
   Than Jesus' blood and righteousness;
 I dare not trust the sweetest frame,
   But wholly lean on Jesus' name;
     On Christ the solid rock I stand;
     All other ground is sinking sand.

2 When darkness seems to veil His face,
   I rest on His unchanging grace;
 In every high and stormy gale,
   My anchor holds within the vail.

3 His oath, His covenant and blood,
   Support me in the whelming flood;
 When all around my soul gives way,
   He then is all my hope and stay.
         Rev. Edward Mote. (1797-.)

739 Ps. xxxi. Isa. xxv. Heb. vi. 9-20. "A place of refuge, and for a covert from storm." C. M.

1 THOU art my Hiding-place, O Lord,
   In Thee I fix my trust;
 Encouraged by Thy holy word,
   A feeble child of dust.

2 I have no argument beside,
   I urge no other plea;
 And 'tis enough: the Saviour died,
   The Saviour died for me.

3 When storms of fierce temptation beat,
   And furious foes assail,
 My refuge is the mercy-seat,
   My hope within the vail.

4 From strife of tongues and bitter words,
   My spirit flies to Thee;
 Joy to my heart the thought affords,
   My Saviour died for me.
         Rev. Thomas Raffles. (1788-1863.)

740 Rom. xiv. 7-9. Gal. ii. 19-21. Ps. xxxvii. 1-11. "I know whom I have believed." C. M.

1 LORD, it belongs not to my care
   Whether I die or live;
 To love and serve Thee is my share,
   And this Thy grace must give.

2 If life be long, I will be glad
   That I may long obey;
 If short, yet why should I be sad
   To soar to endless day?

3 Christ leads me through no darker rooms
   Than He went through before;
 He that unto God's kingdom comes
   Must enter by this Door.

4 My knowledge of that life is small;
   The eye of faith is dim;
 But it's enough that Christ knows all,
   And I shall be with Him.
         Rev. Richard Baxter. (1615-1689.)

741 Rom. iv. 13-25. 1 Thes. ii. Ps. cxli. "He is able to keep." L. M.

1 AWAY, my unbelieving fear!
   Fear shall in me no more have place;
 My Saviour doth not yet appear;
   He hides the brightness of His face.

2 But shall I, therefore, let Him go,
   And basely to the tempter yield?
 No, in the strength of Jesus, no,
   I never will give up my shield.

3 In hope, believing against hope,
   Jesus, my Lord, my God, I claim;
 Jesus, my Strength, shall lift me up;
   Salvation is in Jesus' name.
         Rev. Charles Wesley. (1708-1788.)

742 Acts iv. 1-20. Luke xii. 1-9. Dan. iii. 8-18. "The Lord, the God of hosts, is His name." C. M.

1 I'M not ashamed to own my Lord,
   Or to defend His cause;
 Maintain the honor of His word,
   The glory of His cross.

2 Jesus, my God! I know His name,
   His name is all my trust;
 Nor will He put my soul to shame,
   Nor let my hope be lost.

3 Firm as His throne His promise stands,
   And He can well secure
 What I've committed to His hands,
   Till the decisive hour.

4 Then will He own my worthless name,
   Before His Father's face,
 And, in the new Jerusalem,
   Appoint my soul a place.
         Rev. Isaac Watts.

141

"God hath given rest."

743 "This is my rest." C. M.
Ps. xxv. John iv. 10-15. 2 Cor. iv. 7-18.

1 MY heart is resting, O my God,
   I will give thanks and sing ;
   My heart is at the secret source
   Of every precious thing.

2 Now the frail vessel Thou hast made
   No hand but Thine shall fill ;
   For waters of the earth have failed,
   And I am thirsty still.

3 I thirst for springs of heavenly life,
   And here all day they rise ;
   I seek the treasure of Thy love,
   And close at hand it lies.

4 And a new song is in my mouth,
   To long-loved music set ;
   Glory to Thee for all the grace
   I have not tasted yet.

Miss Anna L. Waring. (1820-.)

746 "On Thee do I wait all the day." C. M.
2 Cor. v. Ps. xvi. Lam. iii. 24-32.

1 MINE be the reverent, listening love
   That waits all day on Thee,
   With service of a watchful heart
   Which no one else can see.

2 The faith that in a hidden way
   No other eye may know,
   Finds all its daily work prepared,
   And loves to have it so.

3 My heart is resting, O my God,
   My heart is in Thy care
   I hear the voice of joy and health
   Resounding everywhere.

4 "Thou art my Portion," saith my soul,
   Ten thousand voices say ;
   The music of their glad Amen
   Will never die away.

Miss Anna L. Waring.

744 "In quietness and in confidence." 11. 8.
Ps. xxiii. Isa. xl. 9-31. Eze. xxxiv. 1 Pet. v. 1-11.

1 THE Lord is my Shepherd, His kindness I know ;
   My wants will be ever supplied :
   He makes me repose where the green pastures grow,
   And waters in gentleness glide.

2 What though I walk through the dark valley of death,
   No evil my spirit will fear ;
   My Shepherd is with me ; His arm is beneath,
   His love and His comfort are near.

3 The hand of His bounty my table supplies,
   My cup of enjoyment o'erflows ;
   He keeps me in safety when troubles arise,
   Nor yields to th' assaults of my foes.

4 His goodness and mercy around me are found,
   His love shall forever endure ;
   Forever I 'll dwell in the house of the Lord ;
   His word of salvation is sure.

Thomas Hastings. (1784-1872.)

745 "Here will I dwell." L. M.
Rom. viii. 31-39. Ps. lvii. Isa. xliii. 1-7.

1 While Thou art intimately nigh,
   Who, who shall violate my rest ?
   Sin, earth, and hell I now defy ;
   I lean upon my Saviour's breast.

2 I rest beneath th' Almighty's shade,
   My griefs expire, my troubles cease ;
   Thou, Lord, on whom my soul is stayed,
   Wilt keep me still in perfect peace.

3 Me for Thine own thou lov'st to take
   In time and in eternity ;
   Thou never, never wilt forsake
   A helpless worm that trusts in Thee.

Rev. Charles Wesley. (1708-1788.)

747 "That good, and acceptable, and perfect will." C. M.
Ps. xl. 7-10. John xiii. 1-17. Heb. x. 1-10.

1 I WORSHIP Thee, sweet Will of God,
   And all Thy ways adore;
   And every day I live I seem
   To love Thee more and more.

2 I love to kiss each print where Thou
   Hast set Thine unseen feet :
   I cannot fear Thee, blessèd Will,
   Thine empire is so sweet.

3 I have no cares, O blessèd Will,
   For all my cares are Thine ;
   I live in triumph, Lord, for Thou
   Hast made Thy triumphs mine.

Rev. Frederick W. Faber. (1814-1863.)

"God hath given rest."

748 "My times are in Thy hand." **S. M.**
Ps. xxxi. Job v. 1-16. Acts xx. 17-37.

1 "MY times are in Thy hand :"
  My God, I wish them there ;
  My life, my soul, my all, I leave
  Entirely to Thy care.

2 "My times are in Thy hand,"
  Whatever they may be :
  Pleasing or painful, dark or bright,
  As best may seem to Thee.

3 "My times are in Thy hand :"
  Why should I doubt or fear ?
  My Father's hand will never cause
  His child a needless tear.

4 "My times are in Thy hand :"
  I'll always trust in Thee.
  Till I possess the promised land,
  And all Thy glory see.
  William F. Lloyd. (1791-1853.)

749 "Under the shadow of Thy wings." **L. M.**
Ps. xix. Rom. i. 19, 20. John xii. 23-46.

1 MY God, what monuments I see
  In all around of Thine and Thee :
  I view Thee in the heavens above,
  More high than these is heavenly love.

2 I mark the strong eternal hill,
  Thy faithfulness is stronger still ;
  I gaze on ocean deep and broad,
  More deep Thy counsels are, O God.

3 The springs of life are all Thine own,
  They flow from Thy eternal throne :
  Light in Thy light alone we see ;
  O save us, for we rest on Thee.
  Rev. Henry F. Lyte. (1793-1847.)

750 "His tender mercies are over all." **L. M.**
Ps. cxix. 65. Heb. xii. 5-11. Luke xxii. 43.

1 MY God, I thank Thee ! May no thought
  E'er deem Thy chastisements severe ;
  But may this heart, by sorrow taught,
  Calm each wild wish, each idle fear.

2 Thy mercy bids all nature bloom ;
  The sun shines bright, and man is gay ;
  Thine equal mercy spreads the gloom
  That darkens o'er his little day.

3 Full many a throb of grief and pain
  Thy frail and erring child must know :
  But not one prayer is breathed in vain,
  Nor does one tear unheeded flow.

4 Thy various messengers employ ;
  Thy purposes of love fulfil ;
  And, mid the wreck of human joy,
  Let kneeling faith adore Thy will.
  Rev. Andrews Norton. (1786-1853.)

751 "Thou compassest my path." **C. M.**
Ps. lxxxvi. Job ii. 1-10. Acts xxvi. 1-29.

1 WHILE Thee I seek, protecting Power !
  Be my vain wishes stilled ;
  And may this consecrated hour
  With better hopes be filled !

2 Thy love the power of thought bestowed ;
  To Thee my thoughts would soar :
  Thy mercy o'er my life has flowed ;
  That mercy I adore.

3 In each event of life, how clear
  Thy ruling hand I see !
  Each blessing to my soul more dear,
  Because conferred by Thee.

4 In every joy that crowns my days,
  In every pain I bear,
  My heart shall find delight in praise,
  Or seek relief in prayer.

5 When gladness wings the favored hour,
  Thy love my thoughts shall fill ;
  Resigned, when storms of sorrow lower,
  My soul shall meet Thy will.

6 My lifted eye, without a tear,
  The gathering storm shall see ;
  My steadfast heart shall know no fear ;
  That heart will rest on Thee.
  Miss Helen M. Williams. (1762-1827.)

752 "O my God, I trust in Thee." **8.**
Prov. iii. 5-26. Ps. cvii. James v. 7-18.

1 HE sendeth sun, He sendeth shower ;
  Alike they're needful for the flower ;
  And joys and tears alike are sent
  To give the soul fit nourishment :
  As comes to me or cloud or sun,
  Father, Thy will, not mine, be done !

2 Can loving children e'er reprove
  With murmurs whom they trust and love ?
  Creator ! I would ever be
  A trusting, loving child to Thee :
  As comes to me or cloud or sun,
  Father, Thy will, not mine, be done !

3 O ne'er will I at life repine !
  Enough that Thou hast made it mine !
  When falls the shadow cold of death,
  I yet will sing, with parting breath —
  As comes to me or shade or sun,
  Father, Thy will, not mine, be done !
  Mrs. Sarah F. Adams. (1805-1848.)

"God hath given rest."

753 "Come . . . and rest awhile."   **7, 6.**
2 Cor. iv. John xxi. 15-18. Ps. xl.

1 O JESUS, Friend unfailing,
   How dear art Thou to me!
   Are cares or fears assailing?
   I find my strength in Thee!
   Why should my feet grow weary
   Of this, my pilgrim way?
   Rough though the path and dreary,
   It ends in perfect day.

2 What fills my soul with gladness?
   'T is Thine abounding grace!
   Where can I look in sadness,
   But, Jesus, on Thy face?
   My all is Thy providing;
   Thy love can ne'er grow cold;
   In Thee, my Refuge, hiding,
   No good wilt Thou withhold.

3 For every tribulation,
   For every sore distress,
   In Christ I 've full salvation,
   Sure help and quiet rest.
   No fears of foes prevailing!
   I triumph, Lord, in Thee!
   O Jesus, Friend unfailing,
   How dear Thou art to me!

Author unknown.

754 "The Lord is the strength of my life." **L. M.**
2 Cor. v. 1 Cor. xv. Ps. lxi.

1 WHEN sins and fears prevailing rise,
   And fainting hope almost expires,
   Jesus, to Thee I lift mine eyes,
   To Thee I breathe my soul's desires.

2 Art Thou not mine, my living Lord?
   And can my hope, my comfort, die,
   Fixed on Thine everlasting word,
   That word which built the earth and sky?

3 If my immortal Saviour lives,
   Then my immortal life is sure;
   His word a firm foundation gives;
   Here let me build, and rest secure.

4 Here let my faith unshaken dwell;
   Immovable the promise stands;
   Nor all the powers of earth or hell
   Can e'er dissolve the sacred bands.

5 Here, O my soul, thy trust repose;
   If Jesus is forever mine,
   Not death itself, that last of foes,
   Shall break a union so divine.

Miss Anne Steele. (1717-1778.)

755 "My soul waiteth upon God." **S. M.**
2 Tim. i. 8-12. Heb. vi. 13-20. Ps. xxxi.

1 MY spirit on Thy care,
   Blest Saviour, I recline;
   Thou wilt not leave me to despair,
   For Thou art Love divine.

2 In Thee I place my trust;
   On Thee I calmly rest:
   I know Thee good, I know Thee just,
   And count Thy choice the best.

3 Whate'er events betide,
   Thy will they all perform;
   Safe in Thy breast my head I hide,
   Nor fear the coming storm.

4 Let good or ill befall,
   It must be good for me,
   Secure of having Thee in all,
   Of having all in Thee.

Rev. Henry F. Lyte. (1793-1847.)

756 "I know that my Redeemer liveth." **C. M.**
Heb. vii. 25-28. John xvii. Job xix. 25-29.

1 I KNOW that my Redeemer lives,
   And ever prays for me;
   A token of His love He gives,
   A pledge of liberty.

2 I find Him lifting up my head;
   He brings salvation near;
   His presence makes me free indeed,
   And He will soon appear.

3 When God is mine, and I am His,
   Of paradise possessed,
   I taste unutterable bliss,
   And everlasting rest.

Rev. Charles Wesley. (1708-1788.)

757 "He is my defence." **L. M.**
Mat. viii 19, 20. Heb. ii. 9-18. Ps. xci.

1 How do Thy mercies close me round!
   Forever be Thy name adored!
   I blush in all things to abound;
   The servant is above his Lord.

2 Inured to poverty and pain,
   A suffering life my Master led;
   The Son of God, the Son of man,
   He had not where to lay His head.

3 But lo! a place He hath prepared
   For me, whom watchful angels keep;
   Yea, He Himself becomes my guard,
   He smooths my bed, and gives me sleep.

4 Jesus protects; my fears, begone:
   What can the Rock of Ages move?
   Safe in Thy arms I lay me down,
   Thine everlasting arms of love.

Rev. Charles Wesley.

"God hath given rest."

758 "He maketh my way perfect." 8. 6.
Ps. lxxi. Isa. xli. 10-14. John xvi. 23-27.

1 FATHER, I know that all my life
 Is portioned out for me ;
 The changes that will surely come
 I do not fear to see :
 I ask Thee for a present mind,
 Intent on pleasing Thee.

2 I ask Thee for a thoughtful love,
 Through constant watching wise,
 To meet the glad with joyful smiles,
 And wipe the weeping eyes ;
 A heart at leisure from itself,
 To soothe and sympathize.

3 I would not have the restless will
 That hurries to and fro,
 Seeking for some great thing to do,
 Or secret thing to know :
 I would be treated as a child,
 And guided where I go.

4 Wherever in the world I am,
 In whatso'er estate,
 I have a fellowship with hearts,
 To keep and cultivate ;
 A work of lowly love to do
 For Him on whom I wait.
  Miss Anna L. Waring. (1820-.)

759 "And blessed be my rock." 8. 6.
Mat vi. 9-13. Phil. iv. 1-13. Ps. cxix. 81-88.

1 I ASK Thee for the daily strength,
 To none that ask denied,
 A mind to blend with outward life,
 While keeping at Thy side ;
 Content to fill a little space,
 If Thou be glorified.

2 And if some things I do not ask
 Among my blessings be,
 I'd have my spirit filled the more
 With grateful love to Thee ;
 More careful, not to serve Thee much,
 But please Thee perfectly.

3 There are set thorns by every path,
 That call for patient care ;
 There is a cross in every lot,
 And an earnest need for prayer ;
 But a lowly heart that leans on Thee
 Is happy anywhere.

4 In service which Thy will appoints
 There are no bonds for me ;
 My inmost heart is taught the truth
 That makes Thy children free ;
 A life of self-renouncing love
 Is one of liberty.
  Miss Anna L. Waring.

760 "I will fear no evil." 8. 7.
Ps. xxiii. Mat. xviii. 12-14. John vi. 35-37.

1 THE King of love my Shepherd is,
 Whose goodness faileth never ;
 I nothing lack if I am His,
 And He is mine forever.
 Where streams of living water flow
 My ransomed soul He leadeth,
 And where the verdant pastures grow,
 With food celestial feedeth.

2 Perverse and foolish, oft I strayed,
 But yet in love He sought me ;
 And on His shoulder gently laid,
 And home rejoicing brought me.
 In death's dark vale I fear no ill,
 With Thee, dear Lord, beside me ;
 Thy rod and staff my comfort still,
 Thy cross before to guide me.

3 Thou spread'st a table in my sight,
 Thy unction grace bestoweth !
 And O the transport of delight
 With which my cup o'erfloweth !
 And so through all the length of days
 Thy goodness faileth never ;
 Good Shepherd, may I sing Thy praise
 Within Thy house forever.
  Sir Henry W. Baker. (1821-1877.).

761 "The word of the Lord endureth." H. M.
Ps. lxv. 2 Cor. i. 1-20. 2 Pet. i. 16-21.

1 THE promises I sing,
 Which sovereign love hath spoke ;
 Nor will the eternal King
 His words of grace revoke :
 They stand secure
 And steadfast still ;
 Not Zion's hill
 Abides so sure.

2 The mountains melt away,
 When once the Judge appears,
 And sun and moon decay,
 That measure mortal years :
 But still the same,
 In radiant lines,
 The promise shines
 Through all the flame.

3 Their harmony shall sound
 Through mine attentive ears,
 When thunders cleave the ground,
 And dissipate the spheres :
 Midst all the shock
 Of that dread scene,
 I stand serene,
 Thy word my rock.
  Rev. Philip Doddridge. (1702-1751.)

"God hath given rest."

762 Ps. cxxxviii. "I will not be afraid." Jer. xvii. 7-17. John xv. 1-14. **7, 6.**

1 IN heavenly love abiding,
   No change my heart shall fear ;
And safe is such confiding,
   For nothing changes here.
The storm may roar without me,
   My heart may low be laid,
But God is round about me,
   And can I be dismayed ?

2 Wherever He may guide me,
   No want shall turn me back ;
My Shepherd is beside me,
   And nothing can I lack.
His wisdom ever waketh,
   His sight is never dim,
He knows the way He taketh,
   And I will walk with Him.

3 Green pastures are before me,
   Which yet I have not seen ;
Bright skies will soon be o'er me,
   Where darkest clouds have been.
My hope I cannot measure,
   My path to life is free,
My Saviour has my treasure,
   And He will walk with me.
      Miss Anna L. Waring. (1820-..)

763 1 Cor. iii. 21-23. 2 Cor. iv. 14-18. Ps. lxxxvii "Possessing all things." **C. M.**

1 IF Christ is mine, then all is mine,
   And more than angels know ;
Both present things and things to come,
   And grace and glory too.

2 If He is mine, I need not fear
   The rage of earth and hell ;
He will support my feeble frame,
   And all their power repel.

3 If He is mine, let friends forsake,
   And earthly comforts flee :
He, the Dispenser of all good,
   Is more than these to me.

4 If He is mine, I 'll fearless pass
   Through death's tremendous vale ;
He 'll be my Comfort and my Stay,
   When heart and flesh shall fail.

5 Let Jesus tell me He is mine ;
   I nothing want beside :
My soul shall at the fountain live,
   When all the streams are dried.
      Rev. Benjamin Beddome. (1717-1795.)

764 Ps. lxxiii. 23-26. "My God, my strength, in whom I will trust." 1 Pet. i. 3-21. John xx. 11-18. **L. M.**

1 O HOLY Saviour, friend unseen !
   Since on Thine arm Thou bid'st me lean,
Help me, throughout life's varying scene,
   By faith to cling to Thee, to Thee.

2 Blest with this fellowship divine,
   Take what Thou wilt, I 'll ne'er repine ;
E'en as the branches to the vine,
   My soul would cling to Thee, to Thee.

3 Though faith and hope may long be tried,
   I ask not, need not, aught beside ;
How safe, how calm, how satisfied,
   The souls that cling to Thee, to Thee !
      Miss Charlotte Elliot. (1789-1871.)

765 Ps lxxi. "My portion forever." Gen. vii. 11-24. Heb. x. 1-22 **8. 7.**

1 THOU my everlasting Portion,
   More than friend or life to me,
All along my pilgrim journey,
   Saviour, let me walk with Thee.
Close to Thee, close to Thee,
   Close to Thee, close to Thee ;
All along my pilgrim journey,
   Saviour, let me walk with Thee.

2 Not for ease or worldly pleasure,
   Nor for fame, my prayer shall be ;
Gladly will I toil and suffer,
   Only let me walk with Thee.

3 Lead me through the vale of shadows,
   Bear me o'er life's fitful sea ;
Then the gate of life eternal
   May I enter, Lord, with Thee.
      Mrs. Frances J. C. Van Alstyne. (1823-..)

766 Gen. viii. 1-11. "She returned unto him into the ark." 1 Pet. iii. 10-22. Heb. xi. 1-10. **S. M.**

1 LIKE Noah's weary dove,
   That soared the earth around,
But not a resting-place above
   The cheerless waters found ;

2 O cease, my wandering soul,
   On restless wing to roam ;
All the wide world, to either pole,
   Has not for thee a home.

3 Behold the ark of God !
   Behold the open door !
Hasten to gain that dear abode,
   And rove, my soul, no more !

4 There, safe thou shalt abide ;
   There, sweet shall be thy rest ;
And every longing satisfied,
   With full salvation blest.
      Rev. William A. Muhlenberg. (1796-1877.)

"God hath given rest."

767 "My help cometh from the Lord." 7. 6. 7.
Ps. cxxiii. 1 Sam. ii. 1-10. Rev. iv.

1 To the hills I lift mine eyes,
   The everlasting hills ;
Streaming thence in fresh supplies,
   My soul the Spirit feels :
Will He not His help afford ?
   Help while yet I ask is given :
God comes down, the God and Lord
   Who made both earth and heaven.

2 Faithful soul, pray always ; pray,
   And still in God confide ;
He thy feeble steps shall stay,
   Nor suffer thee to slide.
Lean on thy Redeemer's breast,
   He thy quiet spirit keeps ;
Rest in Him, securely rest ;
   Thy Watchman never sleeps.
Rev. Charles Wesley. (1708-1788.)

768 "He that keepeth Thee will not slumber." 7. 6. 7.
Ps. cxxi. Deu. xxviii. 1-14. Col. i. 9-29.

1 SEE the Lord, thy Keeper, stand
   Omnipotently near :
Lo, He holds thee by thy hand,
   And banishes thy fear ;
Shadows with His wings thy head,
   Guards from all impending harms ;
Round thee and beneath are spread
   The everlasting arms.

2 Neither sin, nor earth, nor hell,
   Thy Keeper can surprise ;
Careless slumbers cannot steal
   On His all-seeing eyes.
He is Israel's sure Defence,
   Israel all His care shall prove ;
Kept by watchful providence
   And ever waking love.
Rev. Charles Wesley.

769 "The Lord shall preserve thee." L. M.
Ps. xlvi. Mat. vi. 25-34. Luke xii. 11-32.

1 BE still, my heart ! these anxious cares
To thee are burdens, thorns, and snares ;
They cast dishonor on thy Lord,
And contradict His gracious word.

2 Brought safely by His hand thus far,
Why wilt thou now give place to fear ?
How canst thou want if He provide,
Or lose thy way with such a Guide ?

3 Did ever trouble yet befall,
And He refuse to hear thy call ?
And has He not His promise past
That thou shalt overcome at last ?
Rev. John Newton. (1725-1807.)

770 "I will go and return." L. M.
Ps. cxvi. Mal. iii. 7-12. Heb. iv.

1 RETURN, my soul, unto thy rest,
From vain pursuits and maddening cares ;
From lonely woes that wring thy breast,
The world's allurements, Satan's snares.

2 Return unto thy rest, my soul,
From all the wanderings of thy thought ;
From sickness unto death made whole,
Safe through a thousand perils brought.

3 Then to thy rest, my soul, return,
From passions, every hour at strife ;
Sin's works, and ways, and wages spurn ;
Lay hold upon eternal life.

4 God is thy Rest ; with heart inclined
To keep His word, that word believe :
Christ is thy Rest ; with lowly mind
His light and easy yoke receive.
Author unknown.

771 "As thy days so shall thy strength be." 7.
Isa. xli. 10-14. Mark xiii. 1-13. 2 Cor. xii. 9, 10.

1 "As thy day thy strength shall be !"
This should be enough for thee :
He who knows thy frame will spare
Burdens more than thou canst bear.

2 When thy days are veiled in night,
Christ shall give thee heavenly light ;
Seem they wearisome and long,
Yet in Him thou shalt be strong.

3 Cold and wintry though they prove,
Thine the sunshine of His love ;
Or with fervid heat opprest,
In His shadow thou shalt rest.
Miss Frances R. Havergal. (1836-1879.)

772 "It shall be well." S. M.
Isa. iii. 10. Ps. i. 1-3. Mat. v. 1-12.

1 WHAT cheering words are these ;
   Their sweetness who can tell ?
In time and to eternal days
   "'T is with the righteous well !"

2 Well when they see His face,
   Or sink amidst the flood ;
Well in affliction's thorny maze,
   Or on the mount with God.

3 'T is well when joys arise,
   'T is well when sorrows flow ;
'T is well when darkness vails the skies,
   And strong temptations grow.

4 'T is well when Jesus calls,
   "From earth and sin arise.
To join the hosts of ransomed souls,
   Made to salvation wise !"
John Kent. (1766-1843.)

"God hath given rest."

773 "He maketh the storm a calm."
John xvii. 11-22. Job i. Ps. xxxiv. 2 Cor. iv. 8-18.   11. 10.

1 WHEN winds are raging o'er the upper ocean,
   And billows wild contend with angry roar,
'T is said, far down, beneath the wild commotion,
   That peaceful stillness reigneth evermore.

2 Far, far beneath, the noise of tempests dieth,
   And silver waves chime ever peacefully;
And no rude storm, how fierce soe'er it flieth,
   Disturbs the Sabbath of that deeper sea.

3 So to the heart that knows Thy love, O Purest,
   There is a temple, sacred evermore;
And all the babble of life's angry voices
   Dies in hushed stillness at its peaceful door.

4 Far, far away, the roar of passion dieth,
   And loving thoughts rise calm and peacefully;
And no rude storm, how fierce soe'er it flieth,
   Disturbs the soul that dwells, O Lord, in Thee.

Mrs. Harriet B. D. Stowe. (1812-.)

---

774 "Thy sleep shall be sweet."
Ps. cxxvii. 1, 2. Isa. xxxii. 17, 18. Phil. iv. 4-9.   8.

1 OF all the thoughts of God that are
   Borne in upon our souls afar,
Along the Psalmist's music deep,
O tell me if there any is,
For gift or grace surpassing this:
   "He giveth His belovéd sleep."

2 His dews drop mutely on the hill,
His cloud above it saileth still,
   Though on its slope men toil and reap;
More softly than the dew is shed,
Or cloud is floated overhead,
   "He giveth His belovéd sleep."

Mrs. Elizabeth B. Browning. (1809-1861.)

776 "God will enlighten my darkness."
Zech. xiv. 6-11. Isa. xxx. 15-29. Mat. xxiv. 42-47   8.

1 AT evening time let there be light:
   Life's little day draws near its close;
Around me fall the shades of night,
   The night of death, the grave's repose;
To crown my joys, to end my woes,
   At evening time let there be light.

2 At evening time there shall be light,
   For God has spoken, it must be;
Fear, doubt, and anguish take their flight,
   His glory now is risen on me;
Mine eyes shall His salvation see;
   'T is evening time, and there is light.

Author unknown.

---

775 "He shall gently lead."
Ps. xxiii. Eze. xxxiv. 9-31. John x. 11-28. 1 Pet. ii. 11-25.   11.

1 THE Lord is my Shepherd, no want shall I know;
   I feed in green pastures, safe folded I rest;
He leadeth my soul where the still waters flow,
   Restores me when wand'ring, redeems when oppressed.

2 Through the valley and shadow of death though I stray,
   Since Thou art my Guardian, no evil I fear;
Thy rod shall defend me, Thy staff be my stay;
   No harm can befall, with my Comforter near.

3 In the midst of affliction my table is spread;
   With blessings unmeasured my cup runneth o'er;
With perfume and oil Thou anointest my head;
   O what shall I ask of Thy providence more?

4 Let goodness and mercy, my bountiful God,
   Still follow my steps till I meet Thee above;
I seek, by the path which my forefathers trod
   Through the land of their sojourn, Thy kingdom of love.

James Montgomery. (1771-1854.)

"God hath given rest."

777 "Under the shadow of the Almighty." **C. M.**
Ps. xci.   Job v. 17-27.   Rev. iii. 7-12.

1 THERE is a safe and secret place
  Beneath the wings divine,
  Reserved for all the heirs of grace:
  O be that refuge mine !

2 The least and feeblest there may bide,
  Uninjured and unawed ;
  While thousands fall on every side,
  He rests secure in God.

3 He feeds in pastures large and fair
  Of love and truth divine ;
  O child of God, O glory's heir,
  How rich a lot is thine !

4 A hand almighty to defend,
  An ear for every call,
  An honored life, a peaceful end,
  And heaven to crown it all !
                    Rev. Henry F. Lyte.   (1793-1847.)

778 "Peace through the blood of His cross." **S. M.**
Col. i. 9-20.   Isa. liv. 1-10.   Jer. xxxii. 36-44.

1 I HEAR the words of love,
  I gaze upon the blood,
  I see the mighty Sacrifice,
  And I have peace with God.

2 'T is everlasting peace,
  Sure as Jehovah's name ;
  'T is stable as His steadfast throne,
  For evermore the same.

3 I change ; He changes not :
  The Christ can never die ;
  His love, not mine, the resting-place,
  His truth, not mine, the tie.
                    Rev. Horatius Bonar.   (1808-.)

779   "Then am I strong."   **7.**
Ps. lxii.   Mark xiii. 9-13.   2 Cor. xii. 9, 10.

1 WAIT, my soul, upon the Lord ;
  To His gracious promise flee ;
  Laying hold upon His word,
  " As thy days, thy strength shall be."

2 If the sorrows of thy case
  Seem peculiar still to thee,
  God has promised needful grace :
  " As thy days, thy strength shall be."

3 Days of trial, days of grief,
  In succession thou mayst see ;
  This is still thy sweet relief,
  " As thy days, thy strength shall be."

4 Rock of Ages ! I 'm secure,
  With Thy promise, full and free,
  Faithful, positive, and sure,
  " As thy days, thy strength shall be."
                    William F. Lloyd.   (1791-1853.)

780 "Thou wilt keep in perfect peace." **C. M.**
Isa. xxvi. 1-12.   Eph. ii. 11-18.   John xvii. 1-10

1 A MIND at " perfect peace " with God :
  O what a word is this !
  A sinner reconciled through blood :
  O this, indeed, is bliss !

2 By nature and by practice far,
  How very far, from God ;
  Yet now by grace brought nigh to Him,
  Through faith in Jesus' blood.

3 So nigh, so very nigh to God,
  I cannot nearer be ;
  For in the person of His Son,
  I am as near as He.

4 So dear, so very dear to God,
  More dear I cannot be ;
  The love wherewith He loves the Son,
  Such is His love to me.

5 Why should I ever careful be,
  Since such a God is mine ?
  He watches o'er me night and day,
  And tells me, " Mine is thine."
                    Author unknown.

781 "Thou rulest the raging of the sea." **10. 11.**
Mark iv. 35-41.   Isa. xl. 1-8.   Ps. cvii. 23-31.

1 BEGONE, unbelief,
    My Saviour is near ;
  And for my relief
    Will surely appear.
  By prayer let me wrestle,
    And He will perform ;
  With Christ in the vessel,
    I smile at the storm.

2 Though dark be my way,
    Since He is my Guide,
  'T is mine to obey,
    'T is His to provide.
  Though cisterns be broken,
    And creatures all fail,
  The word He has spoken
    Shall surely prevail.

3 Since all that I meet
    Shall work for my good,
  The bitter is sweet,
    The medicine is food :
  Though painful at present,
    'T will cease before long ;
  And then, O how pleasant
    The conqueror's song !
                    Rev. John Newton.   (1725-1807.)

"I will joy in the God of my salvation."

782 2 Sam. xxii. 2)-51. "I will rejoice in the Lord." Hab. iii. Mat. vi. 25-34. **7. 6.**

1 SOMETIMES a light surprises
    The Christian while he sings:
It is the Lord, who rises
    With healing in His wings!
When comforts are declining,
    He grants the soul again
A season of clear shining,
    To cheer it after rain.

2 In holy contemplation,
    We sweetly then pursue
The theme of God's salvation,
    And find it ever new.
Set free from present sorrow,
    We cheerfully can say,
Let the unknown to-morrow
    Bring with it what it may.

3 It can bring with it nothing,
    But He will bear us through;
Who gives the lilies clothing
    Will clothe His people too.
Beneath the spreading heavens,
    No creature but is fed;
And He who feeds the ravens
    Will give His children bread.

4 Though vine nor fig-tree neither
    Their wonted fruit should bear;
Though all the fields should wither,
    Nor flocks nor herds be there:
Yet God the same abiding,
    His praise shall tune my voice;
For while in Him confiding
    I cannot but rejoice.

Rev. John Newton. (1725-1807.)

783 "The fulness of Him that filleth all in all." Isa. ix. 1-8. Jer. xxiii. 1-8. Eph. v. 1-20. **C. M.**

1 THE Saviour! O what endless charms
    Dwell in the blissful sound!
Its influence every fear disarms,
    And spreads sweet comfort round.

2 O the rich depths of love divine,
    Of bliss a boundless store!
Dear Saviour, let me call Thee mine;
    I cannot wish for more.

3 On Thee alone my hope relies,
    Beneath Thy cross I fall:
My Lord, my Life, my Sacrifice,
    My Saviour, and my All.

Miss Anne Steele. (1717-1778.)

784 "I have all and abound." Gen. xxii. Ex. xv. 20 to xvi. 15. Rom. v. **7. 6.**

1 I 'VE found a joy in sorrow,
    A secret balm for pain,
A beautiful to-morrow
    Of sunshine after rain;
I 've found a branch of healing,
    Near every bitter spring,
A whispered promise stealing
    O'er every broken string.

2 I 've found a glad hosanna
    For every woe and wail,
A handful of sweet manna,
    When grapes from Eshcol fail;
I 've found a Rock of Ages,
    When desert wells were dry;
And, after weary stages,
    I 've found an Elim nigh.

3 O'er tears of soft contrition
    I 've seen a rainbow light,
A glory and fruition,
    So near, yet out of sight.
My Saviour, Thee possessing,
    We have the joy, the balm,
The healing and the blessing,
    The sunshine and the psalm.

Mrs. Jane F. Crewdson. (1809-1863.)

785 "In the shadow of Thy wings will I rejoice." Ps. lxxxv. Eze. xi. 14-20. Heb. i. 10-12. **C. M.**

1 O LORD, in whom are all my springs,
    Joyful to Thee I come;
My grateful heart exultant sings
    To know Thou art its home.

2 The shelter of Thy glorious arms,
    How strong and safe and sweet!
From sense and sin, from all alarms,
    I fly to this retreat.

3 Here is my sure and tranquil rest
    In every troubled hour;
Weary, I lean upon Thy breast,
    And feel its soothing power.

4 In that dear place of purest love,
    What wings encircle me!
Naught in the world can ever move
    My trusting heart from Thee.

5 My Lord, if now I find in Thee
    So blest and sweet a home,
What shall my heavenly mansion be,
    When to its door I come?

Rev. Sylvester D. Phelps. (1816-.)

"I will joy in the God of my salvation."

786 "My heart shall rejoice in Thy salvation." **C. M.**
Ps. lxxiii. 25-28. John vii. 37-39. 1 Cor. x. 1-5.

1 O LORD, I would delight in Thee,
And on Thy care depend;
To Thee in every trouble flee,
My best, my only Friend!

2 When all created streams are dried,
Thy fulness is the same;
May I with this be satisfied,
And glory in Thy name.

3 O Lord, I cast my care on Thee,
I triumph and adore;
Henceforth my great concern shall be
To love and praise Thee more.

Rev. John Ryland. (1753-1825.)

787 "How excellent is Thy loving-kindness!" **L. M.**
Ps. cxxxviii. Isa. lxiii. 7-19. Rev. xiv. 1-3.

1 THY loving-kindness, Lord, I sing,
Of grace and life the sacred spring;
The spring o'erflowing, rich and free,
In precious blood, once shed for me.

2 I to Thy mercy-seat repair,
And find Thy loving-kindness there;
And when to Thy sweet word I go,
Thy loving-kindness there I know.

3 Lord, from the moment of my birth
I've nothing known but love on earth;
By day, by night, where'er I be,
Thy loving-kindness follows me.

4 From daily sin and daily woe
Thy loving-kindness saves me now;
And I will praise, for sins forgiven,
Thy loving-kindness all, in heaven.

Rev. George B. Cheever. (1807-.)

788 "I will be glad in the Lord." **C. M.**
Eph. ii. 1-10. 1 Cor. xv. 1-10. Ps. lxxxvi. 1-13.

1 AMAZING grace, how sweet the sound
That saved a wretch like me!
I once was lost, but now am found,
Was blind, but now I see.

2 'T was grace that taught my heart to fear,
And grace my fears relieved;
How precious did that grace appear
The hour I first believed!

3 Through many dangers, toils, and snares,
I have already come;
'T is grace has brought me safe thus far,
And grace will lead me home.

Rev. John Newton. (1725-1807.)

789 "Alway rejoicing." **S. M.**
Ps. xxxiii. Rom. xii. 12-15. John x. 1-5.

1 REJOICE in God alway:
When earth looks heavenly bright,
When joy makes glad the livelong day,
And peace shuts in the night.

2 Rejoice when care and woe
The fainting soul oppress;
When tears at wakeful midnight flow,
And morn brings heaviness.

3 Rejoice in hope and fear;
Rejoice in life and death;
Rejoice when threatening storms are near,
And comfort languisheth.

4 When should not they rejoice
Whom Christ His brethren calls;
Who hear and know His guiding voice,
When on their hearts it falls?

Rev. John Moultrie. (1799-1874.)

790 "Thou hast put gladness in my heart." **C. M.**
Isa. lx. Mal. iv. 2. Rev. xxi. 23 to xxii. 5.

1 MY God, the Spring of all my joys,
The Life of my delights,
The Glory of my brightest days,
And Comfort of my nights!

2 In darkest shades, if He appear,
My dawning is begun;
He is my soul's sweet Morning Star,
And He my rising Sun.

3 The opening heavens around me shine
With beams of sacred bliss,
While Jesus shows His heart is mine,
And whispers I am His.

4 My soul would leave this heavy clay,
At that transporting word;
Run up with joy the shining way,
T' embrace my dearest Lord.

Rev. Isaac Watts. (1674-1748.)

791 "This is the joy of His way." **C. M.**
Mat. vi. 1-6. Isa. xxvi. Ex. xix.

1 How deep and tranquil is the joy
Which Thou hast kindly given
To those who seek Thy presence, Lord,
And tread the path to heaven!

2 'T is here the troubled springs of life
Are calmed to sweetest rest;
The stillness of this hour expels
The tumult of my breast.

3 Far, far above all mortal things,
I walk with God alone;
And while He names celestial joys
I call them all my own.

Rev. Andrew Reed. (1787-1862.)

151

"I will joy in the God of my salvation."

792 "I will offer in His tabernacle sacrifices of joy." 10.
Isa. xxxv. Jer. xxxi. 1-14. Eph. v. 8-20.

1 JOYFULLY, joyfully, onward I move,
Bound to the land of bright spirits above ;
Angelic choristers sing as I come,
Joyfully, joyfully haste to thy home !
Soon, with my pilgrimage ended below,
Home to that land of delight will I go ;
Pilgrim and stranger no more shall I roam,
Joyfully, joyfully resting at home.

2 Sounds of sweet melody fall on my ear ;
Harps of the blessèd, your voices I hear ;
Rings with the harmony heaven's high dome,
Joyfully, joyfully haste to thy home !
Bright will the morn of eternity dawn ;
Death shall be banished, his sceptre be gone :
Joyfully, then, shall I witness his doom,
Joyfully, joyfully, safely at home.

Rev. William Hunter. (1811-1877.)

793 "Thou, Lord, hast made me glad." L. M.
Ps. lxv. Lev. xxvi. 2-13. Rom. xv. 1-17.

1 MY Helper, God, I bless His name ;
The same His power, His grace the same ;
The tokens of His friendly care
Open, and crown, and close the year.

2 Thus far His arm hath led me on,
Thus far I make His mercy known;
And while I tread this desert land
New mercies shall new songs demand.

3 My grateful soul, on Jordan's shore,
Shall raise one sacred pillar more ;
Then bear in His bright courts above
Inscriptions of immortal love.

Rev. Philip Doddridge. (1702-1751.)

794 "My heart greatly rejoiceth." S. M.
Rom. viii. 31-39. John xiv. 1-3. Isa. liv. 1-13.

1 IF Jesus be my Friend,
If God doth love me well,
What matters all my foes intend,
Though strong they be, and fell ?

2 He whispers in my breast
Sweet words of holy cheer ;
How he who seeks in God his rest
Shall ever find Him near.

3 My heart for gladness springs,
It cannot more be sad ;
For very joy it laughs and sings,
Sees naught but sunshine glad.

4 The sun that glads mine eyes
Is Christ, the Lord I love ;
I sing for joy of that which lies
Stored up for us above.

Rev. Paul Gerhardt. (1605-1676.)
Tr. by Miss Catherine Winkworth. 1823.

795 "Thy marvellous loving kindness." L. M.
Ps. cxxxviii. Isa. lxiii. 7-9. Rev. v.

1 AWAKE, my soul, in joyful lays,
And sing thy great Redeemer's praise ;
He justly claims a song from me,
His loving-kindness is so free.

2 He saw me ruined in the fall,
Yet loved me, notwithstanding all ;
And saved me from my lost estate,
His loving-kindness is so great.

3 Through mighty hosts of cruel foes,
Where earth and hell my way oppose,
He safely leads my soul along,
His loving-kindness is so strong.

4 So when I pass death's gloomy vale,
And life and mortal powers shall fail,
O may my last expiring breath
His loving-kindness sing in death.

5 Then shall I mount and soar away
To the bright world of endless day ;
There shall I sing, with sweet surprise,
His loving-kindness in the skies.

Rev. Samuel Medley. (1738-1799.)

796 "To live is Christ." 7.
Phil. i. 19-21. Gal. ii. 16-21. Ps. xxiii.

1 CHRIST, of all my hopes the Ground,
Christ, the Spring of all my joy,
Still in Thee may I be found,
Still for Thee my powers employ.
Fountain of o'erflowing grace,
Freely from Thy fulness give ;
Till I close my earthly race,
May I prove it "Christ to live."

2 When I touch the blessèd shore,
Back the closing waves shall roll;
Death's dark stream shall never more
Part from Thee my ravished soul.
Thus, O thus an entrance give
To the land of cloudless sky ;
Having known it "Christ to live,"
Let me know it "gain to die : "

3 Gain to part from all my grief,
Gain, to bid my sins farewell ;
Gain of all my gains the chief,
Ever with the Lord to dwell.
This Thy people's portion, Lord,
Peace on earth, and bliss on high ;
This their ever-sure reward,
"Christ to live, and gain to die."

Rev. Ralph Wardlaw. (1779-1853.)

"I will joy in the God of my salvation."

797 " I praise and extol . . . the King of heaven." **L. M.**
Ps. civ.   Jer. x. 6-13.   Rev. xix. 1-6.

1 COME, O my soul, in sacred lays
  Attempt thy great Creator's praise :
  But O what tongue can speak His fame,
  What mortal verse can reach the theme ?

2 Enthroned amid the radiant spheres,
  He glory like a garment wears ;
  To form a robe of light divine,
  Ten thousand suns around Him shine.

3 In all our Maker's grand designs
  Almighty power with wisdom shines ;
  His works, through all this wondrous frame,
  Declare the glory of His name.

4 Raised on devotion's lofty wing,
  Do thou, my soul, His glories sing ;
  And let His praise employ thy tongue,
  Till listening worlds shall join the song.
  Rev. Thomas Blacklock. (1721-1791.)

798 " Blessed be the Lord God." **L. M.**
Ps. ciii.   John iii. 14-17.   1 John ii. 1-12.

1 BLESS, O my soul, the living God ;
  Call home thy thoughts that roam abroad :
  Let all the powers within me join
  In work and worship so divine.

2 'T is He, my soul, that sent His Son
  To die for crimes which thou hast done :
  He owns the ransom, and forgives
  The hourly follies of our lives.

3 Bless, O my soul the God of grace ;
  His favors claim thy highest praise :
  Why should the wonders He hath wrought
  Be lost in silence, and forgot ?
  Rev. Isaac Watts. (1674-1748.)

799 " I will praise the name of God with a song." **L. M.**
Ps. xviii.   Dan. iii. 16-30   Acts xx. 17-35.

1 No change of time shall ever shock
  My firm affection, Lord, to Thee ;
  For Thou hast always been my Rock,
  A Fortress and Defence to me.

2 Thou my Deliverer art, my God,
  My trust is in Thy mighty power ;
  Thou art my Shield from foes abroad,
  At home my Safeguard and my Tower.

3 To Thee will I address my prayer,
  To whom all praise we justly owe ;
  So shall I by Thy watchful care
  Be guarded safe from every foe.

4 My God, to celebrate Thy fame
  My grateful voice to heaven I 'll raise :
  And nations, strangers to Thy name,
  Shall learn to sing Thy glorious praise.
  Tate and Brady. 1696.

800 " My soul doth magnify the Lord." **8. 7.**
Ps. cxlv.   Dan. iv. 34-37.   Acts xiv. 8-17.

1 GOD, my King, Thy might confessing,
  Ever will I bless Thy name ;
  Day by day Thy throne addressing,
  Still will I Thy praise proclaim.
  Honor great our God befitteth ;
  Who His majesty can reach ?
  Age to age His works transmitteth,
  Age to age His power shall teach.

2 Nor shall fail from memory's treasure
  Works by love and mercy wrought ;
  Works of love surpassing measure,
  Works of mercy passing thought.
  Full of kindness and compassion,
  Slow to anger, vast in love,
  God is good to all creation ;
  All His works His goodness prove.

3 God is just in all He doeth,
  Kind is He in all His ways ;
  He His ready presence showeth,
  When a faithful servant prays.
  Ever, God of endless praises,
  Shall Thy royal might remain ;
  Evermore Thy brightness blazes,
  Ever lasts Thy righteous reign.
  Bp. Richard Mant. (1776-1848.)

801 " His praise continually in my mouth." **C. M.**
Ps. xxxiv.   Isa. xxxviii. 9-20.   Heb. xiii. 5-15.

1 THROUGH all the changing scenes of life,
  In trouble and in joy,
  The praises of my God shall still
  My heart and tongue employ.

2 Of His deliverance I will boast,
  Till all that are distressed
  From my example comfort take,
  And charm their griefs to rest.

3 O magnify the Lord with me,
  With me exalt His name :
  When in distress to Him I called,
  He to my rescue came.

4 The hosts of God encamp around
  The dwellings of the just ;
  Deliverance He affords to all
  Who on His succor trust.

5 O make but trial of His love :
  Experience will decide
  How blest are they, and only they,
  Who in His truth confide.
  Tate and Brady. 1696.

"I will joy in the God of my salvation."

802 "That my soul may sing praise to Thee." **S. M.**
Ps. ciii. Job xxxiii. 27–30. John iii. 16–18.

1 MY soul, repeat His praise,
    Whose mercies are so great;
  Whose anger is so slow to rise,
    So ready to abate.

2 High as the heavens are raised
    Above the ground we tread,
  So far the riches of His grace
    Our highest thoughts exceed.

3 His power subdues our sins,
    And His forgiving love,
  Far as the east is from the west,
    Doth all our guilt remove.
        Rev. Isaac Watts. (1674–1748.)

803 "I will remember the works of the Lord." **C. M.**
Ps. lxxxix. 1 Chr. xxix. 10–18. Titus ii. 11–14.

1 WHEN all Thy mercies, O my God,
    My rising soul surveys,
  Transported with the view, I 'm lost
    In wonder, love, and praise.

2 O how can words with equal warmth
    The gratitude declare
  That glows within my ravished heart?
    But Thou canst read it there.

3 Ten thousand thousand precious gifts
    My daily thanks employ;
  Nor is the least a cheerful heart
    That tastes those gifts with joy.

4 Through every period of my life
    Thy goodness I 'll pursue,
  And after death in distant worlds
    The glorious theme renew.

5 Through all eternity to Thee
    A joyful song I 'll raise;
  But O eternity 's too short
    To utter all Thy praise.
        Joseph Addison. (1672–1719.)

804 "I will bless the Lord." **S. M.**
Ps. cxlvi. Ex. xv. 1–21. 1 Pet. ii. 24, 25.

1 O BLESS the Lord, my soul;
    Let all within me join,
  And aid my tongue to bless His name,
    Whose favors are divine.

2 'T is He forgives thy sins,
    'T is He relieves thy pain;
  'T is He that heals thy sicknesses,
    And makes thee young again.

3 He crowns thy life with love,
    When ransomed from the grave;
  He that redeemed my soul from hell
    Hath sovereign power to save.
        Rev. Isaac Watts.

805 "Let my mouth be filled with Thy praise." **C. M.**
Ps. lxxi. Jer. xv. 11–21. Jude 24, 25.

1 MY Saviour, my almighty Friend,
    When I begin Thy praise,
  Where will the growing numbers end,
    The numbers of Thy grace?

2 Thou art my everlasting Trust;
    Thy goodness I adore;
  And since I knew Thy graces first
    I speak Thy glories more.

3 My feet shall travel all the length
    Of the celestial road;
  And march with courage, in Thy strength,
    To see my Father, God.

4 Awake, awake, my tuneful powers!
    With this delightful song,
  I 'll entertain the darkest hours,
    Nor think the season long.
        Rev. Isaac Watts.

806 "He that glorieth, let him glory in the Lord." **8, 7.**
Gal. vi. 14–18. Rom. v. 1–11. Isa. liii.

1 IN the cross of Christ I glory,
    Towering o'er the wrecks of time;
  All the light of sacred story
    Gathers round its head sublime.

2 When the woes of life o'ertake me,
    Hopes deceive, and fears annoy,
  Never shall the cross forsake me;
    Lo, it glows with peace and joy.

3 When the sun of bliss is beaming
    Light and love upon my way,
  From the cross the radiance streaming
    Adds more lustre to the day.

4 Bane and blessing, pain and pleasure,
    By the cross are sanctified;
  Peace is there, that knows no measure,
    Joys that through all time abide.
        Sir John Bowring. (1792–1872.)

807 "With Thine honor all the day." **C. M.**
Eze. xxxiv. 20–31. John x. 7–15. Luke xv. 3–7.

1 TO Thee, my Shepherd and my Lord,
    A grateful song I 'll raise;
  O let the meanest of Thy flock
    Attempt to speak Thy praise.

2 My life, my joy, my hope, I owe
    To Thine amazing love;
  Ten thousand thousand comforts here,
    And nobler bliss above.

3 Lead on, dear Shepherd! led by Thee,
    No evil shall I fear;
  Soon shall I reach Thy fold above,
    And praise Thee better there.
        Rev. Ottiwell Heginbotham. (1744–1768.)

154

"I would fly away and be at rest."

808 "Having a desire to depart." **8. P.**
Phil. i. 23. 1 Pet. i. 8. Ps. xvii. 15.

1 To Jesus, the Crown of my hope,
  My soul is in haste to be gone;
  O bear me, ye Cherubim, up,
  And waft me away to His throne;
  My Saviour, whom absent I love,
  Whom not having seen I adore,
  Whose name is exalted above
  All glory, dominion, and power,

2 Dissolve Thou these bands that detain
  My soul from her portion in Thee!
  Ah, strike off this adamant chain,
  And make me eternally free.
  O then shall the vail be removed,
  And round me Thy brightness be poured;
  I shall meet Him whom absent I loved,
  Shall see whom unseen I adored.
                        William Cowper. (1731-1800.)

809 "To be with Christ." **L. M.**
Mark ix. 1-5. John xvii. 11-24. Ruth i. 1-16.

1 LET me be with Thee, where Thou art,
  My Saviour, my eternal Rest;
  Then only will this longing heart
  Be fully and forever blest.

2 Let me be with Thee, where Thou art,
  Thine unveiled glory to behold;
  Then only will this wandering heart
  Cease to be faithless, treacherous, cold.

3 Let me be with Thee, where Thou art,
  Where spotless saints Thy name adore;
  Then only will this sinful heart
  Be evil and defiled no more.

4 Let me be with Thee, where Thou art,
  Where none can die, where none remove;
  Where life nor death my soul can part
  From Thy blest presence and Thy love.
                        Miss Charlotte Elliott. (1789-1871.)

810 "I will lift up mine eyes unto the hills." **S. M.**
Ps. cxxiii. Isa. xxv. 2 Tim. iv. 6-18.

1 How far beyond our mortal sight
  The Lord of glory dwells!
  A vail of interposing night
  His radiant face conceals.

2 O could my longing spirit rise
  On strong, immortal wing,
  And reach Thy palace in the skies,
  My Saviour and my King!

3 Thy presence beams eternal day,
  O'er all the blissful place;
  Who would not drop this load of clay,
  And die, to see Thy face!
                        Miss Anne Steele. (1717-1778.)

811 "As a servant earnestly desireth the shadow." **8. P.**
2 Cor. v. 1 Thes. iv. 13-18. Isa. xxxiii. 17.

1 I LONG to behold Him arrayed
  With glory and light from above;
  The King in His beauty displayed,
  His beauty of holiest love:
  I languish and die to be there,
  Where Jesus hath fixed His abode;
  O when shall we meet in the air,
  And fly to the mountain of God?

2 How happy the people that dwell
  Secure in the city above!
  No pain the inhabitants feel,
  No sickness or sorrow shall prove.
  Physician of souls, unto me
  Forgiveness and holiness give;
  And when from the body set free,
  O then to the city receive.
                        Rev. Charles Wesley. (1708-1788.)

812 "To see Thy power and Thy glory." **8. P.**
Heb. i. Rev. vii. 9-12. Ps. lxv. 1-4.

1 YE angels, who stand round the throne,
  And view my Immanuel's face,
  In rapturous songs make Him known,
  Tune all your soft harps to His praise:
  Ye saints, who stand nearer than they,
  And cast your bright crowns at His feet,
  His grace and His glory display,
  And all His rich mercy relate.

2 O when will the period appear
  When I shall unite in your song?
  I'm weary of lingering here,
  And I to your Saviour belong.
  I want, O I want to be there,
  Where sorrow and sin bid adieu;
  Your joy and your friendship to share,
  To wonder and worship with you.
                        Miss Maria De Fleury. 1791.

813 "As in a strange country." **9. 11. 10.**
Heb. xi. 8-10. Rev. xxi. Gen. xlvii. 1-9.

1 I'M a pilgrim and I'm a stranger;
  I can tarry, I can tarry but a night:
  Do not detain me, for I am going
  To where the fountains are ever flowing.
  I'm a pilgrim, etc.

2 There the glory is ever shining;
  O my longing heart, my longing heart is
      there!
  Here in this country, so dark and dreary,
  I long have wandered, forlorn and weary.

3 There's the city to which I journey;
  My Redeemer, my Redeemer is its light;
  There is no sorrow, nor any sighing,
  Nor any tears there, nor any dying.
                        Mrs. Mary S. B. Dana. (1810-.)

"I would fly away and be at rest."

814 "Labor, therefore, to enter into that rest." 11.
Deu. xii. 9-12. Ps. lv. 1-17. Jer. xxx. 10-22. Heb. vi. 11-20.

1 MY rest is in heaven, my rest is not here;
Then why should I murmur when trials appear?
Be hushed, my dark spirit; the worst that can come
But shortens thy journey, and hastens thee home.

2 It is not for me to be seeking my bliss,
And building my hopes in a region like this;
I ask not my portion, I seek not my rest,
Till I find them, O Lord, in Thy sheltering breast.

Rev. Henry F. Lyte. (1793-1847.)

815 "In my Father's house." L. M.
John xiv. 1-3. Rev. xxi. 10 to xxii. 5. Ps. xlii.

1 THY Father's house! Thine own bright home!
And Thou hast there a place for me!
Though yet an exile here I roam,
That distant home by faith I see.

2 I see its domes resplendent glow,
Where beams of God's own glory fall;
And trees of life immortal grow,
Whose fruits o'erhang the sapphire wall.

3 I know that Thou, who on the tree
Didst deign our mortal guilt to bear,
Wilt bring Thine own to dwell with Thee,
And waitest to receive me there.

4 Thy love will there array my soul
In Thine own robe of spotless hue;
And I shall gaze, while ages roll,
On Thee, with raptures ever new.

5 O welcome day, when Thou my feet
Shalt bring the shining threshold o'er,
A Father's warm embrace to meet,
And dwell at home for evermore!

Rev. Ray Palmer. (1808-.)

817 "He looked for a city." S. M.
Ps. cxxxvii. Job iii. 17-19. 2 Cor. v. 1-9.

1 FAR from my heavenly home,
Far from my Father's breast,
Fainting, I cry, "Blest Spirit, come,
And speed me to my rest!"

2 Upon the willows long
My harp has silent hung;
How should I sing a cheerful song
Till Thou inspire my tongue?

3 My spirit homeward turns,
And fain would thither flee;
My heart, O Zion, droops and yearns,
When I remember thee.

4 To thee, to thee, I press,
A dark and toilsome road;
When shall I pass the wilderness,
And reach the saints' abode?

5 God of my life, be near;
On Thee my hopes I cast:
O guide me through the desert here,
And bring me home at last.

Rev. Henry F. Lyte.

816 "I would not live alway." 11.
Job vii. 1-16. Ps. xxii. 1 Thes. iv. 13 to v. 10. Rev. vii. 9-17.

1 I WOULD not live alway: I ask not to stay
Where storm after storm rises dark o'er the way;
The few lurid mornings that dawn on us here
Are enough for life's woes, full enough for its cheer.

2 I would not live alway, thus fettered by sin,
Temptation without and corruption within;
E'en the rapture of pardon is mingled with fears,
And the cup of thanksgiving with penitent tears.

3 Who, who would live alway away from his God,
Away from yon heaven, that blissful abode:
Where the rivers of pleasure flow o'er the bright plains,
And the noontide of glory eternally reigns;

4 Where the saints of all ages in harmony meet,
Their Saviour and brethren transported to greet;
While the anthems of rapture unceasingly roll,
And the smile of the Lord is the feast of the soul!

Rev. William A. Muhlenberg. (1793-1877.)

"I would fly away and be at rest."

818 "He hath prepared ... a city." **C. M.**
Rev. vii. 2 Cor. iv. Ps. lxxviii. 52–55.

1 GIVE me the wings of faith, to rise
  Within the vail, and see
  The saints above, how great their joys,
  How bright their glories be.

2 Once they were mourning here below,
  And wet their couch with tears;
  They wrestled hard, as we do now,
  With sins, and doubts, and fears.

3 I ask them whence their vic'try came?
  They, with united breath,
  Ascribe their conquest to the Lamb,
  Their triumph to His death.

4 They marked the footsteps that He trod;
  His zeal inspired their breast;
  And, foll'wing their incarnate God,
  Possess the promised rest.
  Rev. Isaac Watts. (1674-1748.)

819 "The Lord shall give thee rest." **S. M.**
Heb. iv. Isa. xxxii. 15–20. Eze. xxxiv. 22–31.

1 AND is there, Lord, a rest,
  For weary souls designed,
  Where not a care shall stir the breast,
  Or sorrow entrance find?

2 Forever blessèd they,
  Whose joyful feet shall stand,
  While endless ages waste away,
  Amid that glorious land!

3 My soul would thither tend,
  While toilsome years are given;
  Then let me, gracious God, ascend
  To sweet repose in heaven.
  Rev. Ray Palmer. (1808–.)

820 "I must put off this my tabernacle." **C. M.**
2 Cor. v. 1–10. Rev. ii. 1–11. Isa. xxxv.

1 AND let this feeble body fail,
  And let it faint or die,
  My soul shall quit the mournful vale,
  And soar to worlds on high;

2 Shall join the disembodied saints,
  And find its long-sought rest,
  That only bliss for which it pants,
  In the Redeemer's breast.

3 O what are all my sufferings here,
  If, Lord, Thou count me meet
  With that enraptured host to appear,
  And worship at Thy feet!

4 Give joy or grief, give ease or pain,
  Take life or friends away,
  I come, to find them all again
  In that eternal day.
  Rev. Charles Wesley. (1708-1788.)

821 "Which hath foundations." **S. M.**
2 Pet. i. 13, 14. John xiv. 1–3. Ps. xiii.

1 I HAVE a home above,
  From sin and sorrow free;
  A mansion, which eternal love
  Designed and formed for me.

2 My Father's gracious hand
  Has built this sweet abode;
  From everlasting it was planned,
  My dwelling-place with God.

3 My Saviour's precious blood
  Has made my title sure;
  He passed through death's dark raging flood,
  To make my rest secure.

4 The Comforter has come,
  The earnest has been given;
  He leads me onward to the home
  Reserved for me in heaven.
  Henry Bennett. (1813-1868.)

822 "My soul shall be satisfied." **6. 8.**
Ps. lxv. 1–4. Heb. xii. 22–24. Rev. iv. 10, 11.

1 'T is heaven begun below
  To hear Christ's praises flow
  In Zion, where His name is known;
  What will it be above
  To sing redeeming love,
  And cast our crowns before His throne!

2 Till that blest period come,
  Zion shall be my home;
  And may I never thence remove,
  Till from the church below
  To that on high I go,
  And there commune in perfect love.
  Rev. Joseph Swain. (1761-1796.)

823 "There is none abiding." **8. 7. P.**
2 Tim. iv. 1–8. Heb. xi. 1–10. Josh. iii.

1 MY days are gliding swiftly by,
  And I, a pilgrim stranger,
  Would not detain them as they fly,
  These hours of toil and danger.

  For O we stand on Jordan's strand,
  Our friends are passing over;
  And, just before, the shining shore
  We may almost discover.

2 Should coming days be cold and dark,
  We need not cease our singing;
  That perfect rest naught can molest
  Where golden harps are ringing.

3 Let sorrow's rudest tempest blow
  Each cord on earth to sever;
  Our King says, "Come," and there 's our home,
  Forever, O forever!
  Rev. David Nelson. (1793-1844.)

"I would fly away and be at rest."

824 *"I will dwell in the house of the Lord forever."* **11.**
Phil. i. 21-26. Job vii. 1-16. Ps. xvii. Heb. iv. 9-16.

1 'MID scenes of confusion and creature complaints,
How sweet to the soul is communion with saints!
To find at the banquet of mercy there 's room,
And feel in the presence of Jesus at home!

2 While here in the valley of conflict I stay,
O give me submission, and strength as my day ;
In all my afflictions to Thee would I come,
Rejoicing in hope of my glorious home.

3 Whate'er Thou deniest, O give me Thy grace,
The Spirit's sure witness, and smiles of Thy face;
Endue me with patience to wait at Thy throne,
And find, even now, a sweet foretaste of home.

4 I long, dearest Lord, in Thy beauties to shine ;
No more as an exile in sorrow to pine ;
And in Thy dear image arise from the tomb,
With glorified millions to praise Thee at home.

Rev. David Denham. (1791-1848.)

825 *"If by any means I might attain."* **L. M.**
1 John ii. 15-17. Mat. vi. 19-24. Prov. iii. 13-26.

1 I SEND the joys of earth away ;
Away, ye tempters of the mind !
False as the smooth, deceitful sea,
And empty as the whistling wind.

2 Now, to the shining realms above,
I stretch my hands and glance mine eyes ;
O for the pinions of a dove,
To bear me to the upper skies !

3 There, from the bosom of my God,
Oceans of endless pleasure roll ;
There would I fix my last abode,
And drown the sorrows of my soul.

Rev. Isaac Watts. (1674-1748.)

827 *"There the prisoners rest together."* **C. M.**
2 Cor. xi. 21-31. 2 Pet. i. 1-11. Ps. lxxxiv.

1 WHEN I can read my title clear
To mansions in the skies,
I bid farewell to every fear,
And wipe my weeping eyes.

2 Let cares like a wild deluge come,
And storms of sorrow fall,
May I but safely reach my home,
My God, my heaven, my all.

3 There shall I bathe my weary soul
In seas of heavenly rest,
And not a wave of trouble roll
Across my peaceful breast.

Rev. Isaac Watts.

826 *"I would hasten my escape from the windy storm."* **11.**
Ps. lxxxvi. Lam. iii. 1-25. Acts vii. 55-60. Jude 20-25.

1 I 'M weary of straying; O fain would I rest
In the far distant land of the pure and the blest ;
Where sin can no longer her blandishments spread,
And tears and temptations forever have fled.

2 I 'm weary of hoping, where hope is untrue,
As fair, but as fleeting, as morning's bright dew ;
I long for that land whose blest promise alone
Is changeless and sure as eternity's throne.

3 I 'm weary of loving what passes away ;
The sweetest, the dearest, alas, may not stay ;
I long for that land where these partings are o'er,
And death and the tomb can divide hearts no more.

4 I 'm weary, my Saviour, of grieving Thy love;
O when shall I rest in Thy presence above ?
I 'm weary, but O let me never repine.
While Thy word, and Thy love, and Thy promise are mine.

Mrs. Sarah E. W. York. 1847.

"I would fly away and be at rest."

828 "I have a goodly heritage." Rev. xxi. Ecc. i. 2-7. 1 Thes. iv. 13-18. **7, 6, 7.**

1 RISE, my soul, and stretch thy wings,
　Thy better portion trace;
Rise, from transitory things,
　Towards heaven, thy native place.
Sun and moon and stars decay,
　Time shall soon this earth remove;
Rise, my soul, and haste away
　To seats prepared above.

2 Rivers to the ocean run,
　Nor stay in all their course;
Fire ascending seeks the sun;
　Both speed them to their source:
So a soul that's born of God
　Pants to view His glorious face;
Upward tends to His abode,
　To rest in His embrace.

3 Cease, ye pilgrims, cease to mourn,
　Press onward to the prize;
Soon our Saviour will return
　Triumphant in the skies.
Yet a season, and you know
　Happy entrance will be given;
All our sorrows left below,
　And earth exchanged for heaven.
　　　　Rev. Robert Seagrave. (1693-1742.)

829 "When I awake with Thy likeness." Isa. xl. 28-31. Deu. viii. 7-10. Rev. xix. 1-16. **L. M.**

1 BEYOND the hills where suns go down,
　And brightly beckon as they go,
I see the land of far renown,
　The land which I so soon shall know.

2 Above the dissonance of time,
　And discord of its angry words,
I hear the everlasting chime
　The music of unjarring chords.

3 I bid it welcome; and my haste
　To join it cannot brook delay;
O song of morning, come at last,
　And ye who sing it, come away!

4 O song of light and dawn and bliss,
　Sound over earth and fill these skies;
Nor ever, ever, ever cease
　Thy soul-entrancing melodies!

5 Glad song of this disburdened earth,
　Which holy voices then shall sing;
Praise for creation's second birth,
　And glory to creation's King!
　　　　Rev. Horatius Bonar. (1808-.)

830 "I am a stranger with Thee." Heb. xi. John xiv. 1-6. 1 Chr. xxix. 10-13. **6. 4. P.**

1 I'M but a stranger here,
　　Heaven is my home;
Earth is a desert drear,
　　Heaven is my home.
Danger and sorrow stand
Round me on every hand;
Heaven is my fatherland,
　　Heaven is my home.

2 What though the tempest rage?
　　Heaven is my home;
Short is my pilgrimage,
　　Heaven is my home.
And time's wild wintry blast
Soon shall be overpast;
I shall reach home at last:
　　Heaven is my home.

3 There, at my Saviour's side,
　　Heaven is my home,
I shall be glorified;
　　Heaven is my home.
There are the good and blest,
Those I love most and best,
And there I too shall rest:
　　Heaven is my home.
　　　　Rev. Thomas R. Taylor. (1807-1835.)

831 "I will behold Thy face in righteousness." Titus ii. 11-14. Acts vii. 55-60. Ps. cxxii. **C. M.**

1 EARTH has engrossed my love too long;
　'T is time I lift mine eyes
Upward, dear Father! to Thy throne,
　And to my native skies.

2 There the blest Man, my Saviour, sits;
　The God, how bright He shines!
And scatters infinite delights
　On all the happy minds.

3 Seraphs, with elevated strains,
　Circle the throne around;
And move, and charm the starry plains,
　With an immortal sound.

4 Jesus, the Lord, their harps employs;
　Jesus, my Love, they sing;
Jesus, the Life of both our joys,
　Sounds sweet from every string.

5 Now let me mount, and join their song,
　And be an angel too;
My heart, my hand, my ear, my tongue,
　Here's joyful work for you.
　　　　Rev. Isaac Watts. (1674-1748.)

"I would fly away and be at rest."

832 John xiv. 1–6. Heb. xi. 1–16 Jer. xxxi. 1–14.   *"His rest shall be glorious."*   8, 7.

1 IN the Christian's home in glory
   There remains a land of rest ;
   There my Saviour's gone before me,
   To fulfil my soul's request.

   There is rest for the weary,
   There is rest for the weary,
   There is rest for the weary,
   There is rest for you ;
   On the other side of Jordan,
   In the sweet fields of Eden,
   Where the tree of life is blooming,
   There is rest for you.

2 He is fitting up my mansion,
   Which eternally shall stand ;
   For my stay shall not be transient
   In that holy, happy land.

3 Sing, O sing, ye heirs of glory;
   Shout your triumph as you go ;
   Zion's gate will ope before ye,
   You shall find an entrance through.
   Rev. Samuel Y. Harmer. (1800–.)

833 Titus ii. 11–14. Mat. xxv. 1–13. Isa. xxv. 1–9.   *"My soul fainteth for Thy salvation."*   8, 7, 4.

1 O'ER the distant mountains breaking
   Comes the reddening dawn of day ;
   Rise, my soul, from sleep awaking,
   Rise and sing, and watch and pray :
      'T is thy Saviour,
   On His bright, returning way.

2 O Thou long-expected, weary
   Waits my anxious soul for Thee ;
   Life is dark, and earth is dreary,
   Where Thy light I do not see :
      O my Saviour,
   When wilt Thou return to me ?

3 Nearer is my soul's salvation,
   Spent the night, the day at hand ;
   Keep me in my lowly station,
   Watching for Thee, till I stand,
      O my Saviour,
   In Thy bright and promised land.

4 With my lamp well trimmed and burning,
   Swift to hear, and slow to roam,
   Watching for Thy glad returning
   To restore me to my home,
      Come, my Saviour,
   O my Saviour, quickly come.
   Rev. John S. B. Monsell. (1811–1875.)

834 Rev. xxii. 1–5. 2 Pet. iii. Ps. xxxvi. 5–9.   *"The light of the sun shall be seven-fold."*   L. M.

1 MY heavenly home is bright and fair,
   Nor pain, nor death, can enter there ;
   Its glittering towers the sun outshine ;
   That heavenly mansion shall be mine.

   I 'm going home, I 'm going home,
   I 'm going home to die no more,
   To die no more, to die no more,
   I 'm going home to die no more.

2 My Father's house is built on high,
   Far, far above the starry sky ;
   When from this earthly prison free,
   That heavenly mansion mine shall be.

3 Let others seek a home below,
   Which flames devour, or waves o'erflow;
   Be mine the happier lot to own
   A heavenly mansion near the throne.

4 Then fail the earth, let stars decline,
   And sun and moon refuse to shine,
   All nature sink and cease to be,
   That heavenly mansion stands for me.
   Rev. William Hunter. (1811–1877.)

835 2 Tim. iv. 1–8. Acts xx. 2 Sam. xxiii. 1–5.   *"I go the way of all the earth."*   7, 6.

1 I JOURNEY forth rejoicing,
      From this dark vale of tears,
   To heavenly joys, and freedom
      From earthly bonds and fears ;
   Where Christ our Lord shall gather
      All His redeemed again,
   His kingdom to inherit :
      Good-night, good-night, till then.

2 I go to see His glory
      Whom we have loved below ;
   I go the blessed angels,
      The holy saints, to know ;
   Our lovely ones departed
      I go to find again,
   And wait for you to join us :
      Good-night, good-night, till then.

3 I hear the Saviour calling,
      The joyful hour has come ;
   The angel guards are ready
      To guide me to my home ;
   Where Christ our Lord shall gather
      All His redeemed again,
   His kingdom to inherit :
      Good-night, good-night, till then.
   Author unknown.

"I would fly away and be at rest."

836 "The heavenly Jerusalem." **C. M.**
Rev. xxi. 1-7. Heb. xii. 22-24. Isa. lx.

1 JERUSALEM, my happy home,
　Name ever dear to me,
When shall my labors have an end,
　In joy, and peace, and thee?
When shall these eyes thy heaven-built
　　walls
And pearly gates behold;
Thy bulwarks, with salvation strong,
And streets of shining gold?

2 O when, thou city of my God,
　Shall I thy courts ascend,
Where congregations ne'er break up,
　And Sabbaths have no end?
There happier bowers than Eden's bloom,
　Nor sin nor sorrow know;
Blest seats, through rude and stormy scenes
　I onward press to you.

3 Apostles, martyrs, prophets, there,
　Around my Saviour stand;
And soon my friends in Christ, below,
　Will join the glorious band.
Jerusalem, my happy home,
　My soul still pants for thee;
Then shall my labors have an end,
　When I thy joys shall see.

　　　　　　　　　Author unknown.

837 "Jerusalem which is above is free." **C. M.**
Ps. lxxxiv. Isa. xxx. 15-29. Rev. xxii. 1-5.

1 O MOTHER dear, Jerusalem,
　When shall I come to thee?
When shall my sorrows have an end?
　Thy joys when shall I see?

2 O happy harbor of God's saints,
　O sweet and pleasant soil,
In thee no sorrow can be found,
　Nor grief, nor care, nor toil.

3 Right through thy streets with pleasing
　　sound
The flood of life doth flow,
And on the banks, on either side,
The trees of life do grow.

4 No dimming cloud o'ershadows thee,
　Nor gloom, nor darksome night;
But every soul shines as the sun,
　For God Himself gives light.

5 O passing happy were my state,
　Might I be worthy found
To wait upon my God and King,
　His praises there to sound.

　　　Rev. Francis Baker. 1616.
　　　Alt. by David Dickson. 1649.

838 "And the Lord shewed him all the land." **C. M.**
Deu. xxxiv. 1-6. 2 Tim. iv. 6-8. Ps. xliii.

1 ON Jordan's stormy banks I stand,
　And cast a wishful eye
To Canaan's fair and happy land,
　Where my possessions lie.
O the transporting, rapturous scene
　That rises to my sight:
Sweet fields arrayed in living green,
　And rivers of delight!

2 All o'er those wide-extended plains
　Shines one eternal day;
There God, the Son, forever reigns,
　And scatters night away.
No chilling winds, or poisonous breath,
　Can reach that healthful shore;
Sickness and sorrow, pain and death,
　Are felt and feared no more.

3 When shall I reach that happy place,
　And be forever blest?
When shall I see my Father's face,
　And in His bosom rest?
Filled with delight, my raptured soul
　Can here no longer stay;
Though Jordan's waves around me roll,
　Fearless I'd launch away.

　　　Rev. Samuel Stennett. (1727-1795.)

839 "The paradise of God." **C. M.**
Ps. cxxi. Isa. xxxiii. 15-24. John xvii. 16-24.

1 O PARADISE, O Paradise,
　Who doth not crave for rest?
Who would not seek the happy land
　Where they that loved are blest?

　Where loyal hearts and true
　　Stand ever in the light,
　All rapture through and through,
　　In God's most holy sight.

2 O Paradise, O Paradise,
　The world is growing old;
Who would not be at rest and free
　Where love is never cold?

3 O Paradise, O Paradise,
　I greatly long to see
The special place my dearest Lord
　In love prepares for me.

4 Lord Jesus, King of Paradise,
　O keep me in Thy love,
And guide me to that happy land
　Of perfect rest above.

　　　Rev. Frederick W. Faber. (1814-1373.)

"I would fly away and be at rest."

840 "In that day shall this song be sung." **12. 8.**
Isa. xlix. 13-23. Jer. xxxi. 1-14. Zeph. iii. 14-20. Rev. v.

1 I WILL sing you a song of that beautiful land,
    The far-away home of the soul,
Where no storms ever beat on the glittering strand,
    While the years of eternity roll.

2 That unchangeable home is for you and for me,
    Where Jesus of Nazareth stands;
The King of all kingdoms forever is He,
    And he holdeth our crowns in His hands.

3 O how sweet it will be, in that beautiful land,
    So free from all sorrow and pain,
With songs on our lips and with harps in our hands,
    To meet one another again!
            Mrs. Ellen M. H. Gates. (1835-.)

841 "There is laid up for me a crown." **8. 7.**
Phil. i. 21-26. Job xiv. 1-14. Ps. xiii.

1 TIME, thou speedest on but slowly,
    Hours, how tardy is your pace,
Ere with Him, the high and holy,
    I hold converse face to face!

2 Here is naught but care and mourning;
    Comes a joy, it will not stay;
Fairly shines the sun at dawning,
    Night will soon o'ercloud the day.

3 Onward, then: not long I wander
    Ere my Saviour comes for me;
And with Him abiding yonder,
    All His glory I shall see.

4 O the music and the singing
    Of the host redeemed by love!
O the hallelujahs ringing
    Through the halls of light above!
            Rev. Johann Georg Albinus. (1624-1679.)
            Tr. by Miss Catherine Winkworth. (1829-.)

843 "This is not your rest." **8. 7.**
Deu. xii. 5-14. Heb. xiii. 14-21. Rev. vii. 9-17.

1 THIS is not my place of resting;
    Mine's a city yet to come;
Onward to it I am hasting,
    On to my eternal home.

2 In it all is light and glory;
    O'er it shines a nightless day;
Every trace of sin's sad story,
    All the curse, hath passed away.

3 There the Lamb, our Shepherd, leads us,
    By the streams of life along;
On the freshest pastures feeds us,
    Turns our sighing into song.

4 Soon we pass this desert dreary,
    Soon we bid farewell to pain;
Nevermore are sad or weary,
    Never, never sin again.
            Rev. Horatius Bonar. (1808-.)

842 "That mortality might be swallowed up of life." **11.**
Ps. lv. 1 John iii. 1-3. Deu. xi. 8-12. Rev. xxi.

1 O HAD I, my Saviour, the wings of a dove,
How soon would I soar to Thy presence above!
How soon would I flee where the weary have rest,
And hide all my cares in Thy sheltering breast!
I flutter, I struggle, I pant to get free;
I feel me a captive while banished from Thee;
A pilgrim and stranger, the desert I roam,
And look on to heaven, and long to be home.

2 Ah, there the wild tempest forever shall cease;
No billow shall ruffle that haven of peace;
Temptation and trouble alike shall depart,
All tears from the eye, and all sin from the heart.
Soon, soon may this Eden of promise be mine;
Rise, bright Sun of glory, no more to decline:
Thy light, yet unrisen, the wilderness cheers;
O what will it be when the fulness appears?
            Rev. Henry F. Lyte. (1793-1847.)

"I would fly away and be at rest."

844   "Jerusalem a rejoicing."   7, 6.
Ps. lxxxiv. Isa. xl. Rev. xv.

1 JERUSALEM, the golden!
   I languish for one gleam
Of all thy glory, folden
   In distance and in dream.
My thoughts, like palms in exile,
   Climb up to look and pray
For a glimpse of that dear country
   That lies so far away.

2 Jerusalem, the golden!
   When the sun sets in the west,
It seems the gate of glory,
   Thou city of the blest;
And midnight's starry torches,
   Through intermediate gloom,
Are waving with their welcome
   To thy eternal home.

3 Jerusalem, the golden!
   I toil on day by day;
Heart-sore each night with longing,
   I stretch my hands and pray
That 'midst Thy leaves of healing
   My soul may find her nest,
Where the wicked cease from troubling,
   The weary are at rest.

Gerald Massey. (1828–.)

846   "Thine eyes shall see the King in His beauty."   7, 6.
2 Tim. iv. 6–8. Isa. xxxv. Rev. vii. 9–17.

1 THE sands of time are sinking,
   The dawn of heaven breaks;
The summer morn I 've sighed for,
   The fair, sweet morn, awakes.
Dark, dark hath been the midnight,
   But dayspring is at hand,
And glory, glory dwelleth
   In Immanuel's land.

2 O Christ, He is the fountain,
   The deep, sweet well of love;
The streams on earth I 've tasted,
   More deep I 'll drink above.
There to an ocean fulness
   His mercy doth expand,
And glory, glory dwelleth
   In Immanuel's land.

3 I 've wrestled on toward heaven
   'Gainst storm and wind and tide;
Now, like a weary traveller,
   That leaneth on his guide,
Amid the shades of evening,
   While sinks life's lingering sand,
I hail the glory dawning
   From Immanuel's land.

Mrs. Anne R. Cousin. 1857.

845   "The time of my departure is at hand."   9, 4.
Gen. xlvii. 27–31. Deu. xxxiv. Acts vii. 55–60.

1 BEYOND the smiling and the weeping
   I shall be soon;
Beyond the waking and the sleeping,
Beyond the sowing and the reaping,
   I shall be soon.
Love, rest, and home! Sweet home!
   Lord, tarry not, but come.

2 Beyond the blooming and the fading
   I shall be soon;
Beyond the shining and the shading,
Beyond the hoping and the dreading,
   I shall be soon;
Love, rest, and home! Sweet home!
   Lord, tarry not, but come.

3 Beyond the parting and the meeting
   I shall be soon;
Beyond the farewell and the greeting,
Beyond the pulse's fever beating,
   I shall be soon;
Love, rest, and home! Sweet home!
   Lord, tarry not, but come.

Rev. Horatius Bonar. (1808–.)

847   "He shall go no more out."   S. M.
1 Thes. iv. 13–18. 1 Cor. xiii. Ps. lxxiii. 23–28.

1 FOREVER with the Lord!
   Amen, so let it be;
Life from the dead is in that word,
   'T is immortality.

2 Here in the body pent,
   Absent from Him I roam,
Yet nightly pitch my moving tent
   A day's march nearer home.

3 Forever with the Lord!
   Father, if 't is Thy will,
The promise of that faithful word
   E'en here to me fulfil.

4 So when my latest breath
   Shall rend the vail in twain,
By death I shall escape from death,
   And life eternal gain.

5 Knowing as I am known,
   How shall I love that word,
And oft repeat before the throne,
   Forever with the Lord!

James Montgomery. (1771–1854.)

"The church of the living God."

848 "Ye my flock, ...and I your God." **C. M.**
1 Tim. iii. 14-16. Isa. lx. Eze. xxxiv.

1 CHURCH of the ever-living God,
   The Father's gracious choice,
   Amid the voices of this earth
   How feeble is thy voice!

2 A "little flock!" 'T is well, 't is well;
   Such be her lot and name :
   Through ages past it has been so,
   And now 't is still the same.

3 But the chief Shepherd comes at length;
   Her feeble days are o'er :
   No more a handful in the earth,
   A "little flock" no more ;

4 No more a lily among thorns,
   Weary and faint and few ;
   But countless as the stars of heaven,
   Or as the early dew.
   Rev. Horatius Bonar. (1808-.)

849 "Happy art thou, O Israel!" **L. M.**
Ps. cxxii. Num. xxiv. Mat. xvi. 12-18.

1 HAPPY the church, thou sacred place,
   The seat of thy Creator's grace ;
   Thy holy courts are His abode,
   Thou earthly palace of our God !

2 Thy walls are strength, and at thy gates
   A guard of heavenly warriors waits ;
   Nor shall thy deep foundations move,
   Fixed on His counsels and His love.

3 Thy foes in vain designs engage,
   Against His throne in vain they rage,
   Like rising waves, with angry roar,
   That dash and die upon the shore.
   Rev. Isaac Watts. (1674-1748.)

850 "As Mount Zion, ... which abideth forever." **C. M.**
Dan. vii. 9-18. Ps. xlv. John xvii. 13-24.

1 O WHERE are kings and empires now,
   Of old that went and came ?
   But, Lord, Thy church is praying yet,
   A thousand years the same.

2 We mark her goodly battlements,
   And her foundations strong ;
   We hear within the solemn voice
   Of her unending song.

3 For not like kingdoms of the world,
   Thy holy church, O God !
   Though earthquake shocks are threatening her,
   And tempests are abroad ;

4 Unshaken as eternal hills,
   Immovable she stands :
   A mountain that shall fill the earth,
   A house not made by hands.
   Bp. Arthur C. Coxe. (1818-.)

851 "The Lord hath chosen Zion." **8. 7.**
Ps. cxxxii. Jer. xxxiii. 9-16. Heb. xii. 22-28.

1 ZION is Jehovah's dwelling,
   There the King of kings appears ;
   Hers is glory far excelling
   All the worldling sees or hears.
   Zion's walls are everlasting,
   Formed through endless years to shine ;
   Strength and beauty, never wasting,
   Show their origin divine.

2 Zion claims peculiar honor,
   High distinction marks her lot ;
   Light eternal shines upon her,
   Hers a sun that faileth not.
   Zion's city hath foundations,
   God Himself has raised her walls ;
   She survives the wreck of nations ;
   Zion stands, whatever falls.

3 Brethren, let the prospect cheer us,
   Fair the lot that 's cast for us ;
   When we call, our God will hear us :
   Happy who are favored thus !
   Let the timid fear no longer ;
   What though earth and hell oppose ?
   He who pleads our cause is stronger,
   Stronger far, than all our foes.
   Rev. Thomas Kelly. (1769-1855.)

852 "O city of God!" **8. 7.**
Ps. lxxxvii. Num. ix. 15-23. Heb. xii. 22-24.

1 GLORIOUS things of thee are spoken,
   Zion, city of our God !
   He whose word cannot be broken
   Formed thee for His own abode.
   On the Rock of Ages founded,
   What can shake thy sure repose ?
   With salvation's walls surrounded,
   Thou mayst smile at all thy foes.

2 See, the streams of living waters,
   Springing from eternal love,
   Well supply thy sons and daughters,
   And all fear of want remove.
   Who can faint, while such a river
   Ever flows their thirst t' assuage ?
   Grace, which, like the Lord, the Giver,
   Never fails from age to age.

3 Round each habitation hovering,
   See the cloud and fire appear,
   For a glory and a covering,
   Showing that the Lord is near.
   Thus deriving from their banner
   Light by night, and shade by day,
   Safe they feed upon the manna
   Which He gives them when they pray.
   Rev. John Newton. (1725-1807.)

164

"The church of the living God."

853 "Thus were the journeyings . . . of Israel." S. M.
Ps. lxxx. Mal. iii. 7 to iv. 6. 2 Thes. ii.

1 FAR down the ages now,
   Much of her journey done,
The pilgrim church pursues her way,
   Until her crown be won.
'T is the same story still
   Of sin and weariness,
Of grace and love yet flowing down
   To pardon and to bless.

2 No wider is the gate,
   No broader is the way,
No smoother is the ancient path,
   That leads to light and day;
No sweeter is the cup,
   Nor less our lot of ill :
'T was tribulation ages since,
   'T is tribulation still.

3 Thus onward still we press
   Through evil and through good,
Through pain and poverty and want,
   Through peril and through blood.
Still faithful to our God,
   And to our Captain true,
We follow where He leads the way,
   The kingdom in our view.
                        Rev. Horatius Bonar. (1808–.)

854 "Fair as the moon, clear as the sun." L. M.
Can. vi. Zech. ix. 9-17. Rev. xix. 1-8.

1 SAY, who is she that looks abroad,
   Like the sweet blushing dawn,
When with her living lights she paints
   The dew-drops of the lawn ?

2 Fair as the moon, when in the skies
   Serene her throne she guides,
And o'er the twinkling stars supreme
   In full-orbed glory rides;

3 Clear as the sun, when from the east
   Without a cloud he springs,
And scatters boundless light and heat
   From his resplendent wings ;

4 Tremendous as an host that moves
   Majestically slow,
With banners wide displayed, all armed,
   All ardent for the foe !

5 This is the church, by Heaven arrayed
   With strength and grace divine ;
Thus shall she strike her foes with dread,
   And thus her glories shine.
                        Rev. Thomas Gibbons. (1720–1785.)

855 "So the Lord is round about His people." 8. 7. 4.
Ps. cxxv. Isa. liv. Rev. ii. 1-11.

1 ZION stands by hills surrounded,
   Zion kept by power divine ;
All her foes shall be confounded,
   Though the world in arms combine.
      Happy Zion,
   What a favored lot is thine !

2 Every human tie may perish,
   Friend to friend unfaithful prove ;
Mothers cease their own to cherish,
   Heaven and earth at last remove ;
      But no changes
   Can attend Jehovah's love.

3 In the furnace God may prove thee,
   Thence to bring thee forth more bright,
But can never cease to love thee ;
   Thou art precious in His sight.
      God is with thee,
   God, thine everlasting light.
                        Rev. Thomas Kelly. (1769–1855.)

856 "The Mount Zion which He loved." L. M.
Ps. lxxxvii. Isa. lx. Rev. xxi.

1 GOD, in His earthly temple, lays
Foundations for His heavenly praise ;
He likes the tents of Jacob well,
But still in Zion loves to dwell.

2 His mercy visits every house
That pay their night and morning vows,
But makes a more delightful stay
Where churches meet to praise and pray.

3 What glories were described of old !
What wonders are of Zion told!
Angels and men shall join to sing
The hill where living waters spring.
                        Rev. Isaac Watts. (1674–1748.)

857 "God is in the midst of her." C. M.
Ps. xlviii. Isa. xi. Eph. ii. 11-22.

1 How honorable is the place
   Where we adoring stand :
Zion, the glory of the earth,
   And beauty of the land !

2 Bulwarks of mighty grace defend
   The city where we dwell ;
The walls, of strong salvation made,
   Defy th' assaults of hell.

3 Here shall you taste unmingled joys,
   And live in perfect peace ;
You that have known Jehovah's name,
   And ventured on His grace.

4 Trust in the Lord, forever trust,
   And banish all your fears ;
Strength in the Lord Jehovah dwells,
   Eternal as His years.
                        Rev. Isaac Watts.

"We have fellowship one with another."

858 "That we should be called the sons of God." **L. M.**
Ps. cxix. 1-8. Rom. iv. 1-7. Rev. xix. 1-9.

1 BLESSÈD are the sons of God :
They are bought with Christ's own blood ;
They are ransomed from the grave ;
Life eternal they shall have :

2 They are justified by grace ;
They enjoy a solid peace ;
All their sins are washed away ;
They shall stand in God's great day :

3 They produce the fruits of grace
In the works of righteousness ;
They are harmless, meek, and mild,
Holy, humble, undefiled :

4 They are lights upon the earth,
Children of a heavenly birth,
One with God, with Jesus one ;
Glory is in them begun.
Rev. Joseph Humphreys. (1720-.)

859 "The peace of Thy children." **L. M.**
Mat. v. 3-6. Isa. lxi. Prov. xi. 1-9.

1 BLEST are the humble souls, that see
Their emptiness and poverty ;
Treasures of grace to them are given,
And crowns of joy laid up in heaven.

2 Blest are the men of broken heart,
Who mourn for sin with inward smart ;
The blood of Christ divinely flows,
A healing balm for all their woes.

3 Blest are the souls that thirst for grace,
Hunger and long for righteousness ;
They shall be well supplied, and fed
With living streams and living bread.
Rev. Isaac Watts. (1674-1748.)

860 "That which is born of the Spirit is spirit." **C. M.**
Heb. x. 1-10. John i. 13, 14. Ps. xl. 6-8.

1 NOT all the outward forms on earth,
Nor rites that God has given,
Nor will of man, nor blood, nor birth,
Can raise a soul to heaven.

2 The sovereign will of God alone
Creates us heirs of grace ;
Born in the image of His Son,
A new, peculiar race.

3 The Spirit, like some heavenly wind,
Blows on the sons of flesh ;
New models all the carnal mind,
And forms the man afresh.

4 Our quickened souls awake, and rise
From the long sleep of death ;
On heavenly things we fix our eyes,
And praise employs our breath.
Rev. Isaac Watts.

861 "As many as are led by the Spirit of God." **C. M.**
Ps. i. 1-3. Jer. xv. 15-21. James i.

1 BLEST is the man who shuns the place
Where sinners love to meet ;
Who fears to tread their wicked ways,
And hates the scoffer's seat ;

2 But in the statutes of the Lord
Has placed his chief delight :
By day he reads or hears the word,
And meditates by night.

3 He like a plant of generous kind,
By living waters set,
Safe from the storms and blasting wind,
Enjoys a peaceful state.

4 Green as the leaf, and ever fair,
Shall his profession shine,
While fruits of holiness appear,
Like clusters on the vine.
Rev. Isaac Watts.

862 "Children of God." **L. M.**
Mat. v. 7-9. Ps. xli. Luke vi. 20-35.

1 BLEST are the men whose hearts do move
And melt with sympathy and love ;
From Christ, the Lord, shall they obtain
Like sympathy and love again.

2 Blest are the pure, whose hearts are clean
From the defiling power of sin ;
With endless pleasure, they shall see
A God of spotless purity.

3 Blest are the men of peaceful life,
Who quench the coals of growing strife ;
They shall be called the heirs of bliss,
The sons of God, the God of peace.
Rev. Isaac Watts.

863 "If a son, then an heir of God." **7.**
Ps. xv. Mat. vii. 24-27. Rev. xiv. 1-5.

1 WHO, O Lord, when life is o'er,
Shall to heaven's blest mansions soar?
Who, an ever-welcome guest,
In Thy holy place shall rest ?

2 He whose heart Thy love has warmed ;
He, whose will to Thine conformed,
Bids his life unsullied run ;
He whose words and thoughts are one ;

3 He who shuns the sinner's road,
Loving those who love their God ;
Who, with hope and faith unfeigned,
Treads the path by Thee ordained ;

4 He who trusts in Christ alone,
Not in aught himself hath done ;
He, great God, shall be Thy care,
And Thy choicest blessings share.
Rev. James Merrick. (1720-1769.)

"We have fellowship one with another."

864 "That they all may be one." 7, 6.
1 Cor. iii. 1–11. Eph. iv. 1–16. Isa. lvii. 15–19.

1 THE church's one Foundation
   Is Jesus Christ, her Lord;
 She is His new creation
   By water and the word.
 From heaven He came and sought her
   To be His holy Bride;
 With His own blood He bought her,
   And for her life He died.

2 Elect from every nation,
   Yet one o'er all the earth;
 Her charter of salvation
   One Lord, one faith, one birth;
 One holy name she blesses,
   Partakes one holy food,
 And to one hope she presses,
   With every grace endued.

3 Yet she on earth hath union
   With God the Three in One,
 And mystic sweet communion
   With those whose rest is won.
 O happy ones, and holy!
   Lord, give us grace that we,
 Like them, the meek and lowly,
   On high may dwell with Thee.
         Rev. Samuel J. Stone. (1839–.)

865 "All one in Christ Jesus." C. M.
Col. i. Mat. iii. 10–12. Mal. iii. 1–12.

1 BLEST be the dear uniting love,
   That will not let us part:
 Our bodies may far off remove,
   We still are one in heart.

2 Joined in one spirit to our Head,
   Where He appoints we go;
 And still in Jesus' footsteps tread,
   And show His praise below.

3 O may we ever walk in Him,
   And nothing know beside;
 Nothing desire, nothing esteem,
   But Jesus crucified.

4 Closer and closer let us cleave
   To His beloved embrace;
 Expect His fulness to receive,
   And grace to answer grace.

5 Partakers of the Saviour's grace,
   The same in mind and heart,
 Nor joy, nor grief, nor time, nor place,
   Nor life, nor death, can part.
         Rev. Charles Wesley. (1708–1788.)

866 "That they may be made perfect in one." C. M.
Col. ii. 1–5. 2 Cor. iii. 1 Sam. xviii. 1–5.

1 OUR souls, by love together knit,
   Cemented, mixed in one,
 One hope, one heart, one mind, one voice,
   'T is heaven on earth begun.

2 Our hearts have often burned within,
   And glowed with sacred fire,
 While Jesus spoke, and fed and blessed,
   And filled th' enlarged desire.

3 And when Thou mak'st Thy jewels up,
   And sett'st Thy starry crown;
 When all Thy sparkling gems shall shine,
   Proclaimed by Thee Thine own;

4 May we, a little band of love,
   We sinners, saved by grace,
 From glory unto glory changed,
   Behold Thee face to face.
         Rev. Henry Miller. 1800.

867 "In the unity of the faith." C. M.
Ps. cxxxiii. 1 John iv. 7–21. 1 Cor. xiii.

1 Lo, what an entertaining sight
   Are brethren that agree;
 Brethren whose cheerful hearts unite
   In bands of piety!

2 When streams of love from Christ, the spring,
   Descend to every soul,
 And heavenly peace, with balmy wing,
   Shades and bedews the whole.

3 'T is pleasant as the morning dews
   That fall on Zion's hill,
 Where God His mildest glory shows,
   And makes His grace distil.
         Rev. Isaac Watts. (1674–1748.)

868 "And all that believed were together." L. M.
Acts x. 24–44. Rom. xiv. Gen. xviii. 1–8.

1 COME in, thou blessèd of the Lord,
   Enter in Jesus' precious name!
 We welcome thee with one accord,
   And trust the Saviour does the same.

2 Those joys which earth cannot afford
   We 'll seek in fellowship to prove;
 Joined in one spirit to our Lord,
   Together bound by mutual love.

3 And while we pass this vale of tears,
   We 'll make our joys and sorrows known;
 We 'll share each other's hopes and fears,
   And count a brother's case our own.

4 Once more our welcome we repeat;
   Receive assurance of our love;
 O may we all together meet
   Around the throne of God above.
         Rev. Thomas Kelly. (1769–1855.)

"We have fellowship one with another."

869 "That they also may be one in us." Col. ii. 1-10. Heb. ii. 14-17. Isa. lxiii. 7-19. **C. M.**

1 LORD Jesus, are we one with Thee?
 O height, O depth of love!
 With Thee we died upon the tree,
 In Thee we live above.

2 Such was Thy grace that, for our sake,
 Thou didst from heaven come down;
 Thou didst of flesh and blood partake,
 In all our sorrows one.

3 Ascended now, in glory bright,
 Still one with us Thou art;
 Nor life, nor death, nor depth, nor height,
 Thy saints and Thee can part.

4 Soon, soon shall come that glorious day
 When, seated on Thy throne,
 Thou shalt to wondering worlds display
 That Thou with us art one.
James G. Deck. (1808-.)

870 "To dwell together in unity." Ps. cxxxiii. Acts ii. 41-47. 1 Thes. iii. **S. M.**

1 BLEST are the sons of peace,
 Whose hearts and hopes are one;
 Whose kind designs to serve and please
 Through all their actions run.

2 Blest is the pious house,
 Where zeal and friendship meet;
 Their songs of praise, their mingled vows,
 Make their communion sweet.

3 Thus on the heavenly hills
 The saints are blest above;
 Where joy, like morning dew, distils,
 And all the air is love.
Rev. Isaac Watts. (1674-1748.)

871 "Daily, with one accord." 1 Sam. xx. 1-17. Rom. xii. 1 John iii. 10-24. **L. M.**

1 O LORD, how joyful 't is to see
 The brethren join in love to Thee!
 On Thee alone their heart relies;
 Their only strength Thy grace supplies.

2 How sweet, within Thy holy place,
 With one accord to sing Thy grace;
 Besieging Thine attentive ear
 With all the force of fervent prayer!

3 O may we love the house of God,
 Of peace and joy the blest abode;
 O may no angry strife destroy
 That sacred peace, that holy joy!

4 Lord, shower upon us, from above,
 The sacred gift of mutual love;
 Each other's wants may we supply,
 And reign together in the sky.
Bantolius Victorinus. (1630-1697.)
Tr. by John Chandler. (1806-.)

872 "By one Spirit . . . baptized into one body." Eph iv. 1-5. John xvii. Gen. xiii. 5-18. **H. M.**

1 ONE sole baptismal sign,
 One Lord below, above;
 Zion, one faith is thine,
 One only watchword, love;
 From different temples though it rise,
 One song ascendeth to the skies.

2 Our Sacrifice is one;
 One Priest before the throne,
 The slain, the risen Son,
 Redeemer, Lord alone:
 Thou who didst raise Him from the dead,
 Unite Thy people in their Head.

3 O may that holy prayer,
 His tenderest and His last,
 His constant, latest care
 Ere to His throne He passed,
 No longer unfulfilled remain,
 The world's offence, His people's stain!

4 Head of Thy church beneath,
 The catholic, the true,
 On all her members breathe,
 Her broken frame renew:
 Then shall Thy perfect will be done,
 When Christians love and live as one.
George Robinson. 1842.

873 "The fellowship of . . . Jesus Christ." 1 Pet. ii. 21-25. John xv. 12-27. Isa. liii. **C. M.**

1 WHAT grace, O Lord, and beauty shone
 Around Thy steps below;
 What patient love was seen in all
 Thy life and death of woe!

2 Forever on Thy burdened heart
 A weight of sorrow hung;
 Yet no ungentle, murmuring word
 Escaped Thy silent tongue.

3 Thy foes might hate, despise, revile,
 Thy friends unfaithful prove;
 Unwearied in forgiveness still,
 Thy heart could only love.

4 O give us hearts to love like Thee;
 Like Thee, O Lord, to grieve
 Far more for others' sins than all
 The wrongs that we receive.

5 One with Thyself, may every eye
 In us, Thy brethren, see
 That gentleness and grace that springs
 From union, Lord, with Thee.
Sir Edward Denny. (1796-.)

"We have fellowship one with another."

874 C. M.
"The church of the first-born."
Heb. xii. 18-24. Ex xix. 16-19. Rev. xix. 1-9.

1 Not to the terrors of the Lord,
  The tempest, fire, and smoke;
  Not to the thunder of that word
  Which God on Sinai spoke ;
  But we are come to Sion's hill,
  The city of our God,
  Where milder words declare His will,
  And spread His love abroad.

2 Behold th' innumerable host
  Of angels clothed in light !
  Behold the spirits of the just,
  Whose faith is turned to sight !
  Behold the blest assembly there,
  Whose names are writ in heaven ;
  And God, the Judge of all, declares
  Their vilest sins forgiven.

3 The saints on earth, and all the dead,
  But one communion make ;
  All join in Christ their living Head,
  And of His grace partake.
  In such society as this,
  My weary soul would rest ;
  The man that dwells where Jesus is,
  Must be forever blest.

  Rev. Isaac Watts. (1674-1748.)

875 S. M.
"Knit together in love."
Gal. vi. 1-5. Acts xx. 17-38. 1 Sam. xviii. 1-4.

1 Blest be the tie that binds
  Our hearts in Christian love;
  The fellowship of kindred minds
  Is like to that above.

2 Before our Father's throne
  We pour our ardent prayers ;
  Our fears, our hopes, our aims are one,
  Our comforts and our cares.

3 We share our mutual woes ;
  Our mutual burdens bear ;
  And often for each other flows
  The sympathizing tear.

4 When we asunder part,
  It gives us inward pain ;
  But we shall still be joined in heart,
  And hope to meet again.

5 From sorrow, toil, and pain,
  And sin we shall be free ;
  And perfect love and friendship reign
  Through all eternity.

  Rev. John Fawcett. (1739-1817.)

876 C. M.
"The whole family in heaven and earth."
Eph. iii. 14-21. John xvii. 20-26. Isa. xxv. 1-9.

1 The glorious universe around,
  The heavens with all their train,
  Sun, moon, and stars, are firmly bound
  In one mysterious chain.

2 In one fraternal bond of love,
  One fellowship of mind,
  The saints below and saints above
  Their bliss and glory find.

3 Here, in their house of pilgrimage,
  Thy statutes are their song ;
  There, through one bright, eternal age,
  Thy praises they prolong.

4 Lord, may our union form a part
  Of that thrice happy whole ;
  Derive its pulse from Thee, the heart,
  Its life from Thee, the soul.

  James Montgomery. (1771-1854.)

877 C. M.
"That He might gather together all in one."
1 Cor. xii. 1-13. Rev. vii. 9-12. Isa. xxvi. 1-12.

1 Happy the souls to Jesus joined,
  And saved by grace alone ;
  Walking in all Thy ways, we find
  Our heaven on earth begun.

2 The church triumphant in Thy love,
  Their mighty joys we know ;
  They sing the Lamb in hymns above,
  And we in hymns below.

3 Thee, in Thy glorious realm, they praise
  And bow before Thy throne ;
  We, in the kingdom of Thy grace :
  The kingdoms are but one.

  Rev. Charles Wesley. (1708-1788.)

878 L. M.
"One body and one spirit."
1 John iv. 7-21. John xv. 8-17. Gen. xliv. 18-34.

1 Still one in life and one in death,
  One in our hope of rest above,
  One in our joy, our trust, our faith,
  One in each other's faithful love ;

2 Yet must we part, and parting weep ;
  What else has earth for us in store ?
  Our farewell pangs, how sharp and deep,
  Our farewell words, how sad and sore !

3 Yet shall we meet again in peace,
  To sing the song of festal joy,
  Where none shall bid our gladness cease,
  And none our fellowship destroy :

4 Where none shall beckon us away,
  Nor bid our festival be done ;
  Our meeting-time the eternal day,
  Our meeting-place the eternal throne.

  Rev. Horatius Bonar. (1808-.)

"We have fellowship one with another."

879 "Of one heart and one soul." **L. M.**
1 Cor. xii. 1-13. Rom. xii. 1 Sam. xx. 1-17.

1 How blest the sacred tie that binds,
   In union sweet, according minds!
   How swift the heavenly course they run,
   Whose hearts, whose faith, whose hopes,
      are one!

2 To each the soul of each how dear!
   What jealous love, what holy fear!
   How doth the generous flame within
   Refine from earth and cleanse from sin!

3 Their streaming eyes together flow
   For human guilt and mortal woe;
   Their ardent prayers together rise,
   Like mingling flames in sacrifice.

4 Nor shall the glowing flame expire,
   When nature droops her sickening fire;
   Then shall they meet in realms above,
   A heaven of joy, a heaven of love.
                        Mrs. Anna L. Barbauld. (1743-1825.)

880 "The bond of perfectness." **S. M.**
Gal. iii. 26-29. 1 Cor. iii. Gen. xiii. 8-18.

1 LET party names no more
   The Christian world o'erspread;
   Gentile and Jew, and bond and free,
   Are one in Christ, their Head.

2 Among the saints on earth
   Let mutual love be found;
   Heirs of the same inheritance,
   With mutual blessings crowned.

3 Thus will the church below
   Resemble that above;
   Where streams of endless pleasure flow,
   And every heart is love.
                        Rev. Benjamin Beddome. (1717-1795.)

881 "Bear ye one another's burdens." **C. M.**
Ps. cxxxix. Rom. xv. 1-14. 1 John iii. 11-24.

1 TRY us, O God, and search the ground
   Of every sinful heart;
   Whate'er of sin in us is found,
   O bid it all depart.

2 If to the right or left we stray,
   Leave us not comfortless;
   But guide our feet into the way
   Of everlasting peace.

3 Help us to help each other, Lord,
   Each other's cross to bear;
   Let each his friendly aid afford,
   And feel his brother's care.

4 Help us to build each other up;
   Our little stock improve;
   Increase our faith, confirm our hope,
   And perfect us in love.
                        Rev. Charles Wesley. (1708-1788.)

882 "Be ye all of one mind;... love as brethren." **L. M.**
Acts ii. 41-47. John xx. 19-29. Ps. cxxii.

1 KINDRED in Christ, for His dear sake,
   A hearty welcome here receive!
   May we together now partake
   The joys which only He can give.
   To you and us by grace 't is given
   To know the Saviour's precious name;
   And shortly we shall meet in heaven,
   Our hope, our way, our end, the same.

2 May He, by whose kind care we meet,
   Send His good Spirit from above;
   Make our communications sweet,
   And cause our hearts to burn with love.
   Forgotten be each worldly theme,
   When Christians see each other thus;
   We only wish to speak of Him
   Who lived, and died, and reigns for us.

3 We 'll talk of all He did and said,
   And suffered for us here below;
   The path He marked for us to tread,
   And what He 's doing for us now.
   Thus, as the moments pass away,
   We 'll love, and wonder, and adore;
   And hasten on the glorious day,
   When we shall meet to part no more.
                        Rev. John Newton. (1725-1807.)

883 "And so fulfil the law of Christ." **C. M.**
Ps. cxxxiii. Eph. iv. 1-16. 1 John iv. 11-19.

1 HOW sweet, how heavenly is the sight,
   When those that love the Lord
   In one another's peace delight,
   And so fulfil His word!

2 When each can feel his brother's sigh,
   And with him bear a part;
   When sorrow flows from eye to eye,
   And joy from heart to heart;

3 When, free from envy, scorn, and pride,
   Our wishes all above,
   Each can his brother's failings hide,
   And show a brother's love;

4 When love, in one delightful stream,
   Through every bosom flows;
   When union sweet and dear esteem
   In every action glows.

5 Love is the golden chain that binds
   The happy souls above;
   And he 's an heir of heaven that finds
   His bosom glow with love.
                        Rev. Joseph Swain. (1761-1796.)

"The oracles of God."

884 "And His name is called the Word of God." 7, 6,
John i. 1-18. Rev. xix. 11-16. Deu. x. 12-22.

1 O WORD of God Incarnate,
    O Wisdom from on high,
  O Truth unchanged, unchanging,
    O Light of our dark sky,
  We praise Thee for the radiance
    That from the hallowed page,
  A lantern to our footsteps,
    Shines on from age to age.

2 The church from Thee, her Master,
    Received the gift divine;
  And still that light she lifteth
    O'er all the earth to shine.
  It is the golden casket
    Where gems of truth are stored;
  It is the heaven-drawn picture
    Of Thee, the living Word.

3 It floateth like a banner
    Before God's host unfurled;
  It shineth like a beacon
    Above the darkling world;
  It is the chart and compass
    That o'er life's surging sea,
  'Mid mists, and rocks, and quicksands,
    Still guide, O Christ, to Thee.
            Rev. William W. How. (1823-.)

885 "The words I speak are spirit and life." C. M.
Ps. cxix. 105. Job. xxiii. 1 John ii. 1-17.

1 LAMP of our feet, whereby we trace
    Our path, when wont to stray;
  Stream from the fount of heavenly grace,
    Brook by the traveller's way;

2 Bread of our souls, whereon we feed,
    True manna from on high;
  Our guide and chart, wherein we read
    Of realms beyond the sky;

3 Pillar of fire through watches dark,
    And radiant cloud by day;
  When waves would whelm our tossing bark
    Our anchor and our stay;

4 Word of the everlasting God,
    Will of His glorious Son;
  Without thee how could earth be trod,
    Or heaven itself be won?

5 Lord, grant us all aright to learn
    The wisdom it imparts;
  And to its heavenly teaching turn
    With simple, child-like hearts.
            Bernard Barton. (1784-1849.)

886 "He may run that readeth." C. M.
Ps. xix. Deu. iv. 1-13. 2 Tim. iii. 14-17.

1 THERE is a book who runs may read,
    Which heavenly truth imparts,
  And all the lore its scholars need,
    Pure eyes and Christian hearts.

2 The works of God, above, below,
    Within us and around,
  Are pages in that book to show
    How God Himself is found.

3 The glorious sky, embracing all,
    Is like the Maker's love,
  Wherewith encompassed, great and small,
    In peace and order move.

4 The Saviour lends the light and heat
    That crowns His holy hill;
  The saints, like stars, around His seat
    Perform their courses still.
            Rev. John Keble. (1792-1866.)

887 "The commandment is a lamp." C. M.
Ps. cxix. 129-136. John xvii. Luke iv. 16-22.

1 HAIL, sacred truth, whose piercing rays
    Dispel the shades of night:
  Diffusing o'er the mental world
    The healing beams of light.

2 Jesus, Thy word, with friendly aid,
    Restores our wandering feet;
  Converts the sorrows of the mind
    To joys divinely sweet.

3 O send Thy light and truth abroad,
    In all their radiant blaze;
  And bid th' admiring world adore
    The glories of Thy grace.
            John Buttress. 1820.

888 "The law is a light." C. M.
2 Pet. i. 16-21. 1 Cor. i. Deu. xxviii. 1-10.

1 BRIGHT was the guiding star that led,
    With mild, benignant ray,
  The Gentiles to the lowly shed
    Where the Redeemer lay.

2 But, lo, a brighter, clearer light
    Now points to His abode;
  It shines through sin and sorrow's night,
    To guide us to our God.

3 O haste to follow where it leads;
    The gracious call obey;
  Be rugged wilds, or flowery meads,
    The Christian's destined way.

4 O gladly tread the narrow path,
    While light and grace are given;
  Who meekly follow Christ on earth
    Shall reign with Him in heaven.
            Miss Harriet Auber. (17--1862.)

"The oracles of God."

889 "Thy Word is a lamp." **C. M.**
Ps. cxix. 97-104. John v. 39-47. 2 Tim. iii.

1 How precious is the book divine,
   By inspiration given!
   Bright as a lamp its doctrines shine,
   To guide our souls to heaven.

2 Its light, descending from above,
   Our gloomy world to cheer,
   Displays a Saviour's boundless love,
   And brings His glories near.

3 It shows to man his wandering ways,
   And where his feet have trod,
   And brings to view the matchless grace
   Of a forgiving God.

4 This lamp, through all the tedious night
   Of life, shall guide our way,
   Till we behold the clearer light
   Of an eternal day.
   Rev. John Fawcett. (1739-1817.)

890 "The light of the glorious gospel of Christ." **L. M.**
Ps. cxix. 89-96. Deu. vi. Rom. viii. 3-11.

1 THE law commands and makes us know
   What duties to our God we owe;
   But 't is the gospel must reveal
   Where lies our strength to do His will.

2 The law discovers guilt and sin,
   And shows how vile our hearts have been;
   Only the gospel can express
   Forgiving love and cleansing grace.

3 My soul, no more attempt to draw
   Thy life and comfort from the law;
   Fly to the hope the gospel gives:
   The man that trusts the promise lives.
   Rev. Isaac Watts. (1674-1748.)

891 "Doth not wisdom cry?" **C. M.**
Isa. lv. Prov. ix. 1-11. Rev. iii. 14-22.

1 LET every mortal ear attend,
   And every heart rejoice;
   The trumpet of the gospel sounds
   With an inviting voice.

2 Eternal wisdom has prepared
   A soul-reviving feast,
   And bids your longing appetites
   The rich provision taste.

3 Ho, ye that pant for living streams,
   And pine away and die!
   Here you may quench your raging thirst
   With springs that never dry.

4 Rivers of love and mercy here
   In a rich ocean join;
   Salvation in abundance flows,
   Like floods of milk and wine.
   Rev. Isaac Watts.

892 "That we ... might have hope." **L. M.**
Isa. lxi. 1-3. 1 Thes. i. 1 Cor. i. 17-31.

1 GOD, in the gospel of His Son,
   Makes His eternal counsels known:
   Where love in all its glory shines.
   And truth is drawn in fairest lines.

2 The prisoner here may break his chains,
   The weary rest from all his pains;
   The captive feel his bondage cease,
   The mourner find the way of peace.

3 Here faith reveals to mortal eyes
   A brighter world beyond the skies;
   Here shines the light which guides our way
   From earth to realms of endless day.

4 O grant us grace, almighty Lord,
   To read and mark Thy holy word;
   Its truth with meekness to receive,
   And by its holy precepts live.
   Rev. Benjamin Beddome. (1717-1795.)
Alt. by Rev. Thomas Cotterill. (1779-1844.)

893 "Men of God spake, ... by the Holy Ghost." **L. M.**
2 Pet. i. 16-21. Eze. iii. Deu. iv. 1-14.

1 'T WAS by an order from the Lord
   The ancient prophets spoke His word:
   His spirit did their tongues inspire,
   And warmed their hearts with heavenly fire.

2 The works and wonders which they wrought
   Confirmed the messages they brought;
   The prophet's pen succeeds his breath,
   To save the holy words from death.

3 Let the false raptures of the mind
   Be lost, and vanish in the wind;
   Here I can fix my hope secure;
   This is Thy word, and must endure.
   Rev. Isaac Watts.

894 "Clean, through the word." **C. M.**
Ps. cxix. 9-16. Prov. vi. 20-23. John xii. 44-50.

1 How shall the young secure their hearts,
   And guard their lives from sin?
   Thy word the choicest rules imparts,
   To keep the conscience clean.

2 When once it enters to the mind,
   It spreads such light abroad,
   The meanest souls instruction find,
   And raise their thoughts to God.

3 'T is like the sun, a heavenly light,
   That guides us all the day;
   And, through the dangers of the night,
   A lamp to lead our way.

4 Thy word is everlasting truth;
   How pure is every page!
   That holy book shall guide our youth
   And well support our age.
   Rev. Isaac Watts.

"The oracles of God."

895 "Thy Word is . . . a light unto my path." **S. M.**
Ps. cxix. 105-112. Mat. vii. 24-29. Deu. xi. 8-21.

1 O LORD, Thy perfect word
  Directs our steps aright;
  Nor can all other books afford
  Such profit or delight.

2 Celestial beams it sheds,
  To cheer this vale below;
  To distant lands its glory spreads,
  And streams of mercy flow.

3 True wisdom it imparts;
  Commands our hope and fear;
  O may we hide it in our hearts,
  And feel its influence there.

  Rev. Benjamin Beddome. (1717-1795.)

896 "The statutes of the Lord are right." **S. M.**
Gen. i. 1-19. Job xxvi. Gal. iii. 24-29.

1 BEHOLD, the lofty sky
  Declares its Maker, God;
  And all His starry worlds on high
  Proclaim His power abroad.

2 The darkness and the light
  Still keep their course the same;
  While night to day, and day to night,
  Divinely teach His name.

3 Ye Christian lands, rejoice!
  Here He reveals His word;
  We are not left to nature's voice
  To bid us know the Lord.

4 His laws are just and pure,
  His truth without deceit;
  His promises forever sure,
  And His rewards are great.

  Rev. Isaac Watts. (1674-1748.)

897 "Thou hast magnified Thy word." **L. M.**
Ps. xix. Isa. xliv. 21-28. Luke i. 68-79.

1 THE heavens declare Thy glory, Lord;
  In every star Thy wisdom shines;
  But when our eyes behold Thy word,
  We read Thy name in fairer lines.

2 Sun, moon, and stars convey Thy praise
  Round the whole earth, and never stand:
  So when Thy truth began its race,
  It touched and glanced on every land.

3 Nor shall Thy spreading gospel rest,
  Till through the world Thy truth has run;
  Till Christ has all the nations blessed
  That see the light, or feel the sun.

4 Great Sun of Righteousness, arise;
  Bless the dark world with heavenly light;
  Thy gospel makes the simple wise,
  Thy laws are pure, Thy judgments right.

  Rev. Isaac Watts.

898 "Christ shall give thee light." **S. M.**
Ps. lxxiv. 12-17. Eph. ii. 1 Pet. i. 17-25.

1 BEHOLD, the morning sun
  Begins his glorious way;
  His beams through all the nations run,
  And life and light convey.

2 But where the gospel comes,
  It spreads diviner light;
  It calls dead sinners from their tombs,
  And gives the blind their sight.

3 How perfect is Thy word,
  And all Thy judgments just!
  Forever sure Thy promise, Lord,
  And men securely trust.

  Rev. Isaac Watts.

899 "My words shall not pass away." **L. M.**
Ps. viii. 2 Pet. iii. 5-14. Isa. xl. 1-8.

1 THE starry firmament on high,
  And all the glories of the sky,
  Yet shine not to Thy praise, O Lord,
  So brightly as Thy written word.

2 The hopes that holy word supplies,
  Its truths divine and precepts wise,
  In each a heavenly beam I see,
  And every beam conducts to Thee.

3 Almighty Lord, the sun shall fail,
  The moon forget her nightly tale,
  And deepest silence hush on high
  The radiant chorus of the sky;

4 But fixed for everlasting years,
  Unmoved, amid the wreck of spheres,
  Thy word shall shine in cloudless day,
  When heaven and earth have passed away.

  Sir Robert Grant. (1785-1838.)

900 "The entrance of Thy words giveth light." **C. M.**
1 Cor. ii. 7-16. Ps. cxix. 130. Luke iv. 16-22.

1 THE Spirit breathes upon the word,
  And brings the truth to sight;
  Precepts and promises afford
  A sanctifying light.

2 A glory gilds the sacred page,
  Majestic, like the sun;
  It gives a light to every age;
  It gives, but borrows none.

3 The hand that gave it still supplies
  The gracious light and heat;
  His truths upon the nations rise;
  They rise, but never set.

4 Let everlasting thanks be Thine
  For such a bright display,
  As makes a world of darkness shine
  With beams of heavenly day.

  William Cowper. (1731-1800.)

"The church in thy house."   "Offerings every morning."

901 "Mercies ... new every morning." L. M.
Ex. xiv.   Isa. xxxiii. 2-6.   Mat. v. 14-24.

1 LORD God of morning and of night,
   We thank Thee for Thy gift of light;
   As in the dawn the shadows fly
   We seem to find Thee now more nigh.

2 Fresh hopes have wakened in the heart
   Fresh force to do our daily part;
   Thy thousand sleeps our strength restore,
   A thousand-fold to serve Thee more.

3 Yet whilst Thy will we would pursue,
   Oft what we would we cannot do;
   The sun may stand in zenith skies,
   But on the soul thick midnight lies.

4 O Lord of lights, 't is Thou alone
   Canst make our darkened hearts Thine own;
   Though this new day with joy we see,
   O dawn of God, we cry for Thee.
   Francis T. Palgrave.   1824-.)

902 "Joy cometh in the morning." C. M.
Ps. xcii.   Ecc. xi. 6-10.   1 Cor. x. 31-33.

1 GIVER and Guardian of our sleep,
   To praise Thy name we wake;
   Still, Lord, Thy helpless servants keep,
   For Thine own mercy's sake.

2 The blessing of another day
   We thankfully receive:
   O may we only Thee obey,
   And to Thy glory live.

3 Upon us lay Thy mighty hand;
   Our words and thoughts restrain;
   And bow our souls to Thy command,
   Nor let our faith be vain.
   Rev. Charles Wesley.   (1708-1788.)

903 "Our Father which art in heaven." S. M.
Mat. vi. 9-13.   1 Chr. xxix. 10-17.   Ps. ix.

1 OUR heavenly Father, hear
   The prayer we offer now:
   Thy name be hallowed far and near;
   To Thee all nations bow.

2 Thy kingdom come; Thy will
   On earth be done in love,
   As saints and seraphim fulfil
   Thy perfect law above.

3 Our daily bread supply,
   While by Thy word we live;
   The guilt of our iniquity
   Forgive, as we forgive.

4 From dark temptation's power,
   From Satan's wiles, defend;
   Deliver in the evil hour,
   And guide us to the end.
   James Montgomery.   (1771-1854.)

904 "Satisfy us early with Thy mercy." L. M.
Ps. lxvii.   Ex. xxix. 38-46.   1 Thes. iii.

1 O THOU great Ruler of the sky,
   Who art, and canst not cease to be,
   Whose power and greatness never die,
   We raise our morning prayer to Thee.

2 In the beginning of the day,
   With the bright rising of the sun,
   Direct the footsteps of our way,
   Nor leave us till the day is done.

3 As hour succeeds to passing hour,
   And duties every moment fill.
   Uphold us by Thy mighty power,
   And guide us by Thy heavenly will.

4 And thus, when all our days shall close,
   And suns for us no more shall shine,
   O may our souls in Thee repose,
   And life and joy be one in Thine.
   Rev. Thomas C. Upham.   (1799-1872.)

905 "The Father of mercies." C. M.
Luke xi. 1-13.   Isa. lxiv.   Ps. xxi.

1 OUR Father, God, who art in heaven,
   All hallowed be Thy name;
   Thy kingdom come; Thy will be done
   In heaven and earth the same.

2 Give us this day our daily bread;
   And as we those forgive
   Who sin against us, so may we
   Forgiving grace receive.

3 Into temptation lead us not;
   From evil set us free;
   And Thine the kingdom, Thine the power
   And glory, ever be.
   Rev. Adoniram Judson.   (1788-1850.)

906 "Thou leddest Thy people like a flock." C. M.
Gen. xxviii.   Deu. xxvi.   John xvii. 15-26.

1 O GOD of Bethel, by whose hand
   Thy people still are fed;
   Who through this weary pilgrimage
   Hast all our fathers led;

2 Our vows, our prayers, we now present
   Before Thy throne of grace;
   God of our fathers, be the God
   Of their succeeding race.

3 Through each perplexing path of life
   Our wandering footsteps guide;
   Give us, each day, our daily bread,
   And raiment fit provide.

4 O spread Thy covering wings around,
   Till all our wanderings cease,
   And at our Father's loved abode
   Our souls arrive in peace.
   Rev. Philip Doddridge.   (1702-1751.)
   Alt. by Michael Bruce.   (1746-1767.)

"The church in thy house."

907 "Thou art good and doest good." C. M.
Ps. cvii. Rom. vii. 12-25. Isa. xxxi.

1 AUTHOR of good, we rest on Thee;
  Thine ever-watchful eye
Alone our real wants can see,
  Thy hand alone supply.

2 In Thine all-gracious providence
  Our cheerful hopes confide;
O let Thy power be our defence,
  Thy love our footsteps guide!

3 And since, by passion's force subdued,
  Too oft, with stubborn will,
We blindly shun the latent good,
  And grasp the specious ill,

4 Not what we wish, but what we want,
  Let mercy still supply;
The good we ask not, Father, grant;
  The ill we ask, deny.
              Rev. James Merrick. (1720-1769.)

908 "We have waited for Thee." C. M.
Ps. lxvi. 1 Chr. xxix. 10-18. John xvii. 20-26

1 BEING of beings, God of love,
  To Thee our hearts we raise;
Thy all-sustaining power we prove,
  And gladly sing Thy praise.

2 Thine, wholly Thine, we pant to be;
  Our sacrifice receive;
Made, and preserved, and saved by Thee,
  To Thee ourselves we give.

3 Come, Holy Ghost, the Saviour's love
  Shed in our hearts abroad;
So shall we ever live, and move,
  And be with Christ in God.
              Rev. Charles Wesley. (1708-1788.)

909 "He led them on safely." S. M.
Hos. xi. 1-4. 1 Thes. iv. Phil. ii. 12, 13.

1 THAT we might walk with God,
  He forms our hearts anew;
Takes us, like Ephraim, by the hand,
  And teaches us to go.

2 He by His Spirit leads
  In paths before unknown;
The work to be performed is ours,
  The strength is all His own.

3 Assisted by His grace,
  We still pursue our way;
And hope at last to reach the prize,
  Secure in endless day.

4 'T is He that works to will,
  'T is He that works to do;
His is the power by which we act,
  His be the glory, too.
              Rev. Benjamin Beddome. (1717-1795.)

"Offerings every morning."

910 "Guide our feet into the way of peace." C. M.
Ps. xvii. Gen. xxii. 1-14. Mat. x. 16-32.

1 FATHER of love, our Guide and Friend,
  O lead us gently on,
Until life's trial-time shall end,
  And heavenly peace be won.

2 If called, like Abraham's child, to climb
  The hill of sacrifice,
Some angel may be there in time;
  Deliverance shall arise.

3 Or if some darker lot be good,
  O teach us to endure
The sorrow, pain, or solitude,
  That make the spirit pure.

4 Christ by no flowery pathway came;
  And we, His foll'wers here,
Must do Thy will and praise Thy name,
  In hope, and love, and fear.
              Rev. William J. Irons. '1812-.)

911 "If any man serve me, let him follow me." C. M.
1 John iv. John xv. 1-17. Jer. xxxi. 1-14.

1 IMMORTAL love, forever full,
  Forever flowing free;
Forever shared, forever whole,
  A never-ebbing sea,

Our outward lips confess the name
  All other names above;
Love only knoweth whence it came
  And comprehendeth love.

2 O Lord and Master of us all,
  Whate'er our name or sign,
We own Thy sway, we hear Thy call,
  We test our lives by Thine.

Our Friend, our Brother, and our Lord,
  What may Thy service be?
Nor name, nor form, nor ritual word,
  But simply following Thee.
              John G. Whittier. (1808-.)

912 "Followers of that which is good." C. M.
Acts x. 34-38. James ii. 1-17. Deu. xv. 7-18.

1 LORD, lead the way the Saviour went,
  By lane and cell obscure;
And let love's treasure still be spent,
  Like His, upon the poor.

2 For Thou hast placed us side by side,
  In this wide world of ill;
And, that Thy followers may be tried,
  The poor are with us still.

3 Mean are all offerings we can make;
  Yet Thou hast taught us, Lord,
If given for the Saviour's sake,
  They lose not their reward.
              Rev. William Croswell. (1804-1854.)

"The church in thy house."

913 "He that hath mercy ... shall lead them." 8. 7.
Ps. lxxx. Deu. xxxii. 1-12. Rev. vii. 9-17.

1 GENTLY, Lord, O gently lead us,
Pilgrims in this vale of tears,
Through the trials yet decreed us,
Till our last great change appears.
When temptation's darts assail us,
When in devious paths we stray,
Let Thy goodness never fail us,
Lead us in Thy perfect way.

2 In the hour of pain and anguish,
In the hour when death draws near,
Suffer not our hearts to languish,
Suffer not our souls to fear;
And when mortal life is ended,
Bid us in Thine arms to rest,
Till, by angel bands attended,
We awake among the blest.
Thomas Hastings. (1784-1872.)

914 "He knoweth." 8. 7. 7.
Heb. v. 1-10. Mat. viii. 16-27. Isa. liii.

1 YES, He knows the way is dreary,
Knows the weakness of our frame,
Knows that hand and heart are weary:
He in all points felt the same.
He is near to help and bless;
Be not weary, onward press.

2 Look to Him who once was willing
All His glory to resign,
That for thee the law fulfilling
All His merit might be thine.
Strive to follow day by day
Where His footsteps mark the way.
Miss Frances R. Havergal. (1830-1879.)

915 "In fire by night ... in a cloud by day." L. M.
Ex. xiv. 15-31. Neh. ix. John viii. 1-12.

1 WHEN Israel, of the Lord beloved,
Out from the land of bondage came,
Her fathers' God before her moved,
An awful Guide, in smoke and flame.

2 By day, along th' astonished lands,
The cloudy pillar glided slow:
By night, Arabia's crimsoned sands
Returned the fiery column's glow.

3 Thus present still, though now unseen,
O Lord, when shines the prosperous day,
Be thoughts of Thee a cloudy screen,
To temper the deceitful ray.

4 And O, when gathers on our path,
In shade and storm, the frequent night,
Be Thou long-suffering, slow to wrath,
A burning and a shining Light.
Sir Walter Scott. (1771-1832.)

"Offerings every morning."

916 "They gathered it every morning." 7.
Ex. xvi. 1-21. Isa. xxxiii. 1-16. Col. iii.

1 EVERY morning mercies new
Fall as fresh as morning dew;
Every morning let us pay
Tribute with the early day;
For Thy mercies, Lord, are sure;
Thy compassion doth endure.

2 Still the greatness of Thy love
Daily doth our sins remove;
Daily, far as east from west,
Lifts the burden from the breast;
Gives unbought to those who pray
Strength to stand in evil day.

3 Let our prayers each morn prevail
That these gifts may never fail;
And, as we confess the sin
And the tempter's power within,
Feed us with the Bread of Life;
Fit us for our daily strife.
Rev. Horatius Bonar. (1808-.)

917 "That our God may lighten our eyes." 8. 6.
Ps. xxxvii. 1-11. Jer. xvii. 7-17. 1 Pet. v. 1-11.

1 O LORD, how happy should we be
If we could cast our care on Thee,
If we from self could rest;
And feel at heart that One above
In perfect wisdom, perfect love,
Is working for the best:

2 Could we but kneel and cast our load,
E'en while we pray, upon our God,
Then rise with lightened cheer;
Sure that the Father, who is nigh
To still the famished raven's cry,
Will hear in that we fear.

3 We cannot trust Him as we should;
So chafes weak nature's restless mood
To cast its peace away;
But birds and flowerets round us preach,
All, all the present evil teach
Sufficient for the day.

4 Lord, make these faithless hearts of ours
Such lessons learn from birds and flowers;
Make them from self to cease,
Leave all things to a Father's will,
And taste, before Him lying still,
E'en in affliction, peace.
Prof. Joseph Anstice. (1808-1836.)

"The church in thy house." "Offerings every morning."

918 "We are Thine." 7,
Ps. c. Eze. xxxiv. 17–31. John x. 11–17.

1 THINE forever! God of love,
Hear us from Thy throne above;
Thine forever may we be
Here and in eternity.

2 Thine forever! Lord of life,
Shield us through the earthly strife;
Thou, the Life, the Truth, the Way,
Guide us to the realms of day.

3 Thine forever! O how blest
They who find in Thee their rest!
Saviour, Guardian, heavenly Friend,
Oh, defend us to the end.

4 Thine forever! Thou our Guide,
All our wants by Thee supplied,
All our sins by Thee forgiven,
Lead us, Lord, from earth to heaven.
Mrs. Mary F. Maude. 1848.

919 "Ye are not your own." S. M.
Luke xvii. 7–10. Mat. xxv. 31–40. Deu. xi. 8–32.

1 WE give Thee but Thine own,
Whate'er the gift may be:
All that we have is Thine alone,
A trust, O Lord, from Thee.

2 To comfort and to bless,
To find a balm for woe,
To tend the lone and fatherless
Is angels' work below.

3 And we believe Thy word,
Though dim our faith may be:
Whate'er for Thine we do, O Lord,
We do it unto Thee.
Rev. William W. How. (1823–.)

920 "Give us this day our daily bread." 7,
Num. xi. 1–9. Deu. xxxiii. 25. Mat. vi. 5–13.

1 DAY by day the manna fell;
O to learn this lesson well!
Still by constant mercy fed,
Give us, Lord, our daily bread.

2 "Day by day" the promise reads,
Daily strength for daily needs;
Cast foreboding fears away,
Take the manna of to-day.

3 Lord, our times are in Thy hand;
All our sanguine hopes have planned
To Thy wisdom we resign,
And would mould our wills to Thine.

4 Thou our daily task shalt give;
Day by day to Thee we live;
So shall added years fulfil
Not our own, our Father's will.
Josiah Conder. (1789–1855.)

921 "Lord, teach us to pray." C. M.
Luke xi. 1–13. Job xiii. 1–16. Col. i. 9–22.

1 LORD! teach us how to pray aright,
With reverence and with fear;
Though dust and ashes in Thy sight,
We may, we must draw near.

2 God of all grace, we come to Thee,
With broken, contrite hearts;
Give, what Thine eye delights to see,
Truth in the inward parts:

3 Patience, to watch, and wait, and weep,
Though mercy long delay;
Courage, our fainting souls to keep,
And trust Thee though Thou slay.

4 Give these, and then, Thy will be done!
Thus strengthened with all might,
We by Thy Spirit and Thy Son
Shall pray, and pray aright.
James Montgomery. (1771–1854.)

922 "Call on the Lord out of a pure heart." C. M.
Isa. lxiv. Ps. xv. 1 Cor. xiii.

1 O THOU who by a star didst guide
The wise men on their way,
Until it came and stood beside
The place where Jesus lay,

2 As yet we know Thee but in part;
But still we trust Thy word,
That blessèd are the pure in heart,
For they shall see the Lord.

3 O Saviour, give us then Thy grace,
To make us pure in heart,
That we may see Thee face to face
Hereafter, as Thou art.
Rev. John M. Neale. (1818–1891.)

923 "Help us, O Lord, . . . for we rest on Thee." C. M.
Mat. viii. 23–27. Mark ix. 14–27. Ps. lxx.

1 O HELP us, Lord, each hour of need
Thy heavenly succor give;
Help us in thought, and word, and deed,
Each hour on earth we live.

2 O help us when our spirits bleed,
With contrite anguish sore;
And when our hearts are cold and dead,
O help us, Lord, the more.

3 If strangers to Thy fold we call,
Imploring at Thy feet
The crumbs that from Thy table fall,
'T is all we dare entreat.

4 O help us, Jesus, from on high:
We know no help but Thee;
O help us so to live and die,
As Thine in heaven to be.
Rev. Henry H. Milman. (1791–1868.)

"The Church in thy House." "Offerings every morning."

924 "Day by day our daily bread." **C. M.**
Mat. xxiv. 42–51. John xii. 20–36. Ps. xc.

1 JESUS, be near us when we wake;
 And, at the break of day,
 With Thy blest touch awake the soul,
 Her meed of praise to pay.

2 The star that heralds in the morn
 Is fading in the skies ;
 The darkness melts : O Thou true Light,
 Once more on us arise.

3 Steep all our senses in Thy beam ;
 The world's false night expel ;
 Purge each defilement from the soul,
 And in our bosoms dwell.

Ambrosian. 5th century.
Tr. by Rev. Edward Caswall. (1814–.)

925 "The Way, the Truth, and the Life." **C. M.**
John xiv. 4–20. Heb. ix. Prov. ix. 1–12.

1 THOU art the Way : to Thee alone
 From sin and death we flee ;
 And he who would the Father seek
 Must seek Him, Lord, by Thee.

2 Thou art the Truth : Thy word alone
 True wisdom can impart ;
 Thou only canst inform the mind,
 And purify the heart.

3 Thou art the Life : the rending tomb
 Proclaims Thy conquering arm,
 And those who put their trust in Thee
 Nor death nor hell shall harm.

4 Thou art the Way, the Truth, the Life ;
 Grant us that Way to know,
 That Truth to keep, that Life to win,
 Whose joys eternal flow.

Bp. George W. Doane. (1799–1859.)

926 "I will draw all men unto me." **L. M.**
Rom. xii. 1 John i. Ps. xxvii.

1 JESUS, our best belovéd Friend,
 Draw out our souls in sweet desire ;
 Jesus, in love to us descend,
 Baptize us with Thy Spirit's fire.

2 Our souls and bodies we resign,
 To fear and follow Thy commands ;
 O take our hearts, our hearts are Thine,
 Accept the service of our hands.

3 Firm, faithful, watching unto prayer,
 May we Thy blesséd will obey ;
 Toil in Thy vineyard here, and bear
 The heat and burden of the day.

4 Yet, Lord, for us a resting-place
 In heaven, at Thy right hand, prepare ;
 And till we see Thee face to face,
 Be all our conversation there.

James Montgomery. (1771–1854.)

927 "The Sun of Righteousness shall arise." **7.**
Ps. v. Mal iv. 2–6. Rev. i.

1 JESUS, Sun of Righteousness,
 Brightest beam of love divine,
 With the early morning rays,
 Do Thou on our darkness shine,
 And dispel, with purest light,
 All our long and gloomy night.

2 Like the sun's reviving ray,
 May Thy love, with tender glow,
 All our coldness melt away,
 Warm and cheer us, forth to go ;
 Gladly serve Thee and obey,
 All our life's short earthly day.

3 Thou, our only hope and guide,
 Never leave us nor forsake ;
 Keep us ever at Thy side,
 Till th' eternal morning break ;
 Moving on to Zion's hill,
 Onward, upward, homeward still.

Christian K. von Rosenroth. (1636–1689.)
Tr. by Miss Jane Borthwick. (18—.)

928 "The light of Thy countenance." **L. M.**
Heb. i. John i. 1–14. Ps. cxix. 81–88.

1 O JESUS, Lord of heavenly grace,
 Thou brightness of Thy Father's face,
 Thou fountain of eternal light,
 Whose beams disperse the shades of night!

2 Come, holy Sun of heavenly love,
 Send down Thy radiance from above,
 And to our inmost hearts convey
 The Holy Spirit's cloudless ray.

3 May He our actions deign to bless,
 And loose the bonds of wickedness ;
 From sudden falls our feet defend,
 And guide us safely to the end.

Ambrose of Milan. (340–397.)
Tr. by Rev. John Chandler. (18—.)

929 "The inward man is renewed day by day." **L. M.**
Ps. cxliii. Can. i. Col. iii.

1 O CHRIST, with each returning morn,
 Thine image to our hearts is borne ;
 O may we ever clearly see
 Our Saviour and our God in Thee.

2 May faith, deep rooted in the soul,
 Subdue our flesh, our minds control ;
 May guile depart and discord cease,
 And all within be joy and peace.

3 O hallowed thus be every day ;
 Let meekness be our morning ray,
 Our faith like noontide splendor glow,
 Our souls the twilight never know.

Ambrose of Milan.
Tr. by Rev. John Chandler.

"The church in thy house."

930 John i. 1-14. 1 John i. 1 to ii. 2. Ps. lxxvii.   "I am the bread of life."   **L. M.**

1 JESUS, Thou Joy of loving hearts,
  Thou Fount of life, Thou Light of men,
From the best bliss that earth imparts,
  We turn unfilled to Thee again.

2 Thy truth unchanged hath ever stood;
  Thou savest those that on Thee call;
To them that seek Thee, Thou art good,
  To them that find Thee, all in all.

3 We taste Thee, O Thou living Bread,
  And long to feast upon Thee still;
We drink of Thee, the Fountain head,
  And thirst, our souls from Thee to fill.

4 Our restless spirits yearn for Thee,
  Where'er our changeful lot is cast;
Glad when Thy gracious smile we see,
  Blest when our faith can hold Thee fast.

5 O Jesus, ever with us stay;
  Make all our moments calm and bright;
Chase the dark night of sin away;
  Shed o'er the world Thy holy light.
Bernard of Clairvaux. (1091-1153.)
Tr. by Rev. Ray Palmer. (1808-.)

931 Heb. ix. 11-28. John xiv. 12-31. Isa. xlix. 1-16.   "He humbled Himself."   **L. M.**

1 O LOVE divine, that stooped to share
  Our sharpest pang, our bitterest tear!
On Thee we cast each earth-born care;
  We smile at pain while Thou art near.

2 Though long the weary way we tread,
  And sorrow crown each lingering year,
No path we shun, no darkness dread,
  Our hearts still whispering, "Thou art near!"

3 On Thee we fling our burdening woe,
  O Love divine, forever dear;
Content to suffer while we know,
  Living and dying, Thou art near!
Oliver W. Holmes. (1809-.)

932 2 Pet. i. John ix. 1-25. Ps. l.   "Until the Day-star arise in our hearts."   **S. M.**

1 WE lift our hearts to Thee,
  Thou Day-star from on high;
The sun itself is but Thy shade,
  Yet cheers both earth and sky.

2 O let Thy rising beams
  Dispel the shades of night;
And let the glories of Thy love
  Come like the morning light.

3 May we this life improve
  To mourn for errors past;
And live this short, revolving day,
  As if it were our last.
Rev. John Wesley. (1703-1791.)

"Offerings every morning."

933 Eph. iii. 14-21. 1 John iii. 1-. Eze. xxxvi. 25-38.   "Herein is love."   **8. 7.**

1 LOVE divine, all loves excelling,
  Joy of heaven, to earth come down!
Fix in us Thine humble dwelling;
  All Thy faithful mercies crown.
Jesus, Thou art all compassion,
  Pure unbounded love Thou art;
Visit us, with Thy salvation;
  Enter every trembling heart.

2 Breathe, O breathe Thy loving spirit
  Into every troubled breast;
Let us all in Thee inherit,
  Let us find the promised rest.
Take away our power of sinning;
  Alpha and Omega be;
End of faith, as its beginning,
  Set our hearts at liberty.

3 Come, almighty to deliver,
  Let us all Thy life receive;
Suddenly return, and never,
  Never more Thy temples leave.
Thee we would be always blessing,
  Serve Thee as Thy hosts above,
Pray, and praise Thee without ceasing,
  Glory in Thy perfect love.

4 Finish, then, Thy new creation,
  Pure and spotless let us be;
Let us see Thy great salvation
  Perfectly restored in Thee.
Changed from glory into glory,
  Till in heaven we take our place,
Till we cast our crowns before Thee,
  Lost in wonder, love, and praise.
Rev. Charles Wesley. (1708-1788.)

934 Ps. lxxx. Eze. xxxiv 11-31. John x. 11-29.   "Thou that leadest Joseph like a flock."   **8. 7. 4.**

1 SHEPHERD of Thine Israel, lead us,
  Pilgrims through this desert land;
Thou who hast from bondage freed us,
  Guard us by Thy mighty hand:
    Daily feed us,
Till we reach the heavenly strand.

2 As Thou didst in wondrous manner
  Guide Thy chosen flock aright,
Let Thy presence be our banner,
  Cloud by day and fire by night:
    Thy protection
Be our shield, Thy word our light.
Josiah Conder. (1789-1855.)

"The church in thy house."   "Offerings every morning."

935 "Be Thou their arm every morning." 7.
Ps. civ. 19-34. Mat. xxi. 17-32. Acts v. 17-32.

1 Now the shades of night are gone,
   Now the morning light is come;
   Lord, may we be Thine to-day;
   Drive the shades of sin away.

2 Fill our souls with heavenly light,
   Banish doubt and clear our sight;
   In Thy service, Lord, to-day,
   May we labor, watch, and pray.

3 Keep our haughty passions bound;
   Save us from our foes around;
   Going out and coming in,
   Keep us safe from every sin.

4 When our work of life is past,
   O receive us then at last;
   Night and sin will be no more,
   When we reach the heavenly shore.
                              Rev. Samson Occum. (1723-1792.)

936 "Let us walk in the light of the Lord." C. M.
Ps. cxliii. 1 Thes v. Titus ii.

1 Now that the sun is gleaming bright,
   Implore we, bending low,
   That He, the uncreated Light,
   May guide us as we go.

2 No sinful word, nor deed of wrong,
   Nor thoughts that idly rove;
   But simple truth be on our tongue,
   And in our hearts be love.

3 And grant that to Thine honor, Lord,
   Our daily toil may tend;
   That we begin it at Thy word,
   And in Thy favor end.
                              Paris Breviary. 1736.
                              Tr. by Rev. John H. Newman. (1801-.)

937 "His own Son in the likeness of sinful flesh." C. M.
Heb. v. 1-9. 1 Cor. xv. 35-49. Ps. xxii. 19-31.

1 O MEAN may seem this house of clay,
   Yet 't was the Lord's abode;
   Our feet may mourn this thorny way,
   Yet here Emmanuel trod.

2 This fleshly robe the Lord did wear;
   This watch the Lord did keep;
   These burdens sore the Lord did bear;
   These tears the Lord did weep.

3 O vale of tears no longer sad,
   Wherein the Lord did dwell;
   O happy robe of flesh that clad
   Our own Emmanuel!

4 O mighty grace, our life to live,
   To make our earth divine;
   O mighty grace, Thy heaven to give
   And lift our life to Thine!
                              Thomas H. Gill. (1819-.)

938 "Let us kneel before the Lord our Maker." S. M.
Ps. lv. 16-23. Dan. vi 4-10. 1 Tim. ii. 1-8.

1 COME at the morning hour,
   Come, let us kneel and pray;
   Prayer is the Christian pilgrim's staff
   To walk with God all day.

2 At noon, beneath the Rock
   Of ages, rest and pray;
   Sweet is that shelter from the sun
   In weary heat of day.

3 At evening, in thy home,
   Around its altar, pray;
   And finding there the house of God,
   With heaven then close the day.

4 When midnight veils our eyes,
   O it is sweet to say,
   I sleep, but my heart waketh, Lord,
   With Thee to watch and pray.
                              James Montgomery. (1771-1854.)

939 "A friend that sticketh closer than a brother." 8. 7.
Prov. xviii. 10-24. John xv. 1-15. Heb. ii. 9-18.

1 ONE there is above all others,
   Well deserves the name of Friend;
   His is love beyond a brother's,
   Costly, free, and knows no end:

2 Which of all our friends, to save us,
   Could or would have shed his blood?
   But our Jesus died to have us
   Reconciled in Him to God.

3 O for grace our hearts to soften;
   Teach us, Lord, at length to love;
   We, alas, forget too often
   What a Friend we have above.
                              Rev. John Newton. (1725-1807.)

940 "Thou shalt make a mercy-seat." L. M.
Isa. iv. Ex. xxv. 17-22. Heb. x. 1-25

1 FROM every stormy wind that blows,
   From every swelling tide of woes,
   There is a calm, a sure retreat;
   'T is found beneath the mercy-seat.

2 There is a place where Jesus sheds
   The oil of gladness on our heads;
   A place than all besides more sweet;
   It is the blood-bought mercy-seat.

3 There is a spot where spirits blend,
   Where friend holds fellowship with friend;
   Though sundered far, by faith they meet
   Around one common mercy-seat.

4 There, there, on eagle wings we soar,
   And time and sense seem all no more;
   And Heaven comes down our souls to greet,
   And glory crowns the mercy-seat.
                              Rev. Hugh Stowell. (1799-1855.)

"The church in thy house."

941 "Who daily loadeth us with benefits." **L. M.**
Lam. iii. 22-41. Isa. xxvi. 1-13. Rom. xii.

1 NEW every morning is the love
Our wakening and uprising prove ;
Through sleep and darkness safely brought,
Restored to life, and power, and thought.

2 New mercies, each returning day,
Hover around us while we pray :
New perils past, new sins forgiven,
New thoughts of God, new hopes of heaven.

3 If on our daily course our mind
Be set to hallow all we find,
New treasures still, of countless price,
God will provide for sacrifice.

4 The trivial round, the common task,
Will furnish all we ought to ask :
Room to deny ourselves, a road
To bring us daily nearer God.

5 Only, O Lord, in Thy dear love
Fit us for perfect rest above ;
And help us, this and every day,
To live more nearly as we pray.
Rev. John Keble. (1792-1866.)

942 "He brought them out of darkness." **L. M.**
Ps. cviii. 1-6. Ecc. xi. 1 Cor. xv. 41-54.

1 THE dawn is sprinkling in the east
Its golden shower, as day flows in ;
Fast mount the pointed shafts of light :
Farewell to darkness and to sin.

2 So, Lord, when that last morning breaks,
Which shrouds in darkness earth and skies,
May it on us, low bending here,
Arrayed in joyful light arise.
Ambrosian. 4th or 5th century.
Tr. by Rev. Edward Caswall. (1814-.)

943 "It is vain for you ... to sit up late." **8. 7.**
Ps. cxxvii. Gen. xi. 1-9. Luke xii. 16-21.

1 VAINLY through night's weary hours,
Keep we watch, lest foes alarm ;
Vain our bulwarks and our towers,
But for God's protecting arm.

2 Vain were all our toil and labor,
Did not God that labor bless ;
Vain, without His grace and favor,
Every talent we possess.

3 Vainer still the hope of heaven,
That on human strength relies ;
But to him shall help be given,
Who in humble faith applies.

4 Seek we, then, the Lord's Anointed ;
He will grant us peace and rest :
Ne'er was suppliant disappointed,
Who through Christ his prayer addressed.
Miss Harriet Auber. (1773-1862.)

"Offerings every morning."

944 "He continued all night in prayer." **S. M.**
Ps. cxi. Mark i. 32-45. Heb. x. 1-14.

1 How sweet the melting lay
Which breaks upon the ear,
When at the hour of rising day
Christians unite in prayer.

2 The breezes waft their cries
Up to Jehovah's throne ;
He listens to their humble sighs,
And sends His blessings down.

3 So Jesus rose to pray
Before the morning light ;
Once on the chilling mount did stay
And wrestle all the night.

4 So Jesus still doth pray
Before the morning bright,
On heavenly mountains far away,
While we toil here in night.

5 Leave, Lord, Thy vigil there,
Descend upon life's wave ;
Come to the bark through midnight air,
The storm shall cease to rave.
Mrs. Phœbe H. Brown. (1783-1861.)

945 "The grace of the Lord Jesus Christ." **C. M.**
1 John iv. Mat. xviii. 12-14. Deu. xxxii. 1-14.

1 THOU grace divine, encircling all,
A soundless, shoreless sea :
Wherein at last our souls shall fall ;
O love of God, most free !

2 When over dizzy steeps we go,
One soft hand blinds our eyes ;
The other leads us, safe and slow,
O love of God, most wise !

3 And though we turn us from Thy face,
And wander wide and long,
Thou hold'st us still in Thine embrace,
O love of God, most strong !

4 The saddened heart, the restless soul,
The toil-worn frame and mind,
Alike confess Thy sweet control,
O love of God, most kind !

5 But not alone Thy care we claim,
Our wayward steps to win ;
We know Thee by a dearer name,
O love of God, within !

6 And filled and quickened by Thy breath,
Our souls are strong and free,
To rise o'er sin, and fear, and death,
O love of God, to Thee !
Miss Eliza Scudder. (1821-.)

"The church in thy house."

946 "Let us run with patience the race." C. M.
Isa. xl. 27-31.   Eph. vi. 10-18.   1 Thes. v.

1 AWAKE, our souls! away, our fears!
   Let every trembling thought be gone;
   Awake, and run the heavenly race,
   And put a cheerful courage on.

2 True, 'tis a strait and thorny road,
   And mortal spirits tire and faint;
   But they forget the mighty God,
   Who feeds the strength of every saint.

3 From Thee, the overflowing spring,
   Our souls shall drink a fresh supply,
   While such as trust their native strength
   Shall melt away, and droop, and die.

4 Swift as an eagle cuts the air,
   We'll mount aloft to Thine abode;
   On wings of love our souls shall fly,
   Nor tire amidst the heavenly road.
   Rev. Isaac Watts. (1674-1748.)

947 "God, even our own God, shall bless us." S. M.
Rom. xii 6-21. James i. 16-27. Deu. x. 12-22.

1 O PRAISE our God to-day,
   His constant mercy bless,
   Whose love hath helped us on our way,
   And granted us success.

2 His arm the strength imparts
   Our daily toil to bear;
   His grace alone inspires our hearts,
   Each other's load to share.

3 Lord, may it be our choice
   This blessèd rule to keep,
   "Rejoice with them that do rejoice,
   And weep with them that weep."
   Rev. Sir Henry W. Baker. (1821-1877.)

948 "I am with you alway." 8. 7.
Mat. xxviii. 18-20. Isa. xliii. 1-7. Deu. viii. 1-10.

1 ALWAYS with us, always with us,
   Words of cheer and words of love;
   Thus the risen Saviour whispers,
   From His dwelling-place above.
   With us when we toil in sadness,
   Sowing much, and reaping none;
   Telling us that in the future
   Golden harvests shall be won.

2 With us when the storm is sweeping
   O'er our pathway dark and drear;
   Waking hope within our bosoms,
   Stilling every anxious fear.
   With us in the lonely valley,
   When we cross the chilling stream;
   Lighting up the steps to glory
   With salvation's radiant beam.
   Rev. Edwin H. Nevin. (1814-.)

"The daily sacrifice."

949 "He shall sustain thee." S. M.
Ps. xxxvii.   Mat. vi. 25-34.   1 Pet. v. 6-10.

1 COMMIT thou all thy griefs
   And ways into His hands,
   To His sure truth and tender care
   Who earth and heaven commands.

2 Who points the clouds their course,
   Whom wind and seas obey,
   He shall direct thy wandering feet,
   He shall prepare thy way.

3 Thou on the Lord rely,
   So safe shalt thou go on;
   Fix on His work thy steadfast eye,
   So shall thy work be done.

4 No profit canst thou gain
   By self-consuming care;
   To Him commend thy cause; His ear
   Attends the softest prayer.

5 And whatso'er Thou will'st
   Thou dost, O King of kings;
   What Thy unerring wisdom chose,
   Thy power to being brings.
   Rev. Paul Gerhardt. (1606-1676.)
Tr. by Rev. John Wesley. (1703-1791.)

950 "Fear none of those things." S. M.
Ex. xiv.   Ps. xlvi.   Mark vi. 45-51.

1 GIVE to the winds thy fears;
   Hope, and be undismayed;
   God hears thy sighs and counts thy tears;
   God shall lift up thy head.

2 Through waves, and clouds, and storms,
   He gently clears thy way;
   Wait thou His time, so shall this night
   Soon end in joyous day.

3 Still heavy is thy heart?
   Still sink thy spirits down?
   Cast off the weight, let fear depart,
   And every care be gone.

4 What though thou rulest not?
   Yet heaven, and earth, and hell
   Proclaim, "God sitteth on the throne,
   And ruleth all things well."

5 Leave to His sovereign sway
   To choose and to command:
   So shalt thou, wondering, own His way,
   How wise, how strong His hand!

6 Far, far above thy thought
   His counsel shall appear,
   When fully He the work hath wrought
   That caused thy needless fear.
   Rev. Paul Gerhardt.
Tr. by Rev. John Wesley.

"The church in thy house."   "The daily sacrifice."

951 "Even there shall Thy hand lead." 7.
John iv. 20-24. 2 Chr. xvi. 1-9. Mal. i. 1-11.

1 THEY who seek the throne of grace
Find that throne in every place ;
If we live a life of prayer,
God is present everywhere.

2 In our sickness and our health,
In our want or in our wealth,
If we look to God in prayer,
God is present everywhere.

3 When our earthly comforts fail,
When the woes of life prevail,
'T is the time for earnest prayer ;
God is present everywhere.

4 Then, my soul, in every strait,
To Thy Father come, and wait ;
He will answer every prayer :
God is present everywhere.
Oliver Holden.

954 "Which came out of great tribulation." C. M.
Heb. xii. 1-14. Isa. liii. Rev. iii. 14-22.

1 Lo, what a cloud of witnesses
Encompass us around ;
Men once like us with suffering tried,
But now with glory crowned.

2 Behold a Witness nobler still,
Who trod affliction's path,
Jesus, the Author, Finisher,
Rewarder of our faith :

3 He, for the joy before Him set,
And moved by pitying love,
Endured the cross, despised the shame,
And now He reigns above.

4 Thither, forgetting things behind,
Press we, to God's right hand ;
There, with the Saviour and His saints,
Triumphantly to stand.
Author unknown.

952 "Faint, yet pursuing." 11.
Judg. vii. 15 to viii. 12. Ps. cxlvi Isa. xl. 1-11. Mark vi. 45-51.

1 THOUGH faint, yet pursuing, we go on our way ;
The Lord is our Leader, His word is our stay ;
Though suffering, and sorrow, and trial be near,
The Lord is our Refuge, and whom can we fear ?

2 He raiseth the fallen, He cheereth the faint ;
The weak and oppressed, He will hear their complaint ;
The way may be weary, and thorny the road,
But how can we falter ? Our help is in God !

3 Though clouds may surround us, our God is our Light ;
Though storms rage around us, our God is our Might ;
So, faint, yet pursuing, still onward we come ;
The Lord is our Leader, and heaven is our home !
Author unknown.

953 "God having provided some better thing." 8. 7.
Phil. iii. 12-21. 1 Cor. ix. 24-27. Isa. l. 7-10.

1 PILGRIMS in this vale of sorrow,
Pressing onward toward the prize,
Strength and comfort here we borrow
From the Hand that rules the skies.

2 'Mid these scenes of self-denial,
We are called the race to run ;
We must meet full many a trial
Ere the victor's crown is won.

3 Love shall every conflict lighten,
Hope shall urge us swifter on,
Faith shall every prospect brighten,
Till the morn of heaven shall dawn.

4 On the eternal Arm reclining,
We at length shall win the day ;
All the powers of earth combining,
Shall not snatch our crown away.
Thomas Hastings. (1784-1872.)

955 "With Him . . . all things." C. M.
Rom. viii. 31-39. Num. xiv. 6-10. Ps. cxviii.

1 O LET triumphant faith dispel
The fears of guilt and woe :
If God be for us, God the Lord,
Who, who shall be our foe ?

2 He who His only Son gave up
To death that we might live,
Shall He not all things freely grant,
That boundless love can give ?

3 Who now His people shall accuse ?
'T is God hath justified :
Who now His people shall condemn ?
The Lamb of God hath died.

4 And He who died hath risen again,
Triumphant from the grave :
At God's right hand for us He pleads,
Omnipotent to save.
Michael Bruce. (1746-1767.)

183

"The church in thy house."   "The daily sacrifice."

956 "God hath sent forth the Spirit." 7.
John xvi. 1-15.   Isa. xxx. 8-21.   Nch. ix. 7-20.

1 HOLY Spirit, faithful Guide,
  Ever near the Christian's side,
  Gently lead us by the hand,
  Pilgrims in a desert land ;
  Weary souls fore'er rejoice,
  While they hear that sweetest voice,
  Whispering softly, Wanderer, come !
  Follow me, I 'll guide thee home.

2 Ever present, truest Friend,
  Ever near Thine aid to lend,
  Leave us not to doubt and fear,
  Groping on in darkness drear ;
  When the storms are raging sore,
  Hearts grow faint and hopes give o'er ;
  Whisper softly, Wanderer, come !
  Follow me, I 'll guide thee home.

3 When our days of toil shall cease,
  Waiting still for sweet release,
  Nothing left but heaven and prayer,
  Wondering if our names were there ;
  Wading deep the dismal flood,
  Pleading naught but Jesus' blood ;
  Whisper softly, Wanderer, come !
  Follow me, I 'll guide thee home.
              M. M. Wells. 1858.

957 "Until the Spirit be poured upon us." C. M.
John xiv.   Acts ii. 1-21.   Eze. xxxix. 23-29.

1 SPIRIT divine, attend our prayers,
    And make this house Thy home ;
  Descend with all Thy gracious powers,
    O come, Great Spirit, come !

2 Come as the light ; to us reveal
    Our sinfulness and woe ;
  And lead us in those paths of life
    Where all the righteous go.

3 Come as the fire, and purge our hearts,
    Like sacrificial flame ;
  Let our whole soul an offering be
    To our Redeemer's name.

4 Come as the dew, and sweetly bless
    This consecrated hour ;
  May barrenness rejoice to own
    Thy fertilizing power.

5 Come as the wind, with rushing sound,
    With Pentecostal grace ;
  And make the great salvation known,
    Wide as the human race.
              Rev. Andrew Reed. (1787-1862.)

958 "The promise of the Father." 7.
Acts i. 1-9.   1 John v.   Zech. iv. 1-10.

1 COME, O promised Comforter,
  Light upon our darkness pour.
  Father of the poor Thou art ;
  Then to us Thy gifts impart.
  Light of everlasting day !
  Lord, direct us on our way.

2 Lord, Thy perfect gifts bestow
  On the fold of Christ below ;
  Crown our days with heavenly grace,
  Help us when we close our race :
  Help us when we look to Thee ;
  Grant us endless joy to see.
              Rev. Arthur T. Russell. (1806 .)

959 "Revealed unto us by His Spirit." L. M.
2 Pet. i. 16-21.   John iii. 1-8.   2 Sam. xxiii. 1-5.

1 COME, Holy Ghost, our hearts inspire,
  Let us Thine influence prove ;
  Source of the old prophetic fire,
  Fountain of light and love !

2 Come, Holy Ghost, for, moved by Thee,
  The prophets wrote and spoke ;
  Unlock the truth, Thyself the key ;
  Unseal the sacred book.

3 Expand Thy wings, celestial Dove !
  Brood o'er our nature's night ;
  On our disordered spirits move,
  And let there now be light.
              Rev. Charles Wesley. (1708-1788.)

960 "We will walk in His paths." 8. 7.
Ex. xxxiii. 12-23.   Ps. lxxvii.   John x. 1-5.

1 LEAD us, heavenly Father, lead us
    O'er the world's tempestuous sea ;
  Guard us, guide us, keep us, feed us,
    For we have no help but Thee ;
  Yet possessing every blessing,
    If our God our Father be.

2 Saviour, breathe forgiveness o'er us ;
    All our weakness Thou dost know ;
  Thou didst tread this earth before us ;
    Thou didst feel its keenest woe ;
  Lone and dreary, faint and weary,
    Through the desert Thou didst go..

3 Spirit of our God, descending,
    Fill our hearts with heavenly joy ;
  Love with every passion blending,
    Pleasure that can never cloy ;
  Thus provided, pardoned, guided,
    Nothing can our peace destroy.
              James Edmeston. (1791-1867.)

"The church in thy house." "The daily sacrifice."

961 "God will provide." 10, 11.
Gen. xxii. 1–14. Luke xii. 22–30. Mat. iv. 1–11. Ps. xlvi.

1 Though troubles assail, and dangers affright,
Though friends should all fail, and foes all unite,
Yet one thing secures us, whatever betide,
The promise assures us, the Lord will provide.

2 The birds, without barn or storehouse, are fed ;
From them let us learn to trust for our bread ;
His saints what is fitting shall ne'er be denied,
So long as 't is written, the Lord will provide.

3 When Satan appears to stop up our path,
And fill us with fears, we triumph by faith ;
He cannot take from us, though oft he has tried,
This heart-cheering promise, the Lord will provide.

4 No strength of our own, or goodness, we claim ;
Yet, since we have known the Saviour's great name,
In this our strong tower for safety we hide :
The Lord is our power, the Lord will provide.

Rev. John Newton. (1725-1807.)

962 "We should live soberly, righteously, godly." L. M.
Titus ii. Mat. v. 1–16. Ex. xix. 1–9.

1 So let our lips and lives express
The holy gospel we profess ;
So let our works and virtues shine,
To prove the doctrine all divine.

2 Thus shall we best proclaim abroad
The honors of our Saviour God,
When His salvation reigns within,
And grace subdues the power of sin.

3 Our flesh and sense must be denied,
Passion and envy, lust and pride ;
While justice, temperance, truth, and love,
Our inward piety approve.

4 Religion bears our spirits up,
While we expect that blessèd hope,
The bright appearance of the Lord,
And faith stands leaning on His word.

Rev. Isaac Watts. (1674-1748.)

964 "Be . . . sober and watch unto prayer." L. M.
Mark xiv. 26–42. Mat. xxv. 1–23. Josh. xiv.

1 They pray the best who pray and watch,
They watch the best who watch and pray ;
They hear Christ's fingers on the latch,
Whether He comes by night or day.

2 Whether they guard the gates and watch,
Or, patient, toil for Him, and wait,
They hear His fingers on the latch,
If early He doth come, or late.

3 With trembling joy they hail their Lord,
And haste His welcome feet to kiss,
While He, well pleased, doth speak the word
That thrills them with unending bliss :

4 " Well done, my servants, now receive,
For faithful work, reward and rest,
And wreaths which busy angels weave
To crown the men who serve me best."

Rev. Edward Hopper. (1816-.)

963 "Spirits sent forth to minister." 11.
Heb. i. Acts x. 1–8. Dan. ix. 20–23. Ps. xxxiv.

1 How dear is the thought, that the angels of God
May bow their bright wings to the world they once trod ;
Will leave the sweet songs of the mansions above,
To breathe o'er our bosoms some message of love !

2 They come, on the wings of the morning they come,
Impatient to lead some poor wanderer home ;
Some sinner to save from his darkened abode,
And lay him to rest in the arms of his God.

3 They come when we wander, they come when we pray,
In mercy to guard us wherever we stray ;
A glorious cloud, their bright witness is given ;
Encircling us here are these angels of heaven.

Author unknown.

"The church in thy house."   "The evening oblation."

965 " He shall give His angels charge."   8. 4.
Ps. cxxi.   Job xxxiii. 14–33.   2 Tim. iv. 1–18.

1 GOD, that madest earth and heaven,
    Darkness and light ;
  Who the day for toil hast given,
    For rest the night :
  May Thine angel-guards defend us,
  Slumber sweet Thy mercy send us,
  Holy dreams and hopes attend us,
    This livelong night.

2 And when morn again shall call us
    To run life's way,
  May we still, whate'er befall us,
    Thy will obey :
  From the power of evil hide us,
  In the narrow pathway guide us,
  Nor Thy smile be e'er denied us,
    The livelong day.

3 Guard us waking, guard us sleeping,
    And when we die,
  May we in Thy mighty keeping
    All peaceful lie :
  When the last dread call shall wake us,
  Do not Thou, our God, forsake us,
  But to reign in glory take us
    With Thee on high.
            Bp. Reginald Heber.   (1783–1826.)
            Abp. Richard Whately.   (1787–1863.)

966 " Let it please Thee to bless the house."   6. 4.
Ps. lxxi.   Isa. lxvi. 1–13.   John xix. 19–28.

1 FATHER of love and power,
  Guard Thou our evening hour,
    Shield with Thy might :
  For all Thy care this day
  Our grateful thanks we pay,
  And to our Father pray,
    Bless us to-night.

2 Jesus Immanuel,
  Come in Thy love to dwell
    In hearts contrite :
  For many sins we grieve,
  But we Thy grace receive,
  And in Thy word believe ;
    Bless us to-night.

3 Spirit of truth and love,
  Life-giving, holy Dove,
    Shed forth Thy light !
  Heal every sinner's smart,
  Still every throbbing heart,
  And Thine own peace impart ;
    Bless us to-night.
            Author unknown.

967 "The same day at evening came Jesus."   8. 7.
Gen. xxxii.   Ps. xxxiv. 1–7.   Acts i. 1–14.

1 SAVIOUR, breathe an evening blessing,
    Ere repose our spirits seal ;
  Sin and want we come confessing,
    Thou canst save, and Thou canst heal.

2 Though destruction walk around us,
    Though the arrow past us fly,
  Angel-guards from Thee surround us,
    We are safe, if Thou art nigh.

3 Though the night be dark and dreary,
    Darkness cannot hide from Thee ;
  Thou art He who, never weary,
    Watchest where Thy people be.

4 Should swift death this night o'ertake us,
    And our couch become our tomb,
  May the morn in heaven awake us,
    Clad in light and deathless bloom.
            James Edmeston.   (1791–1867.)

968 " Even the night shall be light."   8. 7. 7.
Ps. xlii.   1 Chr. xxix. 10–15.   Heb. xi. 1–16.

1 THROUGH the day Thy love has spared us ;
    Now we lay us down to rest.
  Through the silent watches guard us,
    Let no foe our peace molest ;
      Jesus ! Thou our Guardian be ;
      Sweet it is to trust in Thee.

2 Pilgrims here on earth, and strangers,
    Dwelling in the midst of foes,
  Us and ours preserve from dangers ;
    In Thine arms may we repose,
      And when life's short day is past,
      Rest with Thee in heaven at last.
            Rev. Thomas Kelly.   (1769–1855.)

969 " And they sang praises with gladness."   C. M.
Ps. cxli.   Acts xvi. 11–34.   2 Pet. iii.

1 Now, from the altar of our hearts,
    Let incense flames arise ;
  Assist us, Lord, to offer up
    Our evening sacrifice.

2 Minutes and mercies multiplied
    Have made up all this day ;
  Minutes came quick, but mercies were
    More fleet and free than they.

3 New time, new favors, and new joys
    Do a new song require :
  Till we shall praise Thee as we would,
    Accept our heart's desire.

4 Lord of our time, whose hand hath set
    New time upon our score,
  Thee may we praise for all our time,
    When time shall be no more !
            Rev. John Mason.   (–1694.)

"The church in thy house." "The evening oblation."

970 "The darkness hideth not from Thee." 11, 10.
Ps. xc. 1 Chr. xxix. 10–30. 2 Tim. iv. 1–13.

1 FADING, still fading,
　The last beam is shining;
　Father in heaven,
　The day is declining;
　Safety and innocence
　　Fly with the light,
　Temptation and danger
　　Walk forth with the night:
　From the fall of the shade
　Till the morning-bells chime,
　Shield me from danger,
　　Save me from crime.
　　　Father, have mercy,
　　　Father, have mercy,
　　　Father, have mercy,
　Through Jesus Christ our Lord.

2 Father in heaven,
　O hear when we call;
　Hear, for Christ's sake,
　Who is Saviour of all:
　Feeble and fainting
　　We trust in Thy might;
　In doubting and darkness
　　Thy love be our light;
　Let us sleep on Thy breast
　While the night taper burns,
　Wake in Thy arms
　　When morning returns.
　　　　　　　　　Author unknown.

971 "The Lord is our defence." L. M.
Ps. lxxxix. 1–18. Hab. iii. John xvii.

1 LORD of our hearts, belovéd of Thee,
　Weary of earth, we sigh to rest,
　Supremely happy, safe and free,
　Forever on Thy tender breast:

2 To see Thee, love Thee, feel Thee near,
　Nor dread, as now, Thy transient stay;
　To dwell beyond the reach of fear,
　Lest joy should wane or pass away.

3 Children of hope, belovéd Lord,
　In Thee we live, we glory now,
　Our Joy, our Rest, our great Reward,
　Our Diadem of beauty Thou.

4 And when exalted, Lord, with Thee,
　Thy royal throne at length we share,
　To everlasting Thou shalt be
　Our Diadem, our Glory there.
　　　　　　　Sir Edward Denny. (1796—)

972 "I will save my flock." 7.
Ps. iv. Gen. xxxii. John xix. 19–31.

1 ERE the waning light decay,
　God of all, to Thee we pray,
　Thee Thy healthful grace to send,
　Thee to guard us and defend.

2 Guard from dreams that may affright;
　Guard from terrors of the night;
　Guard from foes, without, within;
　Outward danger, inward sin.

3 Mindful of our only stay,
　Duly thus to Thee we pray;
　Duly thus to Thee we raise
　Trophies of our grateful praise.

4 Hear the prayer, almighty King;
　Hear Thy praises while we sing,
　Hymning with Thy heavenly host,
　Father, Son, and Holy Ghost.
　　Ambrose of Milan. (340–397.)
　　Tr. by Bp. Richard Mant. (1776–1848.)

973 "He spreadeth His light upon it." C. M.
Ps. cxxxix. Heb. i. 17–25. Ecc. xi. 6 to xii. 7.

1 GOD of the sunlight hours, how sad
　Would evening shadows be,
　Or night, in deeper sable clad,
　If aught were dark to Thee.

2 How mournfully that golden gleam
　Would touch the thoughtful heart,
　If with its soft, retiring beam,
　We saw Thy love depart.

3 But though the gathering gloom may hide
　Those gentle rays awhile,
　Yet they who in Thy house abide
　Shall ever share Thy smile.

4 Then let creation's volume close,
　Though every page be bright;
　On Thine, still open, we repose
　With more intense delight.
　　　　　Mrs. Maria G. Saffery. (1773–1858.)

974 "The day is far spent." S. M.
Luke xxiv. 13–29. Job xi. 7–19. Mal. iv.

1 THE day, O Lord, is spent,
　Abide with us, and rest;
　Our hearts' desires are fully bent
　On making Thee our Guest.

2 We have not reached that land,
　That happy land, as yet,
　Where holy angels round Thee stand,
　Whose sun can never set.

3 Our sun is sinking now,
　Our day is almost o'er;
　O Sun of Righteousness, do Thou
　Shine on us evermore.
　　　　　Rev. John M. Neale. (1818–1866.)

187

"The church in thy house."

975 " It shall be well with them that fear God."   8. 4.
2 Kings iv. 8-26. 1 Pet. iv. James i. 1-12.

1 THROUGH the love of God our Saviour,
  All will be well;
  Free and changeless is His favor;
  All, all is well.
  Precious is the blood that healed us,
  Perfect is the grace that sealed us;
  Strong the hand stretched out to shield us;
  All must be well.

2 Though we pass through tribulation
  All will be well;
  Ours is such a full salvation
  All, all is well.
  Happy, still in God confiding,
  Fruitful, if in Christ abiding,
  Holy, through the Spirit's guiding,
  All must be well.

3 We expect a bright to-morrow;
  All will be well.
  Faith can sing through days of sorrow,
  All, all is well.
  On our Father's love relying,
  Jesus every need supplying,
  Or in living, or in dying,
  All must be well.

Mrs. Mary B. Peters. (-1850.)

976   " Blessed are they that mourn."   8. 6.
Luke vi. 17-23. 2 Cor. i. 1-7. Isa. xl.

1 O BLESSED are the eyes that see,
    Though silent anguish show
  The love that in their hours of sleep
    Unthanked may come and go;
  And blessed are the ears that hear,
    Though kept awake by woe.

2 Happy are they that learn, in Thee,
    Though patient suffering teach
  The secret of enduring strength,
    And praise too deep for speech;
  Peace that no pressure from without,
    No strife within, can reach.

3 No suffering while it lasts is joy,
    How blest soe'er it be;
  Yet may the chastened child feel glad
    His Father's face to see;
  And O, it is not hard to bear
    What must be borne in Thee.

4 It is not hard to bear by faith,
    In Thy own bosom laid,
  The trial of a soul redeemed
    For Thy rejoicing made.
  Well may the heart in patience rest
    That none can make afraid.

Miss Anna L. Waring. (1820-.)

"The evening oblation."

977   " He satisfieth the longing soul."   11. 12.
Gen. xxii. 1-14. Mat. viii. Ex. xiv. 15-31.

1 IN some way or other
    The Lord will provide;
  It may not be my way
    It may not be thy way;
  And yet, in His own way,
    "The Lord will provide."

2 At some time or other
    The Lord will provide;
  It may not be my time,
    It may not be thy time;
  And yet, in His own time,
    "The Lord will provide."

3 Despond then no longer;
    The Lord will provide;
  And this be the token:
    No word He hath spoken
  Was ever yet broken:
    "The Lord will provide."

4 March on then right boldly;
    The sea shall divide;
  The pathway made glorious,
    With shoutings victorious,
  We'll join in the chorus,
    "The Lord will provide."

Mrs. Martha A. W. Cook. (1807-1874.)

978   " The God of all comfort."   6. 5.
Ps. cxxiv. Isa. lxiii. 2 Cor. iv. 6-18.

1 O LET him whose sorrow
    No relief can find,
  Trust in God, and borrow
    Ease for heart and mind!
  Where the mourner, weeping,
    Sheds the secret tear,
  God his watch is keeping,
    Though none else is near.

2 God will never leave us;
    All our wants He knows;
  Feels the pains that grieve us,
    Sees our cares and woes;
  When in grief we languish,
    He will dry the tear
  Who His children's anguish
    Soothes with succor near.

3 All our woe and sadness
    In this world below
  Equal not the gladness
    We in heaven shall know,
  When our gracious Saviour,
    In the realms above,
  Crowns us with His favor,
    Fills us with His love.

Henry S. Oswald. (1751-1837.)

"The church in thy house."   "The evening oblation."

979 "Thou hast been our dwelling place." C. M.
Ps. lxxvii. Isa. xxx. 15-29. Acts xvi. 25-40.

1 WE praise Thee oft for hours of bliss,
  For days of quiet rest;
  But O how seldom do we feel
  That pain and tears are best!

2 We praise Thee for the shining sun,
  For kind and gladsome ways;
  When shall we learn, O Lord, to sing
  Through weary nights and days?

3 We praise Thee when our path is plain
  And smooth beneath our feet;
  But fain would learn to welcome pain,
  And call the bitter sweet.

4 Teach Thou our weak and wand'ring hearts
  Aright to read Thy way;
  That Thou, with loving hand, dost trace
  Our story every day.
  John P. Hopps.

980 "Thy way is in the sea." C. M.
Ex. xiv. Ps. cvii. 23-31. Mat. xiv. 22-33.

1 THY way is in the deep, O Lord:
  E'en there we'll go with Thee;
  We'll meet the tempest at Thy word,
  And walk upon the sea.

2 Poor tremblers at His rougher wind,
  Why do we doubt Him so?
  Who gives the storm a path will find
  The way our feet shall go.

3 The Lord yields nothing to our fears,
  And flies from selfish care;
  But comes Himself where'er He hears
  The voice of loving prayer.
  Author unknown.

981 "Thou, Lord, wilt bless the righteous." S. M.
Ps. lxvi. 8-20. Rom. xiv. 1-9. Titus ii.

1 BLEST be Thy love, dear Lord,
  That taught us this sweet way,
  Only to love Thee for Thyself,
  And for that love obey.

2 O Thou our souls' chief Hope,
  We to Thy mercy fly;
  Where'er we are, Thou canst protect,
  Whate'er we need, supply.

3 Whether we sleep or wake,
  To Thee we both resign;
  By night we see, as well as day,
  If Thy light on us shine.

4 Whether we live or die,
  Both we submit to Thee;
  In death we live, as well as life,
  If Thine in death we be.
  John Austin. (1613-1669.)

982 "Peace,... like a river." C. M.
Eph. ii. John xiv. 15-29. Isa. lxvi. 5-13.

1 WE bless Thee for Thy peace, O God,
  Deep as the soundless sea,
  Which falls like sunshine on the road
  Of those who trust in Thee.

2 We ask not, Father, for repose
  Which comes from outward rest,
  If we may have through all life's woes
  Thy peace within our breast;

3 That peace which suffers and is strong,
  Trusts where it cannot see,
  Deems not the trial way too long,
  But leaves the end with Thee;

4 That peace which flows serene and deep,
  A river in the soul,
  Whose banks a living verdure keep:
  God's sunshine o'er the whole!

5 Such, Father, give our hearts such peace,
  Whate'er the outward be,
  Till all life's discipline shall cease,
  And we go home to Thee.
  Author unknown.

983 "We walk by faith, not by sight." L. M.
Heb. xi. 1-16. Gen. xii. 1-9. Job ii. 1-10.

1 'T IS by the faith of joys to come,
  We walk through deserts dark as night;
  Till we arrive at heaven, our home,
  Faith is our guide, and faith our light.

2 The want of sight she well supplies;
  She makes the pearly gates appear;
  Far into distant worlds she pries,
  And brings eternal glories near.

3 Cheerful we tread the desert through,
  While faith inspires a heavenly ray;
  Though lions roar and tempests blow,
  And rocks and dangers fill the way.
  Rev. Isaac Watts. (1674-1748.)

984 "God is light." L. M.
1 John i. 1-7. Luke i. 68-79. Zech. xiv. 1-11.

1 O GOD, the Light of all that live,
  Unmoved, who dost all motion sway,
  The times and seasons who dost give,
  And through its changes guide the day,

2 At eventide let there be light!
  So may our souls no sunset see,
  And death to us the portal bright
  To an eternal morning be.

3 This grace on Thy redeemed confer,
  O Father blessed, who, with the Son,
  And Holy Ghost, the Comforter,
  Forever reignest, Three in One!
  Author unknown.

"The church in thy house." "The evening oblation."

985 "God shall wipe away all tears." **11. 10.**
Luke vii. 11-15. John xi. 1-26. Mat. ix. 18-26. 2 Kings iv. 8-26.

1 WE will not weep; for God is standing by us,
   And tears will blind us to the blessed sight:
We will not doubt; if darkness still doth try us,
   Our souls have promise of serenest light.

2 We will not faint; if heavy burdens bind us,
   They press no harder than our souls can bear;
The thorniest way is lying still behind us,
   We shall be braver for the past despair.

3 O not in doubt shall be our journey's ending,
   Sin with its fears shall leave us at the last;
All its best hopes in glad fulfilment blending,
   Life shall be with us when the death is past.

4 Help us, O Father, when the world is pressing
   On our frail hearts that faint without our friend;
Help us, O Father! Let Thy constant blessing
   Strengthen our weakness till the joyful end.
William H. Hurlbut. (1827-)

986 "The word of our God shall stand forever." **11.**
Gen. xxviii. 10-22. Deu. xxxi. 1-8. Josh. xiv. 6-14. 1 Pet. i.

1 How firm a foundation, ye saints of the Lord,
Is laid for your faith in His excellent word!
What more can He say than to you He hath said,
Who unto the Saviour for refuge have fled?

2 In every condition, in sickness and health,
In poverty's vale or abounding in wealth,
At home and abroad, on the land, on the sea,
As thy days may demand shall thy strength ever be.

3 E'en down to old age all my people shall prove
My sov'reign, eternal, unchangeable love;
And when hoary hairs shall their temples adorn,
Like lambs they shall still in my bosom be borne.
George Keith. 1787.

987 "Fear not; for I am with thee." **11.**
Isa. xliii. Ps. cvi. 1-12. Dan. iii. 16-27. Acts xxvi. 1-29.

1 FEAR not, I am with thee, O be not dismayed;
For I am thy God, and will still give thee aid;
I'll strengthen thee, help thee, and cause thee to stand,
Upheld by my righteous, omnipotent hand.

2 When through the deep waters I call thee to go,
The rivers of sorrow shall not overflow;
For I will be with thee, thy troubles to bless,
And sanctify to thee thy deepest distress.

3 When through fiery trials thy pathway shall lie,
My grace, all-sufficient, shall be thy supply;
The flame shall not hurt thee; I only design
Thy dross to consume and thy gold to refine.

4 The soul that on Jesus doth lean for repose,
I will not, I will not desert to His foes;
That soul, though all hell should endeavor to shake,
I'll never, no, never, no, never forsake.
George Keith. 1787.

"The children which God hath graciously given."

988 "Suffer little children to come unto me." **L. M.**
Isa. ix. 1-7,. Luke ii. 1-14. Mat. xix. 13-15.

1 A LITTLE child the Saviour came,
　The mighty God was still His name,
　And angels worshipped, as He lay,
　The seeming infant of a day.

2 He who, a little child, began
　The life divine to show to man,
　Proclaims from heaven the message free,
　"Let little children come to me."

3 O give Thine angels charge, good Lord,
　Them safely in Thy way to guard ;
　Thy blessing on their lives command,
　And write their names upon Thy hand.

4 O Thou, who by an infant's tongue
　Dost hear Thy perfect glory sung,
　May these with all the heavenly host
　Praise Father, Son, and Holy Ghost.
　　　　　Rev. William Robertson. (-1743.)

989 "The children of Thy servants." **S. M.**
Gen. xvii. 1-9. Ps. lxxviii. 1-8. 2 John.

1 O GOD of Abra'm, hear
　The parents' humble cry ;
　In covenant mercy now appear,
　While in the dust we lie.

2 These children of our love
　In mercy Thou hast given,
　That we through grace may faithful prove,
　In training them for heaven.

3 O grant Thy Spirit, Lord,
　Their hearts to sanctify ;
　Remember now Thy gracious word :
　Our hopes on Thee rely.

4 These children now are Thine,
　We give them back to Thee ;
　O lead them by Thy grace divine,
　Along the heavenly way.
　　　　　Thomas Hastings. (1784-1872.)

990 "Forbid them not." **S. M.**
Mark x. 13-16. Gal. iii. 1-9. Gen. xv. 1-6.

1 THE gentle Saviour calls
　Our children to His breast ;
　He folds them in His gracious arms,
　Himself declares them blest.

2 "Let them approach." He cries,
　"Nor scorn their humble claim ;
　The heirs of heaven are such as these,
　For such as these I came."

3 Gladly we bring them, Lord,
　Devoting them to Thee,
　Imploring that, as we are Thine,
　Thine may our offspring be.
　　　　　Bp. Henry U. Onderdonk. (1789-1858.)

991 "He shall be lent to the Lord." **L. M.**
1 Sam. i. Isa. viii. 11-18. Heb. ii. 11-18.

1 GOD of that glorious gift of grace
　By which Thy people seek Thy face,
　When in Thy presence we appear,
　Vouchsafe us faith to venture near.

2 Confiding in Thy truth alone,
　Here, on the steps of Jesus' throne,
　We lay the treasure Thou hast given
　To be received and reared for heaven.

3 Lent to us for a season, we
　Lend him forever, Lord, to Thee :
　Assured that if to Thee he live,
　We gain in what we seem to give.

4 Make him and keep him Thine own child,
　Meek follower of the Undefiled ;
　Possessor here of grace and love,
　Inheritor of heaven above.
　　　　　Rev. John S. B. Monsell. (1811-1875.)

992 "Thy children shall be taught of the Lord." **L. M.**
Acts xvi. 25-34. Ps. ciii. 17, 18. Deu. vii. 6-9.

1 FATHER, in these reveal Thy Son,
　In these for whom we seek Thy face ;
　Adopt and seal them as Thine own,
　By Thy regenerating grace.

2 Jesus, with us Thou always art,
　Now ratify the sacred sign,
　The gift unspeakable impart,
　And bless Thy sacrament divine.

3 Come, Holy Spirit, from on high,
　Baptizer of our spirits, Thou !
　The purifying grace apply
　And witness with the water now.

4 Pour forth Thine energy divine,
　And sprinkle the atoning blood ;
　May Father, Son, and Spirit join
　To seal each child a child of God.
　　　　　Rev. Charles Wesley. (1708-1788.)

993 "Jesus called them unto Him." **L. M.**
Luke xviii. 15-17. 2 Tim. iii. 15. Ex. xxxiv. 7.

1 O LORD, encouraged by Thy grace,
　We bring our infant to Thy throne :
　Give it within Thy heart a place,
　Let it be Thine, and Thine alone.

2 Wash it from every stain of guilt,
　And let this child be sanctified ;
　Lord, Thou canst cleanse it, if Thou wilt,
　And all its native evils hide.

3 We ask not for it earthly bliss,
　Or earthly honors, wealth, or fame.
　The sum of our request is this,
　That it may love and fear Thy name.
　　　　　Miss Anne Steele. (1717-1778.)

"The children which God hath graciously given."

994 "He took them up in His arms." C. M.
Mark x. 16. Acts xvi. 33. Isa. xlix. 13-26.

1 See Israel's gentle Shepherd stand,
   With all-engaging charms !
Hark, how He calls the tender lambs,
   And folds them in His arms !

2 "Permit them to approach," He cries,
   "Nor scorn their humble name ;
For 't was to bless such souls as these,
   The Lord of angels came."

3 We bring them, Lord, in thankful hands,
   And yield them up to Thee ;
Joyful that we ourselves are Thine,
   Thine let our offspring be.

4 Ye little flock, with pleasure hear !
   Ye children, seek his face !
And fly, with transport, to receive
   The blessings of His grace.
                   Rev. Philip Doddridge. (1703-1751.)

995 "He shall lead His flock like a shepherd." 6. 4.
Eze. xxxiv. 23-31. Jer. xxxi. 10. 1 Cor. i. 30

1 SHEPHERD of tender youth,
   Guiding in love and truth
Through devious ways ;
Christ our triumphant King,
We come Thy name to sing ;
Hither our children bring
   To shout Thy praise.

2 Thou art our Holy Lord,
   The all-subduing Word,
      Healer of strife ;
Thou didst Thyself abase,
That from sin's deep disgrace
Thou mightest save our race,
   And give us life.

3 Thou art the great High Priest,
Thou hast prepared the feast
   Of heavenly love ;
While in our mortal pain
None calls on Thee in vain ;
Help Thou dost not disdain,
   Help from above.

4 Ever be Thou our Guide,
   Our Shepherd and our Pride,
      Our Staff and Song ;
Jesus, Thou Christ of God,
By Thy perennial word
Lead us where Thou hast trod,
   Make our faith strong.
                   Clement of Alexandria. (-220.)
                   Tr. by Rev. Henry M. Dexter. (1821-)

996 "He shall gather the lambs with His arm." L. M.
Mat. xix. 13-15. John x. 11-16. Ps. xxiii.

1 WITH thankful hearts our songs we raise
To celebrate the Saviour's praise ;
Yet who but saints in heaven above
Can tell the riches of His love ?

2 He, the good Shepherd, kindly leads
The wanderer, and the hungry feeds ;
Deigns in His arms the lambs to bear,
And makes them His peculiar care.

3 Jesus, to Thy protecting wing
Our helpless little ones we bring ;
O grant them grace and strength, that they
May find and keep the heavenward way.
                   Rev. Edward Bickersteth. (1783-1850.)

997 "They brought young children to Him." 8. 7.
Isa. xl. 9-11. Job i. 1-5. Heb. xiii. 20, 21.

1 SAVIOUR, who Thy flock art feeding,
   With the shepherd's kindest care,
All the feeble gently leading,
   While the lambs Thy bosom share ;

2 Now, these little ones receiving,
   Fold them in Thy gracious arm ;
There, we know, Thy word believing,
   Only there, secure from harm.

3 Never, from Thy pasture roving,
   Let them be the lion's prey ;
Let Thy tenderness, so loving,
   Keep them all life's dangerous way.

4 Then within Thy fold eternal
   Let them find a resting place ;
Feed in pastures ever vernal,
   Drink the rivers of Thy grace.
                   Rev. William A. Muhlenberg. (1796-1877.)

998 "Thy children shall come again." L. M.
Luke xviii. 15-17. Heb. ii. 11-13. Prov. iii.

1 DEAR Saviour, if these lambs should stray
   From Thy secure enclosure's bound,
And, lured by worldly joys away,
   Among the thoughtless crowd be found ;

2 Remember still that they are Thine,
   That Thy dear sacred name they bear ;
Think that the seal of love divine,
   The sign of covenant grace, they wear.

3 In all their erring, sinful years,
   O let them ne'er forgotten be ;
Remember all the prayers and tears
   Which made them consecrate to Thee.

4 And when these lips no more can pray,
   These eyes can weep for them no more,
Turn Thou their feet from folly's way,
   The wanderers to Thy fold restore.
                   Mrs. Ann B. Hyde. (-1872.)

"And children: let them praise."

999 "The children crying in the temple." 7.6
Mat. xxi. 1-16. Ps. viii. Isa. xi. 1-9.

1 WHEN, His salvation bringing,
  To Zion Jesus came,
The children all stood singing
  Hosanna to His name.
Nor did their zeal offend Him,
  But as He rode along,
He let them still attend Him,
  And smiled to hear their song.

2 And since the Lord retaineth
  His love to children still,
Though now as King He reigneth
  On Zion's heavenly hill;
We'll flock around His banner,
  We'll bow before His throne,
And cry aloud, Hosanna
  To David's royal Son.
              Rev. John King. (1788-1858.)

1000 "That the generation to come might know." C. M.
Ps. lxxviii. 1-8. Deu. vi. 6-15. Eph. vi. 1-4.

1 LET children hear the mighty deeds
  Which God performed of old,
Which in our younger years we saw,
  And which our fathers told.

2 Thus shall they learn in God alone
  Their hope securely stands,
That they may ne'er forget His works,
  But practice His commands.
              Rev. Isaac Watts. (1674-1748.)

1001 "Come, ye children, hearken unto me." 8. 7. 4.
Ps. xxxiv. 11. Prov. viii. Mat. vi. 24-34.

1 CHILDREN, hear the melting story
  Of the Lamb that once was slain;
'T is the Lord of Life and Glory:
  Shall He plead with you in vain?
    O receive Him,
  And salvation now obtain.

2 Yield no more to sin and folly,
  So displeasing in His sight:
Jesus loves the pure and holy;
  They alone are His delight:
    Seek His favor,
  And your hearts to Him unite.

3 All your sins to Him confessing
  Who is ready to forgive,
Seek the Saviour's richest blessing,
  On His precious name believe;
    He is waiting,
  Will you not His grace receive?
              Thomas Hastings. (1784-1872.)

13

1002 "I am the good Shepherd." 8. 7. 4.
John x. Eze. xxxiv. 11-16. Deu. xi. 18.

1 SAVIOUR, like a shepherd lead us,
  Much we need Thy tender care;
In Thy pleasant pastures feed us,
  For our use Thy folds prepare.
    Blessèd Jesus,
  Thou hast bought us, Thine we are.

2 We are Thine, do Thou befriend us,
  Be the guardian of our way;
Keep Thy flock, from sin defend us,
  Seek us when we go astray;
    Blessèd Jesus,
  Hear the children when they pray.

3 Thou hast promised to receive us,
  Poor and sinful though we be;
Thou hast mercy to relieve us,
  Grace to cleanse, and power to free;
    Blessèd Jesus,
  Let us early turn to Thee.

4 Early let us seek Thy favor,
  Early let us do Thy will;
Holy Lord, our only Saviour,
  With Thy grace our bosoms fill;
    Blessèd Jesus,
  Thou hast loved us, love us still.
              Miss Dorothy A. Thrupp. (1779-1847.)

1003 "The Lord had called the child." C. M.
Mat. xviii. 1-10. Ps. xxiii. 1 Sam. iii.

1 DEAR Jesus, ever at my side,
  How loving must Thou be,
To leave Thy home in heaven to guard
  A little child like me.

2 I cannot feel Thee touch my hand
  With pressure light and mild,
To check me as my mother did,
  When I was but a child.

3 But I have felt Thee in my thoughts,
  Rebuking sin for me;
And, when my heart loves God, I know
  The sweetness is from Thee.

4 And when, dear Saviour, I kneel down,
  Morning and night, to prayer,
Something there is within my heart
  Which tells me Thou art there.

5 Yes, when I pray, Thou prayest too;
  Thy prayer is all for me;
But when I sleep, Thou sleepest not,
  But watchest patiently.
              Rev. Frederick W. Faber. (1814-1863.)

"And children: let them praise."

1004 " By night on my bed I sought Him." 8, 7,
Luke xviii. 15-17. Isa. xl. 10, 11. Ps. xvi.

1 JESUS, tender Shepherd, hear me,
  Bless Thy little lamb to-night;
  Through the darkness be Thou near me,
  Keep me safe till morning light.

2 All this day Thy hand has led me,
  And I thank Thee for Thy care;
  Thou hast clothed me, warmed and fed me,
  Listen to my evening prayer.

3 Let my sins be all forgiven,
  Bless the friends I love so well;
  Take me, when I die, to heaven,
  Happy there with Thee to dwell.
  Mrs. Mary L. Duncan. (1814-1840.)

1005 " Redeeming the time." 8. 7, 4,
Mat. xxi. 28-32. Mark iv. 1-20. Ruth ii.

1 IN the vineyard of our Father
  Daily work we find to do;
  Scattered gleanings we may gather,
  Though we are but young and few;
  Little clusters
  Help to fill the garners too.

2 Toiling early in the morning,
  Catching moments through the day,
  Nothing small or lowly scorning,
  While we work, and watch, and pray;
  Gathering gladly
  Free-will offerings by the way.

3 Up and ever at our calling,
  Till in death our lips are dumb,
  Or till, sin's dominion falling,
  Christ shall in His kingdom come,
  And His children
  Reach their everlasting home.
  Thomas MacKellar. (1812-.)

1006 " Of such is the kingdom of heaven." 8, 6, 5,
Mal. iii. 17. Mat. xxiv. 42-46. Titus ii. 13.

1 WHEN He cometh, when He cometh
  To make up His jewels,
  All His jewels, precious jewels,
  His loved and His own.

  Like the stars of the morning,
  His bright crown adorning,
  They shall shine in their beauty,
  Bright gems for His crown.

2 He will gather, He will gather
  The gems for His kingdom:
  All the pure ones, all the bright ones,
  His loved and His own.

3 Little children, little children,
  Who love their Redeemer,
  Are the jewels, precious jewels,
  His loved and His own.
  Rev. William O. Cushing. (1823-.)

1007 " They shall walk and not faint." 7,
Mark x. 13-15. Ps. xxiv. Rev. xv. 1-4.

1 LITTLE travellers Zionward,
  Each one entering into rest,
  In the kingdom of your Lord,
  In the mansions of the blest;
  There, to welcome, Jesus waits,
  Gives the crowns His followers win:
  Lift your heads, ye golden gates,
  Let the little travellers in.

2 Who are they whose little feet,
  Pacing life's dark journey through,
  Now have reached that heavenly seat
  They had ever kept in view?
  " I from Greenland's frozen land;"
  " I from India's sultry plain;"
  " I from Afric's barren sand;"
  " I from islands of the main."

3 All our earthly journey past,
  Every tear and pain gone by,
  Here together met at last
  At the portal of the sky:
  Each the welcome, " Come," awaits,
  Conquerors over death and sin;
  Lift your heads, ye golden gates,
  Let the little travellers in.
  James Edmeston. (1791-1867.)

1008 " Hosanna to the Son of David." C. M.
Rev. vii. 9-12. Mat. xix. 14. Ps. cii. 28.

1 AROUND the throne of God in heaven
  Thousands of children stand;
  Children whose sins are all forgiven,
  A holy, happy band,
    Singing, Glory, glory,
    Glory be to God on high.

2 In flowing robes of spotless white
  See every one arrayed;
  Dwelling in everlasting light,
  And joys that never fade.

3 What brought them to that world above,
  That heaven so bright and fair,
  Where all is peace, and joy, and love,
  How came those children there?

4 Because the Saviour shed His blood,
  To wash away their sin;
  Bathed in that pure and precious flood,
  Behold them white and clean.

5 On earth they sought the Saviour's grace,
  On earth they loved His name;
  So now they see His blessèd face,
  And stand before the Lamb.
  Mrs. Anne H. Shepherd. (1809-1857.)

"Give ear, O God of Jacob."

1009 Ps. xcix. "These three are one." Dan. vii. 9-14. Acts i. 1-14.   6. 4.

1 COME, Thou Almighty King,
Help us Thy name to sing,
Help us to praise:
Father, all-glorious,
O'er all victorious,
Come and reign over us,
Ancient of days!

2 Come, Thou Incarnate Word,
Gird on Thy mighty sword;
Our prayer attend:
Come, and Thy people bless,
And give Thy word success;
Spirit of holiness,
On us descend!

3 Come, Holy Comforter,
Thy sacred witness bear,
In this glad hour:
Thou, who almighty art,
Now rule in every heart,
And ne'er from us depart,
Spirit of power!

Rev. Charles Wesley. (1708-1788.)

1010 Ps. xc. "Hear, Lord, the voice of Judah." Luke xi. 1-13. Acts. ix. 17-21.   S. M.

1 OUR Father, who dost lead
The children of Thy grace,
A new-born and believing seed,
Through this wide wilderness:
Thy providential care
In dangers past we own;
Still let Thine arm be ever near;
Still let Thy love be shown.

2 O Saviour, Lamb of God,
Our gracious dying Friend,
Reveal the virtue of Thy blood,
On us Thy mercy send;
Thou art a Master kind,
With voice and person sweet;
Bestow on us a loving mind,
And keep us at Thy feet.

3 Thou, Holy Spirit, art
Of truth the promised seal;
Convincing power Thou dost impart,
And Jesus' grace reveal:
O breathe Thy quickening breath,
And light and life afford;
Instruct us how to live by faith,
And glorify the Lord.

Author unknown.

1011 2 Chr. vi. 1-21. "Hearken Thou to ... Thy people." Dan. ix. 3-19. 1 John v.   7.

1 FATHER, at Thy footstool see
Those who now are one in Thee;
Draw us by Thy grace alone;
Give, O give us to Thy Son.

2 Jesus, Friend of human kind,
Let us in Thy name be joined;
Each to each unite and bless;
Keep us still in perfect peace.

3 Heavenly, all-alluring Dove,
Shed Thine overshadowing love;
Love, the sealing grace, impart,
Dwell within our single heart.

4 Father, Son, and Holy Ghost,
Be to us what Adam lost:
Let us in Thine image rise;
Give us back our Paradise.

Rev. Charles Wesley.

1012 Mat. xxviii. 16-20. "O God of hosts, look down from heaven" John iv. 1-15. Ps. li.   L. M.

1 COME, Father, Son, and Holy Ghost,
Whom one all-perfect God we own,
Restorer of Thine image lost,
Thy various offices make known.

2 Jehovah, in three persons, come,
And draw, and sprinkle us, and seal,
Poor, guilty, dying worms, in whom
Thou wilt eternal life reveal.

3 Our fallen, ruined souls to raise,
The knowledge of Thyself bestow;
Reveal the riches of Thy grace,
And all Thy glorious goodness show.

Rev. Charles Wesley.

1013 John iii. 14-17. "Hear, O our God." Ex. xxx. 11-16. 1 Pet. i.   L. M.

1 FATHER of heaven, whose love profound
A ransom for our souls hath found,
Before Thy throne we sinners bend:
To us Thy pardoning love extend.

2 Almighty Son, incarnate Word,
Our Prophet, Priest, Redeemer, Lord,
Before Thy throne we sinners bend:
To us Thy saving grace extend.

3 Eternal Spirit, by whose breath
The soul is raised from sin and death,
Before Thy throne we sinners bend:
To us Thy quickening power extend.

4 Jehovah, Father, Spirit, Son,
Mysterious Godhead, Three in One,
Before Thy throne we sinners bend:
Grace, pardon, life, to us extend.

John Cooper. 1810.

"Give ear, O God of Jacob."

1014 "Hear Thou in heaven, Thy dwelling." 8. 7. 4.
Mat. xviii. 19, 20. 1 Sam. iii. Ps. lxxxix.

1 IN Thy name, O Lord, assembling,
   We, Thy people, now draw near :
   Teach us to rejoice with trembling ;
   Speak, and let Thy servants hear,
      Hear with meekness,
   Hear Thy word with godly fear.

2 While our days on earth are lengthened,
   May we give them, Lord, to Thee ;
   Cheered by hope, and daily strengthened,
   May we run, nor weary be,
      Till Thy glory
   Without clouds in heaven we see.

3 There in worship purer, sweeter,
   Thee Thy people shall adore ;
   Tasting of enjoyment greater
   Far than thought conceived before ;
      Full enjoyment,
   Full, unmixed, and evermore.
                    Rev. Thomas Kelly. (1769-1855.)

1015 "Hearken unto the prayer." 7.
Ps. lxxxiv. Isa. lvi. 3-7. Heb. xii. 18-24.

1 IN Thy presence we appear;
   Lord, we love to worship here,
   When, within the veil, we meet
   Thee upon Thy mercy-seat.

2 While Thy glorious name is sung,
   Touch our lips, and loose our tongue ;
   Then our joyful souls shall bless
   Thee, the Lord our Righteousness.

3 While to Thee our prayers ascend,
   Let Thine ear in love attend ;
   Hear, for Jesus intercedes ;
   Hear us, for Thy Spirit pleads.

4 While Thy word is heard with awe,
   And we tremble at the law,
   Let Thy gospel's wondrous love
   Every doubt and fear remove.

5 While Thy ministers proclaim
   Peace and pardon through Thy name,
   In their voices let us own
   Jesus, speaking from the throne.

6 From Thy house when we return,
   Let our hearts within us burn ;
   That at evening we may say,
   We have walked with God to-day.
                    James Montgomery. (1771-1854.)

1016 "Hear Thou their supplication." C. M.
Ps. lxxvi. John xx. 19-31. Acts xiii. 44-50.

1 AGAIN our earthly cares we leave,
   And in Thy courts appear;
   Again with joyful feet we come
   To meet our Saviour here.

2 Within these walls let holy peace
   And love and concord dwell :
   Here give the troubled conscience ease,
   The wounded spirit heal.

3 The feeling heart, the melting eye,
   The humble mind, bestow,
   And shine upon us from on high
   To make our graces grow.

4 May we in faith receive Thy word,
   In faith present our prayers,
   And in the presence of our Lord
   Unbosom all our cares.

5 Show us some token of Thy love,
   Our fainting hope to raise,
   And pour Thy blessing from above,
   That we may render praise.
                    Rev. John Newton. (1725-1807.)

1017 "The Lord our God be with us." 6. 5.
2 Chr. vi. Ps. xlvi. Luke i. 68-79.

1 GOD of our salvation,
      Unto Thee we pray ;
   Hear our supplication,
      Be our Strength and Stay.
   Wretched and unworthy,
      Poor, and sick, and blind,
   Prostrate we adore Thee,
      Call Thy grace to mind.

2 He that dwelleth near Thee
      Safely shall abide ;
   Ever love and fear Thee,
      In Thy strength confide.
   Sure is Thy protection,
      Safe is Thy defence,
   While in deep affliction,
      Woe, or pestilence.

3 God of our salvation,
      Saviour, Prince of Peace,
   Boundless Thy compassion,
      Infinite Thy grace.
   While with love unceasing
      Humbly we adore,
   Grant us Thy rich blessing,
      And we ask no more.
                              Author unknown.

"Give ear, O God of Jacob."

1018 "Hear Thou from Thy dwelling-place." **L. M.**
Ps. lxviii. 1-19. Acts x. 30-33. Col. i. 21-29.

1 THY presence, gracious God, afford ;
  Prepare us to receive Thy word ;
  Now let Thy voice engage our ear,
  And faith be mixed with what we hear.

2 Distracting thoughts and cares remove,
  And fix our hearts and hopes above ;
  With food divine may we be fed,
  And satisfied with living bread.

3 To us Thy sacred word apply,
  With sovereign power and energy ;
  And may we, in Thy faith and fear,
  Reduce to practice what we hear.

4 Father, in us Thy Son reveal ;
  Teach us to know and do Thy will ;
  Thy saving power and love display,
  And guide us to the realms of day.
  Rev. John Fawcett. (1739-1817.)

1019 "God be merciful to us and bless us." **C. M.**
Heb. xiii. Ps. cxix. 129. John xiv. 15-26.

1 BEFORE Thy mercy-seat, O Lord,
  Behold Thy servants stand,
  To ask the knowledge of Thy word,
  The guidance of Thy hand.

2 Lord, from Thy word remove the seal,
  Unfold its hidden store ;
  And as we hear, O may we feel
  Its value more and more.

3 Help us to see the Saviour's love
  Beaming from every page ;
  And let the thoughts of joys above
  Our inmost souls engage.

4 Let Thy eternal truths, we pray,
  Dwell richly in each heart ;
  That from the safe and narrow way
  We never may depart.
  Rev. William H. Bathurst. (1796-.)

1020 "Make us glad." **L. M.**
Ps. lxxxiv. Isa. lviii. 13, 14. 1 Cor. ii. 9-16.

1 GREAT God, attend while Zion sings
  The joy that from Thy presence springs ;
  To spend one day with Thee on earth
  Exceeds a thousand days of mirth.

2 God is our Sun, He makes our day ;
  God is our Shield, he guards our way
  From all th' assaults of hell and sin,
  From foes without and foes within.

3 All needful grace will God bestow,
  And crown that grace with glory, too ;
  He gives us all things, and withholds
  No real good from upright souls.
  Rev. Isaac Watts. (1674-1748.)

1021 "O Thou that hearest prayer." **H. M.**
Luke xi. 1-13. John xiv. 1-17. Eze. xxxvi.

1 O THOU that hearest prayer,
  Attend our humble cry ;
  And let Thy servants share
  Thy blessing from on high :
  We plead the promise of Thy word ;
  Grant us Thy Holy Spirit, Lord !

2 If earthly parents hear
  Their children when they cry ;
  If they, with love sincere,
  Their children's wants supply ;
  Much more wilt Thou Thy love display,
  And answer when Thy children pray.

3 Our Heavenly Father, Thou ;
  We, children of Thy grace :
  O let Thy Spirit now
  Descend and fill the place ;
  That all may feel the heavenly flame,
  And all unite to praise Thy name.
  John Burton. (1803-.)

1022 "Let Thy saints rejoice in goodness." **7.**
Neh. i. 1-11. Isa. xxvi. 1-14. Mat. xi. 1-6.

1 LORD, we come before Thee now,
  At Thy feet we humbly bow ;
  O do not our suit disdain,
  Shall we seek Thee, Lord, in vain ?

2 Lord, on Thee our souls depend,
  In compassion now descend ;
  Fill our hearts with Thy rich grace,
  Tune our lips to sing Thy praise.

3 In Thine own appointed way
  Now we seek Thee, here we stay ;
  Lord, we know not how to go,
  Till a blessing Thou bestow.

4 Send some message from Thy word,
  That may joy and peace afford ;
  Let Thy Spirit now impart
  Full salvation to each heart.

5 Comfort those who weep and mourn,
  Let the time of joy return ;
  Those that are cast down lift up,
  Strong in faith, in love, and hope.

6 Grant that those who seek may find
  Thee a God sincere and kind ;
  Heal the sick, the captive free,
  Let us all rejoice in Thee.
  Rev. William Hammond. (1719-1783.)

"We would see Jesus."

1023 "When Thou hearest, forgive." 7.
Heb. ii. 8-18. Ps. xxxii. Acts v. 19-32.

1 SAVIOUR, when in dust to Thee
Low we bend the adoring knee;
When, repentant, to the skies
Scarce we lift our weeping eyes;
O, by all the pains and woe
Suffered once for man below,
Bending from Thy throne on high,
Hear our solemn Litany!

2 By Thy helpless infant years;
By thy life of want and tears;
By Thy days of sore distress
In the savage wilderness;
By the dread, mysterious hour
Of the insulting tempter's power;
Turn, O turn a favoring eye,
Hear our solemn Litany!

3 By Thine hour of dire despair;
By Thine agony of prayer;
By the cross, the nail, the thorn,
Piercing spear, and torturing scorn;
By the gloom that veiled the skies
O'er the dreadful sacrifice;
Listen to our humble cry,
Hear our solemn Litany!

4 By Thy deep expiring groan;
By the sad sepulchral stone;
By the vault, whose dark abode
Held in vain the rising God;
O, from earth to heaven restored,
Mighty reascended Lord,
Listen, listen to the cry
Of our solemn Litany!

Sir Robert Grant. (1785-1838.)

1024 "Where two or three are gathered." L. M.
Mat. xviii. 19, 20. John xx. 19-29. Ps. cxlv.

1 "WHERE two or three, with sweet accord,
Obedient to their sovereign Lord,
Meet to recount His acts of grace,
And offer solemn prayer and praise;

2 "There," says the Saviour, "will I be,
Amid this little company;
To them unveil my smiling face,
And shed my glories round the place."

3 We meet at Thy command, dear Lord,
Relying on Thy faithful word;
Now send Thy Spirit from above;
Now fill our hearts with heavenly love.

Rev. Samuel Stennett. (1727-1795.)

1025 "Desiring to see Thee." L. M.
John iv. 19-26. Acts xvii. 22-28. Mal. i. 1-11.

1 JESUS, where'er Thy people meet,
There they behold Thy mercy-seat;
Where'er they seek Thee, Thou art found,
And every place is hallowed ground.

2 For Thou, within no walls confined,
Inhabitest the humble mind;
Such ever bring Thee where they come,
And, going, take Thee to their home.

3 Dear Shepherd of Thy chosen few,
Thy former mercies here renew;
Here to our waiting hearts proclaim
The sweetness of Thy saving name.

4 Here may we prove the power of prayer
To strengthen faith, and sweeten care,
To teach our faint desires to rise,
And bring all heaven before our eyes.

William Cowper. (1731-1800.)

1026 "Let us worship and bow down." C. M.
1 Kings vii. Ps. lxvi. Luke ix. 24-38.

1 LORD, when we bend before Thy throne,
And our confessions pour,
O may we feel the sins we own,
And hate what we deplore.

2 Our contrite spirits pitying see;
True penitence impart;
And let a healing ray from Thee
Beam peace into each heart.

3 When we disclose our wants in prayer,
May we our wills resign;
And not a thought our bosom share
Which is not wholly Thine.

4 And when, with heart and voice, we strive
Our grateful hymns to raise,
Let love divine within us live,
And fill our souls with praise.

5 Let faith each meek petition fill,
And waft it to the skies,
And teach our hearts 't is goodness still
That grants it, or denies.

Rev. Joseph D. Carlyle. (1750-1801.)

1027 "Come and save us" C. M.
Mat. xx. 29-34. Mark ix. 14-29. Ps. lxxx.

1 HEAL us, Emmanuel; here we stand
Waiting to feel Thy touch:
To wounded souls stretch forth Thy hand;
Blest Saviour, we are such.

2 With wants, and doubts, and fears we come
To touch Thee if we may;
O send us not despairing home,
Send none unhealed away.

William Cowper.

"We would see Jesus."

1028 "We will wait upon Thee." C. M.
Acts i. 13-26. Rev. iii. 18-22. Dan. ix. 3-19.

1 SEE, Jesus, Thy disciples see;
   The promised blessing give;
   Met in Thy name, we look to Thee,
   Expecting to receive.

2 Thee we expect, our faithful Lord,
   Who in Thy name are joined;
   We wait, according to Thy word,
   Thee in the midst to find.

3 With us Thou art assembled here,
   But O, Thyself reveal;
   Son of the living God, appear;
   Let us Thy presence feel.

4 Breathe on us, Lord, in this our day,
   And these dry bones shall live;
   Speak peace into our hearts, and say,
   The Holy Ghost receive.
   Rev. Charles Wesley. (1708-1788.)

1031 "Quicken us, and we will call upon Thy name." C. M.
Ps. xxviii. 1 Pet. i. 3-9. Rev. v

1 COME, Lord, and warm each languid heart,
   Inspire each lifeless tongue,
   And let the joys of heaven impart
   Their influence to our song.

2 Then to the shining seats of bliss
   The wings of faith shall soar,
   And all the charms of paradise
   Our raptured thoughts explore.

3 There shall the foll'wers of the Lamb
   Join in immortal songs;
   And endless honors to His name
   Employ their tuneful tongues.

4 Lord, tune our hearts to praise and love,
   Our feeble notes inspire;
   Till, in Thy blissful courts above,
   We join the heavenly choir.
   Miss Anne Steele. (1717-1778.)

1029 "And sought to see Jesus." 11. 10.
John xii. 20-22. Job x. Ps. xl. 1 Cor. xv. 50-57.

1 WE would see Jesus, for the shadows lengthen
   Across this little landscape of our life;
   We would see Jesus our weak faith to strengthen,
   For the last weariness, the final strife.

2 We would see Jesus, the great Rock foundation,
   Whereon our feet were set by sovereign grace;
   Not life, nor death, with all their agitation,
   Can thence remove us, if we see His face.

3 We would see Jesus; other lights are paling,
   Which for long years we have rejoiced to see;
   The blessings of our pilgrimage are failing,
   We would not mourn them, for we go to Thee.

4 We would see Jesus; this is all we're needing,
   Strength, joy, and willingness come with the sight;
   We would see Jesus, dying, risen, pleading,
   Then welcome day, and farewell mortal night!
   Author unknown.

1030 "Come, Lord Jesus." L. M.
Eph. iii. 14-21. John xiv. Isa. lvii. 15-19.

1 COME, dearest Lord, descend and dwell,
   By faith and love, in every breast;
   Then shall we know, and taste, and feel
   The joys that cannot be expressed.

2 Come, fill our hearts with inward strength,
   Make our enlargéd souls possess,
   And learn the height and breadth and length
   Of Thine unmeasurable grace.

3 Now to the God whose power can do
   More than our thoughts or wishes know,
   Be everlasting honors done,
   By all the church, through Christ, His Son.
   Rev. Isaac Watts. (1674-1748.)

1032 "Jesus in the midst." L. M.
Mat. xviii. 19, 20. Luke ix. 28-36. Ps. lxii.

1 How sweet to leave the world awhile,
   And seek the presence of our Lord!
   Dear Saviour, on Thy people smile,
   And come, according to Thy word.

2 From busy scenes we now retreat,
   That we may here converse with Thee:
   Ah, Lord, behold us at Thy feet;
   Let this the gate of heaven be.

3 Chief of ten thousand, now appear,
   That we by faith may see Thy face;
   O speak, that we Thy voice may hear,
   And let Thy presence fill this place.
   Rev. Thomas Kelly. (1769-1855.)

"We would see Jesus."

1033 "We will run after Thee." C. M.
1 Kings viii. 22-30. Hag. ii. 1 John v.

1 COME, thou Desire of all Thy saints,
  Our humble strains attend,
  While, with our praises and complaints,
  Low at Thy feet we bend.

2 How should our songs, like those above,
  With warm devotion rise !
  How should our souls on wings of love
  Mount upward to the skies !

3 Come, Lord, Thy love alone can raise
  In us the heavenly flame ;
  Then shall our lips resound Thy praise,
  Our hearts adore Thy name.

4 Dear Saviour, let Thy glory shine,
  And fill Thy dwellings here,
  Till life, and love, and joy divine
  A heaven on earth appear.
  Miss Anne Steele. (1717-1778.)

1034 "That we may find grace to help." L. M.
John xiv. 1-19. 2 Cor. iii. 7-18. Ps. lvii.

1 O CHRIST, who hast prepared a place
  For us around Thy throne of grace,
  We pray Thee, lift our hearts above,
  And draw them with the cords of love.

2 Source of all good, Thou, gracious Lord,
  Art our exceeding great Reward ;
  How transient is our present pain,
  How boundless our eternal gain !

3 With open face and joyful heart,
  We then shall see Thee as Thou art :
  Our love shall never cease to glow,
  Our praise shall never cease to flow.

4 Thy never-failing grace to prove,
  A surety of Thine endless love,
  Send down Thy Holy Ghost, to be
  The raiser of our souls to Thee.
  Santolius Victorinus. (1630-1697.)
  Tr. by Rev. John Chandler. (1806-.)

1035 "Cause Thy face to shine." 7.
John i. 1-9. Luke i. 68-79. Ps. cvii. 1-16.

1 LIGHT of life, seraphic fire,
  Love divine, Thyself impart ;
  Every fainting soul inspire ;
  Shine in every drooping heart.

2 Come, in this accepted hour,
  Bring Thy heavenly kingdom in ;
  Fill us with Thy glorious power,
  Rooting out the seeds of sin.

3 Nothing more can we require,
  We will covet nothing less ;
  Be Thou all our heart's Desire,
  All our Joy, and all our Peace.
  Rev. Charles Wesley. (1708-1788.)

1036 "Return that we may look upon Thee." S. M.
John xx. 19-31. Acts i. 1-11. 2 Chr. vi. 1-17.

1 JESUS, we look to Thee,
  Thy promised presence claim ;
  Thou in the midst of us shalt be,
  Assembled in Thy name.

2 We meet the grace to take,
  Which Thou hast freely given ;
  We meet on earth for Thy dear sake,
  That we may meet in heaven.

3 Present we know Thou art,
  But, O Thyself reveal !
  Now, Lord, let every bounding heart
  Thy mighty comfort feel.

4 O may Thy quickening voice
  The death of sin remove ;
  And bid our inmost souls rejoice,
  In hope of perfect love.
  Rev. Charles Wesley.

1037 "Help us... for the glory of Thy name." C. M.
1 Chr. xvi. 1-36. Ps. xcv. Acts x. 30-45.

1 IN Thy great name, O Lord, we come,
  To worship at Thy feet ;
  O pour Thy Holy Spirit down
  On all that now shall meet.

2 We come to hear Jehovah speak,
  To hear the Saviour's voice :
  Thy face and favor, Lord, we seek,
  Now make our hearts rejoice.

3 Teach us to pray, and praise, and hear,
  And understand Thy word ;
  To feel Thy blissful presence near,
  And trust our living Lord.

4 Let sinners, Lord, Thy goodness prove,
  And saints rejoice in Thee ;
  Let rebels be subdued by love,
  And to the Saviour flee.
  Rev. Joseph Hoskins. (1745-1788.)

1038 "Give ear, O Shepherd of Israel." C. M.
2 Chr. vi. 40 to vii. 3. Ps. cxxxii. Acts. ii.

1 BLEST Jesus, come Thou gently down,
  And fill this hallowed place ;
  O make Thy glorious goings known,
  Diffuse around Thy grace.

2 Shine, dearest Lord, from realms of day,
  Disperse the gloom of night ;
  Chase all our clouds and doubts away,
  And turn the shades to light.
  Author unknown.

"That they might receive the Holy Ghost."

1039 "Receive ye the Holy Ghost." S. M.
Acts ii. 1-4. 2 Chr. xxix. 20-36. Joel ii. 15-32.

1 LORD God, the Holy Ghost,
    In this accepted hour,
As on the day of Pentecost,
    Descend in all Thy power.

2 We meet with one accord
    In our appointed place,
And wait the promise of our Lord,
    The Spirit of all grace.

3 Like mighty rushing wind
    Upon the waves beneath,
Move with one impulse every mind,
    One soul, one feeling breathe.

4 The young, the old inspire
    With wisdom from above ;
And give us hearts and tongues of fire
    To pray, and praise, and love.
            James Montgomery. (1771-1854.)

1040 "The earnest of the Spirit." 6. 4.
John xvi. Heb. x. 1-25. 2 Chr. xxxv. 1-18.

1 COME, Holy Ghost, in love,
    Shed on us, from above,
        Thine own bright ray ;
Divinely good Thou art ;
Thy sacred gifts impart,
To gladden each sad heart ;
        O come to-day !

2 Come, tenderest Friend, and best,
    Our most delightful Guest,
        With soothing power ;
Rest, which the weary know ;
Shade, 'mid the noontide glow ;
Peace, when deep griefs o'erflow ;
        Cheer us, this hour !

3 Come, Light serene, and still
    Our inmost bosoms fill ;
        Dwell in each breast ;
We know no dawn but Thine ;
Send forth Thy beams divine,
On our dark souls to shine,
        And make us blest.

4 Come, all the faithful bless ;
    Let all who Christ confess
        His praise employ :
Give virtue's rich reward ;
Victorious death accord,
And, with our glorious Lord,
        Eternal joy !
            Robert II., King of France. (972-1031.)
            Tr. by Rev. Ray Palmer. (1808-.)

1041 "He will guide you into all truth." 7. 5.
Rom. viii. 14-27. 1 Cor. ii. Neh. ix. 19-31.

1 HOLY Ghost, the Infinite,
Shine upon our nature's night
With Thy blessed inward light,
    Comforter Divine !

2 We are sinful, cleanse us, Lord ;
We are faint, Thy strength afford ;
Lost, until by Thee restored,
    Comforter Divine !

3 Like the dew, Thy peace distil ;
Guide, subdue our wayward will,
Things of Christ unfolding still,
    Comforter Divine !

4 In us, for us, intercede,
And with voiceless groaning plead
Our unutterable need,
    Comforter Divine !

5 In us "Abba, Father," cry,
Earnest of our bliss on high,
Seal of immortality,
    Comforter Divine !
            George Rawson. (1807-.)

1042 "Another Comforter." 8. 7.
Acts x. 30-45. John xiv. 15-31. Zech. iv.

1 HOLY Ghost, dispel our sadness,
    Pierce the clouds of sinful night ;
Come, Thou Source of sweetest gladness,
    Breathe Thy life, and spread Thy light :
Come, Thou best of all donations
    God can give, or we implore !
Having Thy sweet consolations,
    We need wish for nothing more.

2 From that height which knows no measure,
    As a gracious shower descend,
Bringing down the richest treasure
    Man can wish, or God can send :
Author of the new creation,
    Come, with unction and with power ;
Make our hearts Thy habitation ;
    On our souls Thy graces shower.

3 Manifest Thy love forever ;
    Fence us in on every side ;
In distress be our Reliever ;
    Guard and teach, support and guide.
Hear, O hear our supplication,
    Loving Spirit, God of peace !
Rest upon this congregation,
    With the fulness of Thy grace !
            Rev. Paul Gerhardt. (1606-1676.)
            Tr. by Rev. Augustus M. Toplady. (1740-1778.)

"That they might receibe the Holy Ghost."

1043 "We through the Spirit wait." C. M.
Ps. li. 10-19. Lam. v. John xiv. 18-31.

1 COME, Holy Spirit, heavenly Dove,
  With all Thy quickening powers,
  Kindle a flame of sacred love
  In these cold hearts of ours.

2 In vain we tune our formal songs,
  In vain we strive to rise;
  Hosannas languish on our tongues,
  And our devotion dies.

3 Dear Lord, and shall we ever live
  At this poor dying rate,
  Our love so faint, so cold to Thee,
  And Thine to us so great?

4 Come, Holy Spirit, heavenly Dove,
  With all Thy quickening powers;
  Come, shed abroad a Saviour's love,
  And that shall kindle ours.
  Rev. Isaac Watts. (1074-1748.)

1044 "He will reprove." L. M.
Eze. xxxvi. 22-38. Ps. cii. 13-22. 2 Cor. iii.

1 COME, Sacred Spirit, from above,
  And fill the coldest heart with love;
  Soften to flesh the rugged stone,
  And let Thy godlike power be known.

2 Speak Thou, and from the haughtiest eyes
  Shall floods of pious sorrow rise;
  While all their glowing souls are borne
  To seek that grace which now they scorn.

3 O let a holy flock await,
  Numerous around Thy temple-gate,
  Each pressing on with zeal to be
  A living sacrifice to Thee.
  Rev. Philip Doddridge. (1702-1751.)

1045 "The Spirit is life." L. M.
John xvi. Isa. xliv. 1-8. 2 Chr. vi. 32-42.

1 COME, O Creator-Spirit blest,
  And in our souls take up Thy rest;
  Come, with Thy grace and heavenly aid,
  To fill the hearts which Thou hast made.

2 Great Comforter, to Thee we cry;
  O highest Gift of God most high,
  Thou in Thy seven-fold gifts art known;
  Thee, finger of God's hand we own.

3 Kindle our senses from above,
  And make our hearts o'erflow with love;
  With patience firm, and virtue high,
  The weakness of our flesh supply.

4 Far from us drive the foe we dread,
  And grant us Thy true peace instead;
  So shall we not, with Thee for Guide,
  Turn from the path of life aside.
  Unknown author of the 7th or 8th century.
Tr. by Rev. Edward Caswall. (1814-1878.)

1046 "He shall teach you." S. M.
1 John v. 1-8. 1 Cor. xii. Num. xi. 16, 17.

1 SPIRIT of faith, come down!
  Reveal the things of God;
  And make to us the Godhead known,
  And witness with the blood.

2 O that the world might know
  The all-atoning Lamb!
  Spirit of faith, descend and show
  The virtue of His name.

3 The grace which all may find,
  The saving power impart;
  And testify to all mankind,
  And speak in every heart.
  Rev. Charles Wesley. (1708-1788.)

1047 "Sealed with that Holy Spirit of promise." C. M.
Ps. lxxx. Isa. xxxii. Rom. viii. 1-21.

1 ETERNAL Spirit, source of truth,
  Our contrite hearts inspire:
  Kindle the flame of heavenly love,
  And feed the pure desire.

2 'T is Thine to soothe the sorrowing mind,
  With Satan's yoke oppressed;
  'T is Thine to bid the dying live,
  And give the weary rest.

3 Subdue the power of every sin,
  Whate'er that sin may be;
  That we, in singleness of heart,
  May worship only Thee.

4 Then with our spirits witness bear
  That we're the sons of God,
  Redeemed from sin, and death, and hell,
  Through Christ's atoning blood.
  Rev. Joseph Hart. (1712-1768.)
Alt. by Rev. Thomas Cotterill. (1779-1823.)

1048 "The Comforter, the Holy Ghost." S. M.
John xiv. 1-17. 1 Kings xix. Joel ii. 21-32.

1 BLEST Comforter Divine,
  Whose rays of heavenly love
  Amid our gloom and darkness shine,
  And point our souls above;

2 Thou, who with "still small voice,"
  Dost stop the sinner's way,
  And bid the mourning saint rejoice,
  Though earthly joys decay;

3 Thou, whose inspiring breath
  Can make the cloud of care,
  And e'en the gloomy vale of death,
  A smile of glory wear;

4 Thou, who dost fill the heart
  With love to all our race;
  Blest Comforter, to us impart
  The blessings of Thy grace.
  Mrs. Lydia H. H. Sigourney. (1791-1865.)

"Praise the Lord ... O ye servants of the Lord."

1049 "Let the saints be joyful in glory." C. M.
Ps. cv. 1–10. Isa. xii. Acts ii. 29–47.

1 COME, we that love the Lord,
  And let our joys be known ;
  Join in a song of sweet accord,
  And thus surround the throne.

2 Let those refuse to sing
  That never knew our God ;
  But favorites of the heavenly King
  May speak their joys abroad.

3 The men of grace have found
  Glory begun below ;
  Celestial fruits on earthly ground
  From faith and hope may grow.

4 Then let our songs abound,
  And every tear be dry ;
  We're marching through Immanuel's ground
  To fairer worlds on high.
  Rev. Isaac Watts. (1674–1748.)

1052 "The high praises of God in their mouth." L. M.
Ps. cxxxvi. Heb. i. Isa. xxxv.

1 GIVE to our God immortal praise ;
  Mercy and truth are all His ways :
  Wonders of grace to God belong ;
  Repeat His mercies in your song.

2 He built the earth, He spread the sky,
  And fixed the starry lights on high :
  Wonders of grace to God belong ;
  Repeat His mercies in your song.

3 He sent His Son with power to save
  From guilt, and darkness, and the grave :
  Wonders of grace to God belong ;
  Repeat His mercies in your song.

4 Through this vain world He guides our feet,
  And leads us to His heavenly seat :
  His mercies ever shall endure,
  When this vain world shall be no more.
  Rev. Isaac Watts.

1050 "His praise in the congregation of the saints." 10. 11.
Ps. xlviii. 1 Chr. xvi. 8–36. Zeph. iii. 8–20. Heb. xii. 18–24.

1 O PRAISE ye the Lord ; prepare your glad voice,
  His praise in the great assembly to sing ;
  In their great Creator let all men rejoice,
  And heirs of salvation be glad in their King.

2 Let them His great name devoutly adore,
  In loud-swelling strains His praises express,
  Who graciously opens His bountiful store,
  Their wants to relieve, and His children to bless.

3 With glory adorned, His people shall sing
  To God, who defence and plenty supplies ;
  Their loud acclamations to Him, their great King,
  Through earth shall be sounded, and reach to the skies.
  Nahum Tate. (1652–1715.)

1051 "O bless our God." C. M.
Isa xl. 9–31. Ps. lxvi. Col. i.

1 LIFT up to God the voice of praise,
  Whose breath our souls inspired ;
  Loud, and more loud, the anthem raise,
  With grateful ardor fired.

2 Lift up to God the voice of praise,
  Whose goodness, passing thought,
  Loads every minute as it flies,
  With benefits unsought.

3 Lift up to God the voice of praise,
  From whom salvation flows,
  Who sent His Son our souls to save
  From everlasting woes.

4 Lift up to God the voice of praise,
  For hope's transporting ray,
  Which lights, through darkest shades of death,
  To realms of endless day.
  Rev. Ralph Wardlaw. (1779–1853.)

1053 "Make the voice of His praise to be heard." L. M.
Ps. xcv. Ex. xv. 1–21. Heb. iv.

1 COME, let our voices join to raise
  A sacred song of solemn praise ;
  God is a sovereign King ; rehearse
  His honors in exalted verse.

2 Come, let our souls address the Lord,
  Who framed our natures with His word ;
  He is our Shepherd, we the sheep ;
  His mercy chose, His pastures keep.

3 Come, let us hear His voice to-day,
  The counsels of His love obey ;
  Nor let our hardened hearts renew
  The sins and plagues that Israel knew.

4 Seize the kind promise while it waits,
  And march to Zion's heavenly gates ;
  Believe, and take the promised rest ;
  Obey, and be forever blessed.
  Rev. Isaac Watts.

"Praise the Lord ... O ye servants of the Lord."

1054 "Let the redeemed of the Lord say so." Isa. xxxv. Hos. xiv. 2 Cor. iv. **C. M.**

1 SING, ye redeeméd of the Lord,
Your great Deliverer sing :
Pilgrims for Zion's city bound,
Be joyful in your King.

2 A Hand divine shall lead you on
Through all the blissful road,
Till to the sacred mount you rise,
And see your smiling God.

3 There garlands of immortal joy
Shall bloom on every head ;
While sorrow, sighing, and distress,
Like shadows, all are fled.

Rev. Philip Doddridge. (1702-1751.)

1057 "Be glad, ye children of Zion." Ps. cxxi. Jer. xxxi. 1-14. Rom. vi. 17-23. **C. M.**

1 COME, let us lift our joyful eyes
Up to the courts above,
And smile to see our Father there,
Upon a throne of love.

2 Now we may bow before His feet,
And venture near the Lord :
No fiery cherub guards His seat,
Nor double flaming sword.

3 The peaceful gates of heavenly bliss
Are opened by the Son :
High let us raise our notes of praise,
And reach the almighty throne.

Rev. Isaac Watts. (1674-1748.)

1055 "O come, let us worship and bow down." Deu. xxvi. Ps. lxvi. Acts xvii. 22-31. Rev. iv. **10, 11.**

1 O WORSHIP the King all-glorious above,
O gratefully sing His power and His love ;
Our Shield and Defender, the Ancient of days,
Pavilioned in splendor and girded with praise.

2 O tell of His might, O sing of His grace,
Whose robe is the light, whose canopy space ;
His chariots of wrath the deep thunder-clouds form,
And dark is His path on the wings of the storm.

3 Thy bountiful care what tongue can recite ?
It breathes in the air, it shines in the light,
It streams from the hills, it descends to the plains,
And sweetly distils in the dew and the rains.

4 Frail children of dust, and feeble as frail,
In Thee do we trust, nor find Thee to fail ;
Thy mercies how tender, how firm to the end !
Our Maker, Defender, Redeemer, and Friend.

Sir Robert Grant. (1785-1838.)

1056 "Praise the Lord, O Jerusalem." Ps. cxlii. 1 Chr. xxix. 10-22. Rev. xv. **L. M.**

1 SERVANTS of God, in joyful lays,
Sing ye the Lord Jehovah's praise :
His glorious name let all adore,
From age to age, for evermore.

2 Blest be that name, supremely blest,
From the sun's rising to its rest ;
Above the heavens His power is known,
Through all the earth His goodness shown.

3 Who is like God ? so great, so high,
He bows Himself to view the sky ;
And yet, with condescending grace,
Looks down upon the human race.

4 He hears the uncomplaining moan
Of those who sit and weep alone ;
He lifts the mourner from the dust,
In Him the poor may safely trust.

James Montgomery. (1771-1854.)

1058 "Praise Thy God, O Zion." Neh. ix. 1-6. Ps. cl. Luke i. 68-79. **S. M.**

1 STAND up, and bless the Lord,
Ye people of His choice !
Stand up, and bless the Lord your God,
With heart, and soul, and voice.

2 Though high above all praise,
Above all blessing high,
Who would not fear His holy name,
And laud, and magnify ?

3 O for the living flame
From His own altar brought,
To touch our lips, our minds inspire,
And wing to heaven our thought !

4 God is our Strength and Song,
And His salvation ours :
Then be His love in Christ proclaimed,
With all our ransomed powers.

James Montgomery.

"Praise the Lord ... all ye people."

1059 "O bless our God, ye people." Ps. c. 2 Chr. v. Rev. xix. 1–6. **L. M.**

1 ALL people that on earth do dwell,
   Sing to the Lord with cheerful voice ;
   Him serve with mirth, His praise forth tell,
   Come ye before Him and rejoice.

2 Know that the Lord is God indeed ;
   Without our aid He did us make ;
   We are His flock, He doth us feed,
   And for His sheep He doth us take.

3 O enter, then, His gates with praise ;
   Approach with joy His courts unto ;
   Praise, laud, and bless His name always,
   For it is seemly so to do.

4 For why ? the Lord our God is good,
   His mercy is forever sure ;
   His truth at all times firmly stood,
   And shall from age to age endure.

Rev. William Kethe. 1502.

1062 "Let the nations be glad and sing." Ps. xcvii. Gen. ii. 1–7. Acts xvii. 22–31. **L. M.**

1 YE nations round the earth, rejoice
   Before the Lord, your sovereign King :
   Serve Him with cheerful heart and voice,
   With all your tongues His glory sing.

2 The Lord is God ; 't is He alone
   Doth life, and breath, and being give ;
   We are His work, and not our own,
   The sheep that on His pastures live.

3 Enter His gates with songs of joy ;
   With praises to His courts repair ;
   And make it your divine employ,
   To pay your thanks and honors there.

4 The Lord is good, the Lord is kind ;
   Great is His grace, His mercy sure ;
   And the whole race of man shall find
   His truth from age to age endure.

Rev. Isaac Watts.

1060 "O clap your hands, all ye people." Ps. lxvi. 1 Chr. xvi. 8–36. Jer. xxxiii 1–16. Rev. xiv. 1–3. **11. 8.**

1 BE joyful in God, all ye lands of the earth ;
   O serve Him with gladness and fear ;
   Exult in His presence with music and mirth,
   With love and devotion draw near.

2 Jehovah is God, and Jehovah alone,
   Creator and Ruler o'er all ;
   And we are His people, His sceptre we own ;
   His sheep, and we follow His call.

3 O enter His gates with thanksgiving and song,
   Your vows in His temple proclaim ;
   His praise with melodious accordance prolong,
   And bless His adorable name.

4 For good is the Lord, inexpressibly good,
   And we are the work of His hand ;
   His mercy and truth from eternity stood,
   And shall to eternity stand.

James Montgomery. (1771-1854.)

1061 "Make a joyful noise, . . . all ye lands." Ps. lxviii. 1 Chr. xxix. 1–18. Mat. vi. 1–13. **L. M.**

1 KINGDOMS and thrones to God belong ;
   Crown Him, ye nations, in your song ;
   His wondrous names and powers rehearse ;
   His honors shall enrich your verse.

2 He shakes the heavens with loud alarms ;
   How terrible is God in arms !
   In Israel are His mercies known,
   Israel is His peculiar throne.

3 Proclaim Him King, pronounce Him blest ;
   He 's your Defence, your Joy, your Rest ;
   When terrors rise, and nations faint,
   God is the Strength of every saint.

Rev. Isaac Watts. (1674-1748.)

1063 "Sing unto the Lord, all the earth." Ps. xcvi. Isa. ii. 1–5. Rev. xx. 1–6. **L. M.**

1 WITH one consent let all the earth
   To God their cheerful voices raise ;
   Glad homage pay, with awful mirth,
   And sing before Him songs of praise :

2 O enter, then, His temple gate,
   Thence to His courts devoutly press ;
   And still your grateful hymns repeat,
   And still His name with praises bless.

3 For He 's the Lord, supremely good ;
   His mercy is forever sure ;
   His truth, which always firmly stood,
   To endless ages shall endure.

Nahum Tate. (1652-1715.)

"Bless ye the Lord, all His hosts ... all His works."

1064 "Rejoice, O ye nations, with His people." **L. M.**
Ps. c. Gen. ii. 1-7. Rev. i. 10-20.

1 BEFORE Jehovah's awful throne,
  Ye nations, bow with sacred joy :
  Know that the Lord is God alone ;
  He can create, and He destroy.

2 His sovereign power, without our aid,
  Made us of clay, and formed us men ;
  And when like wandering sheep we strayed,
  He brought us to His fold again.

3 We'll crowd Thy gates with thankful songs,
  High as the heavens our voices raise ;
  And earth, with her ten thousand tongues,
  Shall fill Thy courts with sounding praise.

4 Wide as the world is Thy command,
  Vast as eternity, Thy love ;
  Firm as a rock Thy truth must stand,
  When rolling years shall cease to move.
  Rev. Isaac Watts. (1674-1748.)

1065 "Make the voice of His praise to be heard." **S. M.**
Ps. cxxxv. Gen. i. Heb. iii. 7-19.

1 COME, sound His praise abroad,
  And hymns of glory sing ;
  Jehovah is the sovereign God,
  The universal King.

2 Come, worship at His throne,
  Come, bow before the Lord ;
  We are His works, and not our own ;
  He formed us by His word.

3 To-day attend His voice,
  Nor dare provoke His rod ;
  Come, like the people of His choice,
  And own your gracious God.
  Rev. Isaac Watts.

1066 "Let all flesh bless His holy name." **L. M.**
Ps. cxvii. Isa. lix. 19-21. Acts ii. 41-47.

1 FROM all that dwell below the skies,
  Let the Creator's praise arise ;
  Let the Redeemer's name be sung
  Through every land, by every tongue.

2 Eternal are Thy mercies, Lord ;
  Eternal truth attends Thy word ;
  Thy praise shall sound from shore to shore
  Till suns shall rise and set no more.

3 Your lofty themes, ye mortals, bring ;
  In songs of praise divinely sing ;
  The great salvation loud proclaim,
  And shout for joy the Saviour's name.

4 In every land begin the song ;
  To every land the strains belong :
  In cheerful sounds all voices raise,
  And fill the world with loudest praise.
  Rev. Isaac Watts.

1067 "Sing, O heavens, and be joyful, O earth." **8. 7.**
Ps. cxlviii. Job xxxviii. Rev. v. 11-14.

1 PRAISE the Lord ! ye heavens, adore Him ;
  Praise Him, angels in the height ;
  Sun and moon, rejoice before Him ;
  Praise Him, all ye stars of light !
  Praise the Lord, for He hath spoken ;
  Worlds His mighty voice obeyed ;
  Laws, which never shall be broken,
  For their guidance He hath made.

2 Praise the Lord, for He is glorious ;
  Never shall His promise fail ;
  God hath made His saints victorious,
  Sin and death shall not prevail.
  Praise the God of our salvation,
  Hosts on high, His power proclaim ;
  Heaven and earth, and all creation,
  Laud and magnify His name.
  Rev. John Kempthorne. (1775-1838.)

1068 "Everything that hath breath praise the Lord." **7.**
Ps. cl. Ex. xv. Luke i. 46-55.

1 PRAISE the Lord, His power confess,
  Praise Him in His holiness ;
  Praise Him as the theme inspires,
  Praise Him as His fame requires.
  Let the trumpet's lofty sound
  Spread its loudest notes around ;
  Let the harp unite, in praise,
  With the sacred minstrel's lays.

2 Let the organ join to bless
  God, the Lord of righteousness ;
  Tune your voice to spread the fame
  Of the great Jehovah's name.
  All who dwell beneath His light,
  In His praise your hearts unite ;
  While the stream of song is poured,
  Praise and magnify the Lord.
  William Wrangham. (-1832.)

1069 "Praise ye Him, all His angels." **8. 7.**
Isa. vi. 1-4. Ex. xl. 34-38. Rev. iv.

1 ROUND the Lord, in glory seated,
  Cherubim and seraphim
  Filled His temple, and repeated
  Each to each the alternate hymn :
  "Lord, Thy glory fills the heaven ;
  Earth is with its fulness stored ;
  Unto Thee be glory given,
  Holy, holy, holy Lord.

2 Heaven is still with glory ringing ;
  Earth takes up the angels' cry,
  "Holy, holy, holy," singing,
  "Lord of hosts, Lord God most high."
  With His seraph train before Him,
  With His holy church below,
  Thus unite we to adore Him ;
  Bid we thus our anthem flow.
  Bp. Richard Mant. (1776-1848.)

"Blessing and honor and glory and power be unto the Lamb."

1070 "Worthy is the Lamb." 6, 4.
Ps. xxxiii. Isa. lxvi. 10–24. Luke i. 68–79.

1 COME, all ye saints of God,
   Publish through earth abroad
     Jesus' fame :
   Tell what His love has done ;
   Trust in His name alone ;
   Shout to His lofty throne,
     " Worthy the Lamb ! "

2 Hence, gloomy doubts and fears !
   Dry up your mournful tears ;
     Join our glad theme ;
   Beauty for ashes bring,
   Strike each melodious string,
   Join heart and voice to sing,
     " Worthy the Lamb ! "

3 Hark ! how the choirs above,
   Filled with the Saviour's love,
     Dwell on His name !
   There, too, may we be found,
   With light and glory crowned,
   While all the heavens resound,
     " Worthy the Lamb ! "
             Rev. James Boden. (1757–1841.)

1071 "And . . . confess that Jesus Christ is Lord." C. M.
Rev. v. 6–14. Phil. ii. 1–11. Ps. lxxii.

1 ALL hail the power of Jesus' name,
   Let angels prostrate fall ;
   Bring forth the royal diadem,
   And crown Him Lord of all.

2 Crown Him, ye martyrs of our God,
   Who from His altar call ;
   Extol the stem of Jesse's rod,
   And crown Him Lord of all.

3 Ye chosen seed of Israel's race,
   Ye ransomed from the fall,
   Hail Him who saves you by His grace,
   And crown Him Lord of all.

4 Sinners, whose love can ne'er forget
   The wormwood and the gall,
   Go, spread your trophies at His feet,
   And crown Him Lord of all.

5 Let every kindred, every tribe,
   On this terrestrial ball,
   To Him all majesty ascribe,
   And crown Him Lord of all.

6 O that with yonder sacred throng,
   We at His feet may fall ;
   We 'll join the everlasting song,
   And crown Him Lord of all.
             Rev. Edward Perronet. (-1792.)

1072 "Crowned with glory and honor." C. M.
Ps. ciii. Dan. vii. 9–14. Rev. i.

1 COME, all harmonious tongues,
   Your noblest music bring ;
   'T is Christ, the everlasting God,
   And Christ, the Man, we sing.

2 Down to the shades of death
   He bowed His awful head ;
   Yet He arose to live and reign
   When death itself is dead.

3 No more the bloody spear,
   The cross and nails no more ;
   For hell itself shakes at His name,
   And all the heavens adore.

4 There the Redeemer sits,
   High on the Father's throne ;
   The Father lays His vengeance by,
   And smiles upon His Son.
             Rev. Isaac Watts. (1674–1748.)

1073 "God also hath highly exalted Him." C. M.
Ps. xlvii. Isa. xxxv. Rev. xv.

1 ARISE, ye people, and adore ;
   Exulting strike the chord ;
   Let all the earth, from shore to shore,
   Confess th' almighty Lord.

2 Hark ! the glad shouts, wide echoing round,
   Th' ascending God proclaim :
   Th' angelic choir respond the sound,
   And shake creation's frame.

3 They sing of death and hell o'erthrown
   In that triumphant hour ;
   And God exalts His conquering Son
   To the right hand of power.
             Miss Harriet Auber. (1773–1862.)

1074 " All the angels of God worship Him." 8, 7.
Rev. vii. Ps. xxiv. Heb. i.

1 HARK the notes of angels, singing,
   " Glory, glory to the Lamb ! "
   All in heaven their tribute bringing,
   Raising high the Saviour's name.

2 Ye, for whom His life was given,
   Sacred themes to you belong ;
   Come, assist the choir of heaven ;
   Join the everlasting song.

3 See th' angelic hosts have crowned Him,
   Jesus fills the throne on high :
   Countless myriads, hovering round Him,
   With His praises rend the sky.

4 Endless life in Him possessing,
   Let us praise His precious name ;
   Glory, honor, power, and blessing,
   Be forever to the Lamb.
             Rev. Thomas Kelly. (1769–1855.)

"Blessing and honor and glory and power be unto the Lamb."

1075 "He hath visited and redeemed His people." **H. M.**
1 Chr. xvi. 28-36. Ps. xxxiv. Eph. iv. 1-16.

1 COME, every pious heart
  That loves the Saviour's name,
  Your noblest power exert
  To celebrate His fame :
  Tell all above, and all below,
  The debt of love to Him you owe.

2 He left His starry crown,
  And laid His robes aside;
  On wings of love came down,
  And wept, and bled, and died :
  What He endured, O who can tell,
  To save our souls from death and hell?

3 From the dark grave He rose,
  The mansion of the dead ;
  And thence His mighty foes
  In glorious triumph led:
  Up through the sky the Conqueror rode,
  And reigns on high, the Saviour, God.
  Rev. Samuel Stennett. (1727-1795.)

1076 "All nations shall call Him blessed." **L. M.**
Rev. iv. 2 Sam. xxii. Col. i. 1-18.

1 WORTHY the Lamb of boundless sway,
  In earth or heaven, the Lord of all !
  Ye princes, rulers, powers, obey,
  And low before His footstool fall.

2 Higher, still higher, swell the strain ;
  Creation's voice the note prolong !
  The Lamb shall ever, ever reign :
  Let hallelujahs crown the song.
  Hon. and Rev. Walter Shirley. (1725-1786.)

1077 "Sing to the Lord, O ye saints of His." **8. 6.**
Col. ii. 1-15. 1 Cor. i. 23-31. Ps. lxvi.

1 COME join, ye saints, with heart and voice,
  Alone in Jesus to rejoice,
    And worship at His feet ;
  Come, take His praises on your tongues,
  And raise to Him your thankful songs,
    "In Him ye are complete !"

2 In Him, who all our praise excels,
  The fulness of the Godhead dwells,
    And all perfections meet :
  The head of all celestial powers,
  Divinely meet, divinely ours ;
    "In Him ye are complete !"

3 Still onward urge your heavenly way,
  Dependent on Him day by day,
    His presence still entreat ;
  His precious name forever bless,
  Your Glory, Strength, and Righteousness,
    "In Him ye are complete !"
  Author unknown.

1078 "Thou crownedst Him." **C. M.**
Ps. cxlvi. Isa. ii. 1-5. 1 Pet. iv. 1-13.

1 COME, ye that love the Saviour's name,
  And joy to make it known ;
  The Sovereign of your hearts proclaim,
  And bow before His throne.

2 Behold your King, your Saviour, crowned
  With glories all-divine ;
  And tell the wondering nations round
  How bright these glories shine.

3 Infinite power and boundless grace
  In Him unite their rays ;
  You that have e'er beheld His face,
  Can you forbear His praise ?
  Miss Anne Steele. (1717-1778.)

1079 "And cast their crowns before the throne." **S. M.**
Rev. xix. 1-16. Ps. cxlvii. Dan. vii.

1 CROWN Him with many crowns,
    The Lamb upon His throne !
  Hark, how the heavenly anthem drowns
    All music but its own.

2 Crown Him the Lord of love !
    Behold His hands and side,
  Rich wounds, yet visible above,
    In beauty glorified.

3 Crown Him the Lord of peace !
    Whose power a sceptre sways,
  From pole to pole, that wars may cease,
    Absorbed in prayer and praise.

4 Crown Him the Lord of heaven!
    One with the Father known,
  And the blest Spirit, through Him given
    From yonder triune throne.
  Matthew Bridges. (1800-1832.)

1080 "Come before His presence with singing." **C. M.**
Rev. v. Ps. cxxviii. Isa. xii.

1 COME, let us join our cheerful songs
  With angels' round the throne ;
  Ten thousand thousand are their tongues,
  But all their joys are one.

2 "Worthy the Lamb that died," they cry,
  "To be exalted thus ! "
  "Worthy the Lamb," our lips reply,
  "For He was slain for us !"

3 Let all that dwell above the sky,
  And air, and earth, and seas,
  Conspire to lift Thy glories high,
  And speak Thine endless praise.

4 The whole creation join in one,
  To bless the sacred name
  Of Him that sits upon the throne,
  And to adore the Lamb.
  Rev. Isaac Watts. (1674-1748.)

"Blessing and honor and glory and power be unto the Lamb."

1081 "Awake, awake, utter a song." S. M.
Rev. xv. Ex. xv. 1, 2. Ps. cxi.

1 AWAKE, and sing the song
   Of Moses and the Lamb;
Wake every heart and every tongue,
   To praise the Saviour's name.
Sing of His dying love ;
   Sing of His rising power ;
Sing how He intercedes above
   For those whose sins He bore.

2 Sing till we feel our hearts
   Ascending with our tongues :
Sing till the love of sin departs,
   And grace inspires our songs.
Sing on your heavenly way,
   Ye ransomed sinners, sing ;
Sing on, rejoicing every day
   In Christ the eternal King.

3 Soon shall ye hear Him say,
   "Ye blessed children, come ; "
Soon will He call you hence away,
   And take His wanderers home.
There shall our raptured tongue
   His endless praise proclaim,
And sweeter voices swell the song
   Of Moses and the Lamb.
Rev. William Hammond. (1719-1783.)
Alt. by Rev. Martin Madan. (1726-1790.)

1082 "The children of Zion be joyful in their King." 7.
Isa. xxxv. Ps. cxxxviii. Luke xii. 31-40.

1 CHILDREN of the heavenly King,
As ye journey, sweetly sing ;
Sing your Saviour's worthy praise,
Glorious in His works and ways.

2 We are travelling home to God,
In the way the fathers trod ;
They are happy now, and we
Soon their happiness shall see.

3 Shout, ye little flock and blest,
You on Jesus' throne shall rest ;
There your seat is now prepared,
There 's your kingdom and reward.

4 Fear not, brethren, joyful stand
On the borders of your land ;
Jesus Christ, your Father's Son,
Bids you undismayed go on.

5 Lord, obediently we go,
Gladly leaving all below ;
Only Thou our Leader be,
And we still will follow Thee.
Rev. John Cennick. (1717-1755.)

1083 "At the name of Jesus every knee should bow." 7.
Ps. cvii. 1-16. Isa. li. 9-23. Rom. v. 1-11.

1 Now begin the heavenly theme,
Sing aloud in Jesus' name ;
Ye, who Jesus' kindness prove,
Triumph in redeeming love.

2 Ye, who see the Father's grace
Beaming in the Saviour's face,
As to Canaan on ye move,
Praise and bless redeeming love.

3 Welcome all, by sin oppressed,
Welcome to His sacred rest !
Nothing brought Him from above,
Nothing but redeeming love.

4 Hither, then, your music bring ;
Strike aloud each joyful string ;
Mortals, join the hosts above,
Join to praise redeeming love.
Rev. Martin Madan.

1084 "Rejoice even with joy and singing." 11.
Luke ii. 1-20. Heb. i. Ps. lxxii.

1 REJOICE and be glad,
   The Redeemer has come !
Go look on His cradle,
   His cross, and His tomb.

   Sound His praises, tell the story
      Of Him who was slain ;
   Sound His praises, tell with gladness,
      He liveth again.

2 Rejoice and be glad !
   For the blood hath been shed ;
Redemption is finished,
   The price hath been paid.

3 Rejoice and be glad !
   For the Lamb that was slain
O'er death is triumphant,
   And liveth again.

4 Rejoice and be glad !
   For our King is on high,
He pleadeth for us on
   His throne in the sky.

5 Rejoice and be glad !
   For He cometh again ;
He cometh in glory,
   The Lamb that was slain.

   Sound His praises, tell the story
      Of Him who was slain ;
   Sound His praises, tell with gladness,
      He cometh again.
Rev. Horatius Bonar. (1808-.)

"Blessing and honor and glory and power be unto the Lamb."

1085 "As they honor the Father." L. M.
Rev. v. John v. 17-31. Isa. xliv. 21-23.

1 WHAT equal honors shall we bring
  To Thee, O Lord our God, the Lamb,
  When all the notes that angels sing
  Are far inferior to Thy name?

2 Worthy is He that once was slain,
  The Prince of Peace that groaned and died,
  Worthy to rise, and live, and reign
  At His almighty Father's side.

3 All riches are His native right,
  Yet He sustained amazing loss;
  To Him ascribe eternal might,
  Who left His weakness on the cross.

4 Blessings forever on the Lamb,
  Who bore the curse for wretched men;
  Let angels sound His sacred name,
  And every creature say, Amen.
  Rev. Isaac Watts. (1674-1748.)

1086 "For Thou wast slain." C. M.
Eph. ii. Isa. viii. 11 to ix. 7. Ps. cxlviii.

1 PLUNGED in a gulf of dark despair,
  We wretched sinners lay,
  Without one cheerful beam of hope,
  Or spark of glimmering day.

2 With pitying eyes the Prince of grace
  Beheld our helpless grief;
  He saw, and, O amazing love!
  He ran to our relief.

3 Down from the shining seats above,
  With joyful haste He fled,
  Entered the grave in mortal flesh,
  And dwelt among the dead.

4 O for this love let rocks and hills
  Their lasting silence break!
  And all harmonious human tongues
  The Saviour's praises speak.
  Rev. Isaac Watts.

1087 "With the angel, ... praising God." C. M.
Luke ii. 1-14. John iii. 16-21. Ps. lxxii.

1 ANGELS rejoiced and sweetly sung,
  At our Redeemer's birth;
  Mortals, awake! let every tongue
  Proclaim His matchless worth.

2 Glory to God, who dwells on high,
  And sent His only Son
  To take a servant's form, and die
  For evils we had done.

3 Good-will to men; ye fallen race,
  Arise, and shout for joy;
  He comes, with rich, abounding grace
  To save, and not destroy.
  Rev. William Hurn. (1754-1829.)

1088 "That He might redeem us." L. M.
Rom. xi. 33-36. Gal. vi. 12-14. Isa. liii.

1 WE sing the praise of Him who died,
  Of Him who died upon the cross;
  The sinner's hope let men deride,
  For this we count the world but loss.

2 Inscribed upon the cross we see,
  In shining letters, "God is Love;"
  He bears our sins upon the tree,
  He brings us mercy from above.

3 The Balm of life, the Cure of woe,
  The Measure and the Pledge of love,
  The sinner's Refuge here below,
  The angels' Theme in heaven above.
  Rev. Thomas Kelly. (1769-1855.)

1089 "Break forth into singing." S. M.
1 John iv. 6-14. Rom. iii. 20-26. Ps. lxxxv.

1 RAISE your triumphant songs
  To an immortal tune;
  Let the wide earth resound the deeds
  Celestial grace has done.

2 Sing how Eternal Love
  Its chief Beloved chose,
  And bade Him raise our wretched race
  From their abyss of woes.

3 'T was mercy filled the throne,
  And wrath stood silent by,
  When Christ was sent, with pardons, down
  To rebels doomed to die.

4 Lord, we obey Thy call;
  We lay an humble claim
  To the salvation Thou hast brought,
  And love and praise Thy name.
  Rev. Isaac Watts.

1090 "Christ, ... over all, God blessed forever." 8. 7.
Rev. xiv. 1-3. Phil. ii. 1-11. Ps. ciii.

1 CROWN His head with endless blessing,
  Who in God the Father's name,
  With compassions never ceasing,
  Comes salvation to proclaim.
  Hail, ye saints, who know His favor,
  Who within His gates are found;
  There on high exalt the Saviour,
  Let His courts with praise resound.

2 Jesus, Thee our Saviour hailing,
  Thee our God in praise we own;
  Highest honors, never failing,
  Rise eternal round Thy throne;
  Now, ye saints, His power confessing,
  In your grateful strains adore;
  For His mercy, never ceasing,
  Flows, and flows for evermore.
  Rev. William Goode. (1762-1816.)

"Blessing and honor and glory and power be unto the Lamb."

1091 "Men shall be blest in Him." L. M.
Rev. v. 1 Tim. vi. 13-16. Isa. xxxii.

1 O CHRIST, the Lord of heaven, to Thee,
  Clothed with all majesty divine,
  Eternal power and glory be,
  Eternal praise of right is Thine.

2 To Thee, the Lamb, our mortal songs,
  Born of deep, fervent love, shall rise ;
  All honor to Thy name belongs,
  Our lips would sound it through the skies.

3 " Jesus ! " all earth shall speak the word;
  " Jesus ! " all heaven resound it still ;
  Immanuel, Saviour, Conqueror, Lord,
  Thy praise the universe shall fill.
  Rev. Ray Palmer. (1808-.)

1092 "I will praise praise Thy name forever." L. M.
Ps. ii. Eph. i. Phil. ii. 5-11.

1 JESUS, Thou everlasting King,
  Accept the tribute which we bring ;
  Accept the well-deserved renown,
  And wear our praises as Thy crown.

2 Let every act of worship be
  Like our espousals, Lord, to Thee ;
  Like the dear hour when, from above,
  We first received Thy pledge of love.

3 The gladness of that happy day,
  Our hearts would wish it long to stay;
  Nor let our faith forsake its hold,
  Nor comfort sink, nor love grow cold.

4 Each foll'wing minute, as it flies,
  Increase Thy praise, improve our joys ;
  Till we are raised to sing Thy name,
  At the great supper of the Lamb.
  Rev. Isaac Watts. (1674-1748.)

1093 "Truly this was the Son of God." 7. 6.
Mark xv. 15-39. 1 Cor. i. Zech. xii. 1-10.

1 O JESUS, we adore Thee,
  Upon the cross, our King ;
  We bow our hearts before Thee ;
  Thy gracious name we sing ;
  That name hath brought salvation,
  That name, in life our stay ;
  Our peace, our consolation
  When life shall fade away.

2 Ah, Lord, our sins arraigned Thee,
  And nailed Thee to the tree :
  Our pride, O Lord, disdained Thee ;
  Yet deign our hope to be.
  O glorious King, we bless Thee,
  No longer pass Thee by;
  O Jesus, we confess Thee
  Our Lord enthroned on high.
  Rev. Arthur T. Russell. (1806-.)

1094 "The Holy One of Israel is our King." C. M.
Isa. ix. 1-7. Mat. xxi. 1-16. John i.

1 O JESUS, King most wonderful,
  Thou Conqueror renowned,
  Thou Sweetness most ineffable,
  In whom all joys are found ;
  When once Thou visitest the heart,
  Then truth begins to shine ;
  Then earthly vanities depart ;
  Then kindles love divine.

2 O Jesus, Light of all below,
  Thou Fount of life and fire,
  Surpassing all the joys we know,
  All that we can desire ;
  Thee may our tongues forever bless ;
  Thee may we love alone ;
  And ever in our lives express
  The image of Thine own.
  Bernard of Clairvaux. (1091-1153.)
Tr. by Rev. Edward Caswall. (1814-.)

1095 "Jesus of Nazareth, the King." 8. 7.
Mat. xxvii. 29-49. Eph. ii. Isa. liii.

1 HAIL, Thou once despiséd Jesus,
  Hail, Thou Galilean King !
  Thou didst suffer to release us,
  Thou didst free salvation bring :
  Hail, Thou agonizing Saviour,
  Bearer of our sin and shame;
  By Thy merits we find favor ;
  Life is given through Thy name.

2 Paschal Lamb, by God appointed,
  All our sins on Thee were laid ;
  By Almighty Love anointed,
  Thou hast full atonement made :
  All Thy people are forgiven
  Through the virtue of Thy blood ;
  Opened is the gate of heaven ;
  Peace is made 'twixt man and God.

3 Jesus, hail, enthroned in glory,
  There forever to abide ;
  All the heavenly hosts adore Thee,
  Seated at Thy Father's side.
  There for sinners Thou art pleading ;
  There Thou dost our place prepare ;
  Ever for us interceding
  Till in glory we appear.

4 Worship, honor, power, and blessing,
  Thou art worthy to receive ;
  Loudest praises, without ceasing,
  Meet it is for us to give.
  Help, ye bright angelic spirits,
  Bring your sweetest, noblest lays ;
  Help to sing our Saviour's merits,
  Help to chant Immanuel's praise.
  Rev. John Bakewell. (1721-1819.)
Alt. by Rev. Augustus M. Toplady. (1740-1778.)

"Blessing and honor and glory and power be unto the Lamb."

1096 "This is Jesus, the King." 6, 4.
Ps. cxlviii. Jer. xxiii. 5, 6. Heb. ii.

1 LET us awake our joys,
　Strike up with cheerful voice,
　　Each creature sing :
　Angels, begin the song,
　Mortals, the strain prolong,
　In accents sweet and strong,
　　"Jesus is King."

2 Proclaim abroad His name,
　Tell of His matchless fame ;
　　What wonders done :
　Shout through hell's dark profound ;
　Let all the earth resound,
　Till the high heavens rebound,
　　"The victory 's won."

3 He vanquished sin and hell,
　And the last foe will quell;
　　Mourner, rejoice !
　His dying love adore,
　Praise Him, now raised in power,
　And triumph evermore,
　　With a glad voice.
　　　　　Rev. William Kingsbury. (1744-1818.)

1097 "Sing, for the Lord hath done it." L. M.
Rev. v. Ps. xcvi. 2 Chr. vii. 1-3.

1 COME, let us sing the song of songs !
　The saints in heaven began the strain,
　The homage which to Christ belongs :
　"Worthy the Lamb, for He was slain ! "

2 Slain to redeem us by His blood,
　To cleanse from every sinful stain,
　And make us kings and priests to God :
　"Worthy the Lamb, for He was slain ! "

3 To Him who suffered on the tree,
　Our souls at His soul's price to gain,
　Blessing, and praise, and glory be :
　"Worthy the Lamb, for He was slain ! "

4 To Him, enthroned by filial right,
　All power in heaven and earth proclaim,
　Honor, and majesty, and might :
　"Worthy the Lamb, for He was slain ! "

5 Come, Holy Spirit from on high,
　Our faith, our hope, our love sustain,
　Living to sing, and dying cry :
　"Worthy the Lamb, for He was slain ! "

6 Long as we live, and when we die,
　And while in heaven with Him we reign,
　This song our song of songs shall be :
　"Worthy the Lamb, for He was slain ! "
　　　　　James Montgomery. (1771-1854.)

1098 "Sing unto the Lord, for He hath triumphed." C. M.
Heb. iv. 9-16. Zech. vi. 9-13. John xvii.

1 COME, let us join in songs of praise
　　To our ascended Priest ;
　He entered heaven, with all our names
　　Engraven on His breast.

2 Below He washed our guilt away,
　　By His atoning blood ;
　Now He appears before the throne,
　　And pleads our cause with God.

3 Nor time, nor distance, e'er shall quench
　　The fervors of His love ;
　For us He died in kindness here,
　　Nor is less kind above.

4 O may we ne'er forget His grace,
　　Nor blush to wear His name ;
　Still may our hearts hold fast His faith,
　　Our mouths His praise proclaim.
　　　　　Rev. Alexander Pirie. (-1804.)

1099 "The Lord hath redeemed." C. M.
1 John iii. Eph. iii. 14-21. Ps. xviii. 27-50.

1 TO our Redeemer's glorious name,
　　Awake the sacred song ;
　O may His love, immortal flame,
　　Tune every heart and tongue !

2 His love what mortal thought can reach ?
　　What mortal tongue display ?
　Imagination's utmost stretch
　　In wonder dies away.

3 O may the sweet, the blissful theme
　　Fill every heart and tongue,
　Till strangers love Thy charming name,
　　And join the sacred song.
　　　　　Miss Anne Steele. (1717-1778.)

1100 "Make a joyful noise unto Him." 7.
Ps. xcv. 1 Chr. xvi. 1-36. Luke xix. 29-40.

1 JOYFUL be the hours to-day ;
　Joyful let the season be ;
　Let us sing, for well we may ;
　Jesus, we will sing of Thee.

2 Joyful are we now to own,
　Rapture thrills us as we trace,
　All the deeds Thy love hath done,
　All the riches of Thy grace.

3 Should Thy people silent be,
　Then the very stones would sing.
　What a debt we owe to Thee,
　Thee our Saviour, Thee our King.

4 Thine the name to sinners dear,
　Thine the name all names before :
　Blessèd here and everywhere ;
　Blessèd now and evermore.
　　　　　Rev. Thomas Kelly. (1769-1855.)

"Blessing and honor and glory and power be unto the Lamb."

1101 Ps. cxxxv. "His kingdom ruleth over all." Isa. xlii. 10–16. 1 Chr. xvi. 8–36. Rev. iv. **10. 11.**

1 YE servants of God, your Master proclaim,
And publish abroad His wonderful name ;
The name all-victorious of Jesus extol ;
His kingdom is glorious, and rules over all.

2 God ruleth on high, almighty to save ;
And still He is nigh, His presence we have ;
The great congregation His triumph shall sing,
Ascribing salvation to Jesus our King.

3 " Salvation to God who sits on the throne,"
Let all cry aloud, and honor the Son ;
The praises of Jesus the angels proclaim,
Fall down on their faces, and worship the Lamb.

4 Then let us adore, and give Him His right,
All glory and power, and wisdom and might,
All honor and blessing, with angels above,
And thanks never ceasing, and infinite love.

Rev. Charles Wesley. (1708-1788.)

1102 "In the midst of the elders stood a Lamb." Rev. v. Heb. ii. Zech. ix. 9-17. **C. M.**

1 BEHOLD the glories of the Lamb,
  Amidst His Father's throne :
Prepare new honors for His name,
  And songs before unknown.

2 Let elders worship at His feet,
  The church adore around,
With vials full of odors sweet,
  And harps of sweeter sound.

3 Now to the Lamb that once was slain
  Be endless blessings paid ;
Salvation, glory, joy remain
  Forever on Thy head.

Rev. Isaac Watts. (1674-1748.)

1104 "To the only wise God, our Saviour." Jude 24, 25. Rom. xvi. 24-27. Dan. iv. 34-37. **S. M.**

1 To God the only wise,
  Our Saviour and our King,
Let all the saints, below the skies,
  Their humble praises bring.

2 'T is His almighty love,
  His counsel and His care,
Preserve us safe from sin and death,
  And every hurtful snare.

3 He will present our souls,
  Unblemished and complete,
Before the glory of His face,
  With joys divinely great.

Rev. Isaac Watts.

1103 "The blessed and only potentate." Rev. i. 1-8. Eph. i. Col. i. Ps. xxix. **10. 11.**

1 OUR Saviour alone, the Lord, let us bless,
Who reigns on His throne, the Prince of our peace ;
Who evermore saves us by shedding His blood :
All hail, holy Jesus, our Lord and our God !

2 We thankfully sing Thy glory and praise,
Thou merciful Spring of pity and grace.
Thy kindness forever to men will we tell ;
And say our dear Saviour redeemed us from hell.

3 Preserve us in love while here we abide :
O never remove Thy presence, nor hide .
Thy glorious salvation, till each of us see,
With joy, the blest vision completed in Thee !

Rev. John Cennick. (1717-1755.)

"Praise unto our God."

1105 "Glorious in holiness, fearful in praises, doing wonders." **11. 12. 10.**
Isa. vi. 1-7. Ps. xcix. Ex. xix. Rev. xv.

1 HOLY, holy, holy, Lord God Almighty !
All Thy works shall praise Thy name, in earth, and sky, and sea ;
Holy, holy, holy, Lord God Almighty,
God in three persons, blessed Trinity !

2 Holy, holy, holy, all the saints adore Thee !
Casting down their golden crowns around the glassy sea ;
Cherubim and seraphim falling down before Thee,
Which wert, and art, and evermore shalt be.

3 Holy, holy, holy, though the darkness hide Thee,
Though the eye of sinful man Thy glory may not see,
Only Thou art holy, there is none beside Thee,
Perfect in power, and love, and purity.

Bp. Reginald Heber. (1783-1826.)

1106 "O Lord, holy and true." **L. M.**
Rev. iv. Ps. lxxii. 2 Cor. xiii. 5-14.

1 O HOLY, holy, holy Lord !
Bright in Thy deeds and in Thy name,
Forever be Thy name adored,
Thy glories let the world proclaim !

2 O Jesus, Lamb once crucified
To take our load of sins away,
Thine be the hymn that rolls its tide
Along the realms of upper day !

3 O Holy Spirit, from above,
In streams of light and glory given,
Thou source of ecstasy and love,
Thy praises ring through earth and heaven !

4 O God Triune, to Thee we owe
Our every thought, our every song ;
And ever may Thy praises flow
From saint and seraph's burning tongue !

Rev. James W. Eastburn. (1797-1819.)

1107 "Unto the King, eternal, immortal, invisible." **6. 4.**
Dan. vii. 9-14. John i. 1-14. Acts ix. 31-43.

1 FATHER of heaven above,
Dwelling in light and love,
Ancient of days,
Light unapproachable,
Love inexpressible,
Thee, the invisible,
Laud we and praise.

2 Christ, the eternal Word,
Christ, the incarnate Lord,
Saviour of all,
High throned above all light,
God of God, Light of Light,
Increate, infinite,
On Thee we call !

3 O God, the Holy Ghost,
Whose fires of Pentecost
Burn evermore,
In this far wilderness,
Leave us not comfortless,
Thee we love, Thee we bless,
Thee we adore.

Rev. Edward H. Bickersteth. (1825-.)

1108 "Sweet counsel together." **7.**
Ps. xcv. 1 John iv. 6-21. Acts ii. 36-47.

1 SWEET the time, exceeding sweet,
When the saints together meet ;
When the Saviour is the theme,
When they join to sing of Him.

2 Sing we then eternal love,
Such as did the Father move :
He beheld the world undone,
Loved the world, and gave His Son.

3 Sing the Son's amazing love :
How He left the realms above,
Took our nature and our place,
Lived and died to save our race.

4 Sing we, too, the Spirit's love :
With our wretched hearts He strove,
Took the things of Christ, and showed
How to reach His blest abode.

Rev. George Burder. (1752-1832.)

1109 "Unto Him that loved us." **L. M.**
John iii. 14-21. Titus iii. 4-7. Ps. lxvi. 8-20.

1 PRAISES to Him whose love has given
In Christ, His Son, the Life of Heaven ;
Who for our darkness gives us light,
And turns to day our deepest night.

2 Praises to Him the chain who broke,
Opened the prison, burst the yoke,
Sent forth its captives glad and free,
Heirs of an endless liberty.

3 Praises to Him who sheds abroad
Within our hearts the love of God ;
The Spirit of all truth and peace,
Fountain of joy and holiness !

4 To Father, Son, and Spirit now
The hands we lift, the knees we bow ;
To Thee, Jehovah, thus we raise
The sinner's endless song of praise.

Rev. Horatius Bonar. (1808-.)

"Praise unto our God."

1110 "We thank Thee and praise Thy glorious name." **11.**
Rev. v. Nch. ix. 1-20. Ps. cvii. 1-16. Hab. iii. 1, 2, 17-19.

1 WE praise Thee, O God, for the Son of Thy love,
For Jesus who died, and is now gone above!
Hallelujah! Thine the glory, Hallelujah! Amen.
Hallelujah! Thine the glory, revive us again.

2 We praise Thee, O God, for Thy Spirit of light,
Who has shown us our Saviour, and scattered our night.

3 All glory and praise to the Lamb that was slain,
Who has borne all our sins, and cleansed every stain.

4 All glory and praise to the God of all grace,
Who has bought us, and sought us, and guided our ways.

5 Revive us again; fill each heart with Thy love;
May each soul be rekindled with fire from above.
Rev. William P. Mackay. (1839-.)

1111 "Peace in heaven and glory in the highest." **7.**
Luke ii. 1-18. Ps. cxlv. Heb. xiii. 7-21.

1 GLORY be to God on high,
God, whose glory fills the sky;
Peace on earth to man forgiven,
Man, the well-beloved of Heaven.
Hail, by all Thy works adored!
Hail, the everlasting Lord!
Thee with thankful hearts we prove,
God of power, and God of love.

2 Christ our Lord and God we own,
Christ, the Father's only Son;
Lamb of God for sinners slain,
Saviour of offending man.
Jesus, in Thy name we pray,
Take, O take our sins away;
Bow Thine ear, in mercy bow,
Hear, the world's atonement, Thou!
Rev. Charles Wesley. (1708-1788.)

1112 "The sons of God shouted for joy." **7.**
Job xxxviii. 4-11. Luke xix. 28-38. Ps. lxxii.

1 SONGS of praise the angels sang,
Heaven with hallelujahs rang,
When Jehovah's work begun,
When He spake, and it was done.

2 Songs of praise awoke the morn
When the Prince of Peace was born;
Songs of praise arose when He
Captive led captivity.

3 Saints below, with heart and voice,
Still in songs of praise rejoice;
Learning here, by faith and love,
Songs of praise to sing above.

4 Borne upon their latest breath,
Songs of praise shall conquer death;
Then, amidst eternal joy,
Songs of praise their powers employ.
James Montgomery. (1771-1854.)

1113 "Who is worthy to be praised." **7. 6. P.**
Isa. vi. Rev. iv. Eph. i.

1 MEET and right it is to sing,
In every time and place,
Glory to our heavenly King,
The God of truth and grace:
Join we, then, with sweet accord,
All in one thanksgiving join:
Holy, holy, holy Lord,
Eternal praise be Thine.

2 Thee the first-born sons of light,
In choral symphonies,
Praise by day, day without night,
And never, never cease:
Thee they sing with glory crowned;
We extol the slaughtered Lamb:
Lower if our voices sound,
Our theme is still the same.
Rev. Charles Wesley.

1114 "The voice of many angels." **C. M.**
Ps. xxiv. Isa. xlii. 5-16. Rev. xiv. 1-3.

1 HARK how the angels sweetly sing!
Their voices fill the sky:
They hail their great victorious King,
And welcome Him on high.

2 We'll catch the note of lofty praise;
Their joys, O may we feel;
Our thankful song with them we'll raise,
And emulate their zeal.

3 Come then, ye saints, and grateful sing
Of Christ, our risen Lord;
Of Christ, the everlasting King;
Of Christ, th' incarnate Word.

4 Hail, mighty Saviour, Thee we hail,
High on Thy throne above:
Till heart and flesh together fail,
We'll sing Thy matchless love.
Rev. Thomas Kelly. (1769-1855.)

"Praise unto our God."

1115 "Thou art worthy, O Lord, to receive glory." **6. 4.**
Ps. cxiii. Acts ii. 22-36. 1 Tim. i. 15-17.

1 GLORY to God on High,
   Let praises fill the sky,
      Praise ye His name!
   Angels His name adore,
   Who all our sorrows bore,
   And saints cry evermore,
      "Worthy the Lamb!"

2 To Him our hearts we raise;
   None else shall have our praise;
      Praise ye His name!
   Him, our exalted Lord,
   By us below adored,
   We praise with one accord,
      "Worthy the Lamb!"

3 Join all the human race,
   Our Lord and God to bless;
      Praise ye His name!
   In Him we will rejoice,
   Making a cheerful noise,
   And say with heart and voice,
      "Worthy the Lamb!"

4 Though we must change our place,
   Our souls shall never cease
      Praising His name;
   To Him we'll tribute bring,
   Laud Him our gracious King,
   And without ceasing sing,
      "Worthy the Lamb!"
         Rev. James Allen. (1734-1804.)

1116 "The whole earth be filled with His glory." **L. M.**
Mat. ii 1-11. Isa. ix. 1-8. John xii. 23-36.

1 ALL praise to Thee, eternal Lord,
   Clothed in the garb of flesh and blood;
   Choosing a manger for Thy throne,
   While worlds on worlds are Thine alone.

2 A little child Thou art our guest,
   That weary ones in Thee may rest;
   Forlorn and lowly is Thy birth,
   That we may rise to heaven from earth.

3 Thou comest in the darksome night
   To make us children of the light,
   To make us, in the realms divine,
   Like Thine own angels round Thee shine.

4 All this for us Thy love hath done;
   By this to Thee our love is won:
   For this we tune our cheerful lays,
   And shout our thanks in ceaseless praise.
         Martin Luther. (1483-1546.)

1117 "Praise Him in the firmament." **7. 6. 7.**
Ps. cl. 1 Chr. xvi. 8-36. Mat. vi. 9-13.

1 PRAISE the Lord, who reigns above,
   And keeps His courts below;
   Praise the holy God of love,
   And all His greatness show;
   Praise Him for His noble deeds;
   Praise Him for His matchless power;
   Him, from whom all good proceeds,
   Let earth and heaven adore.

2 Publish, spread to all around
   The great Immanuel's name;
   Let the trumpet's martial sound
   Him, Lord of Hosts, proclaim.
   Praise Him, every tuneful string;
   All the reach of heavenly art,
   All the powers of music bring,
   The music of the heart.

3 Him, in whom they move and live,
   Let every creature sing;
   Glory to their Maker give,
   And homage to their King:
   Hallowed be His name beneath;
   As in heaven, on earth adored;
   Praise the Lord in every breath;
   Let all things praise the Lord.
         Rev. Augustus M. Toplady. (1740-1778.)

1118 "Bless His holy name." **7.**
Rev. iv. 8-11. Isa. vi. 1-8. Ps. xxx.

1 HOLY, holy, holy Lord,
   Be Thy glorious name adored:
   Lord, Thy mercies never fail;
   Hail, celestial Goodness, hail!

2 Though unworthy, Lord, Thine ear,
   Deign our humble songs to hear;
   Purer praise we hope to bring,
   When around Thy throne we sing.

3 Then with angel-harps again
   We will wake a nobler strain;
   There, in joyful songs of praise,
   Our triumphant voices raise.
         Rev. Benjamin Williams. (1725-1795.)

1119 "Hosanna in the highest." **C. M.**
Mat. xxi. 1-16. Ps. xcvi. Ex. xv. 1-18.

1 HOSANNA to our conquering King!
   All hail, incarnate Love!
   Ten thousand songs and glories wait
   To crown Thy head above.

2 Thy victories, and Thy deathless fame,
   Through the wide world shall run,
   And everlasting ages sing
   The triumphs Thou hast won.
         Rev. Isaac Watts. (1674-1748.)

"The Father, the Word, and the Holy Ghost."

1120   "Sing unto the Lord."   L. M.
Ps. cxv. 18.   Isa. vi. 3.   Rev. iv. 8.

1 GREAT One in Three, great Three in One,
  Thy wondrous name we sound abroad ;
  Prostrate we fall before Thy throne,
  O holy, holy, holy Lord !

2 Thee, Holy Father, we confess !
  Thee, Holy Saviour, we adore !
  And Thee, O Holy Ghost, we bless
  And praise and worship evermore !
  Author unknown.

1121   "Bless His name."   L. M.
Ps. lxvi. 8.   2 Chr. xx. 21.   1 Tim. vi. 15.

1 BLEST Trinity, from mortal sight
  Veiled in Thine own eternal light,
  We Thee confess, in Thee believe,
  To Thee with loving hearts we cleave.

2 Eternal Father, Thee we praise ;
  To Thee, O Son, our hymns we raise ;
  O Holy Ghost, we Thee adore :
  One mighty God for evermore.
  Santolius Maglorianus.   (1624-1684.)
  Tr. by Rev. Sir Henry W. Baker.   (1821-1877.)

1122   "Show forth His salvation."   L. M.
Ps. cxxxv. 19.   Ezra iii. 11.   2 Cor. ii. 14.

1 BLEST be the Father and His love,
  To whose celestial source we owe
  Rivers of endless joy above,
  And rills of comfort here below.

2 Glory to Thee, great Son of God,
  From whose dear wounded body rolls
  A precious stream of vital blood,
  Pardon and life for dying souls.

3 We give the sacred Spirit praise,
  Who, in our hearts of sin and woe,
  Makes living springs of grace arise,
  And into boundless glory flow.
  Rev. Isaac Watts.   (1674-1748.)

1123   "Give to the Lord glory."   C. M.
Ps. xcvi. 2.   Judg. v. 9.   2 Pet. iii. 18.

To Father, Son, and Holy Ghost,
  The God whom we adore,
Be glory, as it was, is now,
  And shall be evermore.
  Tate and Brady.   1695.

1124   "Glory be . . . unto our God."   S. M.
Ps. cxlv. 10.   Isa. lii. 9.   Rom. ix. 5.

To God the Father, Son,
  And Spirit, One in Three,
Be glory, as it was, is now,
  And shall forever be.
  Rev. John Wesley.   (1703-1791.)

1125   "Praise Him in the heights."   L. M.
Ps. cxlvii. 1.   1 Chr. xvi. 23.   Rev. vii. 12.

PRAISE God, from whom all blessings flow ;
Praise Him, all creatures here below ;
Praise Him above, ye heavenly host ;
Praise Father, Son, and Holy Ghost.
  Bp. Thomas Ken.   (1637-1711.)

1126   "Unto praise and honor and glory."   L. M.
Ps. cxli. 10.   Isa. lx. 6.   Rom. xi. 36.

To God the Father, God the Son,
  And God the Spirit, Three in One,
Be honor, praise, and glory given,
By all on earth, and all in heaven ;
As was through ages heretofore,
Is now, and shall be evermore.
  Rev. Isaac Watts.

1127   "Giving glory to God."   8. 6.
Ps. cxlix. 1.   1 Chr. xvi. 4.   Gal. i. 5.

To Father, Son, and Holy Ghost,
The God whom heaven's triumphant host
  And saints on earth adore,
Be glory as in ages past,
As now it is, and so shall last,
  When time shall be no more.
  Tate and Brady.   1696.

1128   "Blessed be the most high God."   8.
Ps. cl. 6.   Zeph. iii. 14.   Eph. v. 20.

Now to the great and sacred Three,
  The Father, Son, and Spirit, be
Eternal praise and glory given,
Through all the worlds where God is known,
By all the angels near the throne,
  And all the saints in earth and heaven.
  Rev. Isaac Watts.

1129   "Blessed forevermore."   6. 8.
Ps. lii. 9.   Jer. xxx. 19.   Jude 25.

O GOD, forever blest,
  To Thee all praise be given ;
Thy name Triune confest
  By all in earth and heaven ;
As heretofore it was, is now,
And shall be so for evermore.
  Rev. Edward H. Bickersteth.   (1825-.)

1130   "Sing praises unto our God."   6. 4.
Ps. cxlviii. 1.   Eze. iii. 12.   1 Thes. v. 18.

To the great One in Three
The highest praises be,
  Hence evermore ;
His sovereign majesty
May we in glory see,
And to eternity
  Love and adore.
  Rev. Charles Wesley.   (1708-1788.)

"The Father, the Word, and the Holy Ghost."

1131 "So will we sing and praise Thy power." 7.
Ps. xcv. 1. Isa. xii. 5. Eph. i. 3.

SING we to our God above
Praise eternal as His love :
Praise Him, all ye heavenly host,
Father, Son, and Holy Ghost.
Rev. Charles Wesley. (1708-1788.)

1132 "Blessed be Thy glorious name." 7.
Ps. cxvii. 1. Deu. viii. 10. Rom. xv. 11.

PRAISE the name of God most high,
Praise Him, all below the sky,
Praise Him, all ye heavenly host,
Father, Son, and Holy Ghost ;
As through countless ages past,
Evermore His praise shall last.
Author unknown. 1827.

1133 "Praise the name of the Lord." 7.
Ps. cxxxiv. 1. Neh. ix. 5. Heb. xiii. 21.

PRAISE our glorious King and Lord,
Angels waiting on His word,
Saints that walk with Him in white,
Pilgrims walking in His light :
Glory to the Eternal One,
Glory to His Only Son,
Glory to the Spirit be
Now, and through eternity.
Rev. Alexander R. Thompson. (1822-.)

1134 "Give glory unto the Lord." 7. 6. 8.
Ps. cxiii 1. Neh. viii. 6. 2 Cor. iv. 15.

FATHER, Son, and Holy Ghost,
Thy Godhead we adore ;
Join we with the heavenly host,
To praise Thee evermore !
Live, by earth and heaven adored,
The Three in One, the One in Three ;
Holy, holy, holy Lord,
All glory be to Thee !
Rev. Charles Wesley.

1135 "Thy saints shall bless Thee." 7. 6.
Ps. cxviii. 1. 1 Chr. xxix. 20. 1 Cor. xv. 57.

To Thee be praise forever,
Thou glorious King of kings !
Thy wondrous love and favor
Each ransomed spirit sings :
We'll celebrate Thy glory
With all Thy saints above,
And shout the joyful story
Of Thy redeeming love.
Rev. Thomas Haweis. (1732-1820.)

1136 "Let heaven and earth praise Him." 7.
Ps. cxlviii. 4. Ex. xv. 21. 1 Pet. i. 3.

PRAISE the Father, earth and heaven,
Praise the Son, the Spirit praise,
As it was, and is, be given
Glory through eternal days.
Author unknown.

1137 "All Thy works shall praise Thee." 8. 7.
Ps. ix. 11. 2 Chr. xxix. 30. 1 Tim. i. 17.

PRAISE the God of our salvation ;
Praise the Father's boundless love ;
Praise the Lamb, our expiation ;
Praise the Spirit from above,
Author of the new creation,
Him by whom our spirits live ;
Undivided adoration
To the one Jehovah given !
Josiah Conder. (1789-1855.)

1138 "Extol Him by His name JAH." 8. 7. 4.
Ps. lxviii. 32. Neh. xii. 27. 1 Pet. v. 11.

GREAT Jehovah, we adore Thee,
God the Father, God the Son,
God the Spirit, joined in glory
On the same eternal throne ;
Endless praises
To Jehovah, Three in One.
Rev. William Goode. (1762-1816.)

1139 "Blessed be the Lord forevermore." 10.
Ps. lxv. 1. 2 Chr. xx. 26. Rev. i. 6.

To Father, Son, and Spirit, ever blest,
Eternal praise and worship be addrest ;
From age to age, ye saints, His name adore,
And spread His fame, till time shall be no more.
Rev. Simon Browne. (1680-1732.)

1140 "Declare His glory." 10. P.
Ps. xlvii. 1. 1 Chr. xvi. 8. Luke ii. 14.

ALL glory to God, the Father and Son,
And Spirit of grace, the great Three in One ;
Let highest ascriptions forever be given
By all the creation on earth and in heaven.
Author unknown.

1141 "They will be still praising Thee." 11.
Ps. viii. 1. Jer. xxxiii. 11. 2 Cor. ix. 15.

O FATHER Almighty, to Thee be addrest,
With Christ and the Spirit, One God ever blest,
All glory and worship, from earth and from heaven,
As was, and is now, and shall ever be given.
Author unknown.

"On the first day shall be a holy convocation."

1142 "The Lord is in His holy temple." 8. 7. 4.
Hab. ii. Ps. xi. Heb. i. 1–3.

1 GOD is in His holy temple,
All the earth, keep silence here;
Worship Him in truth and spirit,
Reverence Him with godly fear;
Holy, holy,
Lord of hosts, our Lord, appear!

2 God in Christ reveals His presence,
Throned upon the mercy-seat:
Saints, rejoice, and sinners, tremble;
Each prepare his God to meet;
Lowly, lowly
Bow adoring at His feet.

3 Hail Him here with songs of praises,
Him with prayers of faith surround;
Hearken to His glorious gospel,
While the preacher's lips expound;
Blessèd, blessèd
They who know the joyful sound.
James Montgomery. (1771–1854.)

1143 "Worship the Lord in the beauty of holiness." 7.
John xx. 19–31. Mat. xviii. 19, 20. Ps. lxi.

1 SWEET and holy is the place,
Where the light. that beams from heaven,
Shows the Saviour's smiling face,
With the joy of sin forgiven.

2 There, with one accord, we meet,
All the words of life to hear;
Bending low at Jesus' feet,
Worshipping with godly fear.

3 Let the world and all its cares
Now retire from every breast;
Let the tempter and his snares
Cease to hinder or molest.
Thomas Hastings. (1784–1872.)

1144 "Even Thine altars." 8.
Ps. xxvii. Job xxiii. John v. 1–9.

1 FORTH from the dark and stormy sky,
Lord, to Thine altar's shade we fly;
Forth from the world, its hope and fear,
Saviour, we seek Thy shelter here;
Weary and weak, Thy grace we pray;
Turn not, O Lord, Thy guests away.

2 Long have we roamed in want and pain,
Long have we sought Thy rest in vain;
Wildered in doubt, in darkness lost,
Long have our souls been tempest-tossed;
Low at Thy feet our sins we lay;
Turn not, O Lord, Thy guests away.
Bp. Reginald Heber. (1783–1826.)

1145 "Strength and beauty are in His sanctuary." H. M.
Ps. lxxxiv. Num. xxiv. 1–6. Acts ii. 46, 47.

1 LORD of the worlds above,
How pleasant and how fair
The dwellings of Thy love,
Thine earthly temples are!
To Thine abode my heart aspires,
With warm desires to see my God.

2 O happy souls who pray,
Where God appoints to hear!
O happy men who pay
Their constant service there!
They praise Thee still; and happy they,
Who love the way to Zion's hill.

3 They go from strength to strength,
Through this dark vale of tears,
Till each arrives at length,
Till each in heaven appears;
O glorious seat, when God, our King,
Shall thither bring our willing feet!
Rev. Isaac Watts. (1674–1748.)

1146 "To the house of God with the voice of joy" S. M.
Ps. cxxxiv. Isa. ii. 1–5. Luke xi. 1–13

1 WITH joy we lift our eyes
To those bright realms above,
That glorious temple in the skies,
Where dwells eternal love.

2 Before Thy throne we bow,
O Thou almighty King!
Here we present the solemn vow,
And hymns of praise we sing.

3 While in Thy house we kneel,
With trust and holy fear,
Thy mercy and Thy truth reveal,
And lend a gracious ear.
Rev. Thomas Jervis. (1748–1793.)

1147 "Joyful in my house of prayer." C. M.
Ps. cxxii. Zech. viii. 20–23. Acts i. 1–14.

1 WITH joy we hail the sacred day,
Which God has called His own;
With joy the summons we obey
To worship at His throne.

2 Thy chosen temple, Lord, how fair,
Where willing votaries throng,
To breathe the humble, fervent prayer,
And pour the choral song.

3 Spirit of grace, O deign to dwell
Within Thy church below;
Make her in holiness excel,
With pure devotion glow.
Miss Harriet Auber. (1773–1862.)

"On the first day shall be a holy convocation."

1148 "And the court was full of the brightness." 7.
Ps. lxxxiv. Num. xxiv. 1-6. Mark ix. 2-10.

1 LORD of hosts, how bright, how fair,
E'en on earth, Thy temples are:
Here Thy waiting people see
Much of heaven, and much of Thee.

2 From Thy gracious presence flows
Bliss that softens all our woes;
While Thy Spirit's holy fire
Warms our hearts with pure desire.

3 Here we supplicate Thy throne;
Here Thou mak'st Thy glories known;
Here we learn Thy righteous ways,
Taste Thy love, and sing Thy praise.

4 Thus with sacred songs of joy
We our happy lives employ;
Love, and long to love Thee more,
Till from earth to heaven we soar.

Rev. Daniel Turner. (1710-1798.)

1151 "Praise waiteth in Zion." L. M.
Ps. lxv. Jer. xxxi. 1-14. Rom. xv. 5-13.

1 PRAISE waits in Zion, Lord, for Thee;
Thy saints adore Thy holy name;
Thy creatures bend the obedient knee,
And humbly now Thy presence claim.

2 Eternal source of truth and light,
To Thee we look, on Thee we call;
Lord, we are nothing in Thy sight,
But Thou to us art all in all.

3 Still may Thy children in Thy word
Their common trust and refuge see;
O bind us to each other, Lord,
By one great bond, the love of Thee.

4 So shall our sun of hope arise,
With brighter still and brighter ray,
Till Thou shalt bless our longing eyes
With beams of everlasting day.

Sir James E. Smith. (1759-1828.)

1149 "The joy of the whole earth is Mount Zion." 11. 9.
Ps. xlviii. Isa. lii. Zech. ii. 3-13. 1 Pet. v. 4-11.

1 O GREAT is Jehovah, and great be His praise;
In the city of God He is King:
Proclaim ye His triumphs in jubilant lays;
On the mount of His holiness sing.

2 The joy of the earth, from her beautiful height,
Is Zion's impregnable hill;
The Lord in her temple still taketh delight;
God reigns in her palaces still.

3 Go, walk about Zion, and measure the length,
Her walls and her bulwarks mark well;
Contemplate her palaces, glorious in strength,
Her towers and their pinnacles tell.

4 Then say to your children, "Our stronghold is tried;
This God is our God to the end;
His people forever His counsels shall guide,
His arm shall forever defend."

James Montgomery. (1771-1854.)

1150 "We will shew forth Thy praise." L. M.
Ps. c. 1 Kings viii. 54-66. 1 Thes. v. 16-24.

1 PRAISE, Lord, for Thee in Zion waits;
Prayer shall besiege Thy temple gates;
All flesh shall to Thy throne repair,
And find, through Christ, salvation there.

2 How blest Thy saints, how safely led,
How surely kept, how richly fed:
Saviour of all in earth and sea,
How happy they who rest in Thee!

3 Lord, on our souls Thy Spirit pour;
The moral waste within restore;
O let Thy love our spring-tide be,
And make us all bear fruit to Thee.

Rev. Henry F. Lyte. (1793-1847.)

1152 "The glory of the Lord filled the house." L. M.
Ps. xxix. 2 Chr. xx. Mat. viii. 23-32.

1 GIVE to the Lord, ye sons of fame,
Give to the Lord renown and power;
Ascribe due honors to His name,
And His eternal might adore.

2 The Lord sits Sovereign on the flood;
The Thunderer reigns forever King;
But makes His church His blest abode,
Where we His awful glories sing.

3 In gentler language there the Lord
The counsels of His grace imparts;
Amid the raging storm His word
Speaks peace and courage to our hearts.

Rev. Isaac Watts. (1674-1748.)

"On the first day shall be a holy convocation."

1153 "The rest of the holy Sabbath." 8.
Gen. ii. 1-3. Ps. cxxxix. 1-18. Luke xxiv. 1-32.

1 GREAT God, this sacred day of Thine
  Demands the soul's collected powers ;
  Gladly we now to Thee resign
  These solemn, consecrated hours ;
  O may our souls adoring own
  The grace that calls us to Thy throne !

2 All-seeing God, Thy piercing eye
  Can every secret thought explore ;
  May worldly cares our bosoms fly,
  And, where Thou art, intrude no more ;
  O may Thy grace our spirits move,
  And fix our minds on things above !

3 Thy Spirit's powerful aid impart,
  And bid Thy word, with life divine,
  Engage the ear and warm the heart :
  Then shall the day indeed be thine ;
  Then shall our souls adoring own
  The grace that calls us to Thy throne.

Miss Anne Steele. (1717-1778.)

1154 "This is the day the Lord hath made." C. M.
Ps. cxviii. Rev. i. 10-20. Mat. xxi. 1-11.

1 THIS is the day the Lord hath made ;
  He calls the hours His own :
  Let heaven rejoice, let earth be glad,
  And praise surround the throne.

2 To-day He rose and left the dead,
  And Satan's empire fell ;
  To-day the saints His triumph spread,
  And all His wonders tell.

3 Hosanna to th' anointed King,
  To David's holy Son :
  Help us, O Lord ! descend, and bring
  Salvation from the throne.

Rev. Isaac Watts. (1074-1748.)

1155 "Not forsaking the assembling of ourselves." C. M.
Ex. xx. 8-11. Ps. lxii. Rev. xxi. 22-27.

1 FREQUENT the day of God returns
  To shed its quickening beams ;
  And yet how slow devotion burns,
  How languid are its flames.

2 Accept our faint attempts to love,
  Our frailties, Lord, forgive ;
  We would be like Thy saints above,
  And praise Thee while we live.

3 Increase, O Lord, our faith and hope,
  And fit us to ascend
  Where the assembly ne'er breaks up,
  The Sabbath ne'er will end.

Rev. Simon Browne. (1680-1732.)

1156 "The Lord ... hallowed it." S. M.
Gen. i. 1-5. Lev. xxiii. John xx.

1 THIS is the day of light :
  Let there be light to-day ;
  O Dayspring, rise upon our night,
  And chase its gloom away.

2 This is the day of rest :
  Our failing strength renew ;
  On weary brain and troubled breast
  Shed Thou Thy freshening dew.

3 This is the day of peace :
  Thy peace our spirits fill ;
  Bid Thou the blasts of discord cease,
  The waves of strife be still.

4 This is the day of prayer :
  Let earth to heaven draw near ;
  Lift up our hearts to seek Thee there ;
  Come down to meet us here.

5 This is the first of days :
  Send forth Thy quickening breath,
  And wake dead souls to love and praise,
  O Vanquisher of death !

Rev. John Ellerton. (1825-.)

1157 "The first day of the week." 7.
Ex. xxxi. 12-17. Ps. cxxii. Acts xiii. 38-51

1 SAFELY through another week
  God has brought us on our way ;
  Let us now a blessing seek,
  Waiting in His courts to-day :
  Day of all the week the best,
  Emblem of eternal rest.

2 While we pray for pardoning grace,
  Through the dear Redeemer's name,
  Show Thy reconciléd face,
  Take away our sin and shame ;
  From our worldly cares set free,
  May we rest, this day, in Thee.

3 Here we come Thy name to praise ;
  May we feel Thy presence near ;
  May Thy glory meet our eyes,
  While we in Thy house appear :
  Here afford us, Lord, a taste
  Of our everlasting feast.

4 May Thy gospel's joyful sound
  Conquer sinners, comfort saints ;
  Make the fruits of grace abound,
  Bring relief for all complaints :
  Thus may all our Sabbaths prove,
  Till we join the church above.

Rev. John Newton. (1725-1807.)

"On the first day shall be a holy convocation."

1158 Nch. viii. 9-12. Isa. xxv. 1-9. Col. iii. 12-17. "My holy day." 7. 6.

1 THY holy day's returning
  Our hearts exult to see ;
And, with devotion burning,
  Ascend, our God, to Thee ;
To-day, with purest pleasure,
  Our thoughts from earth withdraw ;
We search for sacred treasure,
  We learn Thy holy law.

2 We join to sing Thy praises,
  God of the Sabbath day ;
Each voice in gladness raises
  Its loudest, sweetest lay ;
Thy richest mercies sharing,
  O fill us with Thy love,
By grace our souls preparing
  For nobler praise above.
              Rev. Ray Palmer. (1808-.)

1159 Ps. lxxxix. 1 Chr. xxix. 11. Rom. xi. 33-36 "Exalt the Lord our God." S. M.

1 SWEET is the work, O Lord,
  Thy glorious acts to sing,
To praise Thy name, and hear Thy word,
  And grateful offerings bring.

2 Sweet, at the dawning light,
  Thy boundless love to tell ;
And, when approach the shades of night,
  Still on the theme to dwell.

3 Sweet, on this day of rest,
  To join in heart and voice
With those who love and serve Thee best,
  And in Thy name rejoice.

4 To songs of praise and joy
  Be every Sabbath given,
That such may be our blest employ
  Eternally in heaven.
              Miss Harriet Auber. (1773-1862.)

1160 Ps. lxiii. Isa. xii. Acts i. 12-14. "The voice of rejoicing and salvation." L. M.

1 HAIL, morning known among the blest,
Morning of hope, and joy, and love,
Of heavenly peace, and holy rest,
Pledge of the endless rest above !

2 Descend, O Spirit of the Lord,
  Thy fire to every bosom bring ;
Then shall our ardent hearts accord,
  And teach our lips God's praise to sing.
              Rev. Ralph Wardlaw. (1779-1853.)

1161 Heb. iv. 9-16. Isa. lviii. 13, 14. Ps. lxxxiv. "O God, . . . our eyes are upon Thee." L. M.

1 LORD of the Sabbath, hear our vows,
On this Thy day, in this Thy house ;
And own, as grateful sacrifice,
The songs which from the desert rise.

2 Thine earthly Sabbaths, Lord, we love ;
But there 's a nobler rest above ;
To that our laboring souls aspire,
With ardent pangs of strong desire.

3 No more fatigue, no more distress,
Nor sin, nor hell shall reach the place ;
No groans to mingle with the songs
Which warble from immortal tongues.

4 No rude alarms of raging foes,
No cares to break the long repose,
No midnight shade, no clouded sun,
But sacred, high, eternal noon.

5 O long-expected day, begin ;
Dawn on these realms of woe and sin ;
Fain would we leave this weary road,
And sleep in death to rest with God.
              Rev. Philip Doddridge. (1702-1751.)

1162 John xvi. 1 Cor. ii. 7-16. Ex. xxxiii. 12-32. "Thy Spirit is good." C. M.

1 SPIRIT of truth, on this Thy day
  To Thee for help we cry,
To guide us through the dreary way
  Of dark mortality.

2 We ask not, Lord, Thy cloven flame,
  Or tongues of various tone ;
But long Thy praises to proclaim
  With fervor in our own.

3 We mourn not that prophetic skill
  Is found on earth no more ;
Enough for us to trace Thy will,
  In Scripture's sacred lore.

4 No heavenly harpings soothe our ear,
  No mystic dreams we share ;
Yet hope to feel Thy comfort near,
  And bless Thee in our prayer.
              Bp. Reginald Heber. (1783-1826.)

1163 Ps. cxviii. 14-29. Isa. lvi. 2-7. Acts xiii. 44-49. "Rejoice before the Lord thy God." 7.

1 WELCOME, sacred day of rest ;
Sweet repose from worldly care ;
Day above all days the best,
When our souls for heaven prepare.

2 Gracious Lord, we love this day,
When we hear Thy holy word ;
When we sing Thy praise, and pray,
Earth can no such joys afford.
              William Brown. 1823.

"On the first day shall be a holy convocation."

1164 "In the morning, the first day of the week." **7.**
Ps. v. Isa. lvi. 1–7. Mark xvi. 1–11.

1 HAIL, thou bright and sacred morn,
Risen with gladness in thy beams:
Light, which not of earth is born,
From thy dawn in glory streams ;
Airs of heaven are breathed around,
And each place is holy ground.

2 Sad and weary were our way,
Fainting oft beneath our load,
But for thee, thou blessèd day,
Resting-place on life's rough road :
Here flow forth the streams of grace,
Strengthened hence we run our race.

3 Soon, too soon, the sweet repose
Of this day of God will cease ;
Soon this glimpse of heaven will close,
Vanish soon the hours of peace ;
Soon return the toil, the strife,
All the weariness of life.

4 But the rest which yet remains
For Thy people, Lord, above,
Knows nor change, nor fears, nor pains,
Endless as their Saviour's love :
O may every Sabbath here
Bring us to that rest more near.

Mrs. Julia A. Elliott. (–1841.)

1165 "The Sabbath of the Lord thy God." **S. M.**
Gen. ii. 1–3. Ex. xx. 8–11. John iv. 20–24.

1 HAIL to the Sabbath day,
The day divinely given ;
When men to God their homage pay,
And earth draws near to heaven.

2 Lord, in this sacred hour
Within Thy courts we bend,
And bless Thy love, and own Thy power,
Our Father and our Friend.

3 But Thou art not alone
In courts by mortals trod ;
Nor only is the day Thine own
When man draws near to God.

4 Thy temple is the arch
Of yon unmeasured sky;
Thy Sabbath, the stupendous march
Of grand eternity.

5 Lord, may that holier day
Dawn on Thy servants' sight ;
And purer worship may we pay
In heaven's unclouded light.

Rev. Stephen G. Bulfinch. (1809–1870.)

1166 "The Sabbath of rest, holy to the Lord." **7. 6.**
Luke xxiv. 1–12. Heb. iv. 1–10. Ex. xxxv. 1–3.

1 O DAY of rest and gladness,
O day of joy and light,
O balm of care and sadness,
Most beautiful, most bright ;
On thee the high and lowly,
Bending before the throne,
Sing, Holy, holy, holy,
To the great Three in One.

2 On thee, at the creation,
The light first had its birth ;
On thee, for our salvation,
Christ rose from depths of earth ;
On thee, our Lord, victorious,
The Spirit sent from heaven,
And thus on thee, most glorious,
A triple light was given.

3 To-day on weary nations
The heavenly manna falls ;
To holy convocations
The silver trumpet calls,
Where gospel light is glowing
With pure and radiant beams,
And living water flowing
With soul-refreshing streams.

4 New graces ever gaining
From this our day of rest,
We reach the rest remaining
To spirits of the blest :
To Holy Ghost be praises,
To Father and to Son ;
The church her voice upraises
To Thee, blest Three in One.

Bp. Christopher Wordsworth. (1807–.)

1167 "Break forth into singing." **H. M.**
Mat. xxviii. 1–8. Ps. xcv. Rev. i. 10–18.

1 AWAKE, ye saints, awake,
And hail this sacred day ;
In loftiest songs of praise
Your joyful homage pay ;
Come, bless the day that God hath blest,
The type of heaven's eternal rest.

2 All hail, triumphant Lord !
Heaven with hosannas rings,
And earth in humbler strains
Thy praise responsive sings :
Worthy the Lamb, that once was slain,
Through endless years to live and reign.

Miss Elizabeth Scott. (1708–.)
Alt. by Rev. Thomas Cotterill. (1779–1823.)

"At evening ... the first day of the week."

1168 "The same day at evening ... came Jesus." **7.**
Ps. xlviii. 9–14. Phil. iv. 4–7. John xvii. 13–26.

1 SOFTLY fades the twilight ray
Of the holy Sabbath day;
Gently as life's setting sun,
When the Christian's course is run.

2 Peace is on the world abroad;
'Tis the holy peace of God,
Symbol of the peace within
When the spirit rests from sin.

3 Still the Spirit lingers near,
Where the evening worshipper
Seeks communion with the skies,
Pressing onward to the prize.

4 Saviour, may our Sabbaths be
Days of joy and peace in Thee,
Till in heaven our souls repose,
Where the Sabbath ne'er shall close.

Rev. Samuel F. Smith. (1808–.)

1169 "The day goeth away." **8, 7.**
Mark iv. 35–41. 1 Cor. vii. 29–31. Gen. xxviii.

1 Lo, the day of rest declineth,
Gather fast the shades of night;
May the Sun which ever shineth
Fill our souls with heavenly light.

2 While, Thine ear of love addressing,
Thus our parting hymn we sing,
Father, grant Thine evening blessing,
Fold us safe beneath Thy wing.

Rev. Samuel D. Robbins. (1812–.)

1170 "The vision of the evening." **S. M.**
Luke xxiv. 13–29. Isa. lxii. 6–12. Ps. lxxxv.

1 OUR day of praise is done;
The evening shadows fall;
Yet pass not from us with the sun,
True Light that lightenest all.

2 Around the throne on high,
Where night can never be,
The white-robed harpers of the sky
Bring ceaseless hymns to Thee.

3 Too faint our anthems here;
Too soon of praise we tire;
But O the strains, how full and clear,
Of that eternal choir!

4 Yet, Lord, to Thy dear will
If Thou attune the heart,
We in Thine angels' music still
May bear our lower part.

5 'Tis Thine each soul to calm,
Each wayward thought reclaim,
And make our daily life a psalm
Of glory to Thy name.

Rev. John Ellerton. (1826–.)

1171 "As the evening sacrifice." **L. M.**
John xx. 19–23. Acts i. 12–14. Ps. cxli. 1–3.

1 AGAIN, as evening's shadow falls,
We gather in these hallowed walls;
And vesper hymn and vesper prayer
Rise mingling on the holy air.

2 May struggling hearts that seek release
Here find the rest of God's own peace;
And, strengthened here by hymn and prayer,
Lay down the burden and the care.

3 O God, our Light, to Thee we bow;
Within all shadows standest Thou;
Give deeper calm than night can bring;
Give sweeter songs than lips can sing.

4 Life's tumult we must meet again,
We cannot at the shrine remain;
But in the spirit's secret cell
May hymn and prayer forever dwell.

Rev. Samuel Longfellow. (1819–.)

1172 "With one accord." **7.**
1 Kings xviii. 36–39. Dan. ix. 15–22. Heb. iv.

1 ERE another Sabbath's close,
Ere again we seek repose,
Lord, our song ascends to Thee;
At Thy feet we bow the knee.

2 For the mercies of the day,
For this rest upon our way,
Thanks to Thee alone be given,
Lord of earth and King of heaven!

3 While this thorny path we tread,
May Thy love our footsteps lead;
When our journey here is past,
May we rest with Thee at last.

4 Let these earthly Sabbaths prove
Foretastes of our joys above;
While their steps Thy children bend
To the rest which knows no end.

James Montgomery. (1771–1854.)

1173 "Let none that wait on Thee be ashamed." **8, 7, 4.**
Ps. cxi. 2 Pet. i. 2–11. James i. 1–12.

1 KEEP us, Lord, O keep us ever;
Vain our hope, if left by Thee;
We are Thine: O leave us never;
Till Thy glorious face we see;
Then to praise Thee
Through a bright eternity.

2 Precious is Thy word of promise,
Precious to Thy people here;
Never take Thy presence from us,
Jesus, Saviour, still be near;
Living, dying,
May Thy name our spirits cheer.

Rev. Thomas Kelly. (1769–1855.)

"At evening ... the first day of the week."

1174 "The eyes of all wait upon Thee." L. M.
Rom. i. 16-20. John iv. 24. Zech. viii. 22.

1 MILLIONS within Thy court have met,
  Millions this day before Thee bowed;
  Their faces Zionward were set,
  Vows with their lips to Thee they vowed.

2 Soon as the light of morning broke
  O'er island, continent, or deep,
  Thy far-spread family awoke,
  Sabbath all round the world to keep.

3 And not a prayer, a tear, a sigh,
  Hath failed this day some suit to gain;
  To those in trouble Thou wert nigh:
  Not one hath sought Thy face in vain.

4 Yet one prayer more, and be it one
  In which both heaven and earth accord:
  Fulfil Thy promise to Thy Son;
  Let all that breathe the call Jesus Lord.

James Montgomery. (1771-1854.)

1175 "Help us, O God of our salvation." 8. 7. 4.
Ps. lxi. Mat. vi. 9-13. 1 Cor. xiii. 9-13.

1 GOD of our salvation, hear us;
  Bless, O bless us, ere we go!
  When we join the world, be near us,
  Lest we cold and careless grow;
    Saviour, keep us,
  Keep us safe from every foe.

2 As our steps are drawing nearer
  To our best and lasting home,
  May our view of heaven grow clearer,
  Hope more bright of joys to come;
    And, when dying,
  May Thy presence cheer the gloom.

Rev. Thomas Kelly. (1769-1855.)

1176 "Let Israel hope in the Lord." L. M.
Ecc. xi. 6-8. Isa. lviii. 9-14. 2 Pet. iii. 8-13.

1 ANOTHER day has passed along,
  And we are nearer to the tomb;
  Nearer to join the heavenly song
  Or hear the last eternal doom.

2 Sweet is the light of Sabbath eve,
  And soft the sunbeams lingering there;
  For these blest hours the world I leave,
  Wafted on wings of faith and prayer.

3 Season of rest, the tranquil soul
  Feels the sweet calm and melts in love;
  And while these sacred moments roll,
  Faith sees a smiling heaven above.

4 Nor will our days of toil be long;
  Our pilgrimage will soon be trod;
  And we shall join the ceaseless song,
  The endless Sabbath of our God.

James Edmeston. (1791-1867.)

1177 "O that Thou wouldest bless." L. M.
Num. vi. 24-27. Ps. cxxv. 2 Cor. xiii. 11-14.

1 SWEET Saviour, bless us ere we go;
  Thy word into our minds instil,
  And make our lukewarm hearts to glow
  With lowly love and fervent will.

2 The day is done, its hours have run;
  And Thou hast taken count of all,
  The scanty triumphs grace hath won,
  The broken vow, the frequent fall.

3 Grant us, dear Lord, from evil ways
  True absolution and release;
  And bless us, more than in past days,
  With purity and inward peace.

4 Do more than pardon; give us joy,
  Sweet fear, and sober liberty,
  And loving hearts without alloy
  That only long to be like Thee.

5 For all we love, the poor, the sad,
  The sinful, unto Thee we call;
  O let Thy mercy make us glad;
  Thou art our Jesus, and our All.

Rev. Frederick W. Faber. (1814-1863.)

1178 "There is forgiveness with Thee." 8. 7.
Ps. xix. 7-9. 2 Chr. vii. 1-11. 1 Thes. v. 14-24.

1 HEAVENLY Father, grant Thy blessing
  On the teaching of this day;
  That our hearts, Thy fear possessing,
  May from sin be turned away.

2 Have we wandered? O forgive us;
  Have we wished from truth to rove?
  Turn, O turn us, and receive us,
  And incline us Thee to love.

Author unknown.

1179 "The Lord ... shall stablish you." S. M.
Neh. viii. 1 Kings viii. 54-66. Jude 20-25.

1 LORD, at this closing hour
  Establish every heart
  Upon Thy word of truth and power,
  To keep us when we part.

2 Peace to our brethren give;
  Fill all our hearts with love;
  In faith and patience may we live,
  And seek our rest above.

3 Through changes, bright or drear,
  We would Thy will pursue;
  And toil to spread Thy kingdom here,
  Till we its glory view.

4 To God, the only wise,
  In every age adored,
  Let glory from the church arise
  Through Jesus Christ our Lord!

Rev. Eleazar T. Fitch. (1790-1871.)

"At evening ... the first day of the week."

1180 "They were let go in peace." 7.
Acts xx. 17-38. 1 Tim. i. 17. 2 Sam. xxiii. 1-5.

1 CHRISTIANS, brethren, ere we part,
  Every voice and every heart
  Join, and to our Father raise
  One last hymn of grateful praise.

2 Though we here should meet no more,
  Yet there is a brighter shore;
  There, released from toil and pain,
  There we all may meet again.

3 Now to Thee, Thou God of heaven,
  Be eternal glory given;
  Grateful for Thy love divine,
  May our hearts be ever Thine.
  Henry K. White. (1785-1806.)

1181 "He will be our guide." 8. 7.
Ps. xxviii. Eze. xxxiv. John x. 1-28.

1 HEAVENLY Shepherd, guide us, feed us,
  Through our pilgrimage below,
  And beside the waters lead us,
  Where Thy flock rejoicing go.

2 Lord, Thy guardian presence ever,
  Meekly bending, we implore;
  We have found Thee, and would never,
  Never wander from Thee more.
  Rev. John Bickersteth. (1781-1855.)

1182 "The grace that is in Christ Jesus." 8. 7.
2 Cor. xiii. 14. Num. vi. 24-27. Rom. xvi. 24.

1 MAY the grace of Christ, our Saviour,
  And the Father's boundless love,
  With the Holy Spirit's favor,
  Rest upon us from above.

2 Thus may we abide in union
  With each other and the Lord,
  And possess, in sweet communion,
  Joys which earth cannot afford.
  Rev. John Newton. (1725-1807.)

1183 "He shall neither slumber nor sleep." 7.
Heb. xiii. 20, 21. Ps. lxvii. Isa. lvii. 15-19.

1 Now may He who from the dead
  Brought the Shepherd of the sheep,
  Jesus Christ, our King and Head,
  All our souls in safety keep!

2 May He teach us to fulfil
  What is pleasing in His sight;
  Perfect us in all His will,
  And preserve us day and night!

3 To that dear Redeemer's praise,
  Who the covenant sealed with blood,
  Let our hearts and voices raise
  Loud thanksgivings to our God.
  Rev. John Newton.

1184 "Deliver us ... for Thy name's sake." L. M.
Luke xxiv. 49-53. 2 John iii. 1 Chr. xxix.

1 LORD, now we part in Thy blest name,
  In which we here together came;
  Grant us, our few remaining days,
  To work Thy will, and spread Thy praise.

2 Teach us in life and death to bless
  Thee, Lord, our Strength and Righteousness;
  Grant that we all may meet above,
  Where we shall better sing Thy love.
  Rev. John Dracup. (-1755.)

1185 "This God is our God forever." 8. P.
Num. xxiii. 19, 20. Lam. iii. 22-26. Rev. i. 8.

1 THIS God is the God we adore,
  Our faithful, unchangeable Friend;
  Whose love is as large as His power,
  And neither knows measure nor end.

2 'T is Jesus, the First and the Last,
  Whose Spirit shall guide us safe home;
  We'll praise Him for all that is past,
  And trust Him for all that's to come.
  Rev. Joseph Hart. (1712-1768.)

1186 "Peace with God through ... Jesus Christ." L. M.
Phil. iv. 7. John xiv. 27. Isa. xxvi. 3.

1 THE peace which God alone reveals,
  And by His word of grace imparts,
  Which only the believer feels,
  Direct, and keep, and cheer our hearts!

2 And may the holy Three in One,
  The Father, Word, and Comforter,
  Pour an abundant blessing down
  On every soul assembled here.
  Rev. John Newton.

1187 "The very God of peace sanctify you." C. M.
2 Thes. ii. 16. 1 Pet. v. 10. Deu. xxxiii. 27.

1 Now may the God of peace and love,
  Who from th' imprisoning grave
  Restored the Shepherd of the sheep,
  Omnipotent to save;

2 Through the rich merits of that blood
  Which He on Calvary spilt,
  To make th' eternal covenant sure,
  On which our hopes are built;

3 Perfect our souls in every grace,
  To accomplish all His will;
  And all that's pleasing in His sight
  Inspire us to fulfil.

4 For the great Mediator's sake
  We every blessing pray;
  With glory let His name be crowned,
  Through heaven's eternal day.
  Rev. Thomas Gibbons. (1720-1785.)

"At evening ... the first day of the week."

1188 "The seed is the word of God." C. M.
Mark iv. Acts xxvi. 22-29. Ps. xix. 7-14.

1 O GOD, by whom the seed is given,
By whom the harvest blest ;
Whose word, like manna showered from heaven,
Is planted in our breast,

2 Preserve it from the passing feet,
And plunderers of the air ;
The sultry sun's intenser heat,
And weeds of worldly care.

3 Though buried deep, or thinly strown,
Do Thou Thy grace supply :
The hope in earthly furrows sown
Shall ripen in the sky.
Bp. Reginald Heber. (1783-1826.)

1189 "God that giveth the increase." 8. 7. 4.
Acts x. 34-48. 1 Cor. iii. Amos ix. 11-15.

1 COME, Thou soul-transforming Spirit,
Bless the sower and the seed ;
Let each heart Thy grace inherit ;
Raise the weak, the hungry feed :
From the gospel,
Now supply Thy people's need.

2 O may all enjoy the blessing
Which Thy word's designed to give ;
Let us all, Thy love possessing,
Joyfully the truth receive ;
And forever
To Thy praise and glory live.
Rev. Jonathan Evans. (1749-1809.)

1190 "The beauty of the Lord . . . be upon us." 8. 7. 4.
Num. vi. 24. 1 Kings viii. 66. John viii. 32.

1 LORD, dismiss us with Thy blessing,
Fill our hearts with joy and peace ;
Let us each, Thy love possessing,
Triumph in redeeming grace ;
O refresh us,
Travelling through this wilderness.

2 Thanks we give, and adoration,
For Thy gospel's joyful sound ;
May the fruits of Thy salvation
In our hearts and lives abound ;
May Thy presence
With us evermore be found.

3 So, whene'er the signal's given,
Us from earth to call away,
Borne on angels' wings to heaven,
Glad the summons to obey,
May we ever
Reign with Christ in endless day.
Hon. and Rev. Walter Shirley. (1725-1786.)

1191 "It shall not return unto me void." C. M.
Luke viii. 4-15. Isa. lv. Ps. cxix. 89-96.

1 ALMIGHTY God, Thy word is cast
Like seed into the ground ;
O may it grow in humble hearts,
And righteous fruits abound.

2 Let not the foe of Christ and man
This holy seed remove ;
But give it root in praying souls,
To bring forth fruits of love.

3 Let not the world's deceitful cares
The rising plant destroy ;
But may it, in converted minds,
Produce the fruits of joy.

4 Let not Thy word, so kindly sent
To raise us to Thy throne,
Return to Thee, and sadly tell
That we reject Thy Son.
Rev. John Cawood. (1775-1852.)

1192 "Let them not depart." L. M.
Rev. xxii. 18, 19. Deu. iv. 1-9. Mat. xiii.

1 O DO not let the word depart,
And close thine eyes against the light ;
Poor sinner, harden not thy heart ;
Thou wouldst be saved, why not to-night ?

2 To-morrow's sun may never rise
To bless thy long-deluded sight ;
This is the time ! O then be wise !
Thou wouldst be saved, why not to-night ?

3 The world has nothing left to give ;
It has no new, no pure delight ;
O try the life which Christians live !
Thou wouldst be saved, why not to-night ?

4 Our God in pity lingers still,
And wilt thou thus His love requite ?
Renounce at length thy stubborn will ;
Thou wouldst be saved, why not to-night ?

5 Our blessèd Lord refuses none
Who would to Him their souls unite ;
Then be the work of grace begun !
Thou wouldst be saved, why not to-night ?
Rev. Horatius Bonar. (1808-..)

1193 "Feed Thy people." L. M.
Lev. ix. 22. 2 Chr. vi. 40. Rev. iii. 20-22.

1 DISMISS us with Thy blessing, Lord ;
Help us to feed upon Thy word ;
All that has been amiss forgive,
And let Thy truth within us live.

2 Though we are guilty, Thou art good ;
Wash all our works in Jesus' blood ;
Give every fettered soul release,
And bid us all depart in peace.
Rev. Joseph Hart. (1712-1768.)

"Be baptized every one of you in the name of Jesus Christ."

1194 "Teach all nations, baptizing them." L. M.
Mark xvi. 15-20. Heb. x. 19-25. Ps. lxxv.

1 'T WAS the commission of our Lord,
   "Go teach the nations, and baptize!"
   The nations have received the word,
   Since He ascended to the skies.

2 He sits upon th' eternal hills,
   With grace and pardon in His hands,
   And sends His covenant with the seals,
   To bless the distant Christian lands.

3 Our souls He washes in His blood,
   As water makes the body clean;
   And the good Spirit from our God
   Descends like purifying rain.

4 Thus we engage ourselves to Thee,
   And seal our covenant with the Lord;
   O may the great eternal Three
   In heaven our solemn vows record!
   Rev. Isaac Watts. (1674-1748.)

1195 "Not by water only, but by water and blood." S. M.
Col. ii. 1-12. Rev. i. 1-5. Num. viii. 5-22.

1 RITES cannot change the heart,
   Undo the evil done,
   Or with the uttered name impart
   The nature of Thy Son.

2 To meet our desperate want,
   There gushed a crimson flood;
   O from His heart's o'erflowing font
   Baptize this soul with blood!

3 Be grace from Christ our Lord,
   And love from God supreme,
   By the communing Spirit poured
   In a perpetual stream.
   Rev. William M. Bunting. (1805-1866.)

1196 "I will pay my vows unto the Lord." C. M.
1 Tim. vi. 12-16. Neh. ix. 32-38. Ps. xxii.

1 WITNESS, ye men and angels, now,
   Before the Lord we speak;
   To Him we make our solemn vow,
   A vow we dare not break:

2 That long as life itself shall last,
   Ourselves to Christ we yield;
   Nor from His cause will we depart,
   Or ever quit the field.

3 We trust not in our native strength,
   But on His grace rely,
   That, with returning wants, the Lord
   Will all our need supply.

4 O guide our doubtful feet aright,
   And keep us in Thy ways;
   And, while we turn our vows to prayers,
   Turn Thou our prayers to praise.
   Rev. Benjamin Beddome. (1717-1795.)

1197 "Baptized into Jesus Christ." C. M.
Mat. xxviii. 19. Titus iii. 5. Isa. lii. 13-15.

1 O LORD, while we confess the worth
   Of this the outward seal,
   Do Thou the truths herein set forth
   To every heart reveal.

2 Death to the world we here avow,
   Death to each fleshly lust;
   Newness of life our calling now,
   A risen Lord our trust.

3 Baptized into the Father's name,
   We'd walk as sons of God:
   Baptized in Thine, we own Thy claim
   As ransomed by Thy blood.

4 Baptized into the Holy Ghost,
   We'd keep His temple pure,
   And make Thy grace our only boast,
   And by Thy strength endure.
   Mrs. Mary B. Peters. (-1856.)

1198 "Ye shall be baptized with the Holy Ghost." C. M.
Mat. iii Acts xvi. 25-34. Eze. xxxvi. 25-28.

1 WHILE in this sacred rite of Thine
   We yield our spirits now,
   Shine o'er the waters, Dove divine,
   And seal the cheerful vow.

2 All glory be to Him whose life
   For ours was freely given,
   Who aids us in the spirit's strife,
   And makes us meet for heaven.

3 To Thee we gladly now resign
   Our life and all our powers;
   Accept us in the rite divine,
   And bless these hallowed hours.
   Rev. Samuel F. Smith. (1808-.)

1199 "We are buried with Him by baptism." 7, 6.
Rom. vi. Acts viii. 26-40. Ex. xix. 1-6.

1 AROUND Thy grave, Lord Jesus,
   Thine empty grave we stand,
   With hearts all full of praises,
   To keep Thy blest command;
   By faith our souls rejoicing
   To trace Thy path of love,
   Through death's dark angry billows,
   Up to the throne above.

2 Into Thy death baptizéd,
   We own with Thee we died;
   With Thee, our Life, are risen,
   And in Thee glorified;
   From sin, the world, and Satan,
   We're ransomed by Thy blood,
   And now would walk as strangers,
   Alive with Thee to God.
   James G Deck. (1836-.)

"As often as ye eat this bread and drink this cup."

1200 "The same night in which He was betrayed." **L. M.**
1 Cor. xi. 23-26. Ex. xii. 1-14. Ps. xxvi.

1 'T was on that dark, that doleful night,
   When powers of earth and hell arose
   Against the Son of God's delight,
   And friends betrayed Him to His foes;

2 Before the mournful scene began,
   He took the bread, and blessed, and brake :
   What love through all His actions ran,
   What wondrous words of grace He spake.

3 "This is my body, broke for sin ;
   Receive and eat the living food ; "
   Then took the cup, and blessed the wine :
   "'T is the new covenant in my blood."

4 "Do this," He cried, "till time shall end
   In memory of your dying Friend ;
   Meet at my table, and record
   The love of your departed Lord."
   Rev. Isaac Watts. (1674-1748.)

1201 "A feast of fat things." **C. M.**
Can. v. 1, 2. Mat. xxii. 1-4. Prov. ix. 1-5.

1 The King of heaven His table spreads,
   And dainties crown the board ;
   Not paradise, with all its joys,
   Could such delight afford.

2 Millions of souls, in glory now,
   Were fed and feasted here ;
   And millions more, still on the way,
   Around the board appear.

3 All things are ready ; come away,
   Nor weak excuses frame ;
   Crowd to your places at the feast,
   And bless the Founder's name.
   Rev. Philip Doddridge. (1702-1751.)

1202 "Thou preparest a table before me." **L. M.**
Luke xxii. 1-20. Ps. xxiii. 5. Eze. xxxiv. 5.

1 My God, and is Thy table spread ?
   And does Thy cup with love o'erflow ?
   Thither be all Thy children led,
   And let them all its sweetness know.

2 Hail, sacred feast which Jesus makes,
   Rich banquet of His flesh and blood !
   Thrice happy he who here partakes
   That sacred stream, that heavenly food !

3 O let Thy table honored be,
   And furnished well with joyful guests ;
   And may each soul salvation see,
   That here its sacred pledges tastes.

4 Let crowds approach, with hearts prepared ;
   With hearts inflamed let all attend ;
   Nor, when we leave our Father's board,
   The pleasure or the profit end.
   Rev. Philip Doddridge.

1203 "He sat down with the twelve." **C. M.**
Mat. xxvi. 17-29. 2 Chr. v. 11-14. 1 John iv.

1 How sweet and awful is the place
   With Christ within the doors,
   While everlasting love displays
   The choicest of her stores !

2 While all our hearts and all our songs
   Join to admire the feast,
   Each of us cries, with thankful tongue,
   "Lord, why was I a guest ?

3 "Why was I made to hear Thy voice,
   And enter while there 's room,
   When thousands make a wretched choice,
   And rather starve than come ? "

4 'T was the same love that spread the feast
   That sweetly forced us in ;
   Else we had still refused to taste,
   And perished in our sin.
   Rev. Isaac Watts.

1204 "In remembrance of me." **C. M.**
Mark xiv. 12-25. John vi. 27-58. Can. ii. 1-4.

1 In memory of the Saviour's love
   We keep the sacred feast
   Where every humble, contrite heart
   Is made a welcome guest.

2 By faith we take the Bread of life
   With which our souls are fed,
   And cup in token of His blood
   That was for sinners shed.

3 Under His banner thus we sing
   The wonders of His love,
   And thus anticipate by faith
   The heavenly feast above.
   Rev. Thomas Cotterill. (1779-1823.)

1205 "Let a man examine himself." **C. M.**
John xiii. 1-17. 2 Chr. vi. 1-21. 1 Cor. x.

1 O God, unseen, yet ever near,
   Thy presence may we feel ;
   And thus, inspired with holy fear,
   Before Thine altar kneel.

2 Here may Thy faithful people know
   The blessings of Thy love ;
   The streams that through the desert flow,
   The manna from above.

3 We come, obedient to Thy word,
   To feast on heavenly food ;
   Our meat, the body of the Lord ;
   Our drink, His precious blood.
   Edward Osler. (1798-1863.)

"As often as ye eat this bread and drink this cup."

1206 "Man did eat angels' food." 7, 6,
John vi. 27-58. Isa. lv. 1-3. Mat. xxvi. 26-29.

1 O BREAD to pilgrims given,
  O Food that angels eat,
  O Manna sent from heaven,
  For heaven-born natures meet :
    Give us, for Thee long pining,
    To eat till richly filled ;
    Till, earth's delights resigning,
    Our every wish is stilled.

2 O Water, life bestowing,
  From out the Saviour's heart,
  A Fountain purely flowing,
  A Fount of love, Thou art :
    O let us, freely tasting,
    Our burning thirst assuage ;
    Thy sweetness, never wasting,
    Avails from age to age.

3 Jesus, this feast receiving,
  We Thee unseen adore ;
  Thy faithful word believing,
  We take, and doubt no more :
    Give, us, Thou true and loving,
    On earth to live in Thee ;
    Then, death the vail removing,
    Thy glorious face to see.
            Unknown mediæval author.
            Tr. by Rev. Ray Palmer. (1808-.)

1207 "And they made ready." 7.
Ps. lxxxvi. Mat. xviii. 19, 20. Luke xxiv. 13-31.

1 COME, Thou high and lofty Lord,
  Lowly, meek, incarnate Word ;
  Humbly stoop to earth again :
  Come, and visit abject man.

2 Jesus, dear expected Guest,
  Thou art bidden to the feast :
  For Thyself our hearts prepare ;
  Come, and sit, and banquet there.

3 Jesus, we Thy promise claim :
  We are met in Thy great name ;
  In the midst do Thou appear ;
  Manifest Thy presence here.

4 Sanctify us, Lord, and bless ;
  Breathe Thy spirit, give Thy peace ;
  Thou Thyself within us move,
  Make our feast a feast of love.

5 Call, O call us each by name,
  To the marriage of the Lamb ;
  Let us lean upon Thy breast ;
  Love be there our endless feast.
            Rev. Charles Wesley. (1705-1788.)

1208 "He that eateth of this bread shall live." 7,
1 Cor. x. 14-17. Ex. xii. 1-13. 1 Cor. v. 8.

1 SAVIOUR, when Thy bread we break,
  When Thy "cup of blessing" take,
  Fill our souls with life like Thine,
  Thou our bread, and Thou our wine.

2 For us all Thy feast is spread ;
  For us all Thy blood was shed ;
  Thou didst die that all might live ;
  For all sin Thyself didst give.

3 Lowly we, around Thy board,
  Hold communion with the Lord ;
  In our midst Thy form we see,
  And through faith would feed on Thee.

4 Let our guilt be washed away,
  Let our darkness turn to day ;
  May Thy smile upon us rest,
  While we lean upon Thy breast.
            Rev. Samuel D. Robbins. (1812-.)

1209 "Lord, evermore give us this bread." 8. 7.
Mark xiv. 17-25. 1 Pet. i. 3-9. Ps. xvi.

1 WHILE in sweet communion feeding
  On this earthly bread and wine,
  Saviour, may we see Thee bleeding
  On the cross, to make us Thine.
    Now our eyes forever closing
    To this fleeting world below,
    On Thy gentle breast reposing,
    Teach us, Lord, Thy grace to know.

2 Though unseen, be ever near us,
  With the still small voice of love
  Whispering words of peace to cheer us,
  Every doubt and fear remove.
    Bring before us all the story
    Of Thy life and death of woe,
    And, with hopes of endless glory,
    Wean our hearts from all below.
            Sir Edward Denny. (1796-.)

1210 "Let us keep the feast." S. M.
Luke xxii. 7-20. 1 John iii. 1, 2. Ps. xvii. 15.

1 SWEET feast of love divine,
  'T is grace that makes us free
  To feed upon this bread and wine,
  In memory, Lord, of Thee.

2 O if this glimpse of love
  Is so divinely sweet,
  What will it be, O Lord, above,
  Thy gladdening smile to meet ?

3 To see Thee face to face,
  Thy perfect likeness wear,
  And all Thy ways of wondrous grace
  Through endless years declare.
            Sir Edward Denny.

"As often as ye eat this bread and drink this cup."

1211 "Eat, O friends, drink, . . . O beloved." **L. M.**
Ps. lxxvi. 1-13. Mat. xxvi. 20-29. Can. v. 1.

1 DRAW near, O Holy Dove, draw near,
With peace and gladness on Thy wing ;
Reveal the Saviour's presence here,
And light, and life, and comfort bring.

2 "Eat, O my friends, drink, O beloved !"
We hear the Master's voice exclaim :
Our hearts with new desire are moved,
And kindled with a heavenly flame.

3 No room for doubt, no room for dread,
Nor tears, nor groans, nor anxious sighs ;
We do not mourn a Saviour dead,
But hail Him living in the skies.

4 While this we do, remembering Thee,
Dear Saviour, let our graces prove
We have Thy blessed company,
Thy banner over us is love.
Rev. Aaron R. Wolfe. (1821-.)

1212 "Ye do show the Lord's death." **C. M.**
Mark xiv. 12-25. 1 Cor. x. 16-18. Ex. xii.

1 JESUS, at whose supreme command
We now approach to God,
Before us in Thy vesture stand,
Thy vesture dipped in blood.

2 The tokens of Thy dying love,
O let us all receive,
And feel the quick'ning Spirit move,
And sensibly believe.

3 The cup of blessing blest by Thee,
Let it Thy blood impart ;
The bread Thy mystic body be,
To cheer each languid heart.
Rev. Charles Wesley. (1708-1788.)

1213 "We will remember Thy love." **C. M.**
Isa. liii. Mat. iv. 1-11. Heb. v.

1 JESUS, Thy love shall we forget,
And never bring to mind
The grace that paid our hopeless debt,
And bade us pardon find ?

2 Shall we Thy life of grief forget,
Thy fasting and Thy prayer ;
Thy locks with mountain vapors wet,
To save us from despair ?

3 Gethsemane can we forget,
Thy struggling agony,
When night lay dark on Olivet,
And none to watch with Thee ?

4 Life's brightest joys we may forget,
Our kindred cease to love ;
But He who paid our hopeless debt
Our constancy shall prove.
William Mitchell. 1831.

1214 "His banner over me was love." **8. 7.**
Cor. xi. 23-26. Can. ii. 1-4. Phil. ii. 1-11.

1 JESUS spreads His banner o'er us,
Cheers our famished souls with food ;
He the banquet spreads before us
Of His mystic flesh and blood.
Precious banquet ; Bread of heaven ;
Wine of gladness, flowing free :
May we taste it, kindly given,
In remembrance, Lord, of Thee.

2 In Thy holy incarnation,
When the angels sang Thy birth ;
In Thy fasting and temptation ;
In Thy labors on the earth ;
In Thy trial and rejection ;
In Thy sufferings on the tree ;
In Thy glorious resurrection ;
May we, Lord, remember Thee.
Rev. Roswell Park. (1807-1869.)

1215 "Wounded for our transgressions." **C. M.**
Ps. cxvi. Luke xxii. 1-20. 1 John iv. 13-21.

1 IF human kindness meets return,
And owns the grateful tie ;
If tender thoughts within us burn,
To feel a friend is nigh ;

2 O shall not warmer accents tell
The gratitude we owe
To Him who died our fears to quell,
Our more than orphan's woe ?

3 While yet His anguished soul surveyed
Those pangs He would not flee,
What love His latest words displayed,
"Meet, and remember me !"

4 Remember Thee ! Thy death, Thy shame,
Our sinful hearts to share !
O memory, leave no other name
But His recorded there.
Hon. and Rev. Gerard T. Noel. (1782-1851.)

1216 "That bread of life." **7.**
John vi. 32-57. Heb. x. 5-10. Ex. xvi.

1 BREAD of heaven, on Thee I feed,
For Thy flesh is meat indeed ;
Ever may my soul be fed
With this true and living Bread ;
Day by day with strength supplied,
Through the life of Him who died.

2 Vine of heaven, Thy blood supplies
This blest cup of sacrifice ;
'T is Thy wounds my healing give ;
To Thy cross I look and live.
Thou my life, O let me be
Rooted, grafted, built on Thee.
Josiah Conder. (1789-1855.)

"As often as ye eat this bread and drink this cup."

1217 "I am the living bread." 9, 8.
John vi. 51-57. 1 Pet. ii. 21-25. Ps. lxi.

1 BREAD of the world, in mercy broken,
  Wine of the soul, in mercy shed,
  By whom the words of life were spoken,
  And in whose death our sins are dead,

2 Look on the heart by sorrow broken,
  Look on the tears by sinners shed ;
  And be Thy feast to us a token
  That by Thy grace our souls are fed.
  Bp. Reginald Heber. (1783-1826.)

1218 "The love of Christ constraineth us." 7, 6, 7.
Mat. xxvi. 28. Luke xxiii. 33-46. Ps. lxxxv.

1 LAMB of God, whose bleeding love
  We now recall to mind,
  Send the answer from above,
  And let us mercy find ;
  Think on us who think on Thee;
  Every struggling soul release ;
  O remember Calvary,
  And bid us go in peace.

2 By Thine agonizing pain
  And bloody sweat, we pray,
  By Thy dying love to man,
  Take all our sins away;
  Burst our bonds and set us free,
  From iniquity release ;
  O remember Calvary,
  And bid us go in peace.

3 Let Thy blood, by faith applied,
  The sinner's pardon seal ;
  Speak us freely justified,
  And all our sickness heal ;
  By Thy passion on the tree,
  Let our griefs and troubles cease ;
  O remember Calvary,
  And bid us go in peace.
  Rev. Charles Wesley. (1708-1788.)

1219 "So let him eat of that bread." C. M.
Ps. ciii. 1-5. Can. i. 12-17. 1 Cor. x. 16, 17.

1 ALL praise to Him of Nazareth,
  The Holy One who came,
  For love of man, to die a death
  Of agony and shame !

2 In tender mem'ry of His grave,
  The mystic bread we take,
  And muse upon the life He gave
  So freely for our sake.

3 A boundless love He bore mankind ;
  O may at least a part
  Of that strong love descend, and find
  A place in every heart!
  William C. Bryant. (1794-1878.)

1220 "Till He come." 7.
1 Cor. xi. 23-26. 2 Cor. v. 1-15. Isa. li. 1-11.

1 "TILL He come !" O let the words
  Linger on the trembling chords ;
  Let the " little while " between
  In their golden light be seen ;
  Let us think how heaven and home
  Lie beyond that " Till He come !"

2 Clouds and darkness round us press ;
  Would we have one sorrow less ?
  All the sharpness of the cross,
  All that tells the world is loss,
  Death, and darkness, and the tomb,
  Pain us only " Till He come !"

3 See, the feast of love is spread ;
  Drink the wine and eat the bread.
  Sweet memorials, till the Lord
  Call us round His heavenly board,
  Some from earth, from glory some,
  Severed only " Till He come !"
  Rev. Edward H. Bickersteth. (1825-.)

1221 "Our feet shall stand within Thy gates." C. M.
Mark xiv. 12-25. Rev. iii. 20-22. Isa. lv. 1-3.

1 THE Saviour waits ! His presence now
  My thankful heart elates ;
  I hasten at His feet to bow
  Within the temple gates.
  He proffers gifts surpassing all
  The wealth of earth and sea,
  With joy I haste to meet His call;
  The Saviour waits for me.
  The Saviour waits ; for me He waits !
  His presence gilds the sacred gates.

2 The Saviour waits ! O matchless grace !
  He leaves the courts above,
  And comes to spread before my face
  The tokens of His love !
  He kindly calls me to His feast,
  A banquet rich and free ;
  With joys prepared to make me blest,
  The Saviour waits for me.
  The Saviour waits ; for me He waits!
  His presence gilds the sacred gates.
  James C. Odiorne. (1806-1878.)

1222 "My flesh is meat, . . . my blood is drink." C. M.
Luke xxii. 7-20. Acts ii. 44-47. Ex. xii. 1-8

1 HERE at Thy table, Lord, we meet,
  To feed on food divine ;
  Thy body is the bread we eat,
  Thy precious blood the wine.

2 He that prepares this rich repast,
  Himself comes down, and dies ;
  And then invites us thus to feast
  Upon the sacrifice.
  Rev. Samuel Stennett. (1727-1795.)

"The ministers of God."

1223 "Preach the gospel to every creature." **L. M.**
Mark xvi. 15-20. Mat. x. 1-20. Ps. xcvi.

1 Go, preach My gospel, saith the Lord,
   Bid the whole world My grace receive ;
He shall be saved who trusts my word,
   And he condemned who won't believe.

2 I'll make your great commission known ;
   And ye shall prove My gospel true,
By all the works that I have done,
   By all the wonders ye shall do.

3 Teach all the nations My commands ;
   I'm with you till the world shall end ;
All power is trusted in My hands,
   I can destroy, and I defend.
Rev. Isaac Watts. (1674-1748.)

1224 "I have set watchmen upon thy walls." **C. M.**
Isa. lxii. 6-12. Eze. iii. 1-21. Acts ix. 1-19.

1 LET Zion's watchmen all awake,
   And take th' alarm they give ;
Now let them, from the mouth of God,
   Their solemn charge receive.

2 'T is not a cause of small import
   The pastor's care demands ;
But what might fill an angel's heart,
   And filled a Saviour's hands.

3 They watch for souls, for which the Lord
   Did heavenly bliss forego ;
For souls, which must forever live
   In raptures, or in woe.

4 May they that Jesus, whom they preach,
   Their own Redeemer, see ;
And watch Thou daily o'er their souls,
   That they may watch for Thee.
Rev. Philip Doddridge. (1702-1751.)

1225 "That preach the gospel of peace." **S. M.**
Isa. lii. Ps. cxxxii. Rom. x. 14-17.

1 How beauteous are their feet
   Who stand on Zion's hill,
Who bring salvation on their tongues,
   And words of peace reveal !

2 How charming is their voice !
   How sweet the tidings are !
"Zion ! behold thy Saviour-King ;
   He reigns and triumphs here."

3 How happy are our ears,
   That hear this joyful sound,
Which kings and prophets waited for,
   And sought, but never found !

4 The watchmen join their voice,
   And tuneful notes employ ;
Jerusalem breaks forth in songs,
   And deserts learn the joy.
Rev. Isaac Watts.

1226 "Pray ye therefore the Lord of the harvest." **S. M.**
Mat. ix. 36-38. 2 Thes. iii. 3. Ps. lxxix. 9.

1 LORD of the harvest, hear
   Thy needy servants cry ;
Answer our faith's effectual prayer,
   And all our wants supply.

2 On Thee we humbly wait,
   Our wants are in Thy view ;
The harvest truly, Lord, is great,
   The laborers are few.

3 Convert and send forth more
   Into Thy church abroad,
And let them speak Thy word of power,
   As workers with their God.

4 O let them spread Thy name,
   Their mission fully prove ;
Thy universal grace proclaim,
   Thine all-redeeming love.
Rev. Charles Wesley. (1703-1788.)

1227 "Troubled, because there was no shepherd." **L. M.**
Ps. lxxx. Isa. lxiii. 15-19. Acts xvi. 1-13.

1 SHEPHERD of Israel, bend Thine ear,
   Thy servants' prayers indulgent hear ;
Perplexed, distressed, to Thee we cry,
   And seek the guidance of Thine eye.

2 With longing eyes, behold, we wait,
   A suppliant band, at mercy's gate ;
Our drooping hearts, O God, sustain :
   Shall Israel seek Thy face in vain ?

3 O Lord, in ways of peace return,
   Nor let Thy flock neglected mourn ;
May our blest eyes a shepherd see,
   Dear to our souls, and dear to Thee.

4 Fed by his care, our tongues shall raise
   A cheerful tribute to Thy praise,
Our children learn the grateful song,
   And theirs the cheerful notes prolong.
Rev. Philip Doddridge.

1228 "Thy priests be clothed with righteousness." **L. M.**
John xvii. Luke x. 1-20. Eze. xxxiii. 1-19.

1 FATHER of mercies, bow Thine ear,
   Attentive to our earnest prayer ;
We plead for those who plead for Thee :
   Successful pleaders may they be.

2 How great their work, how vast their charge !
   Do thou their anxious souls enlarge ;
To them Thy sacred truth reveal,
   Suppress their fear, inflame their zeal.

3 Teach them aright to sow the seed,
   Teach them Thy chosen flock to feed,
Teach them immortal souls to gain,
   Nor let them labor, Lord, in vain.
Rev. Benjamin Beddome. (1717-1795.)

"The ministers of God."

1229 " Thou hast well done that thou art come." **L. M.**
Acts x. 30-45. 1 Cor. ii. 1-16. Gen. xviii. 1-8.

1 WE bid thee welcome, in the name
  Of Jesus, our exalted Head :
  Come as a servant ; so He came,
  And we receive thee in His stead.

2 Come as a shepherd ; guard and keep
  This fold from hell, and earth, and sin ;
  Nourish the lambs, and feed the sheep,
  The wounded heal, the lost bring in.

3 Come as a teacher, sent from God,
  Charged His whole counsel to declare ;
  Lift o'er our ranks the prophet's rod,
  While we uphold thy hands with prayer.

4 Come as a messenger of peace,
  Filled with the Spirit, fired with love ;
  Live to behold our large increase,
  And die to meet us all above.
  James Montgomery. (1771-1854.)

1230 " The Holy Ghost hath made you overseers." **L. M.**
Isa. lii. Ps. lxvii. 2 Tim. ii. 1-15.

1 SPIRIT of peace and holiness,
  This new-created union bless ;
  Bind each to each in ties of love,
  And ratify our work above.

2 Saviour, who carest for Thy sheep,
  The shepherd of Thy people keep ;
  Guide him in every doubtful way,
  Nor let his feet from duty stray.

3 Gird thou his heart with strength divine :
  Let Christ through all his conduct shine ;
  Faithful in all things may he be,
  Dead to the world, alive to Thee.

4 O Thou, whose love doth never fail,
  Breathe on this dry and thirsty vale ;
  And may it, from this hour, appear
  That Thy reviving power is here.
  Rev. Samuel F. Smith. (1808-.)

1231 " Our sufficiency is of God." **L. M.**
Acts i. 15-26. Ex. iii. 11-18. Eze ii.

1 THE solemn service now is done ;
  The vow is pledged, the toil begun ;
  Seal Thou, O God, the oath above,
  And ratify the pledge of love.

2 The shepherd of Thy people bless ;
  Gird him with thine own holiness ;
  In duty may his pleasure be,
  His glory in his zeal for Thee;

3 Come, Spirit, here consent to dwell ;
  The mists of earth and sin dispel :
  Blest Saviour, Thine own rights maintain ;
  Supreme in every bosom reign.
  Rev. Samuel F. Smith.

1232 " Ministers of the new testament." **7. 6.**
Mat. x. 1-20. Luke x. 1-16. Eze. iii.

1 LORD of the living harvest
  That whitens o'er the plain,
  Where angels soon shall gather
  Their sheaves of golden grain ;
  Accept these hands to labor,
  These hearts to trust and love,
  And deign with them to hasten
  Thy kingdom from above.

2 As laborers in Thy vineyard,
  Send us, O Christ, to be
  Content to bear the burden
  Of weary days for Thee ;
  We ask no other wages,
  When Thou shalt call us home,
  But to have shared the travail
  Which makes Thy kingdom come.

3 Come down, Thou Holy Spirit,
  And fill our souls with light,
  Clothe us in spotless raiment,
  In linen clean and white ;
  Beside Thy sacred altar
  Be with us, where we stand,
  To sanctify Thy people
  Through all this happy land.
  Rev. John S. B. Monsell. (1811-.)

1233 " God shall supply all your need." **L. M.**
Acts ii. 1-21. Joel ii. 28-32. Isa. xxxii. 15-19.

1 POUR out Thy Spirit from on high ;
  Lord, thine assembled servants bless ;
  Graces and gifts to each supply,
  And clothe Thy priests with righteousness.

2 Within Thy temple, when we stand,
  To teach the truth as taught by Thee,
  Saviour, like stars in Thy right hand,
  The angels of the churches be !

3 Wisdom and zeal and faith impart,
  Firmness with meekness from above,
  To bear Thy people on our heart,
  And love the souls whom Thou dost love;

4 To watch and pray, and never faint ;
  By day and night strict guard to keep ;
  To warn the sinner, cheer the saint,
  Nourish Thy lambs, and feed Thy sheep.

5 Then, when our work is finished here,
  In humble hope, our charge resign ;
  When the chief Shepherd shall appear,
  O God, may they and we be Thine.
  James Montgomery.

"Build ye the sanctuary of the Lord."

1234 "We have prepared to build Thee a house." **L. M.**
1 Kings viii. 1-30.   Ezra iii.   Mat. vi. 9-15.

1 THIS stone to Thee in faith we lay;
   To Thee this temple, Lord, we build;
   Thy power and goodness here display,
   And be it with Thy presence filled.

2 Here, when Thy people seek Thy face,
   And dying sinners pray to live,
   Hear Thou in heaven, Thy dwelling-place,
   And when Thou hearest, O forgive.

3 Here, when Thy messengers proclaim
   The blessèd gospel of Thy Son,
   Still by the power of His great name
   Be mighty signs and wonders done.

4 Hosanna, to their heavenly King,
   When children's voices raise that song,
   Hosanna, let their angels sing,
   And heaven with earth the strain prolong.

5 But will, indeed, Jehovah deign
   Here to abide, no transient guest?
   Here will the world's Redeemer reign?
   And here the Holy Spirit rest?

6 That glory never hence depart;
   Yet choose not, Lord, this house alone;
   Thy kingdom come to every heart,
   In every bosom fix Thy throne.
   James Montgomery. (1771-1854.)

1235 "And this stone... shall be God's house." **L. M.**
2 Chr. vi. 1-21.   Ezra v.   1 Cor. iii. 9-23.

1 AN earthly temple here we raise,
   Lord God, our Saviour, to Thy praise;
   O make Thy gracious presence known,
   While now we lay its corner-stone.

2 Within the house Thy servants rear,
   Deign by Thy Spirit to appear;
   On all its walls salvation write,
   From corner-stone to topmost height.

3 And when this temple, "made with hands,"
   Upon its firm foundation stands,
   O may we all, with loving heart,
   In nobler building bear a part:

4 Where every polished stone shall be
   A human soul won back to Thee;
   All resting upon Christ alone,
   The chief and precious Corner-Stone.

5 So, when our toil is o'er at last,
   All labor in both temples passed,
   O may it then by works be shown,
   That faith hath laid this corner-stone.
   Mrs. Katherine H. Johnson. (1835-.)

1236 "The chief corner-stone." **H. M.**
Ps. cxviii. 13-29.   Isa xxviii. 16.   Eph. ii.

1 CHRIST is our Corner-Stone;
   On Him alone we build;
   With His true saints alone
   The courts of heaven are filled;
   On His great love our hopes we place,
   Of present grace and joys above.

2 O then with hymns of praise
   These hallowed courts shall ring;
   Our voices we will raise
   The Three in One to sing,
   And thus proclaim, in joyful song,
   Both loud and long, that glorious name.

3 Here, gracious God, do thou
   For evermore draw nigh;
   Accept each faithful vow,
   And mark each suppliant sigh;
   In copious shower, on all who pray,
   Each holy day, Thy blessings pour.

4 Here may we gain from heaven
   The grace which we implore,
   And may that grace, once given,
   Be with us evermore;
   Until that day when all the blest
   To endless rest are called away.
   Unknown author of the 8th century.
   Tr. by Rev. John Chandler. (1800-1876.)

1237 "Thou hast said, my name shall be there." **L. M.**
Mat. xvi. 13-20.   2 Chr. v.   Ezra vi.

1 O JESUS, our chief Corner-Stone,
   On Thee we rest, on Thee alone!
   The Rock of Ages, Thou; and we,
   As living stones, are built on Thee.

2 In the beginning, Thou wast God;
   The heavens by Thee were spread abroad;
   By Thee was earth's foundation laid;
   Thy power upholds whate'er was made.

3 We bless Thee, O Immanuel,
   Who dost in our own likeness dwell;
   Thy human nature, temple true,
   Wherein the Father's face we view.

4 On hearts in faith confessing Thee,
   The Christ, the Son of God, to be,
   Thy living church Thou dost maintain,
   And gates of death resist in vain.

5 O Lord, accept our off'ring free,
   And may this house be reared for Thee;
   On Thee we build, on Thee alone,
   O Jesus, Thou, our Corner-Stone!
   Rev. Philip Phelps. (1839-.)

"Build ye the sanctuary of the Lord."

1238. "This house is called by Thy name." 7.
1 Kings viii. 1–21.   Ps. lxxxi.   John iv. 21–24.

1 LORD of hosts, to Thee we raise
   Here a house of prayer and praise :
   Thou Thy people's hearts prepare
   Here to meet for praise and prayer.

2 Let the living here be fed
   With Thy word, the heavenly bread ;
   Here, in hope of glory blest,
   May the dead be laid to rest.

3 Here to Thee a temple stand,
   While the sea shall gird the land ;
   Here reveal Thy mercy sure,
   While the sun and moon endure.

4 Hallelujah ! earth and sky
   To the joyful sound reply ;
   Hallelujah ! hence ascend
   Prayer and praise till time shall end.
   James Montgomery. (1771-1854.)

1239. "Will God indeed dwell on the earth?" L. M.
1 Kings viii. 22–30.   Ps. lxxx.   Rom. xii.

1 AND will the great eternal God
   On earth establish His abode ?
   And will He, from His radiant throne,
   Accept our temples for His own ?

2 These walls we to Thy honor raise :
   Long may they echo with Thy praise :
   And Thou, descending, fill the place
   With choicest tokens of Thy grace.

3 Here let the great Redeemer reign,
   With all the graces of His train ;
   While power divine His word attends,
   To conquer foes, and cheer His friends.
   Rev. Philip Doddridge. (1702-1751.)

1240. "They have built Thee a sanctuary." C. M.
2 Chr. vi. 1–21.   Ex. xl.   Eph. vi. 10–18.

1 O THOU, whose own vast temple stands,
   Built over earth and sea,
   Accept the walls that human hands
   Have raised to worship Thee.

2 Lord, from Thine inmost glory send,
   Within these walls t' abide,
   The peace that dwelleth without end
   Serenely by Thy side.

3 May erring minds, that worship here,
   Be taught the better way ;
   And they who mourn, and they who fear,
   Be strengthened as they pray.

4 May faith grow firm, and love grow warm,
   And pure devotion rise,
   While round these hallowed walls the storm
   Of earth-born passion dies.
   William C. Bryant. (1794-1878.)

1241. "Arise, O Lord God, into Thy resting-place." C. M.
2 Chr. vi. 41, 42.   Ps. cxxxii.   Mat. xxi. 1–16.

1 ARISE, O King of grace, arise,
   And enter to Thy rest :
   Lo, Thy church waits with longing eyes,
   Thus to be owned and blest.

2 Enter with all Thy glorious train,
   Thy Spirit and Thy word ;
   All that the ark did once contain
   Could no such grace afford.

3 Here, mighty God, accept our vows,
   Here let Thy praise be spread ;
   Bless the provisions of Thy house,
   And fill Thy poor with bread.

4 Here let the Son of David reign,
   Let God's Anointed shine,
   Justice and truth His court maintain,
   With love and power divine.
   Rev. Isaac Watts. (1674-1748.)

1242. "A place for Thy dwelling." L. M.
Mark xi. 9, 10.   Ps. cxviii. 19–29.   Isa. lx.

1 HOSANNA to the living Lord,
   Hosanna to th' incarnate Word :
   To Christ, Creator, Saviour, King,
   Let earth, let heaven, hosanna sing.

2 O Saviour, with protecting care,
   Return to this, Thy house of prayer,
   Where we Thy parting promise claim,
   Assembled in Thy sacred name.

3 But chiefest in our cleansed breast,
   Eternal, bid Thy Spirit rest,
   And make our secret soul to be
   A temple pure, and worthy Thee.
   Bp. Reginald Heber. (1783-1826.)

1243. "Thine eyes be open, and Thine ears attent." H. M.
2 Chr. v.   Ps. lxxxiv.   Acts ii. 41–47.

1 GREAT King of glory, come,
   And with Thy favor crown
   This temple as Thy home,
   This people as Thine own :
   Beneath this roof, O deign to show
   How God can dwell with men below.

2 Here may Thine ears attend
   Our interceding cries,
   And grateful praise ascend,
   Like incense, to the skies :
   Here may Thy soul-converting word
   With faith be preached, in faith be heard.

3 Here may the listening throng
   Receive Thy truth in love :
   Here Christians join the song
   Of the redeemed above ;
   Till all, who humbly seek Thy face,
   Rejoice in Thy abounding grace.
   Rev. Benjamin Francis. (1734-1799.)

"O Lord, revive Thy work."

1244 "Behold and visit this vine." Ps. lxxx. 1 Kings xviii. 30-46. Acts iv. 1-12.   8. 7.

1 SAVIOUR, visit Thy plantation;
  Grant us, Lord, a gracious rain;
  All will come to desolation,
  Unless Thou return again:
Keep no longer at a distance,
  Shine upon us from on high,
Lest, for want of Thine assistance,
  Every plant should droop and die.

2 Let our mutual love be fervent:
  Make us prevalent in prayers;
Let each one, esteemed Thy servant,
  Shun the world's bewitching snares:
Break the tempter's fatal power,
  Turn the stony heart to flesh,
And begin from this good hour
  To revive Thy work afresh.
  Rev. John Newton. (1725-1807.)

1245 "Always to pray and not to faint." Luke xviii. 1-14. Isa. xlv. 11-19. 2 Chr. xx.   S. M.

1 JESUS, who knows full well
  The heart of every saint,
Invites us all our grief to tell,
  To pray and never faint.

2 He bows His gracious ear,
  We never plead in vain;
Then let us wait till He appear,
  And pray, and pray again.

3 Jesus, the Lord, will hear
  His chosen when they cry;
Yes, though He may awhile forbear,
  He'll help them from on high.

4 Then let us earnest cry,
  And never faint in prayer;
He sees, He hears, and, from on high,
  Will make our cause His care.
  Rev. John Newton.

1246 "Ye know not what shall be on the morrow." James iv. 8. Luke xii. 2 Chr. xxxiv. 14-31.   S. M.

1 TO-MORROW, Lord, is Thine,
  Lodged in Thy sovereign hand;
And, if its sun arise and shine,
  It shines by Thy command.

2 The present moment flies,
  And bears our life away;
O make Thy servants truly wise,
  That they may live to-day.

3 Since on this wingéd hour
  Eternity is hung,
Waken, by Thine almighty power,
  The aged and the young.
  Rev. Philip Doddridge. (1702-1751.)

1247 "Turn us again, O God." Ezra ix. 5-15. Neh. i. Acts ii.   L. M.

1 GREAT Lord of all Thy churches, hear
  Thy ministers' and people's prayer;
Perfumed by Thee, O may it rise,
  Like fragrant incense to the skies.

2 May every pastor from above
  Be new inspired with zeal and love,
To watch Thy flock, Thy flock to feed,
  And sow with care the precious seed.

3 Revive Thy churches with Thy grace;
  Heal all our breaches, grant us peace;
Rouse us from sloth, our hearts inflame
  With ardent zeal for Jesus' name.

4 May young and old Thy word receive,
  Dead sinners hear Thy voice and live,
The wounded conscience healing find,
  And joy refresh each drooping mind.

5 Thus we our suppliant voices raise,
  And, weeping, sow the seed of praise;
In humble hope that Thou wilt hear
  Thy ministers' and people's prayer.
  Rev. William Kingsbury. (1744-1818.)

1248 "O God, lift up Thine hand." Hab. iii. Ps. lxxxv. Acts i. 1-14.   8. 7.

1 HAIL, Thou God of grace and glory,
  Who Thy name hast magnified
By redemption's wondrous story,
  By the Saviour crucified;
Thanks to Thee for every blessing,
  Flowing from the Fount of love;
Thanks for present good unceasing,
  And for hopes of bliss above.

2 Hear us, as thus bending lowly,
  Near Thy bright and burning throne,
We invoke Thee, God most holy,
  Through Thy well-belovéd Son;
Send the baptism of Thy Spirit,
  Shed the pentecostal fire;
Let us all Thy grace inherit,
  Waken, crown each good desire.

3 Bind Thy people, Lord, in union,
  With the sevenfold cord of love;
Breathe a spirit of communion
  With the glorious hosts above;
Let Thy work be seen progressing;
  Bow each heart, and bend each knee,
Till the world, Thy truth possessing,
  Celebrates its jubilee.
  Rev. Thomas W. Aveling. (1815-.)

"O Lord, revive Thy work."

1249 Ps. li. Eze. xxxvi. 22–38. John xvi. 1–15.   "Shine forth."   S. M.

1 COME, Holy Spirit, come;
  Let Thy bright beams arise;
  Dispel the darkness from our minds,
  And open all our eyes.

2 Revive our drooping faith,
  Our doubts and fears remove,
  And kindle in our breasts the flame
  Of never-dying love.

3 Convince us of our sin,
  Then lead to Jesus' blood,
  And to our wondering view reveal
  The secret love of God.

4 'T is Thine to cleanse the heart,
  To sanctify the soul,
  To pour fresh life in every part,
  And new-create the whole.

5 Dwell, therefore, in our hearts,
  Our minds from bondage free;
  Then we shall know, and praise, and love
  The Father, Son, and Thee.
                    Rev. Joseph Hart. (1712–1768.)

1250   "That our God may lighten our eyes."   8. 7.
John i. 1–9. Luke ii. 25–38. Isa. ii.

1 LIGHT of those whose dreary dwelling
  Borders on the shades of death,
  Come, and by Thy love's revealing
  Dissipate the clouds beneath;
  The new heaven and earth's Creator,
  In our deepest darkness rise,
  Scattering all the night of nature,
  Pouring eyesight on our eyes.

2 Still we wait for Thine appearing;
  Life and joy Thy beams impart,
  Chasing all our fears, and cheering
  Every poor, benighted heart;
  Come, and manifest the favor
  God hath for our ransomed race;
  Come, Thou glorious God and Saviour!
  Come, and bring the gospel grace.

3 Save us, in Thy great compassion,
  O Thou mild, pacific Prince!
  Give the knowledge of salvation,
  Give the pardon of our sins;
  By Thine all-sufficient merit
  Every burdened soul release;
  Every weary, wandering spirit
  Guide into Thy perfect peace.
                    Rev. Charles Wesley. (1708–1788.)

1251 Hab. iii. Dan. ix. 3–19. Mat. vi. 9–13.   "Wilt Thou not revive us again?"   S. M.

1 O LORD, Thy work revive,
  In Zion's gloomy hour,
  And let our dying graces live
  By Thy restoring power.

2 O let Thy chosen few
  Awake to earnest prayer;
  Their covenant again renew,
  And walk in filial fear.

3 Thy Spirit then will speak
  Through lips of humble clay,
  Till hearts of adamant shall break,
  Till rebels shall obey.

4 Now lend Thy gracious ear;
  Now listen to our cry;
  O come, and bring salvation near;
  Our souls on Thee rely.
                    Mrs. Phœbe H. Brown. (1783–1861.)

1252   "Till He come and rain righteousness."   C. M.
Hos. xiv. Ps. lxxx. Luke xi. 1–13.

1 GREAT Father of each perfect gift,
  Behold Thy servants wait;
  With longing eyes and lifted hands,
  We flock around Thy gate.

2 O shed abroad that royal gift,
  Thy Spirit from above,
  To bless our eyes with sacred light,
  And fire our hearts with love.

3 Diffuse, O God, those copious showers,
  That earth its fruit may yield,
  And change the barren wilderness
  To Carmel's flowery field.
                    Rev. Philip Doddridge. (1702–1751.)

1253 Ps. lxxxv. Ex. xxxii. 7–32. Acts ii.   "Give us a little reviving."   S. M.

1 REVIVE Thy work, O Lord!
  Thy mighty arm make bare;
  Speak, with the voice that wakes the dead,
  And make Thy people hear.

2 Revive Thy work, O Lord!
  Disturb this sleep of death;
  Quicken the smouldering embers now,
  By Thine almighty breath.

3 Revive Thy work, O Lord!
  Exalt Thy precious name;
  And, by the Holy Ghost, our love
  For Thee and Thine inflame.

4 Revive Thy work, O Lord!
  And give refreshing showers;
  The glory shall be all Thine own,
  The blessing, Lord, be ours.
                    Albert Midlane. (1825–.)

"O Lord, revive Thy work."

1254 "Let us draw near ... in full assurance." C. M.
Heb. xi. Ps. xxxiv. Gen. xxii. 1–14.

1 O FOR a faith that will not shrink
   Though pressed by every foe ;
   That will not tremble on the brink
   Of any earthly woe ;

2 That will not murmur nor complain
   Beneath the chastening rod,
   But, in the hour of grief or pain,
   Will lean upon its God ;

3 A faith that shines more bright and clear
   When tempests rage without ;
   That when in danger knows no fear,
   In darkness feels no doubt ;

4 A faith that keeps the narrow way
   Till life's last hour is fled,
   And with a pure and heavenly ray
   Lights up a dying bed.

5 Lord, give us such a faith as this,
   And then, whate'er may come,
   We'll taste, e'en here, the hallowed bliss
   Of an eternal home.
   Rev. William H. Bathurst. (1796–.)

1255 "O turn Thyself to us again." S. M.
Ps. lxxx. Lam. i. 1–16. 1 Cor. i. 1–10.

1 O FOR the happy hour
   When God will hear our cry ;
   And send, with a reviving power,
   His Spirit from on high !
   We meet, we sing, we pray,
   We listen to the word,
   In vain ; we see no cheering ray,
   No cheering voice is heard.

2 Our prayers are faint and dull,
   And languid all our songs ;
   Where once with joy our hearts were full,
   And rapture tuned our tongues.
   While many seek Thy house,
   How few, around Thy board,
   Meet to recount their solemn vows,
   And bless Thee as their Lord !

3 Thou, Thou alone canst give
   Thy gospel sure success ;
   Canst bid the dying sinner live
   Anew in holiness.
   Come, then, with power divine,
   Spirit of life and love !
   Then shall our people all be Thine,
   Our church, like that above.
   Rev. George W. Bethune. (1805-1862.)

1256 "Increase our faith." C. M.
Luke xvii. 5–19. Mat. viii. 1–13. Job i.

1 INCREASE our faith, belovéd Lord,
   For Thou alone canst give
   The faith that takes Thee at Thy word,
   The faith by which we live.

2 Increase our faith, O Lord, we pray,
   That we may not depart
   From Thy commands, but all obey
   With free and loyal heart.

3 Increase our faith that we may claim
   Each starry promise sure,
   And always triumph in Thy name,
   And to the end endure.

4 Increase our faith, O Saviour dear,
   By Thy sweet, sovereign grace,
   Till, changing faith for vision clear,
   We see Thee face to face.
   Miss Frances R. Havergal. (1836–1879.)

1257 "Remember Thy congregation." L. M.
Ps. lxxiv. Dan. ix. 3–19. 1 Pet. ii.

1 INDULGENT Sovereign of the skies,
   And wilt Thou bow Thy gracious ear ;
   While feeble mortals raise their cries,
   Wilt Thou, the great Jehovah, hear ?

2 How shall Thy servants give Thee rest,
   Till Zion's mouldering walls Thou raise ;
   Till Thine own power shall stand confessed,
   And make Jerusalem a praise ?

3 On all our souls let grace descend,
   Like heavenly dew, in copious showers :
   That we may call our God our Friend ;
   That we may hail salvation ours.
   Rev. Philip Doddridge. (1702-1751.)

1258 "Dry ground into water-springs." 7.
Ps. lxvii. Isa. xliv. 1–8. Acts ii.

1 FOUNT of everlasting love,
   Rich Thy streams of mercy are ;
   Flowing purely from above,
   Beauty marks their course afar.

2 Lo, Thy church, athirst and faint,
   Drinks the full, refreshing tide ;
   Thou hast heard her sad complaint,
   Floods of grace are sweeping wide.

3 God of mercy, to Thy throne
   Now our fervent thanks we bring ;
   Thine the glory, Thine alone,
   Joyous praise to Thee we sing.

4 While we lift our grateful song,
   Let Thy Spirit still descend ;
   Roll the tide of grace along,
   Widening, deepening, to the end.
   Rev. Ray Palmer. (1808–.)

"To seek and to save that which was lost."

1259 " At the last it biteth like a serpent." **L. M.**
Prov. xxiii. 29-35. Isa. xxviii. 1-7. Mat. vi.

1 BONDAGE and death the cup contains;
　Dash to the earth the poisoned bowl!
　Softer than silk are iron chains,
　Compared with those that chafe the soul.

2 Hosannas, Lord, to Thee we sing,
　Whose power the giant fiend obeys :
　What countless thousands tribute bring,
　For happier homes and brighter days !

3 Thou wilt not break the bruiséd reed,
　Nor leave the broken heart unbound ;
　The wife regains a husband freed !
　The orphan clasps a father found !

4 Spare, Lord, the thoughtless ; guide the blind ;
　Till man no more shall deem it just
　To live, by forging chains to bind
　His weaker brother in the dust.
　　　　　　　　　Lucius M. Sargent.　(1786-1867.)

1260 " Considering ... lest thou also be tempted." **C. M.**
Gal. vi. Mat. xviii. 7-22. 2 Sam. xviii.

1 THINK gently of the erring one !
　O let us not forget,
　However darkly stained by sin,
　He is our brother yet !

2 Heir of the same inheritance,
　Child of the self-same God,
　He hath but stumbled in the path
　We have in weakness trod.

3 Speak gently to the erring ones !
　We yet may lead them back,
　With holy words, and tones of love,
　From misery's thorny track.

4 Forget not thou hast often sinned,
　And sinful yet mayst be ;
　Deal gently with the erring heart,
　As God hath dealt with thee.
　　　　　　　　　Miss Fletcher.　1857.

1261 " He that winneth souls is wise." **7.**
1 Cor. i. 17-31. 2 Cor. v. 11-21. Dan. xii. 1-3.

1 WOULD you win a soul to God ?
　Tell him of a Saviour's blood,
　Once for dying sinners spilt,
　To atone for all their guilt.

2 Tell him it was sovereign grace
　Led thee first to seek His face ;
　Made thee choose the better part,
　Wrought salvation in thy heart.

3 Tell him of that liberty
　Wherewith Jesus makes thee free ;
　Sweetly speak of sins forgiven,
　Earnest of the joys of heaven.
　　　　　　　　　Rev. William Hammond.　(-1783.)

1262 " And the land shall mourn." **S. M.**
Jer. ix. 19-21. Joel i. 1 Cor. vi. 9-14.

1 MOURN for the thousands slain,
　The youthful and the strong ;
　Mourn for the wine-cup's fearful reign,
　And the deluded throng.

2 Mourn for the tarnished gem,
　For reason's light divine,
　Quenched from the soul's bright diadem,
　Where God had bid it shine.

3 Mourn for the ruined soul,
　Eternal life and light
　Lost by the fiery, maddening bowl,
　And turned to hopeless night.

4 Mourn for the lost, but call,
　Call to the strong, the free ;
　Rouse them to shun that dreadful fall,
　And to the refuge flee.

5 Mourn for the lost, but pray,
　Pray to our God above,
　To break the fell destroyer's sway,
　And show His saving love.
　　　　　　　　　Author unknown.

1263 " Restore such an one." **11. 10.**
Luke xiv. 15-23. Mat. x. Gen. xviii. 23-33.

1 　RESCUE the perishing,
　　Care for the dying,
　Snatch them in pity from sin and the grave ;
　　Weep o'er the erring one,
　　Lift up the fallen,
　　Tell them of Jesus,
　　The mighty to save.

　　Rescue the perishing,
　　Care for the dying ;
　　Jesus is merciful,
　　Jesus will save.

2 　Though they are slighting Him,
　　Still He is waiting,
　.Waiting the penitent child to receive.
　　Plead with them earnestly,
　　Plead with them gently ;
　　He will forgive
　　If they only believe.

3 　Rescue the perishing,
　　Duty demands it ;
　Strength for thy labor the Lord will provide ;
　　Back to the narrow way
　　Patiently win them ;
　　Tell the poor wanderer
　　A Saviour has died.
　　　　　　　　　Mrs. Frances J. C. Van Alstyne.　(1825-.)

"To seek and to save that which was lost."

1264 "Able to succor them that are tempted." C. M.
Acts iv. 8-22. James iv. Ps. lxxxii.

1 'T IS Thine alone, almighty name,
  To raise the dead to life,
The lost inebriate to reclaim
  From passion's fearful strife.

2 What ruin hath intemperance wrought!
  How widely roll its waves!
How many myriads hath it brought
  To fill dishonored graves!

3 And see, O Lord, what numbers still
  Are maddened by the bowl,
Led captive at the tyrant's will,
  In bondage, heart and soul!

4 Stretch forth Thy hand, O God, our King,
  And break the galling chain;
Deliverance to the captive bring,
  And end th' usurper's reign.
  Rev. Edwin F. Hatfield. (1807-.)

1265 "That ye should do as I have done." C. M.
Luke x. 17-37. James i. 22-27. Lev. xxv.

1 FATHER of mercies, send Thy grace,
  All-powerful from above,
To form, in our obedient souls,
  The image of Thy love.

2 O may our sympathizing breasts
  That generous pleasure know,
Kindly to share in others' joy,
  And weep for others' woe.

3 When the most helpless sons of grief
  In low distress are laid,
Soft be our hearts their pains to feel,
  And swift our hands to aid.
  Rev. Philip Doddridge. (1702-1751.)

1266 "In ... God we will set up our banners." 7, 6.
Ps. cxv. Isa. xxviii. Mal. viii. 16, 17.

1 Now, host with host assembling,
  The victory we win;
Lo! on his throne sits trembling
  That old and giant Sin;
Like chaff by strong winds scattered,
  His banded strength has gone,
His charmèd cup lies shattered,
  And still the cry is "On."

2 Our fathers' God, our Keeper,
  Be Thou our Strength divine!
Thou sendest forth the reaper,
  The harvest all is Thine.
Roll on, roll on this gladness,
  Till, driven from every shore,
The drunkard's sin and madness
  Shall smite the earth no more!
  Rev. Edwin H. Chapin. (1814-1880.)

1267 "Preserve Thou those ... appointed to die." L. M.
Acts xii. 1 Cor. vi. 10. Eze. xxxvii.

1 WHEN, doomed to death, the apostle lay
  At night in Herod's dungeon cell,
A light shone round him like the day,
  And from his limbs the fetters fell.

2 Chains yet more strong and cruel bind
  The victims of that deadly thirst
Which drowns the soul, and from the mind
  Blots the bright image stamped at first.

3 O God of love and mercy, deign
  To look on those with pitying eye
Who struggle with that fatal chain;
  And send them succor from on high!

4 Send down, in its resistless might,
  Thy gracious Spirit, we implore,
And lead the captive forth to light,
  A rescued soul, a slave no more!
  William C. Bryant. (1794-1878.)

1268 "We are risen and stand upright." C. M.
Ps. cvii. 8-22. Rom. v. Titus iii. 3-7.

1 SALVATION! O the joyful sound;
  'T is pleasure to our ears;
A sovereign balm for every wound,
  A cordial for our fears.

2 Buried in sorrow and in sin,
  At hell's dark door we lay;
But we arise, by grace divine,
  To see a heavenly day.

3 Salvation! let the echo fly
  The spacious earth around;
While all the armies of the sky
  Conspire to raise the sound.
  Rev. Isaac Watts. (1674-1748.)

1269 "The snare is broken." L. M.
Ps. cxiii. Isa. xii. Acts xvi. 16-34.

1 WE praise Thee, Lord, if but one soul,
  While the past year prolonged its flight,
Turned shudd'ring from the pois'nous bowl,
  To health, and liberty, and light.

2 We praise Thee, if one clouded home,
  Where broken hearts despairing pined,
Beheld the sire and husband come
  Erect, and in his perfect mind;

3 No more a weeping wife to mock,
  Till all her hopes in anguish end,
No more the trembling mind to shock,
  And sink the father in the fiend.

4 Still give us grace, almighty King,
  Unwavering at our posts to stand;
Till grateful at Thy shrine we bring
  The tribute of a ransomed land.
  Author unknown.

"That glory may dwell in our land."

1270 "Thus shall He deliver... our land." **L. M.**
Ps. lxxxv. Isa. lxiii. 7-19. Luke xxiv. 44-53.

1 LOOK from Thy sphere of endless day,
   O God of mercy and of might;
   In pity look on those who stray,
   Benighted, in this land of light.

2 In peopled vale, in lonely glen,
   In crowded mart, by stream or sea,
   How many of the sons of men
   Hear not the message sent from Thee.

3 Send forth Thy heralds, Lord, to call
   The thoughtless young, the hardened old,
   A scattered, homeless flock, till all
   Be gathered to Thy peaceful fold.

4 Send them Thy mighty word to speak,
   Till faith shall dawn, and doubt depart;
   To awe the bold, to stay the weak,
   And bind and heal the broken heart.

5 Then all these wastes, a dreary scene,
   That make us sadden as we gaze,
   Shall grow with living waters green,
   And lift to heaven the voice of praise.
   William C. Bryant. (1794-1878.)

1271 "Our fathers trusted and Thou didst deliver." **8, 6.**
Deu. xi. 1-25. Josh. xxii. 11-34. Acts i. 1-14.

1 WHEN, Lord, to this our western land,
   Led by Thy providential hand,
   Our wandering fathers came,
   Their ancient homes, their friends in youth,
   Sent forth the heralds of Thy truth,
   To keep them in Thy name.

2 Then, through our solitary coast,
   The desert features soon were lost;
   Thy temples there arose;
   Our shores, as culture made them fair,
   Were hallowed by Thy rites, by prayer,
   And blossomed as the rose.

3 And, O may we repay this debt
   To regions solitary yet,
   Within our spreading land:
   There brethren, from our common home,
   Still westward, like our fathers, roam;
   Still guided by Thy hand.

4 Saviour, we own this debt of love:
   O shed Thy Spirit from above,
   To move each Christian breast;
   Till heralds shall Thy truth proclaim,
   And temples rise to fix Thy name,
   Through all our desert West.
   Bp. Henry U. Onderdonk. (1789-1858.)

1272 "It shall blossom abundantly." **C. M.**
Deu. viii. Ps. lxxix. Mat. iv. 12-17.

1 ON Sion, and on Lebanon,
   On Carmel's blooming height,
   On Sharon's fertile plains, once shone
   The glory, pure and bright:

2 From thence its mild and cheering ray
   Stream'd forth from land to land;
   And empires now behold its day,
   And still its beams expand.

3 But ah, our deserts deep and wild
   See not this heavenly light;
   No sacred beams, no radiance mild,
   Dispel their dreary night.

4 Thou, who didst lighten Sion's hill,
   On Carmel who didst shine,
   Our deserts let Thy glory fill,
   Thy excellence divine.

5 Like Lebanon, in towering pride,
   May all our forests smile;
   And may our borders blossom wide
   Like Sharon's fruitful soil.
   Bp. Henry U. Onderdonk.

1273 "From sea to sea." **7, 6.**
Ps. lxxii. Josh. xxiii. 1-11. Mat. vi. 9-13.

1 FROM ocean unto ocean,
   From hills and plains arise
   The music of devotion
   To God, the only wise;
   Our western home rejoices
   The gospel light to see;
   We raise, O God, our voices
   In grateful thanks to Thee.

2 Take Thou our favored nation
   Beneath Thy fostering care,
   The news of Thy salvation
   Let countless heralds bear;
   Thine are our hearts, believe it,
   We give them to Thee, Lord;
   Thine is our wealth, receive it,
   To spread Thy precious word!

3 From sea to sea obtaining
   A kingdom never moved,
   Within our borders reigning,
   Feared, honored, and beloved;
   North, south, east, west, Thy banner
   Be ever wide unfurled;
   Ten millions sing hosanna
   Throughout our ransomed world.
   Rev. Gardner S. Plumley. (1827-.)

"That glory may dwell in our land."

1274 "Our land shall yield her increase." **C. M.**
Ps. lxxx. Isa. lxiii. 15-19. Acts xvii. 24-31.

1 SHINE on our land, Jehovah, shine,
   With beams of heavenly grace;
  Reveal Thy power through all our coasts,
   And show Thy smiling face.

2 Earth shall confess her Maker's hand,
   And yield a full increase;
  Our God will crown His chosen land
   With fruitfulness and peace.

3 God, the Redeemer, scatters round
   His choicest favors here;
  While the creation's utmost bound
   Shall see, adore, and fear.
   Rev. Isaac Watts. (1674-1748.)

1275 "Go through the gates; prepare ye the way." **7. 6.**
Josh. xviii. 1-6. 2 Chr. xxx. Mat. x. 1-15.

1 OUR country's voice is pleading,
   Ye men of God, arise!
  His providence is leading,
   The land before you lies;
  Day-gleams are o'er it brightening,
   And promise clothes the soil;
  Wide fields, for harvest whitening,
   Invite the reaper's toil.

2 The love of Christ unfolding,
   Speed on from east to west,
  Till all, His cross beholding,
   In Him are fully blest.
  Great Author of salvation,
   Haste, haste the glorious day,
  When we, a ransomed nation,
   Thy sceptre shall obey!
   Mrs. Maria F. Anderson. (1819-.)

1276 "Show us Thy mercy, O Lord." **6. 4.**
Ps. xc. Deu. xxviii. 1-14. Luke i. 68-75.

1 GOD bless our native land;
   Firm may she ever stand,
    Through storm and night;
   When the wild tempests rave,
   Ruler of wind and wave,
   Do Thou our country save
    By Thy great might.

2 For her our prayer shall rise
   To God, above the skies;
    On Him we wait;
   Thou who art ever nigh,
   Guarding with watchful eye,
   To Thee aloud we cry,
    God save the State.
   Rev. John S. Dwight. (1815-.)

1277 "Arise for our help." **C. M.**
Ps. cvi. 1-8, 43-48. Neh. ix. Luke xi. 1-13.

1 LORD, while for all mankind we pray,
   Of every clime and coast,
  O hear us for our native land,
   The land we love the most.

2 O guard our shore from every foe,
   With peace our borders bless,
  With prosperous times our cities crown,
   Our fields with plenteousness.

3 Unite us in the sacred love
   Of knowledge, truth, and Thee,
  And let our hills and valleys shout
   The songs of liberty.

4 Lord of the nations, thus to Thee
   Our country we commend;
  Be Thou her refuge and her trust,
   Her everlasting friend.
   Rev. John R. Wreford. 1837.

1278 "Thy land, O Immanuel." **7.**
Ps. lxii. Isa. lxiv. Heb. i. 1-12.

1 COME, divine Emmanuel, come,
   Take possession of Thy home;
  Now Thy mercy's wings expand,
  Stretch throughout the happy land.

2 Carry on Thy victory,
   Spread Thy rule from sea to sea;
  Take the purchase of Thy blood,
   Bring us to a pard'ning God.

3 O that every soul might be
   Perfectly subdued to Thee;
  O that all in Thee might know
   Everlasting life below.
   Rev. Charles Wesley. (1706-1788.)

1279 "Grant us Thy salvation." **L. M.**
Ps. cvii. Josh. xxiii. 1-11. 1 Tim. i. 17.

1 O GOD, beneath Thy guiding hand,
   Our exiled fathers crossed the sea;
  And when they trod the wintry strand,
   With prayer and psalm they worshipped
     Thee.

2 Thou heard'st, well pleased, the song, the
     prayer.
  Thy blessing came; and still its power
  Shall onward through all ages bear
   The memory of that holy hour.

3 Laws, freedom, truth, and faith in God
   Came with those exiles o'er the waves;
  And where their pilgrim feet have trod,
   The God they trusted guards their graves.

4 And here Thy name, O God of love,
   Their children's children shall adore,
  Till these eternal hills remove,
   And spring adorns the earth no more.
   Rev. Leonard Bacon. (1802-.)

"They that go down to the sea in ships."

1280 "They cry unto the Lord in their trouble." **L. M.**
Job xxxviii. Mat. xiv. 22–36. Gen. i.

1 ETERNAL Father, strong to save,
Whose arm doth bind the restless wave,
Who bidd'st the mighty ocean deep
Its own appointed limits keep ;
O hear us when we cry to Thee
For those in peril on the sea.

2 O Saviour, whose almighty word
The winds and waves submissive heard,
Who walkedst in the foaming deep,
And calm amid its rage didst sleep ;
O hear us when we cry to Thee
For those in peril on the sea.

3 O Sacred Spirit, who didst brood
Upon the chaos dark and rude,
Who bad'st its angry tumult cease,
And gavest light, and life, and peace ;
O hear us when we cry to Thee
For those in peril on the sea.

4 O Trinity of love and power,
Our brethren shield in danger's hour!
From rock and tempest, fire and foe,
Protect them wheresoe'er they go;
Thus evermore shall rise to thee
Glad hymns of praise from land and sea.
William Whiting. (1825–.)

1281 "But He was asleep." **8. 7.**
Ps. xxxiii. Mark iv. 35–41. 2 Cor. xi. 24–31.

1 TOSSED upon life's raging billow,
Sweet it is, O Lord, to know,
Thou didst press a sailor's pillow,
And canst feel a sailor's woe.
Never slumbering, never sleeping,
Though the night be dark and drear,
Thou the faithful watch art keeping,
"All, all 's well," Thy constant cheer.

2 And though loud the wind is howling,
Fierce though flash the lightnings red ;
Darkly though the storm-cloud 's scowling
O'er the sailor's anxious head ;
Thou canst calm the raging ocean,
All its noise and tumult still,
Hush the tempest's wild commotion,
At the bidding of Thy will.

3 Thus my heart the hope will cherish,
While to Thee I lift mine eye,
Thou wilt save me ere I perish,
Thou wilt hear the sailor's cry ;
And though mast and sail be riven,
Life's short voyage will soon be o'er ;
Safely moored in heaven's wide haven,
Storms and tempests vex no more.
Rev. George W. Bethune. (1805–1862.)

1282 "These see the works of the Lord." **L. M.**
Acts xxvii. Mat. viii. 23–27. Jonah i.

1 WHILE o'er the deep Thy servants sail,
Send Thou, O Lord, the prosperous gale;
And on their hearts, where'er they go,
O let Thy heavenly breezes blow.

2 If on the morning's wings they fly,
They will not pass beyond Thine eye :
The wanderer's prayer Thou bend'st to hear,
And faith exults to know Thee near.

3 When tempests rock the groaning bark,
O hide them safe in Jesus' ark ;
When in the tempting port they ride,
O keep them safe at Jesus' side.

4 If life's wide ocean smile or roar,
Still guide them to the heavenly shore ;
And grant their dust in Christ may sleep,
Abroad, at home, or in the deep.
Bp. George Burgess. (1809–1866.)

1283 "Which stilleth the noise of the seas." **L. M.**
Ps. cvii. 23–31. Acts xxviii. Mark vi. 45–51.

1 O GOD, who metest in Thy hand
The waters of the mighty sea,
And barrest ocean with the sand
By Thy perpetual decree ;

2 When they who to the sea go down,
And in the waters ply their toil,
Are lifted on the surge's crown,
And plunged where seething eddies boil ;

3 Rule then, O Lord, the ocean's wrath,
And bind the tempest with Thy will ;
Tread, as of old, the water's path,
And speak Thy bidding, " Peace be still."
Rev. Richard F. Littledale. (1833–.)

1284 "Jesus went unto them walking on the sea." **8. 7. P.**
John vi. 15–21. Jonah ii. Luke viii. 23.

1 STAR of peace, to wanderers weary,
Bright the beams that smile on me ;
Cheer the pilot's vision dreary,
Far, far at sea.

2 Star of hope, gleam on the billow,
Bless the soul that sighs for Thee ;
Bless the sailor's lonely pillow,
Far, far at sea.

3 Star of faith, when winds are mocking
All his toil, he flies to Thee ;
Save him on the billows rocking,
Far, far at sea.

4 Star divine, O safely guide him,
Bring the wanderer home to Thee :
Sore temptations long have tried him,
Far, far at sea.
Mrs. Jane C. B. Simpson. 1810.

"The lost sheep of the house of Israel."

1285 "I will surely gather the remnant of Israel." **L. M.**
Ps. lxxiv. Lam. i. 1-11. Rom. ii.

1 O WHY should Israel's sons, once blest,
  Still roam the scorning world around,
  Disowned by heaven, by man opprest,
  Outcasts from Zion's hallowed ground?

2 Lord, visit Thy forsaken race;
  Back to Thy fold the wanderers bring;
  Teach them to seek Thy slighted grace,
  To hail in Christ their promised King.

3 The veil of darkness rend in twain
  Which hides their Shiloh's glorious light;
  The severed olive-branch again
  Firm to its parent stock unite.

4 Haste, glorious day, expected long,
  When Jew and Greek one prayer shall pour,
  With eager feet one temple throng,
  One God with grateful heart adore.
  Rev. James Joyce. (1781-1850.)

1286 "O that the salvation of Israel were come." **7, 6.**
Ps. xiv. Jer. xvi. 14-21. Heb. viii.

1 O THAT the Lord's salvation
  Were out of Zion come,
  To heal His ancient nation,
  To lead His outcast home.
  How long the holy city
  Shall heathen feet profane?
  Return, O Lord, in pity;
  Rebuild her walls again.

2 Let fall Thy rod of terror,
  Thy saving grace impart;
  Roll back the veil of error,
  Release the fettered heart.
  Let Israel, home returning,
  Her lost Messiah see;
  Give oil of joy for mourning,
  And bind Thy church to Thee.
  Rev. Henry F. Lyte. (1793-1847.)

1287 "My people, my chosen." **S. M.**
Zech. i. Eze. xx. 40-49. Acts ii. 14-47.

1 To bless Thy chosen race,
  In mercy, Lord, incline;
  And cause the brightness of Thy face
  On all Thy saints to shine.

2 Let differing nations join
  To celebrate Thy fame;
  Let all the world, O Lord, combine
  To praise Thy glorious name.

3 O let them shout and sing,
  With joy and pious mirth;
  For Thou, the righteous Judge and King,
  Shalt govern all the earth.
  Nahum Tate. (1652-1715.)

1288 "And I will set a sign among them." **S. M.**
Isa. xi. Zech. xii. Gal. iii.

1 ALMIGHTY God of love,
  Set up th' attracting sign,
  And summon whom Thou dost approve
  For messengers divine.

2 We know it must be done,
  For God hath spoke the word;
  All Israel shall their Saviour own,
  To their first state restored.

3 Send, then, Thy servants forth
  To call the Hebrews home;
  From west and east, and south and north,
  Let all the wanderers come.

4 With Israel's myriads sealed,
  Let all the nations meet;
  And show Thy mystery fulfilled,
  Thy family complete.
  Rev. Charles Wesley. (1708-1788.)

1289 "Bow Thy heavens, O Lord, and come." **L. M.**
Isa. lxi. Eze. xxxvii. Rev. xxii. 17-21.

1 HEAD of the church, whose Spirit fills
  And flows through every faithful soul,
  Unites in mystic love, and seals
  Them one, and sanctifies the whole:

2 Come, Lord, Thy glorious Spirit cries,
  And souls beneath the altar groan;
  Come, Lord, the Bride on earth replies,
  And perfect all our souls in one.

3 Pour out the promised gift on all;
  Answer the universal Come!
  The fulness of the Gentiles call,
  And take Thine ancient people home.

4 To Thee let all the nations flow;
  Let all obey the gospel word;
  Let all their bleeding Saviour know,
  Filled with the glory of the Lord.
  Rev. Charles Wesley.

1290 "Arise, O Lord." **S. M.**
Ps. lxviii. Eze. xxxiv. 22-31. Acts. x. 34-45.

1 O LORD our God, arise!
  The cause of truth maintain;
  And wide o'er all the peopled world
  Extend her blessèd reign.

2 Thou Prince of Life, arise!
  Nor let Thy glory cease;
  Far spread the conquests of Thy grace,
  And bless the earth with peace.

3 Thou Holy Ghost, arise!
  Expand Thy quickening wing,
  And o'er a dark and ruined world
  Let light and order spring.
  Rev. Ralph Wardlaw. (1779-1853.)

"Go ye therefore and teach all nations."

1291 "Come over...and help us." Acts x. 17-33. Mat. iii. 5-12. Ps. lxxii. **7. 6.**

1 FROM Greenland's icy mountains,
　From India's coral strand,
Where Afric's sunny fountains
　Roll down their golden sand:
From many an ancient river,
　From many a palmy plain,
They call us to deliver
　Their land from error's chain.

2 What though the spicy breezes
　Blow soft o'er Ceylon's isle,
Though every prospect pleases,
　And only man is vile:
In vain with lavish kindness
　The gifts of God are strown,
The heathen in his blindness
　Bows down to wood and stone.

3 Can we, whose souls are lighted
　With wisdom from on high,
Can we to men benighted
　The lamp of life deny?
Salvation, O salvation!
　The joyful sound proclaim,
Till each remotest nation
　Has learnt Messiah's name.

4 Waft, waft, ye winds, His story,
　And you, ye waters, roll,
Till, like a sea of glory,
　It spreads from pole to pole;
Till o'er our ransomed nature,
　The Lamb for sinners slain,
Redeemer, King, Creator,
　In bliss returns to reign.
　　　　　Bp. Reginald Heber. (1783-1826.)

1292 "Come up to us quickly and save us." Acts xvi. Mat. xv. 21-28. Zech. viii. 21. **8. 7.**

1 HARK, what mean these lamentations
　Rolling sadly through the sky?
'T is the cry of heathen nations,
　" Come and help us, or we die."
Lost and helpless and desponding,
　Wrapt in error's night they lie;
To their cries your hearts responding,
　Haste to help them ere they die.

2 Hark, again those lamentations
　Rolling sadly through the sky;
Louder cry the heathen nations,
　" Come and help us, or we die."
Hear the heathen's sad complaining;
　Christians, hear their dying cry;
And the love of Christ constraining,
　Join to help them ere they die.
　　　　　Rev. John Cawood. (1775-1852.)

1293 "The people which sat in darkness." Acts xiii. 42-50. Mark i. 1-15. Josh. ix. **8. 7. 4.**

1 SOULS in heathen darkness lying,
　Where no light has broken through,
Souls that Jesus bought by dying,
　Whom His soul in travail knew:
　　Thousand voices
Call us, o'er the waters blue.

2 Christians, hearken: none has taught them
　Of His love so deep and dear;
Of the precious price that bought them;
　Of the nail, the thorn, the spear;
　　Ye who know Him,
Guide them from their darkness drear.

3 Haste, O haste, and spread the tidings
　Wide to earth's remotest strand;
Let no brother's bitter chidings
　Rise against us when we stand
　　In the judgment,
From some far, forgotten land.

4 Lo, the hills for harvest whiten,
　All along each distant shore;
Seaward far the islands brighten;
　Light of nations, lead us o'er;
　　When we seek them,
Let Thy Spirit go before.
　　　　　Mrs. Cecil F. Alexander. (1823-.)

1294 " Now, therefore, arise, go." Ex. xiv. 15-22. Isa. lx. Luke xii. 32-40. **6. 5.**

1 FORWARD! be our watchword,
　Steps and voices joined;
Seek the things before us,
　Not a look behind:
Burns the fiery pillar
　At our army's head;
Who shall dream of shrinking,
　By our Captain led?
Forward through the desert,
　Through the toil and fight:
Jordan flows before us,
　Zion beams with light!

2 Forward, flock of Jesus,
　Salt of all the earth;
Till each yearning purpose
　Spring to glorious birth:
Sick, they ask for healing,
　Blind, they grope for day;
Pour upon the nations
　Wisdom's loving ray.
Forward, out of error,
　Leave behind the night;
Forward through the darkness,
　Forward into light!
　　　　　Rev. Henry Alford. (1810-1871.)

"Go ye therefore and teach all nations."

1295 "Go ye into all the world." L. M.
Mat. xxviii. 19, 20. Mark vi. 7-13. Ps. xcvi.

1 YE Christian heralds, go, proclaim
  Salvation through Immanuel's name ;
  To distant climes the tidings bear,
  And plant the Rose of Sharon there.

2 He'll shield you with a wall of fire,
  With flaming zeal your breast inspire,
  Bid raging winds their fury cease,
  And hush the tempest into peace.

3 And when our labors all are o'er,
  Then we shall meet to part no more ;
  Meet, with the blood-bought throng to fall,
  And crown our Jesus Lord of all.

  Mrs. Voke. 1808.

1296 "Lift ye up a banner." 7. 6.
Luke ix. 1-6. Acts xi. 19-30. Ps. cv.

1 UPLIFT the blood-red banner,
  And shout, with trumpet's sound,
  Deliverance to the captive,
  And freedom to the bound ;
  Earth's jubilee of glory,
  The year of full release :
  O tell the wondrous story,
  Go forth and publish peace.

2 Go forth, confessors, martyrs,
  With zeal and love unpriced,
  And preach the blood of sprinkling,
  And live, or die, for Christ ;
  For Christ claim every nation,
  Your banner wide unfurled ;
  Go forth and preach salvation,
  Salvation for the world.

  Benjamin Gough. (1805-.)

1297 "Many nations shall be joined to the Lord." 8. 7.
Ps. xcvii. Joel ii. Luke xxi. 10-38.

1 WE are living, we are dwelling,
  In a grand and awful time,
  In an age on ages telling ;
  To be living is sublime.
  Hark, the waking up of nations,
  Gog and Magog to the fray.
  Hark, what soundeth ? is creation
  Groaning for its latter day ?

2 Worlds are charging, heaven beholding,
  Thou hast but an hour to fight ;
  Now the blazoned cross unfolding,
  On, right onward for the right !
  On, let all the soul within you
  For the truth's sake go abroad.
  Strike, let every nerve and sinew
  Tell on ages, tell for God.

  Bp. Arthur C. Coxe. (1818-.)

1298 "As ye go, preach." S. M.
Mat. x. Acts xiii. 1-13. Jonah iii.

1 YE messengers of Christ,
  His sovereign voice obey ;
  Arise, and follow where He leads,
  And peace attend your way.

2 The Master whom you serve
  Will needful strength bestow ;
  Depending on His promised aid,
  With sacred courage go.

3 Go, spread a Saviour's fame,
  And tell His matchless grace,
  To the most guilty and depraved
  Of Adam's numerous race.

  Mrs. Voke. (1808.)

1299 "Which stilleth the noise of their waves." 7. 6.
Acts xxvii. Rom. i. 1-15. Ps. xciii.

1 ROLL on, thou mighty ocean ;
  And, as thy billows flow,
  Bear messengers of mercy
  To every land below ;
  Arise, ye gales, and waft them
  Safe to the destined shore ;
  That man may sit in darkness
  And death's black shade no more.

2 O Thou eternal Ruler,
  Who holdest in Thine arm
  The tempests of the ocean,
  Protect them from all harm ;
  Thy presence e'er be with them,
  Wherever they may be ;
  Though far from those who love them,
  Still let them be with Thee.

  James Edmeston. (1791-1867.)

1300 "Let Thy work appear unto Thy servants." C. M.
Acts vi. Luke x. 1-16. Isa. lxi. 1-6.

1 FATHER of mercies, condescend
  To hear our fervent prayer,
  While these our brethren we commend
  To Thy paternal care.

2 Before them set an open door ;
  Their various efforts bless ;
  On them Thy Holy Spirit pour,
  And crown them with success.

3 Endow them with a heavenly mind ;
  Supply their every need ;
  Make them in spirit meek, resigned,
  But bold in word and deed.

4 In every tempting, trying hour,
  Uphold them by Thy grace,
  And guard them by Thy mighty power,
  Till they shall end their race.

  Thomas Morell. (1781-1840.)

"Go ye therefore and teach all nations."

1301 "Put on the whole armor of God." 7.
Mark vi. 7-13. Acts xv. 6-41. Jonah iii.

1 SOLDIERS of the cross, arise !
Gird you with your armor bright ;
Mighty are your enemies,
Hard the battle ye must fight ;

2 O'er a faithless, fallen world,
Raise your banner in the sky,
Let it float there, wide unfurled,
Bear it onward, lift it high.

3 'Mid the homes of want and woe,
Strangers to the living word,
Let the Saviour's herald go,
Let the voice of hope be heard ;

4 To the weary and the worn
Tell of realms where sorrows cease ;
To the outcast and forlorn
Speak of mercy, grace, and peace.

5 Guard the helpless, seek the strayed,
Comfort troubles, banish grief ;
With the Spirit's sword arrayed,
Scatter sin and unbelief.

6 Be the banner still unfurled,
Bear it bravely still abroad,
Till the kingdoms of the world
Are the kingdoms of the Lord.
Rev. William W. How. (1823-.)

1302 "Declare His wonders among all people." 8. 7. 4.
Mat. xxviii. 16-20. Acts i. 1-8. Isa. lviii.

1 MEN of God, go take your stations,
Darkness reigns throughout the earth ;
Go, proclaim among the nations
Joyful news of heavenly birth :
Bear the tidings
Of the Saviour's matchless worth.

2 Of His gospel not ashaméd,
As the power of God to save,
Go where Christ was never naméd,
Publish freedom to the slave :
Blesséd freedom,
Freedom Zion's children have.

3 When exposed to fearful dangers,
Jesus will His own defend ;
Borne afar 'mid foes and strangers,
Jesus will appear your Friend ;
And His presence
Shall be with you to the end.
Rev. Thomas Kelly. (1769-1855.)

1303 "Thou hast given a banner to them." 7. 6.
John iii. 14-21. Luke x. 1-16. Jer. xxxi.10-14.

1 Now be the gospel banner
In every land unfurled,
And be the shout, " Hosanna ! "
Reëchoed through the world :
Till every isle and nation,
Till every tribe and tongue,
Receive the great salvation,
And join the happy throng.

2 What though th' embattled legions
Of earth and hell combine ?
His power, throughout their regions,
Shall soon resplendent shine :
Ride on, O Lord, victorious,
Immanuel, Prince of Peace ;
Thy triumph shall be glorious,
Thine empire still increase.

3 Yes, Thou shalt reign forever,
O Jesus, King of kings :
Thy light, Thy love, Thy favor,
Each ransomed captive sings.
The isles for Thee are waiting,
The deserts learn Thy praise,
The hills and valleys, greeting,
The song responsive raise.
Thomas Hastings. (1784-1872.)

1304 "By the armor of righteousness." S. M.
Eph. vi. 10. 1 Sam. xvii. Ex. xvii. 8-15.

1 SOLDIERS of Christ, arise,
And put your armor on,
Strong in the strength which God supplies
Through His eternal Son.

2 Stand, then, in His great might,
With all His strength endued,
And take, to arm you for the fight,
The panoply of God ;

3 That, having all things done,
And all your conflicts past,
Ye may o'ercome through Christ alone,
And stand entire at last.

4 Leave no unguarded place,
No weakness of the soul ;
Take every virtue, every grace,
And fortify the whole.

5 To keep your armor bright,
Attend with constant care,
Still walking in your Captain's sight,
And watching unto prayer.
Rev. Charles Wesley. (1708-1788.)

"Go ye therefore and teach all nations."

1305 "Go in and possess the land." 6. 5.
Ex. xiv. 15-22. Josh. iii. Luke x. 1-16.

1 ONWARD, Christian soldiers,
  Marching as to war,
With the cross of Jesus
  Going on before.
Christ the royal Master
  Leads against the foe ;
Forward into battle,
  See His banner go.

2 Like a mighty army
  Moves the church of God ;
Brothers, we are treading
  Where the saints have trod ;
We are not divided,
  All one body we,
One in hope and doctrine,
  One in charity.

3 Crowns and thrones may perish,
  Kingdoms rise and wane,
But the church of Jesus
  Constant will remain ;
Gates of hell can never
  'Gainst that church prevail;
We have Christ's own promise,
  And that cannot fail.

Rev. Sabine Baring-Gould. (1834-.)

1307 "Stand up for me." 7. 6.
Luke xxiv. 44-53. Acts iv. 1-20. Isa. xliii.

1 STAND up, stand up for Jesus,
  Ye soldiers of the cross ;
Lift high His royal banner,
  It must not suffer loss :
From victory unto victory
  His army shall He lead,
Till every foe is vanquished,
  And Christ is Lord indeed.

2 Stand up, stand up for Jesus,
  Stand in His strength alone ;
The arm of flesh will fail you,
  Ye dare not trust your own :
Put on the gospel armor
  Each piece put on with prayer ;
Where duty calls, or danger,
  Be never wanting there.

3 Stand up, stand up for Jesus,
  The strife will not be long ;
This day the noise of battle,
  The next the victor's song :
To him that overcometh,
  A crown of life shall be ;
He with the King of Glory
  Shall reign eternally.

Rev. George Duffield, Jr. (1818-.)

1306 "Go and proclaim these words." 6. 4.
Mat. xxviii. 16-20. Mark xvi. 14-20. Ps. cxlv.

1 SOUND, sound the truth abroad,
  Bear ye the word of God,
    Bear ye His name ;
Bear it to every shore,
Regions unknown explore,
  Enter at every door ;
    Silence is shame.

2 Speed on the wings of love ;
Jesus, who reigns above,
    Bids us to fly ;
They who His message bear
Should neither doubt nor fear ;
  He will their Friend appear,
    He will be nigh.

3 Ye who, forsaking all
At your loved Master's call,
    Comforts resign,
Soon will your work be done,
Soon will the prize be won ;
  Brighter than yonder sun
    Then shall ye shine.

Rev. Thomas Kelly. (1769-1855.)

1308 "Lift up an ensign to the nations." L. M.
Isa. xiii. 2, 3. Ex. xvii. 8-15. Acts ii. 1-36.

1 FLING out the banner ! let it float
  Skyward and seaward, high and wide ;
The sun, that lights its shining folds,
  The cross, on which the Saviour died.

2 Fling out the banner ! angels bend
  In anxious silence o'er the sign,
And vainly seek to comprehend
  The wonder of the Love divine.

3 Fling out the banner ! heathen lands
  Shall see from far the glorious sight;
And nations, crowding to be born,
  Baptize their spirits in its light.

4 Fling out the banner ! sin-sick souls,
  That sink and perish in the strife,
Shall touch in faith its radiant hem,
  And spring immortal into life.

5 Fling out the banner ! let it float
  Skyward and seaward, high and wide :
Our glory only in the cross,
  Our only hope, the Crucified.

Bp. George W. Doane. (1799-1859.)

"Go ye therefore and teach all nations."

1309 "His word runneth very swiftly." **6, 4.**
Isa. lv. 8-13. Ps. xix. Mat. xxiv. 34, 35.

1 LORD of all power and might,
  Father of love and light,
  Speed on Thy word :
  O let the gospel sound
  All the wide world around,
  Wherever man is found :
    God speed His word !

2 Our thanks we give to Thee ;
  Thine let the glory be,
    Glory to God !
  Thine was the mighty plan,
  From Thee the work began,
  Away with praise of man,
    Glory to God !

3 Onward shall be our course,
  Despite of fraud and force :
    God bless His word !
  His word erelong shall run
  Free as the noonday sun ;
  His purpose must be done :
    God bless His word !

Rev. Hugh Stowell. (1799-1865.)

1310 "O arm of the Lord, awake." **L. M.**
Isa. li. 9-16. Ps. vii. 6-9. Rev. xi. 17-19.

1 ARM of the Lord, awake, awake ;
  Put on Thy strength, the nations shake ;
  And let the world, adoring, see
  Triumphs of mercy wrought by Thee.

2 No more let human blood be spilt,
  Vain sacrifice for human guilt ;
  But to each conscience be applied
  The blood that flowed from Jesus' side.

3 Almighty God, Thy grace proclaim
  In every clime, of every name,
  Till adverse powers before Thee fall,
  And crown the Saviour Lord of all.

William Shrubsole, Jr. (1750-1829.)

1311 "The Lord shall arise upon thee." **L. M.**
Isa. lx. Ps. xlv. Mat. iv. 12-25.

1 THOUGH now the nations sit beneath
  The darkness of o'erspreading death,
  God will arise with light divine,
  On Zion's holy towers to shine.

2 That light shall shine on distant lands,
  And wandering tribes, in joyful bands,
  Shall come Thy glory, Lord, to see,
  And in Thy courts to worship Thee.

3 O light of Zion, now arise,
  Let the glad morning bless our eyes ;
  Ye nations, catch the kindling ray,
  And hail the splendors of the day.

Rev. Leonard Bacon. (1802-.)

1312 "Hold not Thy peace, O God." **L. M.**
Ps. cii. 13-28. Zech. i. 12-17. Rev. vi.

1 SOVEREIGN of worlds, display Thy power ;
  Be this Thy Zion's favored hour ;
  O bid the morning star arise ;
  O point the heathen to the skies.

2 Set up Thy throne where Satan reigns,
  In western wilds and eastern plains ;
  Far let the gospel's sound be known ;
  Make Thou the universe Thine own.

3 Speak, and the world shall hear Thy voice ;
  Speak, and the desert shall rejoice ;
  Dispel the gloom of heathen night ;
  Bid every nation hail the light.

Mrs. Voke. 1806.

1313 "Be Thou exalted." **L. M.**
Ps. ii. Dan. vii. 9-14. Rev. xii. 10, 11.

1 ASCEND Thy throne, almighty King,
  And spread Thy glories all abroad ;
  Let Thine own arm salvation bring,
  And be Thou known the gracious God.

2 O let the kingdoms of the world
  Become the kingdoms of the Lord ;
  Let saints and angels praise Thy name,
  Be Thou through heaven and earth adored.

Rev. Benjamin Beddome. (1717-1795.)

1314 "Unto Thee shall all flesh come." **S. M.**
2 Chr. vi. 32-42. Hag. ii. 5-9. Luke xi. 1-13.

1 O GOD of sovereign grace,
    We bow before Thy throne ;
  And plead, for all the human race,
    The merits of Thy Son.

2 Spread through the earth, O Lord,
    The knowledge of Thy ways ;
  And let all lands with joy record
    The great Redeemer's praise.

Author unknown.

1315 "He shall judge . . . with righteousness." **C. M.**
Isa. xlv. 5-25. Col. i. Mat. x. 1-20.

1 GREAT God, the nations of the earth
    Are by creation Thine ;
  And in Thy works, by all beheld,
    Thy radiant glories shine.

2 But, Lord, Thy greater love has sent
    Thy gospel to mankind,
  Unveiling what rich stores of grace
    Are treasured in Thy mind.

3 Lord, when shall these glad tidings spread
    The spacious earth around,
  Till every tribe and every soul
    Shall hear the joyful sound ?

Rev. Thomas Gibbons. (1720-1785.)

"Go ye therefore and teach all nations."

1316 "Like rain upon the mown grass." 8. 7.
Isa. lii. John xii. 20-32. Gen. xlix. 1-12.

1 SAVIOUR, sprinkle many nations,
  Fruitful let Thy sorrows be;
  By Thy pains and consolations,
  Draw the Gentiles unto Thee:
  Of Thy cross the wondrous story,
  Be it to the nations told;
  Let them see Thee in Thy glory,
  And Thy mercy manifold.

2 Far and wide, though all unknowing,
  Pants for Thee each mortal breast;
  Human tears for Thee are flowing,
  Human hearts in Thee would rest,
  Thirsting, as for dews of even,
  As the new-mown grass for rain;
  Thee they seek, as God of heaven,
  Thee as man for sinners slain.

3 Saviour, lo, the isles are waiting,
  Stretched the hand, and strained the sight,
  For Thy Spirit, new creating
  Love's pure flame and wisdom's light;
  Give the word, and of the preacher
  Speed the foot, and touch the tongue,
  Till on earth by every creature
  Glory to the Lamb be sung.

  Bp. Arthur C. Coxe. (1818-.)

1317 "The true Light now shineth." C. M.
Ps. lxxxix. Isa. lx. Acts ii.

1 OUR God, our God, Thou shinest here,
  Thine own this latter day;
  To us Thy radiant steps appear:
  We watch Thy glorious way.

2 Thou tookest once our flesh; Thy face
  Once on our darkness shone;
  Yet through each age new births of grace
  Still make Thy glory known.

3 Not only olden ages felt
  The presence of the Lord;
  Not only with the fathers dwelt
  Thy Spirit and Thy word:

4 Doth not the Spirit still descend,
  And bring the heavenly fire?
  Doth not He still Thy church extend,
  And waiting souls inspire?

5 Come, Holy Ghost, in us arise;
  Be this Thy mighty hour;
  And make Thy willing people wise
  To know Thy day of power.

  Thomas H. Gill. (1819-.)

1318 "Not by might nor by power." 8. 7. 4.
Joel ii. 21-32. Ps. lxxxvii. John xvi. 7-16.

1 WHO but Thou, Almighty Spirit,
  Can the heathen world reclaim?
  Men may preach, but till Thou favor,
  Heathens still will be the same:
  Mighty Spirit,
  Witness to the Saviour's name.

2 Thou hast promised by the prophets
  Glorious light in latter days:
  Come, and bless bewildered nations;
  Change our prayers and tears to praise:
  Promised Spirit,
  Round the world diffuse Thy rays.

3 All our hopes and prayers and labors,
  Must be vain without Thy aid;
  But Thou wilt not disappoint us;
  All is true that Thou hast said:
  Gracious Spirit,
  O'er the world Thy influence shed.

  Author unknown.

1319 "I will pour out my Spirit upon all flesh." L. M.
Ps. lxvii. Zech. iv. Mat. vi. 9-13.

1 O SPIRIT of the living God,
  In all Thy plentitude of grace,
  Where'er the foot of man hath trod,
  Descend on our apostate race.

2 Be darkness, at Thy coming, light,
  Confusion, order in Thy path;
  Souls without strength inspire with might;
  Bid mercy triumph over wrath.

3 O Spirit of the Lord, prepare
  All the round earth her God to meet;
  Breathe Thou abroad like morning air,
  Till hearts of stone begin to beat.

4 Baptize the nations; far and nigh
  The triumphs of the cross record;
  The name of Jesus glorify,
  Till every kindred call Him Lord.

  James Montgomery. (1771-1854.)

1320 "By my Spirit, saith the Lord." C. M.
Gen. i. 1-5. Eze. xxxvii. Titus iii. 1-7.

1 SPIRIT of power and might, behold
  A world by sin destroyed;
  Creator, Spirit, as of old,
  Move on the formless void.

2 Give Thou the word: that healing sound
  Shall quell the deadly strife,
  And earth again, like Eden crowned,
  Produce the tree of life.

3 So every kindred, tongue, and tribe,
  Assembling round the throne,
  Thy new creation shall ascribe
  To sovereign love alone.

  James Montgomery.

"Behold, thy King cometh unto thee."

1321 "O Lord, make no tarrying." S. M.
Ps. xciv. Isa. iv. Rev. xxii. 17-21.

1 COME, Lord, and tarry not;
  Bring the long-looked-for day;
  O why these years of waiting here,
  These ages of delay?

2 Come, for Thy saints still wait;
  Daily ascends their sigh;
  The Spirit and the Bride say, Come!
  Dost Thou not hear the cry?

3 Come, and make all things new,
  Build up this ruined earth,
  Restore our faded paradise,
  Creation's second birth.

4 Come and begin Thy reign
  Of everlasting peace;
  Come, take the kingdom to Thyself,
  Great King of righteousness.
  Rev. Horatius Bonar. (1806-.)

1322 "Our soul waiteth for the Lord." L. M.
Ps. xc. Lam. v. 1 Thes. v. 1-10.

1 JESUS, Thy church, with longing eyes,
  For Thine expected coming waits;
  When will the promised light arise,
  And glory beam from Zion's gates?

2 E'en now, when tempests round us fall,
  And wintry clouds o'ercast the sky,
  Thy words with pleasure we recall,
  And deem that our redemption's nigh.

3 O come and reign o'er every land;
  Let Satan from his throne be hurled,
  All nations bow to Thy command,
  And grace revive a dying world.
  Rev. William H. Bathurst. (1796-.)

1323 "Ye shall have a song . . . and gladness." 7. 6.
Isa. lii. Ps. xcviii. Acts xiii. 44-52.

1 WHEN shall the voice of singing
  Flow joyfully along,
  When hill and valley, ringing
  With one triumphant song,
  Proclaim the contest ended,
  And Him, who once was slain,
  Again to earth descended,
  In righteousness to reign?

2 Then from the craggy mountains
  The sacred shout shall fly;
  And shady vales and fountains
  Shall echo the reply;
  High tower and lowly dwelling
  Shall send the chorus round,
  All hallelujah swelling
  In one eternal sound.
  James Edmeston. (1791-1867.)

1324 "Light to them that sit in darkness." C. M.
Num. xxiv. 15-19. Ps. cx. Rom. viii. 19-25.

1 LIGHT of the lonely pilgrim's heart,
  Star of the coming day,
  Arise, and with Thy morning beams,
  Chase all our griefs away.

2 Come, blessed Lord, bid every shore
  And answering island sing
  The praises of Thy royal name,
  And own Thee as their King.

3 Bid the whole earth, responsive now
  To the bright world above,
  Break forth in rapturous strains of joy
  In memory of Thy love.

4 Lord, Lord, Thy fair creation groans,
  The air, the earth, the sea,
  In unison with all our hearts,
  And calls aloud for Thee.
  Sir Edward Denny. (1796-.)

1325 "Peace to the people." 7.
Ps. xlv. Isa. lx. Rom. xv. 8-13.

1 HASTEN, Lord, the glorious time,
  When, beneath Messiah's sway,
  Every nation, every clime,
  Shall the gospel call obey.
  Mightiest kings His power shall own,
  Heathen tribes His name adore;
  Satan and his host o'erthrown,
  Bound in chains, shall hurt no more.

2 Then shall wars and tumults cease,
  Then be banished grief and pain;
  Righteousness, and joy, and peace,
  Undisturbed shall ever reign.
  Time shall sun and moon obscure,
  Seas be dried, and rocks be riven,
  But His reign shall still endure,
  Endless as the days of heaven.
  Miss Harriet Auber. (1773-1862.)

1326 "His glory above the earth and heaven." L. M.
Rev. xi. 15-19. Dan. vii. 9-18. Ps. ii.

1 SOON may the last glad song arise
  Through all the millions of the skies,
  That song of triumph, which records
  That all the earth is now the Lord's.

2 Let thrones, and powers, and kingdoms be
  Obedient, mighty God, to Thee;
  And over land, and stream, and main,
  Wave Thou the sceptre of Thy reign.

3 O that the anthem now might swell,
  And host to host the triumph tell,
  That not one rebel heart remains,
  But over all the Saviour reigns.
  Mrs. Voke. 1806.

"Behold, thy King cometh unto thee."

1327 Isa. lii. Micah iv. 1-8. Mat. xxiv. 1-13. "One that bringeth good tidings." 8, 7, 4.

1 ON the mountain's top appearing,
  Lo, the sacred herald stands,
Welcome news to Zion bearing,
  Zion long in hostile lands;
    Mourning captive,
God Himself will loose thy bands.

2 Has thy night been long and mournful?
  Have thy friends unfaithful proved?
Have thy foes been proud and scornful,
  By thy sighs and tears unmoved?
    Cease thy mourning;
Zion still is well-beloved.

3 God, thy God, will now restore thee;
  He Himself appears thy Friend;
All thy foes shall flee before thee;
  Here their boasts and triumphs end;
    Great deliverance
Zion's King vouchsafes to send.

4 Enemies no more shall trouble:
  All thy wrongs shall be redressed;
For thy shame thou shalt have double,
  In thy Maker's favor blessed;
    All thy conflicts
End in everlasting rest.

Rev. Thomas Kelly. (1769-1855.)

1328 Isa. xlii. 1-16. Eze. xxxvi. 1-11. Luke xxi. "A light to lighten the Gentiles." L. M.

1 ETERNAL Father, Thou hast said,
That Christ all glory shall obtain;
That He who once a sufferer bled
Shall o'er the world a conqueror reign.

2 We wait Thy triumph, Saviour-King;
Long ages have prepared Thy way;
Now all abroad Thy banner fling,
Set time's great battle in array.

3 Thy hosts are mustered to the field;
"The cross! the cross!" the battle-call;
The old grim towers of darkness yield,
And soon shall totter to their fall.

4 On mountain tops the watch-fires glow,
  Where scattered wide the watchmen stand;
Voice echoes voice, and onward flow
The joyous shouts from land to land.

5 O fill Thy church with faith and power,
Bid her long night of weeping cease;
To groaning nations haste the hour
Of life and freedom, light and peace.

6 Come, Spirit, make Thy wonders known,
Fulfil the Father's high decree;
Then earth, the might of hell o'erthrown,
Shall keep her last great jubilee.

Rev. Ray Palmer. (1808-.)

1329 Isa. xxi. 11. 1 Kings xviii. 44. Heb. xii. 22. "Thy watchmen shall lift up the voice." 8, 7,

1 WATCHMAN, tell me, does the morning
  Of fair Zion's glory dawn?
Have the signs that mark its coming
  Yet upon my pathway shone?
Pilgrim, yes; arise, look round thee!
  Light is breaking in the skies;
Gird thy bridal robes around thee,
  Morning dawns, arise, arise!

2 Watchman, see, the light is beaming
  Brighter still upon the way;
Signs through all the earth are gleaming,
  Omens of the coming day.
Pilgrim, yes; the trumpet, sounding,
  Shall awake from earth and sea
All the saints of God now sleeping,
  Clad in immortality.

3 Watchman, hail the light ascending,
  Of the grand Sabbatic year;
All with voices loud proclaiming
  That the kingdom's very near.
Pilgrim, yes; I see just yonder
  Canaan's glorious heights arise;
Salem, too, appears in grandeur,
  Towering 'neath its sunlit skies.

Author unknown.

1330 Isa. lx. Mat. viii. 5-13. Acts x. 19-48. "The morning cometh." 7, 6,

1 THE morning light is breaking;
  The darkness disappears;
The sons of earth are waking
  To penitential tears;
Each breeze that sweeps the ocean
  Brings tidings from afar,
Of nations in commotion,
  Prepared for Zion's war.

2 See heathen nations bending
  Before the God we love,
And thousand hearts ascending,
  In gratitude above;
While sinners, now confessing,
  The gospel call obey,
And seek the Saviour's blessing,
  A nation in a day.

3 Blest river of salvation,
  Pursue thine onward way;
Flow thou to every nation,
  Nor in thy richness stay;
Stay not till all the lowly
  Triumphant reach their home;
Stay not till all the holy
  Proclaim, "The Lord is come."

Rev. Samuel F. Smith. (1808-.)

"Behold, thy King cometh unto thee."

1331 "The bridegroom cometh." 7, 6.
Ps. xlvii. Jer. xxxi. 1–14. Col. iv. 4–9.

1 REJOICE, rejoice, believers,
  And let your lights appear ;
The evening is advancing,
  And darker night is near.
The Bridegroom is arising,
  And soon He will draw nigh ;
Up, pray, and watch, and wrestle,
  At midnight comes the cry.

2 See that your lamps are burning,
  Replenish them with oil ;
Look now for your salvation,
  The end of sin and toil.
The watchers on the mountain
  Proclaim the Bridegroom near ;
Go meet Him as He cometh,
  With hallelujahs clear.

3 Our Hope and Expectation,
  O Jesus, now appear ;
Arise, Thou Sun so longed for,
  O'er this benighted sphere.
With hearts and hands uplifted,
  We plead, O Lord, to see
The day of earth's redemption,
  And ever be with Thee.

Laurentius Laurenti. (1660–1722.)
Tr. by Miss Jane Borthwick. (1825–.)

1332 "King over all the earth." L. M.
Ps. ii. Mal. i. 1–11. Heb. i. 8–14.

1 JESUS shall reign where'er the sun
Does his successive journeys run ;
His kingdom stretch from shore to shore,
Till moons shall wax and wane no more.

2 To Him shall endless prayer be made,
And princes throng to crown His head ;
His name, like sweet perfume, shall rise
With every morning sacrifice.

3 People and realms of every tongue
Dwell on His love with sweetest song ;
And infant voices shall proclaim
Their early blessings on His name.

4 Blessings abound where'er He reigns ;
The prisoner leaps to loose his chains ;
The weary find eternal rest,
And all the sons of want are blest.

5 Let every creature rise and bring
Peculiar honors to our King ;
Angels descend with songs again,
And earth repeat the loud Amen.

Rev. Isaac Watts. (1674–1748.)

1333 "The Desire of all nations shall come." 8, 7.
Gen. iii. 13–15. Isa. ix. 1–7. Luke i. 26–55.

1 COME, Thou long-expected Jesus,
  Born to set Thy people free ;
From our fears and sins release us,
  Let us find our rest in Thee.
Israel's Strength and Consolation,
  Hope of all the earth Thou art ;
Dear Desire of every nation,
  Joy of every longing heart.

2 Born Thy people to deliver,
  Born a Child, and yet a King,
Born to reign in us forever,
  Now Thy gracious kingdom bring.
By Thine own eternal Spirit,
  Rule in all our hearts alone ;
By Thine all-sufficient merit,
  Raise us to Thy glorious throne.

Rev. Charles Wesley. (1708–1788.)

1334 "The coming of the Lord draweth nigh." 8, 7.
Num. xxiv. 12–25. Ps. lxxii. Mat. xxiv.

1 THOU art coming, O my Saviour !
  Thou art coming, O my King !
Every tongue Thy name confessing,
  Well may we rejoice and sing ;
Thou art coming ! rays of glory,
  Through the veil Thy death has rent,
Gladden now our pilgrim pathway,
  Glory from Thy presence sent.

Thou art coming, Thou art coming,
  We shall meet Thee on Thy way,
Thou art coming, we shall see Thee,
  And be like Thee on that day.
Thou art coming, Thou art coming,
  Jesus our belovéd Lord,
O the joy to see Thee reigning,
  Worshipped, glorified, adored.

2 Thou art coming, not a shadow,
  Not a mist, and not a tear,
Not a sin, and not a sorrow,
  On that sunrise grand and clear ;
Thou art coming, Jesus, Saviour,
  Nothing else seems worth a thought ;
O how marvellous the glory
  And the bliss Thy pain hath bought.

3 Thou art coming, we are waiting
  With a hope that cannot fail,
Asking not the day or hour,
  Anchored safe within the vail ;
Thou art coming ! at Thy table
  We are witnesses for this,
As we meet Thee in communion,
  Earnest of our coming bliss.

Arr. fr. Miss Frances R. Havergal. (1836–1879.)

"Behold, thy King cometh unto thee."

1335 Isa. lix. "Behold the day." Ps. xcviii. Acts xi. 1–18. 8, 7, 4.

1 YES, we trust the day is breaking ;
  Joyful times are near at hand ;
God, the mighty God, is speaking
  By His word in every land ;
    Mark His progress !
  Darkness flies, at His command.

2 While the foe becomes more daring,
  While he enters like a flood,
God, the Saviour, is preparing
  Means to spread His truth abroad :
    Every language
  Soon shall tell the love of God.

3 God of Jacob, high and glorious,
  Let Thy people see Thy hand ;
Let the gospel be victorious,
  Through the world, in every land ;
    Let the idols
  Perish, Lord, at Thy command.
        Rev. Thomas Kelly. (1769-1855.)

1336 "Sing unto God, ye kingdoms." Ps. xcvi. Isa. xlix. Mat. iii. 1–12. C. M.

1 SING to the Lord, ye distant lands,
  Ye tribes of every tongue :
His new discovered grace demands
  A new and nobler song.

2 Let heaven proclaim the joyful day,
  Joy through the earth be seen ;
Let cities shine in bright array,
  And fields in cheerful green.

3 Let an unusual joy surprise
  The islands of the sea ;
Ye mountains, sink ; ye valleys, rise ;
  Prepare the Lord His way.

4 Behold He comes, He comes to bless
  The nations as their God ;
To show the world His righteousness,
  And send His truth abroad.
        Rev. Isaac Watts. (1674-1748.)

1337 Isa. xlii. 1–16. "Let the multitude of isles be glad." Eze. xxxvi. 25-38. 1 Thes. i. 7.

1 HARK, the distant isles proclaim
  Glory to Messiah's name ;
Hymns of praise unheard before
  Echo from the farthest shore.

2 Hearts that once were taught to own
  Idol gods of wood and stone,
Now to light and life restored,
  Honor Jesus as their Lord.
        Rev. William H. Bathurst. (1796-.)

1338 Isa. xxi. "Watchman, what of the night?" 11, 12. Zeph. iii. 14-20. Mat. ii. 1–10. 7.

1 WATCHMAN, tell us of the night,
    What its signs of promise are.
  Traveller, o'er yon mountain's height,
    See that glory-beaming star !
  Watchman, does its beauteous ray
    Aught of joy or hope foretell ?
  Traveller, yes ; it brings the day,
    Promised day of Israel !

2 Watchman, tell us of the night ;
    Higher yet that star ascends.
  Traveller, blessedness and light,
    Peace and truth, its course portends.
  Watchman, will its beams alone
    Gild the spot that gave them birth ?
  Traveller, ages are its own ;
    See, it bursts o'er all the earth !

3 Watchman, tell us of the night,
    For the morning seems to dawn.
  Traveller, darkness takes its flight,
    Doubt and terror are withdrawn.
  Watchman, let thy wanderings cease ;
    Hie thee to thy quiet home !
  Traveller, lo, the Prince of Peace,
    Lo, the Son of God, is come!
        Sir John Bowring. (1792-1872.)

1339 "He cometh in the glory of His Father." Ex. xix. Mat. xxvii. 35. 1 Thes. iv. 16. 8, 7, P.

1 THE Lord of might from Sinai's brow
    Gave forth His voice of thunder ;
  And Israel lay on earth below,
    Outstretched in fear and wonder :
  Beneath His feet was pitchy night,
    And at His left hand and His right
  The rocks were rent asunder.

2 The Lord of love, on Calvary,
    A meek and suffering stranger,
  Upraised to heaven His languid eye
    In nature's hour of danger :
  For us He bore the weight of woe,
    For us He gave His blood to flow,
  And met His Father's anger.

3 The Lord of love, the Lord of might,
    The King of all created,
  Shall back return to claim His right,
    On clouds of glory seated ;
  With trumpet-sound, and angel-song,
    And hallelujahs loud and long,
  O'er death and hell defeated.
        Bp. Reginald Heber. (1783-1826.)

"Behold, thy King cometh unto thee."

1340 "Blessed is He that cometh." 7, 6,
Ps. lxxii. Jer. xxiii. 5-8. Luke iv. 16-32.

1 HAIL to the Lord's Anointed,
Great David's greater Son ;
Hail, in the time appointed,
His reign on earth begun.
He comes to break oppression,
To set the captive free ;
To take away transgression,
And rule in equity.

2 He comes with succor speedy
To those who suffer wrong ;
To help the poor and needy,
And bid the weak be strong ;
To give them songs for sighing,
Their darkness turn to light,
Whose souls, condemned and dying,
Were precious in His sight.

3 He shall come down like showers
Upon the fruitful earth ;
And love, joy, hope, like flowers,
Spring in His path to birth ;
Before Him on the mountains
Shall peace, the herald, go,
And righteousness, in fountains,
From hill to valley flow.

4 For Him shall prayer unceasing
And daily vows ascend ;
His kingdom still increasing,
A kingdom without end :
The tide of time shall never
His covenant remove ;
His name shall stand forever,
That name to us is Love.

James Montgomery. (1771-1854.)

1341 "Waters . . . from under the threshold." 8, 7, 4,
Eze. xlvii. Zech. xiv. 8. Rev. xxii. 1.

1 SEE, from Zion's sacred mountain
Streams of living water flow ;
God has opened there a fountain,
That supplies the world below ;
They are blessèd,
Who its sovereign virtues know.

2 Through ten thousand channels flowing,
Streams of mercy find their way,
Life, and health, and joy bestowing,
Making all around look gay :
O ye nations,
Hail the long-expected day.

3 Gladdened by the flowing treasure,
All enriching as it goes,
Lo, the desert smiles with pleasure,
Buds and blossoms as the rose ;
Every object
Sings for joy where'er it flows.

Rev. Thomas Kelly. (1769-1855.)

1342 "He which . . . giveth life unto the world." 6, 4,
2 Cor. v. 11-21. Micah iv. Isa. lxi.

1 CHRIST for the world we sing ;
The world to Christ we bring,
With loving zeal ;
The poor, and them that mourn,
The faint and overborne,
Sin-sick and sorrow-worn,
Whom Christ doth heal.

2 Christ for the world we sing ;
The world to Christ we bring,
With fervent prayer :
The wayward and the lost,
By restless passion tossed,
Redeemed, at countless cost,
From dark despair.

3 Christ for the world we sing ;
The world to Christ we bring,
With joyful song ;
The new-born souls, whose days,
Reclaimed from error's ways,
Inspired with hope and praise,
To Christ belong.

Rev. Samuel Wolcott. (1813-.)

1343 "All nations shall serve Him." 7, 6,
Luke xi. 1-13. Isa. xlii. 1-14. Dan. vii. 1-14.

1 THE whole wide world for Jesus !
Once more, before we part,
Ring out the joyful watchword
From every grateful heart.
The whole wide world for Jesus !
Be this our battle-cry,
The lifted cross our oriflamme,
A sign to conquer by !

2 The whole wide world for Jesus !
From out the Golden Gate,
Through all Pacific's sunny isles
To China's princely state ;
From India's vales and mountains,
Through Persia's land of bloom,
To storied Palestina
And Afric's desert gloom.

3 The whole wide world for Jesus,
Through all its fragrant zones !
Ring out again the watchword
In loftiest, gladdest tones.
The whole wide world for Jesus !
We 'll wing the song with prayer,
And link the prayer with labor,
Till Christ His crown shall wear.

Mrs. Katherine H. Johnson. (1835- .)

"Behold, thy King cometh unto thee."

1344   "Arise, shine."   L. M.
Isa. xi.   Jer. xxxiii.   Rev. xx. 1-6.

1 ARISE, arise! with joy survey
The glory of the latter day;
Already is the dawn begun
Which marks at hand a rising sun.

2 "Behold the way!" ye heralds, cry;
Spare not, but lift your voices high;
Convey the sound from pole to pole,
Glad tidings to the captive soul.

3 The north gives up, the south no more
Keeps back her consecrated store;
From east to west the message runs,
And either India yields her sons.

4 Auspicious dawn, thy rising ray
With joy we view, and hail the day;
Great Sun of Righteousness, arise,
And fill the world with glad suprise.

Rev. Thomas Kelly. (1769-1855.)

1345   "Awake, put on thy strength."   L. M.
Isa. xl.   Joel ii. 21-32.   2 Cor. iii. 7-18.

1 ZION, awake, thy strength renew,
Put on thy robes of beauteous hue;
And let th' admiring world behold
The King's fair daughter clothed in gold.

2 Church of our God, arise and shine,
Bright with the beams of truth divine;
Then shall thy radiance stream afar,
Wide as the heathen nations are.

3 Gentiles and kings thy light shall view;
And shall admire and love thee, too;
They come, like clouds across the sky,
As doves that to their windows fly.

William Shrubsole, Jr. (1759-1829.)

1346   "Your redemption draweth nigh."   L. M.
Isa. xlix.   Joel iii.   Rom. xi.

1 TRIUMPHANT Zion, lift thy head
From dust, and darkness, and the dead;
Though humbled long, awake at length,
And gird thee with thy Saviour's strength.

2 Put all thy beauteous garments on,
And let thy various charms be known;
The world thy glories shall confess,
Decked in the robes of righteousness.

3 No more shall foes unclean invade,
And fill thy hallowed walls with dread;
No more shall hell's insulting host
Their vict'ry and thy sorrows boast.

4 God, from on high, thy groans will hear;
His hand thy ruins shall repair;
Nor will thy watchful Monarch cease
To guard thee in eternal peace.

Rev. Philip Doddridge. (1702-1751.)

1347   "Good tidings."   7. 6.
Rom. x. 4-15.   Isa. lxii.   Ps. cii. 12-28.

1 How beauteous, on the mountains,
The feet of him that brings,
Like streams from living fountains,
Good tidings of good things;
That publisheth salvation,
And jubilee release,
To every tribe and nation,
God's reign of joy and peace!

2 Lift up thy voice, O watchman,
And shout, from Zion's towers,
Thy hallelujah chorus,
"The victory is ours!"
The Lord shall build up Zion
In glory and renown,
And Jesus, Judah's lion,
Shall wear His rightful crown.

3 Break forth in hymns of gladness;
O waste Jerusalem,
Let songs, instead of sadness,
Thy jubilee proclaim;
The Lord, in strength victorious,
Upon thy foes hath trod;
Behold, O earth, the glorious
Salvation of our God!

Benjamin Gough. (1805-.)

1348   "Thy Maker is thine husband."   7. 6.
Isa. li.   Eze. xliii.   Mat. xxv. 1-13.

1 AWAKE, awake, O Zion,
Put on thy strength divine;
Thy garments bright in beauty,
The bridal dress be thine;
Jerusalem the holy,
To purity restored,
Meek Bride, all fair and lowly,
Go forth to meet thy Lord.

2 The Lamb who bore our sorrows
Comes down to earth again;
No Sufferer now, but Victor,
For evermore to reign;
To reign in every nation,
To rule in every zone;
O wide-world coronation,
In every heart a throne.

3 Awake, awake, O Zion,
The bridal day draws nigh,
The day of signs and wonders
And marvels from on high;
Thy sun uprises slowly,
But keep thou watch and ward;
Fair Bride, all pure and lowly,
Go forth to meet thy Lord.

Benjamin Gough.

"Behold, thy King cometh unto thee."

1349 "The days of thy mourning shall be ended." **11. 10.**
Isa. lii. Jer. xxx. 10-24. Eze. xxxvi. Rev. xi. 15-19.

1 WAKE thee, O Zion, thy mourning is ended,
   God, thine own God, hath regarded thy prayer;
   Wake thee, and hail Him, in glory descended,
   Thy darkness to scatter, thy wastes to repair.

2 Wake thee, O Zion, His Spirit of power
   To newness of life is awaking the dead;
   Array thee in beauty, and greet the glad hour
   That brings thee salvation, through Jesus who bled.

3 Saviour, we gladly, with voices resounding,
   Loud as the thunder, our voices would swell;
   Till, from the mountains, its echoes rebounding,
   To all the wide world of salvation shall tell.

Rev. Ray Palmer. (1808-.)

1350 "Sing, O daughter of Zion . . . be glad and rejoice." **11. 10.**
Isa. li. Jer. xxxi. 1-14. Eze. xxviii 24-26. Rev. xii. 10, 11.

1 DAUGHTER of Zion, awake from thy sadness;
   Wake, for thy foes shall oppress thee no more;
   Bright o'er thy hills dawns the day-star of gladness;
   Rise, for the night of thy sorrow is o'er.

2 Strong were thy foes; but the arm that subdued them,
   Scattering their legions, was mightier far;
   They fled, like the chaff, from the scourge that pursued them;
   Vain were their steeds and their chariots of war.

3 Daughter of Zion, the power that has saved thee,
   Praised with the harp and the timbrel should be:
   Shout, for the foe is destroyed that enslaved thee,
   Satan is vanquished, and Zion is free.

Author unknown.

1351 "Glorify ye the Lord . . . in the isles of the sea." **11. 10.**
Ps. lxxii. Isa. xlix. Zeph. iii. 8-20. Mat. xvi. 29-35.

1 LANDS, long benighted, the morning is nearing;
   Lift, with the waves, the glad song of the free;
   He that was promised, in triumph appearing,
   Now wields His sway o'er the land and the sea.

2 Loud from the tops of the mountains sing praises;
   Valleys shall ring with the echoing strain;
   Mighty in war, He the standard upraises,
   Glorious in peace, He advances to reign.

Rev. Charles S. Robinson. 1865.

1352 "Glorious in His apparel, . . . in the greatness of His strength." **12. 11. 8.**
Ps. xxiv. Eze. xxxvii. 21-28. Isa. xii. Mat. xvi. 24-28.

1 THE Prince of Salvation in triumph is riding,
   And glory attends Him along His bright way;
   The tidings of grace on the breezes are gliding,
   And nations are owning His sway.

2 Ride on in Thy greatness, Thou conquering Saviour;
   Let thousands of thousands submit to Thy reign,
   Acknowledge Thy goodness, entreat for Thy favor,
   And follow Thy glorious train.

3 Then loud shall ascend, from each sanctified nation,
   The voice of thanksgiving, the chorus of praise;
   And heaven shall reëcho the song of salvation
   In rich and melodious lays.

Rev. Samuel F. Smith. (1808-.)

"Behold, thy King cometh unto thee."

1353 "As the voice of many waters." 7.
Rev. xi. 15-19. Dan. vii. 9-14. Ps. lxviii.

1 HARK, the song of jubilee,
  Loud as mighty thunders roar,
Or the fulness of the sea,
  When it breaks upon the shore :
Hallelujah ! for the Lord
  God Omnipotent shall reign ;
Hallelujah ! let the word
  Echo round the earth and main.

2 Hallelujah ! hark, the sound,
  From the centre to the skies,
Wakes above, beneath, around,
  All creation's harmonies.
See Jehovah's banners furled,
  Sheathed His sword : He speaks ; 't is done,
And the kingdoms of this world
  Are the kingdoms of His Son.

3 He shall reign from pole to pole
  With illimitable sway ;
He shall reign, when like a scroll
  Yonder heavens have passed away;
Then the end ; beneath His rod
  Man's last enemy shall fall :
Hallelujah ! Christ in God,
  God in Christ, is All in all.

James Montgomery. (1771-1854.)

1354 "With trumpets . . . make a joyful noise." H. M.
Lev. xxv. Isa. lii. Heb. ix. 11-28.

1 BLOW ye the trumpet, blow
  The gladly solemn sound ;
Let all the nations know,
  To earth's remotest bound,
The year of jubilee is come ;
Return, ye ransomed sinners, home.

2 Jesus, our great High Priest,
  Hath full atonement made ;
Ye weary spirits, rest,
  Ye mournful souls, be glad.

3 Extol the Lamb of God,
  The all-atoning Lamb ;
Redemption in His blood
  Throughout the world proclaim ;

4 Ye slaves of sin and hell,
  Your liberty receive,
And safe in Jesus dwell,
  And blest in Jesus live ;

5 The gospel trumpet hear,
  The news of heavenly grace ;
And, saved from earth, appear
  Before your Saviour's face.

Rev. Charles Wesley. (1708-1788.)

1355 "Lift up your heads." 8. 7. 4.
Luke xxi. 7-28. Jude 14-25. Hag. xi. 1-9.

1 LIFT your heads, ye friends of Jesus,
  Partners in His patience here :
Christ, to all believers précious,
  Lord of lords, shall soon appear :
    Mark the tokens
  Of His heavenly kingdom near.

2 Lo, 't is He, our hearts' desire,
  Come for His espoused below ;
Come to join us with His choir,
  Come to make our joys o'erflow :
    Palms of victory,
  Crowns of glory, to bestow.

Rev. Charles Wesley.

1356 "It shall be a jubilee unto you." H. M.
Ps. lxxxi. Isa. li. Titus iii. 3-7.

1 FAIR shines the morning star ;
  The silver trumpets sound,
Their notes reëchoing far,
  While dawns the day around ;
Joy to the slave ; the slave is free :
It is the year of jubilee.

2 Ye, who yourselves have sold
  For debts to justice due,
Ransomed, but not with gold,
  He gave Himself for you ;
The blood of Christ hath made you free :
It is the year of jubilee.

3 Captives of sin and shame,
  O'er earth and ocean, hear
An angel's voice proclaim
  The Lord's accepted year ;
Let Jacob rise, be Israel free :
It is the year of jubilee.

James Montgomery.

1357 "The voice of harpers." 8. 7.
Rev. vii. Heb. i. Ps. xlv.

1 HARK, ten thousand harps and voices
  Sound the note of praise above !
Jesus reigns, and heaven rejoices ;
  Jesus reigns, the God of love ;
See He sits on yonder throne ;
Jesus rules the world alone.

2 King of Glory, reign forever !
  Thine an everlasting crown ;
Nothing from Thy love shall sever
  Those whom Thou hast made Thine own ;
Happy objects of Thy grace,
Destined to behold Thy face.

Rev. Thomas Kelly. (1769-1855.)

"Behold, thy King cometh unto thee."

1358 "The dead in Christ shall rise first." C. M.
1 Thes. iv. 13-18. 1 Cor. xv. 52. 2 Kings ii.

1 Lo, I behold the scattering shades,
  The dawn of heaven appears;
  The sweet immortal morning spreads
  Its blushes round the spheres.

2 I see the Lord of Glory come,
  And flaming guards around;
  The skies divide to make Him room,
  The trumpet shakes the ground.

3 I hear the voice, "Ye dead, arise,"
  And lo, the graves obey;
  And waking saints, with joyful eyes,
  Salute the expected day.

4 They leave the dust, and on the wing
  Rise to the middle air,
  In shining garments meet their King,
  And low adore Him there.
  Rev. Isaac Watts. (1074-1748.)

1359 "Laud Him, all ye people." C. M.
Ps. xcviii. Isa. lv. Mat. xxi. 1-16.

1 Joy to the world, the Lord is come!
  Let earth receive her King;
  Let every heart prepare Him room,
  And heaven and nature sing.

2 Joy to the earth, the Saviour reigns!
  Let men their songs employ;
  While fields and floods, rocks, hills, and plains,
  Repeat the sounding joy.

3 No more let sin, and sorrows grow,
  Nor thorns infest the ground:
  He comes to make His blessings flow
  Far as the curse is found.

4 He rules the world with truth and grace,
  And makes the nations prove
  The glories of His righteousness,
  And wonders of His love.
  Rev. Isaac Watts.

1360 "All kings shall fall down before Him." 7.
Rev. xix. 1-16. Ps. lxxii. Isa. xlii. 1-16.

1 WAKE the song of jubilee;
  Let it echo o'er the sea:
  Now is come the promised hour;
  Jesus reigns with glorious power.

2 All ye nations, join and sing,
  Praise your Saviour, praise your King;
  Let it sound from shore to shore,
  "Jesus reigns for evermore!"

3 Hark, the desert lands rejoice,
  And the islands join their voice:
  Joy! the whole creation sings,
  "Jesus is the King of kings!"
  Rev. Leonard Bacon. (1802-.)

1361 "The tabernacle of God with men." C. M.
Rev. xxi. Mat. xxiv. 29-31. Eze. xliii.

1 Lo, what a glorious sight appears
  To our believing eyes:
  The earth and seas are passed away,
  And the old rolling skies.

2 From the third heaven where God resides,
  That holy, happy place,
  The New Jerusalem comes down,
  Adorned with shining grace.

3 Attending angels shout for joy,
  And the bright armies sing,
  "Mortals, behold the sacred seat
  Of your descending King.

4 "The God of glory down to men
  Removes His blest abode;
  Men, the dear objects of his grace,
  And He the loving God.

5 "His own soft hand shall wipe the tears
  From every weeping eye;
  And pains, and groans, and griefs, and fears,
  And death itself shall die."
  Rev. Isaac Watts.

1362 "The day of the Lord cometh." 8. 7.
Luke xxi. Isa. xxv. 6-9. Rom. xiii. 11-14.

1 "LIFT your heads" with faith: the morrow
  Dawneth brighter than to-day;
  Angel hands will lift the shadows,
  Chase the gathering gloom away.

  "Lift your heads," the day is breaking,
  Soon the morning will appear:
  See the earth from slumber waking;
  "Lift your heads," the day is near.

2 Art thou lonely, sad, and weary,
  Watching through the silent night?
  Dry thy tears, the orient glistens
  Like a thread of silver light.

3 Does the night seem long and weary,
  Dangers threatening 'long the way?
  Joy will soon return to bless thee,
  Soon will dawn a brighter day.

4 Let the heart be cheered with gladness,
  Though the sun is veiled from sight;
  See, the stars are brightly beaming
  Through the shadows of the night.

  Look, e'en now the morn is breaking,
  See, the shadows flee away:
  See, the earth from slumber waking,
  "Lift your heads!" behold the day.
  Author unknown.

"We fasted and besought our God."

1363 "Led up of the Spirit into the wilderness." **L. M.**
Mat. iv. 1-11. Ps. xc. Ezra viii. 15-23.

1 AWHILE in spirit, Lord, to Thee
Into the desert would we flee ;
Awhile upon the barren steep
Thy fast with Thee in spirit keep.

2 Awhile from Thy temptation learn
The daily snares of sin to spurn,
And in our hearts to feel and own
Man liveth not by bread alone.

3 Incarnate Lord, we come to Thee,
Thou knowest our infirmity ;
Be Thou our Helper in the strife,
Be Thou our true, our inward Life.
Rev. Joseph F. Thrupp. 1860.

1364 "Purge away our sins." **7.**
Ps. lxxiv. 1 Kings xviii. 17-46. Heb. viii.

1 CHRIST, by heavenly hosts adored,
Gracious, mighty, sovereign Lord,
God of nations, King of kings,
Head of all created things,
By the church with joy confest,
God o'er all forever blest ;
Pleading at Thy throne we stand,
Save Thy people, bless our land.

2 On our fields of grass and grain
Drop, O Lord, the kindly rain ;
O'er our wide and goodly land
Crown the labors of each hand ;
Let Thy kind protection be
O'er our commerce on the sea ;
Open, Lord, Thy bounteous hand,
Bless Thy people, bless our land.

3 Let our rulers ever be
Men that love and honor Thee ;
Let the powers by Thee ordained
Be in righteousness maintained ;
In the people's hearts increase
Love of piety and peace ;
Thus, united we shall stand
One wide, free, and happy land.
Rev. Henry Harbaugh. (1818-1867.)

1365 "Prayer and supplications with fasting." **C. M.**
Ps. lx. 2 Chr. xxxiv. 14-33. Heb. xii. 6-17.

1 ONCE more the solemn season calls,
A holy fast to keep ;
And now, within the temple walls,
Let priest and people weep.

2 O Father, righteous Judge, and God,
Thy wrath be slow to burn !
Thou givest time to mark the rod,
Give also hearts to turn.
(Lat.) *Prof. Charles Coffin. (1676-1749.)*
Tr. by Rev. William Mercer. 1864.

1366 "Turn us, O God of our salvation." **C. M.**
Ps. x. Neh. ix. James iv. 1-10.

1 SEE, gracious God, before Thy throne,
Thy mourning people bend !
'Tis on Thy sovereign grace alone,
Our humble hopes depend.

2 How changed, alas, are truths divine,
For error, guilt, and shame!
What impious numbers, bold in sin,
Disgrace the Christian name !

3 O turn us, turn us, mighty Lord,
By Thy resistless grace ;
Then shall our hearts obey Thy word,
And humbly seek Thy face.
Miss Anne Steele. (1717-1778.)

1367 "Will the Lord cast off forever?" **L. M.**
Ps. xliv. 2 Chr. xx. 3-13. Jude 1-25.

1 IN prayer together let us fall,
And cry for mercy, one and all,
And weep before the Judge, and say,
O turn from us Thy wrath away.

2 Thy grace have we offended sore
By sins, O God, which we deplore ;
Pour down upon us from above
The riches of Thy pard'ning love.

3 Forgive the sin that we have wrought,
Increase the good that we have sought ;
That we at length, our wanderings o'er,
May please Thee here and evermore.

4 Blest Three in One and One in Three,
Almighty God, we pray to Thee,
That Thou wouldst now vouchsafe to bless
Our fast with fruits of righteousness.
Rev. John M. Neale. (1818-1866.)
Alt. by Rev. Sir Henry W. Baker. (1821-1877.)

1368 "Is not this the fast that I have chosen?" **S. M.**
Isa. lviii. Zech. vii. Mat. vi. 16-18.

1 " Is this a fast for me ?"
Thus saith the Lord our God ;
A day for man to vex his soul
And feel affliction's rod ?

2 " No ; is not this alone
The sacred fast I choose :
Oppression's yoke to burst in twain,
The bands of guilt unloose ?

3 " To nakedness and want
Your food and raiment deal,
To dwell your kindred race among,
And all their sufferings heal ?

4 " Then, like the morning ray,
Shall spring your health and light ;
Before you, righteousness shall shine ;
Behind, my glory bright."
Rev. William H. Drummond. (1772-1854.)

"We fasted and besought our God."

1369 "Remember not against us former iniquities." **7.**
Num. xxi. 1-18. Isa. lxiv. Rom. vii. 14-25.

1 GOD of mercy, God of love,
   Hear our sad repentant song ;
Sorrow dwells on every face,
   Penitence on every tongue.

2 Deep regret for follies past,
   Talents wasted, time misspent,
Hearts debased by worldly cares,
   Thankless for the blessings lent ;

3 These, and every secret fault,
   Filled with grief and shame, we own ;
Humbled at Thy feet we lie,
   Seeking pardon from Thy throne.
Rev. John Taylor. (1694-1761.)

1372 "Let Thy tender mercies speedily prevent us." **L. M.**
Judg. x. 6-16. Ps. lxxx. Heb. x. 1-14.

1 WHILE o'er our guilty land, O Lord,
We view the terrors of Thy sword,
O whither shall the helpless fly ?
To whom but Thee direct their cry ?

2 We plead Thy grace, indulgent God,
We plead Thy Son's atoning blood,
We plead Thy gracious promises ;
And are they unavailing pleas ?

3 These pleas, presented at Thy throne,
Have brought ten thousand blessings down
On guilty lands in helpless woe ;
Let them prevail and help us too.
Rev. Samuel Davies. (1724-1761.)

1370 " O God, Thou art terrible out of Thy holy places." **11. 10. 9.**
Neh. i. Job xxii. Isa. xxxix. Acts xvii. 24-31.

1 GOD, the All-Terrible, Thou who ordainest
   Thunder Thy clarion and lightning Thy sword,
Show forth Thy pity on high where Thou reignest ;
   Give to us peace in our time, O Lord.

2 God, the Omnipotent, Mighty Avenger,
   Watching invisible, judging unheard ;
Save us in mercy, O save us from danger ;
   Give to us peace in our time, O Lord.

3 God, the All-Merciful, earth hath forsaken
   Thy ways all holy, and slighted Thy word ;
Let not Thy wrath in its terror awaken ;
   Give to us pardon and peace, O Lord.

4 So will Thy people, with thankful devotion,
   Praise Him who saved them from peril and sword,
Shouting in chorus from ocean to ocean,
   Peace to the nations, and praise to the Lord.
Henry F. Chorley. (1808-1872.)

1371 " Give us help from trouble." **8. 7.**
1 Sam. vii. Ps. lxxix. Heb. viii. 10-12.

1 DREAD Jehovah, God of nations,
   From Thy temple in the skies,
Hear Thy people's supplications ;
   Now for their deliverance rise.

2 Though our sins, our hearts confounding,
   Long and loud for vengeance call,
Thou hast mercy more abounding :
   Jesus' blood can cleanse them all.

3 Let that love vail our transgression ;
   Let that blood our guilt efface :
Save Thy people from oppression ;
   Save from spoil Thy holy place.

4 Lo ! with deep contrition turning,
   Humbly at Thy feet we bend ;
Hear us, fasting, praying, mourning,
   Hear us, spare us, and defend !
Author unknown.

1373 "Return, O Lord." **7.**
Ps. cvi. 6-48. Amos vii. 1-6. Rom. xi. 1-5.

1 WHY, O Lord, Thy people spurn ?
   Why permit Thy wrath to burn ?
God of mercy, turn once more,
   All our broken hearts restore.

2 Thou hast made our land to quake,
   Heal the sorrows Thou dost make ;
Bitter is the cup we drink,
   Suffer not our souls to sink.

3 Be Thy banner now unfurled,
   Show Thy truth to all the world ;
Save us, Lord ! we cry to Thee,
   Lift Thine arm, Thy chosen free.

4 Give us now relief from pain ;
   Human aid is all in vain ;
We through God shall yet prevail,
   He will help when foes assail.
Rev. Edwin F. Hatfield. (1877--.)

"Thou crownest the year with Thy goodness."

1374 "Go up from year to year to worship." **C. M.**
Ex. xxxiv. 22-26. Ps. viii. Acts xiv. 13-17.

1 GOD of our life, thy various praise
  Let mortal voices sound :
Thy hand revolves our fleeting days,
  And brings the seasons round.

2 To Thee shall annual incense rise,
  Our Father and our Friend !
While annual mercies, from the skies,
  In genial streams descend.

3 In every scene of life, Thy care,
  In every age, we see :
And, constant as Thy favors are,
  So let our praises be.

4 Still may Thy love, in every scene,
  In every age, appear ;
And let the same compassion deign
  To bless the opening year.

  Rev. Ottiwell Heginbotham. (1744-1768.)

1375 "We spend our years as a tale that is told." **C. M.**
Ps. c. Isa. xlii. 10-16. Rom. xiii. 11-14.

1 AWAKE, ye saints, and raise your eyes,
  And raise your voices high :
Awake, and praise that sovereign love
  That shows salvation nigh.

2 On all the wings of time it flies,
  Each moment brings it near ;
Then welcome each declining day,
  Welcome each closing year !

3 Not many years their rounds shall run,
  Nor many mornings rise,
Ere all its glories stand revealed
  To our admiring eyes.

4 Ye wheels of nature, speed your course ;
  Ye mortal powers, decay ;
Fast as ye bring the night of death,
  Ye bring eternal day.

  Rev. Philip Doddridge. (1702-1751.)

1376 "So teach us to number our days." **L. M.**
Ps. ciii. Micah iv. 4, 5. 1 Pet. i. 3-25.

1 ANOTHER year, another year,
  Hath sped its flight on silent wing ;
And all that marked its brief career
  Hath passed from mortal reckoning.

2 Lord, for Thy grace and patient love,
  Unwearied still, and still the same,
For all our hopes of joy above,
  We laud and bless Thy holy name.

3 Still bear with us, and bless us still ;
  And, while in this dark world we stay,
O let us love Thy sacred will,
  O let us keep Thy narrow way.

  Rev. Richard F. Littledale. (1833-.)

1377 "Year by year continually." **7.**
Gen. i. 14-18. Ps. lxv. 1 Thes. v. 14-23.

1 THOU who roll'st the year around,
  Crowned with mercies large and free,
Rich Thy gifts to us abound,
  Warm our thanks shall rise to Thee :
Kindly to our worship bow,
  While our grateful praises swell,
That, sustained by Thee, we now
  Bid the parting year farewell.

2 All its numbered days are sped,
  All its busy scenes are o'er,
All its joys forever fled,
  All its sorrows felt no more :
Mingled with th' eternal past,
  Its remembrance shall decay ;
Yet to be revived at last
  At the solemn judgment-day.

3 All our follies, Lord, forgive ;
  Cleanse each heart and make us Thine ;
Let Thy grace within us live,
  As our future suns decline ;
Then, when life's last eve shall come,
  Happy spirits, let us fly
To our everlasting home,
  To our Father's house on high.

  Rev. Ray Palmer. (1808-.)

1378 "Our heart shall rejoice in Him." **7.**
Ex. xxiii. 15-19. Ps. xc. Eph. v. 14-21.

1 FOR Thy mercy and Thy grace,
  Faithful through another year,
Hear our songs of thankfulness,
  Father and Redeemer, hear.

2 In our weakness and distress,
  Rock of strength, be Thou our Stay ;
In the pathless wilderness
  Be our true and living Way.

3 Who of us death's awful road
  In the coming year shall tread ?
With Thy rod and staff, O God,
  Comfort Thou his dying bed.

4 Keep us faithful, keep us pure,
  Keep us evermore Thine own ;
Help Thy servants to endure,
  Fit us for the promised crown.

5 So within Thy palace gate
  We shall praise, on golden strings,
Thee, the only Potentate,
  Lord of lords, and King of kings.

  Rev. Henry Downton. (1818-.)

"Offer unto the Lord the yearly sacrifice."

1379 "Let Thy mercy, O Lord, be upon us." C. M.
James iv. 13-17. Ps. xxxvii. 1-11. Job vii.

1 OUR Father, through the coming year
  We know not what shall be ;
  But we would leave without a fear
  Its ordering all to Thee.

2 It may be we shall toil in vain
  For what the world holds fair ;
  And all the good we thought to gain
  Deceive and prove but care.

3 It may be it shall darkly blend
  Our love with anxious fears,
  And snatch away the valued friend,
  The tried of many years.

4 It may be it shall bring us days
  And nights of lingering pain ;
  And bid us take a farewell gaze
  Of these loved haunts of men.

5 But calmly, Lord, on Thee we rest ;
  No fears our trust shall move ;
  Thou knowest what for each is best,
  And Thou art Perfect Love.
  Author unknown.

1380 "They are passed away as the swift ships." 7.
Job xiv. 1-14. Ecc. i. 1-11. 1 Cor. vii. 29-31.

1 WHILE with ceaseless course the sun
  Hasted through the former year,
  Many souls their race have run,
  Never more to meet us here.
  Fixed in an eternal state,
  They have done with all below ;
  We a little longer wait,
  But how little none can know.

2 As the wingèd arrow flies
  Speedily the mark to find ;
  As the lightning from the skies
  Darts, and leaves no trace behind ;
  Swiftly thus our fleeting days
  Bear us down life's rapid stream ;
  Upward, Lord, our spirits raise,
  All below is but a dream.

3 Thanks for mercies past receive ;
  Pardon of our sins renew ;
  Teach us henceforth how to live
  With eternity in view.
  Bless Thy word to young and old ;
  Fill us with a Saviour's love ;
  And when life's short tale is told,
  May we dwell with Thee above.
  Rev. John Newton. (1725-1807.)

1381 "Lead . . . into the land of uprightness." 7. 6.
Ps. xxxix. John xxi. 15-25. Phil. iii. 12-21.

1 ANOTHER year is dawning !
  Dear Master, let it be,
  In working or in waiting,
  Another year for Thee ;
  Another year of leaning
  Upon Thy loving breast ;
  Of ever sweet confiding,
  Of quiet, happy rest.

2 Another year of mercies,
  Of faithfulness and grace ;
  Another year of gladness,
  The shining of Thy face ;
  Another year of progress,
  Another year of praise ;
  Another year of proving
  Thy presence "all the days."

3 Another year of service,
  Of witness for Thy love ;
  Another year of training
  For holier work above.
  Another year is dawning !
  Dear Master, let it be,
  On earth or else in heaven,
  Another year for Thee.
  Miss Frances R. Havergal. (1836-1879.)

1382 "They shall sing in the ways of the Lord." L. M.
Ps. cxlvii. Acts xvii. 22-28. Heb. i.

1 GREAT God, we sing that mighty hand,
  By which supported, still we stand ;
  The opening year Thy mercy shows ;
  Let mercy crown it till it close.

2 By day, by night, at home, abroad,
  Still we are guarded by our God ;
  By His incessant bounty fed,
  By His unerring counsel led.

3 With grateful hearts the past we own ;
  The future, all to us unknown,
  We to Thy guardian care commit,
  And peaceful leave before Thy feet.

4 In scenes exalted or depressed,
  Be Thou our Joy and Thou our Rest ;
  Thy goodness all our hopes shall raise,
  Adored through all our changing days.

5 When death shall interrupt our songs,
  And silence these our mortal tongues,
  Our helper, God, in whom we trust,
  In better worlds, our souls shall boast.
  Rev. Philip Doddridge. (1702-1751.)

"He changeth the times and the seasons."

1383 Ps. cxlvii. " He giveth snow like wool." Job xxxvii. 1-14. John xii. 44-50. **C. M.**

1 Now faintly smile day's hasty hours,
   The fields and garden mourn;
   Nor ruddy fruits, nor blooming flowers
   Stern winter's brow adorn.

2 The sun withdraws his vital beams,
   And light and warmth depart;
   And drooping, lifeless nature seems
   An emblem of my heart.

3 Return, O blissful Sun, and bring
   Thy soul-reviving ray!
   This mental winter shall be spring,
   This darkness, cheerful day.

4 Great Source of light, Thy beams display,
   My drooping joys restore,
   And guide me to the seats of day,
   Where winter frowns no more.
   Miss Anne Steele. (1717-1768.)

1384 "Thou makest it soft with showers." Can. ii. Eze. xxxiv. 20-31. Mat. vi. 25-34. **C. M.**

1 While beauty clothes the fertile vale,
   And blossoms on the spray,
   And fragrance breathes in every gale,
   How sweet the vernal day!

2 O let my wondering heart confess,
   With gratitude and love,
   The bounteous hand that deigns to bless
   The garden, field, and grove.

3 That hand in this hard heart of mine
   Can make each virtue live;
   And kindly showers of grace divine
   Life, beauty, fragrance give.

4 O God of nature, God of grace,
   Thy heavenly gifts impart,
   And bid sweet meditation trace
   Spring blooming in my heart.
   Miss Anne Steele.

1385 "Thou visitest the earth." Job v. 8-27. Ps. lxv. Acts xiv. 13-17. **C. M.**

1 Good is the Lord, the heavenly King,
   Who makes the earth His care,
   Visits the pastures every spring,
   And bids the grass appear.

2 The little hills on every side
   Rejoice at falling showers;
   The meadows, dressed in all their pride,
   Perfume the air with flowers.

3 The softened ridges of the field
   Permit the corn to spring,
   The valleys rich provision yield,
   And cheerful laborers sing.
   Rev. Isaac Watts. (1674-1748.)

1386 "Cold and heat, and summer and winter." Gen. viii. 15-22. Ps. lxxiv. 17. Mat. v. 45. **H. M.**

1 Lord of the worlds below,
   On earth Thy glories shine;
   The changing seasons show
   Thy skill and power divine.
   The rolling years are full of Thee;
   In all we see, a God appears.

2 Forth in the flowery spring
   We see Thy beauty move;
   The birds on branches sing
   Thy tenderness and love;
   Wide flush the hills, the air is balm,
   Devotion's calm our bosom fills.

3 Then come, in robes of light,
   The summer's flaming days;
   The sun Thine image bright,
   Thy majesty, displays;
   And oft Thy voice in thunder rolls;
   But still our souls in Thee rejoice.

4 In autumn, a rich feast
   Thy common bounty gives
   To man, and bird, and beast,
   And everything that lives.
   Thy liberal care at morn and noon,
   And harvest moon, our lips declare.

5 In winter, awful Thou,
   With storms around Thee cast!
   The leafless forests bow
   Beneath Thy northern blast.
   While tempests lower, to Thee, dread King,
   We homage bring, and own Thy power.
   Rev. James Freeman. (1759-1835.)

1387 "He appointed the moon for seasons." Ps. civ. Deu. xi. 8-21. 2 Pet. iii. 8-14. **C. M.**

1 Lord, in Thy name Thy servants plead,
   And Thou hast sworn to hear;
   Thine is the harvest, Thine the seed,
   The fresh and fading year.

2 Our hope, when autumn winds blew wild,
   We trusted, Lord, with Thee;
   And still, now spring has on us smiled,
   We wait on Thy decree.

3 The former and the latter rain,
   The summer sun and air,
   The green ear, and the golden grain,
   All Thine, are ours by prayer.

4 So grant the precious things brought forth
   By sun and moon below,
   That Thee, in Thy new heaven and earth,
   We never may forego.
   Rev. John Keble. (1792-1866.)

"Sing unto the Lord with thanksgiving."

1388 "Blessed be the Lord God." L. M.
Gen. viii. 15-22. Ps. cxlvii. Acts xiv. 13-17.

1 ETERNAL Source of every joy,
Well may Thy praise our lips employ,
While, in Thy temple we appear,
Whose goodness crowns the circling year.

2 The flowery spring, at Thy command,
Embalms the air and paints the land;
The summer rays with vigor shine,
To raise the corn and cheer the vine.

3 Thy hand, in autumn, richly pours,
Through all our coasts, redundant stores;
And winters, softened by Thy care,
No more a face of horror wear.

4 Seasons, and months, and weeks, and days,
Demand successive songs of praise;
Still be the cheerful homage paid,
With opening light and evening shade.
Rev. Philip Doddridge. (1702-1751.)

1389 "Serve the Lord with gladness." L. M.
Ps. c. Deu. xii. 5-14. James i. 1-17.

1 ALMIGHTY Sovereign of the skies,
To Thee let songs of gladness rise;
Each grateful heart its tribute bring,
And every voice Thy goodness sing.

2 From Thee our choicest blessings flow,
Life, health, and strength Thy hands bestow;
The daily good Thy creatures share
Springs from Thy providential care.

3 Let every power of heart and tongue
Unite to swell the grateful song;
While age and youth in chorus join,
And praise the majesty divine.
Rev. Nathan Strong. (1748-1816.)

1390 "The earth is full of Thy riches." C. M.
Ps. lxv. Job xxxviii. 4-37. 1 Thes. v. 16-18.

1 'T IS by Thy strength the mountains stand,
God of eternal power;
The sea grows calm at Thy command,
And tempests cease to roar.

2 Thy morning light and evening shade
Successive comforts bring;
Thy plenteous fruits make harvest glad,
Thy flowers adorn the spring.

3 Seasons and times, and moons and hours,
Heaven, earth, and air are Thine;
When clouds distil in fruitful showers,
The Author is divine.

4 The thirsty ridges drink their fill,
And ranks of corn appear;
Thy ways abound with blessings still,
Thy goodness crowns the year.
Rev. Isaac Watts. (1674-1748.)

1391 "His tender mercies are over all." 7.
Ps. cxxxvi. 1 Chr. xvi. 8-36. Luke i. 68-75.

1 LET us, with a gladsome mind,
Praise the Lord, for He is kind:
For His mercies shall endure,
Ever faithful, ever sure.

2 He, with all-commanding might,
Filled the new-made world with light:
For His mercies shall endure,
Ever faithful, ever sure.

3 He hath, with a piteous eye,
Looked upon our misery:
For His mercies shall endure,
Ever faithful, ever sure.

4 All things living He doth feed,
His full hand supplies their need:
For His mercies shall endure,
Ever faithful, ever sure.
John Milton. (1608-1674.)

1392 "Praise is comely." 7.
Ps. cxlv. Deu. iv. 32-40. Rev. v. 13, 14.

1 SWELL the anthem, raise the song,
Praises to our God belong;
Saints and angels, join to sing
Praise to heaven's almighty King.

2 Blessings from His liberal hand
Pour around this happy land:
Let our hearts, beneath His sway,
Hail the bright, triumphant day.

3 Hark, the voice of nature sings
Praises to the King of kings;
Let us join the choral song,
And the heavenly notes prolong.
Rev. Nathan Strong.

1393 "Praise Him for His mighty acts." 7.
Ps. civ. Deu. viii. 1-11. 2 Cor. ix. 8-15.

1 PRAISE, O praise our God and King,
Hymns of adoration sing;
For His mercies still endure,
Ever faithful, ever sure.

2 Praise Him that He made the sun
Day by day his course to run;
And the silver moon by night,
Shining with her gentle light.

3 Praise Him that He gave the rain
To mature the swelling grain;
And hath bid the fruitful field
Crops of precious increase yield.

4 Praise Him for our harvest-store,
He hath filled the garner-floor;
And for richer food than this,
Pledge of everlasting bliss.
Rev. Sir Henry W. Baker. (1821-1877.)

"Sing unto the Lord with thanksgiving."

1394 "Enter into His... courts with praise." **C. M.**
Ps. cxlvii. Job xxxvi. 22-31. 1 Tim. i. 17.

1 WITH songs and honors sounding loud,
   Address the Lord on high ;
   Over the heavens He spreads His cloud,
   And waters vail the sky.
   He sends His showers of blessings down,
   To cheer the plains below ;
   He makes the grass the mountains crown,
   And corn in valleys grow.

2 His steady counsels change the face
   Of the declining year ;
   He bids the sun cut short his race,
   And wintry days appear.
   His hoary frost, his fleecy snow,
   Descend and clothe the ground ;
   The liquid streams forbear to flow,
   In icy fetters bound.

3 He sends His word and melts the snow,
   The fields no longer mourn ;
   He calls the warmer gales to blow,
   And bids the spring return.
   The changing wind, the flying cloud,
   Obey His mighty word :
   With songs and honors sounding loud,
   Praise ye the sovereign Lord.
   Rev. Isaac Watts. (1674-1748.)

1395 "Thy paths drop fatness." **C. M.**
Ps. lxv. Deu. xxxiii. 13-17. Mat. v. 43-48.

1 FOUNTAIN of mercy, God of love,
   How rich Thy bounties are !
   The rolling seasons, as they move,
   Proclaim Thy constant care.

2 When in the bosom of the earth
   The sower hid the grain,
   Thy goodness marked its secret birth,
   And sent the early rain.

3 The spring's sweet influence was Thine,
   The plants in beauty grew ;
   Thou gav'st refulgent suns to shine,
   And mild refreshing dew.

4 These various mercies from above
   Matured the swelling grain ;
   A yellow harvest crowns Thy love,
   And plenty fills the plain.

5 Seed-time and harvest, Lord, alone
   Thou dost on man bestow ;
   Let him not then forget to own
   From whom his blessings flow.
   Mrs. Alice Flowerdew. (1759-1830.)

1396 "Let all the people praise Thee." **H. M.**
Ps. civ. Ex. xxiii. 14-19. 2 Cor. ix. 8-15.

1 LET all the people join,
   To swell the solemn chord ;
   Your grateful notes combine
   To magnify the Lord :
   In lofty songs your voices raise,
   The God of harvest claims your praise.

2 Fair plenty fills the land ;
   His mercies never cease ;
   The husbandman doth smile,
   To see the large increase :
   In lofty songs your voices raise,
   The God of harvest claims your praise.

3 The precious fruits He gives,
   O may we ne'er abuse,
   But, through our future lives,
   To His own glory use,
   Then rise to heaven, and sing His praise,
   In sweeter strains and nobler lays.
   Author unknown.

1397 "O sing praises unto the Lord." **7.**
Ps. cxlviii. Isa. xii. Eph. i. 3-12.

1 PRAISE to God, immortal praise,
   For the love that crowns our days !
   Bounteous Source of every joy,
   Let Thy praise our tongues employ.

2 For the blessings of the field,
   For the stores the gardens yield ;
   For the fruits in full supply,
   Ripened 'neath the summer sky ;

3 All that spring with bounteous hand
   Scatters o'er the smiling land ;
   All that liberal autumn pours
   From her rich, o'erflowing stores ;

4 These to Thee, my God, we owe,
   Source whence all our blessings flow ;
   And for these my soul shall raise
   Grateful vows and solemn praise.

5 Should Thine altered hand restrain
   The early and the latter rain ;
   Blast each opening bud of joy,
   And the rising year destroy ;

6 Yet to Thee my soul should raise
   Grateful vows and solemn praise ;
   And, when every blessing 's flown,
   Love Thee for Thyself alone.
   Mrs. Anna L. Barbauld. (1743-1825.)

"Sing unto the Lord with thanksgiving."

1398 "They joy ... according to the joy in harvest." **6. 4.**
Ps. cxlvii. Ex. xxiii. 14–25. Acts xiv. 13–17.

1 THE God of harvest praise;
   In loud thanksgivings raise
     Hand, heart, and voice;
     The valleys laugh and sing,
     Forests and mountains ring,
     The plains their tribute bring,
   The streams rejoice.

2 Yea, bless His holy name,
   And joyous thanks proclaim
     Through all the earth;
   To glory in your lot
   Is comely; but be not
   God's benefits forgot
     Amidst your mirth.

3 The God of harvest praise;
   Hands, hearts, and voices raise
     With one accord;
   From field to garner throng,
   Bearing your sheaves along,
   And in your harvest song
     Bless ye the Lord.
         James Montgomery. (1771-1854.)

1399 "He giveth to all life ... and all things." **L. M.**
Ps. cvii. Neh. ix. 1–15. 1 Thes. iii. 9–13.

1 SING to the Lord a joyful song;
   Lift up your hearts, your voices raise;
   To us His gracious gifts belong,
   To Him our songs of love and praise.

2 For life and love, for rest and food,
   For daily help and nightly care,
   Sing to the Lord, for He is good,
   And praise His name, for it is fair:

3 For strength to those who on Him wait,
   His truth to prove, His will to do,
   Praise ye our God, for He is great,
   Trust in His name, for it is true:

4 For joys untold that daily move
   Round those who love His sweet employ,
   Sing to our God, for He is love,
   Exalt His name, for it is joy:

5 For life below, with all its bliss,
   And for that life, more pure and high,
   That inner life, which over this
   Shall ever shine, and never die.
         Rev. John S. B. Monsell. (1811-1875.)

1400 "For his merciful kindness is great." **8. 7. P.**
Ps. ciii. 2 Chr. xxx. 13–27. 2 Cor. ix. 8–15.

1 FOR us, O Lord, the year has brought
   Its bloom and harvest glory;
   To us, through changing seasons, taught
   Thy truth, in gospel story.
   Again our voices join in song,
     And bring their glad thanksgiving
   To Thee, to whom all years belong,
     To Thee, the Ever-living.

2 We oft have sung with joy-crowned brow
   Of Thy new love upspringing,
   And some who joined our songs are now
   Amid the angels singing.
   But friends below and friends above
     Unite in glad thanksgiving
   To Thee, whom all Thy children love,
     To Thee, the Ever-living.

3 Thy power in prayer we oft have felt,
   Thy sympathy most tender,
   And seemed to see, as we have knelt,
   Thy face, in vailéd splendor.
   For all these joys from Paradise
     We bring our glad thanksgiving
   To Thee, who every good supplies,
     To Thee, the Ever-living.

4 So may we join from year to year,
   Thy goodness ever singing,
   And each at last with rapture hear
   The bells of glory ringing.
   Then, safe with Thee, again we'll raise
     Our voices in thanksgiving
   To Thee, in more exalted praise,
     To Thee, the Ever-living.
         Hezekiah Butterworth. (1839–.)

1401 "Jesus was called ... to the marriage." **7. 6.**
Gen. ii. 21–24. Ruth iv. 1–12. John ii. 1–10.

1 O LOVE, divine and tender,
   That through our homes dost move,
   Vailed in the softened splendor
   Of holy household love:
   A throne, without Thy blessing,
   Were labor without rest,
   And cottages, possessing
   Thy blessedness, are blest.

2 God bless these hands united,
   God bless these hearts made one;
   Unsevered and unblighted
   May they through life go on:
   Here, in earth's home, preparing
   For the bright home above,
   And there, forever sharing
   Its joy, where "God is love."
         Rev. John S. B. Monsell.

"The land which the Lord our God giveth us."

1402 "A delightsome land." 6. 4.
Ps. lxxxv. Deu. viii. 1-10. 1 Tim. i. 17.

1 My country, 't is of thee,
  Sweet land of liberty,
    Of thee I sing;
  Land where my fathers died,
  Land of the pilgrims' pride,
  From every mountain side
    Let freedom ring.

2 My native country, thee,
  Land of the noble free,
    Thy name I love;
  I love thy rocks and rills,
  Thy woods and templed hills;
  My heart with rapture thrills
    Like that above.

3 Our fathers' God, to Thee,
  Author of liberty,
    To Thee we sing:
  Long may our land be bright
  With freedom's holy light;
  Protect us by Thy might,
    Great God, our King.
                  Rev. Samuel F. Smith. (1808-.)

1403 "The people which Thou hast redeemed." H. M.
Ps. xliv. 1-8. Deu. xi. Rom. xvi. 24-27.

1 Before the Lord we bow,
    The God who reigns above,
  And rules the world below,
    Boundless in power and love;
      Our thanks we bring
      In joy and praise,
      Our hearts we raise
      To heaven's high King.

2 The nation Thou hast blest
    May well Thy love declare,
  From foes and fears at rest,
    Protected by Thy care.
      For this fair land,
      For this bright day,
      Our thanks we pay,
      Gifts of Thy hand.

3 May every mountain height,
    Each vale and forest green,
  Shine in Thy word's pure light,
    And its rich fruits be seen.
      May every tongue
      Be tuned to praise,
      And join to raise
      A grateful song.
                  Francis S. Key. (1779-1843.)

1404 "O land, be glad and rejoice." 6. 4.
Ps. xlvii. Isa. xlix. 13-23. Titus ii. 11-14.

1 Our land, with mercies crowned,
  This wide enchanted ground,
    O God, is Thine;
  Our fathers knew Thy name;
  The trophies of their fame,
  Our heritage, proclaim
    A power divine.

2 Dear native land, rejoice;
  Raise thou thy virgin voice
    To God on high;
  From all thy hills and bays,
  From all thy homes and ways,
  Let symphonies and praise
    Ascend the sky.

3 And Thou Almighty One,
  At whose eternal throne
    She bows the knee,
  In all the coming time
  Bless Thou this favored clime,
  And may her deeds sublime
    Be hymns to Thee!
                  E. T. Winkler. 1871.

1405 "Thou hast guided them in Thy strength." 6. 4.
Ps. cxxxvi. 1 Chr. xvi. 1-36. Eph. iii. 14-21.

1 Auspicious morning, hail!
  Voices, from hill and vale,
    Thy welcome sing:
  Joy on thy dawning breaks;
  Each heart that joy partakes,
  While cheerful music wakes,
    Its praise to bring.

2 Thou, as a shield of power,
  In battle's awful hour,
    Didst round us stand;
  Our hopes were in Thy throne;
  Strong in Thy might alone,
  By Thee our banners shone,
    God of our land!

3 Peace on this day abide,
  From morn till eventide;
    Wake tuneful song;
  Melodious accents raise;
  Let every heart, with praise,
  Bring high and grateful lays,
    Rich, full, and strong.
                  Rev. Samuel F. Smith.

"The things which are seen are temporal."

1406 "Our days on the earth are as a shadow." **C. M.**
Ps. xxxix. Job vii. 1-10. 2 Pet. iii. 8-18.

1 THEE we adore, Eternal Name,
  And humbly own to Thee
How feeble is our mortal frame,
  What dying worms are we.

2 Our wasting lives grow shorter still,
  As days and months increase;
And every beating pulse we tell
  Leaves but the number less.

3 The year rolls round and steals away
  The breath that first it gave;
Whate'er we do, where'er we be,
  We're travelling to the grave.

4 Waken, O Lord, our drowsy sense
  To walk this dangerous road;
And if our souls are hurried hence,
  May they be found with God!
      Rev. Isaac Watts. (1674-1748.)

1407 "As a fading flower." **L. M.**
Job xiv. Ps. ciii. 13-18. 1 Pet. i. 17-25.

1 So fades the lovely blooming flower,
  Frail smiling solace of an hour!
So soon our transient comforts fly,
  And pleasure only blooms to die.

2 Is there no kind, no lenient art,
  To heal the anguish of the heart?
Spirit of grace, be ever nigh,
  Thy comforts are not made to die.

3 Thy powerful aid supports the soul,
  And nature owns Thy kind control;
Hope wipes the tear from sorrow's eye,
  And faith points upward to the sky.
      Miss Anne Steele. (1717-1778.)

1408 "As a morning cloud." **L. M.**
Ps. cix. 21-31. Gen. xlvii. 7-10. 2 Cor. v.

1 How vain is all beneath the skies!
  How transient every earthly bliss!
How slender all the fondest ties,
  That bind us to a world like this!

2 The evening cloud, the morning dew,
  The withering grass, the fading flower,
Of earthly hopes are emblems true,
  The glory of a passing hour.

3 But, though earth's fairest blossoms die,
  And all beneath the skies is vain,
There is a land whose confines lie
  Beyond the reach of care and pain.

4 Then let the hope of joys to come
  Dispel our cares, and chase our fears;
If God be ours, we're travelling home,
  Though passing through a vale of tears.
      Rev. David E. Ford. 1820.

1409 "As the cloud is consumed and vanisheth." **C. M.**
2 Cor. iv. 11-18. Heb. xiii. 14-21. Ps. cii

1 THE roseate hues of early dawn,
  The brightness of the day,
The crimson of the sunset sky,
  How fast they fade away!
O for the pearly gates of heaven!
  O for the golden floor!
O for the Sun of Righteousness,
  That setteth never more!

2 The highest hopes we cherish here,
  How fast they tire and faint!
How many a spot defiles the robe
  That wraps an earthly saint!
O for a heart that never sins!
  O for a soul washed white!
O for a voice to praise our King,
  Nor weary day or night!

3 Here faith is ours, and heavenly hope,
  And grace to lead us higher;
But there are perfectness and peace,
  Beyond our best desire.
O by Thy love and anguish, Lord!
  O by Thy life laid down,
O that we fall not from Thy grace,
  Nor cast away our crown.
      Mrs. Cecil F. Alexander. (1823-.)

1410 "The grace of the fashion of it perisheth." **8. 7.**
Isa. xl. 6-8. Ecc. ii. 1-11. John xi. 1-27.

1 ALL is dying; hearts are breaking
  Which to ours were closely bound;
And the lips have ceased from speaking,
  Which once uttered such sweet sound.

2 Everything we love and cherish
  Hastens onward to the grave;
Earthly joys and pleasures perish,
  And whate'er the world e'er gave.

3 All is fading, all is fleeing;
  Earthly flames must cease to glow,
Earthly beings cease from being,
  Earthly blossoms cease to blow.

4 Yet unchanged while all decayeth,
  Jesus stands beside the dust;
Lean on Me alone, He sayeth;
  Hope and love, and firmly trust.

5 O abide, abide with Jesus,
  Who Himself forever lives,
Who from death eternal frees us,
  Yea, who life eternal gives.
      Rev. Carl J. P. Spitta. (1801-1859.)
      Tr. by Richard Massie.

"The things which are seen are temporal."

1411 James iv. 13-15. Job vii. 6-9. Ps. cii. *"It is even a vapor."* **8. 7. 7.**

1 WHAT is life ? 'T is but a vapor,
   Soon it vanishes away ;
   Life is like a dying taper,
   O my soul, why wish to stay ?
   Why not spread thy wings and fly
   Straight to yonder world of joy ?

2 See that glory, how resplendent !
   Brighter far than fancy paints ;
   There, in majesty transcendent,
   Jesus reigns, the King of saints :
   Spread thy wings, my soul, and fly
   Straight to yonder world of joy.

3 Joyful crowds, His throne surrounding,
   Sing with rapture of His love ;
   Through the heavens His praises sounding,
   Filling all the courts above :
   Spread thy wings, my soul, and fly
   Straight to yonder world of joy.

4 Go, and share His people's glory,
   Midst the ransomed crowd appear ;
   Thine a joyful, wondrous story,
   One that angels love to hear :
   Spread thy wings, my soul, and fly
   Straight to yonder world of joy.

Rev. Thomas Kelly. (1769-1855.)

1412 *"Desiring . . our house . . . from heaven."* Heb. xi. 1-16. 2 Cor. jv. Ps. xvi. **7. 6.**

1 FROM every earthly pleasure,
   From every transient joy,
   From every mortal treasure,
   That soon will fade and cloy ;
   No longer these desiring,
   Upward our wishes tend,
   To nobler bliss aspiring,
   And joys that never end.

2 From every piercing sorrow,
   That heaves our breast to-day,
   Or threatens us to-morrow,
   Hope turns our eyes away ;
   On wings of faith ascending,
   We see the land of light,
   And feel our sorrows ending,
   In infinite delight.

3 'T is true we are but strangers
   And pilgrims here below,
   And countless snares and dangers
   Surround the path we go ;
   Though painful and distressing,
   Yet there 's a rest above ;
   And onward still we 're pressing,
   To reach that land of love.

Rev. Eliel Davis. (1800-1830.)

1413 *"As the stream of brooks they pass away."* Zech. i. 1-6. Job xiv. 1-15. Ps. xvii. **S. M.**

1 How swift the torrent rolls,
   That bears us to the sea !
   The tide that bears our thoughtless souls
   To vast eternity !

2 Our fathers, where are they,
   With all they called their own ?
   Their joys and griefs, and hopes and cares,
   And wealth and honor gone !

3 God of our fathers, hear,
   Thou everlasting Friend !
   While we, as on life's utmost verge,
   Our souls to Thee commend.

4 Of all the pious dead
   May we the footsteps trace,
   Till with them, in the land of light,
   We dwell before Thy face.

Rev. Philip Doddridge. (1702-1751.)

1414 *"Swifter than a post."* Gen. xlvii. 7-10. 1 Pet. i. 2 Sam. xii. 23. **C. M.**

1 LIFE is a span, a fleeting hour,
   How soon the vapor flies ;
   Man is a tender, transient flower,
   That e'en in blooming dies.

2 Hope looks beyond the bounds of time,
   When what we now deplore
   Shall rise in full, immortal prime,
   And bloom to fade no more.

3 Cease, then, fond nature, cease thy tears,
   Religion points on high ;
   There everlasting spring appears,
   And joys that cannot die.

Miss Anne Steele. (1717-1778.)

1415 *"As dying and behold we live."* Ps. cxviii. 14-29. 2 Cor. v. 1-9. Dan. xii. **S. M.**

1 IT is not death to die,
   To leave this weary road,
   And, midst the brotherhood on high,
   To be at home with God.

2 It is not death to close
   The eye long dimmed by tears,
   And wake, in glorious repose
   To spend eternal years.

3 It is not death to fling
   Aside this sinful dust,
   And rise, on strong exulting wing,
   To live among the just.

4 Jesus, Thou Prince of Life,
   Thy chosen cannot die ;
   Like Thee, they conquer in the strife,
   To reign with Thee on high.

Rev. Cæsar H. A. Malan. (1787-1864.)
Tr. by Rev. George W. Bethune. (1805-1862.)

"The things which are not seen are eternal."

1416 "An inheritance incorruptible." **C. M.**
Heb. xi. 32-40. Job xix. Isa. xxxiii. 15-24.

1 THROUGH sorrow's night and danger's path,
  Amid the deepening gloom,
  We, soldiers of an injured King,
  Are marching to the tomb.

2 Our labors done, securely laid
  In this our last retreat,
  Unheeded, o'er our silent dust
  The storms of life shall beat.

3 Yet not thus lifeless, thus inane,
  The vital spark shall lie;
  For o'er life's wreck that spark shall rise
  To seek its kindred sky.

4 These ashes too, this little dust,
  Our Father's care shall keep,
  Till the last angel rise and break
  The long and dreary sleep.

5 Then love's soft dew o'er every eye
  Shall shed its mildest rays,
  And the long-silent dust shall burst
  With shouts of endless praise.
  Henry K. White. (1785-1806.)

1417 "And there shall be no more pain." **6. 8.**
John xi. 1-27. 1 Cor. xv. 12-28. Isa. lxi. 1-7.

1 FRIEND after friend departs:
  Who hath not lost a friend?
  There is no union here of hearts
  That finds not here an end;
  Were this frail world our only rest,
  Living or dying, none were blest.

2 Beyond the flight of time,
  Beyond the vale of death,
  There surely is some blessed clime
  Where life is not a breath;
  Nor life's affections transient fire,
  Whose sparks fly upward to expire.

3 There is a world above,
  Where parting is unknown;
  A whole eternity of love,
  Formed for the good alone;
  And faith beholds the dying here
  Translated to that happier sphere.

4 Thus star by star declines
  Till all are passed away,
  As morning high and higher shines
  To pure and perfect day;
  Nor sink those stars in empty night;
  They hide themselves in heaven's own light.
  James Montgomery. (1771-1854.)

1418 "Neither can they die any more." **7. 6. 7.**
Job vii. 1-10. Ps. xxxix. John xiv. 12-31.

1 TIME is winging us away
  To our eternal home;
  Life is but a winter's day,
  A journey to the tomb.
  Youth and vigor soon will flee,
  Blooming beauty lose its charms;
  All that's mortal soon shall be
  Enclosed in death's cold arms.

2 Time is winging us away
  To our eternal home;
  Life is but a winter's day,
  A journey to the tomb;
  But the Christian shall enjoy
  Health and beauty soon above;
  Far beyond the world's annoy,
  Secure in Jesus' love.
  John Burton. (1803-.)

1419 "He will dwell with them." **L. M.**
1 Cor. ii. 1-10. Mat. xxv. 31-40. Isa. vi. 1-7.

1 DESCEND from heaven, Immortal Dove,
  Stoop down and take us on Thy wings,
  And mount and bear us far above
  The reach of these inferior things.

2 O for a sight, a pleasing sight,
  Of our almighty Father's throne:
  There sits our Saviour crowned with light,
  Clothed in a body like our own.

3 Adoring saints around Him stand,
  And thrones and powers before Him fall;
  The God shines gracious through the Man,
  And sheds sweet glories on them all.
  Rev. Isaac Watts. (1674-1748.)

1420 "They shall be comforted." **L. M.**
Luke vi. 20-23. 2 Cor. vi. 1-10. Ps. xxx.

1 O DEEM not they are blest alone,
  Whose lives a peaceful tenor keep;
  The Power who pities man has shown
  A blessing for the eyes that weep.

2 The light of smiles shall fill again
  The lids that overflow with tears;
  And weary hours of woe and pain
  Are promises of happier years.

3 There is a day of sunny rest
  For every dark and troubled night;
  And grief may bide an evening guest,
  But joy shall come with early light.

4 For God has marked each sorrowing day,
  And numbered every secret tear,
  And heaven's long age of bliss shall pay
  For all His children suffer here.
  William C. Bryant. (1794-1878.)

"Blessed are the dead which die in the Lord."

1421 " Let me die the death of the righteous." L. M.
Rev. xiv. 12, 13. 2 Sam. xxiii. 1–5. Ps. cxvi.

1 How blest the righteous, when he dies,
  When sinks a weary soul to rest;
  How mildly beam the closing eyes,
  How gently heaves th' expiring breast.

2 So fades a summer cloud away;
  So sinks the gale, when storms are o'er;
  So gently shuts the eye of day;
  So dies a wave along the shore.

3 A holy quiet reigns around,
  A calm which life nor death destroys;
  And naught disturbs that peace profound
  Which his unfettered soul enjoys.

4 Life's labor done, as sinks the clay,
  Light from its load the spirit flies;
  While heaven and earth combine to say,
  "How blest the righteous when he dies!"

  Mrs. Anna L. Barbauld. (1743–1825.)

1422 "Through the waters I will be with thee." L. M.
John xvii. 24–26. Phil. i. 19–24. Ps. xxiii.

1 Why should we start and fear to die?
  What timorous worms we mortals are!
  Death is the gate of endless joy;
  And yet we dread to enter there.

2 O if my Lord would come and meet,
  My soul should stretch her wings in haste,
  Fly fearless through death's iron gate,
  Nor feel the terrors as she passed.

3 Jesus can make a dying bed
  Feel soft as downy pillows are,
  While on His breast I lean my head,
  And breathe my life out sweetly there.

  Rev. Isaac Watts. (1674–1748.)

1423 "A tabernacle that shall not be taken down." L. M.
Deu. xxxiv. Phil. iii. 7–21. 2 Tim. iv. 6–8.

1 As when the weary traveller gains
  The height of some o'erlooking hill,
  His heart revives, if 'cross the plains
  He eyes his home, though distant still.

2 So when the Christian pilgrim views,
  By faith, his mansion in the skies,
  The sight his fainting strength renews,
  And wings his speed to reach the prize.

3 The thought of home his spirit cheers;
  No more he grieves for troubles past,
  Nor any future trial fears,
  So he may safe arrive at last.

4 Jesus, on Thee our hope depends
  To lead us on to Thine abode,
  Assured our home will make amends
  For all our toil while on the road.

  Rev. John Newton. (1725–1807.)

1424 "The death of His saints." L. M.
Num. xxiii. 1–10. Gen. l. Heb. xii. 22–24.

1 How sweet the hour of closing day,
  When all is peaceful and serene,
  And the broad sun's retiring ray
  Sheds a mild lustre o'er the scene!

2 Such is the Christian's parting hour,
  So peacefully he sinks to rest;
  When faith, endued from heaven with power,
  Strengthens and cheers his languid breast.

3 Mark but that radiance of his eye,
  That smile upon his wasted cheek!
  They tell us of his glory nigh,
  In language which no tongue can speak.

4 A beam from heaven is sent to cheer
  The pilgrim on his gloomy road;
  And angels are attending near,
  To bear him to their bright abode.

  Rev. William H. Bathurst. (1796–.)

1425 "Willing rather to be absent from the body." L. M.
1 Cor. ii. 9, 10. Heb. iv. Ps. xxi. 5–11.

1 Now let our souls, on wings sublime,
  Rise from the vanities of time,
  Draw back the parting vail, and see
  The glories of eternity.

2 Born by a new celestial birth,
  Why should we grovel here on earth?
  Why grasp at transitory toys,
  So near to heaven's eternal joys?

3 Shall aught beguile us on the road,
  While we are travelling back to God?
  For strangers into life we come,
  And dying is but going home.

  Rev. Thomas Gibbons. (1720–1785.)

1426 "To be present with the Lord." C. M.
Isa. lvii. 1, 2. Ps. xxxvii. Acts vii. 55–60.

1 Behold the western evening light!
  It melts in deepening gloom;
  So calmly Christians sink away,
  Descending to the tomb.

2 How beautiful on all the hills
  The crimson light is shed!
  'T is like the peace the Christian gives
  To mourners round his bed.

3 How mildly on the wandering cloud
  The sunset beam is cast!
  'T is like the memory left behind
  When loved ones breathe their last.

4 But soon the morning's happier light
  Its glory shall restore;
  And eyelids, that are sealed in death,
  Shall wake to close no more.

  Rev. William B. O. Peabody. (1799–1847.)

"Fallen asleep in Christ."

1427 "Whether we live, therefore, or die, we are the Lord's."
Deu. xxxiv. 1 Sam. xii. 1–5. Isa. xxxiii. 15–24. 2 Tim. iv. 6–8. **10.**

1 Go to the grave in all thy glorious prime,
　In full activity of zeal and power;
　A Christian cannot die before his time,
　The Lord's appointment is the servant's hour.

2 Go to the grave; at noon from labor cease;
　Rest on thy sheaves, thy harvest-task is done;
　Come from the heat of battle, and in peace,
　Soldier, go home; with thee the fight is won.

3 Go to the grave, for there thy Saviour lay
　In death's embraces, ere He rose on high;
　And all the ransomed, by that narrow way,
　Pass to eternal life beyond the sky.
　　　　　　　　　　　James Montgomery. (1771–1854.)

1428 "I shall not die, but live." **7.**
Gen. v. 22–24. 2 Kings ii. 1–11. 2 Cor. v. 1–9.

1 DEATHLESS spirit, now arise,
　Soar, thou native of the skies;
　Pearl of price, by Jesus bought,
　To His glorious likeness wrought,
　Go, to shine before His throne;
　Deck His mediatorial crown;
　Go, His triumphs to adorn;
　Made for God, to God return.

2 Angels, joyful to attend,
　Hovering round thy pillow, bend;
　Wait to catch the signal given,
　And escort thee quick to heaven.
　Saints, in glory perfect made,
　Wait thy passage through the shade;
　Ardent for thy coming o'er,
　See, they throng the blissful shore.

3 Shudder not to pass the stream;
　Venture all thy care on Him;
　Him, whose dying love and power
　Stilled its tossing, hushed its roar;
　Lo, He beckons from on high,
　Fearless to His presence fly;
　Thine the merit of His blood;
　Thine the righteousness of God.
　　　　　　　Rev. Augustus M. Toplady. (1740–1778.)

1430 "Yet shall he live." **7.**
Acts vii. 55–60. 1 Cor. xv. 50–57. Ps. xvi.

1 "SPIRIT, leave thy house of clay;
　Lingering dust, resign thy breath;
　Spirit, cast thy chains away;
　Dust, be thou dissolved in death:"
　Thus th' almighty Saviour speaks,
　While the faithful Christian dies;
　Thus the bonds of life He breaks,
　And the ransomed captive flies.

2 "Prisoner, long detained below,
　Prisoner, now with freedom blest,
　Welcome from a world of woe;
　Welcome to a land of rest:"
　Thus the choir of angels sing,
　As they bear the soul on high,
　While with hallelujahs ring
　All the regions of the sky.

3 Grave, the guardian of our dust,
　Grave, the treasury of the skies,
　Every atom of thy trust
　Rests in hope again to rise:
　Hark! the judgment-trumpet calls,
　"Soul, rebuild thy house of clay,
　Immortality thy walls,
　And eternity thy day."
　　　　　　　　　　　　James Montgomery.

1429 "Death is swallowed up in victory" **12. 11.**
1 Cor. xv. 1–28. Rom. v. 12–21. John xiv. 1–19. Dan. xii.

1 THOU art gone to the grave; but we will not deplore thee,
　Though sorrows and darkness encompass the tomb;
　Thy Saviour has passed through its portal before thee,
　And the lamp of His love is thy guide through the gloom.

2 Thou art gone to the grave; but we will not deplore thee;
　Whose God was thy Ransom, thy Guardian and Guide;
　He gave thee, He took thee, and He will restore thee;
　And death has no sting, for the Saviour has died.
　　　　　　　　　Bp. Reginald Heber. (1783–1826.)

"Fallen asleep in Christ."

1431 "Some are fallen asleep." L. M.
1 Thes. iv. 13-18. John xi. Job xix. 23-27.

1 ASLEEP in Jesus: blessèd sleep,
From which none ever wakes to weep;
A calm and undisturbed repose,
Unbroken by the last of foes.

2 Asleep in Jesus : O how sweet
To be for such a slumber meet ;
With holy confidence to sing
That death hath lost his venomed sting !

3 Asleep in Jesus: peaceful rest,
Whose waking is supremely blest ;
No fear, no woe, shall dim that hour
That manifests the Saviour's power.

4 Asleep in Jesus : O for me
May such a blissful refuge be;
Securely shall my ashes lie,
Waiting the summons from on high.
Mrs. Margaret Mackay. (1801-.)

1432 "The joy of thy Lord." S. M.
Mat. xxv. 14-23. Acts vii. 60. Isa. xxv.

1 SERVANT of God, well done !
Rest from thy loved employ ;
The battle fought, the vict'ry won,
Enter thy Master's joy.

2 The pains of death are past ;
Labor and sorrow cease ;
And, life's long warfare closed at last,
His soul is found in peace.

3 Soldier of Christ, well done !
Praise be thy new employ ;
And, while eternal ages run,
Rest in thy Saviour's joy.
James Montgomery. (1771-1854.)

1433 "As the stars forever and ever." C. M.
Mal. iii. 16. Mark xii. 27. Mat. xvii. 3.

1 THE dead are like the stars by day,
Withdrawn from mortal eye,
Yet holding unperceived their way
Through the unclouded sky.

2 By them, through holy hope and love,
We feel, in hours serene,
Connected with a world above,
Immortal and unseen.

3 For death his sacred seal hath set
On bright and bygone hours ;
And they we mourn are with us yet,
Are more than ever ours :

4 Ours by the pledge of love and faith,
By hopes of heaven on high ;
By trust, triumphant over death,
In immortality.
Bernard Barton. (1784-1849.)

1434 "That where I am, there ye may be." 7. 6.
1 Cor. xv. 37-49. Isa. xxxiii. 15-24. Gen. l.

1 THE precious seed of weeping
To-day we sow once more,
The form of one now sleeping,
Whose pilgrimage is o'er.
Ah, death but safely lands him
Where we too would attain ;
Our Father's voice demands him,
And death to him is gain.

2 He has what we are wanting,
He sees what we believe ;
The sins on earth so haunting
Have there no power to grieve:
Safe in his Saviour's keeping,
Who sent him calm release ;
'T is only we are weeping,
He dwells in perfect peace.

3 The crown of life he weareth,
He bears the shining palm ;
The "Holy, holy," shareth,
And joins the angels' psalm :
But we, poor pilgrims, wander
Still through this land of woe,
Till we shall meet him yonder,
And all his joys shall know.
Rev. Carl J. P. Spitta. (1801-1859.)
Tr. by Miss Catherine Winkworth. (1820-.)

1435 "They shall see His face." 8. 7.
Ps. xvi. 8-11. Mat. v. 4. John xvii. 24-26.

1 THINK, O ye who fondly languish
O'er the grave of those you love,
While your bosoms throb with anguish,
They are warbling hymns above.

2 While your silent steps are straying
Lonely through night's deepening shade,
Glory's brightest beams are playing
Round the happy Christian's head.

3 Night, the face of nature veiling,
Rears her sable throne no more
'Mid those spirits pure, inhaling
Life from Him whom they adore.

4 Light and peace at once deriving
From the hand of God most high,
In His glorious presence living,
They shall never, never die.

5 Cease, then, mourner, cease to languish
O'er the grave of those you love ;
Pain, and death, and night, and anguish
Enter not the world above.
Rev. William B. Collyer. (1782-1854.)

"Fallen asleep in Christ."

1436 "Before the throne of God." **L. M.**
John xi. 30-38. Gen. xxiii. Deu. xxxiv.

1 DEAR is the spot where Christians sleep,
   And sweet the strains their spirits pour;
   O why should we in anguish weep?
   They are not lost, but gone before.

2 Secure from every mortal care,
   By sin and sorrow vexed no more,
   Eternal happiness they share,
   Who are not lost, but gone before.

3 To Zion's peaceful courts above,
   In faith triumphant may we soar;
   Embracing in the arms of love
   The friends not lost, but gone before.

4 To Jordan's bank whene'er we come,
   And hear the swelling waters roar,
   Jesus, convey us safely home,
   To friends not lost, but gone before.
   Author unknown.

1437 "That they may rest from their labors." **C. M.**
Rev. xiv. 13. 1 Cor. xv. 12-28. Ps. xci.

1 HEAR what the voice from heaven proclaims
   For all the pious dead:
   Sweet is the savor of their names,
   And soft their sleeping bed.

2 They die in Jesus, and are blessed;
   How kind their slumbers are!
   From sufferings and from sins released,
   And freed from every snare.

3 Far from this world of toil and strife,
   They're present with the Lord;
   The labors of their mortal life
   End in a large reward.
   Rev. Isaac Watts. (1674-1748.)

1438 "That ... we should live ... with Him." **C. M.**
John xiv. 1-3. Eze. xxiv. 15-18. Rev. iii. 21.

1 WHY do we mourn departing friends,
   Or shake at death's alarms?
   'T is but the voice that Jesus sends,
   To call them to His arms.

2 Are we not tending upward, too,
   As fast as time can move?
   Nor would we wish the hours more slow,
   To keep us from our love.

3 Why should we tremble to convey
   Their bodies to the tomb?
   There the dear flesh of Jesus lay,
   And left a long perfume.

4 The graves of all His saints He blessed,
   And softened every bed;
   Where should the dying members rest,
   But with their dying Head?
   Rev. Isaac Watts.

1439 "It is raised in glory." **L. M.**
Gen. l. John xix. 38-42. 1 Cor. xv. 51-58.

1 UNVEIL thy bosom, faithful tomb;
   Take this new treasure to thy trust,
   And give these sacred relics room
   To seek a slumber in the dust.

2 Nor pain, nor grief, nor anxious fear,
   Invade thy bounds; no mortal woes
   Can reach the peaceful sleeper here,
   While angels watch the soft repose.

3 So Jesus slept: God's dying Son
   Passed through the grave, and blest the bed;
   Rest here, blest saint, till from His throne
   The morning break, and pierce the shade.

4 Break from His throne, illustrious morn!
   Attend, O earth, His sovereign word!
   Restore thy trust: a glorious form
   Shall then ascend to meet the Lord.
   Rev. Isaac Watts.

1440 "This mortal must put on immortality." **S. M.**
Num. xxiii. 1-10. Ecc. xii. 7. 1 Thes. iv. 16.

1 O FOR the death of those
   Who slumber in the Lord!
   O be like theirs my last repose,
   Like theirs my last reward!

2 Their bodies in the ground
   In silent hope may lie,
   Till the last trumpet's joyful sound
   Shall call them to the sky.

3 Their ransomed spirits soar
   On wings of faith and love,
   To meet the Saviour they adore,
   And reign with Him above.
   Rev. Samuel F. Smith. (1808-.)

1441 "Is it well with the child? It is well." **7, 8.**
Mark x. 13-16. 2 Sam. xii. 16-23. Isa. xl. 6-11.

1 TENDER Shepherd, Thou hast stilled
   Now Thy little lamb's brief weeping;
   Ah, how peaceful, pale, and mild
   In its narrow bed 't is sleeping!
   And no sigh of anguish sore
   Heaves that little bosom more.

2 In this world of care and pain,
   Lord, Thou wouldst no longer leave it;
   To the sunny heavenly plain
   Thou dost now with joy receive it;
   Clothed in robes of spotless white,
   Now it dwells with Thee in light.
   Rev. Wilhelm Meinhold. (1797-1851.)
   Tr. by Miss Catherine Winkworth. (1829-.)

"Them also which sleep in Jesus will God bring."

1442 "We shall be changed." **C. M.**
1 Cor. xv. 1-20. Ps. l. 1-6. Rev. xx. 11-13.

1 As Jesus died, and rose again
   Victorious from the dead,
So His disciples rise, and reign
   With their triumphant Head.

2 The time draws nigh when from the clouds
   Christ shall with shouts descend ;
And the last trumpet's awful voice
   The heavens and earth shall rend.

3 Then they who live shall changéd be,
   And they who sleep shall wake ;
The graves shall yield their ancient charge,
   And earth's foundations shake.

4 The saints of God, from death set free,
   With joy shall mount on high ;
The heavenly host, with praises loud,
   Shall meet them in the sky.
Michael Bruce. (1746-1767.)

1443 "Changed into the same image." **L. M.**
Ps. xvii. 15. 1 John iii. 1, 2. Rom. vi.

1 What sinners value I resign;
   Lord, 't is enough that Thou art mine :
I shall behold Thy blissful face,
   And stand complete in righteousness.

2 O glorious hour ! O blest abode!
   I shall be near and like my God ;
And flesh and sin no more control
   The sacred pleasures of the soul.

3 My flesh shall slumber in the ground
   Till the last trumpet's joyful sound ;
Then burst the chains with sweet surprise,
   And in my Saviour's image rise.
Rev. Isaac Watts. (1674-1748.)

1444 "This corruptible must put on incorruption." **L. M.**
Isa. xl. 6-8. Gen. xlvii. 8, 9. John x. 27-29.

1 The morning flowers display their sweets,
   And gay their silken leaves unfold,
As careless of the noontide heats,
   As fearless of the evening cold.

2 So blooms the human face divine,
   When youth its pride of beauty shows ;
Fairer than spring the colors shine,
   And sweeter than the virgin rose.

3 Or worn by slowly-rolling years,
   Or broke by sickness in a day,
The fading glory disappears,
   The short-lived beauties die away.

4 Yet these, new rising from the tomb,
   With lustre brighter far shall shine ;
Revive, with ever-during bloom,
   Safe from diseases and decline.
Rev. Samuel Wesley, Jr. (1690-1739.)

1445 "This mortal must put on immortality." **L. M.**
Ps. lxxxviii. 1 Cor. xv. Zech. ix. 12-17.

1 Shall man, O God of light and life,
   Forever moulder in the grave ?
Canst Thou forget Thy glorious work,
   Thy promise, and Thy power to save ?

2 In those dark, silent realms of night,
   Shall peace and hope no more arise ?
No future morning light the tomb,
   No daystar gild the darksome skies ?

3 Cease, cease, ye vain, desponding fears !
   When Christ, our Lord, from darkness sprang,
Death, the last foe, was captive led,
   And heaven with praise and wonder rang.

4 Faith sees the bright eternal doors
   Unfold, to make His children way ;
They shall be clothed with endless life,
   And shine in everlasting day.
Rev. Timothy Dwight. (1752-1817.)

1446 "Fashioned like unto His glorious body." **S. M.**
Job xix. 23-27. Ps. xvi. Phil. iii. 20, 21.

1 And must this body die,
   This mortal frame decay ?
And must these active limbs of mine
   Lie mouldering in the clay ?

2 God, my Redeemer, lives,
   And ever from the skies
Looks down and watches all my dust,
   Till He shall bid it rise.

3 Arrayed in glorious grace
   Shall these vile bodies shine,
And every shape and every face
   Look heavenly and divine.
Rev. Isaac Watts.

1447 "With me where I am." **L. M.**
Rev. v. Mat. xxiii. 31-40. Dan. xii.

1 We sing His love who once was slain,
   Who soon o'er death revived again,
That all His saints, through Him, might have
   Eternal conquests o'er the grave.

2 The saints, who now in Jesus sleep,
   His own almighty power shall keep,
Till dawns the bright, illustrious day,
   When death itself shall die away.

3 How loud shall our glad voices sing,
   When Christ His risen saints shall bring
From beds of dust and silent clay
   To realms of everlasting day !

4 Hasten, dear Lord, the glorious day,
   And this delightful scene display,
When all Thy saints from death shall rise,
   Raptured in bliss beyond the skies.
Rev. Rowland Hill. (1744-1833.)

"The judgment of the great day."

1448 "For the trumpet shall sound." 8. 7. 4.
1 Cor. xv. 51-58. Isa. lxiii. 3. Mat. xvi. 27.

1 HARK! the judgment trumpet sounding
 Rends the skies and shakes the poles;
 Lo, the day, with wrath abounding,
 Breaks upon astonished souls:
  Every creature
 Now the awful Judge beholds.

2 Jesus, Captain of salvation,
 Leads His armies down the skies;
 Every kindred, tribe, and nation,
 From the sleep of death, arise:
  Heaven's loud summons
 Fills the world with dread surprise.

3 Zion's King, His throne ascending,
 Calls His saints before His face;
 Crowns, with glory never ending,
 All the children of His grace:
  Heaven shall echo;
 Songs of triumph fill the place.
Rev. Nathan S. S. Beman. (1785-1871.)

1449 "The hour of His judgment is come." 7.
Mark xiii. 24-37. Mat. xix. 28-30. Dan. xii.

1 DAY of terror, day of doom,
 When the Judge at last shall come;
 Through the deep and silent gloom,
 Shrouding every human tomb,
 Shall the archangel's trumpet tone
 Summon all before the throne.

2 Then shall nature stand aghast,
 Death himself be overcast;
 Then, at her Creator's call,
 Near and distant, great and small,
 Shall the whole creation rise,
 Waiting for the Great Assize.

3 Then the writing shall be read
 Which shall judge the quick and dead;
 Then the Lord of all our race
 Shall appoint to each his place;
 Every wrong shall be set right,
 Every secret brought to light.

4 King of kings, enthroned on high
 In Thine awful majesty,
 Thou who of Thy mercy free
 Savest those who saved shall be,
 Grant forgiveness, Lord, at last,
 Ere the dread account be past.

5 Full of fears and full of dread
 Is the day that wakes the dead;
 Calling all, with solemn blast,
 From the ashes of the past:
 Lord of mercy, Jesus, blest,
 Grant us Thine eternal rest.
Thomas of Celano. c. 1250.
Tr. by Rev. Arthur P. Stanley. (1815-1881.)

1450 "He shall judge … with righteousness." S. M.
Mat. xxiv. 2 Pet. iii. 7-12. Zech. xiv.

1 BEHOLD, the day is come,
 The righteous Judge is near;
 And sinners, trembling at their doom,
 Shall soon their sentence hear.

2 Angels in bright attire
 Conduct Him through the skies;
 Darkness and tempests, smoke and fire,
 Attend Him as He flies.

3 How awful is the sight,
 How loud the thunders roar!
 The sun forbears to give his light,
 And stars are seen no more.

4 The whole creation groans,
 But saints arise and sing;
 They are the ransomed of the Lord,
 And He their God and King.
Rev. Benjamin Beddome. (1717-1795.)

1451 "The great day of His wrath is come." L. M.
Luke xxi. Rev. xx. 11-15. Dan. vii. 9-28.

1 THAT day of wrath, that dreadful day,
 When heaven and earth shall pass away,
 What power shall be the sinner's stay?
 How shall he meet that dreadful day?

2 When, shrivelling like a parchéd scroll,
 The flaming heavens together roll;
 When, louder yet, and yet more dread,
 Swells the high trump that wakes the dead:

3 O on that day, that wrathful day,
 When man to judgment wakes from clay,
 Be thou, O Christ, the sinner's stay,
 Though heaven and earth shall pass away.
Thomas of Celano.
Tr. by Sir Walter Scott. (1771-1832.)

1452 "The great and terrible day of the Lord." L. M.
Mat. xxv. 31-46. Rev. vi. Isa. xiii. 1 14.

1 THAT fearful day, that day of dread,
 When Thou shalt judge the quick and dead,
 O God, I shudder to foresee
 The awful things which then shall be.

2 When Thou shalt come, Thine angels round,
 With legions, and with trumpet sound,
 O Saviour, grant me in the air
 With all Thy saints to meet Thee there.

3 Weep, O my soul, ere that great day,
 When God shall shine in plain array;
 O weep thy sin, that thou mayst be
 In that severest judgment free.

4 O Christ, forgive, remit, protect,
 And set Thy servant with the elect,
 That I may hear the voice that calls
 The righteous to Thy heavenly halls.
Theodore of the Studium. (750-825.)
Tr. by Rev. John M. Neale. (1818-1866.)

"The judgment of the great day."

1453 "Behold, He cometh with clouds." 8. 7. 4.
Mat. xxiv. 29–51. Rev. xx. 11–15. Isa. lxiii.

1 Lo, He comes, with clouds descending,
    Once for favored sinners slain;
    Thousand thousand saints attending
    Swell the triumph of His train:
        Hallelujah!
    God appears on earth to reign.

2 Every eye shall now behold Him,
    Robed in dreadful majesty;
    Those who set at naught and sold Him,
    Pierced and nailed Him to the tree,
        Deeply wailing,
    Shall the true Messiah see.

3 All the tokens of His passion
    Still His dazzling body bears,
    Cause of endless exultation
    To His ransomed worshippers;
        With what rapture
    Gaze we on those glorious scars!

4 Yea, amen; let all adore Thee,
    High on Thine eternal throne:
    Saviour, take the power and glory,
    Claim the kingdom for Thine own.
        O come quickly;
    Hallelujah! come, Lord, come!

Rev. Charles Wesley. (1706–1788.)
Alt. by Rev. Martin Madan. (1726–1790.)

1454 "He that shall come will come." L. M.
1 Thes. iv. 13–18. Rev. i. 1–7. Ps. ii.

1 THE Lord will come, the earth shall quake,
    The hills their fixéd seat forsake,
    And, withering from the vault of night,
    The stars withdraw their feeble light.

2 The Lord will come, but not the same
    As once in lowly form He came,
    A silent Lamb to slaughter led,
    The bruised, the suffering, and the dead.

3 The Lord will come, a dreadful form,
    With wreath of flame and robe of storm,
    On cherub wings, and wings of wind,
    Anointed Judge of human kind.

4 Can this be He who wont to stray
    A pilgrim on the world's highway,
    By power oppressed, and mocked by pride?
    O God, is this the Crucified?

5 Go, tyrants, to the rocks complain;
    Go, seek the mountain's cleft in vain;
    But faith, victorious o'er the tomb,
    Shall sing for joy, "The Lord is come."

Bp. Reginald Heber. (1783–1826.)

1455 "He cometh to judge the earth." 8. 7. 4.
Zeph. i. Isa. xliii. 1–13. Heb. xii. 25–29.

1 Lo, the mighty God appearing,
    From on high Jehovah speaks;
    Eastern lands the summons hearing,
    O'er the west His thunder breaks:
        Earth beholds Him;
    Universal nature shakes.

2 To the heavens His voice ascending,
    To the earth beneath He cries:
    "Souls immortal, now descending,
    Let the sleeping dust arise!
        Rise to judgment;
    Let my throne adorn the skies!

3 "Gather first my saints around me,
    Those who to my covenant stood;
    Those who humbly sought and found me,
    Through the dying Saviour's blood:
        Blest Redeemer!
    Dearest sacrifice to God!"

4 Now the heavens on high adore Him,
    And His righteousness declare;
    Sinners perish from before Him,
    But His saints His mercy share:
        Just His judgment;
    God Himself, the Judge, is there!

Rev. William Goode. (1762–1816.)

1456 "At that day ye shall ask in my name." L. M.
Luke ii. 1–12. Rev. vi. Ps. xciv.

1 WHEN Jesus came to earth of old,
    He came in weakness and in woe;
    He wore no form of angel mould,
    But took our nature, poor and low.
    But when He cometh back once more,
    There shall be set the great white throne,
    And earth and heaven shall flee before
    The face of Him that sits thereon.

2 O Son of God, in glory crowned,
    The Judge ordained of quick and dead;
    O Son of Man, so pitying found
    For all the tears Thy people shed,
    Be with us in this darkened place,
    This weary, restless, dangerous night;
    And teach, O teach us by Thy grace
    To struggle onward into light!

3 Lord, ere the last dread trump be heard,
    And ere before Thy face we stand,
    Look Thou on each accusing word,
    And blot it with Thy bleeding hand;
    And by the love that brought Thee here,
    And by the cross and by the grave,
    Give perfect love for conscious fear,
    And in the day of judgment save.

Mrs. Cecil F. Alexander. (1823–.)

"With white robes, and palms in their hands."

1457 " Arrayed in fine linen, clean and white." 7.
Rev. vii. 13–17. Heb. xi. Isa. lx. 19–22.

1 WHAT are these arrayed in white,
  Brighter than the noonday sun;
Foremost of the sons of light,
  Nearest the eternal throne?
These are they that bore the cross,
  Nobly for their Master stood;
Sufferers in His righteous cause,
  Followers of their Lord and God.

2 Out of great distress they came;
  Washed their robes by faith, below,
In the blood of Christ, the Lamb,
  Blood that washes white as snow:
Therefore are they next the throne,
  Serve their Maker day and night;
God resides among His own,
  God doth in His saints delight.

3 More than conquerors at last,
  Here they find their trials o'er;
They have all their sufferings passed,
  Hunger now and thirst no more.
He that on the throne doth reign,
  Them the Lamb shall always feed;
With the tree of life sustain,
  To the living fountains lead.

Rev. Charles Wesley. (1708-1788.)

1459 " Before the presence of His glory." 7.
Rev. vii. 9–12. Isa. li. 1–16. Jer. xxxi. 1–14.

1 PALMS of glory, raiment bright,
  Crowns that never fade away,
Gird and deck the saints in light,
  Priests, and kings, and conquerors they:
Yet the conquerors bring their palms
  To the Lamb amidst the throne,
And proclaim, in joyful psalms,
  Victory through His cross alone.

2 Kings for harps their crowns resign,
  Crying, as they strike the chords,
" Take the kingdom, it is Thine,
  King of kings, and Lord of lords !"
Round the altar, priests confess,
  If their robes are white as snow,
'T was the Saviour's righteousness,
  And His blood, that made them so.

3 Who were these? On earth they dwelt,
  Sinners once of Adam's race;
Guilt, and fear, and suffering felt,
  But were saved by sovereign grace.
They were mortal, too, like us;
  Ah, when we like them must die,
May our souls, translated thus,
  Triumph, reign, and shine on high.

James Montgomery. (1771-1854.)

1458 " Ten thousand times ten thousand." 7. 6. 8.
Rev. v. Isa. xxxv. Ps. lxviii. 17–35.

1 TEN thousand times ten thousand,
  In sparkling raiment bright,
The armies of the ransomed saints
  Throng up the steeps of light.
'T is finished, all is finished,
  Their fight with death and sin:
Fling open wide the golden gates,
  And let the victors in.

2 What rush of hallelujahs
  Fills all the earth and sky;
What ringing of a thousand harps
  Bespeaks the triumph nigh !
O day, for which creation
  And all its tribes were made ;
O joy, for all its former woes
  A thousand fold repaid !

3 O then what raptured greetings
  On Canaan's happy shore ;
What knitting severed friendships up,
  Where partings are no more !
Then eyes with joy shall sparkle
  That brimmed with tears of late;
Orphans no longer fatherless,
  Nor widows desolate.

Rev. Henry Alford. (1810-1871.)

1460 " Priests of God and of Christ." 7. 6. 7.
Rev. xiv. 1–13. Isa. xlix. 5–16. Ps. xxiii.

1 BLESSED are the dead who die
  In Christ, their glorious Lord ;
They ascend beyond the sky,
  And gain their great reward :
Conquerors in the final hour,
  Death their latest foe o'ercome ;
Safe beyond the tempter's power,
  In heaven, their happy home.

2 They shall never hunger more,
  Nor ever thirst again ;
All their sufferings now are o'er,
  And all their grief and pain.
Now before the throne they stand,
  Clothed in robes of purest white ;
Palms of victory in their hand,
  With all the saints in light.

3 Where the living waters flow
  The Lamb shall gently lead ;
They shall higher raptures know,
  On heavenly manna feed.
God shall wipe away their tears,
  Filled with bliss, their bliss prolong ;
Each a crown of victory wears,
  And sings the victor's song.

Benjamin Gough. (1805-.)

"And they sung a new song."

1461 "The voice of a great multitude." 8. 7.
Rev. xix. 1-10.   Mat. xix. 27-30.   Isa. xxxv.

1 HARK, the sound of holy voices,
   Chanting at the crystal sea:
   Hallelujah, hallelujah,
   Hallelujah, Lord, to Thee!

2 Multitude, which none can number,
   Like the stars in glory stand,
   Clothed in white apparel, holding
   Palms of victory in their hand.

3 They have come from tribulation,
   And have washed their robes in blood,
   Washed them in the blood of Jesus;
   Tried they were, and firm they stood.

4 Gladly, Lord, with Thee they suffered,
   Gladly, Lord, with Thee they died;
   And by death to life immortal
   They were born and glorified.

5 Now they reign in heavenly glory,
   Now they walk in golden light;
   Now they drink, as from a river,
   Holy bliss and infinite.
   Bp. Christopher Wordsworth. (1807-.)

1462 "What are these . . . in white robes?" 7.
Rev. vii. 13-17.   Heb. xi. 32-40.   Job v. 18-27.

1 WHAT are these in bright array,
   This innumerable throng,
   Round the altar night and day,
   Hymning one triumphant song?
   "Worthy is the Lamb, once slain,
   Blessing, honor, glory, power,
   Wisdom, riches, to obtain,
   New dominion every hour."

2 These through fiery trials trod;
   These from great afflictions came;
   Now, before the throne of God,
   Sealed with His almighty name,
   Clad in raiment pure and white,
   Victor palms in every hand,
   Through their dear Redeemer's might,
   More than conquerors they stand.

3 Hunger, thirst, disease, unknown,
   On immortal fruits they feed;
   Them the Lamb amidst the throne
   Shall to living fountains lead.
   Joy and gladness banish sighs,
   Perfect love dispels all fear,
   And forever from their eyes
   God shall wipe away the tear.
   James Montgomery. (1771-1854.)

1463 "Everlasting joy shall be upon their head." 7.
Isa. lx.   Rev. xxi. 1-4.   Heb. iv.

1 HIGH in yonder realms of light
   Dwell the raptured saints above,
   Far beyond our feeble sight,
   Happy in Immanuel's love.

2 Pilgrims in this vale of tears,
   Once they knew, like us below,
   Gloomy doubts, distressing fears,
   Torturing pain, and heavy woe.

3 Happy spirits, ye are fled
   Where no grief can entrance find;
   Lulled to rest the aching head,
   Soothed the anguish of the mind.

4 All is tranquil and serene,
   Calm and undisturbed repose;
   There no cloud can intervene,
   There no angry tempest blows.

5 Every tear is wiped away,
   Sighs no more shall heave the breast;
   Night is lost in endless day,
   Sorrow in eternal rest.
   Rev. Thomas Raffles. (1788-1853)

1464 "The song of songs." L. M.
Rev. v. 11-14.   Isa. li. 1-11.   Ps. cxxvi.

1 HARK, how the choral song of heaven
   Swells, full of peace and joy, above!
   Hark, how they strike their golden harps,
   And raise the tuneful notes of love!

2 No anxious care nor thrilling grief,
   No deep despair nor gloomy woe,
   They feel, while high their lofty strains
   In noblest, sweetest concord flow.

3 When shall we join the heavenly host,
   Who sing Immanuel's praise on high,
   And leave behind our fears and doubts,
   To swell the chorus of the sky?
   Robert S. McAll. 1812.

1465 "Thanksgiving, and the voice of melody." S. M.
Rev. xiv.   Jer. xxxi. 1-14.   John xvi. 16.

1 HARK, hark the voice of praise
   Around Jehovah's throne!
   Songs of celestial joy they raise,
   To mortal lips unknown.

2 In shining robes they stand
   Upon the crystal sea;
   The harps of God are in their hand,
   And all is ecstasy.

3 O for an angel's love,
   A seraph's soaring wing,
   To sing, with thousand saints above,
   The triumphs of our King!
   Author unknown.

"A better country, that is, a heavenly."

1466 "Thy God bringeth thee into a good land." 7. 6.
Rev. xxi. John xi. 11-26. Deu. viii. 7-10.

1 THERE is a land immortal,
　The beautiful of lands;
Beside its ancient portal
　A silent sentry stands:
He only can undo it,
　And open wide the door;
And mortals who pass through it
　Are mortal nevermore.

2 Though dark and drear the passage
　That leadeth to the gate,
Yet grace comes with the message
　To souls that watch and wait;
And at the time appointed
　A messenger comes down,
And leads the Lord's anointed
　From cross to glory's crown.

3 Their sighs are lost in singing,
　They're blessèd in their tears;
Their journey heavenward winging,
　They leave on earth their fears.
Death like an angel seemeth:
　"We welcome thee!" they cry;
Their face with glory beameth,
　'Tis life for them to die!
　　　　　　　Thomas Mackellar. (1812-.)

1467 "The holy city, new Jerusalem." 7. 6.
Rev. xxii. 1 John iii. 2. Isa. xxxiii. 20.

1 THERE is a holy city,
　A happy world above,
Beyond the starry regions,
　Built by the God of love;
An everlasting temple,
　And saints arrayed in white
There serve their great Redeemer,
　And dwell with Him in light.

2 The meanest child of glory
　Outshines the radiant sun;
But who can speak the splendor
　Of that eternal throne
Where Jesus sits exalted,
　In God-like majesty?
The elders fall before Him,
　The angels bend the knee;

3 The hosts of saints around Him
　Proclaim His work of grace;
The patriarchs and prophets,
　And all the godly race,
Who speak of fiery trials
　And tortures on their way,
They came from tribulation
　To everlasting day.
　　　　　　　Author unknown.

1468 "A quiet habitation." 6.
Rev. vii. 9-17. Heb. xii. 18-24. Ps. cvii. 31-36.

1 THERE is a blessèd home
　Beyond this land of woe,
Where trials never come,
　Nor tears of sorrow flow;
Where faith is lost in sight,
　And patient hope is crowned,
And everlasting light
　Its glory throws around.

2 There is a land of peace;
　Good angels know it well;
Glad songs that never cease
　Within its portals swell;
Around its glorious throne
　Ten thousand saints adore
Christ, with the Father one,
　And Spirit, evermore.

3 O joy all joys beyond,
　To see the Lamb who died,
And count each sacred wound
　In hands and feet and side;
To give to Him the praise
　Of every triumph won,
And sing through endless days
　The great things He hath done!
　　　　　　Rev. Sir Henry W. Baker. (1821-1877.)

1469 "Them that had gotten the victory." 7.
Rev. v. 11-14. 1 Cor. xv. 52-58. Isa. xxxv.

1 LIFT your eyes of faith, and see
Saints and angels joined in one;
What a countless company
Stand before yon dazzling throne.
Each before his Saviour stands,
All in milk-white robes arrayed;
Palms they carry in their hands,
Crowns of glory on their head.

2 Saints, begin the endless song,
Cry aloud, in heavenly lays;
Glory doth to God belong,
God, the glorious Saviour, praise.
All salvation from Him came,
Him who reigns enthroned on high;
Glory to the bleeding Lamb,
Let the morning stars reply.

3 Angel powers the throne surround;
Next the saints in glory they;
Lulled with the transporting sound,
They their silent homage pay;
Prostrate on their face, before
God and His Messiah fall;
Then in hymns of praise adore,
Shout the Lamb that died for all.
　　　　　　Rev. Charles Wesley. (1708-1788.)

"A better country, that is, a heavenly."

1470 "They are without fault before the throne." **8. 6.**
Mat. v. 3-9.   Rev. xxii.   Ps. xxiv.

1 THERE is a dwelling-place above ;
  Thither to meet the God of love
  The poor in spirit go.
  There is a paradise of rest ;
  For contrite hearts and souls distrest
  Its streams of comfort flow.

2 There is a goodly heritage,
  Where earthly passions cease to rage ;
  The meek that haven gain.
  There is a board where they who pine,
  Hungry, athirst, for grace divine,
  May feast, nor crave again.

3 There is a voice to mercy true ;
  To them who mercy's path pursue
  That voice shall bliss impart.
  There is a sight from man concealed ;
  That sight, the face of God revealed,
  Shall bless the pure in heart.

4 There is a name in heaven bestowed ;
  That name, which hails them sons of God,
  The friends of peace shall know.
  There is a kingdom in the sky,
  Where they shall reign with God on high
  Who serve Him best below.

  Bp. Richard Mant. (1776-1848.)

1471 " Let the saints be joyful in glory." **C. M.**
Isa. ii. 3-5.   Ps. lxxxvii.   Heb. xi. 1-16.

1 COME, let us join our friends above
  That have obtained the prize,
  And on the eagle wings of love
  To joys celestial rise.

2 Let all the saints terrestrial sing
  With those to glory gone ;
  For all the servants of our King,
  In earth and heaven, are one.

3 One family we dwell in Him,
  One church above, beneath,
  Though now divided by the stream,
  The narrow stream, of death.

4 One army of the living God,
  To His command we bow ;
  Part of His host have crossed the flood,
  And part are crossing now.

5 His militant embodied host,
  With wishful looks we stand,
  And long to see that happy coast,
  And reach the heavenly land.

  Rev. Charles Wesley. (1708-1788.)

1472 " Theirs is the kingdom of heaven." **C. M.**
1 Cor. ii. 9-12.   Isa. xxxiii. 13-24.   Ps. xv.

1 NOR eye has seen, nor ear has heard,
  Nor sense nor reason known,
  What joys the Father has prepared
  For those that love the Son.

2 But the good Spirit of the Lord
  Reveals a heaven to come ;
  The beams of glory in his word
  Allure and guide us home.

3 Pure are the joys above the sky,
  And all the region peace ;
  No wanton lips, nor envious eye,
  Can see or taste the bliss.

4 Those holy gates forever bar
  Pollution, sin, and shame ;
  None shall obtain admittance there
  But followers of the Lamb.

  Rev. Isaac Watts. (1674-1748.)

1473 " A house not made with hands." **S. M.**
2 Cor. v. 1-9.   Heb. iv.   Ps. cxxi.

1 WE know, by faith we know,
  If this vile house of clay,
  This tabernacle, sink below,
  In ruinous decay,

2 We have a house above,
  Not made with mortal hands ;
  And firm as our Redeemer's love
  That heavenly fabric stands.

3 It stands securely high,
  Indissolubly sure ;
  Our glorious mansion in the sky
  Shall evermore endure.

  Rev. Charles Wesley.

1474 " There remaineth, therefore, a rest." **S. M.**
Isa. xl.   Mat. xxv. 34-40.   Heb. xii. 22-24.

1 COME to the land of peace,
  From shadows come away,
  Where all the sounds of weeping cease,
  And storms no more have sway.

2 Fear hath no dwelling here,
  But pure repose and love
  Breathe through the bright, celestial air
  The spirit of the dove.

3 Come to the bright and blest,
  Gathered from every land ;
  For here thy soul shall find its rest,
  Amid the shining band.

4 In this divine abode
  Change leaves no saddening trace ;
  Come, trusting spirit, to thy God,
  Thy holy resting-place.

  Author unknown.

"A better country, that is, a heavenly."

1475 "Ye shall find rest for your souls." 7, 6.
James v. 1-8.   1 Cor. xv. 24-28.   Isa. xxxv.

1 THE world is very evil,
    The times are waxing late;
    Be sober and keep vigil,
    The Judge is at the gate:
    The Judge that comes in mercy,
    The Judge that comes with might,
    To terminate the evil,
    To diadem the right.

2 And when the Sole-Begotten
    Shall render up once more
    The kingdom to the Father,
    Whose own it was before,
    Then glory yet unheard of
    Shall shed abroad its ray,
    Resolving all enigmas,
    An endless Sabbath day;

3 The peace of all the faithful,
    The calm of all the blest:
    Inviolate, unvaried,
    Divinest, sweetest, best:
    Yes, peace, for war is needless;
    Yes, calm, for storm is past;
    And goal from finished labor,
    And anchorage at last.
              Bernard of Cluny. c. 1145.
        Tr. by Rev. John M. Neale. (1818-1866.)

1477 "They shall run and not be weary." 8, 7.
Isa. lx.   Zech. ii.   Rev. xxi. 23-27.

1 HEAR what God, the Lord, hath spoken:
    O my people, faint and few,
    Comfortless, afflicted, broken,
    Fair abodes I build for you!
    Themes of heartfelt tribulation
    Shall no more perplex your ways;
    You shall name your walls "Salvation,"
    And your gates shall all be "Praise."

2 There, like streams that feed the garden,
    Pleasures without end shall flow:
    For the Lord, your faith rewarding,
    All His bounty shall bestow.
    Still in undisturbed possession,
    Peace and righteousness shall reign;
    Never shall you feel oppression,
    Hear the voice of war again.

3 Ye, no more your suns descending,
    Waning moons no more shall see,
    But your griefs, forever ending,
    Find eternal noon in me.
    God shall rise, and, shining o'er you,
    Change to day the gloom of night;
    He, the Lord, shall be your glory,
    God, your everlasting Light.
                        William Cowper. (1731-1800.)

1476 "Sorrow and sighing shall flee away." C. M.
Isa. xxxiii. 15-24.   Ps. xxxvi. 5-10.   Heb. iv.

1 THERE is an hour of peaceful rest,
    To mourning wanderers given;
    There is a joy for souls distressed,
    A balm for every wounded breast,
    'T is found above, in heaven.

2 There is a home for weary souls
    By sin and sorrow driven,
    When tossed on life's tempestuous shoals,
    Where storms arise and ocean rolls,
    And all is drear: 't is heaven.

3 There faith lifts up the tearless eye,
    To brighter prospects given;
    And views the tempest passing by,
    The evening shadows quickly fly,
    And all serene in heaven.

4 There fragrant flowers immortal bloom,
    And joys supreme are given;
    There rays divine disperse the gloom;
    Beyond the confines of the tomb
    Appears the dawn of heaven.
               Rev. William B. Tappan. (1794-1849.)

1478 "The shadow of a great rock." L. M.
John xiv. 1-12.   Rev. xxii.   Deu. viii. 1-10.

1 LORD, Thou wilt bring the joyful day;
    Beyond earth's weariness and pains
    Thou hast a mansion far away,
    Where, for Thine own, a rest remains.

2 No sun there climbs the morning sky,
    There never falls the shade of night;
    God and the Lamb, forever nigh,
    O'er all shed everlasting light.

3 The bow of mercy spans the throne,
    Emblem of love and goodness there;
    While notes, to mortals all unknown,
    Float on the calm, celestial air.

4 Around the throne bright legions stand,
    Redeemed by blood from sin and hell;
    And shining forms, an angel band,
    The mighty chorus join to swell.

5 There, Lord, Thy way-worn saints shall find
    The bliss for which they longed before;
    And holiest sympathies shall bind
    Thine own to Thee for evermore.
                    Rev. Ray Palmer. (1808-.)

"A better country, that is a heavenly."

1479 "Here have we no continuing city." 7. 6.
Ps. cii. Mat. xxv. 1–23. Rev. xxi. 1–7.

1 BRIEF life is here our portion,
 Brief sorrow, short-lived care ;
The life that knows no ending,
 The tearless life, is there.
O happy retribution,
 Short toil, eternal rest :
For mortals and for sinners
 A mansion with the blest.

2 And now we fight the battle,
 But then shall wear the crown
Of full and everlasting
 And passionless renown.
But He whom now we trust in
 Shall then be seen and known ;
And they that know and see Him
 Shall have Him for their own.

3 The morning shall awaken,
 The shadows shall decay,
And each true-hearted servant
 Shall shine as doth the day.
There God, our King and Portion,
 In fulness of His grace,
Shall we behold forever,
 And worship face to face.

Bernard of Cluny. c. 1145.
Tr. by Rev. John M. Neale. (1818–1866.)

1480 "When a few years are come." S. M.
Gen. xlvii. 7–10. Job xiv. James iv. 13–15.

1 A FEW more years shall roll,
 A few more seasons come,
And we shall be with those that rest
 Asleep within the tomb.

2 A few more storms shall beat
 On this wild, rocky shore,
And we shall be where tempests cease,
 And surges swell no more.

3 A few more struggles here,
 A few more partings o'er,
A few more toils, a few more tears,
 And we shall weep no more.

4 A few more Sabbaths here
 Shall cheer us on our way,
And we shall reach the endless rest,
 Th' eternal Sabbath-day.

5 'T is but a little while,
 And He shall come again,
Who died that we might live, who lives
 That we with Him may reign.

Rev. Horatius Bonar. (1808–.)

1481 "At evening time it shall be light." C. M.
Zech. xiv. Gen. ix. 8–17. 1 Cor. xv. 51–58.

1 WE journey through a vale of tears,
 By many a cloud o'ercast ;
And worldly cares and worldly fears
 Go with us to the last.
Not to the last ! Thy word hath said,
 Could we but read aright,
Poor pilgrim, lift in hope thy head ;
 At eve it shall be light !

2 Though earth-born shadows now may
  shroud
 Thy thorny path awhile,
God's blessed word can part each cloud,
 And bid the sunshine smile.
Only believe, in living faith,
 His love and power divine ;
And ere thy sun shall set in death
 His light shall round thee shine.

3 When tempest clouds are dark on high,
 His bow of love and peace
Shines sweetly in the vaulted sky,
 A pledge that storms shall cease.
Hold on thy way, with hope unchilled,
 By faith, and not by sight,
And thou shalt own His word fulfilled,
 At eve it shall be light.

Bernard Barton. (1784–1849.)

1482 "I will bring them again to their folds." C. M.
John x. Eze. xxxiv. 15. Isa. xxxiii. 17.

1 THERE is a fold whence none can stray,
 And pastures ever green,
Where sultry sun, or stormy day,
 Or night, is never seen.

2 Far up the everlasting hills,
 In God's own light, it lies ;
His smile its vast dimension fills
 With joy that never dies.

Bp. John East. 1836.

1483 "Sojourners, as were all our fathers." L. M.
Heb. xiii. 14, 15. Ps. xci. Isa. xxvi. 1–12.

1 WE'VE no abiding city here :
 Sad truth, were this to be our home ;
But let the thought our spirits cheer,
 We seek a city yet to come.

2 We've no abiding city here,
 We seek a city out of sight :
Zion its name, the Lord is there;
 It shines with everlasting light.

3 Zion ! Jehovah is her Strength !
 Secure she smiles at all her foes ;
And weary travellers at length
 Within her sacred walls repose.

Rev. Thomas Kelly. (1769–1855.)

"A better country, that is a heavenly."

1484 Ps. cxliii. "They seek a country." Heb. xii. 18-24. Rev. xxi. **7, 6.**

1 FOR thee, O dear, dear country,
   Mine eyes their vigils keep;
For very love, beholding
   Thy happy name, they weep.
The mention of thy glory
   Is unction to the breast,
And medicine in sickness,
   And love, and life, and rest.

2 The cross is all thy splendor,
   The Crucified thy praise;
His laud and benediction
   Thy ransomed people raise;
And all thine endless leisure
   In sweetest accents sings
The ill that was thy merit,
   The wealth that is thy King's.

3 With jaspers glow thy bulwarks,
   Thy streets with emeralds blaze;
The sardius and the topaz
   Unite in thee their rays;
Thine ageless walls are bonded
   With amethyst unpriced;
Thy saints build up its fabric,
   And the Corner-stone is Christ.

   Bernard of Cluny. c. 1145.
   Tr. by Rev. John M. Neale. (1818-1866.)

1485 Isa. xxxiii. 17. "The land that is very far off." Phil. iii. 20. Rev. xxii. **C. M.**

1 FAR from these narrow scenes of night,
   Unbounded glories rise,
And realms of infinite delight,
   Unknown to mortal eyes.

2 Fair distant land, could mortal eyes
   But half its joys explore,
How would our spirits long to rise,
   And dwell on earth no more!

3 No cloud those blissful regions know,
   Forever bright and fair;
For sin, the source of mortal woe,
   Can never enter there.

4 O may the heavenly prospect fire
   Our hearts with ardent love,
Till wings of faith and strong desire
   Bear every thought above.

5 Prepare us, Lord, by grace divine,
   For Thy bright courts on high;
Then bid our spirits rise and join
   The chorus of the sky.

   Miss Anne Steele. (1717-1778.)

1486 Ps. xlviii. "The glory of God did lighten it." Phil. i. 20-23. John xvii. 20-26. **S. M.**

1 OUR glorious home above,
   The city of our God,
The resting-place of peace and love,
   The pilgrim's sweet abode:

2 O for an angel's wing
   To soar above the skies,
And join the angelic choir who sing
   Their hallowed symphonies!

3 Pure mansions of the blest,
   Prepared by Jesus' hand,
That all His own may sweetly rest
   Safe in Emmanuel's land.

4 May each we love be there,
   From death and darkness free;
Our joy unspeakable to share
   Throughout eternity.

   Rev. D. T. K. Drummond. 1850.

1487 2 Sam. xii. 16-23. "The kingdom of God is nigh at hand." Luke xvii. 21. Rom. xiv. **C. M.**

1 As distant lands beyond the sea,
   When friends go hence, draw nigh,
So heaven, when friends have thither gone,
   Draws nearer from the sky.

2 And as those lands the dearer grow
   When friends are long away,
So heaven itself, through loved ones dear,
   Grows dearer day by day.

3 Heaven is not far from those who see
   With the pure spirit's sight,
But near, and in the very heart
   Of those who see aright.

   Carlos D. Stuart. (1820-1862.)

1488 Ps. cxxvi. "A peaceable habitation." Jer. xxxi. 1-14. Rev. vii. 9-17. **C. M.**

1 THERE is an hour of hallowed peace
   For those with cares distressed,
When sighs and sorrowing tears shall cease,
   And all be hushed to rest.

2 'T is then the soul is freed from fears
   And doubts, which here annoy;
And they who oft have sown in tears
   Shall reap again in joy.

3 There is a home of sweet repose,
   Where storms assail no more;
The stream of endless pleasure flows,
   On that celestial shore.

4 There smiling peace with love appears,
   And bliss without alloy;
There they who once have sown in tears
   Now reap eternal joy.

   Rev. William B. Tappan. (1794-1840.)

"A better country, that is a heavenly."

1489 "And the city was pure gold." 7, 6.
Rev. xxi. 9-24. Mat. xix. 27-30. Isa. lx.

1 JERUSALEM, the golden,
   With milk and honey blest,
Beneath thy contemplation
   Sink heart and voice opprest.
I know not, O I know not,
   What social joys are there;
What radiancy of glory,
   What light beyond compare.

2 They stand, those halls of Zion,
   All jubilant with song,
And bright with many an angel,
   And all the martyr throng.
The Prince is ever in them,
   The daylight is serene;
The pastures of the blessed
   Are decked in glorious sheen.

3 There is the throne of David,
   And there, from care released,
The shout of them that triumph,
   The song of them that feast;
And they who, with their Leader,
   Have conquered in the fight
Forever and forever
   Are clad in robes of white.

Bernard of Cluny.   c. 1145.
Tr. by Rev. John M. Neale.   (1818-1866.)

1490 "The Lamb is the light thereof." 8. 6.
Ps. xix. 1-9.   Isa. vi. 1-7.   Rev. iv.

1 SINCE o'er Thy footstool here below
   Such radiant gems are strown,
O what magnificence must glow,
   Great God, about Thy throne!
So brilliant here these drops of light,
There the full ocean rolls, how bright!

2 If night's blue curtain of the sky,
   With thousand stars inwrought,
Hung, like a royal canopy,
   With glittering diamonds fraught,
Be, Lord, Thy temple's outer vail,
What splendor at the shrine must dwell!

3 The dazzling sun, at noontide hour,
   Forth from his flaming vase
Flinging o'er earth the golden shower,
   Till vale and mountain blaze,
But shows, O Lord, one beam of Thine:
What, then, the day where Thou dost shine!

4 O how shall these dim eyes endure
   That noon of living rays!
Or how our spirits, so impure,
   Upon Thy glory gaze?
Anoint, O Lord, anoint our sight,
And fit us for that world of light.

Rev. William A. Muhlenberg.   (1796-1877.)

1491 "There shall be no night there." C. M.
Ps. xc.   Job iii. 17-19.   2 Pet. iii. 8-13.

1 WHEN brighter suns and milder skies
   Proclaim the opening year,
What various sounds of joy arise,
   What prospects bright appear!

2 Earth and her thousand voices give
   Their thousand notes of praise;
And all that by His mercy live
   To God their offering raise.

3 Thus, like the morning, calm and clear,
   That saw the Saviour rise,
The spring of heaven's eternal year
   Shall dawn on earth and skies.

4 No winter there, no shades of night,
   Obscure those mansions blest,
Where, in the happy fields of light,
   The weary are at rest.

Rev. William B. O. Peabody.   (1799-1847.)

1492 "The former things are passed away." S. M.
Rev. xxii.   John vi. 47-58.   Isa. xxxv.

1 THERE is no night in heaven;
   In that blest world above,
Work never can bring weariness,
   For work itself is love.

2 There is no grief in heaven;
   For life is one glad day,
And tears are of those former things
   Which all have passed away.

3 There is no sin in heaven;
   Behold that blessed throng!
All holy is their spotless robe,
   All holy is their song.

4 There is no death in heaven;
   But, when the Christian dies,
The angels wait his parting soul,
   And waft it to the skies.

Francis M. Knollis.   1800.

1493 "The Lord God giveth them light." 9.
Isa. xxxiii. 15-24.   John xiv.   Rev. vii. 9-17.

1 THERE's a land that is fairer than day,
   And by faith we may see it afar;
For the Father waits over the way,
   To prepare us a dwelling-place there.

2 To our bountiful Father above
   We will offer our tribute of praise,
For the glorious gift of His love,
   And the blessings that hallow our days.

3 We shall meet, we shall sing, we shall reign
   In the land where the saved never die;
We shall rest free from sorrow and pain,
   Safe at home in the sweet by and by.

S. F. Bennett.   1873.

"A better country, that is a heavenly."

1494 "He hath glorified thee." 7. 6.
Rev. vii. Heb. xii. 18-24. Eze. xliii. 1-12.

1 JERUSALEM, the glorious,
   The home of the elect,
O dear and future vision
   That eager hearts expect !
E'en now by faith I see thee,
   E'en here thy walls discern ;
To thee my thoughts are kindled,
   And strive and pant and yearn ;

2 New mansion of new people,
   Whom God's own love and light
Promote, increase, make holy,
   Identify, unite.
And there the band of prophets
   United praise ascribes,
And there the twelve-fold chorus
   Of Israel's ransomed tribes ;

3 And there the Sole-Begotten
   Is Lord in regal state ;
He, Judah's mystic Lion,
   He, Lamb immaculate.
O fields that know no sorrow,
   O state that fears no strife ;
O princely bowers, O land of flowers,
   O realm and home of life !
                Bernard of Cluny. c. 1145.
           Tr. by Rev. John M. Neale. (1818-1866.)

1495 "A great multitude ... before the Lamb" L. M.
John xvii. 22-26. Rev. v. Ps. lxviii. 17-35.

1 O FOR a sweet, inspiring ray,
   To animate our feeble strains,
From the bright realms of endless day,
   The blissful realms where Jesus reigns !

2 There, low before His glorious throne,
   Adoring saints and angels fall ;
And with delightful worship own
   His smile their bliss, their heaven, their all.

3 Immortal glories crown His head,
   While tuneful hallelujahs rise,
And love, and joy, and triumph spread
   Through all th' assemblies of the skies.

4 He smiles, and seraphs tune their songs
   To boundless rapture while they gaze ;
Ten thousand thousand joyful tongues
   Resound His everlasting praise.

5 There, all the favorites of the Lamb
   Shall join at last the heavenly choir ;
O may the joy-inspiring theme
   Awake our faith and warm desire !
                Miss Anne Steele. (1717-1778.)

1496 "A land which the Lord thy God careth for." C. M.
Rev. xxii. Eze. xxviii. 24-26. Deu. xxxiv.

1 THERE is a land of pure delight,
   Where saints immortal reign ;
Infinite day excludes the night,
   And pleasures banish pain.

2 There everlasting spring abides,
   And never-withering flowers ;
Death, like a narrow sea, divides
   This heavenly land from ours.

3 Sweet fields, beyond the swelling flood,
   Stand dressed in living green ;
So to the Jews old Canaan stood,
   While Jordan rolled between.

4 But timorous mortals start and shrink
   To cross this narrow sea ;
And linger, shivering on the brink,
   And fear to launch away.

5 O could we make our doubts remove,
   These gloomy doubts that rise,
And see the Canaan that we love,
   With unbeclouded eyes ;

6 Could we but climb where Moses stood,
   And view the landscape o'er,
Not Jordan's stream, nor death's cold flood,
   Should fright us from the shore.
                Rev. Isaac Watts. (1674-1748.)

1497 "Whither the tribes go up." 7. 6. P.
Num. x. 29-36. Isa. xi. Heb. xiii. 8-15.

1 WE are on our journey home,
   Where Christ, our Lord, is gone ;
We shall meet around His throne,
   When He makes His people one,
   ‖: In the new :‖ Jerusalem.

2 We can see that distant home,
   Though clouds rise dark between ;
Faith views the radiant dome,
   And a lustre flashes keen
   ‖: From the new :‖ Jerusalem.

3 O holy, heavenly home,
   O rest eternal there,
When shall the exiles come,
   Where they cease from earthly care,
   ‖: In the new :‖ Jerusalem ?

4 Our hearts are breaking now
   Those mansions fair to see ;
O Lord, Thy heavens bow,
   And raise us up with Thee
   ‖: To the new :‖ Jerusalem.
                Rev. Charles Beecher. (1815-.)

"The city of the living God."

1498 "Ye shall be comforted in Jerusalem."
Rev. xxi. 1 Cor. xv. 1-28. Isa. xxv.   7. 6.

1 JERUSALEM, the only,
  That look'st from heaven below,
In thee is all my glory,
  In me is all my woe.
I ask not for my merit:
  I seek not to deny
My merit is destruction,
  A child of wrath am I.

2 But yet with faith I venture
  And hope upon my way;
For those perennial guerdons
  I labor night and day.
The best and dearest Father,
  Who made me and who saved,
Bore with me in defilement,
  And from defilement laved.

3 When in His strength I struggle,
  For very joy I leap;
When in my sin I totter,
  I weep, or try to weep:
And grace, sweet grace celestial,
  Shall all its love display,
And David's royal Fountain
  Purge every sin away.

Bernard of Cluny. c. 1145.
Tr. by Rev. John M. Neale. (1818-1866.)

1499 "Come and sing in the height of Zion."
Rev. xxii. 1 Cor. xv. 35-57. Isa. xxvi. 1-12.   7. 6.

1 JERUSALEM, exulting
  On that securest shore,
I hope thee, wish thee, sing thee,
  And love thee evermore!
Thy loveliness oppresses
  All human thought and heart;
And none, O peace, O Syon,
  Can sing thee as thou art.

2 O mine, my golden Syon,
  O lovelier far than gold;
With laurel-girt battalions,
  And safe victorious fold!
O sweet and blessèd country,
  Shall I ever see thy face?
O sweet and blessèd country,
  Shall I ever win thy grace?

3 I have the hope within me
  To comfort and to bless;
Shall I ever win the prize itself?
  O tell me, tell me, yes!
Exult, O dust and ashes,
  The Lord shall be thy Part:
His only, His forever,
  Thou shalt be, and thou art.

Bernard of Cluny. c. 1145.
Tr. by Rev. John M. Neale.

1500 "So shall we be ever with the Lord."
John xvii. 20-26. 1 Cor. iii. 9-13. Isa. xii. Ps. xxiii.   10. 11.

1 SOON and forever, such promise our trust,
  Though ashes to ashes, and dust unto dust;
Soon and forever, our union shall be
Made perfect, our glorious Redeemer, in Thee:
When the sins and the sorrows of time shall be o'er,
Its pangs and its partings remembered no more;
Where life cannot fail, and where death cannot sever,
Christians with Christ shall be soon and forever.

2 Soon and forever, the breaking of day
Shall drive all the night clouds of sorrow away;
Soon and forever, we'll see as we're seen,
And learn the deep meaning of things that have been:
When fightings without us, and fears from within,
Shall weary no more in the warfare of sin;
Where tears, and where fears, and where death shall be never,
Christians with Christ shall be soon and forever.

3 Soon and forever the work shall be done,
The warfare accomplished, the victory won;
Soon and forever the soldier lay down
His sword for a harp, and his cross for a crown.
Then droop not in sorrow, despond not in fear,
A glorious to-morrow is brightening and near,
When, blessèd reward of each faithful endeavor,
Christians with Christ shall be soon and forever.

Rev. John S. B. Monsell. (1811-1875.)

Index of First Lines of Hymns.

	Hymn
Abide with me, fast falls the eventide	600
A broken heart, my God, my King!	187
A charge to keep I have	431
A few more years shall roll	1430
A little child the Saviour came	988
A mind at perfect peace with God	780
A Pilgrim through this lonely world	68
A stranger in the world below	443
According to Thy gracious word	306
Again as evening's shadow falls	1171
Again from calm and sweet repose	678
Again our earthly cares we leave	1016
Ah! how shall fallen man	132
Ah, Jesus, let me hear Thy voice	599
Ah, what avails my strife	178
Ah! whither should I go	179
Alas, and did my Saviour bleed	500
Alas! what hourly dangers rise!	407
All glory to God, the Father and Son (Dox.)	1140
All hail the power of Jesus' name!	1071
All is dying; hearts are breaking	1410
All is o'er, the pain, the sorrow	90
All people that on earth do dwell!	1059
All praise to Him of Nazareth!	1219
All praise to Thee, eternal Lord	1116
All praise to Thee, my God, this night	601
All that I was, my sin, my guilt	249
All things are ready, Come	162
Almighty Father of mankind	721
Almighty God of love	1288
Almighty God, Thy word is cast	1191
Almighty Sovereign of the skies!	1339
Alone, yet not alone	525
Although the vine its fruit deny	730
Always with us, always with us	938
Amazing grace, how sweet the sound	788
Am I a soldier of the cross	415
And can it be that I should gain	243
And can my heart aspire so high	529
And canst thou, sinner, slight	155
And did the Holy and the Just	135
And dost Thou say, "Ask what thou wilt?"	291
And is there, Lord, a rest	819
And let this feeble body fail	820
And must I part with all I have	585
And must this body die	1446
And will the great eternal God	1239
And will the Judge descend?	165
And will the offended God again	288
An earthly temple here we raise	1235
Angel! roll the rock away	91
Angels rejoiced and sweetly sung	1037
Another day has passed along	1176
Another six days' work is done	363
Another year, another year	1376
Another year is dawning!	1381
Approach, my soul, the mercy seat	182
Archangels! fold your wings	101
Arise, arise; with joy survey	1344
Arise, my soul, arise	253
Arise, O King of grace, arise	1241
Arise, ye people! and adore	1073
Arm of the Lord, awake, awake	1310
Around the throne of God in heaven	1008
Around Thy grave Lord Jesus	1199
Art thou weary, art thou languid	527
Ascend Thy throne, almighty King	1313
As distant lands beyond the sea	1487

	Hymn
As Jesus died and rose again	1442
Asleep in Jesus, blessed sleep	1431
As panting in the sultry beam	657
As pants the hart for cooling streams	567
As thy day thy strength shall be	771
As when the weary traveller gains	1423
At evening time let there be light	776
Auspicious morning! hail!	1405
Author of faith, Eternal Word	386
Author of good, we rest on Thee	507
Awake and sing the song	1031
Awake, awake, O Zion	1348
Awake, my soul, and with the sun	677
Awake, my soul, in joyful lays	795
Awake, my soul, lift up thine eyes	411
Awake, my soul! stretch every nerve	429
Awake, my soul, to meet the day	676
Awake, my tongue! thy tribute bring	13
Awake, our souls! away our fears!	946
Awake, ye saints, and raise your eyes	1375
Awake, ye saints, awake	1167
Away, my unbelieving fear	741
Awhile in spirit, Lord to Thee	1363
Before Jehovah's awful throne	1064
Before the Lord we bow	1403
Before Thy mercy-seat, O Lord	1019
Begin, my soul! the exalted lay	238
Begin, my tongue, some heavenly theme	220
Begone unbelief, my Saviour is near	781
Behold! a Stranger's at the door!	160
Behold! I come with joy to do	297
Behold! the blind their sight receive	72
Behold, the day is come	1450
Behold the glories of the Lamb	1102
Behold! the lofty sky	896
Behold the Man! how glorious He	78
Behold! the morning sun	898
Behold the Saviour of mankind	85
Behold the sin atoning Lamb	80
Behold the throne of grace!	403
Behold the western evening light!	1426
Behold what wondrous grace	261
Behold where, in the Friend of man	67
Being of beings. God of love	903
Be joyful in God, all ye lands of the earth	1060
Be still, my heart! these anxious cares	769
Be Thou, O God, exalted high	
Be with me, Lord, where'er I go	598
Beyond the glittering starry skies	107
Beyond the hills where suns go down	833
Beyond the smiling and the weeping	845
Beyond where Kidron's waters flow	74
Blessèd are the dead who die	1470
Blessèd are the sons of God	858
Blessèd Fountain! full of grace	589
Blessèd Jesus, ere we part	
Blessèd Saviour, Thee I love	305
Bless, O my Soul! the living God	708
Blest are the humble souls that see	851
Blest are the men whose hearts do move	852
Blest are the pure in heart	307
Blest are the sons of peace	870
Blest be the dear, uniting love	865
Blest be the Father and His love	1122
Blest be the tie that binds	875
Blest be Thy love, dear Lord!	981
Blest Comforter divine!	1048

Index of First Lines of Hymns.

Blest day of God, most calm, most bright	365
Blest hour when mortal man retires	405
Blest is the man whose softening heart	379
Blest is the man whose spirit shares	377
Blest is the man who shuns the place	861
Blest Jesus! come Thou gently down	1038
Blest Trinity, from mortal sight	1121
Blow ye the trumpet — blow!	1354
Bondage and death the cup contains	1259
Bowed with a burden none can weigh save Thee	546
Bread of heaven, on Thee I feed	1216
Bread of the world, in mercy broken	1217
Brief life is here our portion	1479
Bright and joyful is the morn	55
Bright was the guiding star that led	888
Buried in shadows of the night	127
By faith in Christ I walk with God	387
By faith I view my Saviour dying	216
Call Jehovah thy salvation	43
Calm on the listening ear of night	61
Cast thy burden on the Lord	463
Child of sin and sorrow, filled with	170
Children! hear the melting story	1001
Children of light! arise and shine	855
Children of the heavenly King!	1032
Chosen not for good in me	499
Christ, by heavenly hosts adored	1364
Christ for the world we sing	1342
Christian, seek not yet repose	408
Christian, the morn breaks sweetly o'er thee	
Christians, brethren, ere we part	1180
Christ is our Corner-Stone	1236
Christ, of all my hopes the Ground	796
"Christ, the Lord, is risen to-day!"	94
Christ, whose glory fills the skies	673
Church of the ever-living God	848
Come, all harmonious tongues!	1072
Come, all ye saints of God!	1070
Come at the morning hour	938
Come, blessed Spirit, source of light	488
Come, dearest Lord, descend and dwell	1030
Come, divine Immanuel, come	1278
Come, every pious heart	1075
Come, Father, Son, and Holy Ghost	1012
Come, heavy laden one	173
Come hither, all ye weary souls	138
Come, Holy Ghost, all-quickening fire	491
Come, Holy Ghost! in love	1040
Come, Holy Ghost, my soul inspire	207
Come, Holy Ghost! our hearts inspire	959
Come, Holy Spirit, calm my mind	480
Come, Holy Spirit, come	1249
Come, Holy Spirit, heavenly Dove, My	210
Come, Holy Spirit, heavenly Dove, With	1043
Come in, thou blessed of the Lord	868
Come, Jesus, Redeemer! abide Thou	602
Come join, ye saints, with heart and voice	1077
Come, let our voices join to raise	1053
Come, let us join in songs of praise	1098
Come, let us join our cheerful songs	1080
Come, let us join our friends above	1471
Come, let us lift our joyful eyes	1057
Come, let us sing the song of songs	1097
Come, Lord! and tarry not	1321
Come, Lord! and warm each languid heart	1031
Come, Mighty Spirit, penetrate	211
Come, my Redeemer, come	204
Come, my soul, thy suit prepare	551
Come, O Creator — Spirit blest	1045
Come, O my soul, in sacred lays	797
Come, O promised Comforter	958
Come, sacred Spirit, from above	1044
Come, says Jesus' sacred voice	142
Come, see the place where Jesus lies	88
Come, shout aloud the Father's grace	239
Come, sinner, to the gospel feast	154
Come, sinners, to the gospel feast	156
Come, sound His praise abroad	1065
Come, take His offers now	460
Come, Thou almighty King!	1003
Come, Thou desire of all thy saints!	1033
Come, Thou Fount of every blessing	241
Come, Thou high and lofty Lord	1207
Come, Thou long expected Jesus	1333
Come, Thou soul-transforming Spirit	1189
Come to Calvary's holy mountain	137
Come to Jesus, are you lonely	510
Come to the land of peace	1474
Come unto me when shadows darkly gather	471
Come, weary souls with sin distrest	152
Come, we that love the Lord	1049
Come, ye disconsolate	470
Come, ye saints! look here and wonder	96
Come, ye souls by sin afflicted	140
Come, ye that know and fear the Lord!	33
Come, ye that love the Saviour's name	1078
Commit thou all thy griefs	949
Complete in Thee! no work of mine	301
Crown Him with many crowns	1079
Crown His head with endless blessing	1090
Crowns of glory, ever bright	104
Daughter of Zion, awake from thy sadness	1350
Day by day the manna fell	920
Day divine, when sudden streaming	119
Day of terror, day of doom	1449
Dearest of all the names above	112
Dear is the hallowed morn to me	357
Dear is the spot where Christians sleep	1436
Dear Jesus, ever at my side	1003
Dear Lord and Master mine	248
Dear Refuge of my weary soul	523
Dear Saviour, I am Thine	281
Dear Saviour, if these lambs should stray	998
Deathless Spirit, now arise	1428
Deepen the wound Thy hands have made	663
Deep in the dust before Thy throne	133
Delay not, delay not; O sinner draw near	172
Depth of mercy, can there be	176
Descend from heaven, immortal Dove	1419
Did Christ o'er sinners weep	455
Dismiss us with Thy blessing, Lord!	1193
Do not I love Thee, O my Lord?	310
Does the gospel word proclaim	181
Draw near, O Holy Dove, draw near	1211
Dread Jehovah! God of nations!	1371
Dread Sovereign, let my evening song	701
Drooping souls, no longer mourn	459
Dying souls! fast bound in sin	168
Early, my God, without delay	681
Earth has engrossed my love too long	831
Earth has nothing sweet or fair	312
Encompassed with clouds of distress	642
Equip me for the war	628
Ere another Sabbath's close	1172
Ere God had built the mountains	63
Ere the blue heavens were stretched abroad	62
Ere the waning light decay	972
Eternal beam of light divine	612
Eternal Father, strong to save	1210
Eternal Father, Thou hast said	1328
Eternal Father, when to Thee	487
Eternal God! Almighty Cause	2
Eternal Source of every joy!	1388
Eternal Source of joys divine	346
Eternal Spirit, Source of truth	1047
Eternal Spirit, we confess	123
Eternal Sun of Righteousness	475
Eternal Wisdom! Thee we praise	35
Ever fainting with desire	292
Every morning mercies new	916
Exalt the Lord our God	20
Fade, fade each earthly joy	345
Fading, still fading, the last beam	970
Faint not, Christian, though the road	435
Fair shines the morning star	1356
Faith adds new charms to earthly bliss	390
Faith, hope, and charity, these three	391
Faith is a living power from heaven	385
Far down the ages now	853
Far from my heavenly home	817
Far from my thoughts, vain world, be gone	586
Far from these narrow scenes of night	1485
Far from the world, O Lord, I flee	568
Father, at Thy footstool see	1011

292

Index of First Lines of Hymns.

Father! how wide Thy glory shines!	235
Father, I know that all my life	758
Father, in these reveal Thy Son	992
Father of eternal grace	553
Father of heaven, above	1107
Father of heaven, whose love profound	1013
Father of Jesus Christ my Lord	389
Father of love and power	966
Father of love, our Guide and Friend	910
Father of mercies, bow Thine ear	1228
Father of mercies, condescend	1300
Father of mercies, send Thy grace	1265
Father, Son, and Holy Ghost (Dox.)	1134
Father, Son, and Holy Ghost	285
Father, Thy will, not mine, be done	520
Father, to Thee my soul I lift	555
Father! whate'er of earthly bliss	445
Father, who didst fashion me	209
Fear not, I am with thee — O be not dismayed	987
Fear not, poor weary one	506
Fight the good fight with all thy might	438
Firm as the earth, Thy gospel stands	737
Flee as a bird to your mountain	464
Fling out the banner; let it float	1308
For thee, O dear, dear country!	1484
For Thy mercy and Thy grace	1378
For us, O Lord, the year has brought	1400
For what shall I praise Thee, my God and	536
Forever with the Lord	847
Forth from the dark and stormy sky	1144
Forth in Thy name, O Lord, I go	686
Forward! be our watchword	1294
Fount of everlasting love	1258
Fountain of grace, rich, full, and free	256
Fountain of mercy, God of love	1395
Frequent the day of God returns	1155
Friend after friend departs	1417
From all that dwell below the skies	1066
From Calvary a cry was heard	84
From every earthly pleasure	1412
From every stormy wind that blows	940
From Greenland's icy mountains	1291
From ocean unto ocean	1273
From the cross uplifted high	143
Gently, gently lay Thy rod	479
Gently, Lord, O gently lead us	913
Give me the wings of faith to rise	818
Give thanks to God; He reigns above	29
Give to our God immortal praise	1052
Give to the Lord, ye sons of fame	1152
Give to the winds thy fears	950
Giver and Guardian of our sleep	902
Glorious things of thee are spoken	852
Glory be to God on high	1111
Glory to God on high, Let praises	1115
Go forward, Christian soldier	414
Go, labor on; spend and be spent	418
Go, labor on, while it is day	420
Go, preach my gospel, saith the Lord	1223
Go to the grave in all thy glorious prime	1427
God bless our native land!	1276
God calling yet, shall I not hear?	175
God, in His earthly temple, lays	856
God, in the gospel of His Son	892
God, in the high and holy place	40
God is a Spirit just and wise	493
God is for me! Oh how glorious!	728
God is in His holy temple	1142
God is in this and every place	183
God is Love, His mercy brightens	30
God is my strong Salvation	512
God is the name my soul adores	1
God is the Refuge of His saints	41
God moves in a mysterious way	46
God, my King, Thy might confessing	800
God, my Supporter and my Hope	316
God of all consolation	122
God of almighty love	202
God of almighty power!	14
God of mercy and compassion	519
God of mercy, God of love	1369
God of my life, through all its days	222
God of my life, Thy boundless grace	486
God of my life, to Thee I call	521
God of my life, whose gracious power	632
God of my salvation, hear	481
God of our life! Thy various praise	1374
God of our salvation, hear us	1175
God of our salvation, unto Thee	1017
God of that glorious gift of grace	991
God of the morning, at whose voice	672
God of the sunlight-hours, how sad	973
God, that madest earth and heaven	965
God the all-terrible, Thou who ordainest	1370
God with us! O glorious name!	53
God's holy law transgressed	130
Good is the Lord, the heavenly King	1385
Grace, like an uncorrupted seed	262
Grace! 't is a charming sound	233
Gracious Spirit! Dove divine!	490
Granted is the Saviour's prayer	116
Grant me within Thy courts a place	659
Great Father of each perfect gift	1252
Great God, attend while Zion sings	1020
Great God, how infinite art Thou!	4
Great God, indulge my humble claim	318
Great God, the nations of the earth	1315
Great God, this sacred day of Thine	1153
Great God, to Thee my evening song	690
Great God, we sing that mighty hand	1382
Great God, when I approach Thy throne	253
Great Jehovah! we adore Thee (Dox.)	1138
Great King of glory, come	1243
Great Lord of all Thy churches, hear	1247
Great One in Three, Great Three in One	1120
Great Ruler of all nature's frame!	37
Guide me, O Thou great Jehovah!	630
Had I the tongues of Greeks and Jews	393
Hail, morning known among the blest	1160
Hail, my ever blessed Jesus!	239
Hail, sacred truth, whose piercing rays	887
Hail, sovereign love, that first began	237
Hail, thus bright and sacred morn	1164
Hail, Thou God of grace and glory	1248
Hail, Thou once despised Jesus	1095
Hail to the Lord's Anointed	1340
Hail to the Sabbath day	1165
Hail tranquil hour of closing day!	703
Happy is he that fears the Lord	381
Happy the church, thou sacred place	849
Happy the man, who knows	427
Happy the souls to Jesus joined	877
Hark! hark the voice of praise	1465
Hark, how the angels sweetly sing!	1114
Hark! how the choral song of heaven	1464
Hark, my soul, it is the Lord	468
Hark, ten thousand harps and voices	1357
Hark, the distant isles proclaim	1337
Hark, the glad sound! the Saviour comes	54
Hark, the herald angels sing	60
Hark! the judgment-trumpet sounding	1448
Hark, the notes of angels singing	1074
Hark, the song of jubilee	1353
Hark, the sound of holy voices	1461
Hark, the voice of Jesus calling	419
Hark, the voice of love and mercy	86
Hark, what mean those holy voices	58
Hark, what mean those lamentations	1292
Hast thou, within, a care so deep	509
Hasten, Lord, the glorious time	1325
Hasten, Lord, to my release	478
Hasten, sinner, to be wise	166
Have mercy, Lord, on me	482
Have you sinned as none else in the world have	473
He dies! the Friend of sinners dies!	97
He leadeth me, O blessed thought	534
He lives, the Great Redeemer lives	113
He sendeth sun, He sendeth shower	752
He that goeth forth with weeping	428
He that hath made his refuge God	533
He wills that I should holy be	300
He's come, — let every knee be bent	118
Head of the church, whose Spirit fills	1289
Heal us, Immanuel; here we stand	1027
Hear my prayer, O Heavenly Father	706

293

Index of First Lines of Hymns.

Heart of stone! relent, relent	157
Hear what God, the Lord, hath spoken	1477
Hear what the voice from heaven proclaims	1437
Heavenly Father, grant Thy blessing	1178
Heavenly Father, to whose eye	631
Heavenly Shepherd, guide us, feed us	1181
Help, Lord, to whom for help I fly	616
Here at Thy table, Lord, we meet	1222
High in the heavens, eternal God!	27
High in yonder realms of light	1463
Ho, every one that thirsts, draw nigh	136
Holy and reverend is the name	21
Holy as Thou, O Lord, is none	17
Holy Father! hear my cry	206
Holy Ghost! dispel our sadness	1042
Holy Ghost, the Infinite	1041
Holy Ghost! with light divine	208
Holy, holy, holy Lord Be thy	1118
Holy, holy, holy, Lord God Almighty!	1105
Holy, holy, holy Lord God of Hosts	18
Holy Lamb! who Thee receive	287
Holy Spirit, faithful Guide	956
Hosanna to our conquering King!	1119
Hosanna to the living Lord!	1242
How beauteous are their feet	1225
How beauteous on the mountains	1347
How beauteous were the marks divine	64
How blest the righteous when he dies	1421
How blest the sacred tie that binds	879
How can I sink with such a prop	734
How charming is the place	372
How condescending and how kind	65
How dear is the thought that the angels	962
How deep and tranquil is the joy	791
How did my heart rejoice to hear	364
How do Thy mercies close me round	757
How far beyond our mortal sight	810
How firm a foundation, ye saints of the Lord	986
How gentle God's commands	462
How happy every child of grace	442
How heavy is the night	129
How helpless guilty nature lies	128
How honorable is the name	857
How lost was my condition	217
How oft, alas! this wretched heart	453
How pleasant, how divinely fair	359
How pleased and blest was I	889
How precious is the book divine	180
How sad our state by nature is I	131
How shall the sons of men appear	894
How shall the young secure their hearts	1203
How sweet and awful is the place	883
How sweet, how heavenly is the sight	1424
How sweet the hour of closing day	944
How sweet the me'ting lay	320
How sweet the name of Jesus sounds	1032
How sweet to leave the world awhile	70
How sweetly flowed the gospel's sound	1413
How swift the torrent rolls	338
How tedious and tasteless the hours	1408
How vain is all beneath the skies!	3
How wondrous great, how glorious bright	
I am coming to the cross	197
I am thine, O Lord	661
I asked the Lord that I might grow	502
I ask Thee for the daily strength	759
I bless Thee, Lord, for sorrows sent	532
I cannot always trace the way	34
I did Thee wrong, my God	658
I feel within a want	565
I gave my life for thee	461
I have a home above	821
I have entered the valley of blessing so sweet	547
I hear a voice that comes from far	215
I hear the voice of Jesus say	250
I hear the Saviour say	247
I hear the words of love	778
I journey forth rejoicing	835
I know that my Redeemer lives	756
I lay my sins on Jesus	322
I long to behold Him arrayed	811
I love the Lord: He heard my cries	314
I love the sacred book of God	348
I love the volume of Thy Word	350
I love Thy kingdom, Lord!	1,5
I love to steal awhile away	699
I love to tell the story	339
I need Thee, every hour	571
I need Thee, precious Jesus	582
I need Thy presence every passing hour	601
I see the crowd in Pilate's hall	174
I send the joys of earth away	825
I thank Thee, uncreated Sun	327
I want a heart to pray	611
I want a principle within	615
I was a wandering sheep	234
I will love Thee, all my treasure	304
I will sing you a song of that beautiful land	840
I worship Thee, sweet will of God	747
I would commune with Thee, my God	710
I would love Thee, God and Father	317
I would not live alway: I ask not to stay	816
I've found a joy in sorrow	784
I've found the pearl of greatest price	321
If Christ is mine then all is mine	763
If human kindness meets return	1215
If Jesus be my Friend	794
If life in sorrow must be spent	729
I'm a pilgrim, and I'm a stranger	813
I'm but a stranger here	830
Immortal Love, forever full	911
I'm not ashamed to own my Lord	742
I'm weary of straying; O fain would I rest	826
In all extremes, Lord, Thou art still	667
In all my vast concerns with Thee	12
Increase our faith, beloved Lord	1256
Indulgent sovereign of the skies	1257
In every trying hour	517
In evil long I took delight	251
In heavenly love abiding	762
In memory of the Saviour's love	1204
In prayer together let us fall	1367
In sleep's serene oblivion laid	687
In some way or other the Lord will provide	977
Inspirer and hearer of prayer	696
In the Christian's home in glory	832
In the cross of Christ I glory	806
In Thee I put my steadfast trust	716
In the morning hear my voice	689
In the silent midnight watches	169
In the vineyard of our Father	1005
In this calm impressive hour	683
In Thy great name, O Lord, we come	1037
In Thy name, O Lord, assembling	1014
In Thy presence we appear	1015
In time of fear, when trouble's near	513
In time of tribulation	522
In vain the world's alluring smile	655
Is this a fast for me?	1368
It came upon the midnight clear	59
It is not death to die	1415
It is Thy hand, my God	503
Jehovah, God, Thy gracious power	15
Jehovah reigns; He dwells in light	48
Jehovah reigns; His throne is high	42
Jehovah reigns; let all the earth	25
Jerusalem, exulting	1499
Jerusalem! my happy home	836
Jerusalem the glorious	1494
Jerusalem the golden! I languish	844
Jerusalem the golden, With milk and	1489
Jerusalem, the only	1498
Jesus, and shall it ever be	344
Jesus at whose supreme command	1212
Jesus, be near us when we wake	924
Jesus, engrave it on my heart	581
Jesus, from whom all blessings flow	378
Jesus, full of all compassion	155
Jesus hath died that I might live	608
Jesus, I fain would find	628
Jesus, I fain would walk in Thee	638
Jesus, I live to Thee	298
Jesus, I love Thee evermore	303
Jesus, I love Thy charming name	319
Jesus, I my cross have taken	273
Jesus, in sickness and in pain	504

Index of First Lines of Hymns.

Jesus, in whom the Godhead's rays	622
Jesus, keep me near the cross	620
Jesus, Lamb of God, for me	214
Jesus, let Thy pitying eye	474
Jesus, Lover of my soul	572
Jesus, Master, whom I serve	619
Jesus, Master, whose I am	621
Jesus, merciful and mild	583
Jesus, my all, to heaven is gone	196
Jesus, my heart within me burns	335
Jesus, my Life, Thyself apply	605
Jesus, my Lord, attend	614
Jesus, my Lord, my chief Delight	309
Jesus, my Saviour, Brother, Friend	623
Jesus, my Saviour, look on me	723
Jesus, my Strength, my Hope	610
Jesus, my Truth, my Way	624
Jesus, our best beloved Friend	926
Jesus shall reign where'er the sun	1332
Jesus spreads His banner o'er us	1214
Jesus, Sun of Righteousness	927
Jesus, tender Shepherd, hear me	1004
Jesus, the Life, the Truth, the Way	575
Jesus, these eyes have never seen	308
Jesus, the sinner's Friend, to Thee	184
Jesus, the sinner's Rest thou art	574
Jesus, the very thought of Thee	337
Jesus, Thine all-victorious love	330
Jesus, Thou art my Righteousness	324
Jesus, Thou art the sinner's Friend	191
Jesus, Thou everlasting King!	1092
Jesus, Thou Joy of loving hearts	930
Jesus, Thy blood and righteousness	254
Jesus, Thy boundless love to me	328
Jesus, Thy church, with longing eyes	1322
Jesus, Thy love shall we forget	1213
Jesus, Thy name I love	323
Jesus, we look to Thee	1036
Jesus, where'er Thy people meet	1025
Jesus, who knows full well	1245
Join all the glorious names	232
Joy to the world the Lord is come	1359
Joyful be the hours to-day	1100
Joyfully, joyfully, onward I move	792
Just are Thy ways and true Thy word	24
Just as I am, without one plea	192
Just as thou art, without one trace	150
Just when Thou wilt, O Master call!	724
Keep us, Lord, O keep us ever	1173
Kindred in Christ, for His dear sake	882
Kingdoms and thrones to God belong	1051
Knocking, knocking, who is there?	146
Laborer of Christ, arise	426
Lamb of God for sinners slain	194
Lamb of God, whose bleeding love	1218
Lamp of our feet, whereby we trace	885
Lands, long benighted, the morning is nearing	1351
Lead, kindly light, amid the encircling gloom	636
Lead us, Heavenly Father, lead us	960
Leave God to order all thy ways	503
Let all the people join	1396
Let children hear the mighty deeds	1000
Let every mortal ear attend	891
Let every tongue Thy goodness speak	28
Let me be with Thee where Thou art	809
Let me but hear my Saviour say	725
Let party names no more	880
Let songs of praises fill the sky	120
Let us awake our joys	1096
Let us with a gladsome mind	1391
Let worldly minds the world pursue	244
Let Zion's watchmen all awake	1224
Life is a span, a fleeting hour	1414
Lift up to God the voice of praise	1051
Lift up your heads, ye mighty gates!	276
Lift your eyes of faith and see	1469
Lift your heads with faith, the morrow	1362
Lift your heads, ye friends of Jesus	1355
Light of life, seraphic fire	1035
Light of the lonely pilgrim's heart	1324
Light of those whose dreary dwelling	1250
Like Noah's weary dove	766
Like sheep we went astray	79
Listen, listen, He is there	497
Little travellers Zion-ward	1007
Lo, He comes with clouds descending	1453
Lo, I behold the scattering shades	1358
Lo, the day of rest declineth	1169
Lo, the mighty God appearing	1455
Lo, what a cloud of witnesses	954
Lo, what a glorious sight appears	1361
Lo, what an entertaining sight	867
Long have I seemed to serve Thee	456
Look down, O Lord, with pitying eye	126
Look from Thy sphere of endless day	1270
Look, ye saints, the sight is glorious	103
Lord, am I precious in Thy sight	569
Lord, and is Thine anger gone	501
Lord, as to Thy dear cross we flee	603
Lord, at this closing hour	1179
Lord, dismiss us with Thy blessing	1190
Lord, fill me with an humble fear	613
Lord, forever at Thy side	396
Lord God of morning and of night	901
Lord God, the Holy Ghost	1039
Lord, how mysterious are Thy ways!	718
Lord, I am Thine, entirely Thine	283
Lord, I am vile, conceived in sin	125
Lord, I believe a rest remains	647
Lord, I believe: Thy power I own	645
Lord, I cannot let Thee go	564
Lord, I have made Thy word my choice	349
Lord, I hear of showers of blessing	483
Lord, I know Thy grace is nigh me	212
Lord, in the morning Thou shalt hear	366
Lord, in the strength of grace	264
Lord, in Thy name thy servants plead	1387
Lord, it belongs not to my care	740
Lord Jesus, are we one with Thee?	869
Lord, lead the way the Saviour went	912
Lord, now we part in Thy blest name	1184
Lord of all being; throned afar!	49
Lord of all power and might	1309
Lord of Hosts, how bright, how fair	1148
Lord of hosts, to Thee we raise	1238
Lord of my life, whose tender care	692
Lord of our hearts, beloved of Thee	971
Lord of the harvest, hear	1226
Lord of the living harvest	1232
Lord of the Sabbath, hear our vows	1161
Lord of the worlds above!	1145
Lord of the worlds below!	1386
Lord, take my heart, and let it be	201
Lord! teach us how to pray aright	921
Lord, Thou art my Rock of strength	593
Lord, Thou hast searched and seen me through	556
Lord, Thou hast won: at length I yield	198
Lord, Thou wilt bring the joyful day	1478
Lord, Thou wilt hear me when I pray	695
Lord, we come before Thee now	1022
Lord, when we bend before Thy throne	1026
Lord, while for all mankind we pray	1277
Lord, with glowing heart I'd praise Thee	226
Love divine, all loves excelling	933
Majestic sweetness sits enthroned	284
Make channels for the streams of love	424
Make haste, O man, to live	423
Man's wisdom is to seek	507
Many woes had Christ endured	1
May the grace of Christ our Saviour	1182
Meek and lowly, pure and holy	394
Meet and right it is to sing	1113
Men of God, go take your stations	1302
'Mid scenes of confusion and creature complaints	824
Mighty God, the First, the Last	11
Mighty God, while angels bless Thee	224
Millions within Thy courts have met	1174
Mine be the reverent, listening love	746
Mine eyes and my desire	597
More like Jesus would I be	666
More love to Thee, O Christ	660
Mourn for the thousands slain	1262
Must Jesus bear the cross alone	430
My country, 't is of thee	1402
My days are gliding swiftly by	823

295

Index of First Lines of Hymns.

My dear Redeemer and my Lord	606
My drowsy powers, why sleep ye so	447
My faith looks up to Thee	649
My Father, God! how sweet the sound	257
My Father, when I come to Thee	559
My God, accept my early vows	671
My God, accept my heart this day	268
My God and Father, while I stray	563
My God, and is Thy table spread	1202
My God, how endless is Thy love	682
My God, how wonderful Thou art	22
My God, I know, I feel Thee mine	651
My God, I love Thee; not because	302
My God, is any hour so sweet	404
My God, I thank Thee! may no thought	750
My God, my Father, blissful name	717
My God, my Life, my Love!	313
My God, my Portion, and my Love	711
My God, permit me not to be	550
My God, permit my tongue	560
My God, the covenant of Thy love	720
My God, the Spring of all my joys	790
My God, 't is to Thy mercy-seat	549
My God, what monuments I see	749
My gracious Lord, I own Thy right	280
My gracious Redeemer I love	311
My head is low, my heart is sad	485
My heart is fixed, O God my Strength	557
My heart is resting, O my God	743
My heavenly home is bright and fair	834
My Helper God, I bless His name	793
My hope is built on nothing less	736
My Hope, my All, my Saviour Thou	618
My Jesus, as Thou wilt	540
My Maker and my King	265
My opening eyes with rapture see	353
My prayer to the promise shall cling	552
My precious Lord, for Thy dear name	591
My rest is in heaven, my rest is not here	814
My Saviour, my almighty Friend	805
My Saviour, on the word of truth	668
My Saviour. Thou hast promised rest	644
My soul and all its powers	267
My soul, be on thy guard	412
My soul complete in Jesus stands	246
My soul, for help, on God rely	526
My soul, how lovely is the place	369
My soul, repeat His praise	802
My spirit longs for Thee	576
My spirit looks to God alone	727
My spirit on Thy care	755
My sufferings all to Thee are known	505
My times are in Thy hand	748
My times of sorrow and of joy	542
Nearer, my God, to Thee	650
New every morning is the love	941
No change of time shall ever shock	799
No more, my God, I boast no more	204
No more my own, Lord Jesus	279
No track is on the sunny sky	117
None loves me, Saviour, with Thy love	648
Nor eye has seen, nor ear has heard	1472
Not all the blood of beasts	480
Not all the outward forms of earth	860
Not to the terrors of the Lord	874
Not what I am, O Lord, but what Thou art	652
Now begin the heavenly theme	1083
Now be my heart inspired to sing	229
Now be the gospel banner	1303
Now by the love of Christ, my God	374
Now faintly smile day's hasty hours	1383
Now from labor and from care	694
Now from the altar of our hearts	969
Now, host with host assembling	1266
Now I resolve, with all my heart	266
Now is the accepted time	161
Now let my soul, eternal King	351
Now let our cheerful eyes survey	110
Now let our souls, on wings sublime	1425
Now may He, who from the dead	1183
Now that the sun is gleaming bright	1187
Now the Saviour standeth pleading	144
Now the shades of night are gone	935
Now to the great and sacred Three (Dox.)	1128
Now to the haven of Thy breast	577
Now to the Lord, a noble song!	218
Now to Thy sacred house	365
O blessed are the eyes that see	976
O blessed feet of Jesus	494
O blessed God, to Thee I raise	219
O blessed souls are they	245
O blessed Sun, whose splendor	343
O bless the Lord, my soul, His	240
O bless the Lord, my soul, Let	804
O Bread to pilgrims given	1206
O Christ, the Lord of heaven, to Thee	1091
O Christ, who hast prepared a place	1034
O Christ, with each returning morn	929
O come and mourn with me awhile	81
O come to the merciful Saviour that calls you	472
O could I find from day to day	588
O could I speak the matchless worth	231
O day of rest and gladness	1166
O deem not they are blest alone	1420
O do not let the word depart	1192
O draw me, Father, after Thee	554
O dreadful glory that doth make	16
O eyes that are weary, and hearts that	545
O Father Almighty, to Thee be addrest	1141
O for a closer walk with God	654
O for a faith that will not shrink	1254
O for a heart to praise my God	627
O for a shout of sacred joy	99
O for a sweet inspiring ray	1495
O for a thousand tongues	227
O for the death of those	1440
O for the happy hour	1255
O gift of gifts, O grace of faith!	388
O glorious hope of perfect love	653
O God, beneath Thy guiding hand	1279
O God, by whom the seed is given	1188
O God, forever blest (Dox.)	1129
O God, my God, my all Thou art	669
O God of Abra'm, hear	989
O God of Bethel, by whose hand	906
O God of hosts, the mighty Lord	367
O God of sovereign grace	1314
O God, the Light of all that live	984
O God, Thou art my God alone	670
O God, Thy power is wonderful	19
O God, unseen, yet ever near	1205
O God, what offering shall I give	269
O God, who meltest in Thy hand	1283
O great is Jehovah, and great be His praise	1149
O had I, my Saviour, the wings of a dove	842
O happy day, that fixed my choice	236
O help us, Lord, each hour of need	923
O holy, holy, holy Lord!	1106
O holy Saviour, Friend unseen!	764
O how I love Thy holy law!	347
O how the thought of God attracts	444
O Jesus, Friend unfailing	753
O Jesus, if in days gone by	573
O Jesus, Jesus, dearest Lord	333
O Jesus, King most wonderful	1094
O Jesus, Lord of heavenly grace	928
O Jesus, our chief Corner-Stone	1237
O Jesus, Saviour of the lost	190
O Jesus, Thou art standing	476
O Jesus, Thou the beauty art	336
O Jesus, we adore Thee	1093
O Lamb of God, still keep me	580
O let him whose sorrow	978
O let triumphant faith dispel	955
O Lord, encouraged by Thy grace	993
O Lord, how happy should we be	917
O Lord! how joyful 't is to see	871
O Lord, impart Thyself to me	299
O Lord, in whom are all my springs	785
O Lord, I would delight in Thee	786
O Lord, my best desire fulfil	558
O Lord our God, arise	1290
O Lord, Thou art my Lord	270
O Lord, Thy mercy, my sure hope	38
O Lord, Thy perfect word	895

Index of First Lines of Hymns.

O Lord, Thy work revive	1251	Peace, troubled soul, whose plaintive	466
O Lord, when faith with fixed eyes	77	People of the living God	373
O Lord, when we the path retrace	66	Pilgrim burdened with thy sin	465
O Lord, while we confess the worth	1197	Pilgrims in this vale of sorrow	953
O Love, divine and tender	1401	Pleasant are Thy courts above	360
O Love divine, how sweet Thou art!	325	Plunged in a gulf of dark despair	1086
O Love divine, that stooped to share	931	Pour out Thy spirit from on high	1233
O Love, how cheering is thy ray!	329	Praise God from whom all blessings flow (Dox.)	1125
O Master, it is good to be	587	Praise, Lord, for Thee in Zion waits	1150
O mean may seem this house of clay	937	Praise, my soul, the King of Heaven	230
O Mother dear, Jerusalem	837	Praise, O praise our God and King	1393
O my soul, what means this sadness?	511	Praise our glorious King and Lord (Dox.)	1135
O Paradise, O Paradise	839	Praises to Him whose love has given	1107
O praise our God to-day	947	Praise the Father, earth and heaven (Dox.)	1136
O praise ye the Lord; prepare your glad voice	1050	Praise the God of all creation (Dox.)	1137
O Saviour, whose mercy, severe in its kindness	535	Praise the Lord, His power confess	1068
O Spirit of the living God!	1319	Praise the Lord who reigns above	1117
O Sun of Righteousness, arise	579	Praise the Lord; ye heavens adore Him	1067
O that I could forever dwell	584	Praise the name of God most high (Dox.)	1132
O that I knew the secret place	548	Praise to God, immortal praise	1397
O that my load of sin were gone	641	Praise waits in Zion, Lord, for Thee	1151
O that the Lord's salvation	1286	Prayer is appointed to convey	398
O that the Lord would guide my ways	633	Prayer is the breath of God in man	402
O that Thy statutes every hour	352	Prayer is the soul's sincere desire	401
O the sweet wonders of that cross	252	Prince of Peace, control my will	604
O Thou from whom all goodness flows	544	Prostrate, dear Jesus, at Thy feet	188
O Thou God of my salvation	228	Purer yet and purer	665
O Thou great Ruler of the sky	904		
O Thou in whose presence my soul takes delight	596	Quiet, Lord, my froward heart	640
O Thou that hearest prayer	1021		
O Thou that hear'st the prayer of faith	193	Raise your triumphant songs!	1089
O Thou that hear'st when sinners cry	185	Rejoice and be glad!	1084
O Thou the contrite sinner's Friend	496	Rejoice, believer, in the Lord	440
O Thou to whose all-searching sight	629	Rejoice in God alway	789
O Thou who by a star didst guide	922	Rejoice in Jesus' birth	57
O Thou who camest from above	625	Rejoice, rejoice, believers	1331
O Thou whose mercy guides my way	539	"Repent!" the voice celestial cries	167
O Thou whose own vast temple stands	1240	Rescue the perishing	1263
O Thou whose tender mercy hears	477	Return, my roving heart, return	454
O turn ye, O turn ye, for why will ye die	171	Return, my soul, unto thy rest; From God	271
O what amazing words of grace		Return, my soul, unto thy rest, From vain	770
O what stupendous mercy shines	382	Return, O wanderer! return	141
O where are kings and empires now	850	Return, O wanderer, to thy home	159
O why should Israel's sons, once blest	1285	Revive Thy work, O Lord!	1253
O Word of God Incarnate	884	Rise, glorious Conqueror, rise	98
O worship the King, all-glorious above	1055	Rise, my soul, and stretch thy wings	828
O'er the distant mountains breaking	833	Rise, O my soul, pursue the path	376
Of all the thoughts of God that are	774	Rites cannot change the heart	1195
Of Him who did salvation bring	307	Rock of Ages, cleft for me	199
Once I thought my mountain strong	449	Roll on, thou mighty ocean	1299
Once more before we part		Round the Lord in glory seated	1069
Once more, my soul, the rising day	679		
Once more the solemn season calls	1365	Safely through another week	1157
One cup of healing oil and wine	384	Salvation! O the joyful sound	1268
One more day's work for Jesus	433	Saviour, breathe an evening blessing	967
One prayer I have; all prayers in one	543	Saviour, I follow on	662
One sole baptismal sign	872	Saviour, I look to Thee	609
One there is above all others	939	Saviour, like a Shepherd lead us	1002
On Jordan's stormy banks I stand	838	Saviour, more than life to me	639
On the mountain's top appearing		Saviour, on me the grace bestow	295
On Thee, each morning, O my God	1327	Saviour, sprinkle many nations	1316
On Zion and on Lebanon	684	Saviour, Thy dying love	275
Onward, Christian soldiers	1272	Saviour, visit Thy plantation	1244
Onward, Christian, though the region	1305	Saviour, when in dust to Thee	1023
Our blest Redeemer, ere He breathed	114	Saviour, when night involves the skies	709
Our country's voice is pleading	1275	Saviour, when Thy bread we break	1208
Our day of praise is done	1170	Saviour, who Thy flock art feeding	997
Our Father, God who art in heaven	905	Say, sinner, hath a voice within	164
Our Father through the coming year	1379	Say, who is she that looks abroad	854
Our Father who dost lead	1010	Scorn not the slightest word or deed	425
Our glorious home above	1486	Searcher of hearts, from mine erase	562
Our God, our God, Thou shinest here	1317	See, from Zion's sacred mountain	1341
Our God, our help in ages past	50	See, gracious God, before Thy throne	1366
Our Heavenly Father calls	713	See how the morning sun	674
Our Heavenly Father, hear	903	See Israel's gentle Shepherd stand	994
Our land with mercies crowned	1404	See, Jesus, Thy disciples see	1028
Our Lord is risen from the dead	100	See, the conqueror mounts in triumph	102
Our Saviour alone, the Lord, let us bless	1103	See the Thy Keeper, stand	768
Our souls, by love together knit	866	Servant of God, well done!	1432
		Servants of God, in joyful lays	1056
Pain and toil are over now	89	Shall man, O God of light and life	1445
Palms of glory, raiment bright	1459	Shepherd of Israel, bend Thine ear	1227
Pass me not, O gracious Father!	484	Shepherd of tender youth	995
Peace, peace I leave with you	524	Shepherd of Thine Israel, lead us	934

Index of First Lines of Hymns.

Shine on our land, Jehovah, shine	1274
Show pity, Lord, O Lord, forgive	186
Silently the shades of evening	707
Since all the varying scenes of time	726
Since o'er Thy footstool here below	1490
Sing, my soul, His wondrous love	223
Sing to the Lord a joyful song	1399
Sing to the Lord, ye distant lands	1336
Sing we to our God above (Dox.)	1131
Sing, ye redeemed of the Lord	1054
Sinners, obey the gospel word	151
Sinners, the voice of God regard	139
Sinners, turn, why will you die?	153
So fades the lovely blooming flower	1407
So let our lips and lives express	962
Softly fades the twilight ray	1163
Softly now the light of day	708
Soldiers of Christ, arise	1304
Soldiers of the cross, arise!	1301
Sometimes a light surprises	782
Songs of praise the angels sang	1112
Son of God, to Thee I cry	570
Son of the carpenter, receive	432
Soon and forever, such promise our trust	1500
Soon may the last glad song arise	1336
Souls in heathen darkness lying	1293
Sound, sound the truth abroad	1306
Sovereign of worlds, display Thy power	1312
Sovereign Ruler of the skies	719
Sow in the morn thy seed	422
Spirit divine, attend our prayers	957
Spirit, leave thy house of clay	1430
Spirit of faith, come down!	1046
Spirit of peace and holiness	1230
Spirit of peace, celestial Dove	121
Spirit of power and might, behold	1320
Spirit of truth, on this Thy day!	1162
Stand up, and bless the Lord	1058
Stand up, my soul! shake off thy fears	416
Stand up, stand up for Jesus	1307
Star of peace, to wanderers weary	1284
Stay, Thou insulted Spirit, stay	189
Still one in life and one in death	878
Still, still with Thee, my God	566
Still, still with Thee when purple morning	688
"Stricken, smitten, and afflicted"	82
Sun of my soul, Thou Saviour dear	702
Sweet and holy is the place	1143
Sweet feast of love divine	1210
Sweet hour of prayer	406
Sweet is the memory of Thy grace	315
Sweet is the work, my God, my King	358
Sweet is the work, O Lord	1159
Sweet peace of conscience, heavenly guest	643
Sweet Saviour, bless us ere we go	1127
Sweet the moments, rich in blessing	340
Sweet the time, exceeding sweet	1108
Sweet was the time when first I felt	445
Sweeter sounds than music knows	332
Swell the anthem, raise the song	1392
Take me, O my Father, take me	272
Take my heart, O Father, take it	200
Take, my soul, thy full salvation	274
Take the name of Jesus with you	342
Talk with me, Lord; Thyself reveal	712
Tarry with me, O my Saviour	700
Teach me, my God and King	561
Tell me the old, old story	341
Ten thousand times ten thousand	1458
Tender Shepherd, Thou hast stilled	1441
That day of wrath, that dreadful day	1451
That fearful day, that day of dread	1452
That we might walk with God	909
The bird let loose in eastern skies	656
The busy scenes of day are fled	705
The Christian warrior, see him stand	417
The Church's one foundation	864
The dawn is sprinkling in the East	942
The day is past and gone	697
The day, O Lord, is spent	974
The dead are like the stars by day	1433
The festal morn, my God, is come	356
The floods, O Lord, lift up their voice	45
The gentle Saviour calls	970
The glorious universe around	876
The God of harvest praise	1398
The Great Physician now is near	592
The happy morn is come	92
The harvest dawn is near	439
The head that once was crowned with thorns	106
The heavens declare Thy glory, Lord	897
The King of heaven His table spreads	1201
The King of love my Shepherd is	760
The law commands and makes us know	890
The Lord descended from above	5
The Lord from His celestial throne	124
The Lord Himself, the mighty Lord	731
The Lord! how fearful is His name!	9
The Lord, how wondrous are His ways!	31
The Lord is King, lift up thy voice	6
The Lord is my Shepherd: He makes me	538
The Lord is my Shepherd; His kindness I know	744
The Lord is my Shepherd; no want shall I know	775
The Lord is risen indeed	95
The Lord Jehovah reigns	10
The Lord my pasture shall prepare	736
The Lord my Shepherd is	732
The Lord of glory is my Light	714
The Lord of might from Sinai's brow	1339
The Lord our God is full of might	7
The Lord our God is Lord of all	39
The Lord, the God of glory, reigns	8
The Lord will come, the earth shall quake	1454
The morning dawns upon the place	76
The morning flowers display their sweets	1444
The morning light is breaking	1330
The morning purples all the sky	93
The peace which God alone reveals	1186
The precious seed of weeping	1434
The Prince of Salvation in triumph is riding	1352
The promise of my Father's love	282
The promises I sing	761
The rosente hues of early dawn	1407
The sands of time are sinking	846
The Saviour bids thee watch and pray	407
The Saviour calls: let every ear	145
The Saviour! O what endless charms	783
The Saviour waits! His presence now	1221
The seeds which piety and love	380
The solemn service now is done	1231
The Son of God goes forth to war	413
The spacious firmament on high	36
The Spirit breathes upon the word	900
The Spirit in our hearts	148
The starry firmament on high	899
The thing my God doth hate	289
The twilight falls, the night is near	693
The wanderer no more will roam	260
The whole wide world for Jesus!	1343
The world is very evil	1475
Thee we adore, Eternal Name	1406
There is a blessed home	1468
There is a book that all may read	886
There is a dwelling-place above	1470
There is a fold whence none can stray	1482
There is a fountain filled with blood	225
There is a holy city	1467
There is a land immortal	1466
There is a land of pure delight	1496
There is a name I love to hear	255
There is an eye that never sleeps	399
There is an hour of hallowed peace	1488
There is an hour of peaceful rest	1476
There is a safe and secret place	777
There is none other name than Thine	334
There is no night in heaven	1492
There is no sorrow, Lord, too light	515
There's a land that is fairer than day	1493
They pray the best who pray and watch	964
They who seek the throne of grace	951
Thine forever! God of love	918
Thine, Lord, is wisdom, Thine alone	26
Think gently of the erring one!	1260
Think, O ye who fondly languish	1435
This God is the God we adore	1185
This is not my place of resting	843
This is the day of light	1156

Index of First Lines of Hymns.

This is the day the Lord hath made	1154
This stone to Thee in faith we lay	1234
Thou art coming, O my Saviour	1334
Thou art gone to the grave, but we will not deplore thee	1429
Thou art my Hiding-place, O Lord	739
Thou art the Way; and he who sighs	326
Thou art the Way; to Thee alone	925
Thou Grace divine, encircling all	945
Thou hidden love of God, whose height	293
Thou hidden Source of calm repose	722
Thou Lamb of God, thou Prince of peace	607
Thou my everlasting Portion	765
Thou seest my feebleness	617
Thou Shepherd of Israel, and mine	590
Thou very present Aid	530
Thou who didst on Calvary bleed	205
Thou who dost my life prolong	675
Thou who roll'st the year around	1377
Though faint, yet pursuing, we go	952
Though now the nations sit beneath	1311
Though troubles assail, and dangers	961
Thrice happy man who fears the Lord	383
Throned high is Jesus now	105
Through all the changing scenes of life	801
Through endless years Thou art the same	47
Through sorrow's night and danger's path	1416
Through the day Thy love has spared us	968
Through the love of God our Saviour	975
Thus far the Lord hath led me on	704
Thy ceaseless, unexhausted love	32
Thy Father's house! thine own bright home!	815
Thy holy day's returning	1158
Thy home is with the humble, Lord	305
Thy loving-kindness, Lord, I sing	787
Thy name to me, Thy nature given	290
Thy presence, gracious God, afford	1018
Thy presence, Lord, the place shall fill	296
Thy way is in the deep, O Lord	980
Thy way, not mine, O Lord	635
Thy works, not mine, O Christ	242
"Till He come!" Oh, let the words	1320
Time is winging us away	1418
Time, thou speedest on but slowly	841
Times without number have I prayed	450
'T is by the faith of joys to come	983
'T is by Thy strength the mountains stand	1390
"'T is finished!" so the Saviour cried	87
'T is heaven begun below	822
'T is midnight, and on Olive's brow	75
'T is my happiness below	436
'T is not that I did choose Thee	331
'T is Thine alone, Almighty name	1264
To bless Thy chosen race	1287
To-day the Saviour calls	149
To Father, Son, and Holy Ghost (Dox.)	1123
To Father, Son, and Holy Ghost (Dox.)	1127
To Father, Son, and Spirit, ever blest (Dox.)	1139
To God the Father, God the Son (Dox.)	1126
To God the Father, Son (Dox.)	1124
To God the only wise	1104
To Jesus, the Crown of my hope	808
To our Redeemer's glorious name	1099
To spend one sacred day	370
To Thee be praise forever (Dox.)	1135
To Thee, my God and Saviour	686
To Thee, my Shepherd and my Lord	807
To the great One in Three (Dox.)	1130
To the hills I lift mine eyes	767
To Thy pastures fair and large	637
To Thy temple I repair	371
To us a child of hope is born	56
To whom, my Saviour, shall I go	595
To-morrow, Lord, is Thine	1246
Tossed upon life's raging billow	1281
Triumphant Zion, lift thy head	1346
Try us, O God, and search the ground	581
'T was by an order from the Lord	893
'T was in the watches of the night	715
'T was on that dark, that doleful night	1200
'T was the commission of our Lord	1194
Under Thy wings, my God, I rest	646
Unite, my roving thoughts, unite	528
Unveil thy bosom, faithful tomb	1439
Up to the hills I lift mine eyes	44
Uphold me, Lord, too prone to stray	634
Uplift the blood-red banner	1296
Upward I lift mine eyes	733
Vain, delusive world, adieu	278
Vainly through night's weary hours	943
Wait, my soul, upon the Lord	779
Wait, O my soul, thy Maker's will	23
Wake thee, O Zion, thy mourning is ended	1349
Wake the song of Jubilee	1360
Walk in the light: so shalt thou know	437
Watchman, tell me, does the morning	1329
Watchman tell us of the night	1338
We are living, we are dwelling	1207
We are on our journey home	1497
We bid thee welcome in the name	1229
We bless Thee, for Thy peace, O God	982
We bless the Prophet of the Lord	111
We give Thee but Thine own	919
We journey through a vale of tears	1481
We know, by faith we know	1473
We lift our hearts to Thee	932
We praise Thee, Lord, if but one soul	1269
We praise Thee oft for hours of bliss	979
We praise Thee, O God, for the Son of thy love	1110
We're travelling home to heaven above	158
We sing His love who once was slain	1447
We sing the praise of Him who died	1038
"We've no abiding city here"	1483
We will not weep, for God is standing by us	985
We would see Jesus, for the shadows	1029
Weary of wandering from my God	457
Weary sinner, keep thine eyes	467
Welcome, delightful morn	354
Welcome, O Saviour, to my heart	213
Welcome, sacred day of rest	1163
Welcome, sweet day, of days the best	362
Welcome, sweet day of rest	255
Welcome, welcome, dear Redeemer	277
What are these arrayed in white	1457
What are these in bright array	1462
What cheering words are these	772
What equal honors shall we bring	1085
What grace, O Lord, and beauty shone	873
What is life! 'T is but a vapor	1411
What is our calling's glorious hope	286
What is our God, or what His name	51
What! I never speak one evil word!	664
What shall I render to my God	263
What shall the dying sinner do	134
What sinners value I resign	1443
What though my frail eyelids refuse	698
What various hindrances we meet	400
When all thy mercies, O my God	803
When brighter suns and milder skies	1491
When darkness long has veiled my mind	531
When, doomed to death, the apostle lay	1267
Whene'er the angry passions rise	69
When gathering clouds around I view	518
When God of old came down	115
When He cometh, when He cometh	1006
When His salvation bringing	999
When I can read my title clear	827
When I can trust my all with God	516
When Israel, of the Lord beloved	915
When I survey the wondrous cross	203
When Jesus came to earth of old	1456
When Jesus dwelt in mortal clay	441
When like a stranger on our sphere	71
When, Lord, to this our western land	1271
When, O dear Jesus, when shall I	578
When overwhelmed with grief	514
When shall the voice of singing	1323
When sins and fears prevailing rise	754
When streaming from the eastern skies	685
When Thou, my righteous Judge, shall come	451
When winds are raging o'er the upper ocean	773
When, wounded sore, the stricken soul	498
Where high the heavenly temple stands	108
Where is my God? Does He retire	735
Where two or three, with sweet accord	1024
While beauty clothes the fertile vale	1354

299

Index of First Lines of Hymns.

While in sweet communion feeding	1209
While in this sacred rite of Thine	1198
While o'er our guilty land, O Lord	1372
While o'er the deep thy servants sail	1282
While Thee I seek, protecting Power	751
While Thou art intimately nigh	745
While Thou, O my God, art my Help, and	537
While with ceaseless course the sun	1380
Whither, with this crushing load	495
Who but Thou, Almighty Spirit	1318
Who, O Lord, when life is o'er	863
Why do we mourn departing friends	1438
Why is my heart so far from Thee	448
Why, O God, Thy people spurn?	1373
Why should I murmur or repine	541
Why should the children of a King	492
Why should we start and fear to die?	1422
Why will ye waste on trifling cares	163
With broken heart and contrite sigh	177
With glory clad, with strength arrayed	52
With joy we hail the sacred day	1147
With joy we lift our eyes	1146
With joy we meditate the grace	109
With one consent, let all the earth	1063
With songs and honors sounding loud	1394
With tearful eyes I look around	469
With tears of anguish I lament	452
With thankful hearts our songs we raise	996
Witness, ye men and angels, now	1196
Work, for the night is coming	421
Worthy the Lamb of boundless sway	1076
Would you win a soul to God?	1261
Ye angels who, stand round the throne	812
Ye Christian heralds, go proclaim	1295
Ye messengers of Christ	1293
Ye nations round the earth, rejoice	1062
Ye servants of God, your Master proclaim	1101
Ye servants of the Lord	410
Ye that in His courts are found	458
Ye that pass by, behold the Man	83
Ye wretched, hungry, starving poor	147
Yes, for me, for me He careth	594
Yes! He knows the way is dreary	914
Yes, I will bless Thee, O my God	221
Yes, we trust the day is breaking	1335
Zion, awake, thy strength renew	1345
Zion is Jehovah's dwelling	851
Zion stands with hills surrounded	855

Index of First Lines of Verses.

First Line	Hymn
A beam from	1424
A boundless	1219
A brighter	489
A cloud of	429
A country far	442
A deep and	343
A deeper shade	687
A dying, risen	217
A faith that	1254
A few more	1480
A glory gilds	900
A guilty, weak	180
A hand almigh	777
A hand divine	1054
A heart in	627
A heart re	627
A heart, that	648
A holy quiet	1421
A hope so	261
A horror of	84
A humble, low	627
A land of corn	653
A little child	1116
A little flock!	848
A rest where	647
A second look	251
A song of	246
A thousand a	50
A trusting hea	444
A whispered	425
A word of His	9
Abide with me	702
Above the dis	829
Absent from	477
Accept, O Lord	270
Accept our	1155
Admit Him ere	160
Adoring saints	1419
Against Thee,	482
Against the G	237
Ah! grace into	388
Ah! how shall	132
Ah, Jesus! let	599
Ah, Lord, our	1023
Ah! no, with	595
Ah, there the	842
Ah! what touch	212
Ah, why, by	657
All glory and	1110
All glory be to	1198
All hail, trium	1167
All heaven ab	88
All I ask for is	631
All is fading,	1410
All is tranquil	1463
All its num	1377
All may of Th	561
All my capa	319
All nature sings	35
All needful	1020
All o'er those	83
All our earthly	1007
All our follies	1377
All our hopes,	1318
All our woe and	678
All riches are	1085
All-seeing G	1153
All that being	11
All that I am	734
All that I am	275
All that I am,	249
All that spring	1397
All the tokens	1453
All things are	1201
All things liv	1391
All this day	1034
All this for us	1116
All who dwell	1068
All-wise, Alm	543
All ye nations	1360
All your sins	1001
Almighty God	163
Almighty God	1310
Almighty Lord	877
Almighty Son	1013
Alone with	688
Am I a stranger	347
Amazing love,	167
Among the	830
Among the	263
And a new song	743
And as those	1487
And at my life's	685
And dear to me	357
And death that	64
And duly shall	422
And every vir	114
And filled and	945
And grant that	936
And He has	663
And He who	955
And here Thy	1279
And His that	114
And if some	750
And I have	461
And is it true	215
And, Lord,	253
And may the	1186
And never let	1221
And not a pr	1174
And now we	1479
And of that	174
And O may	1271
And O, when	915
And O, when I	518
And see, O L	1264
And shall my	477
And since by	907
And since the L	999
And there the	1494
And Thou al	1404
And Thou, gr	287
And thus, my	454
And though	381
And though Th	543
And though we	945
And thus,	904
And we believe	919
And what is life	513
And whatsoe'er	949
And when be	247
And when, de	1003
And when ex	971
And when I cl	191
And when I	697
And when mo	965
And when my	405
And when my	534
And when our	1295
And when	306
And when	998
And when the	1475
And when this	1235
And when Th	866
And, when to h	685
And when to	592
And when Thy	17
And when w	1026
And while t.iey	14
And while we	863
And yet this	705
Angels in	1450
Angels joyful	1428
Angel powers	1469
Anon He	107
Another year	1381
Apostles, mar	836
Archangels lea	62
Are darkness	718
Are there no f	415
Are we not ten	1435
Are you sick?	510
Arise, my soul	543
Arm me with	431
Around the	1478
Around the	1170
Around yon cr	174
Arrayed in glo	1446
Art thou lone	1362
Art Thou not	754
Art Thou not	505
As a little child	640
As by the light	244
As from the	211
As hour suc	904
As laborers in	577
As o'er a parch	577
Our steps	1175
As pity dwells	381
As surely as C	440
As the apple of	501
As the clear air	211
As the wingèd	1380
As Thou didst	934
As welcome as	577
As yet we know	922
Ascended now	869
Assist me while	578
Assisted by His	909
Assure my con	402
As evening, in	938
At evening	776
At eventide let	984
At His call the	1449
At last I own	184
At noon, bene	938
At some time	977
At the blest	275
At the name of	342
Attending an	1361
Auspicious	1344
Author and	568
Awake, awake	805
Awake, awake	1348
Awhile from	1363
Bane and bless	806
Baptized into	1197
Baptize the na	1319
Be darkness,	1319
Be earth, with	550
Be faith which	426
Be grace from	1195
Be it according	286
Be my all; in	593
Be the banner	1301
Be this the pur	266
Be this world	434
Be Thou my	606
Be Thou my S	182
De Thou my	618
Be Thou my st	716
Be Thou, O	612
Be Thy ban	1373
Bear witness I	207
Because the S	1008
Before our Fath	875
Before the cross	268
Before the hills	50
Before the mo	1200
Before them	1200
Before Thy th	1146
Behold a Witn	954
Behold He	1336
Behold His pa	33
Behold the ark	766
Behold the h	874
" Behold the	1344
Behold your K	1078
Below He	1098
Beside all wat	422
Better than life	670
Beyond my	375
But if Thy spi	126
Beyond the bl	845
Beyond the fl	1417
Beyond the part	845
Bid the whole	1210
Bind Thy peo	1248
Bless, O my	798
Blessed Sav	375
Blessings abo	1332
Blessings fore	1085
Blessings from	1392
Blest are the	859
Blest are the	862
Blest are the	359
Blest are the pu	862
Blest are these	359
Blest are the so	859
Blest are the so	359
Blest be that	1056
Blest hour for	405
Blest is that	404
Blest is the man	138
Blest is the	870
Blest Jesus!	586
Blest river of	1330
Blest Saviour	429
Blest Three in	1367
Blest Trinity	487
Blest with this	764
Blot out my	482
Born by a new	1425
Born of Him	666
Born Thy	1333
Borne upon	1112
Bow down in	101
Bow to the	139
Bowed down be	182
Bread of our	885
Break forth in	1347
Break from	1439
Break off the	641
Break, sover	452
Breathe, breath	602
Breathe, O	933
Breathe on us	1028
Brethren, let	851
Bright be my	546
Brought forth to	76
Brought safely	769
Bulwarks of	857
Burdened with	253
Buried in sor	1268
Burn, burn, O	333
But ah, our	1272
But calmly, L	1379
But charity	391
But chiefest in	1242
But Christ, the	480
But drops of gr	500
But ere this spa	48
But fixed for ev	899
But God shall	79
But he who	441
But high she	656
But His eternal	31
But I am calm	710
But if at any	424
But I have felt	1003
But in the stat	861
But lo, a bright	858
But lo! a place	757
But lo, He leav	62
But, Lord,	1315
But mightier	45
But not alone	945
But no such	188
But now, when	446
But, O my Lord	531
But O, when g	523
But O, when th	222
But, Saviour,	487
But shall I	741
But soon He'll	85
But soon the	1426
But the chief	848
But the good	1472
But there's a	399
But there's a	180
But the rest	1164
But Thou art	1165
But though	1408
But though the	973
But Thy perfec	47
But timorous	1495
But to draw	316
But to those	1449
But what to	337
But when we	235
But where the	893
But whilst our	133
But will He	160
But wil l in	1234
But yet with	1498
By day, along	915
By day, by	1382
By faith we	386
By faith we	1204
By His own	62
By nature all	124
By nature and	780
By the sealed	88
By the thorn	434
By Thee must	326
By Thee	1433
By Thine ago	1218
By Thine	1023
By Thy deep	1023
By Thy help	1023
Call me away	550
Call, O call us	1207
Calmer yet and	665
Calmly the day	703
Came at length	73
Can aught be	128
Can loving chil	752
Can this be	1454
Can we, whose	1291
Captives of sin	1356
Careless, throu	432
Carry on Thy	1278
Cast care aside	418
Cast thy burden	463
Cast thy guilty	467
Cease, cease	1445
Cease, then	1441
Cease, then	1435
Cease, ye pilgr	828
Celestial beams	895
Chains yet	1267
Chance and	30
Cheered by a	257
Cheerful they	359
Cheerful we	983
Chief of ten	1032
Children of	971
Choose Thou	635
Christ by no	910
Christ hath the	92
Christians hea	1293
Christ is born	58
Christ is my	321
Christ Jesus is	321
Christ leads me	740
Christ our Lor	1111
Christ, the etc	1107

301

Index of First Lines of Verses.

	Hymn		Hymn		Hymn		Hymn		Hymn		Hymn
Christ who now	116	Dear Comfort	395	Fain would I	641	For us all Thy	1208	Glory to Thee	678	Hark, again	1292
Church of our	1345	Dear, dying L	225	Fain would I	680	For voice and	219	Glory to Thee	1122	Hark, how He	85
Clear as the sun	854	Dear Lord, and	248	Faint not, Ch	435	Forward, flock	1294	Go, and share	1411	Hark! how	10, 0
Close and still	90	Dear Lord,	1043	Faint not nor	438	For we must	424	Go forth, Con	1206	Hark, it is the	465
Close by Thy	607	Dear Lord! wh	135	Fair as the	854	For why? the	1059	Go, imitate the	382	Hark, the des	1360
Closer and	865	Dear Name, the	320	Fair distant	1485	Forbid it, Lord	203	Gn, labor on	418	Hark, the glad	1073
Clouds and	1220	Dear native	1404	Fair plenty	1396	Forever blessed	819	Go. spread a	1298	Hark, the	1392
Cold and win	771	Dear Saviour!	1033	Faith feels the	385	Forever firm	27	Go then earthly	273	Hark, those	103
Cold mountains	605	Dear Saviour	1471	Faith finds in	385	Forever on Thy	873	Go, tyrants, to	1454	Harmonious ac	525
Come, all the	1040	Dear Saviour	301	Faith in His	704	Forever shall	48	Go, walk about	1149	Has thy night	1327
Come, almighty	913	Dear Shephe	1025	Faith lends its	356	Forever with	847	Go where the	426	Hast Thou a	310
Come and be	1321	Death may my	281	Faith, mighty	389	Forget not	1260	God bless the	1401	Hast Thou im	4, 9
Come, and	1321	Death to the	1197	Faith sees the	1445	Forget the tri	362	God does His	526	Hast Thou not	733
Come as a sh	1229	Decay then tene	70	Faith, that in	391	Forgive me, L	691	God, from on	1346	Haste, glori	1285
Come as the I	957	Deep regret	1369	Faith to the con	385	Forgive the	1367	God in Christ	1142	Haste, O haste	1293
Come bless the	363	Deep unto deep	557	Faithful amidst	666	Forth in the	1386	God is just in	800	Haste thee on	274
Come blessed	1324	Depend on H	394	Faithful, O Lord	32	Fountain of life	867	God is our Str	1058	Hasten, dear	1447
Come, come to	473	Descend, celes	351	Faithful soul	767	Frail children	1055	God is our Sun	1020	Hasten, mercy	166
Come down	1232	Descend, O Sp	1160	Far and wide	1316	Fresh hopes	901	God is thy Rest	770	Haste, , mortals	58
Come, Father	290	Despond then	977	Far, far above	791	Friend of the	521	God leads me	684	Hasten, sinner	166
Come, fill our	1030	Did ever mour	521	Far, far above	950	From beneath	305	God my Re	1416	Hath God cast	522
Come, for all	469	Did ever troub	769	Far, far away	773	From busy	1012	God of all grace	921	Hath He marks	527
Come, for Thy	1321	Diffuse, O G	1252	Far, far be	773	From daily sin	787	God of Jacob	1335	Have I long in	483
Come, freely	466	Direct, control	677	Far from this	1437	From danger	678	God of mercy	1258	Have we no	81
Come, Holy C	1003	Dispensing good	63	Far from us	1045	From dark	905	God of our fa	1413	Have we wan	1178
Come, Holy G	959	Dissolve Thou	803	Far off I stand	177	From every	1412	God of our sal	1017	He bears their	76
Come, Holy G	1317	Distracting th	1018	Far up the	1482	From every sin	378	God only is the	444	He bids His	39
Come, Holy G	908	Distrest with	544	Farewell mort	345	From evil se	698	God only is the	444	He bows be	74
Come, Holy Sp	992	Do more than	1177	Farewell, ye	345	From Heaven	70	God only know	325	He bows His	1245
Come Holy Sp	1097	Do not I love	310	Father and Son	562	From hell's op	614	God pities all	713	He bows the	40
Come Holy Sp	1043	"Do this," He	1200	Father in heav	970	From morn till	15	God reigns on	1158	He breaks the	227
Come, holy Sun	928	Does the night	1362	Father! in us	1018	From nature	299	God ruleth on	1101	He built the	1052
Come in sorrow	137	Dost Thou not	492	Father! let me	206	From sea to	1273	God, the All-	1370	He by His	909
Come in this	1035	Doth not the	1317	Father-like, He	230	From sin, the	299	God, the bless	209	He came in	114
Come, leave thy	150	Doth sickness	256	Father, make it	200	From sorrow	875	God, the eternal	259	He comes, from	54
Come, let our	1053	Down from	1086	Father of Jesus	22	From strife of	739	God, the ever	116	He comes! He	117
Come, let us	1053	Down to the	1072	Father! save	206	From that	1042	God, the merci	223	He comes the	54
Come, Light	1040	Dwell therefor	1249	Father, Son	1011	From the dark	1075	God, the Om	1270	He comes with	1340
Come, Lord,	1289			Father! Son!	206	From the dis	350	God, the Re	1274	He crowns thy	804
Come, Lord!	1033	Each evening	26	Father, Thy	799	From Thee	1389	God, Thine	229	He dies! the	72
Come near and	702	Each follow	1092	Fear hath no	1474	From Thee that	615	God, thy God	1327	He does my	731
Come, O come	510	Each moment	293	Fear not, bret	1083	From Thee, thr	555	God will never	978	He feeds and	29
Come, sacred S	257	Early let us	1002	Fed by His	1227	From thence	1272	God's guardian	676	He feeds the	777
Come, smiling	63	Earth and her	1471	Feeble, trem	1082	From the sword	43	Good, when He	1246	He feeds thee	240
Come, Spirit l	1231	Earth shall	1274	Fill our souls	935	From the third	1316	Good-will to	1087	He, for the joy	954
Come, Spirit	1328	"Eat, O my	1211	Finish then	1033	From Thy gra	1148	Grace first con	233	He freely is	311
Come, tender	1040	E'en now, to	336	Firm as His	742	From Thy	1015	Grace led my	233	He guides our	44
Come, then, my	1055	E'en now	1322	Firm, faithful	401	Fruitless years	22	Grace! 't is a	208	He has pur	459
Come, then, my	411	E'er since by	225	Fling wide the	276	Full many a	750	Gracious Lord	1163	He has what	1434
Come then, ye	1114	E'en the hour	30	Foes without	205	Full of fears	1449	Grant me now	292	He hath, with	1301
Come, Thou	100	Elect from	854	Foolish, and im	632			Grant one poor	283	He hears the	1056
Come to the	1177	Empty of Him	183	For all we love	1177	Gain, to part	796	Grant that	202	He in the days	109
Come to the liv	136	Endless life in	1074	For death His	1433	Gather, first	1455	Grant these re	291	He in the thick	23
Come, wander	50	Endow them	1300	For every thirs	145	Gentiles and	1345	Grant us, dear	1177	He is fitting up	832
Come, worship	1065	Enemies no	1327	For every tribu	753	Gently with the	675	Gravel the	1430	He is waiting	510
Come, ye bless	1336	Enlightened by	123	For God has	1420	Gethsemane	306	Great Advocate	113	He knows what	548
Comfort those	1022	Enrich me at t	263	For good is	1060	Gethsemane	1213	Great Comfort	1045	He knows	508
Compassion dw	383	Enter His gate	1062	For He indeed	321	Gird thou his	1230	Great God! I	718	He leads me to	732
Confiding in	991	Enter, Incarnate	68	For her my	375	Gird thy heav	408	Great God! let	679	He left His	1075
Confirm the pr	378	Enter thyself	622	For her our	1276	Girt with that	652	Great my sins	705	He like a plant	861
Consecrate me	661	Enter, with all	1041	For He's the	1068	Give joy or	880	Great Prophet	232	He lives and	24
Constant to my	637	Enter, with all	288	For Him shall	1340	Give me a calm	445	Great Source	1383	He lives, He	30
Content with	338	Enthroned ami	797	For joys un	1399	Give me a faith	279	Great Sun of	807	He pardons all	240
Convert and	1226	E'er rolling	58	For life and	1399	Give me a faith	648	Green as the	861	He raiseth the	952
Convince us of	1249	Eternal are	1006	For life below	1379	Give me, O Lo	372	Green pastures	764	He reigns above	1
Correct, reprov	618	Eternal Fath	1121	For lo, the days	59	Give me on Th	610	Guard the hel	1301	He riseth to	427
Could we but	1046	Eternal Soure	151	For nights of	526	Give me Thy	608	Guard us from	972	He rules the	1359
Could we but	917	Eternal Spirit	1013	For not like	850	Give me to bear	680	Guard us wak	965	He sat serene	5
Counting gain	553	Eternal wisdom	891	For nothing	247	Give me to read	291	Guilty, but with	195	He saw my pl	284
Create my natu	185	Eternity with all	4	For sovereign	727	Give me to trust	617	Guilty, forgive	190	He saw me r	795
Creatures no m	244	Even down to	986	For strength	1399	Give thee, and	921			He sends His	1314
Crown Him	1079	Ever be Thou	995	For the bless	1397	Give Thou the	1320	Hail, blessed	118	He sent His	1042
Crown Him ye	1071	Ever let Thy	200	For the bless	1397	Give to mine	327	Hail Him here	1142	He shakes the	1051
Crown the Sav	103	Ever present	956	For Thee my	669	Give us now	1373	Hail, mighty	1114	He shall come	1340
Crowns and th	1305	Every eye	1451	For Thee, the	1277	Give us th's	905	Hail, peaceful	495	He shall reign	1314
		Every human	855	For the grand-	224	Giver of all	562	Hail! sacred	1202	He sits upon	1194
Dark and cheer	673	Everything we	1410	For the great	1187	Glad song of	829	Hail the heaven	60	He smiles and	1405
Dark tempta	478	Every tear is	1463	For the mer	1172	Gladdened by	1341	Hallelujah!	1238	He spake the	51
Darkness and	5	Exalt the Lord	20	For this I sho	1202	Gladly, Lord	1461	Hallelujah!	1322	He speaks and	227
Daughter of Z	1350	Exert Thy	294	For Thou hast	912	Gladly we bring	990	Happy are they	976	He spreads His	379
"Day by day"	920	Expand Thy	959	For Thou to	333	Gladly would I	287	Happy only in	553	He strengthens	538
Days of trial	779	Extol the L	1354	For Thou,	1025	Glory to God!	11	Happy souls!	350	He sunk beneath	65
Dead to the wor	68			For Thy rich	224	Glory to God	1087	Happy spirits	1463	He sweetens	735

302

Index of First Lines of Verses.

	Hymn		Hymn		Hymn		Hymn		Hymn		Hymn
He that drinks	137	Higher, still	1076	How sweet thr	703	I welcome all	720	In Jesus is our	507	"Jesus!" all	1001
He that dwell	1017	Higher yet and	663	How sweet to	703	I will love in	304	In life, Thy	256	Jesus beholds	127
He that pre	1222	Him, in whom	1117	How sweet	871	I would, but	641	In me Thy spir	626	Jesus can	1422
He, the good	996	Him to know	278	How vast His	13	I would forever	252	In one fraternal	876	Jesus, Captain	1448
He took the	135	His arm, the	947	How will my	165	I would love	317	In our sickness	051	Jesus, confirm	625
He vanquish	1036	His comforts	517	Humble, holy	553	I would not be	280	In our weak	1378	Jesus, dear	1207
He wept, that	455	His dews drop	774	Hunger, thirst	1462	I would not h	758	In panoply of	417	Jesus, friend	1011
He whispers	794	His goodness	744	Hushed is each	404	I would not live	816	In peopled	1270	Jesus, hail,	1095
He who, a little	988	His government	57			I would not m	503	In prayer my	446	Jesus! I die to	298
He who for	108	His honor is	737	I am bewilder	723	I would not rise	646	In quietness	644	Jesus Imman	966
He who his	955	His laws are	896	I ask in confi	575	I would see	212	In riches, in	171	Jesus, Master	619
He who shuns	863	His love ex	130	I ask Thee for	758	I would submit	529	In scenes ex	1382	Jesus, Master	621
He whose	863	His love what	1039	I ask them	818	I yield my	682	In service	759	Jesus my all	722
He who trusts	863	His mercy never	28	I bid it wel	820	I'd sing the	231	In shining ro	1465	Jesus, my God	742
He will gather	1006	His mercy vis	856	I breathe my	335	If but my faint	563	In shining wh	105	Jesus, my God	125
He will gird	463	His militant	1471	I call to recol	522	If called, like	910	In spite of all	732	Jesus, my hope	486
He will pre	1104	His name dis	592	I can do all	725	If done to obey	861	In suffering be	329	Jesus, my Hy	713
He will protect	464	His name shall	56	I cannot feel	1003	I fear no foe	601	In suffering be	554	Jesus, my Shep	234
He will teach	666	His name yields	338	I cannot have	303	If earthly par	1021	In tender grass	731	Jesus, on	1423
He, with all-	1391	His oath, His	738	I cannot live	185	If He is mine	763	In tender mem	1219	Jesus, our God	99
He with earthly	30	His own soft	1361	I cannot rest	299	If He our ways	132	In that dear	785	Jesus, our	1354
Head of Thy	872	His power, in	56	I change, He	778	If I ask Him	527	In the ark the	181	Jesus, our only	337
Heal me, for	479	His power subt	802	If delivered thee	468	If I have tasted	623	In the begin	904	Jesus protects	757
Hear the pray	972	His purposes	46	I find Him lift	756	If, in the gloom	39	In the begin	1237	Jesus, Saviour	583
Hear us, as	1248	His sacred limbs	83	I flutter, I strug	842	If I in this dark	620	In The I place	755	Jesus, Saviour	336
Hearer of pray	562	His soul will	383	I give the love	279	If I still hold	527	In the furnace	855	Jesus, the	295
Hearken to my	583	His sovereign	1064	I glory in infir	725	If joy shall at	603	In the hour of	913	Jesus, Thee	1050
Hearts that	1337	His Spirit shall	251	I go to see His	835	If life be long	740	In the last hour	67	Jesus, the Lord	216
Heaven is not	1487	His steady	1194	I have long	176	If life's wide	1282	In the midst of	775	Jesus, the Lord	831
Heaven is still	1063	His terrors keep	42	I have no argu	730	If love to God	393	In Thine all-em	11	Jesus, the Lor	1245
Heaven is thy	14	His the fight	104	I have no cares	747	If my immortal	754	In Thine all gra	907	Jesus, the name	227
Heavenly all-	1011	His touch the	71	I have no skill	632	If, night's blue	1490	In Thine own	1022	Jesus the weary	612
Heir of the	1260	His very word	220	I have the h	1499	If on our daily	941	In this divine	1474	Jesus, this	1206
Hell and thy	416	His work my	280	I have the h	206	If on the morn	1282	In this world	1441	Jesus, Thou	1415
He'll never	109	Hither come	142	I hear the Sav	835	If on the wings	15	In those dark	1445	Jesus, Thy	827
He'll shield	1295	Hither, then	1083	I hear the	1358	If pain afflict	398	In Thy fair	726	Jesus, to Thee	149
Help me to	431	Ho! ye that	8,1	I hold Thee	651	If some poor	702	In Thy holy in	1214	Jesus, to Thy	996
Help us, O	985	Hold Thou	601	I huped that	502	If so poor a	285	In Thy pavil	659	Jesus, to whom	530
Help us throu	603	Holy Ghost!	208	I know His	345	If strangers to	923	In times of gen	381	Jesus triumphs	96
Help us to	881	Holy, holy, holy	18	I know that	815	If such be not	520	In true and in	389	Jesus, we Thy	1207
Help us to help	881	Holy, holy	1105	I know the	721	If tears of sor	188	In us "Abba	1041	Jesus, with us	992
Help us to see	1019	Holy Jesus	209	I know Thy	503	If the sorrows	779	In us, for us	1041	Join all the	1115
Hence, and for	72	Holy Spirit!	208	I lay my body	704	If Thou hadst	198	In vain we s	134	Joined in the	865
Hence, gloom	1070	Hope looks be	1414	I lay my gar	697	If Thou the	541	In vain we tu	1043	Joyful all ye	60
Hence, then, ye	113	Hoping ever	394	I lay my wants	322	If to the right	623	In wakeful	560	Joyful are we	1100
Henceforth to	271	Hosanna to	1151	I lift mine eyes	624	If to the right	615	In want, my	722	Joyful crowds	517
Here, at that	283	Hosanna! to	1234	I long, deare.t	824	If to the right	881	In winter, aw	1386	Joy of the des	470
Here faith is	1407	Hosannas, Lo	1257	I long to be	322	I'll lift my	318	Incarnate L	1363	Joy to the	1359
Here faith re	892	How awful is	1450	I look to my	574	I'll read the his	349	Increase, O L	1155	
Here fix my	713	How beautiful	2	I love by faith	699	I'll speak the	319	Indignant jus	237	Keep me	706
Here, gracious	1236	How beautiful	1416	I love her gates	364	I'll make your	1223	Infinite power	1078	Keep our	935
Here I give my	197	How blest are	201	I love in soli	630	I'm weary of	826	Infinite strength	35	Keep us faith	1378
Here in the	847	How blest	1150	I love the Lord	314	Insatiate to this	30	Kind Author	648
Here, in their	876	How can a soul	253	I love Thy	375	I've found a	284	Inscribed	1088	Kind deeds of	384
Here, in Thy	263	How can I die	734	I love to kiss	747	I've wrestled	846	Inured to pov	757	Kindle our	1045
Here I raise	241	How changed	1366	I love to meat	451	Immortal glory	9	Into tempta	905	Kindled His	176
Here is my	785	How charm	1225	I love to think	699	Immortal glo	1495	Into Thy	1199	King of glory	1357
Here is nought	841	How happy are	430	I mark the	749	In all His toils	107	In all our	797	King of kings	1449
Here it is I find	340	How happy Thy	811	I pass the	731	In all their err	935	Is not Thy	310	Kings for	1459
Here let my	754	How His good	728	I pay this	695	In all my ways	632	Is there a thing	293	Knocking	146
Here let the	1239	How holy is His	20	I plead the	559	In autumn a	135	Is there no	1407	Know that the	1059
Here let the S	1241	How glorious	70	I rest beneath	745	In blessing Th	669	Israel, a name	44	Knowing as I	847
Here may the	1243	How great	1228	I rest upon Thy	610	In darkest	790	It can bring	783	Known to all	277
Here may thi	1243	How happy all	263	I saw One	251	In darkest skies	513	It floateth like	184	Knowledge	392
Here may thy	1205	How happy	1225	I see its domes	815	In each event	751	"It is finished"	86	
Here may we	1236	How happy are	430	I see Thee not	308	In early days	721	It is not as	608	Lamb of God	82
Here may we	1025	How happy the	811	I see the Lord	1358	In every could	986	It is not death	1415	Lamb of God	570
Here mercy's	152	How His good	728	I see the	174	In every dark	113	It is not for me	811	Large are the	471
Here, mighty	1241	How holy is His	20	I see th' ex	663	In every joy	751	It is not hard	976	Laws, freedom	1279
Here my peer	503	How kind are	344	I smite upon	177	In every land	1066	It may be we	1379	Lead me	765
Here, O my	754	How little of	415	I stand upon	710	In every scene	1374	It shows to man	889	Lead me to	210
Here on the	372	How long, dear	452	I strive to	715	In every tempt	1300	It stands se	1473	Lead on, dear	807
Here reach Th	368	How loud	1447	I suffered much	451	In fierce temp	618	It tells me of a	225	Lead, Lord, Th	044
Here see the	470	Howl, winds of	7	I take Thy	532	In flowing	1008	It was Thy love	4	Leave no un	1304
Here shall you	857	How many	388	I thank Thee	295	In gentler lan	1152	Its evils in a mo	443	Leave to His	950
Here's love and	97	How mildly	1426	I thirst for	741	In God my	730	Its garments like	889	Lent to us for	991
Here then my	712	How mournful	971	I thought that	535	In heaven and	23	Its pleasures	244	Less of the	638
Here to Thee	1233	How perfect is	898	I, too, with	299	In Him, who	1077			Less wayward	658
Here we come	1157	How shall	1257	I to thy mercy	787	In holy contem	732	Jehovah, Fath	1013	Let all that	1080
Here we sup	1143	How shall our	1033	I wait till He	285	In holy duties	363	Jehovah in	1012	Let all the	1471
Here, when	1234	How such holy	707	I want a sober	611	In hope below	741	Jehovah is	1060	Let all your	410
High as the	802	How surely	52	I want, with all	611	In it all is light	843	Jehovah's aw	528	Let an unusu	1336
High heaven	236	How sweet the	703	I was not ever	636					Let cares like a	827

303

Index of First Lines of Verses.

First Line	Hymn
Let crowds ap	1202
Let differing	1287
Let elders wor	1102
Let everlasting	900
Let every act	1032
Let every crea	1332
Let every kin	1071
Let every pow	1389
Let every th	678
Let every th	268
Let fall Thy	1286
Let faith each	1026
Let goodness	775
Let good or ill	755
Let grace our	603
Let heaven	1336
Let him that	148
Let Jesus tell	763
Let man, by	238
Let me love	639
Let memory	303
Let me neither	631
Let me never	490
Let mountains	41
Let my sins be	1004
Let none hear	419
Let not the	1191
Let not Thy	1191
Let others seek	834
Let others st	711
Let our guilt	1208
Let our mutu	1244
Let our prayers	916
Let our rulers	1364
Let sinners, L	1037
Let sorrow's	823
Let that love	1371
Let the dumb	84
Let the false	893
Let the heart	1362
Let the living	1238
Let them ap	970
Let them His	1050
Let the organ	1058
Let these	1172
Let the sweet	445
Let the world	1143
Let the world	273
Let this blest	690
Let those re	1043
Let thrones	1326
Let Thy blood	1218
Let Thy eter	1019
Let Thy mer	593
Life and peace	490
Life, like a foun	27
Life's bright	1213
Life's ills with	515
Life's labor	1421
Life's tumult	1171
Lift up Thy bl	478
Lift up Thy co	475
Lift up thy vo	1347
Light	1435
Light, in Thy	475
Like a mighty	1325
Like Him	413
Like Lebanon	1272
Like mighty	1033
Like some	308
Like the dew	1041
Like the sun's	927
Linger not in	163
Linger not, lin	173
Listen to the	58
Listen to the	408
Little children	1006
Little then my	449
Lives again,	94
Living in the	707
Living or dying	208
Lo! glad I	196
Lo! He comes	479

First Line	Hymn
Lo the hills	1293
Lo, Thy chur	1258
Lo 't is He	1355
Lo with deep	1371
Lonely I no	373
Lonely seems	700
Long as I live	267
Long as we	1097
Long have we	1144
Long my im	243
Look as when	474
Look down on	723
Look on the	1217
Look to Him	914
Look up, my	715
Loose all your	100
Lord, arm me	269
Lord, at Thy	178
Lord, be mine	360
Lord, dost	569
Lord, ere the	1456
Lord, for Thy	1376
Lord, from the	787
Lord, from	1240
Lord, from	1019
Lord, give us	1254
Lord, grant us	885
Lord, here we	3
Lord, I address	252
Lord, I am	191
Lord, I believe	645
Lord, I desire	538
Lord! I my	677
Lord, in cease	340
Lord, in this	1165
Lord, I shall	335
Lord, I would	534
Lord Jesus	839
Lord, keep me	697
Lord, Lord	1324
Lord, make	917
Lord, may I	376
Lord, may it	947
Lord, may our	876
Lord, may that	1165
Lord, now in	247
Lord! obedi	1032
Lord of all life	49
Lord of all	312
Lord of glory	570
Lord of our	969
Lord of the	1277
Lord, on our	1150
Lord, on Thee	1022
Lord! our times	920
Lord! search	473
Lord! shall we	447
Lord! shower	871
Lord, this	226
Lord, Thou	619
Lord, Thy	1181
Lord, Thy per	958
Lord, till I	404
Lord! turn our	1031
Lord, uphold	631
Lord, visit Th	1285
Lord, we obey	1089
Lord, when	1315
"Lord, why is	502
Lord, with this	701
Loud from the	1351
Loud may the	41
Love and grief	340
Love is the	883
Love of God	484
Love shall ev	953
Love's redeem	94
Lowly we	1208

First Line	Hymn
Man may troub	273
March on then	977
Mark but that	1424
Mark the sacri	82
May each we	1486
May erring	1240
May every	1403
May every pas	1247
May faith, deep	929
May faith gr	1240
May He, by	882
May He our ac	928
May He teach	1183
May I remem	543
May peace at	361
May strug	1171
May the blood	200
May the dear	268
May they that	1224
May Thy gos	1157
May Thy rich	649
May Thy will	604
May we, a little	866
May we in	1016
May we this	932
May young	1247
Me for Thine	745
Me with that	295
Mean are all	912
Meekly may my	396
Men die in	420
Mercy and	555
Mid the homes	1301
Mid these	953
Midst keen re	67
Mild He lays	60
Millions of	1201
Mindful of our	972
Mine is an un	468
Minutes and	963
More dear than	669
More of myself	207
More of Thy	291
More of Thys	652
More than con	1457
Mortals with joy	42
Mother of cit	335
Multitude	1451
Musing on my	630
Must I be car	415
My cheerful	549
My days, un	690
My dear al	232
My dying Sav	324
My faith would	480
My Father God	259
My Father's	821
My Father's	834
My feet shall	461
My feet shall	733
My feet shall	805
My flesh shall	1443
My flesh would	339
My God! how	27
My God is rec	258
My God, Thy	503
My God! to cel	790
My gracious	227
My grateful	793
My great pro	549
My heart for	794
My heart grows	556
My heart is	746
My heart shall	338
My Hope, my	346
My Jesus ! as	540
My knowledge	740
My life, my joy	807
My lifted eye	751
My lips with	186
My longing	367
My Lord if	785

First Line	Hymn
My Lord on	305
My message as	156
My mind, by	579
My native	1402
My Peace, my	491
My place of	646
My Saviour's	365
My Saviour's	821
My Saviour	784
Myself I can	617
My soul! ask	403
My soul at rest	246
My soul, in	684
My soul its ev	246
My soul lies	187
My soul looks	480
My soul! no	890
My soul obeys	180
My soul shall	364
My soul to	270
My soul to Th	617
My soul with	616
My soul would	790
My soul would	819
My spirit home	817
My spirit in	684
My steadfast	716
My steadfast s	330
My thoughts be	556
My thoughts lie	12
My tongue re	361
My willing soul	335
My wisdom and	624
Name above	334
Near the cross	620
Nearer is my	833
Needful is Thy	581
Night the face	1435
Night unto	679
No act fails	425
No anxious	1464
No bar would I	248
No bleeding	125
No bliss I 'll	729
No cloud	1485
No condemna	243
No dimming	837
No distant Chr	506
No evil tidings	381
No guile within	76
No heavenly	1162
No; I must	564
No; is not this	1368
No; let me	558
No more a lily	848
No more a wan	234
No more a	1269
No more f	1161
No more f	300
No more let h	1310
No more let s	1359
No more shall	1346
No more the	1072
No more the s	167
No nor other name	591
No profit canst	949
No room for	1211
No rude alar	1161
No sin to cloud	656
No sinful word	936

First Line	Hymn
No strength of	961
No suffering	976
No Sun there	1478
No wider is the	853
No winter	1491
No words can	404
Nor alms, nor	177
Nor death, nor	737
Nor doth it yet	861
Nor earth, nor	313
Nor pain, nor	1439
Nor shall fail	800
Nor shall my	221
Nor shall the	879
Nor shall Thy	897
Nor time, nor	1038
Nor voice can	337
Nor will I	221
Nor will our	1176
Nor would I	542
Not a brief	600
Not all our	130
Not all the bl	681
Not all the har	313
Not for ease	765
Not half so far	31
Not half so high	31
Not life itself	681
Not many	1375
Not only olden	1317
Not so your	163
Not the fair	372
Not the labors	199
Not vows	131
Not what we	907
Not with the	302
Nothing have I	431
Nothing he	427
Nothing in my	799
Nothing more	1035
Nothing ye in	136
Now for the	204
Never, from	937
Never weary of	394
Never will He	116
Never will I re	624
Now He 's	144
Now I am	263
Now in Thy	368
Now incline me	176
Now lend Thy	1251
Now let me	831
Now, Lord, I	198
Now, Lord, my	189
Now may the	354
Now may we	1057
Now, O God	285
Now proclaim	104
Now rest my	236
Now shall my	260
Now the frail	743
Now the full	235
Now the heav	1455
Now, then, my	269
Now, these lit	997
Now, they	1461
Now, though H	65
Now to Thee	1150
Now to the G	1030
Now to the L	1102
Now to the sh	825
Now to Thy	366

First Line	Hymn
O abide, abide	1410
O all-sufficient	256
O arm me	628
O be His ser	266
O bid this trif	353
O blessed work	433
O bless the L	40
O cease, my	766
O Christ, for	1452
O Christ, He is	846
O come and	1322
O come, then	472
O come to this	547

First Line	Hymn
O could my	810
O could we	1496
O deathless	279
O enter His	1060
O enter then	1059
O enter then	1063
O Father	1365
O fill Thy	1328
O for an an	1465
O for an an	1486
O for a sight	1419
O for grace our	939
O for the liv	1058
O for this love	1086
O give Thine	988
O give us	873
O gladly tread	888
O glorious	1443
O God of love	1267
O God of na	1384
O God, our	1171
O God, the	1107
O God Triune	1106
O gracious God	409
O grant me to	539
O grant that	328
O grant Thy	989
O grant us	892
O guard our	1277
O guide me	687
O guide our	1196
O hallowed	929
O happy bond	236
O happy, hap	388
O happy harbor	837
O happy heav	569
O happy ser	410
O happy souls	1145
O haste to fol	888
O help us, Jes	923
O help us when	923
O holy, heav	1497
O holy Spirit	569
O holy Spirit	1106
O hope of ev	337
O how benevo	78
O how can	803
O how shall	1490
O how sweet it	840
O if my Lord	1422
O if this	1210
O Jesus, come	588
O Jesus, ever	930
O Jesus, full of	457
O Jesus, Lam	106
O Jesus, Light	1094
O Jesus, Sav	336
O Jesus, Thou	476
O joy all joys	1468
O keep me in	409
O keep my soul	507
O lead me to	514
O let a holy	1044
O let me, Lord	569
O let me, then	531
O let my won	1384
O let the dead	254
O let the k	1313
O let them	1287
O let them sp	1226
O let the saints	29
O let Thy ch	1251
O let Thy grace	265
O let Thy ris	932
O let Thy sac	155
O let Thy ta	1202
O light in dark	333
O light of Zion	1311
O like the sun	672
O long-expect	1161
O Lord accept	1237
O Lord and	911
O Lord, I cast	786

Index of First Lines of Verses.

First Line	Hymn	First Line	Hymn	First Line	Hymn	First Line	Hymn	First Line	Hymn	First Line	Hymn
O Lord, in	1227	O vale of tears	937	Our Heavenly	1021	Ready the Fath	151	See th' angelic	1074	So when the	1423
O Lord, I seek	644	O voice of mer	469	Our Hope and	1331	Reason and con	288	See that glory	1411	So when the	115
O Lord of	901	O wash my soul	186	Our hope wh	1387	Rebel, ye waves	7	See that your	1331	So when Thy	126
O Lord, should	542	O watch and	412	Our labors	1416	Redeemer! com	276	See, the feast	1220	So will Thy	1370
O lovely atti	160	O water, life	1206	Our lives through	4	Refining Fire	330	See the Judge	1449	So, with mild	121
O magnify the	801	O welcome day	815	Our midnight is	49	Regard me	183	See, the stream	852	So, within Thy	1378
O make but	801	O what are all	820	Our prayers	1255	Reign in me, L	605	See, there, His	83	So would I	302
O Master, it is	987	O when His wis	6	Our quickened	860	Reign Thou	335	See where it	218	Sole, self-exist	17
O may all en	1189	O when thou	836	Our reason	3	Rejoice in hope	789	Seed-time and	1395	Soldier of Ch	1432
O may I live	218	O when will	812	Our restless	930	Rejoice when	789	Seek we, then	943	Sometimes mid	534
O may I love	628	O when wilt	432	Our Sacrifice is	872	Rejoice, ye	25	Seize the kind	1053	Songs of prais	1112
O may I never	598	O when wilt	574	Our sins and	80	Rejoicing now	653	Send down in	1267	Soon and for	1500
O may I never	266	O who like Thee	64	Our soaring spir	3	Rejoicing thus	297	Send forth Th	1270	Soon as the eve	36
O may my soul	691	O why should	596	Our souls and	926	Relief alone	130	Send some	1022	Soon as the I	1174
O may our sym	1263	O wondrous	12	Our souls He	1194	Religion bears	962	Send them Th	1270	Soon as the m	446
O may that	872	Obedient faith	389	Our sun is sick	974	Remember still	998	Send, then, Th	1288	Soon as the m	616
O may the h	1485	O'er all the	229	Our thanks we	1307	Remember Th	306	Sent by my L	156	Soon as we	125
O may the least	615	O'er earth	709	Our vows, our	906	Remember Th	1215	Seraphs with	831	Soon, for me	708
O may the right	671	O'er a faithless	1301	Our wasting	1406	Remember Th	191	Serene I laid	674	Soon shall my	580
O may these	556	O'er tears of	784	Ours, by the	1433	Remove this	647	Servant, at	432	Soon shall this	47
O may the s	1099	Of all the	1413	Out of great	1457	Renew my will	563	Set up Thy	1330	Soon shall ye	1081
O may Thy S	1036	Of His deliv	801			Repeated crime	113	Seven times He	81	Soon, soon	869
O may Thy qui	366	Of His gospel	1302	Pardon all my	706	Repent, return	460	Shall aught be	1425	Soon Thou wilt	323
O may we ever	865	Oft I walk be	499	Pardon, O God	676	Rest for my	641	Shall God in	163	Soon, too soon	1164
O may we love	871	Oft the nights	499	Partakers of	865	Retreat bence	507	Shall I with	265	Soon we pass	843
O may we nev	1098	Oft when the	357	Paschal Lamb	1035	Return, O bl	1383	Shall join the	820	Sorrow and fear	530
O might I hear	220	On all our	1251	Pass me not	483	Return, O h	654	Shall we Thy	1213	Soul of my soul	289
O mighty grace	937	On all the	1375	Patient Suffer	495	Return unto	770	Shine, dearest	1058	Sounds of	792
O mine, O	1499	On cherubim and	5	Patience to	921	Revive our	1249	Shine, Lord!	642	Source of all	1034
O my Saviour	332	On earth they	1008	Peace from the	379	Revive Thy	1247	Should cunning	823	Sow thy seed	428
O ne'er will I	752	On hearts in	1227	Peace is on	1168	Revive us	1110	Should I dis	303	Spare, Lord	1259
O never let	549	On Him the Sp	54	Peace on earth	58	Ride on in Th	1352	Should strong	504	Speak, and the	1312
O not in doubt	985	On mountain	1328	Peace on this	1405	Rise, bright	842	Should swift	967	Speak gently	1260
O on that day	1451	On our fields	1364	Peace to our	1179	Rise, Saviour	446	Should Thine	1307	Speak Thou	1044
O passing hap	837	On Thee alone	783	People and	1332	Riven the Rock	662	Should Thy	1100	Speak Thy par	400
O sacred heart	494	On thee, at	1166	Perfect our	1372	Rivers of love	891	Should Thy	631	Speak to my	612
O Sacred Spir	1280	On Thee my	709	Permit them to	994	Rivers to the	828	Shout ye lit	1082	Speed on the	1306
O Saviour, give	922	On Thee, O	300	Perpetual bless	701	Rock of Ages!	779	Shout, ye saints	91	Spirit of glory	486
O Saviour in	485	On Thee we f	1226	Perverse and	760	Room in the	147	Shows me the	390	Spirit of grace	1147
O Saviour, La	1010	On Thee we h	931	Pilgrim, see	1329	Round each	852	Shew us some	1016	Spirit of our	960
O Saviour wh	1280	On the Eternal	953	Pilgrims here	68	Rule then, O	1283	Shudder not to	1428	Spirit of truth	966
O Saviour wi	1242	Once again, be	305	Pilgrims in	1456	Rule Thou in	294	Sin hath bruised	89	Spread for the	143
O send Thy	368	Once a sinner	564	Pillar of fire	885	Run the straig	438	Sin nor death	593	Spread throug	1314
O send Thy	887	Once earthly	660	Pity and heal	184			Since all, that	781	Spread Thy great	2
O send Thy S	633	Once more our	868	Pity dwelleth	394	Sad and wea	1164	Since from His	284	Sprinkled afres	701
O shall not	1217	Once safe in	190	Pity the weep	382	Had to his toil	439	Since ef Thy	731	Sprinkled now	143
O shed abroad	1252	Once the	272	Place on the	512	Safe the dreary	637	Since ef Thy	38	Spurn not the	164
O shine on this	477	Once they were	818	Plenteous grace	572	Saints, begin	1469	Since, on this	1246	Stand, then, in	1304
O side from	494	Once with	239	Poor though I	521	Saints below	1112	Since Thou	560	Standing alone	723
O song of light	829	One army of	1471	Poor tremblers	980	Salvation! let	1268	Sing how eter	1089	Standing now	481
O Son of God	1456	One family	1471	Pour forth Thi	992	Salvation to	1101	Sing, my soul	223	Star divine, O	124
O Spirit of the	1319	One more day's	433	Pour out the	1289	Sanctify us, L	1207	Sing, O sing	832	Star of faith	128
O spread Thy	906	One narrow	810	Praise Him	1393	Save me from	622	Sing the Son's	1108	Star of hope	1284
O tell of His	1055	One privilege	714	Praise, my soul	226	Save us in Th	1250	Sing till we	1081	Stay with us	336
O that every	1278	One with Thy	873	Praise the L	1067	Saved! the	195	Sing, we, then	1108	Steep all our	924
O that I could	278	Only, O Lord	941	Praises to H	1109	Saviour! at Th	604	Sing, we, too	1108	Still bear with	1376
O that I now	647	Only thy rest	508	Pray thou	434	Saviour! breath	960	Sinner, it was	164	Still give us	1269
O that my ten	613	Onward shall	1307	Prayer is the	401	Saviour! I long	621	Sinners!	1071	Still heavy is	950
O that our	363	Onward, then	841	Prayer makes	400	Saviour, look	519	Slain in the	963	Still let Him	623
O that the an	1326	Open now the	630	Precious is the	459	Saviour, lo	1316	Slain to re	1097	Still looking to	545
O that the w	1046	Or if on joyful	630	Precious is Th	1173	Saviour of souls	985	Smile, Lord	1315	Still may Thy	1151
O that to Thee	613	Or if some dark	910	Prepare us, L	1485	Saviour, may	1168	So blooms the	1444	Still may Thy	1374
O that with all	663	Or worn by	144	Present we	1056	Saviour, Prince	474	So dear, so very	70	Still my feet	675
O that with	1071	Order my foot	633	Preserve it	1188	Saviour, shine	449	So every kin	1330	Still onward	1077
O the lost, the	707	Other knowl	278	Preserve us in	1103	Saviour! we	1349	So fades a sum	1421	Still, restless na	1
O the music	841	Other lords	621	Prevent me	598	Saviour! we	1271	So grant me, L	636	Still the great	916
O then, blessed	602	Other refuge	57	Prevent, pre	451	Saviour! where	629	So grant the	1387	Still the Spirit	1168
O then what	1488	Our blessed	1192	Prince of Life	570	Saviour, who	1230	So here I lay	603	Still, through	59
O then, with	1	Our children's	47	Prisoner!	1430	Say not 't is thy	169	So Jesus rose	944	Still, to the	397
O the rich	783	Our contrite	1026	Proclaim abro	1096	Scatter the last	605	So Jesus slept	1439	Still we wait	1250
O this is life	710	Our daily	95	Proc'aim Him	1061	Seal my for	690	So Jesus still	944	Straight I up	533
O Thou by	401	Our fallen, ru	1012	Promises how	728	Searcher of	179	So long Thy	636	Stretch forth	1264
O Thou dear	83	Our fathers' G	1266	Prostrate bow	168	Season of rest	1176	So, Lord, when	942	Strong were	1350
O Thou eter	1299	Our fathers' G	1402	Protect me	577	Seasons, and	1388	So may we	1400	Stronger His	325
O Thou, long-ex	833	Our fathers w	1413	Publish, sprea	1117	Seasons and	1390	So nigh, so ve	780	Subdue the	1047
O Thou, our	951	Our fellow-suf	108	Pure are the	1472	Secure from	1436	So shall it be	688	Subdued and	535
O Thou, who	988	Our flesh and	962	Pure man	1486	Seen from His	203	So shall our	1151	Submissive	541
O Thou wh	1230	Our glad hosan	54	Put all thy	1346	See heathen	1336	So shall you	426	Such, Father	982
O Thou who	667	Our God in	1192			See Him set	156	So sweet the	773	Such guests	38
O to be	516	Our guilty souls	127	Quick as the	615	See, Jesus	147	So when e'er	1100	Such is the	1424
O to grace how	241	Our guilty sp	129			See, low before	477	So when I pass	705	Such seeds of	124
O Trinity of	1280	Our hearts are	1497	Raised on de	797	See me, Sav	474	So when my	847	Such was Thy	606
O turn us	1366	Our hearts have	866	Ready for all	625	See my utter	501	So, when our	1235	Sun, moon, and	897

305

Index of First Lines of Verses.

	Hymn		Hymn		Hymn		Hymn		Hymn		Hymn
Sun of our life	49	The crown of	1434	The present	1246	Then in a no	225	There shall I w	416	Thou art our	995
Sure as Thy	375	The cup of	1212	The prisoner	892	Then is my	404	There shall my	221	Thou art the e	492
Sure, I must	415	The darkness	896	The powers of	129	Then let crea	973	There shall th	1031	Thou art the g	309
Sure, never tell	251	The darkness of	249	The rising God	97	Then let my	416	There shed	262	Thou art the g	995
Sure the Holy	119	The day is	1177	The saddened	945	Then let our	1049	There smiling	1488	Thou art the s	313
Sure there was	452	The dazzling	1490	The saints of	1442	Then let the	1408	There the	831	Thou, as a	1405
Surely Christ	467	The dearest	654	The saints on	874	Then let us ad	1101	There the glory	813	Thou blessed	323
Sweet as home	140	The deepest	21	The saints wh	1447	Then let us ea	1245	There the L	843	Thou callest me	712
Sweet as the	121	The dying thief	225	The Saviour	886	Then, like the	1368	There the great	369	Thou canst fit	583
Sweet, at the	1159	The evening	1408	The Saviour	1221	Then loud	1352	There the Re	1072	Thou canst not	422
Sweet book! in	348	The evil of my	249	The scourge, the	84	Then love's	1416	There, there, on	940	Thou comest	1116
Sweet fields	1496	The faith that	746	The seeds are	25	Then, my soul	951	There, what	351	Thou givest me	514
Sweet is the d	338	The Father h	258	The shelter of	785	Then needful	581	There, with	1143	Thou God of	271
Sweet is the l	1176	The Father, S	151	The shepherd	1231	Then, O my soul	23	Therefore in	721	Thou God of	643
Sweet on this	1159	The feeling	1016	The Shepherd	234	Then say to	1149	There 's a song	547	Thou Great and	318
Sweet truth	531	The few that	378	The shining an	93	Then shall I m	795	There 's room	154	Thou hast b	604
Swift as an ea	946	The fires that	115	The sinner's	377	Then shall l s	358	There 's the	813	Thou hast h	564
Swift to its	600	The flowery	1388	The softened	1385	Then shall my	294	These ashes	1416	Thou hast kept	675
		The forests in	40	The Son of	455	Then shall my	655	These, and	1369	Thou hast m	1373
Take all the	573	The former	1387	The sorrow	77	Then shall my	660	These children	989	Thou hast my	269
Take His easy	740	The gladness	1092	The soul that	987	Then shall my	346	These clouds	579	Thou hast	1318
Take my soul	285	The glorious	886	The sovereign	860	Then shall na	1449	These pleas	1372	Thou hast	1002
Take the name	342	The God of g	1361	The spacious	51	Then shall w	1325	These through	1462	Thou heard'st	1279
Take Thou	1273	The God of h	1398	The Spirit and	150	Then snatch	193	These to Thee	1397	Thou Holy Gh	1290
Teach all the	1223	The good, the	422	The Spirit, by	120	Then, then	545	These various	1395	Thou holy God l	21
Teach me to	403	The gospel	1354	The Spirit calls	149	Then the writ	1449	These walls	1239	Thou, Holy S	1010
Teach them	1228	The grace	1046	The Spirit cam	117	Then they	1442	They are justi	858	Thou knowest	693
Teach Thou	979	The graves of	148	The Spirit, like	860	Then, though	539	They are lights	858	Thou knowest	668
Teach us in	1184	The hand of	744	The springs	749	Then, through	1271	They climbed	413	Thou knowest	457
Teach us, O	441	The hand that	900	The spring's	1395	Then, to the	1031	They come, on	963	Thou know'st	310
Teach us to	1037	The highest h	1407	The star that	924	Then, to Thy e	353	They die in	1437	Thou mine	478
Tell him, it	1261	The highest pl	106	The sun that	794	Then, to thy r	770	They find ac	262	Thou my De	799
Tell him of	1261	The hopes that	899	The sun with	1383	Then what	583	They go from	1145	Thou my life	292
Tell me, faint	495	The hosts of G	801	The task Thy	680	Then when	1233	They have	1461	Thou, O Christ	572
Tell me the	341	The hosts of s	1467	The terror and	411	Then why, O	302	They leave	1359	Thou, O my	302
Tell of His	220	The humble	402	The things of	220	Then will He	742	They marked	818	Thou on the	949
Tempest-tossed	181	The joyful news	288	The things un	386	Then will I say	533	They mourn	245	Thou our daily	920
Tempt not my	345	The joy of all	106	The thirsty	1390	Then will I	187	They produce	858	Thou our only	927
Temptations	544	The joy of the	1149	The thought	1423	Then will I tell	196	They shall find	138	Thou Prince	1290
Ten thousand	803	The joy of Thy	596	The thunders of	10	Then, with an	1118	They shall nev	1460	Thou shalt see	468
Ten thousand	846	The joy Thy	482	The tide of crea	51	Then, within	997	They sing of	1073	Thou spread'st	760
Ten thousand	585	The kingdom	635	The time	1442	Then, with my	650	They sing the	105	Thou spread'st	682
Tender and	374	The King Him	355	The tokens of	1212	Then, with our	1047	They stand	1489	Thou, Thou	1255
Thankful I	612	The King of	193	The trivial	941	Then, with the	454	They watch	1224	Thou tookest	1317
Thanks for	1380	The Lamb	1345	The troubled	123	There all the	1495	Thine all-sur	12	Thou to the	118
Thanks we	1250	The law dis	890	The unwearied	36	There are	661	Thine earthly	1161	Thou tread'st	411
That blessed	289	The least and	777	The veil of	1285	There are set	759	Thine image	403	Thou waitest to	32
That deeper	687	The light of	1420	The want of	830	There, at my	830	Thine inward	488	Thou, who	1272
That eye is	399	The light of tr	210	The watch	1225	There everlast	1496	Thine the na	1100	Thou, who dost	209
That glory	1234	The little hills	1385	The way to	158	There faith	1476	Thine, wholly	908	Thou, who hast	515
That hand in	1384	The Lord be	314	The whole cre	1450	There, for me	175	Thine would I	283	Thou, whose	708
That, having	1304	The Lord His	370	The whole cre	1080	There fragrant	1476	Think of Thy	188	Thou, whose	1048
That light	1311	The Lord is	1062	The work begun	33	There, from the	825	This day must	365	Thou wilt my	723
That long as	1196	The Lord is King	6	The works and	893	There gar	1054	This day shall	61	Thou wilt not	505
That love, this	532	The Lord of	1339	The works of	886	There He helps	116	This fleshly	937	Thou wilt not	1259
That man may	441	The Lord sits	1152	The world and	213	There His tri	100	This grace on	934	Thou wondrous	191
That peace	982	The Lord sup	28	The world has	1192	There, if Thy	568	This heavenly	363	Tho' dark be	751
That power is	399	The Lord, the	8	The world re	595	There, in wor	1014	This is employ	362	Though buri	1189
That rich aton	403	The Lord will	1454	The world shut	584	There is a day	1420	This is My	1200	Though careful	297
That tender	68	The Lord yiel	980	The wounded	390	There is a voi	1470	This is salva	130	Though cloth	260
That truth	532	The love of	775	The year rolls	1406	There is a h	1476	This is the h	854	Though clouds	952
That unchang	840	The martyr first	413	The young	1039	There is a h	1488	This is the day	1156	Though dark	1466
That when my	697	The Master	1278	Thee at all	719	There is a l	1468	This is the first	1156	Though dead	376
That will not	1254	The meanest	1467	Thee, Holy	1120	There is an	399	This is the gr	392	Though des	967
The atonement	324	The men of	1049	Thee, in the	670	There is a p	1495	This is the hid	584	Though dis	511
The balm of	1088	The mighty God	57	Thee, in Thy	877	There is a place	940	This is the pil	134	Though earth	1481
The best relief	349	The mite my	380	Thee the first	1113	There is a stream	41	This is the r	565	Though faith	764
The birds, with	961	The more I	196	Thee we ex	1038	There is a w	1417	This is the way	196	Though fields	730
The blessing of	902	The morning	327	Thee will I	327	There is no gr	1492	This lamp	889	Though from	730
The bliss Thou	299	The morning	391	Their bodies	1440	There is no se	515	This only can	717	Though high	1058
The bounties of	732	The mountains	1132	Their harmony	761	There is no sin	1492	This only this	378	Though I have	185
The bow of	1478	The mountains	761	Their ransom	1440	There is peace	547	This precious	33	Though I have	189
The breezes	944	The nation	110	Their sighs	1466	There is the	1489	This spotless	254	Though in the	736
The church fr	884	The nation	1403	Their stream	879	There Jesus	351	This was com	65	Though like	650
The church tri	877	The north	1344	Then all these	1270	There let it for	625	This will I do	271	Though long	931
The cloud and	634	The old, old	1081	Then bless the	240	There let the	650	Thither, forget	954	Though many	506
The Comforter	821	The opening	790	Then blessed	576	There, like an	471	This, like an	1477	Though many	440
The consecrate	430	The pains of	1432	Then, come in	1386	There, Lord!	1478	Those charac	110	Though now	108
The consola	574	The peaceful	1057	Then come to	472	There, low be	1495	Those holy	1572	Though oft	335
The creature of	265	The peace of	1475	Then dear to	357	There safe thou	766	Those joys	863	Though oft Th	541
The cross He	106	The peace that	552	Then fall the	834	"There," says	1024	Thou all our	555	Though snares	387
The cross is	1484	The precious	1396	Then from the	1323	There shall l b	827	Thou art my	805	Though our	1371
The crowd of	388	The precious	309	Then garlands	1054	There shall I	714	Thou art my	746	Though some	440

306

Index of First Lines of Verses.

Hymn		Hymn		Hymn		Hymn		Hymn		Hymn
Though ten	511	Thy love by	66	'T is to my Sav	280	Under His	1204	We'll crowd	1064	When pain o'er 607
Though the	967	Thy love can	529	'T is true we	1412	Under the	50	We'll talk of	882	When peni	498
Though they	1263	Thy love it	343	'T is well when	772	Unholy and im	127	Well done	964	When rising	629
Though uns	1209	Thy love, O	602	'T is what I	652	Unite us in	1277	Well might the	500	When satan ap 961
Though unseen 228		Thy love the	751	'T is when thy	506	Unless it come	576	Well, the de	231	When satan, by 496
Though unw	1118	Thy love will	815	To chase the	128	Unshaken as	850	Well, when	772	When shall I	838
Though vine	782	Thy mercy bids 750		To comfort and 919		Until I find, O 668		Weep, O my	1452	When shall we 1464
Though we ar 1193		Thy mercy-seat 523		To-day a par	155	Unwearied may 328		Were I in heav 316		When should	789
Though we h	1180	Thy mercy st	715	To-day attend 1065		Up and ever	1005	Were I inspir	393	When shrivel	1451
Though we m	1115	Thy mercy tem	37	To-day He	1154	Up, then, with	423	Were I posses	711	When sinks the 688
Though we pas 975		Thy mighty	722	To-day on	1166	Up to the hills	386	Were the whole 203		When sorrow	518
Thrice holy	26	The minister	696	To do his heav	69	Uphold me, S	638	We 've no abid 1483		When sorrow	498
Through all et 803		Thy ministers	126	To each the	879	Upon the wil	817	What are our	201	When storms	739
Through all His 10		Thy morning	1390	To Father, S	1109	Upon us lay	902	What brought 1008		When streams	867
Through all His 42		Thy nature be	289	To gentle offi	379	Upon your	382	What can these 508		When tempest 1481
Through all my 504		Thy nature	627	To God direct	362			What fills my	753	When tem	1282
Through all th 701		Thy never fail 1034		To God, the	1179	Vain every	237	What glories	856	When the full	496
Through all the 454		Thy only will	296	To guide me	559	Vain searchers	16	What greater	118	When the m	1265
Through chan 1179		Thy pardoning 453		To heaven, the 284		Vain the stone	94	What if the	316	When the roun 689
Through each	13	Thy power and 123		To Him, en	1097	Vain were all	943	What I hope	589	When the soft	702
Through each	906	Thy powerful	1407	To Him I owe 284		Vainer still the 943		What I possess 667		When the sun	806
Through every 803		Thy power in	1400	To Him our	1115	Veiled in flesh	60	What is it keep 179		When the woes 806
Through many 788		Thy power is in 15		To Him shall	1332	Victor o'er death 98		What is my	280	When they	1283
Through might 795		Thy power un	17	To Him who	1097	Vine of heav	1216	What peaceful 654		When Thou	1452
Through paths	71	Thy presence	810	To Jordan's	1436	Visit them	673	What secret	16	When through 987
Through ten	1341	Thy promise, L	52	To keep your	1304			What shall I	271	When thy days 771
Through the	689	Thy promise is 182		To meditate	352	Waft, waft ye	1291	What shall I	184	When to the	306
Through the	1187	Thy ransom'd	264	To meet our	1105	Wake, and lift	677	What ruin	1264	When unto	323
Through the	775	Thy sinless	604	To mine illu	488	Wake thee, O	1349	What rush of	1458	When, weary	496
Through this	639	Thy sins I bore 150		To-morrow's	1192	Waken, O L	1406	What though I 744		When we, asun 875
Through this	1052	Thy sovereign	270	To nakedness	1368	Wash it from	993	What though	1303	When we dis	1026
Through waves 950		Thy sovereign	717	To our bounti 1493		Wash me, and	324	What though	1291	Where am I	456
Thus doth the	72	Thy Spirit, O	578	To please	456	Wash out its	629	What though	830	Where about Th 596
Thus far His	793	Thy Spirit's	1153	To save a guilty 80		Was it for	500	What though	950	Where every	1235
Thus life with	211	Thy Spirit	1251	To scorn the	561	Watch by the	702	What Thou	640	Where love in	883
Thus, like the	1491	Thy temple is 1165		To see Thee	1210	Watch, for	498	Whate'er ev	755	Where none	878
Thus may we	1182	Thy threaten	350	To see Thee	971	Watchman	1329	Whate'er I say 202		Where sin did	133
Thus might I	500	Thy throne eter	4	To serve the	431	Watch o'er my 671		Whate'er the	509	Where the liv	1460
Thus my heart 1281		Thy truth un	930	To songs of	1159	Watch! 't is	410	Whate'er Thou 824		Where the sain 816
Thus on the	870	Thy various	750	To spread the	67	We ask not, F 982		Whate'er Thy	717	Wherever earth 14
Thus onward	853	Thy victories	1119	To that dear	1183	We ask not for	993	When against	469	Wherever He	762
Thus present	915	Thy voice pro	1	To that Jerusa 443		We ask not L	1162	When all cre	786	Wherever in	758
Thus preserved 640		Thy walls are	849	To Thee alone	2	We are sinful	1041	When all is	382	Whether they	964
Thus shall	1000	Thy will by me 575		To Thee, dea	1500	We are Thine	1002	When anxious	222	Whether to live 298
Thus shall we	962	Thy word is	894	To Thee, I still	281	We are travel	1082	When cares	504	Whether we	981
Thus star by	1417	Thy word has	552	To Thee, I tell	523	We bless Th	1237	When darkness 758		Which of all	939
Thus strong in 417		Thy worship	696	To Thee let	1289	We bring them 994		When death	222	While all our	1203
Thus, till my	681	Thy wounds	24	To Thee shall 1374		We cannot	917	When death	1382	While He nf	732
Thus we en	1194	Till that blest	832	To Thee, tho	1091	We can see	1497	When death	308	While here in	824
Thus we our	1247	Till then, nor	344	To Thee, to	817	We come, obe 1205		When each can 883		While He tho	93
Thus, when li	699	Till Thou anew 613		To Thee we	1198	We come to	1037	When ends	649	While I am a	551
Thus, when the 704		Time is wing	1418	To Thee will	799	We expect a	975	When ends	640	While I con	245
Thus while His 251		Times of sick	719	To the heav	1455	We, for whom	447	When evening	684	While I draw	199
Thus will the	880	'T is a broad	349	To them the	106	We, for whose 447		When exposed 1302		While I hear	371
Thus wisdom's	63	'T is but a lit	1480	To the weary	1301	We give the	1122	When fear her	34	While I lay	715
Thus with my	695	'T is by the	112	To this dear	282	We have a	1473	When, free	883	While in Thy 1146
Thus with sac 1148		'T is done! O	88	To Thy benign	65	We have not	974	When from the 254		While I sit in	212
Thus would I	584	'T is done; the 236		To us Thy	1018	We honor our	111	When gladness 751		While Jews on 112
Thus would my 674		'T is done, the	85	To watch and 1233		We join to	1158	When God in	402	While life's	649
Thy blood	131	'T is everlast	778	To Zion's	1436	We know it	1268	When God is	756	While looking	545
Thy bountiful 1055		'T is God's all	429	Too faint our	1179	We mark her	850	When groaning 514		While our	1014
Thy bright ex	432	'T is He for	804	Too long my	270	We meet at	1024	When He came 332		While the an	228
Thy chosen	1147	'T is He, my	795	Together in Hi 617		We meet the	1036	When I faint	507	While the foe 1335
Thy covenant	720	'T is here the	791	Toil on, and in 418		We meet with 1039		When I have	496	While the pr	371
Thy cross, not 242		'T is He that	24	Toil on; faint	420	We mourn not 1162		When in flow	499	While, Thine 1169
Thy death, not 242		'T is He that	909	Toiling early 1005		We oft have	1400	When in His	1498	While this th	1172
Thy favor all	558	'T is His al	1104	Touched with a 109		We plead Thy 1372		When in the	1395	While this we 1211
Thy foes in	849	'T is Jesus' bl	498	Trembling arm 495		We praise Th	979	When in the	691	While through 488
Thy foes might 873		'T is Jesus the 1183		Tremendous as 354		We praise Th	1269	When in the	876	While Thy do 371
Thy gifts, alas 608		'T is like the	894	Trials make	436	We praise Th	1110	When I touch	796	While Thy gl 1015
Thy glories	35	'T is my most	565	Trials must and 436		We reverence	11	When I tread	630	While we fill 1258
Thy glorious be	2	'T is not a	1224	True, 't is a	946	We shall meet 1493		When Jesus	286	While we pray 1157
Thy grace first 249		'T is only in	580	True wisdom	895	We share our	75	When like a	63	While with	214
Thy grace hav 1367		'T is pleasant as 867		Trust Him, ye	727	We sing Thine 133		When midnight 938		While yet His 1209
Thy grace still 129		'T is prayer	298	Trust in the L	857	We taste Thee 930		When mystery	34	While your si 1435
Thy hand, how	35	'T is Thee I	307	Turn to Christ 458		We thankfully 1103		When my trials 397		Whilst all the	36
Thy hand, in	1388	'T is then the	1488	'T was grace	788	We trust not	1196	When nature	347	Whither, O	632
Thy Holy Spir 539		'T is there	590	'T was I that	174	We wait Thy	1328	When noon her 709		Who are they	1007
Thy hosts are	1328	'T is the Sav	91	'T was mercy 1089		We will not	985	When once it	844	Who best can	413
Thy justice is	19	'T is Thine	1170	'T was sover	331	Weak is the el	320	When our days 956		Who can behold	1
Thy justice like 38		'T is Thine the 128		'T was the	1203	Weak as you	404	When our	501	Who is like	1056
Thy kingdom	903	'T is Thine to 1249		'T was through 376		Welcome all	1083	When our work 735		Who made this 395
Thy light, and	282	'T is Thine to 1047				We'll catch	1114	When our dizzy 945		Who now His	955

307

Index of First Lines of Verses.

First Line	Hymn
Who of us	1378
Who points the	949
Who were	1459
Who, who	816
Who, within	470
Whose breast	379
Whose grace is	219
Why should I	780
Why should I	558
Why should my	448
Why should my	550
Why should th	462
Why should we	726
Why should w	1438
Why was I	1203
Why will you	171
Wide as the	1064
Wide as they	37
Wide it unveils	390
Wilt Thou cast	194
Wilt thou let	157
Wilt thou not	155
Wilt Thou not	572
Wisdom and	1233
With cold affec	77
With fraudless	607
With gentle	74
With glory	1050
With God, the	122
With grateful	1382
With heart and	318
With Him	387
With His rich	369
With holy joy	356
With humble	597
With Israel's	1288
With jaspers	1484
With longing	1227
With longing	315
With my bur	551
With my lamp	833
With open	1034
Without Thee	602
With pitying	1086
With prayer	692
With sacred awe	21
With strong de	646
With such, I	215
With tears of	705
With Thee con	712
With Thee, in	566
With the morn	683
With trembling	964
With us Thou	1028
With us, when	948
With wants	1027
Withdraw not	482
Within that	485
Within the	1235
Within these	1016
Within Thy cir	556
Within Thy pr	514
Within Thy	1233
Without Thee	602
Wonderful in	55
Wonderful the	728
Word of the	885
Work in me, L	644
Work on, des	425
Worlds are	1297
Worldly good	194
Worship, hon	1095
Worthy is He	101
Worthy is He	1085
Worthy the L	1080
Wretch that I	448
Ye chosen	1071
Ye Christian	896
Ye fearful saints	46
Ye for whom	1074
Ye little flock	994
Ye nations bend	7
Ye, no more	1477
Ye sinners, c	145
Ye sinners, s	165
Ye slaves of	1354
Ye weary, heav	158
Ye wheels of	1375
Ye who, for	1306
Ye who see	1083
Ye, who tossed	142
Ye, who your	1356
Yea, amen; let	1453
Yea, bless His	1398
Yea, in the	260
Yea, into noth	591
Yes, for me He	594
Yes, God is	546
Yes, God is love	34
Yes, I believe	645
Yes, I must and	204
Yes, in me, in	594
Yes, let it go	535
Yes, the Ro	135
Yes, Thou art	537
Yes, Thou art	319
Yes, thy sins	157
Yes, when I	1003
Yes, whosoever	148
Yet, Lord, for	926
Yet, Lord, to	1170
Yet more than	19
Yet must we	878
Yet gracious	523
Yet not the love	174
Yet not thus	1416
Yet now the	450
Yet one prayer	1174
Yet, O the chief	189
Yet save a trem	186
Yet she on	864
Yet shall we	878
Yet sovereign	453
Yet the morn	89
Yet these, new	1444
Yet, though I	308
Yet through	670
Yet to Thee	1397
Yet unchang	1410
Yet whilst Thy	901
Yield no more	1001
Your lofty	1066
Zion claims	851
Zion! Jeho	1483
Zion thrice	361
Zion's King	1448

308

Index of Scripture Texts.

GENESIS.
Chap. i. ver. 1: hymn 1, 8, 35, 62, 896. 2: 117, 1280, 1320.
5: 672. 14: 1377. 26: 444. — ii. 1: 1153. 3: 354, 365, 1165.
7: 1062, 1064. 24: 1401. — iii. 8: 1338. — v. 24: 724, 1428.
— vi. 5: 124. — vii. 16: 5, 765. — viii. 9: 181, 776. 22: 1386,
1388. — ix. 13: 1481. — xi. 8: 943. — xii. 4: 983. — xiii. 8:
872, 880. — xv. 6: 389, 990. — xvii. 1: 300. 7: 989. —
xviii. 3: 277, 600, 868, 1229. 23: 1263. 26: 25. — xix. 2:
700. 15: 172. 17: 168. — xxii. 1: 910. 8: 061, 977. 10: 1254.
13: 784. — xxiii. 20: 1436. — xxvii. 38: 484. — xxviii.
11: 706, 1169. 15: 986. 16: 183, 525. 17: 650. 18: 676,
689. 19: 906. 20: 400. — xxxii. 11: 972. 26: 564, 651,
967. — xliv. 33: 878. — xlv. 10: 147. — xlvii. 9: 813,
1408, 1414, 1444, 1480. 30: 845. — xlix. 10: 1316. — l.
13: 1434, 1439. 26: 1424.

EXODUS.
Chap. iii. ver. 5: hymn 525. 12: 1231. 14: 1, 51. — xii. 3: 82.
6: 1222. 13: 1208. 14: 1200. 22: 390, 1212. 23: 86. — xiii.
21: 636. — xiv. 13: 950. 15: 414, 1294, 1305. 19: 915. 21:
977. 22: 980. 29: 901. 31: 429. — xv. 1: 1068, 1081. 2:
512, 804. 11: 19. 18: 1119, 21: 784, 1023. — xvi. 4: 1216.
21: 916. — xvii. 3: 657. 6: 664. 9: 1304. 15: 1308. —
xix. 5: 20, 1199. 6: 962. 18: 115, 874, 1105, 1339. 20:
791. — xx. 10: 1155, 1165. — xxiii. 11: 381. 16: 1378,
1396, 1398. — xxiv. 13: 710. — xxv. 17: 940. 22: 370,
549. — xxviii. 12: 110. — xxix. 38: 904. — xxx. 7: 678,
16: 1013. — xxxi. 13: 357. 17: 1157. xxxii. 7: 126.
12: 1253. 32: 189, 374, 394. — xxxiii. 13: 552. 15: 573,
598, 960, 1162. 17: 30, 630. 18: 590. 20: 27. 22: 199. —
xxxiv. 6: 26. 7: 33, 973. 22: 1374. 29: 587. — xxxv.
2: 1166. — xl. 34: 1069, 1240. 35: 3. 38: 296.

LEVITICUS.
Chap. iii. ver. 8: hymn 130. — v. 6: 182. — ix. 22: 1193. —
xi. 44: 21. — xiii. 45: 177. — xvi. 15: 480. — xix. 2:
286. 10: 425. 18: 391. — xxiii. 3: 1156. — xxv. 35: 426.
36: 1265. — xxvi. 13: 793.

NUMBERS.
Chap. iii. ver. 10: hymn 410. — vi. 24: 1177, 1190. 27: 1182.
— viii. 15: 852. 17: 664. — x. 29: 158, 1497.
— xi. 9: 920. 17: 1046. — xiv. 8: 376, 955. — xx. 11:
199. — xxi. 7: 1369. 8: 166. 9: 217. — xxiii. 10: 1424,
1440. 19: 1185. — xxiv. 5: 849, 1145, 1148. 17: 1324, 1334.

DEUTERONOMY.
Chap. iv. ver. 1: hymn 893. 5: 1102. 6: 886. 7: 20. 37: 1392.
— vi. 2: 890. 7: 1000. — vii. 7: 302, 331. 9: 992. — viii.
2: 717, 948, 1478. 3: 29. 7: 271, 653, 829, 1272, 1466. 10:
1393, 1402. 18: 282. — x. 12: 310. 13: 884. 17: 24. 18:
947. — xi. 1: 155. 2: 1271. 8: 895. 12: 842, 1403. 14:
1387. 16: 6. 21: 1002. 27: 918. — vii. 8: 913. 13: 1389.
— xv. 7: 382, 912. 10: 424. 11: 377. — xviii. 15: 111. —
xxiii. 23: 460. — xxvi. 10: 1055. 11: 906. — xxviii. 1:
768, 888, 1275. — xxx. 11: 462. — xxxi. 7: 986. 8: 463. —
xxxii. 4: 107, 945. 9: 259. 12: 913. 14: 730. — xxxiii.
3: 682. 16: 1305. 25: 920. 27: 50, 537, 1187. — xxxiv.
1: 838, 845, 1423, 1496. 4: 406. 5: 1427. 6: 724, 1436.

JOSHUA.
Chap. i. ver. 2: hymn 414. — iii. 6: 1305. 17: 823. — ix.
9: 1293. — x. 13: 7. — xiv. 9: 540. 10: 376, 986. 11:
597. 12: 964. — xviii. 13: 1275. — xx. 4: 464. — xxii.
22: 1271. — xxiii. 9: 1273. 10: 38. 11: 1279. — xxiv.
14: 244. 15: 266. 17: 315. 19: 383.

JUDGES.
Chap. v. ver. 9: hymn 1123. — viii. 4: 952. — x. 15: 272,
1372.

RUTH.
Chap. i. ver. 16: hymn 373, 809. — ii. 7: 1005. — iv. 9: 1401.

I. SAMUEL.
Chap. i. ver. 28: hymn 991. — ii. 1: 580, 767. — iii. 10: 1003,
1014. 18: 503, 516, 558. — vii. 6: 1371. 12: 704. — xii. 2:
1427. 24: 149. — xiv. 6: 438. — xv. 22: 384. — xvii. 37:
716. 40: 417, 1304. — xviii. 1: 866. 3: 875. — xx. 4: 871.
17: 879.

II. SAMUEL.
Chap. vii. ver. 12: hymn 241. 14: 262. 28: 635. — x. 12:
415. — xii. 13: 173, 473. 20: 529, 543. 23: 1414, 1441,
1487. — xv. 26: 563. — xviii. 33: 1260. — xxii. 2: 238.
17: 1076. 20: 265. 29: 782. 33: 43. — xxiii. 2: 959 4:
343, 579, 1180, 1421. 5: 535, 720, 835.

I. KINGS.
Chap. iii. ver. 5: hvmn 403. 7: 601. 9: 562, 612. — viii. 12:
16. 21: 1238. 22: 710. 27: 1239. 28: 551, 1033. 29:
1234. 30: 368, 1026. 50: 152. 54: 1179. 56: 263, 1150.
66: 371, 1190. — ix. 4: 170. — xviii. 25: 40. 36: 1172.
37: 670, 1244. 43: 1329, 1364. — xix. 10: 712. 11: 15, 528
12: 1048.

II. KINGS.
Chap. ii. ver. 11: hymn 1358, 1428. — iv. 26: 506, 603, 975,
985. — vi. 17: 212, 386. — xix. 35: 400. — xx. 3: 456.

I. CHRONICLES.
Chap. xvi. ver. 1: hymn 1037. 8: 1117. 9: 1100, 1405. 10:
1050, 1101. 14: 1060. 31: 49. 34: 1075, 1391. — xvii. 1:
659. — xxix. 10: 903, 1159, 1184. 11: 908, 1056. 12: 830.
15: 968, 970. 17: 13. 22: 367.

II. CHRONICLES.
Chap. i. ver. 10: hymn 209, 291, 491. 11: 236. — v. 1: 1237,
1243. 13: 1059. 14: 1203. — vi. 1: 1240. 17: 1017, 1036.
18: 288. 19: 1205. 21: 372, 1011, 1235. 24: 544. 32: 1314.
41: 98, 602, 1038, 1045, 1241. 42: 1193. — vii. 3: 1007. 10:
1178. 12: 401. — xvi. 9: 195. — xx. 3: 1367. 6: 607. 11:
1245. 21: 1121. 27: 1152. — xxix. 10: 268. 11: 803.
29: 362, 1039. — xxx. 2: 1400. 9: 1275. 19: 667. 21:
264. — xxxii. 8: 728. — xxxiii. 13: 260, 454. — xxxiv.
19: 186. 21: 352, 435, 1365. 31: 611, 1246. — xxxv. 6:
681. 15: 1040.

EZRA.
Chap. iii. ver. 10: hymn 1234. 11: 1122. — v. 8: 1235. — vi.
15: 1237. — viii. 21: 1363. — ix. 5: 695. 6: 496. 15:
201, 1247.

Index of Scripture Texts.

NEHEMIAH.

Chap. i. ver. 5: hymn 1370. 6: 1022, 1247. 9: 133. 11: 249.—
iv. 4: 478. 16: 411.— v. 19: 432.— viii. 9: 1158. 10:
358: 12: 1179.— ix. 5: 1058, 1399. 6: 698. 12: 534, 915.
15: 630. 17: 32. 19: 529. 20: 121, 210, 488, 956, 1041,
1110. 31: 1277. 32: 1366. 38: 1195.— xiii. 14: 544.

ESTHER.

Chap. v. ver. 3: hymn 551.

JOB.

Chap. i. ver 5: hymn 671, 997. 21: 502, 516, 536, 543, 546, 585,
726, 1256. 22: 773.— ii. 10: 503, 559, 751, 983.— iii. 17:
817, 1491.— v. 10: 777, 1385. 11: 542. 17: 721. 21: 1462.
— vii. 1: 1379. 6: 1406, 1411, 1418. 10: 423. 16: 816.—
viii. 20: 38.— ix. 10: 46.— x. 2: 179. 9: 1029.— xi. 7:
718. 18: 974. 19: 690.— xiii. 3: 921. 15: 385. 16: 191.
— xiv. 1: 1380, 1480. 2: 1407. 15: 1413.— xv. 17: 139.—
xviii. 5: 128.— xix. 25: 306, 756, 1431. 26: 1446. 27:
1416.— xxii. 23: 1370. 25: 508.— xxiii. 3: 523, 548,
596, 735, 1144. 10: 183, 635. 12: 650, 885.— xxvi. 11:
42. 13: 896. 14: 22, 37.— xxviii. 13: 321.— xxix. 3:
446. 13: 379.— xxxi. 20: 381.— xxxiii. 3: 358. 5: 965.
18: 240. 24: 253. 26: 527. 28: 802.— xxxiv. 21: 12,
556.— xxxvi. 5: 39, 610. 27: 1394.— xxxvii. 5: 9. 23:
24.— xxxviii. 4: 1067. 7: 1112. 10: 1383. 11: 7, 1280.
12: 1390.— xlii. 5: 632. 6: 187, 658.

PSALMS.

Psalm i. ver. 1: hymn 427, 442, 772, 861. 2: 932.— ii. 6: 63,
101, 104, 1092, 1454. 8: 1313, 1326, 1332.— iii. 112, 296.
—iv. 4: 21. 8: 683, 690, 972.— v. 3: 366, 677, 685, 689,
927, 1164.— vi. 1: 479. 4: 450.— vii. 6: 1310.— viii.
1: 235, 897, 1374. 2: 999.— ix. 1: 627. 2: 903. 9: 521.—
x. 1: 1366.— xi. 1: 464. 4: 1142.— xii. 1: 616.— xiii.
5: 190, 521.— xiv. 2: 1286.— xv. 1: 397, 863.
2: 922.— xvi. 1: 469, 700, 704, 1004. 5: 309. 7: 746. 9:
1435. 10: 92. 11: 633, 1209, 1412, 1425, 1430, 1446.—
xvii. 12. 15: 617, 910. 7: 113. 8: 697. 15: 543, 644,
808, 1210, 1413, 1443.— xviii. 1: 304, 327. 2: 274, 593.
3: 219. 6: 194. 9: 5. 29: 554. 35: 628. 46: 94, 799, 1099.
— xix. 1: 36, 749, 886, 897, 1400. 2: 679. 5: 674. 7: 1309.
9: 1178.— xxi. 1: 188.— xxi. 7: 546. 13: 905.— xxii. 1: 84,
816. 2: 04. 19: 75, 1196. 22: 67, 937.— xxiii. 1: 588,
637, 711, 732, 744, 760, 773, 906, 1003. 2: 531, 1460. 4:
1422. 5: 1202. 6: 796, 1500.— xxiv. 4: 1470. 7: 72, 96,
276, 1074, 1114, 1352. 8: 1007. 9: 100.— xxv. 1: 552, 597,
676, 2: 23, 743. 4: 712. 5: 578, 604. 7: 185. 8: 1362. 20:
646.— xxvi. 1: 451. 3: 1200. 6: 370.— xxvii. 1: 256, 512,
702, 714. 3: 435. 4: 584, 1144. 8: 926. 11: 636, 652, 673.
— xxviii. 1: 486, 1031. 7: 574. 9: 1181.— xxix. 1: 1152.
3: 528. 11: 1103.— xxx. 1: 487. 4: 1118. 5: 1420. 8:
85.— xxxi. 1: 739. 2: 194, 695. 3: 601. 5: 243, 755. 15:
542, 719, 748.— xxxii. 1: 245. 2: 615. 5: 622, 1023. 7:
705.— xxxiii. 1: 789, 1070. 7: 1281.— xxxiv. 1: 801,
1254. 2: 344. 3: 1075. 7: 963, 967. 8: 472. 11: 1001. 14:
158. 17: 182. 22: 773.— xxxv. 1: 522.— xxxvi. 5: 27.
8: 1476. 9: 475, 718, 834. 10: 560.— xxxvii. 5: 508, 1379.
8: 138. 37: 1426. 39: 652.— xxxviii. 1: 195, 481. 4:
174. 5: 917, 949. 6: 740. 12: 68. 16: 485.— xxxix. 4:
1381, 1406. 5: 1418. 7: 431.— xl. 1: 699, 1029. 3: 228.
6: 860. 8: 66, 267, 297, 747. 17: 648, 753.— xli. 1: 379.
511. 8: 968.— xliii. 1: 210, 519. 3: 838. 4: 371. 5:
448. 11: 1360.— xliv. 8: 1403. 23: 1367.— xlv. 1: 229.
2: 282. 3: 328. 4: 1357. 6: 52. 9: 1311. 13: 850.—
xlvi. 1: 41, 504, 530, 961, 1017. 2: 950. 7: 517. 11: 769.
— xlvii. 4: 1331. 5: 95, 99, 1073. 6: 1404. 10: 40.—
xlviii. 1: 367, 1149. 2: 857, 1486. 9: 1050, 1168. 10:
241.— l. 3: 144.— li. 1: 176, 186, 206, 474, 482. 2: 483.
5: 125. 10: 1012. 11: 636. 12: 184, 1043, 1240. 17: 187,
272.— lv. 1: 445, 634. 2: 409. 4: 620. 7: 6: 814, 842.
13: 1359. 16: 938. 17: 687, 693, 709. 22: 462.— lvi. 3:
537. 4: 247.— lvii. 1: 577, 745, 914. 7: 557.—
lix. 16: 246.— lx. 3: 1365.— lxi. 1: 706, 1175, 1217. 2:
514. 3: 794. 4: 754, 1143. 5: 323.— lxii. 1: 1032, 1155.
2: 526, 727. 5: 444. 6: 396. 7: 725. 8: 1278.— lxiii.
1: 313, 565, 651, 670, 681, 1160. 3: 303. 4: 285. 6: 715.
8: 660, 666.— lxv. 1: 822, 1151. 2: 761, 793. 4: 812. 10:

1385. 11: 1377. 12: 1395.— lxvi. 1: 908, 1055, 1060. 2:
231. 8: 1051, 1109, 1121. 9: 1077. 13: 357, 368, 1026. 17:
222. 20: 981.— lxvii. 1: 553, 904, 1258. 2: 1230, 1319.
7: 1183.— lxviii. 1: 1290. 4: 1353. 8: 1018. 17: 107.
18: 1458, 1495. 32: 1061.— lxix. 16: 34.— lxx. 1: 478,
923. 5: 624.— lxxi. 1: 569, 696, 716, 765. 3: 214, 966. 5:
591, 619. 6: 758. 9: 324. 15: 248, 381, 805.— lxxii. 1:
779. 2: 1340. 8: 1273. 9: 1351. 10: 1291. 11: 1360. 14:
1087. 17: 56, 93, 336, 1084. 18: 1071. 19: 1106, 1112,
1334.— lxxiii. 3: 658. 13: 571. 24: 764. 25: 290, 308,
345, 581, 595, 618, 786. 26: 316, 573, 639, 711, 847. 28:
621.— lxxiv. 1: 1364. 2: 1257, 1285. 12: 39. 16: 898.
17: 1386.— lxxv. 1: 1194. 7: 128.— lxxvi. 2: 1016. 8:
46, 541.— lxxviii. 5: 1000. 7: 989. 20: 960. 55: 818.—
lxxix. 8: 1371. 9: 1226, 1272.— lxxx. 1: 590, 913, 934,
1227, 1239, 1244. 3: 1027, 1047, 1252, 1274. 8: 853. 14:
1255, 1372.— lxxxi. 1: 307, 1238. 3: 1356.— lxxxii. 4:
1264.— lxxxiv. 1: 359, 372, 844, 1145, 1243. 2: 356, 837,
1015, 1161. 4: 1148. 6: 547. 8: 278. 10: 362, 1020.—
lxxxv. 1: 501. 4: 1218, 1248. 6: 1253. 7: 785, 1170. 8:
599. 9: 1270. 12: 1402. 13: 1089.— lxxxvi. 1: 200, 571,
1207, 1211. 5: 685. 6: 188. 7: 515. 11: 588. 12: 283.
13: 788. 15: 751.— lxxxvii. 1: 856. 3: 852, 1318. 7:
763, 1471.— lxxxviii. 1: 74. 10: 1445.— lxxxix. 1:
218, 803, 1150. 2: 26. 5: 1014. 15: 458, 717, 1317. 18:
257, 971. 24: 334. 46: 154.— xc. 1: 50, 659, 662, 729, 970,
1010. 2: 4. 8: 1363. 9: 1378. 13: 1322. 14: 924. 15:
1491. 16: 90. 17: 423, 1276.— xci. 1: 533, 777. 2: 43,
299. 4: 757, 1173. 7: 414. 16: 1437, 1483.— xcii. 1: 358.
2: 675, 920.— xciii. 1: 10, 48. 3: 45, 1299.— xciv. 1:
1321. 12: 476. 14: 1456.— xcv. 1: 319, 355, 1053, 1100,
1108, 1167. 2: 360. 6: 1037. 7: 170. 8: 164.— xcvi. 1:
1063, 1097. 3: 1119, 1223, 1295. 6: 369. 13: 1336.—
xcvii. 1: 25, 1062, 1297. 2: 16.— xcviii. 2: 57, 1335.
4: 1359. 7: 1323.— xcix. 1: 42, 1009. 5: 17. 9:
1105.— c. 1: 1059, 1066. 2: 223, 405. 3: 918. 4: 1150,
1375, 1389.— ci. 1: 275. 2: 1200, 654. 3: 298.— cii.
11: 1409, 1479. 12: 47. 13: 1312. 16: 1347. 17: 1044.
28: 1008, 1411.— ciii. 1: 798, 802. 2: 230, 240, 328.
3: 510. 4: 1072, 1376, 1406. 8: 31, 713. 13: 1027. 17:
535, 992, 1090.— civ. 1: 312, 797. 14: 1396. 19: 1387.
23: 694, 935. 24: 1393. 31: 51. 34: 337, 404.— cv. 1:
1296. 3: 1049.— cvi. 1: 1373. 12: 987. 47: 498, 1277.—
cvii. 1: 28, 29, 226, 907. 2: 1083, 1110. 6: 1279. 7: 752.
8: 1268. 14: 1036. 22: 1399. 23: 1283. 28: 980. 29: 781.
36: 1468.— cviii. 2: 13, 669, 678, 942. 4: 198.— cix.
21: 292. 23: 518, 1408.— cx. 1: 105, 1324. 4: 111.—
cxi. 3: 944. 9: 202, 1081.— cxii. 1: 363.— cxiii. 1:
1056. 5: 111. 7: 1269.— cxv. 1: 1366. 9: 346. 18: 1120.
cxvi. 1: 333, 1215. 5: 318. 7: 363, 454, 770. 9: 271. 12:
263, 269. 13: 203, 213. 15: 1412. 16: 297.— cxvii. 1:
1: 1066.— cxviii. 5: 317, 513. 6: 734, 955. 17: 1415.
18: 536. 19: 311. 20: 1242. 22: 1236. 24: 1332, 1154,
1163.— cxix. 1: 858. 5: 352, 633, 641. 9: 894. 10: 268.
20: 351. 25: 863. 27: 341. 28: 576. 29: 497. 34: 612.
39: 456. 41: 549. 49: 575. 57: 273, 653. 58: 611. 65:
750. 81: 520, 759. 88: 330, 928. 89: 349, 1191. 94: 661.
96: 890. 97: 547. 103: 889. 105: 885, 895. 113: 289,
348. 117: 611. 129: 1360. 130: 857, 900, 1019. 146: 614.
147: 446. 174: 668. 175: 490, 608. 176: 234.— cxx. 7:
643.— cxxi. 1: 44, 153, 189, 879. 2: 473. 4: 698. 5:
586. 6: 876. 8: 882.— cxxiii. 1: 775, 767, 810. 2: 889.—
cxxiv. 7: 737. 8: 978.— cxxv. 2: 885, 4: 1117.— cxxvi.
2: 1464. 5: 1488. 6: 380, 422, 428, 439.— cxxvii. 2: 774,
943.— cxxviii. 1: 392.— cxxx. 1: 572. 2: 610. 4: 452.
5: 185.— cxxxi. 1: 205, 509, 677, 815. 2: 287, 335. 5:
1038, 1241. 9: 1255. 13: 851.— cxxxiii. 1: 867, 872, 883.—
cxxxiv. 2: 406, 1114.— cxxxv. 1: 1066, 1101, 1122.—
cxxxvi. 1: 1391. 3: 49. 4: 37. 6: 1052. 13: 1405.—
cxxxvii. 6: 375, 817.— cxxxviii. 1: 787. 2: 319. 5:
449, 1082. 6: 395. 7: 762. 8: 236. 9: 795.— cxxxix. 1:
493, 556, 629, 881. 2: 12, 290, 566. 3: 688, 726, 1153. 7:
179. 4: 561. 8: 741.— cxliii. 1: 708. 3: 562, 598. 5: 77.
— cxliii. 6: 506. 7: 625, 642. 8: 929, 936. 9:
656. 10: 723, 1484.— cxliv. 1: 416.— cxiv. 1: 339, 800.
2: 684, 691, 703. 3: 979. 9: 1111. '12: 1106. 16: 1372. 17: 19.
18: 1024.— cxlvi. 1: 804. 2: 221, 686. 8: 952, 1078.—
cxlvii. 3: 315, 1070. 4: 1388, 1394. 8: 1.
14: 1388, 1308.— cxlviii. 1: 224, 238, 1067. 2: 1096. 4:
1050. 14: 1086. 15: 1397.— cxlix. 1: 1127.— cl. 1: 1058,
1068, 1117. 6: 227.

Index of Scripture Texts.

PROVERBS.
Chap. i. ver. 23 : hymn 144. 24 : 160. 28 : 169. — iii. 12 : 502, 532, 539. 13 : 655. 15 : 321. 26 : 998. — vi. 6 : 447. 23 : 350, 894. — viii. 1 : 156, 348. 3 : 146, 476. 20 : 70. 22 : 63. 29 : 10. 32 : 1001. — ix. 5 : 147, 151, 162, 925, 1201. 10 : 891. — xi. 25 : 424. 30 : 441. — xiii. 20 : 412. — xv. 8 ; 664. — xvi. 3 : 859. 9 : 509. — xviii. 24 : 939. — xxiii. 29 : 1259.

ECCLESIASTES.
Chap. i. ver. 4 : hymn 1380. 7 ; 828. — ii. 11 : 1410. — iii. 1 : 684, 693, 719. 15 : 418. — ix. 17 : 420. — xi. 1 : 1176. 6 : 422, 428, 687, 697. 7 : 902, 942, 973. 8 : 421. 9 : 163. — xii. 1 : 170. 7 ; 1440.

SOLOMON'S SONG.
Chap. i. ver. 7 : hymn 596, 929. 12 : 1219. — ii. 4 : 340, 1204, 1214. 12 : 1384. — v. 1 : 1201, 1211. 2 : 146, 497. — vi. 10 : 854.

ISAIAH.
Chap. i. ver. 8 : hymn 393, 511. 16 : 629. 18 : 258. — ii. 2 : 1063. 3 : 361, 1146. 5 : 437, 1078, 1250. 15 : 1471. — iii. 10 : 772. — iv. 2 : 1321. 6 : 940. — vi. 1 : 3, 276, 1419, 1490. 3 : 18, 1069, 1105, 1113, 1118, 1120. 8 : 419. — vii. 14 : 53. — viii. 18 : 991. — ix. 4 : 1086. 5 : 1333. 6 : 55, 58, 232, 255, 320, 332, 542, 570, 988, 1094, 1116. 7 : 788 — xi. 6 : 999. 9 : 857. 10 : 1288, 1344, 1497. — xii. 1 : 1269. 2 : 228, 675, 1500. 3 : 1160. 4 : 1049. 5 : 1080. 6 : 239, 1352. 12 : 1397. — xiii. 2 : 1308. 13 : 1452. — xiv. 1 : 143. — xvi. 5 : 460. — xxi. 11 : 1329, 1338. — xxv. 1 : 669, 1158. 4 : 572, 739. 8 : 810, 833, 1432, 1498. 9 : 137, 701, 876. — xxvi. 1 : 293, 513, 560, 827. 3 : 780, 701. 4 : 199, 593. 8 : 565, 588, 941, 1022. 9 : 290, 469, 582, 607. 12 : 71. 13 : 270, 555, 621. 20 : 471, 507. 21 : 262, 351. — xxviii. 4 : 1483, 1499. 7 : 1259. 16 : 1236. 29 : 1266. — xxx. 15 : 644. 19 : 837. 20 : 979. 21 : 623, 956. 29 : 776. — xxxi. 2 : 907. — xxxii. 1 : 1091. 2 : 237. 15 : 489, 1047, 1233. 18 : 41, 774, 819. 32 : 577. — xxxiii. 2 : 901, 916. 15 : 1427. 16 : 1434. 17 : 308, 333, 811, 839, 1416, 1427, 1482, 1485, 1493. 20 : 1469, 1496. — xxxv. 6 : 1052. 8 : 198. 9 : 1475. 10 : 443, 792, 820, 845, 1054, 1073, 1082, 1458, 1461, 1462, 1492. — xxxviii. 3 : 479. 16 : 674. 20 : 509, 801. — xxxix. 8 : 1370. — xl. 1 : 976. 6 : 1410. 7 : 1444. 8 : 781, 899. 9 : 844, 1051, 1345, 1474. 11 : 734, 736, 744, 952, 997, 1004, 1441. 12 : 36. 28 : 2. 31 : 404, 407, 653, 656, 665, 829, 946. — xli. 10 : 129, 463, 506, 758. 13 : 771. 17 : 521. — xliii. 1 : 606. 3 : 109, 505. 4 : 1343. 10 : 1101, 1337, 1375. 15 : 1328, 23 : 148. — xliii. 1 : 458. 2 : 732, 745, 948, 987. 4 : 569. 6 : 1455. 10 : 1114, 1307. 15 : 1328. — xliv. 3 : 116, 211, 1045, 1235. 6 : 4, 11. 23 : 61, 227, 1085. 24 : 897. — xlv. 5 : 23. 9 : 132. 11 : 1245. 12 : 1315. 15 : 722. 22 : 139, 164, 216, 465, 649. — xlvii. 12 : 144. 16 : 250. — xlix. 1 : 1336. 10 : 1460. 12 : 1351. 13 : 59, 220, 224, 1346. 15 : 468. 16 : 931. 25 : 994. — l. 6 : 461, 558. 10 : 527, 053. — li. 1 : 467. 3 : 1220. 6 : 47. 9 : 1310. 10 : 122. 11 : 1083, 1356, 1459, 1464. 15 : 9. 17 : 1348, 1350. — liii. 1 : 677, 1349. 6 : 1354. 7 : 1225, 1230, 1327. 9 : 91. 14 : 495. 15 : 1316, 1323. — liii. 3 : 65, 78, 1207. 4 : 322, 873. 5 : 242, 914. 6 : 79. 7 : 69. 9 : 89. 10 : 1088. 11 : 738, 959, 1249. 12 : 494, 806, 1095. 15 : 1197. 37 : 500. — liv. 8 : 247. 10 : 778. 11 : 466. 13 : 794. 17 : 855. — lv. 1 : 136, 510, 891, 1206. 3 : 1221. 6 : 161, 180. 11 : 1191, 1309. — lvi. 2 : 353, 1163. 7 : 359, 369, 1075, 1164. — lvii. 2 : 168. 15 : 119, 395, 487, 864, 1030. 19 : 524, 1183. — lviii. 1 : 1302. 5 : 1368. 10 : 172, 567. 13 : 201. 14 : 318, 363, 1020, 1161, 1176. — lix. 2 : 157. 20 : 83, 1065, 1335. 21 : 215. — lx. 1 : 1330. 2 : 700, 1311, 1325. 4 : 1294. 11 : 1242. 13 : 1477. 14 : 848, 856. 19 : 702, 1463. 20 : 360, 1457, 1489. 21 : 836. — lxi. 1 : 54, 892. 2 : 70. 3 : 850. 4 : 1300. 6 : 1289. 7 : 1417. 10 : 254. 11 : 1342. — lxii. 1 : 137. 5 : 364, 1370, 1234, 1347. — lxiii. 1 : 102, 103, 413, 1453. 3 : 1448. 7 : 226, 787, 795. 9 : 978. 15 : 1257, 1274. 16 : 869. 17 : 1270. 19 : 499. — lxiv. 1 : 1278. 5 : 922. 8 : 905. 9 : 1369. — lxvi. 2 : 966. 12 : 982, 1070. 13 : 470.

JEREMIAH.
Chap. i. ver. 6 : hymn 634. — ii. 13 : 172. — iii. 12 : 140, 142, 258, 465, 472. 23 : 44. — vi. 16 : 471. — viii. 22 : 466, 592. —

— ix. 1 : 430. 19 : 1262. 23 : 204. 24 : 305. — x. 6 : 797. — xii. 5 : 131, 165. — xiii. 21 : 132. — xiv. 7 : 193. 8 : 294, 600. — xv. 1 : 168. 16 : 805. 21 : 861. — xvi. 15 : 1286. 19 : 522. — xvii. 7 : 317, 387, 762, 917. 8 : 547. 14 : 530. — xx. 13 : 533. — xxi. 8 : 173. — xxiii. 5 ; 783. 6 : 232, 320, 334, 538, 1340. 24 : 13 — xxix. 13 : 298. — xxx. 10 : 470, 526, 814, 1349. — xxxi. 3 : 554, 911. 7 : 1057, 1331. 10 : 995, 1303. 12 : 439, 792, 832, 840, 1151, 1350, 1465. 13 : 1450. 14 : 313, 1488. 20 : 141. 33 : 633. 34 : 279. — xxxii. 19 : 11. 40 : 778 — xxxiii. 5 : 1096. 9 : 1060. 16 : 127, 301, 851, 1344. — l. 20 : 28.

LAMENTATIONS.
Chap. i. ver. 4 : hymn 1255. 6 : 1285. — iii. 21 ; 65. 23 : 682, 941. 24 : 346, 576, 746. 25 : 34, 1185. 55 : 73. 56 : 189. — v. 21 : 642, 1043, 1322.

EZEKIEL.
Chap. ii. ver. 1 : hymn 416. 3 : 1231. — iii. 1 : 893. 4 : 1232. 17 : 1224. 23 : 941. — iv. 4 : 135. — xi. 16 : 785. — xx. 40 : 1287. 43 : 131. — xxiv. 17 : 1438. — xxxiii. 2 : 1350. 25 : 1496. 26 : 45. — xxxiii. 2 ; 1228. 7 : 407. 11 : 153, 167, 171. 19 : 175. — xxxiv. 2 : 1290. 5 : 934. 11 : 744. 12 : 234, 736, 1002, 1181. 14 : 237, 637, 775. 15 : 1202, 1482. 23 : 807, 995. 25 : 819. 26 : 1384. 31 : 843, 918. — xxxvi. 8 : 1328. 25 : 639, 933, 1198, 1337. 26 : 1044. 27 : 114, 627, 1021, 1249, 1349. — xxxvii. 1 : 126. 9 : 1267, 1289, 1320. 25 : 1352. — xxxix. 29 : 957. — xliii. 2 : 1348, 1494. 7 : 1361. — xlvii. 1 : 137, 1341.

DANIEL.
Chap. ii. ver. 4 : hymn 56. — iii. 17 : 389, 742, 709. 27 : 987. — iv. 34 : 2, 230, 800, 1104. 37 : 399. — vi. 10 : 568, 683, 700, 938. — vii. 9 : 235, 1009, 1107. 10 : 1451. 13 : 1072. 14 : 752, 1079, 1213, 1326, 1341, 1353. 18 : 850. — ix. 3 : 1011. 5 : 133. 8 : 531. 9 : 249. 17 : 1251. 19 : 378, 1028, 1257. 21 : 708, 963, 1172. 26 : 87. — xii. 3 : 1261, 1415, 1429, 1447, 1449.

HOSEA.
Chap. ii. ver. 10 : hymn 261. — vi. 4 : 455. 6 : 150, 1054. — xi. 8 : 141, 153, 155, 200, 472. — xiii. 9 : 140. 14 : 88. — xiv. 1 : 413, 477, 1252. 2 : 1054. 8 : 181.

JOEL.
Chap. i. ver. 5 : hymn 1262. — ii. 2 : 1297. 11 : 8. 12 : 154, 470. 21 : 1345. 28 : 120, 148, 1039, 1048, 1233, 1318. — iii. 1 : 1346.

AMOS.
Chap. v. ver. 6 : hymn 145, 171. — vii. 2 ; 1373. — ix. 6 : 14. 13 : 1189.

JONAH.
Chap. i. ver. 51 : hymn 1282. — ii. 2 : 448. 3 : 1284. — iii. 2 : 1298, 1301. 10 : 32.

MICAH.
Chap. iv. ver. 1 : 59, 1327. 2 : 654, 1342. 4 : 647, 1376. 5 : 680. — v. 2 : 60. — vi 6 : 457. — vii. 7 : 646, 714, 727. 18 : 31, 388.

HABAKKUK.
Chap. i. ver. 12 : hymn 17. — ii. 20 : 1142. — iii. 2 : 1110, 1248, 1251. 3 : 52, 115. 17 : 325, 329, 730, 782. 18 : 316, 338, 445, 971.

ZEPHANIAH.
Chap. i. ver. 7 : hymn 1455. — iii. 9 : 150. 14 : 1050, 1351. 17 : 1388.

HAGGAI.
Chap. ii. ver. 7 : hymn 288, 1033, 1314, 1355.

ZECHARIAH.
Chap. i. ver. 3 : hymn 159. 5 : 1413. 12 : 1287, 1312. 17 :

Index of Scripture Texts.

326.—ii. 10: 103, 1149. 13: 1477.—iv. 6: 123, 958, 1042. 1330. 7: 233.—vi. 12: 108. 13: 1078.—vii. 5: 1368.—viii. 21: 1147. 22: 1174, 1292.—ix. 12: 180, 467. 16: 854. 17: 1102.—xii. 10: 80, 216, 251, 402, 1073, 1288.—xiii. 1: 225, 589, 620. 6: 76, 81, 157.—xiv. 1: 1450. 7: 707, 776, 984, 1481. 8: 1341.

MALACHI.

Chap. i. ver. 11: hymn 951, 1025, 1332.—iii. 1: 54. 3: 330, 541, 865. 7: 459, 477, 770. 16: 257, 1433. 17: 514, 853, 1006.—iv. 2: 60, 343, 475, 579, 673, 790, 927, 974.

MATTHEW.

Chap. i. ver. 21: hymn 232, 255, 320. 23: 53.—ii. 1: 61. 11: 1116.—iii. 3: 1336. 16: 1291. 12: 865. 13: 1198. 16: 114, 354.—iv. 1: 1363. 2: 1213. 4: 961. 6: 1272. 16: 1311. 22: 540—v. 3: 205, 392, 859, 1470. 4: 1435. 6: 772. 7: 379, 862. 8: 21. 10: 476. 12: 442. 14: 211, 901. 16: 266, 420, 619, 962, 1368. 20: 289. 46: 1386, 1395. 48: 300.—vi. 5: 791. 6: 406, 586. 9: 575, 903, 1117, 1175. 10: 1214, 1251, 1273, 1319. 11: 759, 920. 13: 409, 1061, 1259. 25: 623. 30: 29, 769. 31: 387, 782. 32: 949, 1384. 33: 512, 1001.—vii. 7: 308, 401. 24: 593, 805. 25: 738, 863.—viii. 2: 292. 3: 217. 8: 177, 599. 10: 1256, 1330. 17: 477, 914, 977, 1266. 19: 396, 607. 20: 68, 757. 22: 173. 24: 1282. 25: 572, 923. 27: 1152.—ix. 13: 592. 18: 492. 22: 386. 25: 985. 27: 574, 723. 36: 506. 38: 1226.—x. 5: 1275, 1208. 6: 1263. 7: 421, 1223, 1315. 16: 910, 1232. 22: 621. 25: 621: 42, 384, 425.—xi. 2: 1338. 5: 72, 1022. 28: 138, 142, 152, 173, 250, 459, 464, 471, 510, 527.—xii. 36: 664, 50: 594.—xiii. 8: 428. 9: 1192.—xiv. 12: 517, 505. 14: 504. 15: 604. 24: 950. 25: 696, 715, 1280. 30: 617, 638.—xv. 22: 184, 1292. 30: 71. 32: 515.—xvi. 18: 849, 1237. 27: 1152, 1448.—xvii. 2: 284. 3: 1433. 4: 369, 405, 587. 20: 645.—xviii. 2: 1003. 5: 640. 11: 79 12: 760, 945, 1260. 20: 14, 1014, 1022, 1024, 1143, 1207.—xix. 13: 996. 14: 988, 1008. 17: 71. 21: 303, 585. 28: 1449, 1461, 1489. 29: 380.—xx. 15: 25. 30: 206, 1027. 31: 187.—xxi. 5: 1241. 9: 57, 224, 1094, 1119, 1154, 1350.—xxii. 14: 128, 935, 1005. 37: 144.—xxii. 3: 151, 410. 4: 147, 156, 162, 1201.—xxiii. 33: 205. 34: 1447. 37: 153, 160.—xxiv. 3: 1309, 1327, 1334. 30: 3351, 1361, 1450, 1453. 46: 476, 1006.—xxv. 6: 174. 8: 178. 11: 169. 13: 410, 833. 21: 1119, 1432, 1479. 31: 451, 1419, 1452. 32: 165. 34: 1474. 40: 919.—xxvi. 13: 924. 20: 1203, 1218. 26: 1211. 28: 1206. 36: 74. 41: 407. 42: 434. 67: 78. 70: 450. 75: 457.—xxvii. 1: 76. 14: 67 29: 81, 106, 1095. 32: 420. 35: 85, 494. 46: 1339. 55: 340. 60: 89.—xxviii. 1: 365, 1167. 2: 91. 6: 94. 19: 1012, 1197, 1295, 1302, 1306. 20: 525, 948.

MARK.

Chap. i. ver. 5: hymn 1293. 9: 135. 15: 167. 18: 236. 20: 271. 25: 366, 944.—iv. 19: 1005. 14: 1189. 35: 1160. 37: 781. 38: 577, 1281. 39: 7.—v. 12: 2. 353. 3: 432. 4: 1283. 7: 1205, 1301. 31: 699. 32: 705. 50: 950. 51: 642, 952.—viii. 34: 413. 38: 344—ix. 5: 355, 566, 803, 1148. 10: 688. 22: 1077.—xii. 24: 104, 614, 641, 645.—x. 13: 1007. 14: 583, 990, 994, 1441. 28: 277, 540. 47: 484, 48: 186, 193, 105, 277, 564.—xi. 9: 1243.—xii. 33: 394. 43: 49.—xiii. 13: 771, 779. 26: 1449.—xiv. 17: 1209, 1212, 1221. 24: 1282. 32: 73. 34: 673. 38: 964.—xv. 24: 79, 203. 34: 84. 36: 1073. 37: 500. 47: 89.—xvi. 2: 1164. 6: 88, 92. 15: 1223, 1306. 16: 1194. 19: 97.

LUKE.

Chap. i. ver. 33: hymn 56. 46: 218. 47: 1068. 49: 1333. 68: 220, 1058, 1070, 1308. 71: 1276. 79: 897, 984, 1035.—ii. 11: 55. 12: 1456. 13: 988. 14: 58, 321, 1084, 1087. 1111. 25: 458. 32: 61, 1250. 77: 1007.—iv. 18: 54. 887, 909, 1320. 30: 70.—v. 28: 267. 40: 175.—vi. 12: 606. 20: 862. 21: 976, 1420.—vii. 14: 985. 22: 108. 38: 275. 43: 327. 47: 230, 304, 402, 681. 48: 498.—viii. 11: 1191. 24: 523, 1284. 38: 637. 39: 339. 55: 592.—ix. 2: 1296. 23: 410. 28: 1032. 31: 1026. 33: 586, 710. 57: 161. 59: 1: 1300, 1303, 1304. 2: 1228. 1212. 3: 410, 433. 17: 427, 1265. 21: 28. 39: 335, 345, 584. 42: 581.—xi 1: 921, 1010. 2: 559, 905, 1146, 1277, 1314, 1343. 9: 551. 13: 209, 1021, 1252.—xii. 1: 742.

21: 943. 24: 508, 961. 22: 732, 769, 1082, 1294. 35: 247, 476 36: 1246. 40: 170.—xiii. 24: 164, 171.—xiv. 16: 116. 17: 143, 154, 161, 420. 23: 1263. 27: 524.—xv. 2: 141. 4: 234. 7: 807. 14: 173. 18: 159, 260, 464. 20: 141. 21: 200, 272, 435, 614.—xvii. 5: 1256. 10: 919. 14: 71. 21: 1487.—xviii. 7: 564. 13: 177, 188, 401, 482. 14: 305. 15: 998. 16: 993, 1004. 28: 273. 38: 1,0, 212.—xix. 6: 213, 576. 8: 263, 280, 674. 38: 1100, 1112. 41: 453. 42: 149.—xxi. 3: 380. 25: 1207. 27: 1461. 28: 1128, 1355, 1362.—xxii. 14: 1202, 1210, 1222. 19: 1215. 39: 75. 41: 546. 42: 520. 43: 750. 51: 69. 61: 501. 62: 176, 474. 66: 76.—xxiii. 4: 97. 33: 82, 251, 620. 34: 1218. 42: 191, 198, 544, 649. 43: 473. 45: 72. 46: 66, 84. 53: 90.—xxiv. 1: 355, 1153, 1166. 6: 93. 15: 712. 17: 545. 29: 204, 600, 700, 974, 1170, 1207. 34: 95. 47: 1270, 48: 1307. 50: 1184.

JOHN.

Chap. i. ver. 1: hymn 53, 62, 341, 884, 1107. 3: 860. 4: 211, 245, 312, 579, 636, 928, 930, 1035, 1250. 9: 673. 16: 301. 29: 80. 36: 214, 570. 46: 158. 49: 1044.—ii. 2: 1401.—iii. 5: 959. 13: 694. 14: 467, 1303. 15: 253. 16: 34, 798, 1013, 1087, 1109. 17: 217, 802. 18: 385.—iv. 14: 172. 15: 567, 573, 743, 1012. 21. 1238. 23: 951, 1025, 1174. 24: 493, 1165. 34: 69, 297. 35: 418. 42: 330. 47: 483.—v. 3: 1144. 7: 582. 17: 421. 24: 155. 26: 1085. 39: 889.—vi. 15: 703. 19: 1284. 34: 1206. 35: 760. 38: 66. 47: 711, 1492. 51: 168, 1216, 1243. 58: 1204. 63: 349, 491. 68: 178, 197, 498, 504, 530.—vii. 37: 136, 145, 150, 786.—viii. 12: 915. 32: 1199. 36: 299.—ix. 5: 932. 11: 624. 36: 505. 38: 201, 213, 335.—x. 3: 534, 1002. 4: 736, 789, 969, 1181. 11: 467, 803, 807, 934, 996. 14: 324. 16: 731, 1482. 27: 584, 632, 775. 28: 550, 500, 918, 1444. 29: 737.—xi. 11: 1431. 15: 40. 21: 734. 25: 985. 26: 1410, 1417, 1466. 28: 470, 548. 31: 437, 714. 36: 1034, 1116. 46: 678, 749, 1383. 50: 894.—xiii. 8: 23. 9: 324, 747. 15: 67, 603. 17: 1205.—xiv. 1: 471, 1438. 2: 815, 821, 1034, 1493. 3: 545, 704, 830, 832. 6: 1247, 653, 925. 7: 1478. 14: 1021. 16: 1116, 957, 1048. 18: 602. 19: 1418, 1429. 23: 931, 1030. 26: 118, 488, 1019, 1044, 1403. 27: 406, 982, 1186.—xv. 4: 571, 581. 5: 247, 659, 688 6: 507. 7: 291, 566, 762. 12: 382, 873. 13: 939. 16: 131, 713. 17: 878, 401.—xvi. 7: 114, 1045. 8: 1249 13: 348, 499, 956, 1049, 1152. 14: 1318. 15: 120, 208. 16: 1465. 23: 758. 33: 122.—xvii. 1: 533. 4: 87. 6: 887. 9: 756, 780, 1098. 11: 773. 13: 27. 14: 1228. 21: 283, 872, 876, 908. 22: 378, 1455. 23: 329. 24: 697, 800, 839, 906, 1168, 1224, 1435, 1468, 1500. 33: 860.—xviii. 1: 74. 11: 563. 27: 473.—xix. 5: 78, 83. 17: 405. 19: 196, 286. 28: 215, 972. 30: 86. 34: 199, 223. 40: 68. 41: 1430. 42: 90.—xx. 1: 309, 1156. 2: 96. 16: 764. 17: 100. 19: 357, 405, 697, 968, 992, 882, 1016, 1024, 1036, 1143, 1171. 26: 705. 28: 622.—xxi. 15: 304, 333, 467, 501, 660. 16: 450. 17: 185, 310, 327, 753. 18: 1381.

ACTS.

Chap. i. ver. 5: hymn 958, 1009. 8: 625, 1271, 1302. 9: 99. 11: 1036. 13: 1147. 14: 568, 967, 1028, 1160, 1171, 1248. 26: 1231.—ii. 1: 1038, 1039, 1253, 1247. 2: 115. 3: 957. 4: 119. 5: 1000. 17: 1233, 1258, 1317. 23: 85. 24: 92. 32: 1308. 33: 286. 36: 229, 1115. 38: 156, 459, 472. 39: 1287. 44: 870, 882. 46: 1107, 1222. 47: 1049, 1066, 1145, 1243.—iii. 9: 358, 570. 19: 142, 157, 460. 26: 135, 237, 471.—iv. 12: 334, 1244, 1264. 20: 742, 1307. 31: 117, 118. 32: 244.—v. 3: 493. 6: 232. 21: 935. 29: 248. 31: 103, 1023. 41: 730.—vi. 6: 1100.—vii. 59: 683, 831, 845. 60: 1426, 1430, 1434.—viii. 31: 349. 37: 276, 522. 38: 1199.—ix. 6: 105, 212, 280, 414, 525. 15: 1294. 17: 1010. 31: 1107.—x. 3: 963. 22: 1291. 25: 868. 30: 708. 33: 1018, 1037, 1042, 1229. 34: 912. 38: 441. 44: 126, 1180. 45: 1200, 1304. 47: 285.—xi. 18: 1335. 22: 1206.—xii. 7: 243, 606, 1367.—xiii. 2: 1298. 34: 196. 33: 123. 38: 160. 42: 134, 1293. 44: 364, 1016, 1157. 48: 1163.—xiv. 7: 1374. 17: 1, 30, 208, 800, 1185, 1388, 1308.—xv. 28: 1269. 25: 166, 979. 30: 134, 482. 31: 170. 33: 281, 902, 994, 1198. 34: 104.—xvii. 11: 31, 2, 241. 22: 247, 1370. 28: 42, 555, 1382. 30: 167.—xx. 20: 431. 24: 513, 748. 25: 537, 835. 28: 426. 31: 375, 546. 32: 1180. 35: 799. 36: 875.—xxi. 13: 307, 520, 543, 557, 563, 635, 724.—

Index of Scripture Texts.

xxii. 7: 661. 8: 251, 487. 10: 190, 196, 452. — xxiv. 16: 615, 643. — xxvi. 9: 449. 18: 129, 19: 198, 250. 22: 704. 23: 691. 29: 137, 535, 658, 751, 987, 1188.— xxvii. 1: 1299. 11: 1282. 23: 706, 715. 24: 15. 25: 528.— xxviii. 11: 1283.

ROMANS.

Chap. i. ver. 15: hymn 1299. 16: 344, 415. 19: 749. 20: 36, 1174. 21: 128. 32: 133.— ii. 8: 130. 24: 1285.— iii. 10: 180. 12: 124. 24: 607. 26: 1089.— iv. 5: 389. 7: 245, 858. 18: 741.— v. 1: 524, 547, 646. 2: 784. 3: 532, 539. 6: 65, 214. 8: 184. 10: 223. 11: 806. 21: 1268, 1429.— vi. 2: 270. 4: 1199. 5: 666, 1443. 8: 655. 9: 95. 10: 267. 11: 295. 17: 230. 18: 285. 23: 242, 1057.— vii. 5: 127. 12: 347. 15: 641. 18: 409. 19: 181. 22: 448, 654. 23: 604. 24: 578. 25: 723, 907, 1369.— viii. 1: 243. 2: 287, 299. 3: 19. 4: 121, 890. 9: 262. 10: 491. 15: 206, 402. 16: 117, 1047. 17: 166. 21: 449. 22: 1322. 27: 1041. 31: 745, 955. 32: 468. 34: 246. 35: 704. 37: 338, 719. 38: 737. 39: 325, 328, 648, 663.— ix. 15: 132. 26: 259.— x. 4: 385. 13: 597. 15: 1225, 1347.— xi. 2: 1373. 22: 275. 26: 83, 1346. 33: 30, 453, 721. 36: 26, 1088, 1150.— xii. 1: 289, 585, 626, 679. 689, 1239. 2: 244, 926. 3: 612. 6: 941. 10: 871, 879. 11: 947. 12: 222, 789.— xiii. 11: 447, 1362, 1375.— xiv. 7: 281. 8: 298, 685, 729, 740, 981. 17: 1487. 19: 868.— xv. 1: 603, 881. 9: 1325. 11: 1151. 13: 123. 17: 793.— xvi. 1: 374. 24: 1182. 27: 18, 1104, 1403.

I. CORINTHIANS.

Chap. i. ver. 10: hymn 514, 1255. 18: 892. 20: 127. 23: 1093. 24: 888, 1261. 30: 112, 256, 526, 591, 935, 1077.— ii. 1: 1229. 2: 77, 252, 278, 303. 9: 1020, 1472. 10: 396, 488, 900, 1041, 1419, 1425. 12: 1162.— iii. 7: 1189. 9: 880. 11: 601, 864, 1235. 16: 119, 277, 296, 550. 22: 763.— iv. 5: 556. 10: 197, 607.— v. 8: 1208.— vi. 10: 1269. 11: 1267. 20: 264, 279.— vii. 31: 1169, 1380.— viii. 6: 626.— ix. 26: 412, 953. 26: 447. 27: 615.— x. 4: 786. 16: 1205, 1208, 1212, 1219. 31: 202, 561, 902.— xi. 23: 1200, 1214. 26: 1220.— xii. 4: 877. 10: 617. 12: 281. 13: 879, 1046.— xiii. 3: 456. 7: 867. 10: 1175. 12: 847, 923, 1500. 13: 329, 391.— xv. 3: 288. 9: 174, 249, 473. 10: 589, 788. 20: 94, 754, 1437, 1442. 21: 1417, 1498. 22: 1429. 24: 104, 1475. 26: 1445. 28: 537. 37: 1434. 49: 937. 52: 1358, 1448. 53: 1430. 54: 942, 1439, 1469, 1481. 55: 38. 57: 1029, 1499. 58: 721.

II. CORINTHIANS.

Chap. i. ver. 3: hymn 219, 240, 529. 4: 519. 5: 976. 12: 588, 643. 20: 44, 761. 22: 201.— ii. 10: 122. 14: 1122.— iii. 2: 866. 11: 618. 16: 1345. 18: 183, 1034, 1044.— iv. 4: 129. 6: 616, 753. 7: 743. 10: 264, 287, 434. 11: 204. 13: 390. 15: 763. 16: 773. 17: 978, 1054. 18: 222, 656, 818, 1040, 1412.— v. 1: 820, 1428, 1473. 2: 1415. 4: 811. 8: 817. 9: 746, 1408. 14: 302, 444. 16: 86, 279, 298, 1220. 17: 734, 754. 19: 1342. 20: 161. 21: 131, 469. 1261.— vi. 7: 671. 10: 557, 1420. 16: 290, 294, 690. 17: 274, 397.— ix. 6: 381, 424. 8: 441. 13: 1400. 15: 1393, 1396.— xi. 23: 269, 429, 619. 24: 306. 25: 1281. 30: 652, 670.— xii. 8: 502. 9: 292, 771, 779. 10: 248, 310, 536, 624, 725. 11: 226.— xiii. 14: 1106, 1177, 1182.

GALATIANS.

Chap. i. ver. 23: hymn 452.— ii. 16: 387. 20: 570, 664, 740, 796.— iii. 9: 990. 24: 896. 26: 261. 28: 880. 1388.— iv. 6: 257. 15: 449.— v. 2: 547. 16: 210. 22: 121, 302.— vi. 2: 377, 875, 1260. 9: 439, 669. 14: 252, 591, 806, 1088.

EPHESIANS.

Chap. i. ver. 3: hymn 219, 1113. 6: 652. 7: 125, 1103. 12: 583, 634. 13: 492. 17: 313, 1397. 18: 286. 20: 1092. 21: 220. 16: 722.— ii. 1: 898. 4: 93. 5: 499. 7: 311. 8: 233, 265, 388, 788. 9: 242. 12: 1086. 13: 215, 361, 486, 620. 14: 481, 780, 982. 20: 738, 1095, 1236. 21: 857. 22: 207.— iii. 14: 112. 16: 315. 16: 123. 17: 856, 1030. 18: 663. 19: 293 305, 328, 337, 582, 933, 1099, 1405.

20: 702.— iv. 1: 613, 679. 3: 605. 4: 864, 883. 5: 872. 8: 96, 1075. 15: 698. 23: 627.— v. 2: 691. 8: 437. 14: 411, 475, 677. 16: 1378. 20: 783, 792.— vi. 4: 1000. 10: 946, 1240, 1304. 11: 417. 13: 616. 14: 203. 17: 408. 18: 611.

PHILIPPIANS.

Chap. i. ver. 4: hymn 374. 21: 281, 432, 796, 1422. 23: 578, 808, 1486.— ii. 5: 553, 666. 7: 109. 9: 342. 10: 143, 323, 336, 1071, 1090. 11: 1092. 13: 909. 15: 628.— iii. 7: 204, 535, 565, 573. 8: 196, 278, 305, 542, 618. 9: 254, 318. 10: 319, 605, 660. 12: 953, 1381. 13: 345, 14: 1423. 21: 1446, 1485.— iv. 6: 297, 509, 686, 692. 7: 489, 1168, 1186. 8: 562. 9: 346, 774. 12: 631. 13: 610, 725, 759.

COLOSSIANS.

Chap. i. ver. 3: hymn 1103. 9: 665. 11: 316, 921. 12: 768, 1051. 16: 63, 1315. 17: 865. 18: 265, 312, 1076. 19: 256. 20: 288, 332, 495, 722, 778. 24: 1018.— ii. 2: 866, 869. 6: 680. 10: 246, 1077. 12: 1105. 15: 100 — iii. 1: 672, 727, 916, 929. 3: 293. 10: 301. 16: 1158. 17: 561.— iv. 2: 366. 5: 1331.

I. THESSALONIANS.

Chap. i. ver. 5: hymn 892. 9: 1337.— ii. 12: 741.— iii. 1: 1226. 4: 909. 9: 1399. 12: 870, 904.— iv. 1: 274, 684. 3: 650. 14: 811, 1431. 16: 828, 1339, 1368, 1440, 1454. 17: 816, 847.— v. 5: 682. 6: 411, 1322. 7: 126. 9: 946. 10: 130, 701. 14: 426. 16: 440, 686. 21: 1150. 22: 936. 23: 613, 1178, 1377.

II. THESSALONIANS.

Chap. ii. ver. 1: hymn 853. 13: 122. 16: 50, 1187.— iii. 1: 1226.

I. TIMOTHY.

Chap. i. ver. 7: hymn 1115. 13: 174. 14: 205. 15: 239. 17: 1180, 1279, 1394, 1402.— ii. 8: 938.— iii. 15: 848. 16: 53, 91, 107.— vi. 11: 438. 12: 412, 417. 13: 1196. 15: 1121. 16: 27, 48, 342, 1091.

II. TIMOTHY.

Chap. i. ver. 7: hymn 651. 9: 233, 625, 733, 755.— ii. 3: 415, 438. 12: 685. 15: 1230.— iii. 14: 408. 15: 993. 16: 347, 886, 889. 17: 270.— iv. 1: 431. 5: 416. 6: 338, 835, 846. 8: 367, 716, 810, 838, 1423, 1427. 18: 445, 965, 970. 26: 823.

TITUS.

Chap. i. ver. 2: hymn 52.— ii. 7: 962. 12: 550. 13: 803, 831, 833, 1006. 14: 558, 936, 981, 1404.— iii. 5: 188, 490, 499, 1197, 1268, 1320, 1356. 6: 192, 1109.

HEBREWS.

Chap. i. ver. 2: hymn 1052. 3: 284, 928. 6: 60, 812, 1074, 1142, 1357. 8: 223, 1084, 1278, 1332. 9: 229, 235. 11: 785. 12: 48, 1382. 14: 963. 35: 973.— ii. 8: 1102. 9: 89, 99, 494, 757, 1096. 13: 928. 14: 869, 991. 17: 111, 905. 18: 517, 939, 1023.— iii. 7: 139, 149. 14: 181. 18: 166.— iv. 3: 819. 4: 1166, 1172. 9: 363, 644, 647, 1161, 1425, 1463, 1473, 1476. 10: 693, 770. 11: 1053. 12: 350. 13: 11. 14: 258. 15: 108, 518.— v. 2: 515, 914, 937. 7: 75, 455, 1213. 24: 64.— vi. 1: 362, 446. 10: 244, 422. 13: 31. 17: 552. 18: 755. 19: 241, 603, 739, 814. 20: 110.— vii. 19: 466, 521, 756. 27: 306, 594.— viii. 1: 3, 586, 822. 12: 31, 1364, 1371.— ix. 4: 1354. 6: 326. 11: 113. 12: 191.— x. 4: 102. 26: 216. 28: 80, 635, 931.— x. 4: 870. 7: 418, 747. 10: 1216. 12: 944, 1372. 14: 695. 15: 1040. 22: 183, 268, 401, 454, 481, 549, 765, 940, 1194. 25: 360.— xi. 1: 386, 1254. 3: 35. 10: 706, 831, 931. 13: 295, 613, 968, 983, 1457. 16: 443, 630, 707, 830, 832, 1412. 25: 373. 33: 413. 27: 504, 1142.— xii. 1: 19, 105, 532, 536. 12: 479. 13: 1365. 18: 874. 22: 442, 836, 851, 1015, 1329, 1424. 23: 359, 371, 822, 852, 1050, 1468, 1494. 27: 1455. 29: 1484.— xiii.

Index of Scripture Texts.

14: 1409, 1483, 1497. 15: 221, 259, 358, 368, 801, 1111. 16: 1019. 20: 538, 720, 997, 1183. 21: 604.

JAMES.

Chap. I. ver. 2: hymn 436. 3: 1389. 5: 291. 12: 516, 541, 975, 1173. 17: 49, 555. 21: 633. 25: 531, 861. 27: 383, 947, 1265. — ii. 1: 912. 24: 648. — iii. 2: 664. — iv. 8: 149, 154, 166, 1246. 10: 1366. 11: 1264. 13: 1480. 14: 423, 1411. 15: 1379. — v. 7: 427, 752. 8: 1475. 17: 398.

I. PETER.

Chap. I. ver. 3: hymn 228. 7: 764. 8: 308, 317, 337, 580, 808, 1031, 1209. 9: 390, 12: 62. 13: 661, 687. 17: 1376. 18: 202. 19: 192, 589, 608. 23: 1013. 24: 1407, 1414. 25: 898, 986. — ii. 6: 231, 309. 7: 310, 9: 260, 266, 1257. 10: 560. 11: 286. 12: 672. 21: 64, 606, 873. 24: 77, 1217. 25: 443, 775, 804. — iii. 15: 667. 18: 81. 21: 766. 22: 101. — iv. 1: 628. 7: 163. 13: 73, 975, 1078. 14: 486. 19: 559. — v. 4: 744. 7: 138, 463, 917, 949. 8: 435. 10: 640, 1149. 16: 1187.

II. PETER.

Chap. I. ver. 3: hymn 300, 608. 5: 565, 11: 1173. 14: 821, 18: 587. 19: 351, 761, 888, 932. 21: 893, 959. — ii. 9: 32. — iii. 5: 899. 7: 1450. 8: 1491. 9: 47. 11: 171, 1406. 13: 834, 1176, 1287. 14: 407, 451, 703. 18: 657.

I. JOHN.

Chap. I. ver. 5: hymn 984. 7: 225, 245, 713, 926, 930. 9: 176, 324, 457, 496, 574. — ii. 2: 735, 798. 8: 885. 10: 377. 15: 163. 17: 423, 647. — iii. 1: 261, 933. 2: 1210, 1443, 1467. 3: 397, 1184, 9: 362. 11: 301, 871. 12: 842. 14: 881. 16: 461, 1099. 20: 13. — iv. 2: 207. 7: 867, 878. 8: 30, 393, 911. 9: 1089, 1108. 10: 302, 303, 314, 331, 945, 1203. 11: 382, 883. 18: 711. 19: 323, 1215 — v. 3: 462.

4: 1033. 6: 489. 7: 958, 1011. 8: 1046. 12: 601. 14: 399.

II. JOHN.

Ver. 3: hymn 271. 4: 983. 8: 675.

JUDE.

Ver. 14: hymn 1355. 16: 125. 20: 1367. 25: 43, 805, 1104, 1179.

REVELATION.

Chap. I. ver. 4: hymn 1454. 5: 927, 1103, 1195. 8: 4, 1185. 10: 1154, 1167. 13: 104, 365, 1072; 17: 1064. 18: 113, 134. — ii. 5: 152. 10: 435, 629, 820, 855. — iii. 2: 150, 410, 676. 726. 5: 110. 8: 554. 10: 569, 668, 777. 12: 38. 14: 954. 18: 254. 20: 146, 160, 169, 175, 465, 476, 497, 1028, 1221. 21: 602, 1193, 1438. 22: 891. — iv. 1: 165, 767, 3: 191. 5: 1490. 8: 18, 1060, 1106, 1113, 1118, 1120. 10: 218. 11: 3, 10, 822, 1055, 1076, 1101. — v. 1: 795. 6: 22, 105, 311. 9: 220, 1031, 1085, 1110, 1447. 11: 227, 1080, 1458, 1464, 1469, 1495. 12: 55, 1091, 1097. 13: 840, 1067, 1102, 1392. — vi. 10: 1312. 14: 1456. 17: 1452. — vii. 4: 1494. 9: 816, 846, 877, 913, 1008, 1459, 1493. 11: 812, 1074. 12: 1357. 13: 1457, 1462. 14: 818. 15: 1468. 17: 843. — x. 1: 37. — xi. 15: 1326, 1349, 1353. 17: 6, 57, 1310. — xii. 10: 1313, 1350. — xiv. 1: 98, 370. 2: 1465. 3: 221, 787, 1060, 1099, 1114, 1460. 5: 863. 13: 1421, 1437. — xv. 2: 844, 1007. 3: 9, 13, 24, 45, 718, 1056, 1073, 1081. 4: 20, 1105. — xix. 1: 797, 653, 829. 6: 1050, 1360, 1461. 7: 844, 858. 9: 874. 11: 884. 12: 1079. 16: 5, 58, 102, 255. 17: 107. xx. 6: 1063, 1344. 11: 1453. 12: 1442, 1451. — xxi. 1: 828, 1466, 1498. 2: 836, 842, 1361. 3: 59, 1463. 6: 145. 7: 1479. 9: 856. 11: 815. 18: 1480. 19: 1184, 22: 1155. 23: 343, 790, 813. 24: 1477. — xxii. 1: 1341. 2: 837, 842, 1496. 3: 1467, 1478, 1485, 1499. 5: 41, 51, 834, 1492. 14: 1470. 17: 136, 148, 1289. 19: 1192. 21: 1321. 23: 8.

Index of Authors.

ADAMS, REV. NEHEMIAH, D. D. (1806-.)
Hymn 460.
ADAMS, MRS. SARAH FLOWER. (1805-1848.)
Hymns 650, 752.
ADDISON, JOSEPH. (1672-1719.)
Hymns 36, 736, 803.
ALBINUS, REV. JOHANN GEORG. (1624-1679.)
Hymn 841.
ALEXANDER, MRS. CECIL FRANCES. (1823-.)
Hymns 89, 498, 1293, 1409, 1456.
ALFORD, REV. HENRY, D. D. (1810-1871.)
Hymns 1294, 1458.
ALLEN, REV. JAMES. (1734-1804.)
Hymns 340, 1115.
AMBROSE OF MILAN. (340-397.)
Hymns 93, 928, 929, 972.
AMBROSIAN. (5th century.)
Hymns 924, 942.
ANDERSON, MRS. MARIA FRANCES. (1819-.)
Hymn 1275.
ANSTICE, PROF. JOSEPH. (1808-1836.)
Hymn 917.
AUBER, MISS HARRIET. (1773-1862.)
Hymns 114, 888, 943, 1073, 1147, 1159, 1325.
AUSTIN, JOHN. (1613-1669.)
Hymn 981.
AVELING, REV. THOMAS WILLIAM. (1815-.)
Hymn 1248.

BACON, REV. LEONARD, D. D. (1802-.)
Hymns 703, 1279, 1311, 1360.
BAKER, REV. FRANCIS. 1616.
Hymn 837.
BAKER, REV. AND SIR HENRY WILLIAMS. (1821-1877.)
Hymns 209, 230, 760, 947, 950, 1121, 1367, 1393, 1468.
BAKEWELL, REV. JOHN. (1721-1819.)
Hymn 1095.
BARBAULD, MRS. ANNA LÆTITIA. (1743-1825.)
Hymns 142, 379, 411, 879, 1397, 1421.
BARING-GOULD, REV. SABINE. (1834-.)
Hymn 1305.
BARTON, BERNARD. (1784-1849.)
Hymns 437, 885, 1433, 1481.
BATHURST, REV. WILLIAM HILEY. (1796-.)
Hymns 1019, 1254, 1322, 1337, 1424.
BAXTER, MRS. LYDIA. (1809-1874.)
Hymn 342.
BAXTER, REV. RICHARD. (1615-1691.)
Hymn 740.
BEDDOME, REV. BENJAMIN. (1717-1795.)
Hymns 23, 130, 270, 309, 402, 455, 488, 542, 585, 763, 880, 892, 895, 909, 1196, 1228, 1313, 1450.
BEECHER, REV. CHARLES. (1819-.)
Hymn 1497.
BEMAN, REV. NATHAN SIDNEY SMITH, D. D. (1786-1871.)
Hymn 1448.
BENEDICT, ERASTUS CORNELIUS. (1800-.)
Hymn 303.
BENNETT, HENRY. (1813-1868.)
Hymn 821.
BENNETT, S. FILLMORE. 1873.
Hymn 1493.
BERNARD OF CLAIRVAUX. (1091-1153.)
Hymns 307, 336, 337, 930, 1094.
BERNARD OF CLUNY. Ab. 1145.
Hymns 1475, 1479, 1484, 1489, 1494, 1498, 1499.

BETHUNE, REV. GEORGE WASHINGTON. (1805-1862.)
Hymns 1255, 1281, 1415.
BICKERSTETH, REV. EDWARD. (1786-1850.)
Hymn 996.
BICKERSTETH, REV. EDWARD HENRY. (1825-.)
Hymns 190, 1107, 1129, 1220.
BICKERSTETH, REV. JOHN. (1781-1855.)
Hymn 1181.
BLACKLOCK, REV. THOMAS, D. D. (1721-1791.)
Hymn 797.
BODEN, REV. JAMES. (1757-1841.)
Hymn 1070.
BOEHM, REV. ANTHONY WILHELM. (1673-1722.)
Hymn 307.
BONAR, REV. HORATIUS, D. D. (1808-.)
Hymns 174, 206, 211, 234, 242, 249, 250, 322, 418, 420, 423, 594, 635, 652, 658, 778, 829, 843, 845, 848, 853, 878, 916, 1054, 1109, 1192, 1321, 1480.
BONAR, MRS. JANE CATHERINE. (1808-.)
Hymn 345.
BORTHWICK, MISS JANE. (1825-.)
Hymns 175, 304, 540, 927, 1331.
BOURNE, REV. HUGH. (1772-1852.)
Hymn 213.
BOWDLER, REV. JOHN. (1783-1815.)
Hymn 657.
BOWRING, SIR JOHN, LL. D. (1792-1872.)
Hymns 30, 70, 806, 1338.
BREWER, REV. JEHOIADA. (1752-1817.)
Hymn 237.
BRIDGES, MATTHEW. (1800-1852.)
Hymns 98, 268, 1079.
BROWN, MRS. PHŒBE HINSDALE. (1783-1861.)
Hymns 699, 944, 1251.
BROWN, WILLIAM. 1822
Hymn 1163.
BROWNE, REV. SIMON. (1680-1732.)
Hymns 2, 210, 362, 1139, 1153.
BROWNING, MRS. ELIZABETH BARRETT. (1809-1861.)
Hymn 774.
BRUCE, MICHAEL. (1746-1767.)
Hymns 108, 721, 906, 955, 1442.
BRYANT, WILLIAM CULLEN. (1794-1878.)
Hymns 1219, 1240, 1267, 1270, 1420.
BRYDGES, SIR SAMUEL EGERTON. (1762-1837.)
Hymn 101.
BULFINCH, REV. STEPHEN GREENLEAF. (1809-1870.)
Hymn 1165.
BUNTING, REV. WILLIAM MACLARDIE. (1805-1866.)
Hymn 1195.
BURDER, REV. GEORGE. (1752-1832.)
Hymns 33, 1108.
BURGESS, BP. GEORGE, D. D. (1809-1866.)
Hymns 45, 439, 1282.
BURNHAM, REV. RICHARD. (1749-1810.)
Hymn 191.
BURNS, REV. JAMES DRUMMOND. (1823-1864.)
Hymns 205, 566.
BURTON, JOHN. (1803-.)
Hymns 1021, 1418.
BUTTERWORTH, HEZEKIAH. (1839-.)
Hymn 1400.
BUTTRESS, JOHN. 1820
Hymn 887.
BYROM, JOHN. (1691-1763.)
Hymn 576.

Index of Authors.

CARLYLE, REV. JOSEPH DACRE. (1759-1804.)
Hymn 1026.
CASWALL, REV. EDWARD. (1814-1878.)
Hymns 302, 336, 337, 924, 942, 1045, 1094.
CAWOOD, REV. JOHN. (1775-1852.)
Hymns 58, 1191, 1292.
CENNICK, REV. JOHN. (1717-1755.)
Hymns 196, 578, 598, 1082, 1103.
CHANDLER, REV. JOHN. (1806-1876.)
Hymns 871, 928, 929, 1034, 1236.
CHAPIN, REV. EDWIN HUBBELL, D. D. (1814-1880.)
Hymn 1266.
CHEEVER, REV. GEORGE BARRELL, D. D. (1807-.)
Hymn 787.
CHORLEY, HENRY FOTHERGILL. (1808-1872.)
Hymn 1370.
CLARK, BENJAMIN.
Hymn
CLARKE, REV. JAMES FREEMAN, D. D. (1810-.)
Hymn 949.
CLEMENT OF ALEXANDRIA. (-220.)
Hymn 995.
CLEVELAND, BENJAMIN. 1790.
Hymn 588.
CODNER, MRS. ELIZABETH. 1860.
Hymns 483, 484.
COFFIN, CHARLES. (1676-1749.)
Hymn 1365.
COKE, BP. THOMAS, LL. D. (1747-1814.)
Hymn 618.
COLLYER, REV. WILLIAM BENZO, D. D. (1782-1854.)
Hymns 141, 1435.
CONDER, JOSIAH. (1789-1855.)
Hymns 6, 331, 516, 631, 920, 934, 1137, 1216.
COOK, MRS. MARTHA ANN WALKER. (1807-1874.)
Hymn 977.
COOK, REV. RUSSELL STURGIS. (1814-1864.)
Hymn 150.
COOPER, JOHN. 1818.
Hymn 1013.
COTTERILL, REV. THOMAS. (1779-1823.)
Hymns 120, 892, 1047, 1167, 1204.
COUSIN, MRS. ANNE ROSS. 1857.
Hymn 846.
COWPER, WILLIAM. (1731-1800.)
Hymns 46, 63, 225, 400, 436, 468, 507, 521, 531, 558, 568, 654, 808, 900, 1025, 1027, 1477.
COX, CHRISTOPHER C., M. D. (1816-.)
Hymn 707.
COX, MISS FRANCES ELIZABETH. 1841.
Hymn 312.
COXE, BP. ARTHUR CLEVELAND, D. D. (1818-.)
Hymns 64, 169, 850, 1297, 1316.
CRABBE, REV. GEORGE. (1754-1832.)
Hymn 465.
CREWDSON, MRS. JANE FOX. (1809-1863.)
Hymns 515, 784.
CROSWELL, REV. WILLIAM, D. D. (1804-1854.)
Hymn 912.
CUNNINGHAM, REV. JOHN WILLIAM. (1780-1861.)
Hymns 84, 357.
CUSHING, REV. WILLIAM ORCUTT. (1823-.)
Hymn 1006.

- DANA, MRS. MARY SCHINDLER BARBER. (1810-.)
Hymns 464, 604, 813.
DAVIES, REV. SAMUEL. (1724-1761.)
Hymns 283, 1372.
DAVIS, REV. ELIEL. (1800-1830.)
Hymn 1412.
DECK, JAMES GEORGE. (1808-.)
Hymns 66, 323, 503, 580, 869, 1199.
DE FLEURY, MISS MARIA. 1791.
Hymn 812.
DENHAM, REV. DAVID. (1791-1848.)
Hymn 824.
DENNY, SIR EDWARD. (1796-.)
Hymns 68, 646, 873, 971, 1209, 1210, 1324.
DEXTER, REV. HENRY MARTYN, D. D. (1821-.)
Hymn 995.
DICKSON, DAVID. 1649.
Hymn 837.
DOANE, BP. GEORGE WASHINGTON, D. D. (1799-1859.)
Hymns 708, 925, 1308.

DOBELL, JOHN. (1757-1840.)
Hymn 161.
DOBER, MRS. ANNA SCHINDLER. (1713-1739.)
Hymn 287.
DODDRIDGE, REV. PHILIP, D. D. (1702-1751.)
Hymns 37, 54, 110, 126, 163, 165, 167, 222, 233, 236, 257, 280, 281, 310, 319, 380, 410, 429, 454, 462, 528, 676, 713, 720, 761, 793, 906, 994, 1044, 1054, 1161, 1201, 1202, 1224, 1227, 1239, 1246, 1252, 1257, 1265, 1346, 1375, 1382, 1388, 1413.
DOWNTON, REV. HENRY. (1818-.)
Hymn 1378.
DRACUP, REV. JOHN. (-1795.)
Hymn 1184.
DRUMMOND, REV. D. T. K. 1850.
Hymn 1486.
DRUMMOND, REV. WILLIAM HAMILTON. (1772-1856.)
Hymns 384, 1368.
DUFFIELD, REV. GEORGE, JR., D. D. (1818-.)
Hymns 305, 1307.
DUNCAN, MRS. MARY LUNDIE. (1814-1840.)
Hymn 1004.
DWIGHT, REV. JOHN SULLIVAN. (1812-.)
Hymn 1276.
DWIGHT, REV. TIMOTHY, D. D. (1752-1817.)
Hymns 368, 375, 1445.
DYER, REV. SIDNEY. (1814-.)
Hymn 421.

EAST, REV. JOHN. 1836.
Hymn 1482.
EASTBURN, REV. JAMES WALLIS. (1798-1819.)
Hymn 1106.
EDMESTON, JAMES. (1791-1867.)
Hymns 256, 539, 960, 967, 1007, 1176, 1299, 1323.
ELLERTON, REV. JOHN. (1826-.)
Hymns 1156, 1170.
ELLIOTT, MISS CHARLOTTE. (1789-1871.)
Hymns 192, 404, 469, 496, 503, 764, 809.
ELLIOTT, MRS. JULIA ANNE. (-1841.)
Hymn 1164.
ELVEN, REV. CORNELIUS. (1797-.)
Hymn 177.
ENFIELD, REV. WILLIAM, D. D. (1741-1797.)
Hymn 67.
ESLING, MRS. CATHARINE H. (1812-.)
Hymn 471.
EVANS, REV. JAMES HARRINGTON. (1785-1840.)
Hymn 435.
EVANS, REV. JONATHAN. (1749-1809.)
Hymns 86, 1189.

FABER, REV. FREDERICK WILLIAM. (1815-1863.)
Hymns 19, 22, 81, 117, 333, 388, 395, 444, 472, 473, 573, 747, 839, 1003, 1177.
FANCH, REV. JAMES. 1776.
Hymn 107.
FAWCETT, REV. JOHN, D. D. (1739-1817.)
Hymns 80, 139, 511, 875, 839, 1018.
FITCH, REV. ELEAZER T., D. D. (1790-1871.)
Hymn 1179.
FLETCHER, MISS. 1857.
Hymn 1260.
FLOWERDEW, MRS. ALICE. (1759-1830.)
Hymn 1395.
FORD, REV. DAVID EVERARD. 1828.
Hymn 1408.
FRANCIS, REV. BENJAMIN. (1734-1799.)
Hymns 311, 344, 1243.
FRANK, JOHANN. (1618-1677.)
Hymn
FRANKE, REV. AUGUST HERMANN. (1663-1727.)
Hymn 593.
FREEMAN, REV. JAMES. (1759-1835.)
Hymn 593.
FURNESS, REV. WILLIAM HENRY, D. D. (1802-.)
Hymn 565.

GALLAUDET, THOMAS HOPKINS, LL. D. (1789-1851.)
Hymn 504.
GANSE, REV. HERVEY DODDRIDGE. (1822-.)
Hymns 212, 487.
GASKELL, MRS. ELIZABETH CLEGHORN. (1810-1865.)
Hymn 11.

Index of Authors.

GATES, MRS. ELLEN M. HUNTINGTON. (1835-.)
Hymn 840.
GERHARDT, REV. PAUL. (1606-1676.)
Hymns 328, 329; 794, 949, 950, 1042.
GIBBONS, REV. THOMAS, D. D. (1720-1785.)
Hymns 382, 441, 854, 1187, 1315, 1425.
GILL, THOMAS HORNBLOWER. (1819-.)
Hymns 16, 119, 248, 937, 1317.
GILMORE, REV. JOSEPH HENRY. (1834-.)
Hymn 534.
GISBORNE, REV. THOMAS. (1758-1846.)
Hymn 709.
GOODE, REV. WILLIAM. (1762-1816.)
Hymns 1090, 1138, 1455.
GOUGH, BENJAMIN. (1805-.)
Hymns 1296, 1347, 1348, 1460.
GRANT, SIR ROBERT. (1785-1838.)
Hymns 518, 535, 899, 1023, 1055.
GRIGG, REV. JOSEPH. (1728-1768.)
Hymns 160, 344.
GURNEY, REV. JOHN HAMPDEN. (1802-1862.)
Hymn 603.
GUYON, MME. JEANNE M. B. DE LA M. (1648-1717.)
Hymns 317, 729.

HALL, MRS. ELVIRA M. (1818-.)
Hymn 247.
HAMMOND, REV. WILLIAM. (1719-1783.)
Hymns 1022, 1081, 1261.
HANKEY, MISS KATHERINE. 1865.
Hymns 339, 341.
HANKINSON, REV. THOMAS EDWARDS. (1805-1843.)
Hymn 88.
HARBAUGH, REV. HENRY. (1818-1867.)
Hymns 298, 1364.
HARMER, REV. SAMUEL YOUNG. (1809-.)
Hymn 832.
HART, REV. JOSEPH. (1712-1768.)
Hymns 72, 398, 1047, 1185, 1193, 1249.
HASTINGS, THOMAS, D. M. (1784-1872.)
Hymns 159, 168, 170, 172, 407, 428, 459, 470, 513, 524, 583, 609, 683, 686, 694, 744, 913, 953, 989, 1001, 1143, 1303.
HATFIELD, REV. EDWIN FRANCIS, D. D. (1807-.)
Hymns 1264, 1373.
HAVERGAL, MISS FRANCES RIDLEY. (1836-1879.)
Hymns 461, 619, 621, 724, 771, 856, 914, 1256, 1334, 1381.
HAWEIS, REV. THOMAS, M. D. (1732-1820.)
Hymns 92, 143, 544, 1135.
HAWES, MISS ANNIE SHERWOOD. (1835-.)
Hymn 571.
HAWKESWORTH, JOHN, LL. D. (1715-1773.)
Hymn 687.
HAYWARD, ——. 1806.
Hymn 354.
HEATH, GEORGE. (1781-.)
Hymn 412.
HEBER, BP. REGINALD, D. D. (1783-1826.)
Hymns 413, 965, 1105, 1144, 1162, 1188, 1217, 1242, 1291, 1339, 1429, 1454.
HEGINBOTHAM, REV. OTTIWELL. (1744-1768.)
Hymns 221, 259, 351, 643, 807, 1374.
HERBERT, REV. GEORGE. (1593-1632.)
Hymn 561.
HERVEY, REV. JAMES. (1714-1758.)
Hymn 726.
HILL, REV. ROWLAND. (1744-1833.)
Hymns 458, 463, 1447.
HINSDALE, MRS. GRACE W. 1865.
Hymn 246.
HOLDEN, OLIVER.
Hymn 951.
HOLMES, OLIVER WENDELL, M. D. (1809-.)
Hymns 50, 931.
HOPKINS, REV. JOSIAH, D. D. (1786-1862.)
Hymn 171.
HOPPER, REV. EDWARD. (1818-.)
Hymn 964.
HOPPS, JOHN PAGE.
Hymn 979.
HOSKINS, REV. JOSEPH. (1745-1788.)
Hymn 1037.
HOW, REV. WILLIAM WALSHAM. (1823-.)
Hymns 408, 476, 884, 919, 1301.

HUMPHREYS, REV. JOSEPH. (1720-.)
Hymn 858.
HUNTER, REV. WILLIAM, D. D. (1811-1877.)
Hymns 592, 792, 834.
HUNTINGDON, SELINA SHIRLEY, COUNTESS OF. (1707-1791.)
Hymn 451.
HURLBUT, WILLIAM HENRY. (1827-.)
Hymn 985.
HURN, REV. WILLIAM. (1754-1829.)
Hymn 1087.
HUTTON, JAMES. (1715-1795.)
Hymn 353.
HYDE, MRS. ANN BEADLEY. (-1872.)
Hymns 155, 164, 998.

IRONS, REV. WILLIAM JOSIAH, D. D. (1812-.)
Hymn 910.

JERVIS, REV. THOMAS. (1748-1793.)
Hymn 1146.
JOHNSON, MRS. CATHERINE HARDENBERGH. (1835-.)
Hymns 1235, 1343.
JOHNSON, REV. SAMUEL. (1822-.)
Hymn 434.
JOYCE, REV. JAMES. (1781-1850.)
Hymn 1285.
JUDKIN, REV. THOMAS JAMES. (1788-1871.)
Hymn 105.
JUDSON, REV. ADONIRAM, D. D. (1788-1850.)
Hymn 905.
JUKES, R. 1842.
Hymn 216.

KEBLE, REV. JOHN. (1792-1866.)
Hymns 115, 397, 702, 886, 941, 1387.
KEITH, GEORGE. 1787.
Hymns 986, 987.
KELLY, REV. THOMAS. (1769-1855.)
Hymns 72, 82, 95, 96, 103, 104, 106, 215, 348, 589, 851, 855, 863, 968, 1014, 1032, 1074, 1088, 1100, 1114, 1173, 1175, 1302, 1306, 1327, 1335, 1341, 1344, 1357, 1411, 1483.
KEMPTHORNE, REV. JOHN. (1775-1838.)
Hymn 1067.
KEN, BP. THOMAS. (1637-1711.)
Hymns 677, 691, 1125.
KENT, JOHN. (1766-1843.)
Hymn 772.
KETHE, REV. WILLIAM. (1561-.)
Hymn 1059.
KEY, FRANCIS SCOTT. (1779-1843.)
Hymns 226, 1403.
KING, REV. JOHN. (1788-1858.)
Hymn 999.
KINGSBURY, REV. WILLIAM. (1744-1818.)
Hymns 1096, 1247.
KIPPIS, REV. ANDREW, D. D. (1725-1795.)
Hymn 684.
KNOLLIS, FRANCIS MINDEN. 1860.
Hymn 1492.
KNOX.
Hymn 538.
KRÜGER, JOHN. 1640.
Hymn 157.

LANGE, REV. ERNEST. (1650-1727.)
Hymn 26.
LANGE, REV. JOACHIM. (1670-1744.)
Hymn 269.
LAURENTIUS, LAURENTII. (1660-1722.)
Hymn 1331.
LELAND, REV. JOHN. (1754-1841.)
Hymn 697.
LITTLEDALE, REV. RICHARD FREDERICK. (1833-.)
Hymns 1283, 1376.
LLOYD, WILLIAM FREEMAN. (1791-1853.)
Hymns 748, 779.
LONGFELLOW, REV. SAMUEL. (1819-.)
Hymn 1171.
LUTHER, MARTIN. (1483-1546.)
Hymn 1116.
LYTE, REV. HENRY FRANCIS. (1793-1847.)
Hymns 121, 230, 273, 274, 360, 377, 479, 567, 600, 601, 634, 749, 755, 777, 814, 817, 842, 1150, 1286.

317

Index of Authors.

MCALL, ROBERT STEVENS. 1812.
Hymn 1464.
MCCHEYNE, REV. ROBERT MURRAY. (1813-1843.)
Hymn 499.
MCDONALD, REV. WILLIAM. (1820-.)
Hymn 197.
MACDUFF, JOHN R., D. D. (-1820.)
Hymn 723.
MACKAY, MRS. MARGARET. (1801-.)
Hymn 1431.
MACKAY, REV. WILLIAM PATON. (1839-.)
Hymn 1110.
MACKELLAR, THOMAS. (1812-.)
Hymns 1005, 1466.
MADAN, REV. MARTIN. (1726-1790.)
Hymns 1081, 1083, 1453.
MALAN, REV. CÆSAR HENRY ABRAHAM, D. D. (1787-1864.)
Hymn 1415.
MANT, BP. RICHARD, D. D. (1776-1848.)
Hymns 570, 800, 972, 1069, 1470.
MARCH, REV. DANIEL. (1816-.)
Hymn 419.
MASON, REV. JOHN. (-1694.)
Hymns 321, 365, 969.
MASON, REV. WILLIAM. (1725-1797.)
Hymn 277.
MASSEY, GERALD. (1828-.)
Hymn 844.
MASSIE, RICHARD. (1800-.)
Hymns 343, 1410.
MAUDE, MRS. MARY FAWLER. 1848.
Hymn 918.
MEDLEY, REV. SAMUEL. (1738-1799.)
Hymns 231, 581, 795.
MEINHOLD, REV. JOHN WILHELM. (1797-1851.)
Hymn 1441.
MERCER, REV. WILLIAM. 1864.
Hymn 1365.
MERRICK, REV. JAMES. (1720-1769.)
Hymns 356, 637, 863, 907.
MIDLANE, ALBERT. (1825-.)
Hymns 162, 1253.
MILLER, REV. HENRY. 1809.
Hymn 866.
MILMAN, REV. HENRY HART, D. D. (1791-1868.)
Hymn 923.
MILTON, JOHN (1608-1674.)
Hymn 1391.
MITCHELL, REV. WILLIAM. 1831.
Hymn 1213.
MONSELL, REV. JOHN SAMUEL BEWLEY, LL. D (1811-1875.)
Hymns 433, 485, 833, 991, 1232, 1399, 1401, 1500.
MONTGOMERY, JAMES. (1771-1854.)
Hymns 18, 40, 43, 55, 71, 76, 137, 271, 306, 371, 373, 391, 396, 401, 417, 422, 478, 512, 520, 522, 543, 553, 650, 670, 689, 775, 847, 876, 903, 921, 926, 938, 1015, 1039, 1056, 1058, 1060, 1097, 1112, 1142, 1149, 1172, 1174, 1229, 1233, 1234, 1238, 1319, 1320, 1340, 1353, 1356, 1398, 1417, 1427, 1430, 1432, 1459, 1462.
MOORE, THOMAS. (1779-1852.)
Hymns 470, 636.
MORELL, THOMAS. (1781-1840.)
Hymn 1300.
MORRIS, GEORGE PERKINS. (1802-1864.)
Hymn 562.
MORRISON, REV. JOHN, D. D. (1749-1798.)
Hymn 56.
MOTE, EDWARD. (1797-.)
Hymn 738.
MOULTRIE, REV. JOHN. (1799-1874.)
Hymns 208, 789.
MUHLENBERG, REV. WILLIAM AUGUSTUS, D. D. (1796-1877.)
Hymns 766, 816, 997, 1490.

NEALE, REV. JOHN MASON. (1818-1866.)
Hymns 527, 922, 974, 1367, 1452, 1475, 1479, 1484, 1489, 1494, 1498, 1499.
NEEDHAM, REV. JOHN. 1768.
Hymns 13, 21, 376.
NELSON, REV. DAVID, M. D. (1793-1844.)
Hymn 823.
NETTLETON, REV. ASAHEL. (1783-1844.)
Hymn 207.

NEVIN, REV. EDWIN H. (1814-.)
Hymn 948.
NEUMARK, GEORG. (1621-1681.)
Hymn 508.
NEWMAN, REV. JOHN HENRY. (1801-.)
Hymns 636, 936.
NEWTON, REV. JOHN. (1725-1807.)
Hymns 181, 182, 198, 217, 244, 251, 291, 320, 332, 338, 387, 403, 440, 446, 449, 502, 551, 564, 640, 769, 781, 782, 788, 852, 882, 939, 961, 1016, 1157, 1182, 1183, 1186, 1244, 1245, 1380, 1423.
NOEL, HON. AND REV. GERARD THOMAS. (1782-1851.)
Hymn 1215.
NORTON, REV. ANDREWS, D. D. (1786-1853.)
Hymn 750.

OCCUM, REV. SAMSON. (1723-1792.)
Hymn 935.
ODIORNE, JAMES C. (1802-1879.)
Hymn 1221.
OGILVIE, REV. JOHN, D. D. (1733-1814.)
Hymn 238.
OLIVERS, REV. THOMAS. (1725-1799.)
Hymn 228.
ONDERDONK, BP. HENRY USTICK. (1789-1858.)
Hymns 148, 730, 990, 1271, 1272.
OSLER, EDWARD. (1798-1863.)
Hymn 1205.
OSWALD, HENRY SIGISMUND. (1751-1837.)
Hymn 978.

PALGRAVE, FRANCIS TURNER. (1824-.)
Hymn 901.
PALMER, REV. RAY, D. D. (1808-.)
Hymns 214, 272. 308, 335, 602, 640, 815, 819, 930, 1040, 1091, 1168, 1206, 1258, 1328, 1349, 1377, 1478.
PARK, REV. ROSWELL, D. D. (1807-1869.)
Hymn 1214.
PARR, MISS HARRIET. 1856.
Hymn 706.
PEABODY, REV. WILLIAM BOURN OLIVER, D. D. (1799-1847.)
Hymns 1426, 1491.
PERRONET, REV. EDWARD. (1792-.)
Hymn 1071.
PETERS, MRS. MARY BOWLEY. (-1856.)
Hymns 975, 1197.
PHELPS, REV. PHILIP, D. D. (1826-.)
Hymn 1237.
PHELPS, REV. SYLVESTER DRYDEN, D. D. (1816-.)
Hymns 275, 728, 785.
PHILPOT, REV. CHARLES. (1831-.)
Hymn 678.
PIRIE, ALEXANDER. (-1804.)
Hymn 1098.
PLUMLEY, REV. GARDNER SPRING. (1827-.)
Hymn 1273.
PRENTISS, MRS. ELIZABETH PAYSON. (1818-1869.)
Hymn 660.

QUARLES, JOHN. (-1665.)
Hymn 667.

RAFFLES, REV. THOMAS, D. D. (1788-1863.)
Hymns 405, 739, 1463.
RANKIN, REV. JEREMIAH EAMES. (1828-.)
Hymn 497.
RAWSON, GEORGE. (1807-.)
Hymns 463, 1041.
REED, REV. ANDREW, D. D. (1787-1862.)
Hymns 28, 294, 584, 599, 791, 957.
RICHTER, CHRISTIAN FRIEDRICH. (1676-1711.)
Hymn 607.
ROBBINS, REV. SAMUEL DOWSE. (1812-.)
Hymns 1169, 1208.
ROBERT II. OF FRANCE. (972-1031.)
Hymn 1040.
ROBERTSON, REV. WILLIAM. (-1743.)
Hymn 988.
ROBINSON, REV. CHARLES S., D. D. 1862.
Hymns 662, 1351.
ROBINSON, GEORGE. 1842.
Hymn 872.

Index of Authors.

ROBINSON, REV. ROBERT. (1735-1790.)
  Hymns 224, 241.
ROSENROTH, CHRISTIAN KNORR, VON. (1636-1689.)
  Hymn 927.
RUSSELL, REV. ARTHUR TOZER. (1806-.)
  Hymns 958, 1093.
RYLAND, REV. JOHN, D. D. (1753-1825.)
  Hymns 719, 786.

SAFFERY, MRS. MARIA GRACE. (1773-1858.)
  Hymn 973.
SANTOLIUS, MAGLORIANUS. (1624-1684.)
  Hymn 1121.
SARGENT, LUCIUS MANLIUS. (1786-1867.)
  Hymn 1259.
SCHEFFLER, JOHANN ANGELUS. (1624-1677.)
  Hymns 304, 312, 327.
SCHMOLKE, REV. BENJAMIN. (1672-1737.)
  Hymn 540.
SCOTT, MISS ELIZABETH. Ab. 1764.
  Hymns 674, 1167.
SCOTT, REV. THOMAS. (1700-1776.)
  Hymns 91, 166.
SCOTT, SIR WALTER. (1771-1832.)
  Hymns 915, 1451.
SCUDDER, MISS ELIZA. (1821-.)
  Hymn 945.
SEAGRAVE, REV. ROBERT. (1693-1742.)
  Hymn 828.
SEARS, REV. EDMUND HAMILTON, D. D. (1810-1876.)
  Hymns 50, 61.
SHEPHERD, MRS. ANNE HOULDITCH. (1809-1857.)
  Hymn 1008.
SHEPHERD, THOMAS. (1665-1739.)
  Hymn 430.
SHIPTON, MISS ANNA.
  Hymns 279, 510.
SHIRLEY, HON. AND REV. WALTER. (1725-1786.)
  Hymns 340, 466, 1076, 1190.
SHRUBSOLE, WILLIAM, JR. (1759-1829.)
  Hymns 685, 1310, 1345.
SIGOURNEY, MRS. LYDIA HUNTLEY. (1791-1865.)
  Hymns 426, 1048.
SIMPSON, MRS. JANE CROSS BELL. 1830.
  Hymn 1284.
SLINN, MISS SARAH. 1779.
  Hymn 53.
SMITH, MRS. CAROLINE SPRAGUE. 1856.
  Hymn 700.
SMITH, SIR JAMES EDWARD, M. D. (1759-1828.)
  Hymn 1151.
SMITH, REV. SAMUEL FRANCIS, D. D. (1808-.)
  Hymns 74, 149, 1168, 1198, 1230, 1231, 1330, 1352, 1402, 1405, 1440.
SPITTA, REV. CARL JOHANN PHILIP, D. D. (1801-1859.)
  Hymns 343, 1410, 1434.
STANLEY, REV. ARTHUR PENRHYN, D. D. (1815-1881.)
  Hymn 587, 1449.
STEELE, MISS ANNE. (1716-1778.)
  Hymns 8, 69, 113, 128, 135, 145, 147, 152, 265, 266, 346, 409, 445, 453, 477, 523, 529, 549, 655, 690, 717, 718, 735, 754, 783, 810, 993, 1031, 1033, 1078, 1099, 1153, 1366, 1383, 1384, 1406, 1407, 1414, 1485, 1495.
STENNETT, REV. JOSEPH, D. D. (1663-1713.)
  Hymn 363.
STENNETT, REV. SAMUEL, D. D. (1727-1795.)
  Hymns 87, 131, 188, 284, 288, 372, 452, 838, 1024, 1075, 1222.
STEPHEN OF ST. SABAS. (725-794.)
  Hymn 527.
STERNHOLD, THOMAS. (-1549.)
  Hymn 5.
STOCKER, JOHN. Ab. 1776.
  Hymn 490.
STONE, REV. SAMUEL JOHN. (1839-.)
  Hymn 864.
STOWE, MRS. HARRIET ELIZABETH BEECHER. (1812-.)
  Hymns 146, 688, 773.
STOWELL, REV. HUGH. (1799-1865.)
  Hymns 940, 1309.
STRONG, REV. NATHAN, D. D. (1748-1816.)
  Hymns 1389, 1392.
STUART, CARLOS D. (1820-1862.)
  Hymn 1487.

SWAIN, REV. JOSEPH. (1761-1796.)
  Hymns 140, 596, 822, 883.
TAPPAN, REV. WILLIAM BINGHAM. (1794-1849.)
  Hymns 75, 1476, 1488.
TATE, NAHUM. (1652-1715.)
  Hymns 367, 1050, 1063, 1287.
TATE AND BRADY. 1696.
  Hymns 25, 38, 47, 52, 482, 526, 567, 716, 731, 799, 801, 1123, 1127.
TAYLOR, REV. JOHN. (1694-1761.)
  Hymn 1369.
TAYLOR, REV. THOMAS RAWSON. (1807-1835.)
  Hymn 830.
TERSTEEGEN, GERHARDT. (1697-1769.)
  Hymns 175, 293, 629.
THEODORE OF THE STUDIUM. (759-826.)
  Hymn 1452.
THOMAS OF CELANO. Ab. 1250.
  Hymn 1451.
THOMPSON, REV. ALEXANDER RAMSAY. (1822-.)
  Hymn 93.
THOMSON, REV. JOHN, D. D. (1782-1841.)
  Hymn 15.
THRUPP, MISS DOROTHY ANN. (1779-1847.)
  Hymn 1002.
THRUPP, REV. FRANCIS JOSEPH. (1827-1867.)
  Hymn 1363.
TOPLADY, REV. AUGUSTUS MONTAGUE. (1740-1778.)
  Hymns 193, 199, 574, 642, 696, 698, 1042, 1095, 1117, 1428.
TRENCH, ARCHBISHOP, RICHARD CHENEVIX. (1807-.)
  Hymn 424.
TURNER, REV. DANIEL. (1710-1798.)
  Hymns 195, 390, 1148.
TUTTIETT, REV. LAWRENCE. (1825-.)
  Hymn 414.

UPHAM, REV. THOMAS COGSWELL. (1799-1872.)
  Hymns 427, 506, 904.

VAN ALSTYNE, MRS. FRANCES JANE CROSBY. (1823-.)
  Hymns 620, 639, 661, 666, 765, 1263.
VICTORINUS, SANTOLIUS. (1630-1697.)
  Hymns 871, 1034.
VOKE, MRS. AB 1806.
  Hymns 1295, 1298, 1312, 1326.

WALFORD, REV. WILLIAM W. 1846.
  Hymn 406.
WALKER, MRS. MARY JANE. Ab. 1847.
  Hymn 260.
WALLACE, REV. JOHN AIKMAN. (1802-1870.)
  Hymn 399.
WARDLAW, REV. RALPH, D. D. (1779-1853.)
  Hymns 796, 1051, 1160, 1290.
WARING, MISS ANNA LÆTITIA. (1820-.)
  Hymns 546, 552, 557, 646, 668, 743, 746, 758, 759, 762, 976.
WARNER, MISS ANNA.
  Hymn 433.
WATTS, REV. ISAAC, D. D. (1674-1748.)
  Hymns 1, 3, 4, 9, 10, 12, 20, 24, 27, 28, 29, 31, 35, 41, 42, 44, 48, 49, 51, 62, 65, 72, 79, 97, 99, 109, 111, 112, 123, 124, 125, 127, 129, 132, 133, 134, 138, 180, 185, 186, 187, 203, 204, 218, 220, 229, 232, 235, 240, 245, 252, 261, 262, 263, 282, 313, 314, 315, 316, 318, 347, 349, 350, 355, 358, 359, 361, 364, 366, 369, 370, 374, 381, 383, 392, 393, 415, 416, 447, 448, 480, 492, 493, 500, 514, 533, 548, 550, 556, 560, 586, 597, 606, 633, 671, 672, 679, 681, 682, 695, 701, 704, 711, 714, 715, 725, 727, 732, 733, 734, 737, 742, 790, 798, 802, 804, 805, 818, 825, 827, 831, 849, 856, 857, 859, 861, 862, 867, 870, 874, 890, 891, 893, 894, 896, 897, 898, 946, 962, 983, 1000, 1020, 1030, 1043, 1049, 1052, 1053, 1057, 1061, 1062, 1064, 1065, 1066, 1072, 1080, 1085, 1086, 1089, 1092, 1104, 1119, 1122, 1126, 1128, 1145, 1152, 1154, 1194, 1200, 1203, 1223, 1225, 1241, 1268, 1274, 1332, 1336, 1358, 1359, 1361, 1385, 1390, 1394, 1406, 1419, 1422, 1437, 1438, 1439, 1443, 1446, 1472, 1496.
WEBB, REV. EDWARD. (1818-.)
  Hymn 495.
WEISSEL, REV. GEORG. (1590-1635.)
  Hymn 276.

Index of Authors.

WELLS, M. M. 1858.
Hymn 956.
WESLEY, REV. CHARLES. (1708-1788.)
Hymns 17, 32, 57, 60, 83, 94, 100, 116, 122, 136, 151, 153, 156, 157, 176, 178, 179, 183, 184, 189, 194, 202, 227, 243, 258, 264, 267, 278, 285, 286, 289, 290, 292, 295, 296, 297, 299, 300, 324, 325, 330, 378, 386, 389, 431, 432, 442, 443, 450, 456, 457, 460, 474, 475, 481, 491, 501, 505, 530, 555, 572, 575, 577, 590, 605, 608, 610, 611, 612, 613, 614, 615, 616, 617, 622, 623, 624, 625, 626, 627, 628, 632, 638, 641, 647, 651, 653, 663, 664, 673, 680, 712, 722, 741, 745, 756, 757, 767, 768, 811, 820, 865, 877, 881, 902, 908, 933, 959, 992, 1009, 1011, 1012, 1028, 1035, 1036, 1046, 1101, 1111, 1113, 1130, 1131, 1134, 1207, 1212, 1218, 1226, 1250, 1278, 1285, 1289, 1304, 1333, 1354, 1355, 1453, 1457, 1469, 1471, 1473.
WESLEY, REV. JOHN. (1703-1791.)
Hymns 26, 97, 201, 254, 269, 287, 293, 327, 328, 329, 579, 607, 629, 669, 932, 949, 950, 1124.
WESLEY, REV. SAMUEL. (1662-1735.)
Hymn 85.
WESLEY, REV. SAMUEL, JR. (1690-1739.)
Hymn 1444.
WHATELY, ARCHBISHOP RICHARD. (1787-1863.)
Hymn 965.
WHITE, HENRY KIRKE. (1785-1806.)
Hymns 7, 30, 1180, 1416.
WHITFIELD, REV. FREDERICK. (1829-.)
Hymns 255, 582.
WHITING, WILLIAM. (1825-.)
Hymn 1280.
WHITTIER, JOHN GREENLEAF. (1808-.)
Hymn 911.
WILLIAMS, REV. BENJAMIN. (1725-1795.)
Hymn 1113.
WILLIAMS, MISS HELEN MARIA. (1762-1827.)
Hymn 751.
WILLIAMS, REV. PETER. (1719-1796.)
Hymn 630.

WILLIAMS, REV. WILLIAM. (1717-1791.)
Hymn 630.
WILSON, MRS. CAROLINE FRY. (1787-1846.)
Hymn 536.
WINGROVE, JOHN. 1806.
Hymn 239.
WINKLER, E. T. 1871.
Hymn 1404.
WINKWORTH, MISS CATHERINE. (1829-1878.)
Hymns 276, 503, 794, 841, 1434, 1441.
WINSLOW, MISS MARGARET ELIZABETH. (1836-.)
Hymn 494.
WITTENMEYER, MRS. ANNIE. 1868.
Hymn 547.
WOLCOTT, REV. SAMUEL, D. D. (1813-.)
Hymn 1342.
WOLFE, REV. AARON ROBARTS. (1821-.)
Hymns 301, 1211.
WORDSWORTH, BP. CHRISTOPHER, D. D. (1807-.)
Hymns 102, 554, 1166, 1461.
WRANGHAM, WILLIAM. (-1832.)
Hymn 1068.
WREFORD, REV. JOHN REYNELL, D. D. 1837.
Hymns 645, 1277.

XAVIER, FRANCIS. (1506-1552.)
Hymn 302.

YESUDASAN. (A Tamil Christian.)
Hymn 495.
YORK, MRS. SARAH EMILY WALDO. (1847)
Hymn 826.
YOUNG, REV. WILLIAM. (-1757.)
Hymn 537.

ZINZENDORF, COUNT NICOLAUS LUDWIG. (1700-1760.)
Hymns 201, 254.

Authors Unknown.

Hymns 14, 34, 77, 118, 144, 154, 158, 172, 200, 209, 219, 223, 253, 326, 334, 385, 394, 425, 467, 486, 509, 517, 519, 525, 532, 545, 559, 569, 591, 595, 644, 648, 665, 667, 675, 692, 693, 705, 710, 753, 770, 776, 780, 835, 836, 952, 954, 963, 966, 970, 980, 982, 984, 1010, 1017, 1029, 1038, 1077, 1120, 1132, 1136, 1140, 1141, 1178, 1206, 1262, 1269, 1314, 1318, 1329, 1350, 1362, 1371, 1379, 1396, 1436, 1465, 1467, 1474.

www.ingramcontent.com/pod-product-compliance
Lightning Source LLC
Chambersburg PA
CBHW030735230426

43667CB00007B/717